THE CHANGING CHARACTER OF INTERNATIONAL DISPUTE SETTLEMENT

The international dispute settlement system is currently facing many challenges regarding the authority, effectiveness, and legitimacy of its methods and mechanisms and their co-ordination. These challenges cut across different fields of international law and relations such as investment, trade, human rights, water resources, the law of the sea, the environment, international peace and security, disaster law, space, and cyberspace. New technologies also have an impact on the scope of existing disputes and their settlement, which leads to the emergence of new disputes and ways of settling them.

This book offers insightful reflections by academics and practitioners on such challenges and how they can be addressed as well as on how the international dispute settlement system should adapt to attain its aim of maintaining peace and international legality. It deals with many contemporary issues and is wide-ranging in scope. It is suitable for students, scholars, and practitioners of international dispute settlement, international law, and international relations.

Russell Buchan is Professor of International Law at the University of Reading. Russell has published widely in the field of public international law, including three monographs: *International Law and the Construction of the Liberal Peace* (Hart, 2013), *Cyber Espionage and International Law* (Hart, 2018), and *Regulating the Use of Force in International Law: Stability and Change* (with Nicholas Tsagourias; Edward Elgar, 2021). He is also a co-editor of the *Research Handbook on International Law and Cyberspace* (with Nicholas Tsagourias; Edward Elgar, 2021) and a co-editor-in-chief of the *Journal of International Humanitarian Legal Studies*.

Daniel Franchini is Lecturer in International Law and Deputy Director of the Sheffield Centre for International and European Law at the University of Sheffield. He is the convenor of International Dispute Settlement and International Investment Law and Arbitration at the School of Law. His research focuses on the role of unilateral measures in the settlement of international disputes. He obtained his DPhil from the University of Oxford (2021) and has published, among others, in the *Virginia Journal of International Law*.

Nicholas Tsagourias is Professor of International Law at the University of Sheffield. He has published widely on international law and the use of force, humanitarian law, and the law and cyberspace. Among his publications are the books *International Humanitarian Law: Cases, Materials and Commentary* (with Dr Alasdair Morrison; Cambridge University Press, 2023), the *Research Handbook on International Law and Cyberspace* (with Russell Buchan; Edward Elgar, 2021) and the *Research Methods in International Law: A Handbook* (with Dr Rossana Deplano; Edward Elgar, 2021). He is general editor of the Elgar International Law and Technology series (with Dr Russell Buchan).

The Changing Character of International Dispute Settlement

CHALLENGES AND PROSPECTS

Edited by

RUSSELL BUCHAN

University of Reading

DANIEL FRANCHINI

University of Sheffield

NICHOLAS TSAGOURIAS

University of Sheffield

CAMBRIDGE
UNIVERSITY PRESS

CAMBRIDGE
UNIVERSITY PRESS

Shaftesbury Road, Cambridge CB2 8EA, United Kingdom

One Liberty Plaza, 20th Floor, New York, NY 10006, USA

477 Williamstown Road, Port Melbourne, VIC 3207, Australia

314–321, 3rd Floor, Plot 3, Splendor Forum, Jasola District Centre, New Delhi – 110025, India

103 Penang Road, #05-06/07, Visioncrest Commercial, Singapore 238467

Cambridge University Press is part of Cambridge University Press & Assessment, a department of the University of Cambridge.

We share the University's mission to contribute to society through the pursuit of education, learning and research at the highest international levels of excellence.

www.cambridge.org
Information on this title: www.cambridge.org/9781316513903

DOI: 10.1017/9781009076296

First published 2024

A catalogue record for this publication is available from the British Library

Library of Congress Cataloging-in-Publication Data
NAMES: Buchan, Russell, 1983- editor. | Franchini, Daniel, editor. | Tsagourias, Nikolaos K., editor.
TITLE: The changing character of international dispute settlement : challenges and prospects / edited by Russell Buchan, University of Reading; Daniel Franchini, University of Sheffield; Nicholas Tsagourias, University of Sheffield.
DESCRIPTION: Yes. | Cambridge, United Kingdom ; New York, NY : Cambridge University Press, 2023. | Includes index.
IDENTIFIERS: LCCN 2023025417 (print) | LCCN 2023025418 (ebook) | ISBN 9781316513903 (hardback) | ISBN 9781009074964 (paperback) | ISBN 9781009076296 (epub)
SUBJECTS: LCSH: Dispute resolution (Law) | Pacific settlement of international disputes. | International criminal law. | International law and human rights.
CLASSIFICATION: LCC K2390 .C425 2023 (print) | LCC K2390 (ebook) | DDC 347/.09–dc23/eng/20230608
LC record available at https://lccn.loc.gov/2023025417
LC ebook record available at https://lccn.loc.gov/2023025418

ISBN 978-1-316-51390-3 Hardback

Contents

PART III NEW OPPORTUNITIES AND THE FUTURE OF INTERNATIONAL DISPUTE SETTLEMENT

Contributors

Eric De Brabandere is Professor of International Dispute Settlement Law and Director of the Grotius Centre for International Legal Studies. He is also Attorney-at-Law at the Brussels Bar (with DMDB Law) practising in international law and investment arbitration and is Visiting Professor of International Investment Law and Arbitration at the University of Makeni, Sierra Leone. Eric is a general international lawyer, with special expertise in international investment law and arbitration and international dispute settlement. He is the author and editor of several books and edited collections, including *Merrills' International Dispute Settlement* (7th ed.) (with the late Professor John Merrills; Cambridge University Press, 2022), *Investment Treaty Arbitration as Public International Law: Procedural Aspects and Implications* (Cambridge University Press, 2014), and, as editor, *International Procedure in Interstate Litigation and Arbitration: A Comparative Approach* (Cambridge University Press, 2021).

Russell Buchan is Professor of International Law at the University of Reading, UK. Russell has published widely in the field of public international law, including three monographs: *International Law and the Construction of the Liberal Peace* (Hart, 2013), *Cyber Espionage and International Law* (Hart, 2018), and *Regulating the Use of Force in International Law: Stability and Change* (with Nicholas Tsagourias; Edward Elgar, 2021). He is also co-editor of the *Research Handbook on International Law and Cyberspace* (with Nicholas Tsagourias; Edward Elgar, 2021) and *The Rights to Privacy and Data Protection in Times of Armed Conflict* (with Asaf Lubin; CCDCOE, 2022). He is co-editor-in-chief of the *Journal of International Humanitarian Legal Studies*.

Richard Collins is Professor of Law at Queen's University Belfast, where he also currently serves as the Dean of Internationalisation and Engagement in the Faculty of Arts, Humanities, and Social Sciences. Previously he was an associate professor in the Sutherland School of Law, University College Dublin, and prior to that a lecturer in the School of Law at the University of Sheffield. He has held visiting positions at a number of universities, including the University of Sydney, Monash University, York University (Toronto), iCourts Centre of Excellence (Copenhagen), and the University of Amsterdam. His research interests span international legal theory, the law of the sea, and international organisations, and his published work includes *The Institutional Problem in Modern International Law* (Hart, 2016) and *International Organisations and the Idea of Autonomy* (co-edited with Nigel D. White; Routledge, 2011). He is also co-editor-in-chief of the *Irish Yearbook of International Law*.

Rossana Deplano is Associate Professor and Co-Director of the Centre for European Law and Internationalisation at the University of Leicester. She has been a visiting scholar at Georgetown University, the University of Cambridge's Lauterpacht Centre for International Law, and the US Library of Congress. Rossana is author of *Empirical and Theoretical Perspectives on International Law: How States Use the UN General Assembly to Create International Obligations* (Cambridge University Press, 2022), and co-editor of *Research Methods of International Law: A Handbook* (with Nicholas Tsagourias; Edward Elgar, 2021). She is the recipient of a UKRI/AHRC Innovation Scholar fellowship to carry out an interdisciplinary research project in the field of international space law (2023/24).

Sir Malcolm D. Evans, KCMG, is Principal of Regent's Park College, Oxford, and Honorary Professor at the University of Bristol. He is a former member, and chair, of the UN Subcommittee on Prevention of Torture. His work has a particular focus on human rights, in particular the prevention of torture and the freedom of religion or belief. He is the editor of *International Law* (5th ed., Oxford University Press, 2018) and author and editor of numerous books and edited collections, including, most recently, the *Research Handbook on Torture* (Edward Elgar, 2020) and *Islands, Law and Context: The Treatment of Islands in International Law* (with Dr Reece Lewis; Edward Elgar, 2023). He is also Co-General Editor of the *International and Comparative Law Quarterly* and the *Oxford Journal of Law and Religion*. In 2021, he was elected as Associate Member of the Institut de Droit International and a fellow of the Learned Society of Wales.

Malgosia Fitzmaurice is Professor of Public International Law at the Department of Law, Queen Mary University of London. Since 2019, she has been elected an associate member of the Institut de Droit International, and in 2021, she was awarded the Doctorate Honoris Causa of the University of Neuchâtel. She specialises in international environmental law, the law of treaties, and Indigenous peoples. She publishes widely on these subjects. She has delivered a lecture on the international protection of the environment at The Hague Academy of International Law. Professor Fitzmaurice was invited as a visiting professor to and has lectured at various universities such as Berkeley Law School, the University of Kobe, and Panthéon-Sorbonne, Paris I. She is the editor-in-chief of the *International Community Law Review* journal and of the book series Queen Mary Studies in International Law (Brill/Nijhoff).

Daniel Franchini is Lecturer in International Law and Deputy Director of the Sheffield Centre for International and European Law at the University of Sheffield. He is the convenor of International Dispute Settlement and International Investment Law and Arbitration. His research focuses on the role of unilateral measures in the settlement of international disputes. He obtained his DPhil from the University of Oxford (2021) and has published, among others, in the *Virginia Journal of International Law*.

Tarcisio Gazzini is Professor of International Law at the University of Padua, Italy. He has also taught at the Universities of Glasgow and VU Amsterdam. Between 2014 and 2017, he co-directed a research project financed by the Swiss National Science Foundation on Foreign Investment in Africa – Gaining Development Momentum. His research interests include foreign investment law, the law of State responsibility, use of force, and the law of international organisations. He is the author of *Interpretation of Investment International Treaties* (Hart, 2016) and a founding member of the book series International Investment Law (Brill).

Aris Georgopoulos is Assistant Professor in Public Law and European Law at the School of Law of the University of Nottingham and Head of the Research Unit for Innovation, AI, Strategic, and Defence Procurement of the Public Procurement Research Group. He is also co-lead of the Research Unit on Public Procurement, Human Rights, and Social Sustainability. He has acted as expert advisor to companies and national authorities in the field of regulatory compliance and to international organisations and institutions (such as the OECD, World Bank, European Central Bank, European Court of Auditors, and USAID) in the field of regulatory reform.

Maria A. Gwynn is a member of the governing council of the binational entity ITAIPU and a senior research fellow of the Institute of International Law, University of Bonn, Germany. She is a professor at the Institute for

Strategic Studies of Paraguay and an international arbitrator at the Court of Arbitration for Sport, Switzerland. She was selected for the United Nations Leaders' Summit and, on behalf of ITAIPU, received the 2022 UN Sustainable Development Goal Recognition. Dr Gwynn is also a member of the National Climate Change Commission of Paraguay and has represented both Paraguay and ITAIPU at the COP26 and COP27 as well as at international events such as the 2023 UN Water Conference, the World Water Forum, World Energy Council, and others. A former Oxford–Princeton Global Leaders Fellow, Gwynn holds a PhD from the Bergische Universität Wuppertal, a Magister Juris from the University of Oxford, and an LLB Honours from the Faculty of Law, National University of Asuncion. She is the author of *Adapting Watercourse Agreements to Developments in International Law: The Case of the Itaipu Treaty* (Brill, 2019), 'South American Countries' Bilateral Investment Treaties: A Structuralist Perspective' (*Journal of International Dispute Settlement*, 2015); 'Balancing the State's Right to Regulate with Foreign Investment Protection' (*Groningen Journal of International Law*, 2018), and *The Uses of Common and Shared Natural Resources: A Tragedy or a Chance for Governance?* (Unweltrechtliche Beiträge aus Wissenschaft und Praxis, 2020).

Massimo Lando is an assistant professor at the Faculty of Law of the University of Hong Kong. He served as Associate Legal Officer at the International Court of Justice (2017–20) and obtained his PhD from the University of Cambridge (2019). His research interests are in general international law, especially the law of the sea, international dispute settlement, and sources of international law. He is a member of the Bar of England and Wales (Gray's Inn).

Petros C. Mavroidis is Edwin B. Parker Professor of Law at Columbia Law School, New York City. He has acted as chief reporter for the American Law Institute study 'Principles of Trade Law: The WTO'. His latest publications include *The WTO Dispute Settlement System: How? Why? Where?* (Edward Elgar, 2022) and *China and the WTO: Why Multilateralism Still Matters* (with Andre Sapir; Princeton University Press, 2021).

James Mehigan is Senior Lecturer in Law at the University of Canterbury and a barrister at Garden Court Chambers in London. He is the general editor of the *New Zealand Yearbook of International Law*. His research interests are in international criminal law, criminology, human rights, and domestic criminal law.

Fiona Middleton is a PhD candidate at the University of Sheffield School of Law.

Therese O'Donnell is a reader in the Law School at the University of Strathclyde in Glasgow, Scotland. She has particular expertise in public international law, human rights law, and international disaster law. Her research has a significant interdisciplinary dimension and ranges across law's encounters with history and critical geography. She has published extensively regarding a disaster-affected State's right to refuse aid, duties of cooperation, the coincidence of disaster aid and security issues, and the question of whether there is (or should be) an emerging legal duty to offer aid. More theoretically, she interrogates what disaster response law reveals about solidarity, how opportunities to develop more sophisticated understandings of vulnerability have been missed (and might be rescued), how disaster law recontours the role of NGOs, and how disaster law itself may be reconceived.

Alessandra Pietrobon is Professor of Public International Law and Humanitarian Law at the University of Padova, Italy. She has been the Director of the LM in International Relations and Diplomacy and the Coordinator of the PhD programme in International Law and Private and Labour Law. Her latest research interests include international arbitration and arms control and disarmament. She has published several articles on these subjects and a book concerning inter-State arbitration, focusing on procedure and applicable law (*Il Giudizio nell'arbirtrato fra Stati*; Editoriale scientifica, 2016).

Antonio Segura Serrano is Professor of International Law and EU Law at the University of Granada. His research interests include cyberspace law, international economic law, trade law, humanitarian law, and EU law. He has published extensively on different topics in the field of public international law and EU law and is also the author or editor of several books and edited collections, including *Global Cybersecurity and International Law* (Routledge, 2024), *The Challenge of Global Cybersecurity* (Tirant lo Blanch, 2023, in Spanish), and *The Reform of International Economic Governance* (Routledge, 2016).

Jacob Smith leads the UK Accountability Programme at Rights & Security International and is an associate lecturer at the University of Surrey. Jacob specialises in the application of international law and human rights law to the national security space, with particular focus on counterterrorism and counterextremism measures. His research interests also include public law and transitional justice in Northern Ireland.

Kimberley N. Trapp is Professor of Public International Law at the University College London Faculty of Law. She collaborates as an academic advisor on issues of international humanitarian and human rights law with various NGOs and government departments; has published in leading academic journals and edited collections on issues relating to the use of force, State responsibility, international humanitarian law, terrorism suppression, and the settlement of international disputes; and has presented related scholarship in various forums, including the annual meetings of the CCIL, ASIL, and ANZIL. Kimberley is co-editor of the OUP's Elements of International Law book series and a member of the board of various journals, including *Cambridge International Law Journal*, the *Journal on the Use of Force and International Law*, and *McGill Journal of International Law & Legal Pluralism*.

Nicholas Tsagourias is Professor of International Law at the University of Sheffield. His teaching and research interests are in the fields of international law and the use of force, international humanitarian law, international criminal law, international constitutional law, and cybersecurity. Among his recent publications are *Regulating the Use of Force in International Law: Stability and Change* (with Dr Russell Buchan; Edward Elgar, 2021), *Research Handbook on International Law and Cyberspace* (with Dr Russell Buchan; Edward Elgar, 2021), and *Research Methods on International Law: A Handbook* (with Dr Rossana Deplano; Edward Elgar, 2021). Professor Tsagourias sits on the editorial boards of the *Journal of Conflict and Security Law* and the *Journal on the Use of Force and International Law*. He is also general editor of the Elgar International Law and Technology series (with Dr Russell Buchan).

Nigel D. White is currently Professor of Public International Law at the University of Nottingham and formerly Professor of International Law at the University of Sheffield. He is the sole author of *The United Nations and the Maintenance of International Peace and Security* (Manchester University Press, 1990), *Keeping the Peace* (Manchester University Press, 1997), *The UN System: Toward International Justice* (Manchester University Press, 2002), *The Law of International Organisations* (3rd ed., Manchester University Press, 2017), *Democracy Goes to War* (Oxford University Press, 2009), *The Cuban Embargo under International Law* (Routledge, 2015), and *Military Justice: The Rights and Duties of Soldiers and Government* (Edward Elgar, 2022). He is also co-author and co-editor of a number of other books on international law and has published a large number of essays and articles primarily in the areas of peacekeeping law, law of international organisations, sanctions, embargoes, collective security law, and military justice. He has been a visiting professor at the University of Uppsala, Australian National University, and Kobe University. He has been the co-editor of the *Journal of Conflict and Security Law* since its founding in 1995.

Sir Michael Wood, KC, is a barrister at Twenty Essex, London, where he practises in the field of public international law, including before international courts and tribunals. He was a legal advisor to the UK Foreign and Commonwealth Office between 1999 and 2006, having joined as an assistant legal advisor in 1970. Sir Michael was a member of the UN International Law Commission from 2008 to 2022 and its Special Rapporteur on the identification of customary international law. He is a senior fellow of the Lauterpacht Centre for International Law at the University of Cambridge.

Foreword

Few disciplines are so all-encompassing and central to the study and practice of international law as the settlement of international disputes. In this important field, few voices have stood out as much as that of Professor John Merrills. Throughout his entire academic career at the University of Sheffield, John published extensively, and his work greatly advanced our understanding of this complex area. His textbook *International Dispute Settlement* is a staple for students, academics, and practitioners.

One of John's many contributions was to draw our attention to the fact that international dispute settlement is a continuously evolving discipline due to political, economic, social, and legal changes within the international community. All this means that the actors among which disputes arise and the fora in which these disputes are dealt with continue to mutate. John's many publications track these developments and examine their implications. For example, the consolidation of China as a global superpower and the rise of non-State actors, such as multinational corporations, have a profound impact on dispute settlement.

Other developments concern the type of disputes that are currently litigated at the international level and, even more so, those that do not form the subject of judicial proceedings before international courts and tribunals. Questions such as the extent to which individual recourse to human rights remedies and investor–State arbitration is changing the character of international adjudication are now accompanied by more radical attempts to reimagine classic principles of international dispute settlement in new areas such as cyberspace.

Yet, at its heart, the system of international dispute settlement is a resilient one, and its basic features have stood the test of time. Many of the 'new' challenges of today, such as the competition and co-ordination of an ever-increasing plethora of international dispute settlement mechanisms, resemble similar challenges of past eras. Thus, looking back may occasionally provide viable solutions to contemporary challenges.

By tackling these questions in a thorough and sophisticated manner and from theoretical as well as practical perspectives, this book offers a welcome addition to international legal scholarship on the settlement of international disputes. This collection stands out for the breadth of the analysis covering the most salient issues of international dispute settlement today as well as for venturing into new areas in which the role of international dispute settlement is still underexplored. It features remarkable contributions from a variety of fields and an innovative conversation that will satisfy the curiosity of both researchers and policymakers wishing to engage in the debate over the present and future role of dispute settlement within the international legal system. By continuing the tradition of excellence in international dispute settlement scholarship, the book is also a commendable and lasting tribute to the memory of Professor John Merrills.

Judge James Crawford
The Hague

Acknowledgements

This book is dedicated to the memory of Professor John Merrills, a trusted friend and colleague who worked at the University of Sheffield School of Law for over forty years. John was a leading scholar in the field of international dispute settlement and published widely in this area. In the months following his death, we thought it would be a fitting tribute to John to organise a memorial conference exploring the prospects and challenges for international dispute settlement. The conference was held at the University of Sheffield in December 2019 and generously supported by a grant from the Society of Legal Scholars. This edited collection expands on the themes and issues presented at the conference.

We wish to thank the contributors for their excellent chapters. We also wish to thank the late Judge James Crawford for writing a foreword for this collection while expressing our sadness at his death in late May 2021. Additionally, we wish to thank Tina Coetzer for her excellent editorial assistance, Cambridge University Press for their patience and hard work, the Sheffield Centre for International and European Law at the University of Sheffield for its institutional and financial support, and John's family for their kindness throughout the project.

Table of Cases

ARBITRATION INSTITUTE OF THE STOCKHOLM CHAMBER OF COMMERCE

Charanne B.V. and Construction Investments S.A.R.L. v. *Spain* (Final Award of 21 January 2016) SCC Case No. 062/2012
Limited Liability Company AMTO v. *Ukraine* (Award of 26 March 2008) SCC Case No. 080/2005
Petrobart Limited v. *Kyrgyz Republic* (Award of 29 March 2005) SCC Case No. 126/2003

COURT OF JUSTICE OF THE EUROPEAN UNION

Case 11/70, *Internationale Handelsgesellschaft mbH* v. *Einfuhr- und Vorratsstelle für Getreide und Futtermittel* [1970] ECR 114
Case 120/78, *Rewe-Zentral AG* v. *Bundesmonopolverwaltung für Branntwein* [1979] ECR 649
Case 26/62, *NV Algemene Transport-en Expeditie Onderneming van Gend & Loos* v. *Netherlands Inland Revenue Administration* [1963] ECR 1
Case 6/64, *Flaminio Costa* v. *ENEL* [1964] ECR 585
Case 8/74, *Procureur du Roi* v. *Dassonville* [1974] ECR 837
Case 120/78, *Rewe-Zentral AG* v. *Bundesmonopolverwaltung für Branntwein* [1979] ECR 42
Case 333/14, *Scotch Whisky Association and Others* v. *Lord Advocate and the Advocate General for Scotland* [2015] ECR 845

EUROPEAN COURT OF HUMAN RIGHTS

Agrotexim and Others v. *Greece* App. No. 14807/89 (Judgment of 24 October 1995)

Al-Adsani v. *The United Kingdom*, App. No. 35763/97 (ECtHR, 21 November 2011)
Amat-G Ltd and Mebaghishvili v. *Georgia* App. No. 2507/03 (Judgment of 27 September 2005)
Animal Defenders International v. *The United Kingdom*, App. No. 48876/08 (ECtHR, 22 April 2013)
Baumann v. *Austria*, App. No. 76809/01 (ECtHR, 7 October 2004)
Calcerrada Fornieles and Cabeza Mato v. *Spain* 17512/90 (Decision of 6 July 1992) DR 73
Celniku v. *Grèce* App. No. 21499/04 (Judgment of 5 October 2007)
Cereceda Martin and Others v. *Spain* App. No. 16358/90 (Decision of 12 October 1992)
Chagos Islanders v. *United Kingdom*, App. No. 35622/04 (ECHR, 11 December 2012)
De Pace v. *Italy*, App. No, 22728/03 (1 December 2008)
Decision on the Competence of the Court to Give an Advisory Opinion (Decision of 2 June 2004) ECHR 2004-VI
Demir and Baykara v. *Turkey*, App. No. 34503/97 (ECtHR, 12 November 2008)
Ebanks v. *The United Kingdom*, App. No. 36822/06 (ECtHR, 26 January 2010)
ECtHR, *Advisory Opinions Concerning the Recognition in Domestic Law of a Legal Parent–Child Relationship between a Child Born through a Gestational Surrogacy Arrangement Abroad and the Intended Mother*, Request No. P16-2018-001 (Advisory Opinion of 10 April 2019)
Fédération Hellénique des Syndicats des Employés du Secteur Bancaire (OTOE) v. *Grèce*, Aoo. No. 72808/10 (Judgment of 6 December 2011)
Feldman and Slovyanskyy Bank v. *Ukraine*, App. No. 42758/05 (Judgment of 21 December 2017)
G.J. v. *Luxembourg*, App. No. 21156/93 (Judgment of 26 October 2000)
Gürdeniz v. *Turkey*, App. No. 59715/10 (Judgment of 18 March 2014)
International Bank for Commerce and Development AD and Others v. *Bulgaria*, App. No. 7031/05 (Judgment of 2 June 2016)
James and Others v. *The United Kingdom*, App. No. 8793/79 [1986] ECHR 2 (21 February 1986)
Jones and Others v. *The United Kingdom*, App. Nos. 34356/06 and 40528/06 (14 January 2014)
Joseph Peraldi v. *France*, App. No. 2096/05 (Judgment of 7 April 2009)
Jovanović v. *Serbia*, App. No. 32299/08 (ECtHR, 2 October 2012)
Karoussiotis v. *Portugal*, App. No. 23205/08 (Judgment of 1 February 2011)
Lalmahomed v. *The Netherlands*, App. No. 26036/08 (ECtHR, 22 February 2011)
Lautsi and Others v. *Italy*, App. No. 30814/06 (ECtHR, 18 March 2011)
Lekić v. *Slovenia*, App. No. 36480/07 (Judgment of 11 December 2018)

Mata Estevez v. *Spain*, App. No. 56501/00 (ECtHR, 10 May 2001)
Meltex Ltd and Mesrop Movsesyan v. *Armenia*, App. No. 32283/04 (Judgment of 17 June 2008)
Naït-Liman v. *Switzerland*, App. No. 51357/07 (ECtHR, 15 March 2018)
OAO Neftyanaya Kompaniya Yukos v. *Russian Federation*, App. No. 14902/04 (Admissibility, 23 April 2004)
OAO Neftyanaya Kompaniya Yukos v. *Russian Federation*, App. No. 14902/04 (Judgment of 20 September 2011)
OAO Neftyanaya Kompaniya Yukos v. *Russian Federation* , App. No. 14902/04 (Just Satisfaction of 31 July 2014)
Patera v. *Czech Republic*, App. No. 25326/03 (Judgment of 10 January 2006)
Pauger v. *Austria*, App. No. 24872/94 (Decision of 9 January 1995) DR 80A
Perez v. *France*, App. No. 47287/99 (ECtHR, 12 February 2004)
Pretty v. *The United Kingdom*, App. No. 2346/02 (ECtHR, 29 April 2002)
Professional Trades Union for Prison, Correctional and Secure Psychiatric Workers and Others (POA and Others) v. *United Kingdom*, App. No. 59253/11 (Decision of 21 May 2013)
Savda v. *Turquie*, App. No. 42730/05 (Judgment of 12 June 2012)
Schalk and Kopf v. *Austria*, App. No. 30141/04 (ECtHR, 24 June 2010)
Selahattin Demirtaş v. *Turkey* (No. 2), App. No. 14305/17 (Judgment of 22 December 2020)
Smirnova v. *Russia*, App. No. 46133/99 and 48183/99 (3 October 2002)
Strand Lobben and Others v. *Norway*, App. No. 37283/13 (ECtHR, 10 September 2019)
Tomić and Others v. *Montenegro*, App. Nos. 18650/09, 18676/09, 18679/09, 38855/09, 38859/09, 38883/09, 39589/09, 39592/09, 65365/09 and 7316/10 (ECtHR, 17 April 2012)
Vesa Peltonen v. *Finland* (dec.), App. No. 19583/92 (20 February 1995)
VgT Verein gegen Tierfabriken v. *Switzerland*, App. No. 24699/94 (ECtHR, 28 June 2001)
Vladimirova v. *Russia*, App. No. 21863/05 (Judgment of 10 April 2018)

FRANCE

Cour de Cassation (France), Chambre Sociale, 24 Janvier 2001, 98-45.055

INTER-AMERICAN COURT OF HUMAN RIGHTS

Almonacid Arellano v. *Chile*, Judgment, IACtHR Series C No. 154 (26 September 2006)
Case of Genie Lacayo v. *Nicaragua*, Merits, IACtHR Series C No. 30 (13 September 1997)

INTERNATIONAL ARBITRATIONS

INTERNATIONAL CENTRE FOR SETTLEMENT OF INVESTMENT DISPUTES ARBITRATION

Apotex Holdings Inc. and Apotex Inc. v. *United States* (Award of 15 August 2014) ICSID ARB(AF)/12/1
Asian Agricultural Products Limited v. *Republic of Sri Lanka* (Award of 27 June 1990) ICSID ARB/87/3
BP America Production Co. and Others v. *Argentine Republic* (Decision on Preliminary Objections of 27 July 2006) ICSID ARB/04/8
El Paso Energy International Company v. *Argentine Republic* (Decision on Jurisdiction of 27 April 2006) ICSID ARB/03/15
Electrabel S.A. v. *Republic of Hungary* (Decision on Jurisdiction, Applicable Law and Liability of 30 November 2012) ICSID ARB/07/19
H&H Enterprises Investments, Inc. v. *Egypt* (Award of 6 May 2014) ICSID ARB/09/15
Impregilo S.p.A. v. *Islamic Republic of Pakistan* (Decision on Jurisdiction of 22 April 2005) ICSID ARB/03/3
M.C.I. Power Group L.C. and New Turbine Inc. v. *Republic of Ecuador* (Decision on Annulment of 19 October 2009) ICSID ARB/03/6
Mondev International Ltd. v. *United States* (Award of 11 October 2002) ICSID ARB(AF)/99/2
Orascom TMT Investments S.àr.l. v. *Algeria* (Award of 31 May 2017) ICSID ARB/12/35
Orascom TMT Investments S.àr.l. v. *Algeria* (Decision on Annulment of 17 September 2020) ICSID ARB/12/35
Pan American Energy LLC and BP Argentina Exploration Company v. *Argentine Republic* (Decision on Preliminary Objections, 27 July 2006) ICSID ARB/03/13
Pantechniki S.A. Contractors & Engineers v. *Albania* (Award of 30 July 2009) ICSID ARB/07/21
Phoenix Action, Ltd v. *The Czech Republic* (Award of 15 April 2009) ICSID ARB/06/5
Rumeli Telekom A.S. v. *Kazakhstan* (Award of 29 July 2008) ICSID ARB/05/16
Saipem v. *People's Republic of Bangladesh* (Award of 30 June 2009) ICSID ARB/05/7
Salini Costruttori S.p.A. and Italstrade S.p.A. v. *Jordan* (Decision on Jurisdiction of 9 November 2004) ICSID ARB/02/13
Sempra Energy International v. *Argentine Republic* (Award of 28 September 2007) ICSID ARB/02/16
SGS Société Générale de Surveillance S.A. v. *Republic of the Philippines* (Decision on Jurisdiction of 29 January 2004) ICSID ARB/02/6
Supervision y Control S.A. v. *Costa Rica* (Award of 18 January 2017) ICSID ARB/12/4
Técnicas Medioambientales Tecmed, S.A. v. *Mexico* (Award of 29 May 2003) ICSID ARB (AF)/00/2

Tradex Hellas S.A. v. *Republic of Albania* (Decision on Jurisdiction of 24 December 1996) ICSID ARB/94/2
Unión Fenosa Gas, S.A. v. *Arab Republic of Egypt* (Award of 31 August 2018) ICSID ARB/14/4
Vattenfall AB and Others v. *Federal Republic of Germany* (Recommendation on the Proposal to Disqualify the Tribunal of 4 March 2019) ICSID ARB/12/12
Venezuela Holdings BV (Formerly Mobil Corporation) v. *Bolivarian Republic of Venezuela* (Decision on Jurisdiction of 10 June 2010) ICSID ARB/07/27
Víctor Pey Casado and President Allende Foundation v. *Republic of Chile* (Award of 8 May 2008) ICSID ARB/98/2*Ampal-American Israel Corporation and Others* v. *Egypt* (Jurisdiction of 1 February 2016) ICSID ARB/12/11

PERMANENT COURT OF INTERNATIONAL JUSTICE AND INTERNATIONAL COURT OF JUSTICE

Accordance with International Law of the Unilateral Declaration of Independence in Respect of Kosovo (Advisory Opinion) [2010] ICJ Rep. 403
Aerial Incident of 10 August 1999 (Pakistan v. *India)* (Jurisdiction, Judgment) [2000] ICJ Rep. 12
Ahmadou Sadio Diallo (Republic of Guinea v. *Democratic Republic of the Congo)* (Merits, Judgment) [2010] ICJ Rep. 639
Allegations of Genocide under the Convention on the Prevention and Punishment of the Crime of Genocide (Ukraine v. *Russian Federation)* (Request for the Indication of Provisional Measures, Order), 16 March 2022
Alleged Violations of Sovereign Rights and Maritime Spaces in the Caribbean Sea (Nicaragua v. *Colombia)* (Preliminary Objections, Judgment) [2016] ICJ Rep. 32
Alleged Violations of the 1955 Treaty of Amity, Economic Relations, and Consular Rights (Islamic Republic of Iran v. *United States of America)* (Preliminary Objections, Judgment) [2021] ICJ Rep. 9
Application of the Convention on the Prevention and Punishment of the Crime of Genocide (Bosnia and Herzegovina v. *Serbia and Montenegro)* (Judgment) [2007] ICJ Rep. 43
Application of the Convention on the Prevention and Punishment of the Crime of Genocide (Bosnia and Herzegovina v. *Serbia and Montenegro)* (Order) [1993] ICJ Rep. 325
Application of the Convention on the Prevention and Punishment of the Crime of Genocide (Croatia v. *Serbia)* (Preliminary Objections, Judgment) [2008] ICJ Rep. 412
Application of the Convention on the Prevention and Punishment of the Crime of Genocide (The Gambia v. *Myanmar)* (Application Instituting Proceedings and Request for the Indication of Provisional Measures), 11 November 2019

Application Instituting Proceedings and Application for Provisional Measures (Republic of Armenia v. *Republic of Azerbaijan*) Vol. I, 16 September 2021

Application of the Interim Accord of 13 September 1995 (Former Yugoslav Republic of Macedonia v. *Greece)* (Judgment) [2011] ICJ Rep. 644

Application of the International Convention on the Elimination of All Forms of Racial Discrimination (Georgia v. *Russian Federation)* (Preliminary Objections, Judgments) [2011] ICJ Rep. 70

Application of the International Convention on the Elimination of All Forms of Racial Discrimination (Qatar v. *United Arab Emirates)* (Preliminary Objections, Judgment) [2021] ICJ Rep. 71

Application of the International Convention on the Elimination of All Forms of Racial Discrimination (Qatar v. *United Arab Emirates)* (Provisional Measures, Order) [2018] ICJ Rep. 406

Application of the International Convention on the Elimination of All Forms of Racial Discrimination (Qatar v. *United Arab Emirates)* (Provisional Measures, Order of 14 June 2019) [2019] ICJ Rep. 361

Application of the International Convention for the Suppression of the Financing of Terrorism and of the International Convention on the Elimination of All Forms of Racial Discrimination (Ukraine v. *Russian Federation)* (Application Instituting Proceedings), 16 January 2017

Application of the International Convention on the Suppression of International Terrorism and of the International Convention on the Elimination of All Forms of Racial Discrimination (Ukraine v. *Russian Federation)* (Preliminary Objections, Judgment) [2019] ICJ Rep. 558

Application of the International Convention on the Suppression of International Terrorism and of the International Convention on the Elimination of All Forms of Racial Discrimination (Ukraine v. *Russian Federation)* (Provisional Measures, Order) [2017] ICJ Rep. 104

Arbitral Award of 3 October 1899 (Guyana v. *Venezuela)* (Jurisdiction of the Court, Judgment) [2020] ICJ Rep. 455

Armed Activities on the Territory of the Congo (New Application: 2002) (Democratic Republic of the Congo v. *Rwanda)* (Jurisdiction and Admissibility, Judgment) [2002] ICJ Rep. 6

Asylum Case (Colombia v. *Peru)* (Judgment) [1950] ICJ Rep. 266

Border and Transborder Armed Actions (Nicaragua v. *Honduras)* (Jurisdiction and Admissibility, Judgment) [1988] ICJ Rep. 69

Case of Certain Norwegian Loans (France v. *Norway)* (Preliminary Measures) [1957] ICJ Rep. 9

Case Concerning Armed Activities on the Territory of the Congo (Democratic Republic of the Congo v. *Uganda)* (Judgment) [2005] ICJ Rep. 168

Case Concerning Certain German Interests in Polish Upper Silesia (Germany v. *Polish Republic)* (The Merits) [1926] PCIJ Rep. Series A No. 7

Case Concerning the Factory at Chorzow (Germany v. *Poland)* (Merits) [1928] PCIJ Rep. Series A No. 9

Case Concerning the Gabčíkovo-Nagymaros Project (Hungary v. *Slovakia)* (Judgment) [1997] ICJ Rep. 7

Case Concerning the Land and Maritime Boundary between Cameroon and Nigeria (Cameroon v. *Nigeria: Equatorial Guinea Intervening)* (Preliminary Objections, Judgment) [1998] ICJ Rep. 315

Case Concerning Military and Paramilitary Activities in and against Nicaragua (Nicaragua v. *United States of America)* (Merits, Judgment) [1986] ICJ Rep. 14

Case Concerning the Northern Cameroons (Cameroon v. *United Kingdom)* (Judgment) [1963] ICJ Rep. 15

Case Concerning Oil Platforms (Islamic Republic of Iran v. *United States of America)* (Judgment) [2003] ICJ Rep. 161

Case Concerning Pulp Mills on the River Uruguay (Argentina v. *Uruguay)* (Judgment) [2010] ICJ Rep. 14

Case of the Free Zones of Upper Savoy and the District of Gex (Order of 19 August 1929) PCIJ Rep. Series A No. 22

Certain Activities Carried Out by Nicaragua in the Border Area (Costa Rica v. *Nicaragua)* (Compensation, Judgment) [2018] ICJ Rep. 1

Certain Activities Carried Out by Nicaragua in the Border Area (Costa Rica v. *Nicaragua) and Construction of a Road in Costa Rica along the San Juan River (Nicaragua* v. *Costa Rica)* [2015] ICJ Rep. 665

Certain Expenses of the United Nations (Advisory Opinion) [1962] ICJ Rep. 151

Certain German Interests in Polish Upper Silesia (Germany v. *Poland)* [1926] PCIJ Rep. Series A No. 7

Certain German Interests in Polish Upper Silesia (Germany v. *Poland)* (Preliminary Objections, Judgment of 25 August 1925) PCIJ Rep. Series A No. 6

Certain German Interests in Polish Upper Silesia (Preliminary Objections, Judgment of 25 August 1925) PCIJ Rep. Series A No. 6

Certain Phosphate Lands in Nauru (Nauru v. *Australia)* (Preliminary Objections) [1992] ICJ Rep. 240

Certain Phosphate Lands in Nauru (Nauru v. *Australia)* (Preliminary Objections, Judgment) [1992] ICJ Rep. 240

Certain Property (Liechtenstein v. *Germany)* (Judgment) [2005] ICJ Rep. 6

Certain Questions of Mutual Assistance in Criminal Matters (Djibouti v. *France)* (Judgment) [2008] ICJ Rep. 177

Conditions of Admission of a State to Membership in the United Nations (Advisory Opinion) [1948] ICJ Rep. 57

Continental Shelf (Libya v. *Malta)* (Application by Italy for Permission to Intervene) [1984] ICJ Rep. 3

Corfu Channel Case (United Kingdom of Great Britain and Northern Ireland v. *Albania)* (Judgment) [1949] ICJ Rep. 4
Dispute over the Status and Use of the Waters of the Silala (Chile v. *Bolivia)* (Judgment of 1 December 2022) ICJ (to be published)
East Timor (Portugal v. *Australia)* (Judgment) [1995] ICJ Rep. 90
Electricity Company of Sofia and Bulgaria (Belgium v. *Bulgaria)* (Preliminary Objections, Judgment) [1939] PCIJ Rep. Series A/B No. 77
Factory at Chorzów [1928] PCIJ Rep. Series A No. 17
Fisheries Jurisdiction (Spain v. *Canada)* (Jurisdiction, Judgment) [1998] ICJ Rep. 432
Fisheries Jurisdiction Case (United Kingdom v. *Iceland)* (Merits, Judgment) [1974] ICJ Rep. 3
Frontier Dispute (Burkina Faso v. *Niger)* (Judgment) [2013] ICJ Rep. 44
Gabčikovo-Nagymaros Project (Hungary v. *Slovakia)* [1997] ICJ Rep. 7
Interpretation of the Agreement of 25 March 1951 between the WHO and Egypt (Advisory Opinion) [1980] ICJ Rep 73
Interpretation of Judgments Nos. 7 and 8 (The Chorzów Factory) [1927] PCIJ Rep. Series A No. 13
Interpretation of Peace Treaties (Second Phase) (Advisory Opinion) [1950] ICJ Rep. 221
Interpretation of Peace Treaties with Bulgaria, Hungary and Romania (Advisory Opinion) (First Phase) [1950] ICJ Rep. 65
Jadhav Case (India v. *Pakistan)* (Judgment) [2019] ICJ Rep. 418
Jurisdictional Immunities of the State (Germany v. *Italy, Greece Intervening)* (Judgment) [2012] ICJ Rep. 99
Legal Consequences of the Construction of a Wall in the Occupied Palestinian Territory (Advisory Opinion) [2004] ICJ Rep. 136
Legal Consequences of the Separation of the Chagos Archipelago from Mauritius in 1965 (Advisory Opinion) [2019] ICJ Rep. 95
Legal Consequences for States of the Continued Presence of South Africa in Namibia (South West Africa) Notwithstanding Security Council Resolution 276 (1970) (Advisory Opinion) [1971] ICJ Rep. 16
Legality of the Threat or Use of Nuclear Weapons (Advisory Opinion) [1996] ICJ Rep. 226
Maritime Delimitation in the Black Sea (Romania v. *Ukraine)* (Judgment) [2009] ICJ Rep. 61
Maritime Delimitation in the Indian Ocean (Somalia v. *Kenya)* (Judgment) [2021] ICJ Rep. 206
Maritime Delimitation and Territorial Questions between Qatar and Bahrain (Qatar v. *Bahrain)* (Jurisdiction and Admissibility, Judgment) [1994] ICJ Rep. 112
Mavrommatis Palestine Concessions (Greece v. *Great Britain)* (Judgment) [1924] PCIJ Rep. Series A No. 2

Monetary Gold Removed from Rome in 1943 (Italy v. *France, United Kingdom and United States of America)* (Preliminary Question) [1954] ICJ Rep. 19
Nationality Decrees Issued in Tunis and Morocco (Advisory Opinion) [1923] PCIJ Rep. Series B No. 4
North Sea Continental Shelf (Federal Republic of Germany v. *Denmark; Federal Republic of Germany* v. *Netherlands)* (Judgment) [1969] ICJ Rep. 3
Nuclear Tests (New Zealand v. *France)* (Judgment) [1974] ICJ Rep. 457
Obligation to Negotiate Access to the Pacific Ocean (Bolivia v. *Chile)* (Judgment) [2018] ICJ Rep. 507
Obligations Concerning Negotiations Relating to Cessation of the Nuclear Arms Race and to Nuclear Disarmament (Marshall Islands v. *United Kingdom)* (Preliminary Objections, Judgment) [2016] ICJ Rep. 833
Oil Platforms (Islamic Republic of Iran v. *United States of America)* (Preliminary Objections, Judgment) [1996] ICJ Rep. 13
Phosphates in Morocco (Italy v. *France)* (Preliminary Objections, Judgment) [1938] PCIJ Rep. Series A/B No. 74
Pulp Mills on the River Uruguay (Argentina v. *Uruguay)* [2010] ICJ Rep. 14
Question of the Delimitation of the Continental Shelf between Nicaragua and Colombia beyond 200 Nautical Miles from the Nicaraguan Coast (Nicaragua v. *Colombia)* (Preliminary Objections, Judgment) [2016] ICJ Rep. 100
Questions Relating to the Obligation to Prosecute or Extradite (Belgium v. *Senegal)* (Judgment) [2012] ICJ Rep. 442
Questions Relating to the Obligation to Prosecute or Extradite (Belgium v. *Senegal)* (Order on Provisional Measures) [2009] ICJ Rep 139
Relocation of the United States Embassy to Jerusalem (Palestine v. *United States of America)* (Order of 15 November 2018) [2018] ICJ Rep. 708
Request for Interpretation of the Judgment of 15 June 1962 in the Case Concerning the Temple of Preah Vihear (Cambodia v. *Thailand)* (Judgment) [2013] ICJ Rep. 281
Request for Interpretation of the Judgment of 31 March 2004 in the Case Concerning Avena and Other Mexican Nationals (Mexico v. *United States of America*) (Provisional Measures) [2008] ICJ Rep. 3
Right of Passage over Indian Territory (Portugal v. *India)* (Merits, Judgment) [1960] ICJ Rep. 6
South West Africa Cases (Ethiopia v. *South Africa; Liberia* v. *South Africa) Second Phase* (Judgment) [1966] ICJ Rep. 6
South West Africa Cases (Ethiopia v. *South Africa; Liberia* v. *South Africa)* (Preliminary Objections, Judgment) [1962] ICJ Rep. 319
Sovereignty over Pedra Branca/Pulau Batu Puteh, Middle Rocks and South Ledge (Malaysia v. *Singapore)* (Judgment) [2008] ICJ Rep. 12
Status of Eastern Carelia (Advisory Opinion) [1923] PCIJ Rep. Series B No. 5
Western Sahara (Advisory Opinion) [1975] ICJ Rep. 12

Whaling in the Antarctic (Australia v. *Japan: New Zealand Intervening)* [2014] ICJ Rep. 226

INTERNATIONAL CRIMINAL COURT

Situation in Darfur, Sudan, The Prosecutor v. *Omar Hassan Ahmad Al-Bashir* (Judgment in the *Jordan Referral re Al-Bashir* of 6 May 2019) ICC-02/05-01/09-397

Situation in the Democratic Republic of the Congo, Prosecutor v. *Bosco Ntaganda* (Corrigendum to the 'Defence submissions on the scheduled oral hearing', 5 May 2020, ICC-01/04-02/06-2524) ICC-01/04-02/06

Situation in the Republic of Mali, Prosecutor v. *Al Hassan* (Registry's observations on methods of work to minimise the impact of COVID-19 and related measures on the conduct of proceedings (ICC-01/12-01/18-776), 20 May 2020) ICC-01/12-01/18

INTERNATIONAL CRIMINAL TRIBUNAL FOR THE FORMER YUGOSLAVIA

Prosecutor v. *Dražen Erdemović* (Sentencing Judgment) ICTY-96-22-T*bis* (5 March 1998)

Prosecutor v. *Kordić and Čerkez* (Judgment) ICTY-95-14/2-A (17 December 2004)

Prosecutor v. *Milorad Krnojelac* (Judgment) ICTY-97-25-T (15 March 2002)

Prosecutor v. *Tadić* (Decision on Interlocutory Motion on Jurisdiction) ICTY-94-1 (2 October 1995)

INTERNATIONAL TRIBUNAL FOR THE LAW OF THE SEA

ARA *Libertad Case (Argentina* v. *Ghana)* (Provisional Measures, Order of 15 December 2012) ITLOS Reports 2012, 332

The 'Arctic Sunrise' Case (Kingdom of the Netherlands v. *Russian Federation), Provisional Measures* (Order of 22 November 2013), ITLOS Reports 2013, 230

Delimitation of the Maritime Boundary between Mauritius and Maldives in the Indian Ocean (Mauritius v. *Maldives)* (Judgment on Preliminary Objections, Judgment of 28 January 2021) (to be published)

Dispute Concerning Delimitation of the Maritime Boundary in the Bay of Bengal (Bangladesh v. *Myanmar)* (Judgment of 14 March 2012) ITLOS Reports 2012, 4

Dispute Concerning Delimitation of the Maritime Boundary between Ghana and Côte d'Ivoire in the Atlantic Ocean (Ghana v. *Côte d'Ivoire)* ITLOS Reports 2015, 122

M/V 'Louisa' Case (Saint Vincent and the Grenadines v. *Spain)* (Judgment of 28 May 2013) ITLOS Reports 2013, 4

M/V 'Norstar' Case (Panama v. *Italy)* (Preliminary Objections, Judgment of 4 November 2016) ITLOS Reports 2016, 44

M/V 'Norstar' Case (Panama v. *Italy)* (Judgment of 10 April 2019) ITLOS Reports 2018–19, 10

M/V 'Saiga' (No. 2) (Saint Vincent and the Grenadines v. *Guinea)* (Judgment of 1 July 1999) ITLOS Reports 1999, 10

M/V 'Virginia G' (Panama v. *Guinea-Bissau)* (Judgment of 14 April 2014) ITLOS Reports 2014, 4

MOX *Plant Case (Ireland* v. *United Kingdom)* (Provisional Measures, Order of 3 December 2001) ITLOS Reports 2001, 95

Request for Advisory Opinion Submitted by the Sub-regional Fisheries Commission (Advisory Opinion of 2 April 2015) ITLOS Reports 2015, 4

Responsibilities and Obligations of States Sponsoring Persons and Entities with Respect to Activities in the Area (Advisory Opinion of 1 February 2011) ITLOS Reports 2011, 10

Southern Bluefin Tuna Cases (New Zealand v. *Japan; Australia* v. *Japan)* (Provisional Measures, Order of 27 August 1999) ITLOS Reports 1999, 280

IRAN–UNITED STATES CLAIMS TRIBUNAL

Yeager v. *Islamic Republic of Iran*, 17 Iran-U.S. Cl. Trib. Rep. 92 (1987)

PERMANENT COURT OF ARBITRATION

The Arctic Sunrise Arbitration (Kingdom of the Netherlands v. *The Russian Federation)* (Award on Merits of 14 August 2015) PCA Case No. 2014-02

Chagos Marine Protected Area Arbitration (Mauritius v. *United Kingdom)* (Final Award of 18 March 2015) PCA Case No. 2011-03

Chagos Marine Protected Area Arbitration (Mauritius v. *United Kingdom)* (Dissenting and Concurring Opinion of Judges Kateka and Wolfrum of 18 March 2015) PCA Case No. 2011-03

Dispute Concerning Coastal State Rights in the Black Sea, Sea of Azov, and Kerch Strait (Ukraine v. *The Russian Federation)* PCA Case No. 2017-06 (pending)

Dispute Concerning the Detention of Ukrainian Naval Vessels and Servicemen (Ukraine v. *the Russian Federation)* PCA Case No. 2019-28

The 'Enrica Lexie' Incident (The Italian Republic v. *The Republic of India)* (Award of 21 May 2020) PCA Case No. 2015-28

The 'Enrica Lexie' Incident (The Italian Republic v. *The Republic of India)* (Concurring and Dissenting Opinion – Dr Sreenivasa Rao Pemmaraju of 21 May 2020) PCA Case No. 2015-28

The 'Enrica Lexie' Incident (The Italian Republic v. *The Republic of India)* (Dissenting Opinion – Judge Patrick Robinson of 21 May 2020) PCA Case No. 2015-28

Hulley Enterprises Ltd v. *Russian Federation* PCA Case No. 2005-03/AA226

Iron Rhine Arbitration (Belgium v. *Netherlands)* (Award of 24 May 2005) PCA Case No. 2003-2

MOX Plant Case (Ireland v. *United Kingdom)* (Order No. 3 of 24 June 2003) PCA Case No. 2002-01

MOX Plant Case (Ireland v. *United Kingdom)* (Order No. 6 of 6 June 2008) PCA Case No. 2002-01

Nord Stream 2 AG v. *European Union* (Claimant's Response to the EU's Request for a Preliminary Phase on Jurisdiction and Bifurcation of 16 October 2020) PCA Case No. 2020-07

Nord Stream 2 AG v. *European Union* (EU Memorial on Jurisdiction and Request for Bifurcation of 15 September 2020) PCA Case No. 2020-07

Nord Stream 2 AG v. *European Union* (Procedural Order No. 4 of 31 December 2020) PCA Case No. 2020-07

Philip Morris Asia Limited v. *The Commonwealth of Australia* (Award on Jurisdiction and Admissibility of 17 December 2015) PCA Case No. 2012-12

Republic of Ecuador v. *United States of America* (Award of 29 September 2012) PCA Case No. 2012-5

South China Sea Arbitration (Philippines v. *China)* (Award on Jurisdiction and Admissibility of 29 October 2015) PCA Case No. 2013-19

South China Sea Arbitration (Philippines v. *China)* (Award on Merits of 12 July 2016) PCA Case No. 2013-19

Timor Sea Conciliation (Timor-Leste v. *Australia)* (Decision on Australia's Objections to Competence of 19 September 2016) PCA Case No. 2016-10

Timor Sea Conciliation (Timor-Leste v. *Australia)* (Report and Recommendations of the Compulsory Conciliation Commission of 9 May 2018) PCA Case No. 2016-10

Veteran Petroleum Ltd v. *Russian Federation* PCA Case No. 2005-05/AA228

Yukos Universal Limited (Isle of Man) v. *Russian Federation* (Interim Award on Jurisdiction and Admissibility of 30 November 2009) PCA Case No. 2005-04/AA227

Yukos Universal Limited (Isle of Man) v. *Russian Federation* (Final Award of 18 July 2014) PCA Case No. 2005-04/AA227

UNCITRAL AD HOC TRIBUNAL

BG Group Plc. v. *The Republic of Argentina* (Final Award of 24 December 2007) UNCITRAL

CME Czech Republic B.V. v. *The Czech Republic* (Partial Award of 13 September 2001) UNCITRAL

CME Czech Republic B.V. v. *The Czech Republic* (Legal Opinion by Christoph Schreuer and August Reinisch of 20 June 2002) UNCITRAL

Glamis Gold, Ltd. v. *United States* (Final Award of 8 June 2009) NAFTA (UNCITRAL)

Methanex Corporation v. *The United States of America* (Decision of the Tribunal on Petitions form Third Persons to Intervene as 'Amici Curiae' of 15 January 2001) UNCITRAL

National Grid plc v. *The Argentine Republic* (Award of 3 November 2008) UNCITRAL

Ronald S. Lauder v. *The Czech Republic* (Final Award of 3 September 2001) UNCITRAL

THE UNITED KINGDOM

Benkharbouche v. *Secretary of State for Foreign and Commonwealth Affairs* [2017] UKSC 62

Chagos Islanders v. *Attorney-General and BIOT Commissioner* [2003] EWHC 2222 (QB)

Hutchinson v. *Newbury Magistrates' Court* (2000) ILR 499

Johnson v. *Gore Wood & Co.* [2002] 2 AC 1 (House of Lords)

R. v. *Bow Street Stipendiary Magistrate and Others, Ex Parte Pinochet Ugarte (Amnesty International and Others Intervening) (No. 3)* [1999] UKHL 17, [1999] 2 All ER 97

R. v. *Gul* [2012] EWCA Crim 280

R. v. *Jones (Margaret)* [2006] UKHL 16

R. v. *Secretary of State for the Home Department, Ex Parte Mullen* [2004] UKHL 18

R (Bancoult) v. *Secretary of State for Foreign and Commonwealth Affairs and Another (No. 1)* [2000] EWHC 413 (Admin)

R (Bancoult) v. *Secretary of State for Foreign and Commonwealth Affairs (No. 2)* [2008] UKHL 61

R (Bancoult) v. *Secretary of State for Foreign and Commonwealth Affairs (No. 3)* [2018] UKSC 3

R (Hoareau and Bancoult) v. *Secretary of State for Foreign and Commonwealth Affairs* [2020] EWCA Civ 1010

The Red Crusader Inquiry (Denmark v. *United Kingdom)* (1962) 35 ILR 485

THE UNITED STATES

Puerto Rico Maritime Shipping v. *Star Lines Ltd.*, 454 F. Supp. 368 (SDNY 1978)

Spector Motor Service Inc. v. *Walsh* 139 F. 2d 809 (2d Cir. 1944)

United States of America v. *Park Jin Hyok*, United States District Court for the Central District of California, Case No. MJ 18-1479, Criminal Complaint (8 June 2018)

United States of America v. *Yuriy Sergeyevich Andrienko et al.*, United States District Court for the Western District of Pennsylvania, Case No. 20-CR-316 (15 October 2020)

Willis-Knighton Medical Center v. *Caddo-Shreveport Sales and Use Tax Commission* 903 So. 2d 1071 (La. 2005)

WORLD TRADE ORGANIZATION

WTO, *Dominican Republic – Measures Affecting the Importation and Internal Sale of Cigarettes*, WT/DS302/AB/R (25 April 2005)

WTO, *European Communities – Measures Affecting Asbestos and Asbestos-Containing Products*, WT/DS135/AB/R (12 March 2001)

WTO, *European Communities – Measures Prohibiting the Importation and Marketing of Seal Products*, DS401/AB/R (22 May 2014)

WTO, *European Communities and Certain Member States – Measures Affecting Trade in Large Civil Aircraft*, WT/DS316/AB/R (18 May 2011)

WTO, *Japan – Taxes on Alcoholic Beverages II, Report of the Appellate Body* , WT/DS8/AB/R, WT/DS8/AB/R, WT/DS11/AB/R (4 October 1996)

WTO, *Korea – Measures Affecting Imports of Fresh, Chilled and Frozen Beef*, WT/DS169/AB/R (11 December 2000)

WTO, *United States – Import Prohibition of Certain Shrimp and Shrimp Products*, WT/DS58/AB/R (12 October 1998)

WTO, *United States – Measures Concerning the Importation, Marketing and Sale of Tuna and Tuna Products*, WT/DS381/AB/R (16 May 2012)

WTO, *United States – Stainless Steel (Mexico), Report of the Appellate Body* WT/DS344/AB/R (20 May 2008)

Table of International Instruments

Aarhus Convention (United Nations Economic Commission for Europe Convention on Access to Information, Public Participation in Decision-Making and Access to Justice in Environmental Matters), Aarhus, 25 June 1998, 2161 UNTS 447; (1999) 38 ILM 517

Acuerdo Tripartito Referente al Aprovechamiento hidroeléctrico del río Paraná (Argentina, Brazil, Paraguay: Agreement on Parana River Projects), 19 October 1979; (1980) 19 ILM 615

African Charter on Human and Peoples' Rights, Nairobi, 27 June 1981, 1520 UNTS 217

Agreement on the Co-operation for the Sustainable Development of the Mekong River Basin, Chiang Rai, 5 April 1995, 2069 UNTS 3

Agreement on the Establishment of the ASEAN Co-ordinating Centre for Humanitarian Assistance on Disaster Management, Bali, 17 November 2011

Agreement for the Establishment of the Commission of Small Island States on Climate Change and International Law, Edinburgh, 31 October 2021 (UN Registration No. 56940)

Agreement on the Establishment of the Zambezi Watercourse Commission, Kasane, 13 July 2004

Agreement Governing Activities of States on the Moon and Other Celestial Bodies, New York, 5 December 1979, 1363 UNTS 3

Agreement on the Guarani Aquifer between Argentina, Brazil, Paraguay, and Uruguay, San Juan, 2 August 2010

Agreement for the Implementation of the Provisions of the United Nations Convention on the Law of the Sea of 10 December 1982 Relating to the Conservation and Management of Straddling Fish Stocks and Highly Migratory Fish Stocks, New York, 4 August 1995, 2167 UNTS 88

Agreement on the Nile River Basin Co-operative Framework, Sharm el Sheikh, 13 April 2010 (not yet in force)

Agreement for the Prosecution and Punishment of the Major War Criminals of the European Axis, London, 8 August 1945, 82 UNTS 280

Agreement between the Republic of Kazakhstan, the Kyrgyz Republic, the Republic of Tajikistan, Turkmenistan, and the Republic of Uzbekistan on Co-operation in the Field of Joint Management on Utilisation and Protection of Water Resources from Interstate Sources, Almaty, 18 February 1992

Agreement on the Rescue of Astronauts, the Return of Astronauts, and the Return of Objects Launched into Outer Space, Washington, Moscow, London, 19 December 1967, 672 UNTS 119

Agreement to Resolve the Controversy over the Frontier between Venezuela and British Guiana, Geneva, 17 February 1966 (UN Registration No. 8192)

Agreement on Trade Facilitation, 27 November 2014, WT/L/940

Agreement on Trade-Related Aspects of Intellectual Property Rights, Marrakesh, 15 April 1994, 1869 UNTS 299

American Convention on Human Rights, San José, 22 November 1969, 1144 UNTS 143

American Treaty on Pacific Settlement, Bogota, 30 April 1948, 30 UNTS 55

The Antarctic Treaty, Washington, 1 December 1959, 402 UNTS 71

ASEAN Agreement on Disaster Management and Emergency Response, Vientiane, 26 July 2005

ASEAN Declaration on Mutual Assistance on Natural Disasters, Manila, 26 June 1976

ASEAN Protocol on Enhanced Dispute Settlement Mechanism, Vientiane, 29 November 2004

ASEAN Treaty on Amity and Co-operation in Southeast Asia, Bali, 24 February 1976, 1025 UNTS 297

Basel Convention on the Control of Transboundary Movements of Hazardous Wastes and Their Disposal, Basel, 22 March 1989, 1673 UNTS 126; (1989) 28 ILM 657

Charter of the Organisation of African Unity, Addis Ababa, 25 May 1963, 479 UNTS 39

Charter of the Organisation of American States, Bogota, 20 April 1948, 119 UNTS 3

Charter of the United Nations, San Francisco, 26 June 1945, 1 UNTS 16

Consolidated Versions of the Treaty on the Functioning of the European Union, Rome, 25 March 1957, [2012] OJ C326/47

Convention on Conciliation and Arbitration within the Conference on Security and Co-operation in Europe, Stockholm, 15 December 1992, 1842 UNTS 151

Convention for the Conservation of Southern Bluefin Tuna, Canberra, 10 May 1993, 1819 UNTS 359

Convention on Co-operation for the Protection and Sustainable Use of the Danube River, Sofia, 29 June 1994

Convention on Cybercrime, Budapest, 23 November 2001, ETS 185, 2296 UNTS 167

Convention on the Elimination of All Forms of Discrimination against Women, New York, 18 December 1979, 1249 UNTS 13
Convention Establishing an International Relief Union, Geneva, 12 July 1927, 135 UNTS 247
Convention for the Establishment of a European Space Agency, Paris, 30 May 1975, (1975) 14 ILM 864
Convention on International Liability for Damage Caused by Space Objects, Washington, Moscow, London, 29 March 1972, 961 UNTS 187
Constitution of the International Telecommunications Union, Geneva, 22 December 1992, 1825 UNTS 31251
Convention on International Trade in Endangered Species of Wild Fauna and Flora, Geneva, 3 March 1973, 993 UNTS 243; (1973) 12 ILM 1085; 27 UST 1087
Convention on the Law of the Non-navigational Uses of International Watercourses, New York, 21 May 1997, 2999 UNTS 77
Convention on the Law of the Sea Referring to United Nations Convention on the Law of the Sea, Montego Bay, 10 December 1982, 1833 UNTS 397
Convention on Long-Range Transboundary Air Pollution, Geneva, 13 November 1979, 1302 UNTS 217
Convention for the Pacific Settlement of International Disputes, The Hague, 29 July 1899, (1899) 187 CTS 410
Convention on the Prevention of Marine Pollution by Dumping of Wastes and Other Matters, London, 29 December 1972, 1046 UNTS 120; (1972) 11 ILM 1294
Convention on the Prevention and Punishment of the Crime of Genocide, Paris, 9 December 1948, 78 UNTS 277
Convention on the Prohibition of the Development, Production, Stockpiling, and Use of Chemical Weapons and on Their Destruction, Geneva, 3 September 1992, 1974 UNTS 45
Convention for the Protection of Human Rights and Fundamental Freedoms, Rome, 4 November 1950, 213 UNTS 221
Convention on the Protection of the River Rhine, Berne, 12 April 1999, L289 European Union Treaties Office 31
Convention on the Protection and Use of Transboundary Watercourses and International Lakes, Helsinki, 17 March 1992, 1936 UNTS 269
Convention on Registration of Objects Launched into Outer Space, New York, 12 November 1974, 1023 UNTS 15
Convention on the Rights of the Child, New York, 20 November 1989, 1577 UNTS 3
Convention on the Rights of Persons with Disabilities, New York, 13 December 2006, 2515 UNTS 3
Convention on the Settlement of Investment Disputes between States and Nationals of Other States, Washington DC, 18 March 1965, 575 UNTS 159; 17 UST 1270

Convention for the Suppression of Unlawful Acts against the Safety of Civil Aviation, Montreal, 23 September 1971, 974 UNTS 178

Convention against Torture and Other Cruel, Inhuman, or Degrading Treatment or Punishment, New York, 10 December 1984, 1465 UNTS 85

Council of Europe, Second Additional Protocol to the Cybercrime Convention Adopted by the Committee of Ministers of the Council of Europe, 17 November 2021

Covenant of the League of Nations, Versailles, 28 June 1919, (1919) 225 CTS 195

Cuenca del Plata Treaty, Brasilia, 23 April 1969

Energy Charter Treaty, Lisbon, 17 December 1994, 2080 UNTS 95

European Convention on Human Rights, Rome, 4 November 1950, 213 UNTS 222

European Union–Vietnam Free Trade Agreement (Hanoi, 30 June 2019) L 186 of 12 June 2020 OJ, 3-1400

Framework Agreement on the Sava River Basin, Kranjska Gora, 13 December 2002, UNTS 479

Framework Convention on Civil Defence Assistance, Geneva, 22 May 2000, 2172 UNTS 213

General Act of Arbitration (Pacific Settlement of International Disputes), Geneva, 26 September 1928, 93 LNTS 343

General Agreement on Tariffs and Trade, Geneva, 30 October 1947, 55 UNTS 187

Geneva Convention Relative to the Protection of Civilian Persons in Time of War, Geneva, 12 August 1949, 72 UNTS 287

Hague Convention on the Pacific Settlement of International Disputes, The Hague, 29 July 1899

Hague Convention on the Pacific Settlement of International Disputes, The Hague, 18 October 1907, (1907) 205 CTS 277

Indus Waters Treaty 1960 between the Government of India, the Government of Pakistan, and the International Bank for Reconstruction and Development, Karachi, 19 September 1960, 419 UNTS 125

International Covenant on Civil and Political Rights, New York, 16 December 1966, 999 UNTS 171

International Covenant on Economic, Social, and Cultural Rights, New York, 16 December 1966, 993 UNTS 3

International Convention on the Elimination of All Forms of Racial Discrimination, New York, 21 December 1965, 660 UNTS 195

International Convention for the Protection of All Persons from Enforced Disappearances, New York, 20 December 2006, 2716 UNTS 3

International Convention on the Protection of the Rights of All Migrant Workers and Members of Their Families, New York, 18 December 1990, 2220 UNTS 3

International Convention for the Regulation of Whaling, Washington, DC, 2 December 1946, 161 UNTS 72
Israeli–Palestinian Interim Agreement on the West Bank and the Gaza Strip, Washington, DC, 28 September 1995
Joint Declaration on ASEAN–UN Collaboration in Disaster Management, Ha Noi, 30 October 2010
Kyoto Protocol to the United Nations Framework Convention on Climate Change, Kyoto, 11 December 1997, 2303 UNTS 162
Marrakesh Agreement Establishing the World Trade Organization, Marrakesh, 15 April 1994, 1867 UNTS 154 (including the General Agreement on Trade in Services, Annex IB, and the Understanding on Rules and Procedures Governing the Settlement of Disputes, Annex 2)
Montreal Protocol on Substances That Deplete the Ozone Layer, Montreal, 16 September 1987, 1522 UNTS 3
Nile Basin Initiative Agreement, Entebbe, 22 February 1999
North American Free Trade Agreement, 17 December 1992, (1993) 32 ILM 296 and 605
Optional Protocol on the Compulsory Settlement of Disputes Relating to the Constitution of the International Telecommunications Union and to the Administrative Regulations, Geneva, 22 December 1992, 1825 UNTS 31251
Optional Protocol to the Convention against Torture and Other Cruel, Inhuman, and Degrading Treatment or Punishment, New York, 18 December 2002, 2375 UNTS 237
Paris Agreement, Paris, 12 December 2015, UN Doc. FCCC/CP/2015/L.9/Rev/1
Proclamation Defining Terms for Japanese Surrender, Potsdam, 26 July 1945 (Department of State Bulletin, XIII(318), 29 July 1945)
Protocol 1 to the Convention for the Protection of Human Rights and Fundamental Freedoms, Paris, 20 March 1952, ETS 9, 213 UNTS 262
Protocol Additional to the Geneva Conventions of 12 August 1949, and Relating to the Protection of Victims of International Armed Conflicts (Protocol I), Geneva, 8 June 1977, 1125 UNTS 3
Protocol Additional to the Geneva Conventions of 12 August 1949, and Relating to the Protection of Victims of Non-international Armed Conflicts (Protocol II), Geneva, 8 June 1977, 1125 UNTS 609
Protocol No. 11 to the Convention for the Protection of Human Rights and Fundamental Freedoms Restructuring the Control Machinery Established Thereby, Strasbourg, 11 May 1994, 2061 UNTS 12, 3 ETS 155
Ramsar Convention on Wetlands of International Importance Especially as Waterfowl Habitat, Ramsar, 2 February 1971, 996 UNTS 245; (1972) 11 ILM 963
Revised Protocol on Shared Watercourses of the South African Development Community, Windhoek, 7 August 2000

Rome Statute of the International Criminal Court, Rome, 17 July 1998, 2187 UNTS 3

Singapore Convention on Mediation/United National Convention on International Settlement Agreements Resulting from Mediation, New York, 20 December 2018

Statute of the International Atomic Energy Agency, New York, 26 October 1956, 276 UNTS 3

Statute of the International Court of Justice, San Francisco, 26 June 1945, 33 UNTS 993

Statutes of the International Red Cross and Red Crescent Movement, Geneva, October 1986

Tampere Convention on the Provision of Telecommunication Resources for Disaster Mitigation and Relief Operations, Tampere, 18 Jun 1998, 2296 UNTS 5

Treaty between Brazil and Paraguay Concerning the Hydroelectric Utilisation of the Water Resources of the Parana River Owned in Condominium by the Two Countries, from and Including the Salto Grande de Sete Quedas or Salto del Guairâ, to the Mouth of the Iguassu River, Brasilia, 26 April 1973 (UN Registration No. 13164)

Treaty between the Democratic Republic of Timor-Leste and Australia Establishing Their Maritime Boundaries in the Timor Sea, New York, 6 March 2018

Treaty on the Lesotho Highlands Water Project between the Government of the Kingdom of Lesotho and the Government of the Republic of South Africa, Maseru, 24 October 1986, 1462 UNTS 24808

Treaty on Principles Governing the Activities of States in the Exploration and Use of Outer Space, Including the Moon and Other Celestial Bodies, Washington, Moscow, London, 27 January 1967, 610 UNTS 205

Treaty of the South African Development Community, Windhoek, 17 August 1992

Treaty of Yacyreta between the Republic of Paraguay and the Argentine Republic, Asunción, 3 December 1973 (UN Registration No. 23141)

United Nations Convention on the Law of the Sea, Montego Bay, 10 December 1982, 1833 UNTS 397

United Nations Framework Convention on Climate Change, New York, 9 May 1992, 1771 UNTS 107; (1992) 31 ILM 849

Vienna Convention on the Law of Treaties, Vienna, 23 May 1969, 1155 UNTS 331; (1969) 8 ILM 679

Vienna Convention on the Protection of the Ozone Layer, Vienna, 22 March 1985, 1513 UNTS 323; (1987) 26 ILM 1529

Warsaw Treaty of Friendship, Co-operation, and Mutual Assistance, Warsaw, 14 May 1955, 219 UNTS 3

WTO, 'Multi-party interim appeal arbitration arrangement' (30 April 2020) WTO Doc JOB/DSB/1/ADD.12

Table of Legislation

LUXEMBOURG

Law of 20 July 2017 on the Exploration and Use of Space Resources, Official Journal, Mémorial A No. 674 (28 July 2017)

THE UNITED KINGDOM

Criminal Justice Act 1988
Human Rights Act 1998
Supreme Court Act 1981

THE UNITED STATES

Clarifying Lawful Overseas Use of Data Act of 2018, Public Law 115–141 (23 March 2018)
Commercial Space Launch Competitiveness Act of 2015, Public Law 114–90 (25 November 2015)

Abbreviations

AADMER	ASEAN Agreement on Disaster Management and Emergency Response
ABAJ	*American Bar Association Journal*
ACHPR	African Charter on Human and Peoples' Rights
ACWL	Advisory Centre on WTO Law
ADR	alternative dispute resolution
AHA/AHA Centre	ASEAN Co-ordinating Centre for Humanitarian Assistance
AIA	autonomous institutional arrangement
AJIL	*American Journal of International Law*
Am Econ Rev	*American Economic Review*
Am Pol Sc Rev	*American Political Science Review*
AMC	Asteroid Mining Corporation Ltd (UK)
Arb Int'l	*Arbitration International*
ARSIWA	Articles on the Responsibility of States for Internationally Wrongful Acts
ASEAN	Association of Southeast Asian Nations
Asian JIL	*Asian Journal of International Law*
ASIL Proceedings	*Proceedings of the Annual Meeting* (American Society of International Law)
ASR	Articles on State Responsibility
ATF	Agreement on Trade Facilitation
Aus YBIL	*Australian Yearbook of International Law*
Aust ILJ	*Australian International Law Journal*
BCL Rev	*Boston College Law Review*
Berkeley J Int'l L	*Berkeley Journal of International Law*

BiH	Bosnia and Herzegovina
BIOT	British Indian Ocean Territory
BIT	bilateral investment treaty
Brook J Int'l L	*Brooklyn Journal of International Law*
Buff Hum Rts L Rev	*Buffalo Human Rights Law Review*
Buff L Rev	*Buffalo Law Review*
BYBIL	*British Yearbook of International Law*
CAT	Committee against Torture
CED	Committee on Enforced Disappearances
CEDAW	Committee on the Elimination of Discrimination against Women
CERD	International Convention on the Elimination of All Forms of Racial Discrimination
CERD Committee	Committee on the Elimination of Racial Discrimination
CESCR	Committee on Economic, Social, and Cultural Rights
Chi-Kent L Rev	*Chicago-Kent Law Review*
Chinese JIL	*Chinese Journal of International Law*
CIL	customary international law
CITES	Convention on International Trade in Endangered Species of Wild Fauna and Flora
CJEU	Court of Justice of the European Union
CJICL	*Cambridge Journal of International and Comparative Law*
CLCS	UN Commission on the Limits of the Continental Shelf
CLP	Current Legal Problems
CLRTAP	Convention on Long-Range Transboundary Air Pollution
CMW	Committee on Migrant Workers
Colum J Transnat'l L	*Columbia Journal of Transnational Law*
Colum L Rev	*Columbia Law Review*
Conn J Int'l L	*Connecticut Journal of International Law*
Contemp Sec Pol'y	*Contemporary Security Policy*
COP	Conference of the Parties
COPUOS	UN Committee on the Peaceful Uses of Outer Space
Cornell Int'l L J	*Cornell International Law Journal*
CRC	Committee on the Rights of the Child

CRPD	Committee on the Rights of Persons with Disabilities
DePaul L Rev	*DePaul Law Review*
DR	*Reports of Judgments and Decisions*
DRC	Democratic Republic of the Congo
DSB	dispute settlement body
DSU	dispute settlement understanding
Duke J Comp & Int'l L	*Duke Journal of Comparative and International Law*
Duke L J	*Duke Law Journal*
EC	European Commission
ECCC	Extraordinary Chambers in the Courts of Cambodia
ECHR	European Convention on Human Rights
ECOSOC	UN Economic and Social Council
ECT	Energy Charter Treaty
ECtHR	European Court of Human Rights
EEZ	exclusive economic zone
EGAS	Egyptian Natural Gas Holding Company
EGPC	Egyptian General Petroleum Corporation
EIA	environmental impact assessment
EJC	*European Journal of Criminology*
EJIL	*European Journal of International Law*
ELJ	*European Law Journal*
EPL	*European Public Law*
ESA	European Space Agency
EU	European Union
Fed Law	*The Federal Lawyer*
FET	fair and equitable treatment
FFM	fact-finding mechanism
Fordham Int'l L J	*Fordham International Law Journal*
Fordham L Rev	*Fordham Law Review*
FPS	full protection and security
FRD	Declaration on Principles of International Law Concerning Friendly Relations and Co-operation among States in Accordance with the Charter of the United Nations (Friendly Relations Declaration)
FTA	free trade area
FYBIL	*Finnish Yearbook of International Law*

Ga J Int'l & Comp L	*Georgia Journal of International and Comparative Law*
Ga L Rev	*Georgia Law Review*
GATS	General Agreement on Trade in Services
GATT	General Agreement on Tariffs and Trade
Geo Wash Int'l L Rev	*George Washington International Law Review*
Geo Wash L Rev	*George Washington Law Review*
GSO	Global Space Organisation
Hague YB Int'l L	*Hague Yearbook of International Law*
Harv Int'l L J	*Harvard International Law Journal*
Harv J L & Tech	*Harvard Journal of Law and Technology*
Harv L Rev	*Harvard Law Review*
H R L Rev	*Human Rights Law Review*
HRA	Human Rights Act
HRC	UN Human Rights Committee
HRLJ	*Human Rights Law Journal*
Hum Rts Q	*Human Rights Quarterly*
IACHR	Inter-American Commission of Human Rights
IACtHR	Inter-American Court of Human Rights
IAEA	International Atomic Energy Agency
IBA	International Bar Association
ICASA	International Court of Aviation and Space Arbitration
ICC	International Criminal Court
ICCBA	International Criminal Court Bar Association
ICCPR	International Covenant on Civil and Political Rights
ICESCR	International Covenant on Economic, Social, and Cultural Rights
ICJ	International Court of Justice
ICL	*International Criminal Law*
ICLQ	*International and Comparative Law Quarterly*
ICRC	International Committee of the Red Cross
ICS	Investment Court System
ICSID	International Centre for Settlement of Investment Disputes
ICTR	International Criminal Tribunal for Rwanda
ICTY	International Criminal Tribunal for the Former Yugoslavia

ICWC	International Centre for Water Cooperation
IDL	International Disaster Law
IDRL	International Disaster Response Law
IDS	International Dispute Settlement
IFRC	International Federation of Red Cross and Red Crescent Societies
IGO	Intergovernmental Organisation
IHL	International Humanitarian Law
IIIC	International Independent Investigative Committee
IIIM	International, Impartial, and Independent Mechanism to Assist in the Investigation and Prosecution of Persons Responsible for the Most Serious Crimes under International Law Committed in the Syrian Arab Republic since March 2011
IIT	Investigation and Identification Team
ILA	International Law Association
ILC	International Law Commission
ILR	*International Law Reports*
IMT	International Military Tribunal
Ind J Global Legal Studies	*Indiana Journal of Global Legal Studies*
Int C L Rev	*International Community Law Review*
Int'l J Hum Rts	*International Journal of Human Rights*
Int'l Org	*International Organization*
IOLR	*International Organizations Law Review*
IP	Internet Protocol
ISA	International Seabed Authority
ISDS	Investor–State Dispute Settlement System
Israel L Rev	*Israel Law Review*
Ital YB Int'l L	*Italian Yearbook of International Law*
ITLOS	International Tribunal for the Law of the Sea
ITU	International Telecommunications Union
J Common Mkt Stud	*Journal of Common Market Studies*
J Conflict Resol	*Journal of Conflict Resolution*
J Disp Resol	*Journal of Dispute Resolution*
J Int'l Arb	*Journal of International Arbitration*
J Int'l Econ L	*Journal of International Economic Law*
J L Econ & Org	*Journal of Law, Economics, and Organization*
J Peace Res	*Journal of Peace Research*

J Space L	*Journal of Space Law*
JC & SL	*Journal of Conflict and Security Law*
JEL	*Journal of Environmental Law*
JICJ	*Journal of International Criminal Justice*
JIDS	*Journal of International Dispute Settlement*
JILIR	*Journal of International Law and International Relations*
La L Rev	*Louisiana Law Review*
LCP	*Law and Contemporary Problems*
LHDA	Lesotho Highlands Development Authority
LHU	Lancaster House Undertakings
LJIL	*Leiden Journal of International Law*
Loy LA Int'l & Comp L Rev	*Loyola of Los Angeles International and Comparative Law Review*
Loy U Chi Int'l L Rev	*Loyola University Chicago International Law Review*
LPICT	*Law and Practice of International Courts and Tribunals*
LQR	*Law Quarterly Review*
MC12	12th WTO Ministerial Conference
MEA	Multilateral Environmental Agreement
MIC	Multilateral Investment Court
Mich J Intl L	*Michigan Journal of International Law*
Mich L Rev	*Michigan Law Review*
MINUSCA	UN Multidimensional Stabilisation Mission in the Central African Republic
MINUSMA	UN Multidimensional Integrated Stabilisation Mission in Mali
MLAT	Mutual Legal Assistance Treaty
MLR	*Modern Law Review*
MOP	Meeting of the Parties
MPA	Marine Protected Area
MPIA	Multiparty Interim Agreement
MSU	Mediation Support Unit
NAFTA	North American Free Trade Agreement
NASA	National Aeronautics and Space Administration
NATO	North Atlantic Treaty Organisation
NC J Int'l L & Com Reg	*North Carolina Journal of International Law and Commercial Regulation*

NC L Rev	*North Carolina Law Review*
NCP	Non-compliance Procedure
NCSC	National Cyber Security Centre
NGO	Non-governmental Organisation
NILR	*Netherlands International Law Review*
NSA	National Security Agency
NYIL	*Netherlands Yearbook of International Law*
NYU J Int'l L & Pol	*New York University Journal of International Law and Politics*
OAS	Organisation of American States
Ocean Dev & Int'l L	*Ocean Development and International Law*
ODR	Online Dispute Resolution
OECD	Organisation for Economic Cooperation and Development
OEWG	Open-Ended Working Group
OHCHR	UN Office of the High Commissioner for Human Rights
Ohio St J on Disp Resol	*Ohio State Journal on Dispute Resolution*
OJ	*Official Journal of the European Union*
OJLS	*Oxford Journal of Legal Studies*
OLA	UN Office of Legal Affairs
OPCW	Organisation for the Prohibition of Chemical Weapons
OSCE	Organisation for Security and Cooperation in Europe
OSIF	Open Source Information
OSINT	Open Source Intelligence
PCA	Permanent Court of Arbitration
PCIJ	Permanent Court of International Justice
Pol Res Q	*Political Research Quarterly*
Quest Int'l L	*Questions of International Law*
RBDI	*Revue Belge de Droit International*
Rev Fr Dr Const	*Revue Française de Droit Constitutionnel*
Rev Quebec Droit Int'l	*Revue Québécoise de Droit International*
RGDIP	*Revue General de Droit International Public*
SADC	Southern African Development Community
SCSL	Special Court for Sierra Leone
SPT	Subcommittee on Prevention of Torture
Stan L Rev	*Stanford Law Review*
TCTA	Trans-Caledon Tunnel Authority

Temp Int'l & Comp L J	*Temple International and Comparative Law Journal*
Tex Int'l L J	*Texas International Law Journal*
TRIPS	Agreement on Trade-Related Aspects of Intellectual Property Rights
TTIP	Transatlantic Trade and Investment Partnership
Tul Eur & Civ LF	*Tulane European and Civil Law Forum*
U Miami Inter-Am L Rev	*University of Miami Inter-American Law Review*
UAE	United Arab Emirates
UN	The United Nations
UN GGE	UN Group of Governmental Experts
UN OLA	UN Office of Legal Affairs
UNCAT	UN Convention against Torture and Other Cruel, Inhuman, and Degrading Treatment or Punishment
UNCITRAL	UN Commission on International Trade Law
UNCLOS	UN Convention on the Law of the Sea
UNCTAD	UN Conference on Trade and Development
UNDKPO	UN Department of Peacekeeping Operations
UNDRO	Office of the UN Disaster Relief Co-ordinator
UNECE	UN Economic Commission for Europe
UNESCAP	UN Economic and Social Commission for Asia and the Pacific
UNFCCC	UN Framework Convention on Climate Change
UNGA	UN General Assembly
UNISDR	UN Office for Disaster Risk Reduction
UNOCHA	UN Office for the Co-ordination of Humanitarian Affairs
UNODC	UN Office on Drugs and Crime
UNOOSA	UN Office for Outer Space Affairs
UNSC	UN Security Council
UNSG	UN Secretary-General
UNTAG	UN Transition Assistance Group
UNYBILC	*UN Yearbook of the International Law Commission*
USSR	Union of Soviet Socialist Republics
Va J Int'l L	*Virginia Journal of International Law*

Va L Rev	*Virginia Law Review*
Vand L Rev	*Vanderbilt Law Review*
VCLT	Vienna Convention on the Law of Treaties
Vill L Rev	*Villanova Law Review*
Wash L Rev	*Washington Law Review*
Windsor Y B Access Just	*Windsor Yearbook of Access to Justice*
World Dev	*World Development*
WTO	World Trade Organization
Yale J Int'l L	*Yale Journal of International Law*
Yale J World Pub Ord	*Yale Journal of World Public Order*
Yale L J	*Yale Law Journal*
ZaöRV	*Zeitschrift für Ausländisches Öffentliches Recht und Völkerrecht*

Introduction

RUSSELL BUCHAN, DANIEL FRANCHINI, AND NICHOLAS TSAGOURIAS

In the last solo-authored edition of his seminal book, *International Dispute Settlement*, the late Professor John Merrills wrote that 'the peaceful settlement of international disputes is the most critical issue of our time'.[1] To the casual reader, this statement may seem an exaggeration. Surely the environment and climate change, collective security, global health, human rights, and international trade and finance, among others, may appear to be more pressing issues today. And yet, having devoted most of his professional life to the advancement of legal scholarship on international dispute settlement, Merrills was acutely aware that the study of this discipline offers the most effective litmus test to assess the strengths and limitations of international law at any given time. International disputes naturally arise whenever international law subjects disagree on matters of law or fact. Alongside disputes concerning territory and the use of force, today we witness an exponential growth of disputes on issues as diverse as human rights, environment, trade, and investment. Disputes are also becoming more complex, involving multiple parties, norms, and dispute settlement mechanisms (diplomatic or adjudicatory). At the same time, international disputes and the process of dispute settlement can act as a catalyst for the enforcement but also the development of international law. Dispute settlement and its institutions reaffirm existing norms and stabilise legal relations, but can also contribute to the crystallisation of new norms or new interpretations of existing norms because international disputes and their processes of settlement may evidence gaps or shortcomings of existing norms.

[1] John G. Merrills, *International Dispute Settlement* (Cambridge: Cambridge University Press, 2017), p. 328. This statement has been retained in John G. Merrills and Eric De Brabandere, *Merrills' International Dispute Settlement* (Cambridge: Cambridge University Press, 2022), p. 437.

The settlement of international disputes is not a static phenomenon. It mutates according to the needs of its users – States and increasingly non-State actors[2] – and the needs of the international society, but is also influenced by the broader dynamics of world politics and international relations. Likewise, the scholarship on international dispute settlement is in constant evolution. The origins of international dispute settlement as a discrete field of international legal study – which occurred only in recent times,[3] also thanks to Merrills' work – coincided with the emergence of an unprecedented number of international courts and tribunals. The 'proliferation of international courts' quickly became a 'familiar trope' and brought with it increased interest in the process of 'judicialisation' of international law.[4] At present, the academic discourse largely focuses on the systematisation of the 'mosaic'[5] of international dispute settlement and on the assessment of the impact this would have on international law as a whole.[6] One of its central preoccupations is the effectiveness of the system of international adjudication.[7] The main challenge is the multiplication of international courts and tribunals, which can invariably increase the risk of conflicting outcomes and fragmentation, the avoidance of which requires some means of harmonisation.[8] Implicit also in scholarship is the conviction that the process of judicialisation of international

2 See Eric De Brabandere, 'Non-State actors and the proliferation and individualization of international dispute settlement', in Bob Reinalda (ed.), *The Ashgate Research Companion to Non-State Actors* (Oxford: Routledge, 2011), p. 347.

3 Thomas Schultz, 'Editorial' (2010) 1 J. Int'l Disp. Settlement 1–2 ('International dispute settlement has come to light in recent years as a new field of study').

4 Charles N. Brower and Daniel Litwin, 'Navigating the judicialization of international law in troubled waters: Some reflections on a generation of international lawyers' (2019) 37 Berkeley J Int'l L 171–92. See also Cesare P. R. Romano, 'The proliferation of international judicial bodies: The pieces of the puzzle' (1999) 31 JILP 709–51; Gleider Hernandez, 'The judicialization of international law: Reflections on the empirical turn' (2014) 25 EJIL 919–34.

5 See John G. Merrills, 'The mosaic of international dispute settlement procedures: Complementary or contradictory?' (2007) 54 NILR 361–93.

6 See, e.g., Duncan French, Matthew Saul, and Nigel D. White (eds.), *International Law and Dispute Settlement: New Problems and Techniques* (Oxford: Hart, 2010); Cesare P. R. Romano, Karen J. Alter, and Yuval Shany (eds.), *The Oxford Handbook of International Adjudication* (Oxford: Oxford University Press, 2013).

7 See, e.g., Yuval Shany, *Assessing the Effectiveness of International Courts* (Oxford: Oxford University Press, 2014); Karen J. Alter, *The New Terrain of International Law: Courts, Politics, Rights* (Princeton, NJ: Princeton University Press, 2014).

8 See Laurence Boisson De Chazournes, 'Plurality in the fabric of international courts and tribunals: The threads of a managerial approach' (2017) 28 EJIL 13–72; Yuval Shany, 'Plurality as a form of (mis)management of international dispute settlement: Afterword to Laurence Boisson de Chazournes' Foreword' (2017) 28 EJIL 1241–49.

law will ultimately have a positive effect as it will strengthen the legalisation of international governance.[9]

Yet, more recent publications have been characterised by a less optimistic outlook on the system of international adjudication.[10] The growth and diversification of international courts and tribunals regarding their subject matter jurisdiction, membership, and locus standi have gradually given rise to concerns about their 'authority' and, more broadly, their 'legitimacy'.[11] Critics have lamented the circumvention of democratic principles and questioned the opportunity of international adjudicators dealing with issues involving public interests such as health, the environment, and human rights. As Romano pointed out, this new preoccupation with questions of authority and legitimacy is not only 'the logical next step of an intellectual evolution' but 'may be the result of a fundamental anxiety caused by a radically changed context, one that has become considerably more hostile to the [international courts] enterprise'.[12] Fuelled by the resurgence of nationalism and protectionism and the fact that international dispute settlement is par excellence consensual, the mounting hostility towards the system of international adjudication has already exacted a price, resulting in the paralysis of the appellate body of the World Trade Organization (WTO).

The difficulties that international dispute settlement is currently facing, however, should not be overstated. If the system is in crisis, this may very well represent an opportunity to rethink some of its features and construct a more balanced system.[13] As will be seen, this may also bring about a renewed appreciation for non-judicial means of dispute settlement. Furthermore, it can invite us to reconsider the merits or demerits of jurisdictional substitution or of parallel proceedings. It can make us reflect more deeply on the role of domestic courts in international dispute settlement. It can finally direct our attention to consider the techniques that courts can use to maintain their authority and legitimacy. In our opinion, there is strategic unity in

9 See Hernandez, 'The judicialization', 923.

10 See, e.g., Andreas Føllesdal and Geir Ulfstein (eds.), *The Judicialization of International Law: A Mixed Blessing?* (Oxford: Oxford University Press, 2018).

11 See Karen J. Alter, Laurence R. Helfer, and Mikael Rask Madsen (eds.), *International Court Authority* (Oxford: Oxford University Press, 2018); Nienke Grossman, Harlan G. Cohen, Andreas Føllesdal, and Geir Ulfstein (eds.), *Legitimacy and International Courts* (Cambridge: Cambridge University Press, 2018); Freya Baetens (ed.), *Legitimacy of Unseen Actors in International Adjudication* (Cambridge: Cambridge University Press, 2019).

12 Cesare P. R. Romano, 'Legitimacy, authority, and performance: Contemporary anxieties of international courts and tribunals' (2020) 114 AJIL 149–63, 162.

13 See Robert McDougall, 'The crisis in WTO dispute settlement: Fixing birth defects to restore balance' (2018) 52 J World Trade 867–96.

international dispute settlement notwithstanding certain problems of coordination or the appearance of competition. There is no reason thus to doubt the resiliency of the system of international dispute settlement as a whole, which, for all its changes, has offered elements of continuity throughout its history.[14]

In the light of these developments, the editors of this volume set out to pay tribute to the life and work of John Merrills by investigating the dynamics of change and stability that have characterised, and continue to characterise, international dispute settlement. Our enquiry has three objectives. First, it takes stock of the changes that international dispute settlement underwent in recent years as a result of the multiplication and institutionalisation of various means of international dispute settlement as well as the ensuing challenges concerning fragmentation, coordination, and legitimacy.

Second, through the analysis of questions cutting across different regimes (law of the sea, environment, transboundary waters, investment, collective security, human rights, international criminal law, and international trade), this volume examines the evolving relationship between different means of dispute settlement, the degree of control that States exercise on how disputes are settled, the perception of individual institutions as to their role in the system of international dispute settlement, and the extent to which existing dispute settlement mechanisms have satisfactorily addressed the needs for which they were created.

Third, this volume sheds a light on the future of international dispute settlement. Contributors were asked to identify ways and make proposals as to how the system of international dispute settlement can address the challenges it is currently facing and how it can evolve and adapt in order to preserve peace and international legality. Several contributions have also been dedicated to examining whether the expansion of international law to new areas (disaster assistance, new technologies, space, and cyber) is creating the need for new dispute settlement institutions or the adaptation of existing ones.

This collection contains seventeen chapters and is structured in three parts. **Part I** examines recent trends and cross-cutting issues in international dispute settlement. In **Chapter 1**, Daniel Franchini and Russell Buchan examine the status, nature, content, and scope of the obligation of peaceful dispute settlement. This chapter traces the emergence of this obligation under customary and conventional international law, analyses the conditions that trigger its engagement, and explores what measures disputants must take in order to discharge this obligation. This chapter maintains that the peaceful settlement

[14] James Crawford, 'Continuity and discontinuity in international dispute settlement: An inaugural lecture' (2010) 1 J Int Disput Settl 3–24.

obligation is an interstitial norm insofar as it influences the interpretation and application of other rules of international law relevant to the peaceful settlement of disputes.

In **Chapter 2**, Tarcisio Gazzini and Alessandra Pietrobon focus on parallel proceedings in investment and human rights claims. This chapter examines how tribunals coordinate the exercise of their jurisdictions, how they should deal with the merits (including applicable law and issues of interpretation), and how they should avoid double recovery. The complex disputes related to *Yukos* are discussed with a view to formulating some tentative recommendations on how to manage parallel proceedings before the European Court of Human Rights and investment arbitral tribunals.

In **Chapter 3**, Kimberley N. Trapp and Jacob Smith examine the role of domestic courts in international dispute settlement. This chapter maps the variety of engagements by international dispute settlement bodies with the decisions and processes of domestic courts and explores how the particular institutional nature and contexts of international dispute settlement bodies may colour the nature and degree of that engagement. The chapter situates this engagement on a spectrum of deference to greater intrusion. It also provides an illustration of the factors that determine this engagement, including the degree of penetration of the international legal framework in domestic legal systems, the expectations that States have when submitting to means of dispute settlement, and the socio-legal context.

In **Chapter 4**, Massimo Lando focuses on the advisory jurisdiction of international courts and tribunals. This chapter explains that traditionally advisory opinions are not seen as a means of inter-State dispute settlement. However, it argues that recent developments justify reassessing this traditional view. This chapter claims that the most significant development in this context is the judgment on preliminary objections delivered by the Special Chamber of the International Tribunal for the Law of the Sea in the maritime dispute between Mauritius and Maldives, which gave binding effect to the determinations made by the International Court of Justice in its 2019 advisory opinion concerning the decolonisation of Chagos. This chapter evaluates the Special Chamber's decision by considering its impact on the *Eastern Carelia* doctrine and the *Monetary Gold* principle, as well as its implications for the legal effects of advisory opinions and for the legitimacy of exercising the advisory function.

Part II delves deeper into specific areas of dispute settlement, focusing on the challenges that several institutions have faced regarding their effectiveness, authority, and legitimacy. These contributions also investigate possible reforms to address these challenges. In **Chapter 5**, Richard Collins assesses the contribution of the United Nations Convention on the Law of the Sea's dispute settlement procedures to the resolution of maritime disputes. In particular, this chapter explains that recent decisions of the International Tribunal for the Law of the Sea (ITLOS) have grappled with a range of international legal issues that are not directly related to the law of the sea, including sovereignty, human rights, and sovereign immunities. This chapter observes that this development has led some commentators to criticise ITLOS for jurisdictional overreach. This chapter pushes back against this criticism. It argues that ITLOS' engagement with international law regimes going beyond the law of the sea is a necessary recognition of the integrated and interconnected nature of the modern international legal system and, ultimately, leads to a strengthening of the rule of law.

In **Chapter 6**, Malgosia Fitzmaurice examines the procedures and mechanisms for the peaceful settlement of environmental disputes. This chapter deals with the issue of classical settlement of environmental disputes and the relatively new and still evolving phenomenon of so-called non-compliance procedures, which are an element of the legal structure of the Multilateral Environmental Agreements and administered by the Conferences of the Parties/Meetings of the Parties. This chapter explores the legitimacy of these procedures and focuses in particular on the question of State consent. It explains that, while classical means of dispute settlement do not present questions of legitimacy, their inherent bilateralism is ill-suited for the protection of the environment. Non-compliance procedures may be a more effective tool in light of their multilateral nature, and recent trends based on co-operative efforts may eliminate questions of legitimacy to some degree.

In **Chapter 7**, Sir Malcolm D. Evans examines the role and legitimacy of international human rights mechanisms of dispute settlement. This chapter argues that the relationship between international dispute settlement and the work of the UN human rights treaty bodies is demonstrated by a series of cases brought by Qatar against the United Arab Emirates before both the International Court of Justice (ICJ) and the UN Committee on the Elimination of Racial Discrimination (CERD). This chapter explores some of the tensions which have been revealed concerning the interplay between the work of the CERD and that of the ICJ and how each responded to them. It notes that the multifaceted and *sui generis* nature of their work means that they do not operate in a single 'conceptual space' and that the nature of the treaty bodies, their role and function, and the environment in which they work need to be borne in mind if their work is to be properly appreciated, understood, and engaged with.

In **Chapter** 8, Maria A. Gwynn focuses on the settlement of water-related disputes in international law. This chapter evaluates agreements governing transboundary water resources from different regions of the world and highlights the different mechanisms of dispute settlement they provide. It argues that joint or international commissions play a key role in the settlement of water-related disputes. This chapter explores how the complementarity of different treaties, on the one hand, and international law, on the other, coupled with States' willingness to co-operate with one another, enables States to negotiate and resolve disputes amicably and according to the principles contained in the 1997 UN Watercourses Convention.

In **Chapter** 9, Eric De Brabandere zeroes in on the settlement of disputes in the context of investment arbitration. This chapter accepts that the case law of the current investor–State dispute settlement system is inconsistent and unpredictable and requires reform. However, this chapter claims that the problems associated with the dispute settlement system for investment arbitration cannot be isolated from broader questions on the coherence of general international law, the determinacy of legal norms, and the role of arbitral tribunals in the interpretation of these norms. The chapter argues that coherence can be seen as existing on a spectrum and that a 'middle ground' might be to consider that international investment law forms a part of international law, which is a coherent legal system from the perspective of the sources of the secondary norms of international law. Consistency, on the other hand, is not completely achievable in the current investment landscape, given its lack of uniformity in terms of substantive law and *ad hoc* method of dispute settlement. Consistency must be sought through different options, such as redrafting investment treaties to ensure better balance and predictability of outcomes.

In **Chapter** 10, Aris Georgopoulos and Petros C. Mavroidis examine the contribution of the WTO's dispute settlement body to the resolution of trade disputes. This chapter documents the problems and challenges faced by the WTO's dispute settlement body and reveals their debilitating impact on its work. This chapter then puts forward concrete proposals for the establishment of a new WTO Court and explains why such a course of action has a realistic chance of breaking the current impasse and creating an effective dispute settlement body for trade disputes.

In **Chapter** 11, Nigel D. White assesses the contribution of the UN's collective security system to the settlement of international disputes. This chapter tests the assumption that the Security Council's impartial law-based dispute settlement is neither achievable because of its political nature nor required by the UN Charter. This chapter analyses the provisions of the

Charter and the practices of the Security Council, looks for evidence of impartiality in both inter-State and intra-State disputes, as well as assesses the influence of peacekeeping mandated by the Council upon impartiality. This analysis shows that the concept of impartiality in peaceful settlement has largely disappeared and asks, in the conclusion, whether it is possible and desirable to (re)turn to impartiality.

In **Chapter 12**, James Mehigan focuses on the contribution of international criminal law (ICL) to the peaceful settlement of international disputes. More specifically, this chapter looks at the aims of ICL and analyses how effective it has been at achieving its international law and criminal law objectives. It argues that ICL has not made a broader contribution to dispute settlement as many commentators hoped for because ICL provides a form of retributive justice that does not necessarily engender a sense of justice for victims nor contribute to reconciliation or fact-finding. After looking at the impact of ICL in the former Yugoslavia, this chapter concludes that there is little evidence to show that ICL has achieved any of its aims other than individualising guilt and punishing offenders – in other words, ICL's contribution to the settlement of international disputes is minimal and should not be overstated.

Part III explores the opportunities for dispute settlement in new and fast developing fields. In **Chapter 13**, Therese O'Donnell brings together research literature from international law, disaster studies, and the mediation field to investigate the possibilities that mediation offers in the context of disaster assistance. This chapter argues that mediation is an untapped resource in the disaster milieu given its capacity for widening participation, contextual sensitivity and discretion, and proven success rate even in the most fraught environments. This chapter claims that mediation has the potential to facilitate partnered dispute resolution and create the conditions for paying heed to international legal standards of protection while reflecting notions of solidarity. Most importantly, it contends that mediation offers a route to avoid unhelpful political confrontation while ensuring that the needs of disaster-stricken populations are met in sustainable ways.

In **Chapter 14**, Rossana Deplano focuses on the peaceful settlement of outer-space disputes. This chapter argues that traditionally States have resorted to diplomatic, as opposed to legal, means for the settlement of disputes related to space activities. However, with the growing privatisation and commercialisation of space activities, this chapter avers that the current treaty framework for the settlement of space disputes is inadequate to cope with the demands of the present space industry. This chapter examines the principles governing the treaty framework for the settlement of space disputes as well as the existing dispute settlement mechanisms. It evaluates whether the apparently unstructured character of the UN treaty framework for dispute settlement is sufficient to deal with traditional and emerging space disputes, especially those stemming from space mining operations. An argument is made that, although there is no all-encompassing and binding dispute settlement process, a specialised dispute settlement system endowed with enforcement powers is not desirable.

In **Chapter 15**, Nicholas Tsagourias and Fiona Middleton examine the role of fact-finding in ascertaining the facts supporting cyber attribution claims. More specifically, the chapter considers the modalities of fact-finding, discusses the challenges it is encountering in the context of cyber attribution, and assesses the proposed cyber attribution mechanisms. It concludes by identifying certain key features a fact-finding mechanism should exhibit to perform its tasks effectively and contribute to the settlement of cyber attribution disputes.

In **Chapter 16**, Antonio Segura Serrano examines the potential for using new and emerging technologies to settle international disputes. This chapter considers how digital evidence can be gathered and evaluated by dispute settlement bodies. This chapter also analyses what role online dispute settlement bodies can play in the settlement of international disputes. In doing so, it assesses the practice of dispute resolution systems already in place for online transactions among individuals (both private and public systems) in order to identify any features that can be transposed to inter-State dispute settlement. This chapter concludes by explaining that these systems, in particular their use of algorithms and artificial intelligence, offer some important lessons for inter-State dispute settlement.

By way of conclusion to this edited collection, **Chapter 17** by Sir Michael Wood examines the future of international dispute settlement system. The core claim of this chapter is that continuity is, and will continue to be, this system's defining feature. The chapter observes that the fundamentals of inter-State disputes have changed little since 1920. Most notably, consent to third-party dispute settlement remains at the heart of the system, as does a widespread reluctance by sovereign States to give that consent prior to disputes arising. The Optional Clause, for example, remains unchanged after a hundred years, as does States' unwillingness to accept it or do so without extensive reservations. That said, and reflecting on the other chapters contained in this collection, this chapter accepts that there have been new and important developments in the international dispute settlement system in recent years, and providing their promise is realised, they will perform a critical function in maintaining peace, security, and stability in an increasingly contested world order.

Several common themes emerge from these contributions. To begin with, problems of coordination and fragmentation remain very much present in the current system of international dispute settlement and, to some extent, have been exacerbated by the availability of different fora for the settlement of complex disputes that straddle the subject matter specialisation of several institutions (Chapter 2). In fact, we are witnessing an increased tendency of dispute settlement bodies, such as ITLOS, to push the boundaries of their jurisdiction (Chapter 5). This only compounds questions of coordination of different means of dispute settlement as seen in the use of ICJ's advisory opinions by ITLOS (Chapter 4), in the engagement of IDS bodies with domestic court decisions (Chapter 3), and in the relationship between dispute settlement and the work of human right treaty bodies (Chapter 7). As the discussion on investment arbitration shows (Chapter 9), it can even be questioned whether consistency is a desirable objective under all circumstances and whether individual courts and tribunals are sufficiently equipped to achieve this.

All these issues raise questions as to the degree of control that States continue to exercise on how their disputes are settled and the legitimacy of the system of dispute settlement. These concerns are very much at the heart of the current crisis of WTO's dispute settlement system, and any credible prospect of reform must take them into account (Chapter 10). At the same time, recent developments may question whether the complete faith in the process of judicialisation of international law, which has characterised the dispute settlement discourse of the past decades, should be reconsidered. It is not at all clear that the perceived benefits in terms of effectiveness, predictability, and impartiality have fully materialised. This does not mean that the efforts to create a court-based system for the settlement of international disputes are devoid of merits, particularly when compared to the shortcomings of political means of dispute settlement such as the UN's collective security system (Chapter 11). However, not all international disputes must be decided by a court, and it may very well be the case that certain international courts, such as international criminal courts, are not engaged in any meaningful dispute settlement as traditionally intended (Chapter 12).

The backlash against international courts and tribunals has, to some extent, led to a renewed appreciation for non-judicial means of dispute settlement and other informal mechanisms to monitor compliance with international norms. This is particularly evident in the case of multilateral disputes concerning the environment (Chapter 6) and shared watercourses (Chapter 8), where a clear tendency has emerged privileging mechanisms that are more likely to lead to amicable settlement. The same tendency can be registered in new and emerging fields, where the creation of specialised dispute settlement bodies with compulsory powers may not always be desirable – such as in the case of space law (Chapter 14) – and where a key role can be played by diplomatic means of dispute settlement, such as mediation in disaster relief (Chapter 13) and fact-finding in cyber law (Chapter 15). The emergence of new technologies (Chapter 16) will likely push the search for creative dispute settlement solutions even further.

Far from being mutually exclusive, judicial and non-judicial means of dispute settlement must work synergically towards the common objectives behind the enterprise of dispute settlement, which is the maintenance of international peace and security (Chapter 1). After all, this has been the guiding principle of dispute settlement since its inception, and the 'fundamentals' of this system remain unchanged (Chapter 17). This does not mean that the system of international dispute settlement is impervious to change (*plus ça change* . . .), but that the system constantly evolves to serve the common interests of the international community. In this sense, it is difficult not to share the optimism that Merrills expressed on the subject: 'The magnitude of current international problems appears a little less dispiriting in the light of the unimagined progress of the last 100 years in the furtherance of such interests through treaties and international institutions'.[15] In this spirit, the changing character of international dispute settlement appears less as a threat and more as a promise for the future of international law.

[15] John G. Merrills, *Anatomy of International Law* (London: Sweet & Maxwell, 1981), p. 132.

PART I

Recent Trends and Cross-Cutting Issues in International Dispute Settlement

1

The Obligation of Peaceful Settlement of International Disputes

Status, Nature, Content, and Scope

DANIEL FRANCHINI AND RUSSELL BUCHAN

1.1 INTRODUCTION

As sovereign entities in pursuit of their domestic and foreign policy objectives, States invariably fall into dispute. The existence of disputes is not in and by itself a weakness of the international society – in fact, disputes can be an indicator of a vibrant, energetic, and healthy society.[1] That said, disputes run the risk of disrupting international relations and creating threats to international peace and security.[2] What is critical is that the international society puts in place measures, mechanisms, and means to ensure that disputes are resolved peacefully. Indeed, where disputes are settled peacefully this can be a driver of positive change within the international society, for example, by forging a closer sense of community between its members and by developing new norms and rules that set acceptable standards of behaviour.[3]

In order to maintain international peace and security, States have developed a range of political and legal methods to facilitate the peaceful settlement of their disputes, including negotiation, conciliation, mediation,

[1] John G. Collier and Vaughan Lowe, *The Settlement of Disputes in International Law: Institutions and Procedures* (Oxford: Oxford University Press, 2000), pp. 1–2.

[2] As an arbitral tribunal explained, it is 'essential to the well-being of the community of nations' that the parties to a dispute resolve it peacefully; *Case Concerning Claims Arising out of Decision of the Mixed Graeco-German Arbitral Tribunal Set Up under Article 304 in Part X of the Treaty of Versailles (Greece v. Germany)* (1972) 19 RIAA 25, para. 62.

[3] See Manfred Lachs, 'Some reflections on the settlement of international disputes' (1974) 68 ASIL Proc 323–31 at 324.

and arbitration, among others.[4] One of the cornerstones of this system is the obligation to settle disputes peacefully.[5]

The scholarship on peaceful dispute settlement has traditionally adopted an 'institutional' approach to the subject,[6] with its focus being on the *means and methods* that can be used to settle disputes rather than on the *substance* of the peaceful settlement obligation itself. The reason for this is because the obligation to settle disputes peacefully is usually seen as the flip side of the prohibition on the threat or use of force,[7] meaning that the peaceful settlement obligation does no more than require States to refrain from the threat or use of force when seeking to resolve disputes. By effectively flattening the obligation to settle disputes peacefully into a reiteration of the duty to avoid force in international relations, this approach precludes an in-depth investigation into the content of the obligation of peaceful dispute settlement as an autonomous rule of international law.

This chapter rejects the conflation of the principles of non-use of force and peaceful dispute settlement and separates them out by examining the status, nature, content, scope, and consequences of the latter. In doing so, this chapter adheres to the following structure: Section 1.2 traces the emergence of the obligation of peaceful dispute settlement under international law and establishes its status as a binding rule of treaty and customary law. Section 1.3 examines the conditions for the engagement of the obligation to settle disputes peacefully. Section 1.4 explores what measures disputants must take in order to discharge their obligation to settle disputes peacefully. This section argues that the obligation of peaceful dispute settlement is dynamic in nature and, as such, the conduct it requires from disputing parties varies depending on the circumstances of each case. This section also shows that the obligation operates as an interstitial norm insofar as it influences the interpretation and application of other rules of international law relevant to the peaceful settlement of disputes. Section 1.5 offers some concluding remarks on the utility of

4 As Sohn explains, 'adequate means for settling international disputes are indispensable for the maintenance of international peace and security'; Louis B. Sohn, 'Peaceful settlement of disputes and international security' (1987) 3 Negot J 155–66 at 155.

5 Robert Barnidge, 'The international law as a means of negotiation settlement' (2013) 36 Fordham Int'l L J 545–74 at 546.

6 See Eric De Brabandere, *Merrills' International Dispute Settlement*, 7th ed. (Cambridge: Cambridge University Press, 2022), preface; Duncan B. Hollis and Eneken Tikk, 'Peaceful settlement and international law: A *jus ad pacem*', Temple University Legal Studies Research Paper No. 2021-37, 2021, https://dx.doi.org/10.2139/ssrn.3908182 (accessed 27 September 2022), 30.

7 E.g., Alain Pellet, 'Peaceful settlement of international disputes', in Anne Peters (ed.), *Max Planck Encyclopaedia of International Law* (Oxford: Oxford University Press, 2013), para. 5.

the obligation of peaceful dispute settlement in contemporary international relations.

1.2 THE OBLIGATION OF PEACEFUL DISPUTE SETTLEMENT: HISTORY AND STATUS

The obligation of peaceful dispute settlement has a long history in international law and can be traced back at least as far as the 1899 Hague Convention on the Peaceful Settlement of Disputes.[8] This Convention requires State parties 'to use their best efforts to insure the pacific settlement of international differences'[9] and identifies a range of methods they can use to help settle their disputes peacefully, including good offices, commissions of inquiry, mediation, and arbitration.[10]

The obligation of peaceful dispute settlement has been confirmed in numerous treaties since the adoption of the Hague Convention in 1899.[11] Given its (almost) universal membership, the United Nations (UN) is most significant in this regard. Article 1 of the Charter sets out the UN's overarching aims and objectives and, according to Article 1(1), one of its main purposes is to

> maintain international peace and security, and to that end ... to bring about by peaceful means, and in conformity with the principles of justice and international law, adjustment or settlement of international disputes or situations which might lead to a breach of the peace.[12]

While Article 1 identifies the UN's purposes, Article 2 enumerates its guiding principles and, with a view to maintaining international peace and security, Article 2(3) of the Charter provides that 'all Member States shall settle their

[8] Although Hollis and Tikk claim that the obligation of peaceful dispute settlement has its origins in the Treaty of Westphalia of 1648; Hollis and Tikk, 'Peaceful settlement and international law', 10.

[9] Art 1 of the Hague Convention on the Pacific Settlement of International Disputes, The Hague, 29 July 1899, in force 4 September 1900.

[10] Ibid., Arts 2, 9, and 15.

[11] See, e.g., Art 1 of the Hague Convention on the Pacific Settlement of International Disputes, The Hague, 18 October 1907, in force 26 January 1910, (1907) 205 CTS 277; Art 13 of the Covenant of the League of Nations, Versailles, 28 June 1919, in force 10 January 1920, (1919) 225 CTS 195; Art III(g)–(i) of the Charter of the Organization of American States, Bogota, 20 April 1948, in force 13 December 1951, 119 UNTS 3; Art 1 of the Warsaw Treaty of Friendship, Cooperation, and Mutual Assistance, Warsaw, 14 May 1955, in force 6 June 1955, 219 UNTS 3 (the Warsaw Pact); Art XIX of the Charter of the Organization of African Unity, Addis Ababa, 25 May 1963, in force 13 September 1963, 479 UNTS 39.

[12] See further Leland M. Goodrich, 'Pacific settlement of disputes' (1945) 39 Am Pol Sc Rev 956–70 at 956.

international disputes by peaceful means in such a manner that international peace and security, and justice, are not endangered'.

Article 2(3) is framed in binding terms: by using the imperative 'shall', UN members must settle their disputes peacefully as a matter of international law.[13] Article 33(1) of the UN Charter – located in Chapter VI titled 'Pacific Settlement of Disputes' – reaffirms the obligation upon member States to settle their disputes peacefully (again, note Article 33(1)'s use of the imperative 'shall') and provides a list of political and legal methods they can use to help realise this objective.[14] Article 33(1) therefore 'complements'[15] Article 2(3) and reads:

> The parties to any dispute, the continuance of which is likely to endanger the maintenance of international peace and security, shall, first of all, seek a solution by negotiation, enquiry, mediation, conciliation, arbitration, judicial settlement, resort to regional agencies or arrangements, or other peaceful means of their own choice.

Depending on the extent of their obligations under international law, States may be compelled to participate in certain forms of dispute settlement – for example, States may accept the jurisdiction of the International Court of Justice (ICJ) under Article 36(2) of the Statute of the ICJ, or incorporate a compromissory clause within a treaty that grants the ICJ jurisdiction in relation to disputes emerging under that agreement. However, absent such a rule of international law, a corollary of the principle of the sovereign equality of States is the principle of free choice of means, which means that States are free to decide for themselves which peaceful means and methods to use to settle their disputes or, put differently, States cannot be compelled to participate in a dispute settlement process unless they have given their consent.[16]

[13] Pellet explains that the obligation of peaceful dispute settlement contained in Arts 2(3) and 33 (1) of the Charter of the United Nations (San Francisco, 26 June 1945, in force 24 October 1945, 1 UNTS 16) is 'indisputably a legally binding obligation'; Pellet, 'Peaceful settlement of international disputes', para. 2.

[14] On the distinction between diplomatic and legal means, see Anne Peters, 'International dispute settlement: A network of cooperational duties' (2003) 14 EJIL 1–34 at 4.

[15] David D. Caron and Christian Tomuschat, 'Article 2, para. 3 UN Charter', in Andreas Zimmermann et al. (eds.), *The Statute of the International Court of Justice* (Oxford: Oxford University Press, 2019), p. 125.

[16] *Status of Eastern Carelia* (Advisory Opinion) [1923] PCIJ Rep. Series B No. 5 at 27; *Fisheries Jurisdiction (Spain* v. *Canada)* (Jurisdiction, Judgment) [1998] ICJ Rep. 432 at para. 56; *Obligation to Negotiate Access to the Pacific Ocean (Bolivia* v. *Chile)* (Judgment) [2018] ICJ Rep. 507 at para. 165. See also UNGA, 'Declaration on principles of international law concerning friendly relations and cooperation among States in accordance with the Charter of the United Nations' (24 October 1970) UN Doc. A/RES/2625(XXV) (the Friendly Relations

In fact, the methods listed in Article 33(1) are not exhaustive, with this provision explaining that States can settle their disputes through 'other peaceful means of their own choice'. For instance, States often use good offices to help resolve their disputes and, while this method is not mentioned in Article 33(1), it is referred to in the 1899 Hague Convention and the UN General Assembly's (UNGA) Manila Declaration. States can also combine methods and create bespoke processes aimed at settling their disputes.[17] Under Article 37 of the UN Charter, if States are unable to settle a dispute by peaceful means, they must refer it to the UN Security Council (UNSC).

The obligation of peaceful dispute settlement has undoubtedly acquired the status of customary international law.[18] This status is supported by the near-universal membership of the UN Charter,[19] together with the fact that the obligation is embedded in a number of successive treaties.[20] The customary law status of the obligation is also confirmed by its inclusion

Declaration, or FRD), para 5; UNGA, 'Manila declaration on the peaceful settlement of international disputes' (15 November 1982) UN Doc. A/RES/37/10 (the Manila Declaration), para. 3; Art 3 of the American Treaty on Pacific Settlement, Bogota, 30 April 1948, in force 6 May 1949, 30 UNTS 55 (the Pact of Bogota); and Art 280 of the Convention on the Law of the Sea referring to United Nations Convention on the Law of the Sea, Montego Bay, 10 December 1982, in force 16 November 1994, 1833 UNTS 397 (UNCLOS).

17 Joe Verhoeven, *Droit International Public* (Brussels: Larcier, 2000), p. 696.

18 *Case Concerning Military and Paramilitary Activities in and against Nicaragua (Nicaragua* v. *United States of America)* (Merits, Judgment) [1986] ICJ Rep. 14 at para. 290. See also *Request for Interpretation of the Judgment of 15 June 1962 in the Case Concerning the Temple of Preah Vihear (Cambodia* v. *Thailand)* (Judgment) [2013] ICJ Rep. 281 at paras 105–6.

19 The ICJ has explained that the 'very widespread and representative participation' in a treaty can be evidence of its customary law character; *North Sea Continental Shelf (Federal Republic of Germany* v. *Denmark; Federal Republic of Germany* v. *Netherlands)* (Judgment) [1969] ICJ Rep. 3 at para. 73; *Legality of the Threat or Use of Nuclear Weapons* (Advisory Opinion) [1996] ICJ Rep. 226 at para. 82 (citing 'the extent of the accession' to the Hague and Geneva Treaties as confirming their customary international law status); ILC, 'Draft conclusions on identification of customary international law, with commentaries', in *Yearbook of the International Law Commission. 2018, Volume II, Part Two: Report of the Commission to the General Assembly on the Work of Its Seventieth Session* (New York: UN, 2018), Draft Conclusion 11, commentary, para. 3 ('The number of parties to a treaty may be an important factor in determining whether particular rules set forth therein reflect customary international law; treaties that have obtained near-universal acceptance may be seen as particularly indicative in this respect').

20 'In some cases it may be that frequent repetition in widely accepted treaties evinces a recognition by the international community as a whole that a rule is one of general, and not just particular, law'; ILA, *Committee on Formation of Customary (General) International Law: Final Report* (London: International Law Association, 2000), Rule 25, commentary, para. 5. See also Institut de Droit International, 'Problems arising from a succession of codification conventions on a particular subject', 1 September 1995, www.idi-iil.org/app/uploads/2017/06/1995_lis_01_en.pdf (accessed 28 September 2022), Rule 12; UNGA Res. 73/203 (20 December 2018) UN Doc. A/RES/73/203 (the ILC's 'Identification of customary international

in multiple resolutions of the UNSC[21] and declarations of the UNGA.[22] Importantly, the obligation of peaceful dispute settlement is contained in the 1970 Friendly Relations Declaration (FRD),[23] whose adoption by the UNGA without the need for a vote 'may be understood as an acceptance of the validity of the rule or set of rules declared by the resolution by themselves'.[24] The FRD explains:

> Every State shall settle its international disputes with other States by peaceful means in such a manner that international peace and justice are not endangered.
>
> States shall accordingly seek early and just settlement of their international disputes by negotiation, inquiry, mediation, conciliation, arbitration, judicial settlement, resort to regional agencies or arrangements or other peaceful means of their choice. In seeking such a settlement the parties shall agree upon such peaceful means as may be appropriate to the circumstances and nature of the dispute.

Additionally, the UNGA adopted the Manila Declaration on the Peaceful Settlement of International Disputes in 1982, which was also adopted without the need for a vote.[25] This Declaration explains that

law'), Conclusion 11(2); Yoram Dinstein, 'The interaction between customary international law and treaties' (2006) 322 Recueil des Cours 242–428 at 299–300.

21 See, e.g., UNSC Res. 1318 (7 September 2000) UN Doc. S/RES/1318; UNSC Res. 1366 (30 August 2001) UN Doc. S/RES/1366; UNSC Res. 1809 (6 April 2008) UN Doc. S/RES/1809.

22 See, e.g., the FRD; Manila Declaration; UNGA Res. 40/9 (6 November 1985) UN Doc. A/RES/40/9; UNGA Res. 43/51 (5 December 1988) UN Doc. A/RES/43/51; UNGA Res. 46/59 (9 December 1991) UN Doc. A/RES/46/59; UNGA Res. 47/120 (18 December 1992) UN Doc. A/RES/47/120; UNGA Res. 57/26 (19 November 2002) UN Doc. A/RES 57/26; UNGA, '2005 World Summit Outcome' (24 October 2005) UN Doc. A/RES/60/1; and UNGA Res. 67/1 (30 November 2012) UN Doc. A/RES/67/1. In the cyber context, in separate UN processes, States have affirmed that they 'shall seek the settlement of disputes by peaceful means such as negotiation, enquiry, mediation, conciliation, arbitration, judicial settlement, and resort to regional agencies or arrangements, or other peaceful means of their own choice'; UNGA, 'Open ended working group on developments in the field of information and telecommunications in the context of international security: Final substantive report' (10 March 2021) UN Doc. A/AC.290/2021.CRP.2, para. 35. In 2021, a UN Group of Governmental Experts confirmed that international law applies to cyberspace, including the principle of the 'settlement of international disputes by peaceful means in such a manner that international peace and security and justice are not endangered'; UNGA, 'Report of the Group of Governmental Experts on advancing responsible State behaviour in cyberspace in the context of international security' (14 July 2021) UN Doc. A/76/135, para. 69.

23 UNGA, 'Declaration on principles of international law concerning friendly relations' (the FRD).

24 *Nicaragua* v. *United States of America*, para. 188.

25 'The [Manila] *Declaration* has since become a normative benchmark, with repeated subsequent calls by the UNGA for Member States to observe its terms'; Hollis and Tikk, 'Peaceful settlement and international law', 14.

> States shall seek in good faith and in a spirit of cooperation an early and equitable settlement of their international disputes .... In seeking such a settlement, the parties shall agree on such peaceful means as may be appropriate to the circumstances and the nature.

The international society has developed a sophisticated system of peaceful dispute settlement that comprises a dense patchwork of principles, rules, procedures, and institutions. The obligation of peaceful dispute settlement is a critically important feature of this system and, while it represents an ontologically distinct obligation under international law, it sits alongside other international legal rules that work together to ensure the maintenance of international peace and security.[26] Take, for example, the principles of non-intervention and non-use of force. The principle of non-intervention is 'part and parcel of customary international law' and prohibits States from coercively intervening in the *domaine réservé* of other States.[27] The principle of non-use of force prohibits States from engaging in acts of violence (and threats thereof) against other States and is embedded in a number of treaties as well as customary law.[28] Most notably, this principle is enshrined in Article 2(4) of the UN Charter, which reads:

> All Members shall refrain in their international relations from the threat or use of force against the territorial integrity or political independence of any state, or in any other manner inconsistent with the Purposes of the United Nations.

Action amounting to a breach of the non-intervention and non-use of force principles may also constitute a breach of the obligation of peaceful dispute settlement on the basis that it involves the use of a non-peaceful means to resolve a dispute.[29] Importantly, however, the obligation of peaceful dispute settlement goes beyond prohibiting the use of non-peaceful means to resolve disputes and imposes an 'affirmative duty' on States to work together to find a peaceful means to settle their disputes.[30] This was recognised by the ICJ in the

[26] How these principles interact with each other will be addressed in Section 1.4.

[27] *Nicaragua* v. *United States of America*, para. 202.

[28] Ibid., para. 34.

[29] 'Any measure taken in violation of the principle of non-use of force qualifies as non-peaceful and therefore contrary to Art. 2 para 3. Actions infringing Art. 2 para 4 UN Charter infringe at the same time Art. 2 para 3'; Caron and Tomuschat, 'Article 2, para. 3', 131. See also Pellet, 'Peaceful settlement of international disputes', para. 4.

[30] '[The obligation contained in Article 2(3) of the UN Charter] extends beyond a requirement not to settle disputes through force – the point of Article 2(4). Rather, it represents an affirmative duty (though one of conduct, not result) to settle their dispute in a certain manner';

Nicaragua judgment when it held that the obligation to settle disputes peacefully is 'complementary to the principles of a prohibitive nature' found in international law such as the principles of non-intervention and non-use of force.[31] Yet, to determine the content of the obligation of peaceful dispute settlement, it is first necessary to investigate the conditions for its engagement. The next section turns to this issue.

1.3 CONDITIONS FOR THE ENGAGEMENT OF THE OBLIGATION OF PEACEFUL DISPUTE SETTLEMENT

Establishing the conditions for the engagement of the obligation of peaceful dispute settlement entails answering three questions: (1) when does a dispute come into existence; (2) whether a dispute should present certain features to engage the obligation; and (3) what parties are subject to the obligation. Each issue is addressed in turn.

1.3.1 *Existence of a Dispute*

The existence of a dispute is the trigger of the obligation of peaceful dispute settlement.[32] Yet, there is considerable uncertainty regarding what situations qualify as a 'dispute', or even whether a unitary definition of 'dispute' exists in international law.[33] The term 'dispute' appears in several international conventions and is not used consistently.[34] Indeed, the notion of a dispute may have different implications depending on the purpose for which it is sought.

Steven Ratner, 'The aggravating duty of non-aggravation' (2020) 31 EJIL 1307–42 at 1310. See also Caron and Tomuschat, 'Article 2, para. 3', 126.

31 *Nicaragua* v. *United States of America*, para. 290. 'The principle of the peaceful settlement of international disputes is linked to various other principles of international law [such as non-intervention and non-use of force] ... [These principles] are interrelated in their interpretation and application and each principle should be construed in the context of other principles'; UN OLA, *Handbook on the Peaceful Settlement of Disputes between States* (New York: UN, 1992), p. 4.

32 Hollis and Tikk, 'Peaceful settlement and international law', 18.

33 Paolo Palchetti, 'Dispute', in Anne Peters (ed.), *Max Planck Encyclopaedia of International Law* (Oxford: Oxford University Press, 2018), para. 10.

34 E.g., 'a dispute ... under Article 60 of the Statute ... does not need to satisfy the same criteria as would a dispute ... as referred to in Article 36, paragraph 2': *Request for Interpretation of the Judgment of 31 March 2004 in the Case Concerning Avena and Other Mexican Nationals (Mexico* v. *United States of America*) (Provisional Measures) [2008] ICJ Rep. 3 at para. 53. It may also be noted that, while the English text of the ICJ Statute (Statute of the International Court of Justice, San Francisco, 26 June 1945, in force 24 October 1945, 33 UNTS 993) uses the unitary term 'disputes', the French text uses several terms, such as 'conflits' (Art 4), 'différends' (Art 36(2)), 'contestation' (Art 60).

The existence of a dispute is often the precondition for the exercise of jurisdiction by an international court or tribunal.[35] In this regard, most international courts and tribunals define disputes by reference to the *Mavrommatis* case, where the Permanent Court of International Justice (PCIJ) held that a dispute is 'a disagreement on a point of law or fact, a conflict of legal views or of interests between two persons'.[36] It is questionable, however, whether this definition is satisfactory for the purpose of the obligation of peaceful settlement. First, international courts and tribunals are only ever concerned with 'justiciable' disputes, that is, disputes that 'can be resolved by the application of rules of law by judicial (including arbitral) processes'.[37] Second, the *Mavrommatis* definition is formulated in such general terms that, at best, it provides very little guidance when it comes to identifying specific disputes and, at worst, it may be overinclusive.[38] Indeed, the ICJ, followed by

[35] See Palchetti, 'Dispute', para. 2. For instance, the jurisdiction of a court may be limited to disputes arising only after a certain date; see, e.g., *Phosphates in Morocco (Italy* v. *France)* (Preliminary Objections, Judgment) [1938] PCIJ Rep. Series A/B No. 74; *Electricity Company of Sofia and Bulgaria (Belgium* v. *Bulgaria)* (Preliminary Objections, Judgment) [1939] PCIJ Rep. Series A/B No. 77; *Right of Passage over Indian Territory (Portugal* v. *India)* (Merits, Judgment) [1960] ICJ Rep. 6.

[36] *Mavrommatis Palestine Concessions (Greece* v. *Great Britain)* (Judgment) [1924] PCIJ Rep. Series A No. 2 at 11. For references to this case by other courts, see, e.g., *Right of Passage over Indian Territory*, 34; *South West Africa Cases (Ethiopia* v. *South Africa; Liberia* v. *South Africa)* (Preliminary Objections, Judgment) [1962] ICJ Rep. 319 at 328; *Southern Bluefin Tuna Cases (New Zealand* v. *Japan; Australia* v. *Japan)* (Provisional Measures, Order of 27 August 1999) ITLOS Reports 1999, 280 at 293; *M/V 'Norstar' Case (Panama* v. *Italy)* (Preliminary Objections, Judgment of 4 November 2016) ITLOS 2016, 44; *Republic of Ecuador* v. *United States of America* (Award of 29 September 2012) PCA Case No. 2012-5 at para. 212. See, most recently, ICJ, *Allegations of Genocide under the Convention on the Prevention and Punishment of the Crime of Genocide (Ukraine* v. *Russian Federation)* (Request for the Indication of Provisional Measures, Order), 16 March 2022, www.icj-cij.org/public/files/case-related/182/182-20220316-ORD-01-00-EN.pdf (accessed 29 September 2022) at para. 28. See also Michael Waibel, '*Mavrommatis Palestine Concessions (Greece* v *Great Britain)* (1924–27)', in Eirik Bjorge and Cameron Miles (eds.), *Landmark Cases in Public International Law* (Oxford: Hart, 2017), p. 56.

[37] Collier and Lowe, *Settlement of Disputes*, 10. See also Christoph Schreuer, 'What is a legal dispute?', in Isabelle Buffard et al. (eds.), *International Law between Universalism and Fragmentation: Festschrift in Honour of Gerhard Hafner* (Leiden: Martinus Nijhoff, 2008), p. 965.

[38] For instance, it can be questioned whether a conflict of interests with no tangible effects on the conduct of the parties qualifies as a dispute. See Gerhard Hafner, 'The physiognomy of disputes and the appropriate means to resolve them', in United Nations (ed.), *International Law as a Language for International Relations. Proceedings of the United Nations Congress on Public International Law* (The Hague: Kluwer Law, 1995), pp. 560, 567; Yoshifumi Tanaka, *The Peaceful Settlement of International Disputes* (Cambridge: Cambridge University Press, 2021), p. 8. See also Robert Y. Jennings, 'Reflections on the term "dispute"', in Ronald St. J. Macdonald (ed.), *Essays in Honour of Wang Tieya* (Leiden: Brill, 1993), p. 402; Sienho Yee,

other international courts and tribunals,[39] has added several qualifications to this definition, stating in particular that a dispute comes into existence when 'the claim of one party is positively opposed by the other',[40] and that this 'opposition' may 'be inferred from the failure of a State to respond to a claim in circumstances where a response is called for'.[41]

These qualifications are also helpful when establishing the existence of a dispute for the purpose of the obligation of peaceful settlement, in that they shift the focus from the 'conflict of views or interests' (in itself a subjective condition) to the *externalisation* of such conflict through the conduct of the parties (which is capable of objective determination[42]). This notion was best captured by Judge Morelli, who described the essence of a dispute as the 'contrast between the respective attitudes of the parties in relation to a certain conflict of interests'.[43] To be more precise, Judge Morelli found that the existence of a dispute requires 'a manifestation of the will, at least of one of the parties, consisting in the making of a claim or of a protest'.[44] The opposition to this manifestation of will may take the form of a (counter-) claim, in which one party rejects the claim(s) put forward by the other party. It may also be inferred from the conduct of one party, so long as it is incompatible with the claim(s) advanced by the other parties.[45]

'Article 40', in Andreas Zimmermann et al. (eds.), *The Statute of the International Court of Justice: A Commentary*, 3rd ed. (Oxford: Oxford University Press, 2019), p. 1047.

39 E.g., *Texaco* v. *Libya* (Preliminary Award of 27 November 1975) (1979) 53 ILR 389 at 416; *Southern Bluefin Tuna Cases*, para. 44; *Impregilo S.p.A.* v. *Islamic Republic of Pakistan* (Decision on Jurisdiction of 22 April 2005) ICSID ARB/03/3 at para. 302.

40 *South West Africa Cases*, 328.

41 *Application of the International Convention on the Elimination of All Forms of Racial Discrimination (Georgia* v. *Russian Federation)* (Preliminary Objections, Judgment) [2011] ICJ Rep. 70 at para. 30. See also *Case Concerning the Land and Maritime Boundary between Cameroon and Nigeria (Cameroon* v. *Nigeria: Equatorial Guinea Intervening)* (Preliminary Objections, Judgment) [1998] ICJ Rep. 315 at para. 89. Similarly, emphasis on the lack of response by a party to the claims of the other has been placed by investment tribunals; see, e.g., *Tradex Hellas S.A.* v. *Republic of Albania* (Decision on Jurisdiction of 24 December 1996) ICSID ARB/94/2 at 68–69; *Asian Agricultural Products Limited* v. *Republic of Sri Lanka* (Award of 27 June 1990) ICSID ARB/87/3 at 251.

42 The ICJ has reiterated time and again that the existence of a dispute must be established objectively; see, e.g., *Interpretation of Peace Treaties with Bulgaria, Hungary and Romania* (Advisory Opinion) (First Phase) [1950] ICJ Rep. 65 at 74.

43 *South West Africa Cases*, 567 (Dissenting Opinion of Judge Morelli).

44 Ibid.

45 See Gaetano Morelli, 'Nozione ed elementi constitutivi della controversia internazionale' (1960) 43 Rivista di diritto internazionale 405–26 at 406–9; *South West Africa Cases*, 567 (Dissenting Opinion of Judge Morelli); *Case Concerning the Northern Cameroons (Cameroon* v. *United Kingdom)* (Judgment) [1963] ICJ Rep. 15 at 133 (Separate Opinion of Judge Morelli).

The claims of (at least one of) the parties are thus an essential element for the establishment of a dispute. Through their claims, the parties control not only the moment at which the conflict of views or interests materialises but also, depending on the type of arguments used to support them, the content and nature of the dispute.[46] For instance, the use of 'moral' or 'historical' arguments will maintain the dispute in the 'political' sphere, but the move towards 'legal' arguments by one of the parties will give rise to a 'legal' dispute. Whether this has an impact on the engagement of the obligation of peaceful settlement will be explored in Section 1.3.2. For now, it is worth noting that, if the claims of the parties determine the existence and content of a dispute, some communications between the parties seem to be a necessary precondition for the emergence of a dispute (and thus for the engagement of the obligation of peaceful settlement). As Schreuer puts it, 'the matter must have been taken up with the other party, which must have opposed the claimant's position if only indirectly'.[47] At the same time, this should not imply that a particular 'threshold' of communications must be reached before it can be said that a dispute has arisen. In this regard, the ICJ has sparked debate – and criticism[48] – with its decision in the *Nuclear Arms and Disarmament* cases, where it held that 'a dispute exists when it is demonstrated, on the basis of the evidence, that the respondent was aware, or could not have been unaware, that its views were "positively opposed" by the applicant' and that this must have occurred 'at the time of their submission' to the Court.[49] Yet, the emphasis the ICJ placed on the time of the submission suggests that the Court was preoccupied not so much with disputes *tout court* but with specific disputes subject to the jurisdiction of the Court.[50]

46 Schreuer, 'What is a legal dispute?', 978.

47 Ibid., 962.

48 *Obligations Concerning Negotiations Relating to Cessation of the Nuclear Arms Race and to Nuclear Disarmament (Marshall Islands v. United Kingdom)* (Preliminary Objections, Judgment) [2016] ICJ Rep. 833 at 866, paras 21–22 (Dissenting Opinion of Judge Yusuf); and 1093, para. 1 (Dissenting Opinion of Judge Crawford); Beatrice I. Bonafé, 'Establishing the existence of a dispute before the International Court of Justice: Drawbacks and implications' (2017) 45 Quest Int'l L 3–32 at 19; Tullio Treves, 'Litigating global crises: What role for international courts and tribunals in the management of climate change, mass migration and pandemics?' (2021) 85 Quest Int'l L 5–15 at 12. See also contributions to the 'Symposium on the *Marshall Islands* case' (2017) 111 AJIL Unbound 62–102. For a defence of the court's position, see Hugh Thirlway, 'Establishing the existence of a dispute: A response to Professor Bonafé's criticisms of the ICJ' (2017) 45 Quest Int'l L 53–63 at 55.

49 *Obligations Concerning Negotiations Relating to Cessation of the Nuclear Arms Race*, paras 41–43.

50 See Bonafé, 'Establishing the existence of a dispute', 16 ('the awareness requirement is not so much about the existence of the dispute but rather about the intention of the applicant to seize the Court').

The existence of a dispute as the trigger of the obligation of peaceful dispute settlement is a different issue compared to its suitability for adjudication by international courts and tribunals. The externalisation of a conflict of views or interests through the claims of one of the parties is sufficient to give rise to a dispute so long as these claims are incompatible with the claims or conduct of the other party.[51] Such claims can be made in several ways and require no formalities;[52] they can be raised through diplomatic exchanges but also through more informal means of communication between the parties.[53] A parallel can be drawn between the dynamics by which a dispute arises and the means by which a State can invoke the responsibility of another State for internationally wrongful acts. As the International Law Commission (ILC) has highlighted, the invocation of responsibility may occur through 'diplomatic contacts ... [which] involve specific claims by the State concerned, such as for compensation for a breach affecting it, or specific action such as the filing of an application before a competent international tribunal, or even the taking of countermeasures'.[54] Indeed, with the exception of the *Nuclear Arms and Disarmament* cases, international courts and tribunals have rarely, if ever, declined jurisdiction on the basis of the non-existence of a dispute, particularly if, 'at the latest by the date when the Court decides on its jurisdiction', the applicant would be entitled 'to bring fresh proceedings'.[55]

[51] According to the PCIJ, 'a difference of opinion does exist as soon as one of the Governments concerned points out that the attitude adopted by the other conflicts with its own views': *Certain German Interests in Polish Upper Silesia (Germany* v. *Poland)* (Preliminary Objections, Judgment of 25 August 1925) PCIJ Rep. Series A No. 6 at 14.

[52] See *Application of the International Convention on the Elimination of All Forms of Racial Discrimination*, para. 30: 'the matter is one of substance, not of form'; *Alleged Violations of Sovereign Rights and Maritime Spaces in the Caribbean Sea (Nicaragua* v. *Colombia)* (Preliminary Objections, Judgment) [2016] ICJ Rep. 32 at para. 72: 'a formal diplomatic protest' is not required. See also *Channel Tunnel Group Limited and France-Manche SA.* v. *United Kingdom and France* (Partial Award of 30 January 2007) (2008) 132 ILR 1 at para. 142: 'international tribunals have been willing to discern a dispute from general exchanges of correspondence manifesting a difference of view without requiring the claim to have been made out with any particularity'.

[53] See e.g., *Certain Phosphate Lands in Nauru (Nauru* v. *Australia)* (Preliminary Objections, Judgment) [1992] ICJ Rep. 240 at para. 36.

[54] The ILC's *Articles on State Responsibility for Internationally Wrongful Acts, with Commentaries*, contained in 'Draft articles on responsibility of states for internationally wrongful acts', in *Yearbook of the International Law Commission. 2001, Volume II, Part Two: Report of the Commission to the General Assembly on the Work of Its Fifty-Third Session* (New York: UN, 2008), p. 117, commentary to Art 42, https://legal.un.org/ilc/texts/instruments/english/commentaries/9_6_2001.pdf.

[55] *Application of the Convention on the Prevention and Punishment of the Crime of Genocide (Croatia* v. *Serbia)* (Preliminary Objections, Judgment) [2008] ICJ Rep. 412 at para. 85. See also Thirlway, 'Establishing the existence of a dispute', 62 ('the existing proceedings would

This is not to say that communications between the parties are not necessary for the settlement of a dispute. However, the extent to which the parties should engage in exchanges to fulfil the obligation of peaceful settlement is a separate issue, which pertains to the content of the obligation.[56] As far as the engagement of the obligation is concerned, once a dispute has come into existence, what remains to be asked is whether such a dispute should possess certain features to give rise to the obligation of peaceful settlement. The next subsection turns to this.

1.3.2 *Character of the Dispute*

As Merrills stated, 'international disputes can be about almost anything'.[57] It may thus be asked whether all disputes trigger the obligation of peaceful settlement or whether the latter should be reserved only for certain classes of disputes. In this regard, it is important to recall the function the obligation of peaceful dispute settlement serves under the UN Charter and general international law. The premise is that disputes, if left unchecked, may cause friction in international relations and have the potential to escalate, thereby threatening international peace and security. As will be further explored below, the obligation of peaceful dispute settlement aims at reducing this risk by compelling the States to 'manage' their disputes and ensure these do not spiral out of control. Although the potential for escalation may be very different in practice, in principle all disputes present such a risk. Thus, Article 33 of the UN Charter mandates member States to seek a solution to a dispute 'the continuance of which is likely to endanger the maintenance of international peace and security'. To be sure, other provisions in the UN Charter appear to add qualifications to the obligation. In particular, Article 2 (3) restricts the obligation of peaceful settlement to 'international disputes'. This provision must be read in conjunction with Article 2(7), which provides that member States are not required to submit to settlement 'matters which are essentially within the[ir] domestic jurisdiction'. The obligation of peaceful dispute settlement is thereby limited to disputes that are

have created the necessary "awareness" in the respondent'). See also *Certain Polish Interests in Polish Upper Silesia*, 14: 'Even if, under Article 23, the existence of a definite dispute were necessary, this condition could at any time be fulfilled by means of unilateral action on the part of the applicant Party'. For similar statements in arbitral practice, see Schreuer, 'What is a legal dispute?', 978.

[56] See further Section 1.4.

[57] John G. Merrills, 'The means of dispute settlement', in Malcolm D. Evans (ed.), *International Law*, 5th ed. (Oxford: Oxford University Press, 2018), p. 549.

'international' in the sense of not being 'purely internal'.[58] Yet, the scope of this limitation is not static; the very notion of essential domestic jurisdiction excluding the international character of a dispute has shrunk over time.[59] Domestic jurisdiction can only be defined in the negative as the area in which a State has not taken up international obligations.[60] This, coupled with the growing number of inward-looking norms (i.e. 'norms that aim to regulate State conduct within the domestic jurisdiction'[61]), means that several disputes once regarded as purely internal are now unquestionably international in character – with human rights disputes being the most visible example.

The existence of a dispute concerning matters that are regulated by international law is therefore necessary for the engagement of the obligation of peaceful dispute settlement. At the same time, this does not imply that the arguments of the parties must be based on international law, as suggested by Peters.[62] As discussed above, the claims of the parties are key to the characterisation of the dispute. If the parties use international law in support of their claims, the dispute will be unquestionably 'international' in character, thereby giving rise to the obligation of peaceful settlement. Similarly, the choice of using legal arguments – and even more so the choice of some legal arguments to the exclusion of others[63] – will have implications for the means available for its settlement. However, the risk of placing too much emphasis on the arguments used by the parties is to limit the obligation to legal disputes, ignoring those in which the parties rely on extra-legal (e.g. political, moral, historical) arguments.[64] Disputes of the latter kind, if left unchecked, may very well spiral out of control and threaten international peace and security as much as any legal dispute.[65] Thus, limiting the ambit of the obligation of

[58] Caron and Tomuschat, 'Article 2, para. 3', 130.

[59] Ibid., 130–1.

[60] *Nationality Decrees Issued in Tunis and Morocco* (Advisory Opinion) [1923] PCIJ Rep. Series B No. 4 at 24: 'The question whether a certain matter is or is not solely within the jurisdiction of a State is an essentially relative question; it depends upon the development of international relations.'

[61] Antonios Tzanakopoulos, 'Domestic courts in international law: The international judicial function of national courts' (2011) 34 Loy LA Int'l & Comp L Rev 133–68 at 138.

[62] Peters, 'International dispute settlement', 3.

[63] This is particularly relevant when the jurisdictional basis is narrow and covers only part of a broader dispute; see Callista Harris, 'Claims with an ulterior purpose: Characterising disputes concerning the "interpretation or application" of a treaty' (2019) 18 LPICT 279–99.

[64] The obligation of peaceful settlement is not limited to legal disputes: UNGA, '2005 World Summit Outcome', para. 73. See also Caron and Tomuschat, 'Article 2, para. 3', 131.

[65] Moreover, as Lauterpacht argued, 'all international disputes are, irrespective of their gravity, disputes of a legal character in the sense that, so long as the rule of law is recognized, they are capable of an answer by the application of legal rules'; see Hersch Lauterpacht, *The Function*

peaceful dispute settlement to specific classes of disputes seems unwarranted. If a dispute pertains to matters that are regulated by international law, the obligation of peaceful dispute settlement is triggered for the simple fact that the issue is one of international concern. Further qualifications may contribute to shaping the content of the obligation of peaceful dispute settlement by determining the steps that should be taken to fulfil it. For instance, Article 36 of the UN Charter provides that 'legal disputes' should as a general rule be referred to the ICJ, while Article 52 suggests that 'local disputes' may involve settlement through regional agencies or agreements. However, the content of the obligation should not be conflated with the conditions for its engagement. If the 'international' character of a dispute is not only a necessary but also a sufficient condition for the engagement of the obligation, the question is whether international dispute settlement exclusively concerns disputes among States,[66] or whether the ever-growing phenomenon of 'mixed' disputes involving State and non-State actors is also affecting the scope of the obligation. The next subsection turns to this.

1.3.3 *Subjects of the Obligation*

The PCIJ's definition of a dispute in the *Mavrommatis* case referred to 'a disagreement ... *between two persons*'.[67] This choice of words was almost certainly intended as a reference to 'international legal persons', which at the time equalled States.[68] This is reinforced by the fact that, under the system created by the 1899 Hague Convention, dispute settlement was essentially a matter of inter-State relations. Even disputes involving non-State actors acquired international relevance only to the extent that a State raised the issue against another State. Notably, the PCIJ held that 'by taking up the case of one of its subjects and by resorting to diplomatic action or international judicial proceedings on his behalf, a State is in reality asserting its own

of Law in the International Community, rev. ed. (Oxford: Oxford University Press, 1933/2011), p. 172. See also Hans Kelsen, *Peace through Law* (Chapel Hill: University of North Carolina, 1944), pp. 23–24.

66 In this sense, see Christian Tomuschat, 'Article 2(3)', in Bruno Simma et al. (eds.), *The Charter of the United Nations: A Commentary*, 3rd ed. (Oxford: Oxford University Press, 2012), p. 193.

67 *Mavrommatis Palestine Concessions*, 11 (emphasis added).

68 But see James Crawford, 'Continuity and discontinuity in international dispute settlement: An inaugural lecture' (2010) 1 JISD 3–24 at 9: 'Even in reliance on decisions from the period of classical dualism, the boundaries between the international and the national, the public and the private, turn out to be more permeable than it might have been thought'.

rights'.[69] In the following decades, States, acting as 'gatekeepers' of the international legal system,[70] have recognised limited forms of international legal personality over non-State actors, such as international organisations, individuals, and corporations.[71] In several instances, these actors have been granted direct access to international judicial bodies for the settlement of disputes that affect them, particularly in human rights and investment matters.[72] The 'proliferation'[73] of international courts and tribunals competent to settle disputes involving both States and non-State actors has led some to question whether 'international dispute settlement properly so-called' should be confined to cases involving States.[74] This question has an obvious impact on the extent to which the obligation of peaceful dispute settlement applies to State and non-State actors alike.

The starting point is that the obligation of peaceful dispute settlement is first and foremost an obligation binding on States. While instruments such as the 1970 FRD compel States to settle 'international disputes with other States', other instruments do not contain such limitations. Notably, Article 2(3) of the UN Charter sets out an obligation of the member States to settle 'their international disputes', and Article 33 of the UN Charter refers to 'any dispute, the continuance of which is likely to endanger the maintenance of international peace and security'. It is reasonable to assume that, if a dispute may endanger international peace and security, the States remain under an obligation to seek a solution regardless of whether the other party is a State or non-State entity.[75] Whether non-State entities, in turn, bear an obligation in this sense is a more difficult question.

It is well known that the UN and other international organisations may have a significant role to play as settlers of international

69 *Mavrommatis Palestine Concessions*, 12.

70 Thomas D. Grant, 'The "open system" and its gatekeepers: From *Complexity in International Law*, a seminar in honour of James Crawford' (2002) 13 JISD 41–53.

71 William Thomas Worster, 'Relative international legal personality of non-State actors' (2016) 42 Brook J Int'l L 207–73 at 212.

72 Cesar P. Romano, 'The proliferation of international judicial bodies: The pieces of the puzzle' (1999) 31 NYU J Int'l L & Pol 709–51 at 710. As an implicit acknowledgement of these changing dynamics, reference to the *Mavrommatis* definition in more recent cases has been interpolated to read 'a disagreement ... between *parties*'; see, e.g., *East Timor (Portugal* v. *Australia)* (Judgment) [1995] ICJ Rep. 90 at 100; *Certain Property (Liechtenstein* v. *Germany)* (Judgment) [2005] ICJ Rep. 6 at para. 24.

73 John G. Merrills, 'The mosaic of international dispute settlement procedures: Complementary or contradictory?' (2007) 54 NILR 361–93 at 362.

74 E.g., Crawford, 'Continuity and discontinuity', 4.

75 Caron and Tomuschat, 'Article 2, para. 3', 126.

disputes.[76] Increasingly, however, international organisations may themselves be parties to international disputes concerning, for instance, the responsibility arising from their activities vis-à-vis member States, third States, and non-State parties (individuals, other organisations, etc.).[77] Considering that the obligation of peaceful dispute settlement exists as a matter of customary international law, international organisations are in principle bound by the same obligation with respect to the settlement of their disputes.[78] To be sure, access to the means of dispute settlement may be significantly more limited in cases involving international organisations.[79] Thus, what international organisations must do in order to fulfil their obligation may be different from what is required of States. At the same time, some of the steps explored further in Section 1.4 can be expected also from international organisations. This is a fast-evolving area of international law which has been recently added to the long-term programme of work for the ILC and therefore requires further scrutiny in the future.[80]

[76] For instance, the UN Security Council can make recommendations as to how a dispute is to be settled under Art 36 of the UN Charter. See Matthew Saul and Nigel D. White, 'Legal means of dispute settlement in the field of collective security: The quasi-judicial powers of the Security Council', in Duncan French, Matthew Saul, and Nigel D. White (eds.), *International Law and Dispute Settlement: New Problems and Techniques* (Oxford: Hart, 2011), pp. 191–224. International organisations, such as the EU, may also play an important role as mediators; see Jacob Bercovitch and Judith Fretter, 'Studying international mediation: Developing data sets on mediation, looking for patterns, and searching for answers' (2007) 12 Int Negot 145–73.

[77] See the ILC's *Articles on the Responsibility of International Organisations and Their Commentaries*, contained in 'Draft articles on the responsibility of international organizations, with commentaries', in *Yearbook of the International Law Commission, 2011, Volume II, Part Two: Report of the Commission to the General Assembly on the Work of Its Sixty-Third Session* (New York: UN, 2011), https://legal.un.org/ilc/texts/instruments/english/commentaries/9_11_2011.pdf. See also Jan Klabbers, *An Introduction to International Organizations Law*, 3rd ed. (Cambridge: Cambridge University Press, 2015), p. 306; Nigel D. White, *The Law of International Organisations*, 2nd ed. (Manchester: Manchester University Press, 2017), p. 230.

[78] 'International organizations are subjects of international law and, as such, are bound by any obligations incumbent upon them under general rules of international law': *Interpretation of the Agreement of 25 March 1951 between the WHO and Egypt* (Advisory Opinion) [1980] ICJ Rep 73 at para. 37. These are deemed to encompass at least 'those rules of customary international law that are relevant to the activities of the international organisation': Guglielmo Verdirame, *The UN and Human Rights: Who Guards the Guardians?* (Cambridge: Cambridge University Press, 2011), p. 72.

[79] 'There is no general dispute settlement mechanism to handle disputes involving international organizations'; Pierre Schmitt, *Access to Justice and International Organizations: The Case of Individual Victims of Human Rights Violations* (Cheltenham: Edward Elgar, 2017), p. 135. See generally Karel Wellens, *Remedies against International Organisations* (Cambridge: Cambridge University Press, 2009).

[80] See August Reinisch, 'International organizations and dispute settlement: A new topic for the International Law Commission' (2018) 15 IOLR 1–7.

Under customary international law, other non-State actors may be right-holders or duty-bearers in relation to the settlement of disputes.[81] Whether these obligations include the general obligation of peaceful dispute settlement depends on the circumstances of the specific entity. Some non-State actors, such as national liberation movements (particularly when exercising territorial control), may be bound by the general rules of international law that are not exclusively directed to the States.[82] Obligations pertaining to international dispute settlement would certainly fall within this category given the prominent role these actors play in the settlement of international disputes. The UNSC has frequently called on them to enter negotiations with their government opponents to achieve a settlement of their disputes.[83] These actors may have access not only to diplomatic means of dispute settlement but also to judicial means as demonstrated by the *Abyei* arbitration.[84] As to individuals in general, their international legal standing in the settlement of disputes is more limited compared to that of other international legal subjects. And yet, once individuals are granted direct access to international courts and tribunals (particularly if they are acting for the protection of a right of their own that is distinct from that of the State[85]), there are, in principle, no reasons to exclude them from the general rules of international law governing the settlement of international disputes to the extent applicable to them.[86] Once again, the key question is one not of engagement but of the content of the obligation of peaceful settlement.

1.4 CONTENT AND EFFECTS OF THE OBLIGATION OF INTERNATIONAL DISPUTE SETTLEMENT

Having identified the conditions that trigger the application of the obligation of peaceful dispute settlement, the immediate question is what this obligation

[81] The Manila Declaration states that 'peoples' as holders of the right to self-determination should benefit from the mechanisms available for the peaceful settlement of disputes: Annex, ch. I, para. 12.

[82] See Antal Berkes, *International Human Rights Law beyond State Territorial Control* (Cambridge: Cambridge University Press, 2021), s. 4.2.1.1.

[83] For a recent example, see UNSC, 'Security Council press statement on Yemen truce announcement, SC/14853', United Nations, 4 April 2022, www.un.org/press/en/2022/sc14853.doc.htm (accessed 2 October 2022).

[84] *The Government of Sudan* v. *The Sudan People's Liberation Movement/Army* (2009) 30 RIAA 145. For a critical appraisal, see Gary B. Born and Adam Raviv, 'The Abeyi Arbitration and the rule of law' (2017) 58 Harv Int'l L J 177–224.

[85] See Zachary Douglas, 'The hybrid foundations of investment treaty arbitration' (2004) 74 BYBIL 151–289 at 182.

[86] See Caron and Tomuschat, 'Article 2, para. 3', 130–31; Pellet, 'Peaceful settlement of international disputes', para. 25.

entails. To fully grasp the content of the obligation of peaceful dispute settlement, it is first necessary to identify the setting in which it operates, that is, to flesh out the character of the process of a peaceful dispute settlement (Subsection 1.4.1). This analysis will reveal that, given that the obligation operates in a dynamic context, its content is itself dynamic and varies depending on the circumstances of each case (Subsection 1.4.2). While the obligation has a normative content of its own and imposes specific conduct on the parties to a dispute, it will be shown that the obligation can also operate as an interstitial norm and influence the content of other obligations (Subsection 1.4.3).

1.4.1 *Situating the Obligation in the Dynamic Process of International Dispute Settlement*

As 'historical facts', disputes arise at a given moment, persist for a certain duration, and, if settled, come to an end.[87] It is therefore commonplace to think of the obligation of peaceful dispute settlement as operating in a linear fashion. However, this linear understanding of dispute settlement makes it extremely difficult to give any meaningful content to the obligation of peaceful dispute settlement.

The first obstacle is that the obligation of peaceful dispute settlement is one of conduct, not of result.[88] This is the case also when the obligation is formulated in seemingly strict terms such as those of Article 33 of the UN Charter ('shall ... seek a solution'). Because one party alone cannot settle a dispute without the agreement of the other party – lest the obligation mandates one of the parties to give up its claims – the obligation can only impose a duty to 'undertake efforts towards that purpose'.[89] That the obligation cannot be one of result is also evidenced by the fact that the submission of a dispute to a means of dispute settlement is no guarantee that 'settlement' – in itself a vague concept[90] – will be reached. This is evident in the case of diplomatic

[87] See Morelli, 'Nozione ed elementi constitutivi della controversia internazionale', 413.

[88] See Pellet, 'Peaceful settlement of international disputes', para. 2; Robert Kolb, *The International Court of Justice* (Oxford: Hart, 2013), p. 23.

[89] David D. Caron and Christian Tomuschat, 'Article 33', in Andreas Zimmermann et al. (eds.), *The Statute of the International Court of Justice* (Oxford: Oxford University Press, 2019), p. 167.

[90] Morelli distinguished between the 'termination' of a dispute – which occurs when one of its constitutive elements ceases to exist – and its 'settlement' – which results from a judicial determination of the conflict of interests; see Gaetano Morelli, 'Estinzione e soluzione di controversie internazionali', in *Scritti Giuridici in Onore di Francesco Carnelutti, Vol. IV – Diritto Pubblico e Storia del Diritto* (Padova: CEDAM, 1950), p. 99.

methods (negotiation, good offices, mediation, inquiry, and conciliation), where, in the absence of binding outcomes (unless the parties have made stipulations to this end),[91] settlement is completely reliant on extra-legal factors which may be outside the control of any individual party. Yet, even the submission to a judicial means of dispute settlement does not necessarily ensure that the disagreement at the heart of a dispute will be resolved.[92] In other words, regardless of the means chosen, the settlement of a dispute requires concerted and concordant action on behalf of all disputing parties – a 'result' that is beyond the exclusive control of a single party at any given moment.

Even when the obligation of peaceful dispute settlement is seen as one of conduct, it is not immediately evident what conduct it requires. As we saw above, it is a well-established principle that the parties to a dispute, unless they have agreed otherwise, are under no obligation to submit it to a *specific* means of dispute settlement. The absence of a specific course of action the parties must undertake to fulfil the obligation gives them a 'wide margin of discretion' and can even lead to an impasse.[93] Because States are not bound to submit to any specific means of dispute settlement, it may seem that they cannot be compelled to do anything concrete to settle their disputes despite being subject to an obligation to this end.

If States cannot be compelled to settle their disputes, it may be argued that, at the very least, they should be bound to refrain from engaging in acts that would aggravate the dispute.[94] However, the parties to a dispute may deem it necessary to resort to limited forms of escalation in order to persuade a recalcitrant counterparty to submit to a means of dispute settlement. It is generally accepted that unfriendly but lawful acts do not run into conflict with the obligation of peaceful dispute settlement.[95] These include measures of retorsion (such as the expulsion of diplomats) and countermeasures (which are breaches of international obligations whose wrongfulness is precluded by virtue of their function as a means to implement the international responsibility of wrongdoing States). The risk is that these exceptions may swallow the

[91] Tanaka, *Peaceful Settlement of International Disputes*, 20–21.
[92] 'A judicial decision in and of itself does not always remove the causes underlying the controversy. In general, adjudication that peacefully resolves disputes is supported by political efforts'; Caron and Tomuschat, 'Article 2, para. 3', 123.
[93] Peters, 'International dispute settlement', 11.
[94] See Ratner, 'Aggravating duty of non-aggravation', 1310.
[95] See Tomuschat, 'Article 2(3)', 196; Caron and Tomuschat, 'Article 2, para. 3', 132; Ratner, 'Aggravating duty of non-aggravation', 1330.

rule, given that States taking aggravating measures will almost always claim that they have valid reasons to do so.[96]

A more meaningful effort to conceptualise the obligation of peaceful dispute settlement should therefore begin by acknowledging that disputes are not static phenomena; they arise, evolve, and mutate in response to the conduct of the parties. As seen above, the existence of a dispute can only be ascertained by contrasting the claims of a party with the action and/or claims of another party. The context continues to inform the required conduct of the parties as the dispute develops. Further claims or actions by either party may contribute to the evolution of the dispute by specifying its terms, or may create new disputes concerning the legality of the reaction or connected incidents. These steps cannot be seen in isolation; the legality of the conduct of the parties to a dispute is necessarily influenced by the context and must take into account their past and (possible) future interactions.

This is of particular significance when seeking to ascertain whether the continuance of a dispute is likely to endanger international peace and security under Article 33 of the UN Charter. A disagreement of a relatively minor character between two States with a history of friendly relations is unlikely to threaten international peace and security. In such a context, the parties to the dispute have significant leeway in deciding how to deal with it: they can set it aside temporarily to preserve their friendly relations in other fields; they can attempt to settle it via peaceful means; or they can take unfriendly measures in the form of retorsion or countermeasures that will be unlikely to endanger international peace and security. The same cannot be said when disputes arise between two States that are already experiencing hostile relations – in this environment, acts of escalation may spiral out of control. In fact, it may be argued that all unsettled disputes have the potential of escalating over time and threatening international peace and security. For this reason, Cassese reasoned that 'the obligation of peaceful settlement might concern all disputes'.[97] The consequence is that the obligation of peaceful dispute settlement must be seen as a dynamic one, whose content varies according to the circumstances of the dispute.[98] In particular, as the next subsection shows, the

[96] See James Crawford, 'Counter-measures as interim measures' (1994) 5 EJIL 65–76 (explaining that '[countermeasures] can tend to exacerbate disputes'). See also Monica Hakimi, 'Unfriendly unilateralism' (2014) 55 Harv Int'l L J 105–50 at 117.

[97] Paola Gaeta, Jorge E. Viñuales, and Salvatore Zappalá, *Cassese's International Law*, 3rd ed. (Oxford: Oxford University Press, 2020), p. 277.

[98] Ratner, 'Aggravating duty of non-aggravation', 1320 ('Not all unlawful acts are aggravations of a dispute, as suggested by the Security Council's selectivity in identifying acts as aggravating. And not all aggravations of a dispute are otherwise unlawful').

greater the threat to international peace and security posed by a dispute, the more demanding the obligation becomes.

1.4.2 *Dynamic Content of the Obligation*

As seen above, the obligation of peaceful dispute settlement does not just proscribe the use of non-peaceful means to resolve disputes, but also imposes a positive duty upon the States to engage with each other and work together with a view to settling their disputes. That the obligation of peaceful dispute settlement requires 'active efforts'[99] from the States is indicated by the language of Article 33(1) of the UN Charter, which explains that the UN members must 'seek a solution' to their disputes. In a similar vein, the FRD explains that 'States shall accordingly seek early and just settlement of their international disputes', and the Manila Declaration provides that 'States shall seek in good faith and in a spirit of cooperation and early and just settlement of the international disputes'. All these authorities point to the fact that States cannot remain inert or inactive in the face of a dispute.[100] However, when it comes to identifying the concrete steps that States must take when faced with a dispute, the picture is more nuanced.

A number of commentators have interpreted the obligation of peaceful dispute settlement broadly. For them, this obligation does not just require the States to work together to identify a peaceful means that can be used to settle their disputes, but it imposes a more arduous duty to enter into negotiations and attempt to resolve the *substance* of the dispute itself.[101] In this context, the duty to negotiate requires, as a baseline minimum, the disputants to listen to the arguments of the opposing parties, reflect on their own positions in light of these arguments, and engage in meaningful dialogue in an attempt to resolve the dispute.[102]

99 Tomuschat, 'Article 2(3)', 190.

100 '[States are under an] obligation to settle their disputes by peaceful means. The choice of those means admittedly rests with the parties under Article 33 of the United Nations Charter. They are nonetheless under an obligation to seek such settlement'; *Aerial Incident of 10 August 1999 (Pakistan* v. *India)* (Jurisdiction, Judgment) [2000] ICJ Rep. 12 at para. 53.

101 'A general (but context-bound) duty to cooperate with a view to settlement is inherent in the customary law obligation to settle disputes peacefully, because resolution of a dispute would otherwise be impossible. This general obligation comprises the duty at least to negotiate, as it would otherwise be meaningless': Peters, 'International dispute settlement', 29. 'The choice of a particular means of settlement necessarily involves some kind of negotiation at a time or another': Pellet, 'Peaceful settlement of international disputes', para. 69. See also Caron and Tomuschat, 'Article 2, para. 3', 126.

102 The ICJ has held that negotiation requires that parties 'should pay reasonable regard to the interests of the other'; *Application of the Interim Accord of 13 September 1995 (Former Yugoslav Republic of Macedonia* v. *Greece)* (Judgment) [2011] ICJ Rep. 644 at para. 132.

This interpretation of the obligation of peaceful dispute settlement is problematic. In the *Bolivia* v. *Chile* case, Bolivia maintained that Chile had failed to comply with its duty to negotiate an agreement that granted Bolivia access rights through Chile's territory to the Pacific Ocean.[103] Reaffirming its previous jurisprudence,[104] the Court held that an obligation to negotiate can only arise where the parties have expressed an intention to be legally bound.[105] Bolivia argued that Chile's intention to be bound by a duty to negotiate could be derived from the obligations to settle disputes peacefully as contained in Articles 2(3) and 33(1) of the UN Charter, but the Court rejected this interpretation when it held that 'there is no indication ... that the parties to a dispute are required to resort to a specific method of settlement, such as negotiation'.[106] Correctly in our view, the Court justified this conclusion on the basis that a duty to negotiate is at odds with the principle of free choice of a means of dispute settlement.[107]

Despite this, there is a grain of truth in the argument that, without a minimum conduct baseline, the obligation to settle disputes peacefully would be devoid of any meaning.[108] While the States cannot be compelled to submit their disputes to a specific means of dispute settlement, the fact that they are required, in principle, to seek to settle their disputes by peaceful means and to do so in good faith[109] entails that they must, at the very least, engage in a meaningful exchange of views.[110] This is not the same as an obligation to negotiate the substance of the dispute; it concerns 'the ways in which the dispute will be settled rather than ... the merits of the dispute'.[111] The difference is most evident in the UN Convention on the Law of the Sea,

[103] *Obligation to Negotiate Access to the Pacific Ocean* case.

[104] *Maritime Delimitation and Territorial Questions between Qatar and Bahrain (Qatar* v. *Bahrain)* (Jurisdiction and Admissibility, Judgment) [1994] ICJ Rep. 112.

[105] *Obligation to Negotiate Access to the Pacific Ocean*, para. 91.

[106] Ibid., para. 165.

[107] The language of the Manila Declaration also rules out the duty to negotiate: 'States should, without prejudice to the right of free choice of means, bear in mind that direct negotiations are a flexible and effective means of peaceful settlement of their disputes. When they chose to resort to direct negotiations, States should negotiate meaningfully': para. 10.

[108] Peters, 'International dispute settlement', 11.

[109] 'States shall seek in good faith and in a spirit of cooperation an early and just settlement of their international disputes': Manila Declaration, para 5. '[States are under an] obligation to settle their disputes by peaceful means ... and to do so in good faith': *Aerial Incident of 10 August 1999*, para. 53.

[110] Although this may give rise to 'meta-disputes', that is, disputes as to which means of dispute settlement, if any, should be resorted to, such phenomenon is a necessary consequence of the dynamic nature of the obligation and may be indicative of the fact that the dispute is coming to maturity.

[111] De Brabandere, *Merrills' International Dispute Settlement*, 264.

where the obligation to exchange views is a precondition for access to the dispute settlement mechanism of the Convention.[112] As mentioned above, the very existence of a dispute requires a minimum baseline of communication that allows the parties to be aware of the nature and scope of their disagreement. An exchange of views is also necessary to give meaningful content to the obligation of peaceful dispute settlement, because in order to settle a dispute, the parties must at least assess whether dispute settlement mechanisms would be practically available.

As an obligation of conduct rather than result, where the States have co-operated in good faith and that, after all reasonable efforts have been exhausted, they are still unable to agree on a means for resolving their disputes, they do not have to consult ad infinitum.[113] The reason for this is because some disputes may be so entrenched and adversarial that it is practically impossible for the parties to agree on which means to use to resolve their disputes. In these circumstances, forcing the States to continue to discuss their disputes when it is clear that no agreement can be reached may be counter-productive and may actually exacerbate the dispute. Instead, the parties may be under an obligation to freeze the dispute and pause discussions until an environment emerges that is more conducive to a peaceful settlement of the dispute.[114] But given the dynamic nature of the obligation of dispute settlement, where there is a material change in circumstances surrounding the dispute – for example, the political climate improves because there is a change in government in one or all of the disputing States – the duty to seek a peaceful settlement is reactivated, and the disputants must resume their consultations and again work together in an attempt to find a means to settle their dispute.

[112] Art 283 of UNCLOS. As the tribunal in the *Chagos Marine Protected Area* arbitration stated, the obligation 'requires the Parties to exchange views regarding the means for resolving their dispute; it does not require the Parties to in fact engage in negotiations or other forms of peaceful dispute resolution': *Chagos Marine Protected Area Arbitration (Mauritius* v. *United Kingdom)* (Final Award of 18 March 2015) PCA Case No. 2011-03 at para. 378. See also Mariano J. Aznar Gómez, 'The obligation to exchange views before the International Tribunal for the Law of the Sea: A critical appraisal' (2014) 47 RBDI 237–54.

[113] See *ARA Libertad Case (Argentina* v. *Ghana)* (Provisional Measures, Order of 15 December 2012) ITLOS Reports 2012, 332 at para. 71 ('A State Party is not obliged to continue with an exchange of views when it concludes that the possibilities of reaching an agreement have been exhausted'). See also *MOX Plant Case (Ireland* v. *United Kingdom)* (Provisional Measures, Order of 3 December 2001) ITLOS Reports 2001, 95 at para. 60.

[114] The most notorious example of a frozen dispute is perhaps that concerning the territorial claims over Antarctica; see Martin Lishexian Lee, 'The 1959 Antarctic Treaty: The "freezing and bifocalism" formula' (2000) Aust ILJ 200–14.

On top of this, the obligation of peaceful dispute settlement has a role to play in preventing disputes from escalating and spiralling out of control. As seen above, limited forms of escalation are, in principle, permissible in the context of a dispute so long as they involve lawful measures (retorsion or countermeasures). At the same time, this freedom must be reconciled with the duty of the parties to a dispute to 'refrain from any action which may aggravate the Situation so as to endanger the maintenance of international peace and security'.[115] The obligation of peaceful dispute settlement therefore includes a principle of non-aggravation that proscribes acts of escalation under certain circumstances.[116]

The principle of non-aggravation inherent in the obligation of peaceful dispute settlement has an element of vagueness and indeterminacy.[117] However, it is in the interaction with other norms that the obligation most visibly exercises its normative pull. From this perspective, the obligation may colour the legality of the conduct of the parties by informing the content of other rules of international law, which in turn proscribe acts antagonistic to the settlement of disputes. In other words, the obligation of peaceful dispute settlement, alongside its status as a self-standing rule of international law, may also share some features with what Lowe describes as 'interstitial norms'.[118]

1.4.3 *Interstitial Character of the Obligation*

According to Lowe, interstitial norms are 'normative concepts operating in the interstices between ... primary norms'[119] and 'direct the manner in which competing or conflicting norms that do have their own normativity should interact in practice'.[120] For the reasons mentioned above, the obligation of

[115] The Manila Declaration repeats this provision of the FRD, para. 8. See also Ratner, 'Aggravating duty of non-aggravation', 1319 ('[The duty of non-aggravation] is legally grounded in the UN Charter and authoritative interpretations thereof (including the FRD, Manila Declaration and Security Council resolutions)').

[116] See Merrills, 'Means of dispute settlement', 549 ('The obligation is not just to give peaceful methods a try but to persevere as long as necessary, while at the same time avoiding action which could make things worse. In other words, if a dispute cannot be settled, States must at least manage it and keep things under control').

[117] Ratner, 'Aggravating duty of non-aggravation', 1321.

[118] Vaughan Lowe, 'The politics of law-making: Are the method and character of norm creation changing?' in Michael Byers (ed.), *The Role of Law in International Politics: Essays in International Relations and International Law* (Oxford: Oxford University Press, 2001), pp. 207–26.

[119] Ibid., 213.

[120] Ibid., 216.

peaceful dispute settlement does have a normative charge of its own. However, this does not exhaust the normative pull of the obligation, which can also be appreciated by looking at its effects on other rules of international law. International law provides several norms which are inextricably linked to the process of dispute settlement and whose content is dependent on the circumstances of each case. Two examples are particularly emblematic in this regard.

The first concerns the regulation of countermeasures under the law of State responsibility. There is a clear connection between countermeasures and dispute settlement; as Simma noted, 'recourse to counter-measures not involving the threat or use of force is in itself a peaceful means of settling a dispute arising from an internationally wrongful act'.[121] Yet, as Arangio-Ruiz pointed out, countermeasures are evidently 'non-amicable' when compared to other means of dispute settlement and thus have the potential of aggravating the dispute.[122] In his capacity as the ILC Special Rapporteur on State Responsibility, Arangio-Ruiz proposed to subject resorting to countermeasures to the 'prior ... exhaustion of all the amicable settlement procedures available under general international law, the Charter of the United Nations or any other dispute settlement instrument to which it [the reactor State] is a party'.[123] This proposal was deemed unrealistic by other ILC members and was ultimately rejected.[124] After several iterations, the ILC finally settled on the text of Article 52(1) of the Articles on State Responsibility, 2001 (ASR), which requires an injured State to 'call on the responsible State ... to fulfil its obligations' and to 'notify the responsible State of any decision to take countermeasures and offer to negotiate with that State'. Even the mere 'offer' to negotiate as a precondition to the taking of countermeasures gave rise to 'lively

[121] Bruno Simma, 'Counter-measures and dispute settlement: A plea for a different balance' (1994) 5 EJIL 102–5 at 103.

[122] Gaetano Arangio-Ruiz, 'Counter-measures and amicable dispute settlement means in the implementation of State responsibility: A crucial issue before the International Law Commission' (1994) 5 EJIL 20–53 at 21.

[123] ILC, 'Fourth report on State responsibility by Mr. Gaetano Arangio-Ruiz, Special Rapporteur', in *Yearbook of the International Law Commission. 1992, Volume II, Part One: Report of the Commission to the General Assembly on the Work of Its Forty-Fourth Session* (New York: UN, 1992), p. 22, para. 52 (Draft Art 12(1)(a)).

[124] See Yuji Iwasawa and Naoki Itwatsuki, 'Procedural conditions', in James Crawford, Alain Pellet, and Simon Ollerson (eds.), *The Law of International Responsibility* (Oxford: Oxford University Press, 2010), p. 1151. Concerns were also voiced about the unfair advantage this would give to the wrongdoing State, which would be able to avoid the application of countermeasures by maintaining the appearance of engagement with a means of dispute settlement; see David J. Bederman, 'Counterintuiting countermeasures' (2002) 96 AJIL 817–32 at 824.

debates' within the ILC, evidencing a 'central disagreement' on the point.[125] Still, the fact remains that, in the normative conflict between the rules allowing the taking of countermeasures and those protecting the sovereignty of the target State, the obligation of peaceful dispute settlement exercises its normative pull. The injured State wishing to resort to countermeasures must first ensure that reasonable attempts to settle the dispute have been made. What is reasonable depends on the circumstances of the case and is tempered by the exception for 'urgent' countermeasures pursuant to Article 52(2) of the ASR.[126] Still, measures taken without any consideration for the settlement of the dispute will likely run counter to customary international law.

The continuing normative pull of the obligation of peaceful dispute settlement on the law of countermeasures is further demonstrated by Article 50(2)(a) of the ASR, according to which 'a State taking countermeasures is not relieved from fulfilling its obligations ... under any dispute settlement procedure applicable between it and the responsible State' and, most importantly, by Article 52(3)(b) of the ASR, which provides that 'countermeasures may not be taken, and if already taken must be suspended without undue delay if ... the dispute is pending before a court or tribunal which has the authority to make decisions binding on the parties'. This is an important aspect of the connection between the legality of countermeasures and the dynamic nature of the obligation of peaceful dispute settlement. Where a means of dispute settlement has been selected, 'for so long as the dispute settlement procedure is being implemented in good faith, unilateral action by way of countermeasures is not justified';[127] any countermeasure would constitute in and of itself an aggravation of the dispute running counter to the obligation of dispute settlement. As the ILC commentary explains, this is because 'once the parties submit their dispute to such a court or tribunal for resolution, the injured State may request it to order provisional measures to protect its rights'.[128] At the same time, the obligation of peaceful dispute settlement continues to expand or contract according to the evolving circumstances. Thus, the ASR go on to specify that this limitation on the taking of countermeasures 'does not apply if the responsible State fails to implement the dispute settlement

[125] Maurice Kamto, 'The time factor in the application of countermeasures', in James Crawford, Alain Pellet, and Simon Ollerson (eds.), *The Law of International Responsibility* (Oxford: Oxford University Press, 2010), p. 1171.

[126] Ibid.

[127] ILC, *Articles on State Responsibility*, 136, commentary to Art 52.

[128] Ibid. But see Bederman, 'Counterintuiting countermeasures', 825 ('The fact that a tribunal might ostensibly have the power to indicate provisional measures, even while lacking actual jurisdiction over the dispute, raises concerns about the reading of Article 52 (3)').

procedures in good faith'.[129] Once again, the obligation is flexible enough to allow a party to resort to unilateral measures when the conduct of the other party is thwarting the peaceful settlement of a dispute.[130]

An even more striking example of the normative pull exercised by the obligation of peaceful dispute settlement is the notion that, under certain circumstances, resorting to a judicial means of dispute settlement may be antagonistic to the settlement of a dispute and should therefore be deemed unlawful. This idea is captured in the principles of 'abuse of right' and 'abuse of process', which, according to Kolb, consist of 'the use of procedural instruments or rights by one or more parties for purposes that are alien to those for which the procedural rights are established, especially for a fraudulent, procrastinatory or frivolous purpose, for the purpose of causing harm or obtaining an illegitimate advantage, for the purpose of reducing or removing the effectiveness of some other available process or for purposes of pure propaganda'.[131]

Dispute settlement bodies have been reluctant to find that an abuse of process has occurred for multiple reasons.[132] Chief among them is the fact that the threshold for an abuse of process is high and a party often has several reasons to institute judicial proceedings; this makes it difficult for the other party to prove that proceedings have been improperly used.[133] The ICJ has never recognised as well-founded a claim of this kind and, on several occasions, has stated that 'it cannot concern itself with the political motivation which may lead a State at a particular time, or in particular circumstances, to choose judicial settlement'.[134] Despite this, there is little doubt that abuse of

[129] ILC, *Articles on State Responsibility*, Art 52(4).

[130] The ILC's commentary lists 'various possibilities, ranging from an initial refusal to cooperate in the procedure, for example by non-appearance, through non-compliance with a provisional measures order . . . through to refusal to accept the final decision of the court or tribunal'; ILC, *Articles on State Responsibility*, 137, commentary to Art 52.

[131] Robert Kolb, 'General principles of procedural law', in Andreas Zimmermann et al. (eds.), *The Statute of the International Court of Justice* (Oxford: Oxford University Press, 2019), p. 998. See also Alexandre Kiss, 'Abuse of rights', in Anne Peters (ed.), *Max Planck Encyclopedia of Public International Law* (Oxford: Oxford University Press, 2006).

[132] Andrew D. Mitchell and Trina Malone, 'Abuse of process in inter-State dispute resolution', in Anne Peters (ed.), *Max Planck Encyclopedia of International Procedural Law* (Oxford: Oxford University Press, 2018), para. 5.

[133] See Marie Lemey, 'Incidental proceedings before the International Court of Justice: The fine line between "litigation strategy" and "abuse of process"' (2021) 20 LPICT 5–29 at 24.

[134] *Border and Transborder Armed Actions (Nicaragua* v. *Honduras)* (Jurisdiction and Admissibility, Judgment) [1988] ICJ Rep. 69 at para. 52. See also *Alleged Violations of the 1955 Treaty of Amity, Economic Relations, and Consular Rights (Islamic Republic of Iran* v. *United States of America)* (Preliminary Objections, Judgment) [2021] ICJ Rep. 9 at para. 95.

process is firmly rooted in the general principle of good faith and, as such, is part of international law.[135] States have continued to plead abuse of process before international courts and tribunals in recent years,[136] and the claim has encountered some success before investment tribunals.[137]

The notion of abuse of process is another way in which the obligation of international dispute settlement acquires a concrete normative dimension. It is imbued with the idea that the context in which the actions of a party to a dispute take place ultimately determines their legality. As seen above, the dynamic nature of the obligation means that certain steps that would be permissible (or even desirable) under different circumstances become impermissible when a party to a dispute is no longer seeking in good faith to achieve the peaceful settlement of that dispute.

1.5 CONCLUSION

The obligation to settle disputes peacefully is a critical element of the international society's dispute settlement system and is embedded in multiple treaties as well as customary law. To date, the academic literature has largely focused on the means and methods to settle disputes without inquiring into the content of the peaceful dispute settlement obligation itself other than to the extent to which it prohibits resorting to force. To fill this gap in the literature, this chapter has elaborated on the conditions that activate this obligation and on the substance of the obligation. In doing so, this chapter has demonstrated that the obligation of peaceful dispute settlement is a complex and multifaceted rule that exercises 'an immense gravitational pull' both on its own terms and on the rules that surround it.[138] At a minimum, it requires a degree of communication that allows the disputing parties to be

[135] Mitchell and Malone, 'Abuse of process', para. 7.

[136] In fact, claims of abuse of process have been on the rise; see Freya Baetens, 'Abuse of process and abuse of rights before the ICJ: Ever more popular, ever less successful?', *EJIL: Talk!*, 15 October 2019, www.ejiltalk.org/abuse-of-process-and-abuse-of-rights-before-the-icj-ever-more-popular-ever-less-successful (accessed 2 October 2022).

[137] Arbitration claims have been dismissed on the grounds that the investor underwent corporate restructuring solely for the purpose of accessing arbitration; see, e.g., *Phoenix Action, Ltd* v. *The Czech Republic* (Award of 15 April 2009) ICSID ARB/06/5 at para. 144; *Venezuela Holdings BV (Formerly Mobil Corporation)* v. *Bolivarian Republic of Venezuela* (Decision on Jurisdiction of 10 June 2010) ICSID ARB/07/27 at para. 190; *Philip Morris Asia Limited* v. *The Commonwealth of Australia* (Award on Jurisdiction and Admissibility of 17 December 2015) PCA Case No. 2012-12 at para. 588. See also Jorun Baumgartner, *Treaty Shopping in International Investment Law* (Oxford: Oxford University Press, 2016), p. 12.

[138] Lowe, 'Politics of law-making', 217.

aware of the nature and scope of their disagreement and to assess the viability of a potential means to settle it. Even when no agreement concerning the settlement of a dispute can be reached, the obligation of peaceful dispute settlement continues to guide the behaviour of the disputing parties, and as a dynamic norm, its content changes in line with the mutating circumstances.

This chapter has also demonstrated that the obligation of peaceful dispute settlement operates as an interstitial norm insofar as it informs the interpretation and application of other rules of international law linked with the process of dispute settlement. Understood in this way, the obligation of peaceful dispute settlement ensures that the conduct of the disputing parties, even when not bound by obligations concerning specific means of dispute settlement, remains within tolerable boundaries and does not stray too far from the goal of peaceful dispute settlement. Far from being a mere duplicate of the prohibition on the threat or use of force, the obligation of peaceful dispute settlement is rich in normative content and plays an essential role in preventing disputes from spiralling out of control and maintaining international peace and security more generally.

2

Parallel Proceedings Concerning Investment and Human Rights Claims

TARCISIO GAZZINI AND ALESSANDRA PIETROBON

2.1 INTRODUCTION

The proliferation of specialised tribunals in different areas of international law, each with its own characteristics, is a positive development in a decentralised or horizontal legal order such as international law. However, it has some side effects, particularly the risk of parallel proceedings, which may lead to inconsistent decisions.

This essay discusses a peculiar category of parallel proceedings, namely those originating from the same matrix of facts brought before one or more investment arbitral tribunals as well as before the European Court of Human Rights (ECtHR). Sections 2.2 to 2.6 concisely discuss the doctrines of *res judicata*, *lis pendens*, *forum non conveniens*, and abuse of process from the standpoint of international law. Those doctrines are intended to coordinate and manage parallel proceedings with a view to minimising the associated risks of different and potentially conflicting outcomes as well as double or multiple recovery.

Sections 2.7 to 2.9 zoom in on parallel proceedings before the ECtHR and investment tribunals. Due to overlapping substantive rules, this type of parallel proceedings may be expected to proliferate in the future, even if some case proceedings before the ECtHR or investment tribunals may be precluded on jurisdictional grounds. The disputes related to *Yukos* before the ECtHR and several investment tribunals provide an excellent case study to examine this peculiar type of parallel proceedings and formulate some considerations on how they can be managed.

2.2 PARALLEL PROCEEDINGS IN INTERNATIONAL LAW

For the purpose of this chapter, parallel proceedings is 'a generic term referring to a wide range of situations in which disputes that are linked in some ways, or which have some similarities are brought before different adjudicators'.[1]

Parallel proceedings may occur in a multitude of forms at the domestic, transnational, and international levels. They are considered undesirable for several reasons, most prominently because of the risk of different and potentially conflicting outcomes, the risk of double or multiple recovery, and, ultimately, the unavoidably negative impact on legal predictability and certainty.[2]

The peculiar situation in which more proceedings on the same matter are pending is described as *lis alibi pendens*, meaning that two (or more) tribunals are simultaneously required to adjudicate. As soon as one tribunal delivers a final decision settling all aspects of the dispute, the other tribunal(s) must refrain from exercising their jurisdiction by virtue of the *res judicata* principle.

The rules concerning *res judicata* and *lis pendens* serve the same objectives – in particular judicial economy (by preventing costly parallel litigation), legal security (by avoiding conflicting judgments), and protection of defendants (from oppressive litigation tactics).[3] However, while the former principle is well settled in international law (see Section 2.3), the latter remains uncertain (Section 2.4).[4]

1 Gilles Cuniberti, 'Parallel litigation and foreign investment disputes settlement' (2006) 21 ICSID Rev 381–426 at 382. Likewise, see Hanno Wehland, *The Coordination of Multiple Proceedings in Investment Treaty Arbitration* (Oxford: Oxford University Press, 2013), para. 1.20. In the ILA, *Final Report on Lis Pendens and Arbitration* (72nd ILA Conference on International Commercial Arbitration, Toronto, 4–8 June 2006), footnote 3, however, the Committee on International Commercial Arbitration of the International Law Association took a pragmatic approach and considered the term 'parallel proceedings' as interchangeable with *lis pendens*. It explained that 'there was a debate within the Committee whether it would be preferable to use the phrase "parallel proceedings" in this report, but it was decided that use of Latin was acceptable to describe parallel litigation because the phrase is well recognised and customarily used in that context; nevertheless, the phrase "parallel proceedings" is adopted in the recommendations'.

2 Vaughan Lowe, 'Overlapping jurisdiction in international tribunals', (1999) 20 Aus YBIL 191–204 at 203, has pointed out that *lis alibi pendens*, abuse of process, and *res judicata* relate to the 'good order of judicial proceedings'. See also Gilbert Guillaume, 'The future of international judicial institutions' (1995) 44 ICLQ 848–62 at 862. The need to avoid multiplicity of legal proceedings is recognised in some domestic legal systems: see, for instance, the United Kingdom Supreme Court Act 1981, s. 49(2).

3 Phillip Janig and August Reinisch, 'General principles and the coherence of international investment law: Of *res judicata*, *lis pendens* and the value of precedents', in Mads Tønnesson Andenæs et al. (eds.), *General Principles and the Coherence of International Law* (Leiden: Brill, 2019), p. 249.

4 For a detailed discussion, see Luiz E. Salles, *Forum Shopping in International Adjudication: The Role of Preliminary Objections* (Cambridge: Cambridge University Press, 2014), pp. 277–81.

2.3 *RES JUDICATA*

The principle of *res judicata* is commonly considered as part of the general principles of international law.[5] The concept is twofold: on the one hand, it refers to the binding authority of the judgment on the parties. Such authority, granted by the law in domestic systems, has equal standing in international law where it is based, first and foremost, on the consent of the parties to the jurisdiction of the court (or tribunal).[6] On the other hand, the same principle implies that no further litigation will be allowed on the same matter. The application of the second tenet might be controversial, since it requires a definition of the concept of 'same dispute'.[7]

Moreover, determining which part of the first judgment is to be considered as *res judicata* – preventing further litigation – may present additional challenges. While the operative part of the judgment will not be subject to further scrutiny, the extent to which incidental decisions on preliminary questions should be excluded from new judicial consideration is more debatable. To this purpose, a general principle requires the separation of fundamental steps in the legal reasoning that logically supports the decision – which shall not be rediscussed – from secondary issues that, to the contrary, might be submitted again to a different judge.[8]

As emphasised by the International Court of Justice (the ICJ), the principle of *res judicata* in international law serves two purposes: the first – common to domestic law – is to safeguard the interests of the parties in avoiding an issue that has already been adjudicated to be argued again. The second purpose is essential to the stability of an international legal system that requires termination of disputes by peaceful means[9] This latter purpose is mirrored by the

[5] In literature, see Bin Cheng, *General Principles of Law as Applied by International Courts and Tribunals* (London: Stevens, 1953), pp. 336–37; William S. Dodge, 'Res judicata', in *Max Planck Encyclopedia of Public International Law* (Oxford: Oxford University Press, 2006).

[6] According to the Hague Convention on the Pacific Settlement of International Dispute (The Hague, 29 July 1899, in force 4 September 1900), 'the Arbitration Convention implies the engagement to submit loyally to the Award' (Art 18).

[7] The issue will be dealt with below, as application of rules based on *lis pendens* calls into question the same problem.

[8] A further elaboration on the issue is beyond the scope of this study. The principle, derived from domestic procedural systems, also belongs to international law, as argued by Judge Anzilotti: see *Interpretation of Judgments Nos. 7 and 8 (The Chorzów Factory)* [1927] PCIJ Rep. Series A No. 13 at p. 24 (Dissenting Opinion by Anzilotti).

[9] *Application of the Convention on the Prevention and Punishment of the Crime of Genocide (Bosnia and Herzegovina* v. *Serbia and Montenegro)* (Judgment) [2007] ICJ Rep. 43 at para. 116. In *Question of the Delimitation of the Continental Shelf between Nicaragua and Colombia beyond 200 Nautical Miles from the Nicaraguan Coast (Nicaragua* v. *Colombia)* (Preliminary Objections, Judgment) [2016] ICJ Rep. 100 at para. 58, the ICJ reiterated that the

final character of arbitral awards or judgments in inter-State disputes that rules out any possibility of appeal before a different judge.

The relevance of this principle can be traced back to ancient Greece, as witnessed by inscriptions on the temple of Athena in Rhodos, representing a sort of *procès-verbal* of a long-lasting dispute between the two Greek city States of Samo and Priene.[10] The two cities had been litigating for centuries over the possession of the region of Dryoussa and the fortress of Kairon, located at their common border. Several arbitral awards on the issue were rendered since 323 BC, providing alternative solutions. In fact, after some years, the losing city used to reject the unfavourable judgment by claiming to relitigate the same issue. Eventually, the parties appointed the Roman Senate as arbitrator, which was able to provide the final settlement, precisely by reference to the principle of *res judicata* (135 BC): they held that a further judicial assessment was precluded, upholding the previous judgment rendered by the arbitrators in Rhodos (196–192 BC).[11] The memory of this case provides good evidence of how much the stability of international relations as well as the certainty of international law are still owing to the Roman law principle of *res judicata*.

2.4 *LIS PENDENS*

Domestic systems provide specific rules to manage parallel proceedings, determining which tribunal must stay proceedings or waive jurisdiction, leaving competence to a different judge. They may rely on several legal assumptions, ultimately concerning the role of the judiciary. In civil law

principle 'protects, at the same time, the judicial function of a court or tribunal and the parties to a case which has led to a judgment that is final and without appeal'. In investment arbitration, see, for instance, *Apotex Holdings Inc. and Apotex Inc.* v. *United States* (Award of 15 August 2014) ICSID ARB(AF)/12/1 at para. 7.11. In *Petrobart Limited* v. *Kyrgyz Republic* (Award of 29 March 2005) SCC Case No. 126/2003 at p. 64, the tribunal referred also to procedural fairness. As far as commercial arbitration is concerned, in *Puerto Rico Maritime Shipping* v. *Star Lines Ltd.*, 454 F. Supp. 368 (SDNY 1978) at 372, the tribunal held that 'it is the general rule with regard to the confirmability of arbitration awards that, in order to be "final" and "definite", the award must both resolve all the issues submitted to arbitration, and determine each issue fully so that no further litigation is necessary to finalize the obligations of the parties under the award'.

[10] Wolfgang Preiser, 'History of international law' Ancient times to 1648', in *Max Planck Encyclopedia of Public International Law* (Oxford: Oxford University Press, 2006); Anna Magnetto, 'Interstate arbitration and foreign judges', in Edward M. Harris and Mirko Canevaro (eds.), *The Oxford Handbook of Ancient Greek Law* (Oxford Academic, 2016), http://dx.doi.org/10.1093/oxfordhb/9780199599257.013.20.

[11] See Jan Hendrik Willem Verzijl, *International Law in Historical Perspective* (Leiden: Sijthoff, 1968), p. 545.

systems, the rules preventing parallel proceedings are basically conceived on the premise that each dispute must be adjudicated by its *natural judge*, to be identified according to precise legal criteria – that, sometimes, may even provide for a possible choice between different alternative fora. In common law systems, attention rather goes to the specific dispute to be dealt with, leaving to each judge the possibility to waive jurisdiction if they find that a different court would be in a better position to decide on the matter. Therefore, a common law court could consider itself as a *forum non conveniens*, waiving jurisdiction to a different court better posed, for instance, to collect pieces of evidence or hear witnesses.[12]

General criteria to manage parallel proceedings are lacking in international law. This comes as no surprise, since a proper international procedural law *system* is not conceivable due to the lack of any authority responsible for the efficiency of the 'judiciary' as a whole, as it happens in domestic law. Every international court or arbitral tribunal is rather established and functions on a consensual basis, and no general authority could be vested with adequate coordination powers. Besides, in the international legal order, 'neither the equality nor the legitimacy of all adjudicators should be assumed. The issue of parallel litigation can therefore be addressed by discriminating between the competing adjudicators on very substantive grounds'.[13]

Neither the Permanent Court of Justice[14] nor the ICJ has taken a definitive position on the role of the *lis pendens* principle in international law.[15] Some mixed-claim commissions have acknowledged situations of *lis alibi pendens*, mostly concerning parallel claims contemporarily pending before the claim commissions themselves and domestic courts. However, the issue was dealt with in different ways. In *Santa Rosa Mining*, for instance, the British-Mexican Commission held that it was not prevented from exercising jurisdiction.[16] The French-Italian Commission in *SAIMI* took the opposite view, refusing to consider the merits unless a parallel claim before a municipal court

[12] For an overview on the solutions in different domestic systems and in the EU law, see ILA, *Final Report on Res Judicata and Arbitration* (72nd ILA Conference on International Commercial Arbitration, Toronto, 4–8 June 2006), para. 2.

[13] Cuniberti, 'Parallel litigation', 383.

[14] See, in particular, *Certain German Interests in Polish Upper Silesia* (Preliminary Objections, Judgment of 25 August 1925) PCIJ Rep. Series A No. 6 at p. 20.

[15] According to Judge *ad hoc* Cot (Dissenting Opinion) para. 3 in *Application of the International Convention on the Elimination of All Forms of Racial Discrimination (Qatar* v. *United Arab Emirates)* (Provisional Measures, Order of 14 June 2019) [2019] ICJ Rep. 361, 'the status of the doctrine of *lis pendens* in public international law is not entirely clear'.

[16] *The Santa Rosa Mining Company (Ltd.) (Great Britain)* v. *United Mexican States* (Decision 92 of 3 August 1931) 5 RIAA 252 at p. 252.

was discontinued.[17] It is worth pointing out that both Commissions were perfectly aware of the need to avoid double recovery, an issue that will be discussed below.

Due to the growing number of possible adjudicators, parallel proceedings are becoming more frequent in the international legal order, sometimes leading to blatantly conflicting judgments, as revealed by the *Lauder/CME* cases.[18] The need to address issues arising from parallel proceedings is becoming more and more evident. As for scholarly opinions, some authors argue that the principle of *lis pendens* precludes instituting new international proceedings if litigation between the same parties and involving the same dispute is already pending.[19] According to other scholars, on the contrary, 'there are serious doubts as to whether *lis pendens* can be applied as a principle of general international law'.[20] Others contend that '*lis pendens* may operate as a discretion to decline jurisdiction, rather than a binding rule'.[21]

It would be unwise, at the moment, to assume that some general rules on *lis pendens* already exist in international law.

2.5 DEALING WITH PARALLEL PROCEEDINGS

Studies on *lis pendens* and *res judicata* in international law have intensified in recent years, proposing to address the problem according to different rules or mechanisms. The first preliminary issue to be solved, however, is the identification of the cases that would trigger the application of those rules and mechanisms. The crux of the matter remains this: under what conditions should proceedings before a tribunal be precluded due to parallel proceedings already pending before, or decided by, another tribunal? The solutions

[17] *Différend SAIMI (Società per Azioni Industriale Marmi d'Italia) – Décisions Nos. 4, 11, 19, 38 et 70* (1948–50) 13 RIAA 43 at p. 45.

[18] *Ronald S. Lauder* v. *The Czech Republic* (Final Award of 3 September 2001) UNCITRAL; *CME Czech Republic B.V.* v. *The Czech Republic* (Partial Award of 13 September 2001) UNCITRAL. According to Christoph Schreuer, 'Multiple proceedings', in Andrea Gattini, Attila Tanzi, and Filippo Fontanelli (eds.), *General Principles of Law and International Investment Arbitration* (Leiden: Brill, 2018), p. 157, these decisions are 'one of the more embarrassing episodes in the history of arbitration'.

[19] See, for instance, Janig and Reinisch, 'General principles', 254; Kaj Hobér, '*Res judicata* and *lis pendens* in international arbitration' (2014) 366 Recueil des Cours 99–405 at 330.

[20] Wehland, *Coordination of Multiple Proceedings*, 194. See Yuval Shany, *Regulating Jurisdictional Relations between National and International Courts* (Oxford: Oxford University Press, 2007), p. 158; Cuniberti, 'Parallel litigation', 282–83; Giovanni Zarra, *Parallel Proceedings in Investment Arbitration* (Torino: Giappichelli, 2016), pp. 117–21.

[21] Campbell McLachlan et al., *International Investment Arbitration* (Oxford: Oxford University Press, 2008), para. 4.37.

proposed can be divided between those based on objective criteria, being suitable for (almost) automatic application, and those leaving a larger margin of appreciation to the interpreter.

2.5.1 *Objective Criteria: The Triple Test*

Objective criteria rely on the so-called triple test based on 'the three traditional elements for identification of a dispute: *persona, petitum, causa petendi*'.[22] This test assumes that the rules concerning *lis pendens* and *res judicata* should apply if three conditions are cumulatively met, namely, identity of the parties, the cause of action, and the relief sought. More recently, the ICJ referred to 'the same parties, object and legal ground'.[23] According to Schreuer and Reinisch, 'identical "object" (*petitum*) means that the same type of relief is sought in different proceedings. Identical "ground" (*causa petendi*) means that the same legal arguments are relied upon in different proceedings'.[24]

In theory, this method could be followed without hesitation, considering how the same test works in many domestic legal systems, particularly in civil law countries. In practice, lacking general co-ordination norms, the complexity of the international law scenario requires a less strict approach.[25] In some cases, the same kind of relief might be sought on the basis of different, independent legal instruments, each of them providing a separate legal ground for the request. For instance, relevant rights might be grounded, on the one side, on an investment agreement and, on the other side, on a human rights instrument. As will be discussed below, in case of an unlawful expropriation, the investment tribunal would focus on the violations of relevant investment law provisions, while the court of human rights would consider the right to property. Each of them would retain jurisdiction based on a *different* cause of action, even if the events at the origin of the proceedings are actually the same. According to the triple test, the dispute would *not* be the same and, therefore, double recovery would seemingly be lawful.

[22] *Interpretation of Judgments Nos. 7 and 8* (Dissenting Opinion by Anzilotti), p. 23.

[23] *Question of the Delimitation of the Continental Shelf* (Preliminary Objections, Judgment), para. 59.

[24] *CME Czech Republic B.V. v. The Czech Republic* (Legal Opinion by Christoph Schreuer and August Reinisch of 20 June 2002) UNCITRAL at p. 16, para. 43. For the ILA, *Interim Report: Res Judicata and Arbitration* (71st ILA Conference on International Commercial Arbitration, Berlin, 20 August 2004), p. 7, cause of action 'comprises all the facts and circumstances necessary to give rise to a right to relief. Generally, all claims arising from a single event and relying on the same evidence will be treated as the same cause of action'.

[25] See Zarra, *Parallel Proceedings*, ch. 3.

Moreover, in investment disputes, the same interests are often shared by different subjects, and each of them may be entitled to bring the dispute before a different judge. In this situation, the relief sought and the cause of action might be the same — that is, a company and its shareholders start different proceedings based on the same facts and seek the same relief. In this case, reference to the triple test would preclude the possibility of declaring one of the two applications inadmissible, because the parties are not the same. The test would thus be unsuitable to prevent the formation of conflicting judgments to the detriment of the certainty of rights and the sound administration of justice.[26]

2.5.2 *Non-objective Criteria*

As objective tests are easy to manage but not always effective, attention should be paid to other possible means to deal with the issues of *lis pendens* and *res judicata*. The recommendation adopted by the International Law Association (ILA) defines 'parallel proceedings' in terms of parties and issues that are 'the same or substantially the same'. This reflects the ILA Committee's view that *lis pendens* in arbitration is largely a matter of management rather than the application of rigid criteria.[27]

The *forum non conveniens* doctrine may provide a solution, according to which a judge could decline jurisdiction on the assumption that a different court would be better placed to deal with the issue, in the interest not only of the parties but also of a better administration of justice. At the international level, considerations in the line of *forum non conveniens* should include the different expertise and level of legitimacy or support of the different court or tribunal that could retain jurisdiction.[28] However, this is a highly discretionary and unpredictable doctrine, whose application will depend on the personal attitude of the judge. Moreover, the judge declining jurisdiction is not supposed to assess whether the more *conveniens* court would find itself competent or not.

Comity among the courts could also play a prominent role, as shown by the *MOX Plant* case, in which the arbitral tribunal suspended the proceedings in

[26] As a matter of fact, *lis pendens* exceptions are often dismissed by courts, precisely because the test proves too strict: see Cuniberti, 'Parallel litigation'.

[27] ILA, *Final Report on Lis Pendens*, para. 5.6.

[28] Joost Pauwelyn and Luiz Eduardo Salles, 'Forum shopping before international tribunals: (Real) concerns, (im)possible solutions' (2009) 42 Cornell Int'l L J 77–118 at 115.

order to consider the forthcoming decision of the European Court of Justice in a related proceeding.[29]

A further possible ground for denial of jurisdiction, in case of multiple proceedings, is abuse of process. The term does not imply any illegal conduct, but rather an alleged unfair behaviour of the applicant that initiates multiple proceedings without any genuine need for doing so, only for maximising its chances of success.[30] Realising that such a strategy is being put in place, the judge could deny its jurisdiction to avoid the duplication of proceedings already pending before a different tribunal. Needless to say, this way of dealing with a situation of *lis alibi pendens* will equally be left to the appreciation of the judge on a case-by-case basis as the concept of abusive behaviour would escape any objective definition.

Compared to the triple test, these criteria can prove more effective, but the outcome of their application could be less predictable. Scholars actually strive to give a rational standing to erratic jurisprudence, highlighting the criteria applied to prevent issues related to parallel proceedings. Present case studies are fundamental for understanding the principles underlying each possible legal tool, its practical relevance, and its limits. However, from a general perspective, the same studies confirm how the present solutions – due to the inorganic, fragmented nature of international law – cannot be easily arranged into a system of procedural rules. Some authors conclude by suggesting – *de lege ferenda* – that future investment agreements should explicitly consider the issue and set out tailored rules to prevent parallel proceedings in relation to the specific matter of each agreement.[31]

2.6 DOUBLE RECOVERY

Successful parallel proceedings can lead to double or multiple recovery for the same wrong. Such an outcome could hardly conform to justice. The victim, being already afforded appropriate redress by a first judgment, must not be

[29] The arbitral tribunal held that 'considerations of mutual respect and comity which should prevail between judicial institutions both of which may be called upon to determine rights and obligations as between two States': see *MOX Plant Case (Ireland* v. *United Kingdom)* (Order No. 3 of 24 June 2003) PCA Case No. 2002-01 at para. 28. However, the issue was not exactly one of *lis pendens*, but rather of connected proceedings.

[30] In investment disputes, the respondent (the State) is often forced to defend itself before different courts and shall be successful only after winning in all the separate trials, while the applicant (the investor) could take advantage even from success in one single proceeding. See Emmanuel Gaillard, 'Abuse of process in international arbitration' (2017) 32 ICSID Rev 17–37 at 22.

[31] See Pauwelyn and Salles, 'Forum shopping'.

allowed to take further advantage from a different judgment substantially concerning the same dispute. At the same time, the losing party must be protected against the burden of double condemnation, imposing twice the compensation for the same wrongdoing.

The principle that double recovery should be avoided is well settled in international law. In the *Alabama* arbitration, the tribunal held that 'in order to arrive at an equitable compensation for the damages which have been sustained, it is necessary to set aside all double claims for the same losses'.[32] The PCIJ and ICJ jurisprudence is equally clear since the *Chorzow* case, when the Court held that the same compensation could not be 'awarded twice over'.[33] In literature, it has been argued that double recovery may be avoided, or at least minimised, by resorting to 'consolidation, pro rata awards, a flexible application of *lis pendens* and *res judicata* as well as other methods'.[34]

Furthermore, the International Law Commission's (ILC) Articles on State Responsibility clearly preclude double recovery in case of plurality of responsible States by providing that a State cannot recover by way of compensation more than the damage it has suffered (Article 47(2)(a)). In case of plurality of injured States under Article 46, the concerned States are 'expected to coordinate their claims so as to avoid double recovery'.[35] Indeed, it has been observed that 'the very notion and rationale of full compensation implies that double recovery has to be avoided. Offset of benefits is also determined by considerations of equity which are inherently part of any damage calculation.'[36]

There are no precise guidelines for the avoidance of double recovery in investment arbitration.[37] However, the need is clearly perceived by the tribunals. In *Orascom* v. *Algeria*, for instance, the tribunal held that if the harm incurred by one entity in a corporate chain is fully repaired in one arbitration,

[32] *Alabama Claims of the United States* v. *Great Britain* (Award of 14 September 1872) 29 RIAA 125 at p. 133. In the same vein, in *Affaire du Guano (Chili* v. *France)* (Award of 8 January 1901) 15 RIAA 77 at p. 117, the tribunal concluded that 'le Pérou n'est pas exposé à payer deux fois'.

[33] *Factory at Chorzów* [1928] PCIJ Series A No. 17 at pp. 29, 59.

[34] Christoph Schreuer, 'Shareholder protection in international investment law' (2005) 2 TDM 1–12 at 1.

[35] ILC, 'Commentary to Article 46', in *Yearbook of the International Law Commission. 2001, Volume II, Part Two: Report of the Commission to the General Assembly on the Work of Its Fifty-Third Session* (New York: UN, 2007), p. 124.

[36] Emily Sipiorski and Christian Tietje, 'Offset of benefits in damages calculation in international investment arbitration' (2012) 29 J Int'l Arb 545–66.

[37] David V. Rivkin, 'The impact of parallel and successive proceedings on the enforcement of arbitral awards', in Bernardo M. Cremades and Julian D. M. Lew (eds.), *Parallel State and Arbitral Procedures in International Arbitration* (Alphen aan den Rijn: Kluwer, 2005), p. 278.

the claims brought by other entities belonging to the same chain in other arbitral proceedings may become inadmissible.[38]

2.7 PARALLEL PROCEEDINGS BEFORE ECTHR AND INVESTMENT ARBITRAL TRIBUNALS

Investment law and human rights are fertile grounds for parallel proceedings due to the significant overlap of the respective substantive provisions.[39] The obvious examples are fair and equitable treatment (FET) and expropriation. The human rights content of FET is demonstrated by the concrete principles on the basis of which arbitral tribunals have fleshed out the meaning of the standard. The concrete principles indicated in *Rumeli* v. *Kazakhstan*,[40] and especially those of due process and non-discrimination, reflect to a large extent substantive human rights protected in most human rights instruments. Likewise, the provisions on expropriation in investment law and on the right of property in human rights treaties, including in the ECHR, tend to overlap.[41] It is no coincidence that some investment tribunals have looked at the ECtHR jurisprudence in search of indications useful to draw the line dividing non-compensable exercise of normative powers and compensable indirect expropriation. For instance, a tribunal has found inspiration in the 'reasonable

[38] *Orascom TMT Investments S.à r.l.* v. *Algeria* (Award of 31 May 2017) ICSID ARB/12/35 at para. 495.

[39] As pointed out by Martins Paparinskis, 'Analogies and other regimes of international law', in Zachary Douglas, Joost Pauwelyn, and Jorge E. Viñuales (eds.), *The Foundations of International Investment Law. Bringing Theory into Practice* (Oxford: Oxford University Press, 2014), pp. 79–80, 'the particular substantive rights provided by human rights and investment protection seem substantively similar'. Christoph Schreuer and Ursula Kriebaum, 'The concept of property in human rights law and international investment law', in Stephan Breitnemoser (ed.), *Human Rights, Democracy and the Rule of Law. Liber Amicorum Wildhaber* (Baden-Baden: Nomos, 2007), p. 743; Ursula Kriebaum, 'Is the European Court of Human Rights an alternative to investor-State arbitration?' in Pierre-Marie Dupuy, Ernst-Ulrich Petersmann, and Franceso Francioni (eds.), *Human Rights in International Investment Law and Arbitration* (Oxford: Oxford University Press, 2009), p. 219; Maria Fanou and Vassilis P. Tzevelekos, 'The shared territory of the ECHR and international investment law', in Yannick Radi (ed.), *Research Handbook on Human Rights and Investment* (Cheltenham: Edward Elgar, 2018), p. 93.

[40] *Rumeli Telekom A.S.* v. *Kazakhstan* (Award of 29 July 2008) ICSID ARB/05/16 at para 609. The tribunal held that 'the State must act in a transparent manner; the State is obliged to act in good faith; the State's conduct cannot be arbitrary, grossly unfair, unjust, idiosyncratic, discriminatory, or lacking in due process; the State must respect procedural propriety and due process. The case law also confirms that to comply with the standard, the State must respect the investor's reasonable and legitimate expectations'.

[41] Art 1 of Protocol 1 to the Convention for the Protection of Human Rights and Fundamental Freedoms, Paris, 20 March 1952, in force 18 May 1954, ETS 9, 213 UNTS 262.

relationship of proportionality between the means employed and the aim sought to be realised' elaborated by the ECtHR.[42]

After all, qualifying investment agreements as human rights agreements has been more than a provocation. Chapter XI of the North American Free Trade Agreement (NAFTA), dealing with the protection of foreign investment, is defined as 'a human rights treaty for a special-interest group',[43] namely, natural and legal persons falling in the treaty definition of investors.

The risk of proliferation of parallel proceedings instituted in accordance with relevant investment treaties, legislation, or contracts, on the one hand, and under human rights agreements such as the ECHR, on the other hand, is therefore real. Nonetheless, such a risk may be reduced by some important differences concerning the jurisdiction of investment tribunals and the ECtHR.

In the first place, remedies available in the host State must be exhausted before filing an application under the ECHR. The exhaustion of domestic remedies is not required in investment arbitration, unless so provided by the relevant legal instrument. It is then possible that a potential applicant before the ECtHR may be satisfied with the decision rendered by domestic tribunals of the host State, or with the award an investment arbitral tribunal may have delivered in the meantime.

Second, nationality (or lack thereof) is irrelevant for the ECHR, but crucial in investment arbitration. Parallel proceedings before the ECtHR and investment tribunals can therefore be instituted only by natural or legal persons entitled to protection in accordance with the definition of nationality contained in the relevant investment instrument.

Third, shareholders can be applicants before the ECtHR only in exceptional circumstances,[44] whereas in investment arbitration, shareholders and even minority shareholders may be permitted to institute arbitral proceedings.[45]

[42] *Técnicas Medioambientales Tecmed, S.A.* v. *Mexico* (Award of 29 May 2003) ICSID ARB (AF)/00/2 at para. 122 (footnote omitted), quoting *James and Others* v. *The United Kingdom* 8793/79 [1986] ECHR 2 (21 February 1986) at pp. 19–20. In *Mondev International Ltd.* v. *United States* (Award of 11 October 2002) ICSID ARB(AF)/99/2 at para. 144, the tribunal observed more prudently that decisions rendered by the ECtHR can 'at most . . . provide guidance by analogy as to the possible scope of NAFTA's guarantee of treatment in accordance with international law, including fair and equitable treatment and full protection and security'.

[43] José E. Alvarez, 'Critical theory and the North American Free Trade Agreement's Chapter Eleven' (1996) 28 U Miami Inter-Am L Rev 303–12 at 307. At p. 308, NAFTA is described as the 'most bizarre human rights treaty ever conceived'.

[44] See Section 2.9.2.

[45] See Gabriel Bottini, *Admissibility of Shareholder Claims under Investment Treaties* (Cambridge: Cambridge University Press, 2020). See also Daniela Páez-Salgado, 'Settlements

Normally, therefore, parallel proceedings may be instituted before arbitral tribunals and the ECtHR only by enterprises.

Regarding the jurisdiction of the ECtHR and of arbitral tribunals dealing with investor–State disputes under the Energy Charter Treaty (the ECT), as in the *Yukos* case, the key provisions are, respectively, Article 35(2)(b) of the ECHR and Article 26(3)(b)(i) of the ECT.

Under Article 35(2)(b) of the ECHR, the Court cannot deal with an application that 'is substantially the same as a matter that . . . has already been submitted to another procedure of international investigation or settlement'. The purpose of the provision is to avoid a plurality of proceedings before international bodies relating to substantially the same case, because this would be incompatible with the spirit and letter of the Convention.[46] The Court must apply Article 35(2)(b) on its own motion.[47]

The ECtHR has clarified that the procedure referred to in Article 35(2)(b) must offer 'an adversarial procedure enabling each party to be informed of and to reply to the other party's submissions'.[48] It has also indicated the characteristics of such procedure, which must be public, international, independent, judicial, or quasi-judicial, and be capable of both determining the responsibilities of the concerned State and bringing the violation to an end by offering appropriate redress.[49]

Arbitral tribunals satisfy these procedural requirements. Incidentally, in *AMTO* v. *Ukraine*, the tribunal convincingly described arbitral tribunals as 'supra national Courts'.[50] Concerning the publicity requirement, the Court seems to have understood it as related to the participation to the procedure

in investor–State arbitration: Are minority shareholders precluded from having its treaty claims adjudicated?' (2016) 8 JIDS 101–24; David Gaukrodger, 'Investment treaties and shareholder claims for reflective loss: Insights from advanced systems of corporate law', OECD Working Papers – International Investment 2014/02, www.oecd.org/investment/investment-policy/WP-2014_02.pdf (accessed 5 June 2022); Lukas Vanhonnaeker, *Shareholders' Claims for Reflective Loss in International Investment Law* (Cambridge: Cambridge University Press, 2020).

46 See, amongst many, *Calcerrada Fornieles and Cabeza Mato* v. *Spain* 17512/90 (Decision of 6 July 1992) DR 73 at p. 223; *Pauger* v. *Austria* 24872/94 (Decision of 9 January 1995) DR 80A at p. 170; *Smirnova* v. *Russia* 46133/99 and 48183/99 (3 October 2002); *Professional Trades Union for Prison, Correctional and Secure Psychiatric Workers and Others* (*POA and Others*) v. *United Kingdom* 59253/11 (Decision of 21 May 2013) at para. 27.

47 *POA and Others* (Decision), para. 27.

48 *Selahattin Demirtaş* v. *Turkey (No. 2)* 14305/17 (Judgment of 22 December 2020) at para. 185.

49 See *Fédération Hellénique des Syndicats des Employés du Secteur Bancaire (OTOE)* v. *Grèce* 72808/10 (Judgment of 6 December 2011) at para. 35; and *Demirtaş* v. *Turkey* (Judgment), para. 183, as well as the decisions referred to.

50 *Limited Liability Company* AMTO v. *Ukraine* (Award of 26 March 2008) SCC Case No. 080/2005 at para. 71.

and access of the related documents by the applicant, rather than publicity from the standpoint of the general public.[51]

Regarding the co-ordination of applications under the ECHR and the other international procedures, the ECtHR has embraced two different interpretations of the term 'submitted' contained in Article 35(2)(b). In several decisions, it has understood Article 35.2(b) as reflecting the principle of *lis pendens*.[52] Accordingly, the Court must refrain from exercising its jurisdiction with regard to 'any application which has already been investigated or is *being* investigated by an international body'.[53]

In other decisions, the ECtHR has held that Article 35(2)(b) is triggered when a request 'has already been examined by an international body' (in the French text: 'une requête ayant déjà fait l'objet d'un examen de la part d'une instance internationale'),[54] which means that 'the element to be taken into account is the prior existence of a decision on the merits at the time the Court considers the case' (in the French text: 'l'élément à prendre en compte étant l'existence préalable d'une décision rendue sur le fond au moment où la Cour examine l'affaire').[55] This interpretation would substantially reduce the scope of application of Article 35(2)(b) to the *res judicata* principle, as its functioning requires a prior decision on the merits rendered by the international body.

The first interpretation is more convincing. Article 35(2)(b) precludes the ECtHR from exercising its jurisdiction if another international body had already rendered a decision on the same matter or is in the process of delivering it, which presupposes that such a body has considered itself competent. By requiring a matter '*being* investigated', such interpretation indicates

[51] In *Demirtaş* v. *Turkey* (Judgment), para. 180, the court stressed that each party needs to be informed to participate in the proceedings, while the international body must respond to individual application by making its decisions public and stating the reasons for them. See also *Celniku* v. *Grèce* 21499/04 (Judgment of 5 October 2007) at para. 40 regarding the so-called Procedure 1503 within the United Nations. On transparency and public access in investment arbitration, see Eric De Brabandere, *Investment Treaty Arbitration as Public International Law: Procedural Aspects and Implications* (Cambridge: Cambridge University Press, 2014), ch. V.

[52] *Demirtaş* v. *Turkey* (Judgment), para. 180.

[53] See, for instance, *Calcerrada Fornieles and Cabeza Mato* v. *Spain* (Decision), p. 223; *Smirnova* v. *Russia*, p. 10; *Karoussiotis* v. *Portugal* 23205/08 (Judgment of 1 February 2011) at para. 62 (emphasis added). See also *Decision on the Competence of the Court to Give an Advisory Opinion* (Decision of 2 June 2004) ECHR 2004-VI at p. 11, referring to applications which have already been submitted to another procedure.

[54] See, for instance, *Patera* v. *Czech Republic* 25326/03 (Judgment of 10 January 2006) at para. 2.1; *De Pace* v. *Italy* 22728/03 (1 December 2008) at para. 25; *Joseph Peraldi* v. *France* 2096/05 (Judgment of 7 April 2009) at p. 10; *Celniku* v. *Greece* (Judgment), para. 39; *OTOE* v. *Grèce* (Judgment), para. 32.

[55] See, in particular, *Peraldi* v. *France* (Judgment), p. 10; *OTOE* v. *Grèce* (Judgment), para. 32.

that Article 35(2)(b) does not apply if the international body has not yet established its jurisdiction. Otherwise, there is a risk that neither the ECtHR nor the international body would eventually consider the application.

Concerning the meaning of 'substantially the same' application, the ECtHR has generally interpreted it as requiring that the 'facts, parties and the complaints are identical'.[56] From this perspective, it has tailored its own triple identity test. The decisions on this matter rendered by the Court, however, reveal a certain reluctance towards abstract rulings on the principle of *lis pendens* and a certain propension to operate 'strictly on a case-by-case basis',[57] and take a 'functional approach without insisting on full textual similarities of the two legal instruments'.[58]

Article 26 of the ECT is a rather different provision. It does not deal directly with the question of parallel proceedings. It provides that the parties give their *unconditional* consent to the submission of disputes arising out of Part III of the treaty ('Investment promotion and protection') to international arbitration or conciliation.[59] It nonetheless offers to the parties the possibility to exclude from the scope of their expression of consent such disputes the investor has already submitted to the tribunals of the host State, or to 'previously agreed dispute settlement procedure'.[60] The parties that have availed themselves of this partial opting-out mechanism are listed in Annex 1D (which includes the Russian Federation).[61]

Regarding the parties listed in Annex 1D, therefore, an arbitral tribunal must refrain from exercising its jurisdiction, inter alia, if the dispute has already been submitted to a previously agreed dispute settlement procedure.

[56] See, for instance, *Peraldi* v. *France* (Judgment), p. 10; *Savda* v. *Turquie* 42730/05 (Judgment of 12 June 2012) at para. 68; *Gürdeniz* v. *Turkey* 59715/10 (Judgment of 18 March 2014), para 41; *Demirtaş* v. *Turkey* (Judgment), para. 181. In *OTOE* v. *Grèce* (Judgment), para. 39, the court took a more articulated view and held that it has to consider the identity of the parties in the two proceedings, the legal provisions on which they relied, the nature of their grievances, and the nature of the relief they are seeking. In *POA and Others* (Decision), para. 28, the court held that 'the complaint under the Convention is the same in substance. Indeed, it is virtually identical, the essence of their argument in both sets of international proceedings'.

[57] Nina Vajić and Vadim Pak, 'Avoiding plurality of international proceedings in the European Court of Human Rights', in Rüdiger Wolfrum, Maja Seršić, and Trpimir M. Šošić (eds.), *Contemporary Developments in International Law: Essays Vukas* (Leiden: Brill, 2016), p. 634.

[58] Ibid., 623.

[59] Art 26(3)(a) of the Energy Charter Treaty, Lisbon, 17 December 1994, in force 16 April 1998, 2080 UNTS 95.

[60] Art 26(3)(b)(i) of the ECT.

[61] See the ECT Annex ID: List of contracting parties not allowing an investor to resubmit the same dispute to international arbitration at a later stage under Art 26. The Russian Federation has not issued any statement in relation to Annex 1D.

Like in the case of Article 35(2)(b) of the ECHR, this raises two preliminary questions. The first question relates to the qualification of a procedure under Article 34 of the ECHR as 'a previously agreed dispute settlement procedure'. In *Charanne* v. *Spain*, the tribunal held *obiter dicta* that the ECtHR does not fall within the scope of Article 26(3)(b)(i) of the ECT since there is no previous agreement between the parties.[62] While the text of Article 26(3)(b)(i) of the ECT supports such a view, the meaning of the provision must be established through a holistic process that goes beyond the literal analysis. From this perspective, excluding the ECtHR from the scope of Article 26(3)(b)(i) of the ECT seems to run against the object and purpose of such provision, which is clearly intended to avoid the difficulties and risks related to parallel proceedings by different judicial or quasi-judicial bodies. Thus, the fact that the procedure before the ECtHR may be initiated by an individual without a previous agreement with the State cannot be a decisive argument.

The second question regards the term 'submitted'. As in the case of Article 34 of the ECHR, the interpretation requiring that the previously agreed dispute settlement procedure has declared itself competent seems more convincing. Requiring a decision on the merits rendered by the previously agreed dispute settlement would run against the literal tenor of Article 26(3)(b)(i) of the ECT and be reminiscent of the *res judicata* principle, which does not require a treaty provision. Furthermore, interpreting Article 26(3)(b)(i) of the ECT as requiring merely the filing of the application may deprive the investor of any effective remedy if the previously agreed dispute settlement procedure eventually declines to exercise its jurisdiction. This is hardly persuasive if the purpose of Article 26(3)(b)(i) of the ECT is to prevent parallel proceedings or, in other words, to offer investors one and only one remedy.

2.8 DECISIONS IN THE *YUKOS* CASE

The proceedings arising out of the events leading to the liquidation of the Russian energy giant Yukos offer an interesting case study from the standpoint of the management of parallel proceedings before the ECtHR and investment tribunals. The following analysis focuses on the case brought by OAO Neftyanaya Konpaniya Yukos (hereinafter *OAO Neftyanaya Konpaniya Yukos* v. *Russian Federation*) before the ECtHR[63] and the three cases brought before three identically composed investment tribunals established under the

[62] *Charanne B.V. and Construction Investments S.A.R.L.* v. *Spain* (Final Award of 21 January 2016) SCC Case No. 062/2012 at para. 409 (in Spanish).

[63] *OAO Neftyanaya Kompaniya Yukos* v. *Russian Federation* 14902/04.

auspices of the Permanent Court of Arbitration (PCA) and functioning under UNCITRAL Rules.[64] Space restraints make it impossible to deal with other related investment cases, other decisions rendered by the ECtHR, domestic litigation, or the plethora of domestic decisions that followed the final awards rendered by the PCA. Yet, the ECtHR decision in *Yukos* and the three PCA awards contain the essential legal issues for a reflection on the parallel proceedings under discussion.

2.8.1 *Proceedings before the ECtHR*

Yukos filed an application under Article 34 of the ECHR against the Russian Federation on 23 April 2004, and the ECtHR delivered its decision on admissibility on 29 January 2009. Meanwhile, Yukos had ceased to exist due to a domestic bankruptcy decision delivered on 12 November 2007, and the Russian Federation requested the ECtHR to discontinue the case.

In the admissibility decision, after noting the agreement between the parties that the application had been validly filed by Yukos, the ECtHR held that striking out the application could encourage governments to deprive companies of the legal protection they are entitled to under the Convention. It stressed the 'moral dimension' of human rights cases and that the issue at stake 'transcends the interests of the company'.[65]

The ECtHR discussed the question of parallel proceedings in the judgment, rendered on 20 September 2011. Meanwhile, majority shareholders representing over 60 per cent of shares had resorted to investment arbitration (2 November 2004) and obtained a favourable decision on jurisdiction (30 November 2009; see Subsection 2.8.2).

The Russian Federation argued that following the liquidation of the company, the same shareholders before the investment tribunals were behind the application before the ECtHR and would be the beneficiaries of any eventual award. According to the Russian Federation, this would trigger the application

[64] *Yukos Universal Limited (Isle of Man)* v. *Russian Federation* PCA Case No. 2005-04/AA227; *Hulley Enterprises Ltd* v. *Russian Federation* PCA Case No. 2005-03/AA226; *Veteran Petroleum Ltd* v. *Russian Federation* PCA Case No. 2005-05/AA228. The decisions on jurisdiction and admissibility (30 November 2009) and the final awards (18 July 2014) being virtually identical, references will be made in this chapter to the first case. In literature, see, in particular, Eric De Brabandere, '*Yukos Universal Limited (Isle of Man)* v *The Russian Federation*. Complementarity or conflict? Contrasting the *Yukos* case before the European Court of Human Rights and investment tribunals' (2015) 30 ICSID Rev 344–55 at 345.

[65] *OAO Neftyanaya Kompaniya Yukos* v. *Russian Federation* (Admissibility, 23 April 2004) 14902/04 at paras 440, 443, 444.

of Article 35(2)(b) of the ECHR and prevent the Court from exercising its jurisdiction.

The Court reiterated that Article 35(2)(b) is meant to avoid a plurality of international proceedings relating to the same case[66] and usually requires a comparison of the parties in the respective proceedings, the relevant legal provisions relied on by them, the scope of their claims, and the types of the redress sought.[67] It held:

> Despite certain similarities in the subject-matters of the present case and of the arbitration proceedings, the claimants in those arbitration proceedings are the applicant company's shareholders acting as investors, and not the applicant company itself, which at that moment in time was still an independent legal entity ... the parties ... are different and therefore the two matters are not 'substantially the same' within the meaning of Article 35 § 2 (b) of the Convention.[68]

The finding attracted the dissent of one judge, according to whom:

> Article 35 § 2 (b) of the Convention, in referring to the substance of the matter, primarily concerns the merits (the substantial part) of the dispute, i.e. those criteria that the Court chose not to consider in the case at hand. Were it otherwise, it would be too simple to overcome the restriction set out in Article 35 § 2 (b) of the Convention by, for example, assigning rights to an affiliate, or submitting identical applications in the name of different stakeholders, etc.[69]

Regarding the decision on the merits, the ECtHR found that the Russian Federation had violated Articles 6.1 and 3(b) in relation to the 2000 Tax Assessment (six votes to one) as well as Article 1 of Protocol 1 in relation to both the 2000–2001 Tax Assessments (four votes to three) and the enforcement proceedings (five votes to two).

On 24 June 2014, the ECtHR eventually deliberated on just satisfaction, which it globally quantified as approximately 1,866 billion EUR, including

[66] *OAO Neftyanaya Kompaniya Yukos* v. *Russian Federation* (Judgment of 20 September 2011) 14902/04 at para. 520.

[67] Ibid., para. 521, relying on *Vesa Peltonen* v. *Finland* (Decision) 19583/92 (20 February 1995); *Cereceda Martin and Others* v. *Spain* 16358/90 (Decision of 12 October 1992); *Smirnova* v. *Russia*, and *Decision on the Competence of the Court to Give an Advisory Opinion*, para. 31.

[68] *Yukos* v. *Russian Federation* (Judgment), paras 524–25. The court did not find it necessary to decide whether the investment arbitration is 'another procedure of international investigation or settlement' for the purpose of Art 35.2(b).

[69] *Yukos* v. *Russian Federation* (Judgment), Partly Dissenting Opinion of Judge Bushev, joined in part by Judge Hajiyev, para. 4.3.

interest (five votes to two). This amount was to be distributed to the applicant company's shareholders and their legal successors and heirs. For that purpose, the Court suggested using the list of shareholders at the date of company's liquidation.[70] It summarily dismissed the concern expressed by the Russian Federation about parallel proceedings simply by mentioning two investment arbitration awards rendered by the Stockholm Chamber of Commerce as well as the three PCA pending proceedings.[71] The Court ordered the Russian Federation to produce, in cooperation with the Committee of Ministers, a comprehensive plan and timeframe for the execution of the decision on just satisfaction.

Two judges dissented with the decision on just satisfaction. In their opinion, the extraordinary level of compensation disregarded the requirement of equity, also considering that the decision – contrary to the investment arbitration awards – neglected the applicant's contribution to the damage sustained by the company.[72]

Even more important for the purpose of this chapter, they criticised the Court for failing to consider stakeholders other than shareholders, the latter normally not holding any additional privilege in the distribution of the company's assets in case of bankruptcy. Furthermore, they observed that shareholders have no rights under the ECHR save in exceptional circumstances and on the assumption that they have 'decisive and ultimate power in the company's governance'.[73]

On 1 October 2020, the Committee of Ministers noted that 'no comprehensive plan, including a binding time frame, for distribution of the award of just satisfaction has been produced in six years, despite the Court's clear indications. The main just satisfaction award and the default interest for the belated payment of the costs and expenses remain outstanding to date'.[74]

[70] OAO *Neftyanaya Kompaniya Yukos* v. *Russian Federation* (Just Satisfaction of 31 July 2014) 14902/04 at para. 38.

[71] Ibid., para. 43.

[72] *Yukos* v. *Russian Federation* (Just Satisfaction), Partly Dissenting Opinion of Judge Bushev, joined in part by Judge Hajiyev. At p. 26, in particular, they observed that 'placing the entire burden of compensation on only one party among several others which contributed to the damage would breach a principle of (just) equity'. On the decision on this point in the investment award, see note 80.

[73] Ibid., para. 1.1.

[74] Committee of Ministers, '1383rd Meeting, 29 September–1 October 2020 (DH), Notes', https://rm.coe.int/090000168009f8f52 (accessed 6 June 2022). See also Committee of Ministers, 'Interim Resolution CM/ResDH(2020)', and the letter dated 25 February 2015 from the law firm representing the applicant in *Yukos* v. *Russian Federation* and acting on behalf of Hulley Enterprises Ltd and Yukos Universal Ltd, urging the execution of the ECtHR judgment

2.8.2 *Proceedings before Arbitral Tribunals*

Three requests for arbitration were filed on 2 November 2004 by three major Yukos shareholders against the Russian Federation for alleged violations of the ECT.

The Russian Federation submitted that the investment tribunals should decline to exercise their jurisdiction. In its opinion, a dispute for the purpose of Article 26(3)(b)(i) of the ECT must be understood as 'a dispute between essentially the same parties relating to the same material facts or injuries that constitute the basis of the dispute before the Arbitral Tribunal'.[75] In the opinion of the Russian Federation, this was the case of the proceedings concerning *Yukos* before the arbitral tribunals and ECtHR.

The tribunals referred to the triple test, which was apparently considered as applicable by the parties, but failed to offer any thoughtful examination on any of the three prongs of the test. They dismissed the objection in a remarkably summarily fashion in just three paragraphs. In the first paragraph, they confined themselves to opine – without any legal argumentation – that the so-called triple identity test was not satisfied and therefore the 'fork-in-the-road' provision contained in Article 26(3)(b)(i) of the ECT could not be relied upon by the respondent. The remaining two paragraphs discussed Article 26(3)(b)(i) of the ECT from the standpoint of Russian courts and are consequently immaterial for the purpose of the present chapter.[76]

At the merits phase, the respondent attempted to raise again the objection to the tribunals' jurisdiction based on Article 26(3)(b)(i) of the ECT. The tribunals refused to 'reopen' this issue.[77] The issue was not raised before Dutch tribunals during an unsuccessful attempt by the Russian Federation to have the awards set aside.

on just satisfaction. On 19 January 2017, the Russian Constitutional Court held that the judgment on just satisfaction in the *Yukos* case was not enforceable as it was contrary to the Constitution of the Russian Federation. Art 79 of the Constitution was amended in 2020 and now reads: 'Decisions of interstate bodies adopted based on the provisions of international treaties ratified by Russia in their interpretation that is contrary to the Constitution of the Russian Federation will not be subject to enforcement', 'Amendments to the 1993 Constitution of the Russian Federation concerning international law' (2020), 60 ILM 341, with introductory note by Paul Kalinichenko and Dimitry Vladimirovich Kochenov.

[75] *Yukos Universal Limited (Isle of Man)* v. *Russian Federation* (Interim Award on Admissibility and Jurisdiction of 30 November 2009) PCA Case No. 2005-04/AA227 at para. 590.

[76] Ibid., paras 598–600.

[77] *Yukos Universal Limited (Isle of Man)* v. *Russian Federation* (Final Award of 18 July 2014) PCA Case No. 2005-04/AA227 at para. 1271.

The tribunals found the Russian Federation in breach of Article 13 of the ECT (indirect expropriation). With regard to the four requirements for lawful expropriation, they found that: (1) it was 'profoundly questionable' whether the Russian authorities acted in the public interest; (2) there was no need for a decision on the discriminatory nature of those measures; (3) due process of law was not respected as Russian courts bent to the will of the Russian government; and (4) no compensation whatsoever was provided to the applicants.[78]

They further held that after having found the respondent in breach of its obligation related to expropriation under Article 13 of the ECT, it was not indispensable to also adjudicate alleged breaches of the FET standard under Article 10 of the ECT.[79]

Finally, they discussed at length the material and significant misconduct of the claimants which, according to the tribunal, contributed to the extent of 25 per cent to the prejudice they suffered as a result of the respondent's destruction of Yukos and therefore justified a reduction of the compensation accordingly.[80]

2.9 ANALYSIS OF THE *YUKOS* CASE

2.9.1 *General Considerations*

The first element of note that is common to the decisions under discussion is how easily the ECtHR and the arbitral tribunals have disposed of the question of parallel proceedings. The arbitral tribunals dismissed the objections raised by the respondent regarding the proceedings before the ECtHR in just one paragraph of less than eighty words. Paragraph 598 contains a bare declaration that Article 26(3)(b)(i) of the ECT (the 'fork-in-the-road' provision) is not triggered by the proceedings before the ECtHR. No legal argument is offered to support such a conclusion.[81]

The ECtHR's decision on the question is equally brief. In two key paragraphs, the Court did not go beyond finding that the parties before it were different from those before the arbitral tribunals.[82] The conclusion is fortified

[78] Ibid., paras 1581–84.
[79] Ibid., para. 1585.
[80] Ibid., Section X, Part E (paras 1594–637).
[81] See note 76.
[82] *Yukos* v. *Russian Federation* (Judgment), paras 524–25.

by the policy argument that dismissing the case may offer governments an opportunity to escape their responsibilities under the Convention.

The lightness showed by the arbitral tribunals and the ECtHR is rather shocking given the complexity of the question, the length of the decisions,[83] and the financial interests at stake (not necessarily only those of the company and the shareholders). Yet, no decision seriously discusses the allegation made by the Russian Federation that 'the very same economic interests'[84] were behind and controlled all proceedings.

The second element relates to the inadequate level, or even the complete lack, of coordination between the ECtHR and the investment tribunals, all limiting themselves to take note of each other's decisions without seriously considering the related legal arguments, however sketchy the latter were.[85] Even when a temporal interval of more than three years elapsed, as between the decisions on the merits rendered by the investment tribunals and the ECtHR, there is little elaboration on previous respective decisions.

2.9.2 *Proceedings before the ECtHR*

The decision on admissibility delivered by the ECtHR has been welcomed in literature as 'surely correct'.[86] Yet, this decision does not stand up to scrutiny. The Court conflates three related yet independent questions, namely: (1) the status of a victim for the purpose of Article 34 ECHR; (2) the existence of parallel proceedings from the standpoint of Article 35(2)(b) ECHR; and (3) the question of double recovery.

Starting with the status of a victim, the case before the ECtHR could have been seen as the perfect situation in which shareholders were exceptionally allowed to appear before the Court. In a leading case, the Court admitted that

[83] Incidentally, in *OAO Neftyanaya Kompaniya Yukos* v. *Russian Federation* (Judgment), the ECtHR delivered itself in a massive exercise of copy and paste, which resulted in almost seventy pages reproducing, with some minor changes, the first eighty-five pages of the 2009 decision on admissibility.

[84] *Yukos Universal Limited (Isle of Man)* v. *Russian Federation* (Final Award), para. 1268.

[85] In *Ampal-American Israel Corporation and Others* v. *Egypt* (Liability and Heads of Loss of 21 February 2017) ICSID ARB/12/11 at para. 252, for instance, the tribunal directed the parties 'to keep it fully informed as to the decisions of the other tribunals'.

[86] David John Harris et al., *Law of the European Convention on Human Rights*, 4th ed. (Oxford: Oxford University Press, 2018), p. 74. They have explained that the decision 'is entirely consistent with the Court's settled case law that majority shareholders cannot claim to be victims of an alleged violation of the company's rights under the Convention and that an exception will only be made to that rule when it is clearly established that it is impossible for the company to apply to the Court through the organs set up under its articles of incorporation or, in the event of liquidation, through its liquidators'.

the piercing of the 'corporate veil', or the disregarding of a company's legal personality, will be justified only in exceptional circumstances, in particular where it has been clearly established that it is impossible for the company to apply to the Convention institutions through the organs set up under its articles of incorporation or – in the event of liquidation – through its liquidators.[87]

Although these decisions related to disputes in which shareholders were allowed to file the application under Article 34 of the ECHR, the principle should apply – still exceptionally – *a fortiori* when the application has been filed by a company that subsequently ceased to exist, as in the case of *Yukos* due to the bankruptcy decision. Furthermore, even if the Court has felt obviously more comfortable in applying this principle in the case of a sole shareholder or overwhelming control by a shareholder over the company,[88] nothing in the Court's jurisprudence seems to militate against the possibility of admitting an application submitted by majority shareholders.

In *OAO Neftyanaya Konpaniya Yukos* v. *Russian Federation*, piercing the corporate veil would have been fully justified by the factual control the shareholders maintained throughout the proceedings despite the unaltered denomination of the applicant. This had been certified by the formal declaration by the shareholders in the investment arbitration proceedings that 'should any pecuniary damages be awarded to Yukos in the ECtHR proceedings, and should the Claimants receive any payments, such payments would be deducted from the amounts claimed in these arbitrations'.[89]

[87] *Agrotexim and Others* v. *Greece* 14807/89 (Judgment of 24 October 1995). The court added that 'the Supreme Courts of certain member States of the Council of Europe have taken the same line. This principle has also been confirmed with regard to the diplomatic protection of companies by the International Court of Justice'. In *Lekić* v. *Slovenia* 36480/07 (Judgment of 11 December 2018) at para. 111, the court further held that 'since companies had a distinct legal personality from shareholders, it was the former and not the latter who could lodge complaints of violations of Article 1 of Protocol No. 1 with the Court, unless, due to exceptional circumstances, the company was not in a position to do so'. See also *Amat-G Ltd and Mebaghishvili* v. *Georgia* 2507/03 (Judgment of 27 September 2005) at para. 33; *Meltex Ltd and Mesrop Movsesyan* v. *Armenia* 32283/04 (Judgment of 17 June 2008) at para. 66; *International Bank for Commerce and Development AD and Others* v. *Bulgaria* 7031/05 (Judgment of 2 June 2016) at paras 89–92; *Feldman and Slovyanskyy Bank* v. *Ukraine* 42758/05 (Judgment of 21 December 2017) at para. 26; *Vladimirova* v. *Russia* 21863/05 (Judgment of 10 April 2018) at para. 40.

[88] In *G.J.* v. *Luxembourg* 21156/93 (Judgment of 26 October 2000) at para. 24, the applicant held 90 per cent of the shares.

[89] Letter from the claimants to the Arbitral Tribunal of 1 April 2010, as quoted by the tribunal in *Yukos* v. *Russian Federation*, Award; see note 77, para. 1266.

Furthermore, admitting that the shareholders could continue the proceedings initiated by the company would make the policy argument advanced by the Court redundant, namely the risk of permitting governments to circumvent their obligations under the Convention.

Finally, and quite logically, the shareholders were eventually the beneficiaries of the compensation granted by the Court. Piercing the veil at the admission stage would have permitted the Court to avoid a rather incoherent approach based on the legal fiction that an extinguished company could complete the proceedings for the benefit of the shareholders.

Neither the fact that the shareholders involved in the proceedings, that is, Hulley Enterprises Limited and Yukos Universal Limited, represented roughly 60 per cent of the shares,[90] nor the risk of different opinions amongst shareholders, undermine the argument that the Court should have treated the shareholders – and not the defunct company – as applicants. Instead, the Court ended up allowing Hulley Enterprises Limited and Yukos Universal Limited to proceed on behalf of all shareholders.

Had the Court allowed the shareholders to appear before it under exceptional circumstances, the next question would have concerned the existence of parallel proceedings. At this point the Court would have compared the proceedings before it and those pending before the arbitral tribunals. The focus would have been first and foremost on the subject matter of the proceedings.

In the *Southern Bluefin Tuna* case, the International Tribunal for the Law of the Sea held that the very same dispute had arisen between the parties under both the Convention for the Conservation of Southern Bluefin Tuna and the Convention on the Law of the Sea. Conversely, to consider that there were two distinct disputes arising under the two conventions would have been 'artificial'.[91]

Thus, the ECtHR should have compared the claims brought before it and the investment tribunals with a view to establishing whether or to what extent they related to the same dispute. This would have required a comparison of the claims from the standpoint of relevant provisions of the ECHR and ECT.

Yet, it would have been plausible for the ECtHR to exercise its jurisdiction in spite of the existence of parallel proceedings before investment tribunals on the basis of the argument – effectively put forward by the Court – that

[90] See note 77, para. 69.

[91] *Southern Bluefin Tuna (New Zealand* v. *Japan, Australia* v. *Japan)* (Jurisdiction and Admissibility, Award of 4 August 2000) (2000) 23 RIAA 45 at para. 54.

applications under Article 34 of the ECHR possess a moral dimension and the interests at stake transcend those of the applicants themselves.[92] The special nature of the ECHR – so often celebrated by the Court as the foundation of an European public order – would have justified parallel proceedings and even prevailed over considerations of efficiency, judicial economy, and coherence.

The third question would have arisen had the Court exercised its jurisdiction and found the respondent in breach of the Convention. At that point, the Court could have moved to just satisfaction and possibly needed to consider double recovery of the damages. To the extent that the damage had already been compensated by investment tribunals, the ECtHR should have refrained from granting any pecuniary compensation. If appropriate, the decision certifying the violation would have been considered as offering per se adequate satisfaction to the applicant. Importantly, the ECtHR would have fully achieved its objectives in line with the moral dimension of the Convention. If, on the contrary, the decision on the quantum by arbitral tribunals was still pending before the investment tribunals at the time of the decision on just satisfaction by the ECtHR, the ECtHR could have considered postponing its own decision.

From this perspective, the principle preventing double recovery would function as a safeguard against compensation beyond the damage suffered, which would be contrary not only to the very essence of compensation but also to the principles of equity and unjust enrichment. Besides, the concept of punitive damages is hardly acceptable in international law.[93]

2.9.3 *Proceedings before* Yukos *Arbitral Tribunals*

The *Yukos* arbitral tribunals have refrained from seriously discussing the implications of proceedings before the ECtHR in the decisions on jurisdiction and admissibility, as well as in the decision on the merits. It is true that when the first decision was rendered, the ECtHR had already found that the applicant in the proceedings before it was the company, and not its shareholders. Regardless of the persuasiveness of the finding by the ECtHR, however, the arbitral tribunals were obliged to make their own determination from the standpoint of the 'fork-in-the-road' provision contained in the ECT. The crux of the matter was indeed the interpretation and application of the 'fork-in-the-

92 See note 65.

93 Stephan Wittich, 'Punitive damages', in James Crawford, Alain Pellet, and Simon Olleson (eds.), *The Law of International Responsibility* (Oxford: Oxford University Press, 2010), pp. 667ff.

road' provision, which precludes the submission of the same dispute before an arbitral tribunal constituted under the ECT and 'any previously agreed dispute settlement procedure'.

If it is accepted that the proceedings before the ECtHR could trigger the application of the 'fork-in-the-road' provision, the tribunal should have determined the existence of a single 'dispute'. The mechanical application of the triple test by the tribunals remains unpersuasive, even if shared by the parties.

The identity of the disputes before the ECtHR and the arbitral tribunals must be determined by looking at the parties and the subject matter. Regarding the parties, it was necessary to discuss whether the applicant before the ECtHR was the company – as maintained by the ECtHR itself – or its shareholders. This would have required an inquiry into whether 'the very same economic interests' were behind both the proceedings.

It has been suggested in literature that an 'economic approach' should be adopted when dealing with parallel proceedings whereby 'strict legal distinctions, not reflecting the underlying economic realities, may be disregarded'.[94] From this perspective, investment tribunals should not satisfy themselves with the formal name of the applicant before the ECtHR, nor the determination of the ECtHR itself. Instead, they should consider whether the same economic interests are behind all proceedings or, in other words, determine the 'substantial identity' of the applicants in terms of the decision-making process.[95]

Moving to the subject matter, the tribunals could have looked at 'whether claimed entitlements have the same normative basis',[96] or, put differently, 'whether the claims share the same fundamental basis'.[97] Such a case-by-case and flexible approach is fully consistent with the aim and purpose of the 'fork-in-the-road' provision. In the words of a tribunal, what matters for the

94 *CME Czech Republic B.V.* v. *The Czech Republic* (Legal Opinion by Schreuer and Reinisch), para. 22. August Reinisch, 'The issues raised by parallel proceedings and possible solutions', in Michael Waibel et al. (eds.), *The Backlash against Investment Arbitration* (The Hague: Kluwer, 2010), p. 122, further argued that 'the recognition of shareholders as potential claimants with individual standing, necessarily leads to a multiplication of the opportunities to bring investment claims. In such a situation, it may be more appropriate to focus on issues and facts of a dispute rather than on the parties and causes of actions when applying the triple identity test. Under this more flexible test, special attention should be given to the corporate structure of foreign investors'.

95 *Charanne* v. *Spain* (Final Award), para. 408.

96 *Pantechniki S.A. Contractors & Engineers* v. *Albania* (Award of 30 July 2009) ICSID ARB/07/21 at para. 62. In the same vein, in *H&H Enterprises Investments, Inc.* v. *Egypt* (Award of 6 May 2014) ICSID ARB/09/15 at para. 368, the tribunal held that what matters is whether 'the two relevant proceedings . . . have the same normative source and pursue the same aim'.

97 *H&H Enterprises Investments* (Award), para. 368.

application of 'fork-in-the-road' clauses is that 'the two relevant proceedings under examination have the same normative source and pursue the same aim'.[98]

The argument has been echoed by the EU in the *Nord Stream* case:

> This approach involves an inquiry into whether the claims have the same fundamental basis, i.e. whether the disputes have the same 'subject matter', regardless of whether the formal cause of action may be differently expressed (depending on whether it is pursued under a treaty or as a breach of contract) and/or that the formal parties are distinct (i.e. attempting to sue the State under a bilateral investment treaty while at the same time suing a State-owned company under a contract, relying on the same facts).[99]

Such an approach implies a 'comparison of the pleas in law as set out' in all proceedings.[100] The idea behind this is to prevent the proliferation of proceedings that substantially replicate the same claims related to the same factual matrix. This does not necessarily mean that a party cannot initiate proceedings before different fora in order to effectively protect its rights, especially when the jurisdiction of those tribunals is not obvious. Yet, as recently pointed out by a tribunal, pursuing parallel proceedings in the merits after the jurisdiction of a tribunal has been established would amount to the abuse of process.[101] From a different perspective, a balance must be struck between ensuring an effective remedy to the applicant without exposing the respondent as well as the whole system to the negative consequences and risks of parallel proceedings.[102]

From a domestic perspective, it has been held that

> if the shareholder is allowed to recover in respect of [indirect] loss, then either there will be double recovery at the expense of the defendant or the

98 *Supervision y Control* S.A. v. *Costa Rica* (Award of 18 January 2017) ICSID ARB/12/4 at para. 330.

99 *Nord Stream 2 AG* v. *European Union* (EU Memorial on Jurisdiction and Request for Bifurcation of 15 September 2020) PCA Case No. 2020-07 at para. 42. According to the claimant's response to the EU Request for a Preliminary Phase on Jurisdiction and Bifurcation of 16 October 2020, para. 31, the argument is not supported by jurisprudence. In the Procedural Order No. 4 of 31 December 2020, para. 48, the tribunal has noted that the matter is complex, imposes an analysis which considers 'the complete picture', and may be 'intertwined with aspects of the merits'.

100 *Nord Stream* v. *EU* (EU Memorial), para. 227.

101 *Ampal-American Israel Corporation and Others* v. *Egypt* (Jurisdiction of 1 February 2016) ICSID ARB/12/11 at para. 331.

102 According to Zarra, *Parallel Proceedings*, 147, 'it seems … completely unreasonable to consider two claims as having different *causae petendi* only because the sources under which the same standard is invoked are formally different'.

> shareholder will recover at the expense of the company and its creditors and other shareholders. Neither course can be permitted. This is a matter of principle; there is no discretion involved . . .. Justice to the defendant requires the exclusion of one claim or the other; protection of the interests of the company's creditors requires that it is the company which is allowed to recover to the exclusion of the shareholder.[103]

In investment arbitration, a tribunal held that

> the existence of several legal foundations for arbitration does not necessarily mean that the various entities in the shareholder chain could make use of the existing arbitration clauses to assail the same measures and to recover the same economic loss under any circumstances. Indeed, the purpose of investment treaty arbitration is to grant full reparation for the injuries that a qualifying investor may have suffered as a result of a host state's wrongful measures.[104]

Yet, an investor who controls several entities in a vertical chain of companies commits an abuse of process if it resorts to arbitration in relation to the same alleged violations and harm by relying on different investment treaties.[105] Accordingly, the tribunal declared the inadmissibility of the claims due to the peculiar facts of the case, in which (1) the group of companies of which the claimant was a part was organised as a vertical chain; (2) the entities in the chain were under the control of the same shareholder; (3) the measures complained of by the various entities in the chain were the same and thus the dispute notified to Algeria by those entities was in essence identical; and (4) the damage claimed by the various entities was in its economic essence the same.[106]

In the *Yukos* case, investment tribunals should also have compared the claims brought before them and before the ECtHR, most importantly from the standpoint of FET and expropriation. Regarding expropriation, the respondent argued that

> the ECHR and ECT claims both aim to obtain compensation for the purported expropriation of Yukos and 'have the same normative source', as Article 13(1) of the ECT and Article 1 of Protocol No. 1 ECHR do not lay

[103] *Johnson* v. *Gore Wood & Co.* [2002] 2 AC 1 (House of Lords) at 62.
[104] *Orascom* v. *Algeria* (Award), para. 495.
[105] Ibid., para. 542.
[106] Ibid., para. 546. The entire award survived the annulment proceedings; *Orascom TMT Investments S.à r.l.* v. *Algeria* (Decision on Annulment of 17 September 2020) ICSID ARB/12/35.

> down independent standards by which Respondent's conduct is to be judged.[107]

A comparison between the two standards goes beyond the purpose of this chapter. What is worth noting, however, is that in the jurisdiction decision, investment tribunals completely neglected the question and confined themselves to refer to previous decisions related to Yukos bankruptcy and the 'wide margin of appreciation' enjoyed by the ECtHR in that matter.

The perspective changed when the investment tribunals delivered the decision on the merits. It was not a matter of 'reopening' the question of *lis pendens* as held by the tribunals. Such a question had hardly been considered in the decision on jurisdiction. Even more importantly, after the decision on the merits rendered by the ECtHR on the claims against the Russian Federation, the question had potentially become one of *res judicata*.

It is argued that at this point the investment tribunals should have compared the ECtHR decision on the merits with the claims pending before them (rather than comparing two pending claims as at the admissibility and jurisdiction stage). The purpose of the comparison would have been to determine to what extent, if any, the claims pending before the investment tribunals had already been settled by the ECtHR and acquired the status of *res judicata*. This would have prevented the risk of overlapping and possibly conflicting decisions, on the one hand, and excluded the possibility of double recovery, on the other hand.

2.10 CONCLUSION

The *Yukos* case confirms the risk of parallel proceedings before the ECtHR and investment tribunals. The decisions considered in this chapter are arguably unsatisfactory, as no legal argument on parallel proceedings has been sufficiently articulated by the ECtHR or investment tribunals.

For this type of parallel proceedings – perhaps more than parallel proceedings in commercial arbitration or investment arbitration – case management, rather than the application of a set of rigid criteria, appears to be more suitable.[108] From this perspective, the crux of the matter would be considering whether the claims have been put forward by substantially the same parties in relation to substantially equivalent measures.[109]

[107] As reported by the tribunal, *Yukos Universal Limited (Isle of Man)* v. *Russian Federation* (Final Award), para. 1261.

[108] ILA, *Interim Report*, text note 24. See also the conclusions on the triple identity test with respect to *res judicata* in ILA, *Final Report on Res Judicata*, paras 41–49.

[109] Regarding the co-ordination of claims in international trade, see, for instance, Art 15.24(2) of the Free Trade Agreement between the EU and Vietnam (Hanoi, 30 June 2019, in force

When considering the parties, managing parallel proceedings may require a flexible approach based on economic reality. In a complex legal framework where different applicants – legal persons or shareholders – may initiate parallel proceedings, the tribunals need to look behind formal denominations and examine the overlapping claims brought by the same economic interests in terms of control and decision-making process.

When considering the subject matter, the tribunals should compare the different claims duly considering the specific provisions in the ECHR and the relevant investment-related legal instrument. Normally such a comparison may be made at the admissibility/admission stage from the standpoint of *lis pendens*. The risk here is that a tribunal may refrain from exercising jurisdiction in relation to a claim pending before a different tribunal, which has declared itself competent to adjudicate but eventually decides not to (possibly as a matter of judicial restraint). This occurred in the *Yukos* case with regard to the FET claims before the investment tribunals.

The applicants can still institute parallel proceedings, especially when the jurisdiction of the seized tribunals is not uncontroversial. Yet, continuing parallel proceedings after one tribunal has decided to exercise its jurisdiction may amount to the abuse of process. The tribunals' efforts to secure the equality of arms between the parties should include limiting the possibility for one of them to take advantage of parallel proceedings. The principle of equality, which normally applies *within* a single procedure, is considered here as a tool to prevent unfair litigation by the party seeking double or multiple relief before different tribunals.

In the case of the ECtHR, nonetheless, the peculiar nature or moral public order dimension of the obligations stemming from the ECHR may justify parallel proceedings. If the ECtHR decides to proceed in parallel with investment tribunals, double recovery functions as a safety valve.

More generally, double recovery is excluded by the principle of unjust enrichment, or rather unjust impoverishment of the party who has already been condemned to pay compensation. Its application can be seen as a means to protect the economy and prerogatives of the State against the proliferation of claims concerning the very same conduct. The condemnation by the

1 August 2020, L 186 of 12 June 2020 OJ, 3-1400), which reads: 'A Party shall not, for a particular measure, seek redress for the breach of a substantially equivalent obligation under this Agreement and under the WTO Agreement or in any other international agreement to which both Parties are parties in the relevant fora.' See also UNCITRAL, 'Concurrent proceedings in investment arbitration. Note by the Secretariat' (17 April 2015) UN Doc. A/CN.9/848, p. 3.

ECtHR would in this case be considered as adequate reparation, and no compensation should be awarded.

Once a tribunal has delivered a final decision, the matter becomes one of *res judicata*. If properly applied, the principle ensures that substantially the same claims are not adjudicated twice, with all the implications thereof. In the *Yukos* case, one may even speculate that the finding of the ECtHR on the violations of due process may not be extraneous to the decision of the investment tribunal not to deal with the alleged violations of FET under the ECT.

It can be concluded that dealing with parallel proceedings is a matter of case management, rather than the mechanical application of a set of criteria, and that general principles may assist tribunals.

3

The Mosaic of International Dispute Settlement

The Role of Domestic Courts in International Dispute Settlement

KIMBERLEY N. TRAPP AND JACOB SMITH

3.1 INTRODUCTION

A purely horizontal system of public international law, governing the conduct of States as between themselves on the international plane, would offer up very few opportunities for overlap between the domestic and the international spheres.[1] Faced with such a system, interrogating the role of domestic courts in international dispute settlement (IDS) would make little sense.[2] But if there ever was an era of international law as a purely horizontal legal system, it is evidently no more. Indeed, long-standing international wrongs which regulate State conduct vis-à-vis natural or legal persons, such as 'denial of justice', strongly suggest that there was no 'once upon a time' during which the domestic legal sphere was impenetrable. In any event, from the second half of the twentieth century, States have consented to more and more

[1] See Machiko Kanetake, 'The interfaces between the national and international rule of law: A framework paper', in Machiko Kanetake and André Nollkaemper (eds.), *The Rule of Law at the National and International Levels: Contestations and Deference* (Oxford: Hart, 2016), p. 1, noting the increasing substantive overlap between national and international law and the opportunities for 'mutual self-reflection' created thereby.

[2] There are cases in which 'purely' or at least principally horizontal international law is addressed within a domestic judicial context. For example, in *R.* v. *Jones (Margaret)* [2006] UKHL 16, the UK courts had occasion to consider the prohibition of aggression. But in such cases, the international norm is not being applied as an inter-State norm, but as a norm which informs or should be reflected in domestic law, often in the form of a defence to criminal charges. In its horizontal guise, it would otherwise be non-justiciable. For a relatively early discussion of the doctrines and techniques that domestic courts rely on in avoiding engagement with horizonal norms *qua* horizontal norm, see Eyal Benvenisti, 'Judicial misgivings regarding the application of international law: An analysis of attitudes of national courts' (1993) 4 EJIL 159–83. See further Eyal Benvenisti, 'Reclaiming democracy: The strategic uses of foreign and international law by national courts' (2008) 102 AJIL 241–74; Mattias Kumm, 'International law in national courts: The international rule of law and the limits of the internationalist model' (2003–2004) 44 Va J Int'l L 19–32.

international law which goes further than this purely horizontal dynamic by reaching into their domestic legal systems – law which either sets standards against which to measure the adequacy of substantive and procedural protections afforded by those systems, or otherwise governs States' relationships with persons and property subject to their jurisdiction.[3] Subject to particularities around the reception of international law into a domestic legal sphere, the substance of these primary obligations may come before domestic courts in a number of ways, including by way of enforcing relevant rights or protections directly against the State, or by way of judicially reviewing the conduct of State organs. With States consenting to dispute settlement mechanisms or treaty-monitoring mechanisms which evaluate compliance with these international law obligations – which are designed to sound in or shape the domestic legal system and conduct of States – the role of domestic courts in IDS (or more particularly on international law as articulated and applied by dispute settlement bodies) becomes an ever more interesting, complex, and – in some instances – controversial question.[4]

3 While EU law very evidently 'reaches into' the domestic legal systems of member States, this chapter does not address it as a species of international law given the rather unique or *sui generis* nature of this particular regional system and its dispute settlement. On the interaction between the European Court of Justice and the domestic courts of member States, see Walter Mattli and Anne-Marie Slaughter, 'Revisiting the European Court of Justice' (1998) 52 Int'l Org 177–209. See also Tommaso Pavone and R. Daniel Keleman, 'The evolving judicial politics of European integration: The European Court of Justice and national courts revisited' (2019) 25 ELJ 352–73; Thomas Horsley, 'Subsidiarity and the European Court of Justice: Missing pieces in the subsidiarity jigsaw?' (2011) 50 J Common Mkt Stud 267–82; Juan A. Mayoral, 'In the CJEU judges trust: A new approach in the judicial construction of Europe' (2016) 55 J Common Mkt Stud 551–68. Otherwise, there are any number of ways to categorise or characterise international law which is designed to sound in and shape the domestic legal systems and conduct of States bound by relevant primary obligations, including by the nature of the primary obligation (positive or negative obligation, obligation of conduct or result), or their content or subject matter (substantive rights, procedural rights, criminal law enforcement, regulatory regimes in pursuance of particular aims). See generally Phillipe Gautier, 'On the classification of obligations in international law', in Holger P. Hestermeyer et al. (eds.), *Coexistence, Cooperation and Solidarity: Liber Amicorum Rüdiger Wolfrum* (Leiden: Brill Nijhoff, 2012), pp. 854–79. See also Dinah Shelton and Ariel Gould, 'Positive and negative obligations', in Dinah Shelton (ed.), *The Oxford Handbook of International Human Rights Law* (Oxford: Oxford University Press, 2013), pp. 562–84; Pierre-Marie Dupuy, 'Reviewing the difficulties of codification: On Ago's classification of obligations of means and obligations of result in relation to State responsibility' (1999) 10 EJIL 371–85; Thomas Kleinlein, 'The procedural approach of the European Court of Human Rights: Between subsidiarity and dynamic evolution' (2019) 68 ICLQ 91–110. See further Section 3.4.2.

4 One way of framing this question might be to consider whether domestic courts, in adjudicating upon these norms, are *themselves* engaging in IDS (framed in normative rather than institutional terms). See Antonios Tzanakopoulos, 'Domestic courts in international law:

There has been a good deal of academic engagement with this question, but it is often approached from the perspective of a particular forum of IDS – the International Court of Justice (ICJ) in Professor Nollkaemper's work,[5] the European Court of Human Rights (ECtHR) in Professor McGoldrick's[6] and Judge Mahoney's work,[7] and the inter-American human rights system (consisting of the Inter-American Commission of Human Rights (IACHR) and the Inter-American Court of Human Rights (IACtHR)) in Judge Mac-Gregor's work.[8] Where there has been engagement with the broader question of domestic courts and IDS, we are generally invited to think of the relationship in terms of judicial dialogue and cooperation.[9]

The purpose of this chapter is not to reinvent these wheels. Rather, it is to honour Professor Merrills' work on IDS: his work engaged analytically with the broad and varied landscape of dispute settlement bodies – in all their different institutional frameworks and contexts. The editors also invited the authors to map the ways in which IDS has changed as a result of developments in various fields of international law. To do both these things, this chapter will explore the relationship between domestic courts and IDS at a certain level of abstraction. First, Sections 3.2 and 3.3 will sketch the different circumstances in which IDS bodies might engage with domestic court decisions, and then Section 3.4 turns to a series of factors which might affect the

The international judicial function of national courts' (2011) 34 Loy LA Int'l & Comp L Rev 133–68 at 145–54 for such a discussion.

5 André Nollkaemper, 'The role of domestic courts in the case law of the International Court of Justice' (2006) 5 Chinese JIL 301–22; André Nollkaemper, 'Conversations among courts: Domestic and international adjudicators', in Cesare P. R. Romano, Karen J. Alter, and Yuval Shany (eds.), *The Oxford Handbook of International Adjudication* (Oxford: Oxford University Press, 2013), pp. 523–49.

6 Dominic McGoldrick, 'A defence of the margin of appreciation and an argument for its application by the Human Rights Committee' (2016) 65 ICLQ 21–60; Dominic McGoldrick, 'Religious rights and the margin of appreciation', in Petr Agha (ed.), *Human Rights between Law and Politics: The Margin of Appreciation in Post-National Contexts* (Oxford: Hart, 2017), pp. 145–68.

7 Paul Mahoney, 'Judicial activism and judicial self-restraint: Two sides of the same coin' (1990) 11 HRLJ 57–89; Paul Mahoney, 'The relationship between the Strasbourg Court and the national courts' (2014) 130 LQR 568–87.

8 Eduardo Ferrer Mac-Gregor, 'What do we mean when we talk about judicial dialogue? Reflections of a judge of the Inter-American Court of Human Rights' (2017) 30 Harv Hum Rts J 89–127; Eduardo Ferrer Mac-Gregor, 'Conventionality control: The new doctrine of the Inter-American Court of Human Rights' (2015) 109 AJIL Unbound 93–99.

9 Among others, see Anne-Marie Slaughter, 'Judicial globalization' (1999–2000) 40 Va J Int'l L 1103–24; David S. Law and Wen-Chen Chang, 'The limits of global judicial dialogue' (2011) 86 Wash L Rev 523–78; Philip M. Moreman, 'National court decisions as State practice: A transnational judicial dialogue' (2006) 32 NC J Int'l L & Com Reg 259–309; Mac-Gregor, 'What do we mean when we talk about judicial dialogue?'

nature and degree of engagement with domestic court decisions by IDS bodies. Many of the examples relied on by way of the analysis in this chapter will focus on the ECtHR. This is both because that Court is one of the most prolific and long-standing human rights courts and is an institutionally mature example of IDS, and because human rights law is, par excellence, one of the bodies of international law which is designed to penetrate the domestic legal sphere (both substantively and procedurally).

In conceptualising the different ways in which IDS might engage with domestic court decisions, the sections below rely on a rather straightforward distinction: whether the international court is being asked to rely upon domestic jurisprudence generally to ascertain or develop international law, or whether the respondent State's own courts' decisions are, in some manner, at issue in or relevant to the international dispute. This chapter first addresses the former in Section 3.2 and the latter in Section 3.3.

3.2 ASCERTAINMENT AND DEVELOPMENT OF INTERNATIONAL LAW

Domestic courts frequently reference, interpret, and apply international law when deciding disputes before them,[10] a practice that has only increased as the breadth of international law has widened and the number of international agreements steadily proliferated. In many instances, application will itself be required as an international legal obligation – and not infrequently a domestic or a constitutional one[11] – or will be deemed an uncontroversial interpretive aid for the court. The inverse relationship is, however, much less clear-cut. What is the impact of domestic court judgments on international law? This section notes two contrasting ways in which IDS bodies may engage with domestic court decisions – the first as data points or relevant facts in the

[10] To the extent that international law is not directly effective in the domestic legal sphere, domestic courts are often applying the domestic 'translation' of an international norm (which is formally binding only as between States and therefore inapplicable in domestic proceedings, at least insofar as the *ratione personae* scope of the source international norm is concerned). On translation in the context of international law on immunities, see Roger O'Keefe, 'The doctrine of incorporation revisited' (2009) 79 BYBIL 7–85 at 58.

[11] For instance, the German Federal Constitutional Court generally grants treaties the same status as the implementing Act, with the exception of the European Convention on Human Rights (ECHR), which 'has assumed quasi-constitutional rank'; see Stefan Kadelbach, 'International treaties and the German Constitution', in Curtis A. Bradley (ed.), *The Oxford Handbook of Comparative Foreign Relations Law* (Oxford: Oxford University Press, 2019), pp. 173–90. In the UK, there is certainly an arguable case that the Human Rights Act (HRA) has likewise assumed constitutional status; see Liberty, *A Parliamentarian's Guide to the Human Rights Act* (London: Liberty, 2010).

ascertainment of international law (Section 3.2.1), and the second as sources of potentially influential legal reasoning in the development of international law (Section 3.2.2).

3.2.1 *CIL Data Points*

Classically, decisions of domestic courts can be the 'stuff' of a customary international law (CIL) analysis. As a State organ capable of contributing to both State practice and *opinio juris*, domestic court decisions can act as CIL data points. In such cases, these decisions will have their impact on IDS – or perhaps more aptly on international law as articulated by dispute settlement bodies. A good example of this is domestic court decisions on immunities treated as facts by IDS bodies – evidence of a practice which does or does not contribute to the formation or development of CIL.[12]

We have seen the same approach in some judicial articulations of general principles of law (to the extent that we understand general principles to be principles common to the major legal systems of the world).[13] In either case, on a classical or black letter account of international law sources, when IDS bodies determine the existence and substance of CIL norms (or indeed general principles of law), they would principally be tallying the decisions 'for' and 'against' a particular norm as evidence of the consistency and duration of a given practice.[14] And given the possibility that domestic court

[12] In *Jones and Others* v. *The United Kingdom*, App. Nos 34356/06 and 40528/06 (14 January 2014) at paras 112–49, the ECtHR listed decisions of American, Canadian, Italian, Greek, Polish, French, and Slovenian courts, in considering whether a '*jus cogens* exception to State immunity' had developed. The court ultimately held it need not examine developments in those decisions in any detail, because the ICJ had settled the international law question in *Jurisdictional Immunities of the State (Germany* v. *Italy, Greece Intervening)* (Judgment) [2012] ICJ Rep. 99 at paras 197–98.

[13] In *Certain Phosphate Lands in Nauru (Nauru* v. *Australia)* (Preliminary Objections) [1992] ICJ Rep. 240 at paras 47–54, and the *Case Concerning Oil Platforms (Islamic Republic of Iran* v. *United States of America)* (Judgment) [2003] ICJ Rep. 161 at para. 73, Judges Shahabuddeen and Simma, respectively, note that domestic case law on joint and several liability might be used to infer a general principle of law.

[14] The ICJ has framed the identification of CIL variously as a search for practice which is 'constant and uniform' (*Asylum Case (Colombia* v. *Peru)* (Judgment) [1950] ICJ Rep. 266 at p. 277); 'both extensive and virtually uniform' (*North Sea Continental Shelf (Federal Republic of Germany* v. *Denmark; Federal Republic of Germany* v. *Netherlands)* (Judgment) [1969] ICJ Rep. 3 at p. 43, para. 74). The ILC concludes that 'practice must be general, meaning that it must be sufficiently widespread and representative' ('Draft conclusions on identification of customary international law, with commentaries', in *Yearbook of the International Law Commission 2018, Volume II, Part Two: Report of the Commission to the General Assembly on the Work of Its Seventieth Session* (New York: UN, 2018), conclusion 8), while making

decisions reflect both the practice of a State and an indication that the norm in question is considered legally binding (to the extent that the court is in effect 'enforcing' translated international law in the domestic sphere),[15] in principle they can satisfy both the State practice and *opinio juris* elements of a CIL analysis[16] as a feature of CIL ascertainment.[17]

There is nevertheless a sense of shallowness in respect of these classical or black letter accounts of the role domestic court decisions might play in IDS,[18] not least because a 'tallying approach' does not require international courts or treaty-monitoring bodies to engage in any depth substantively with the reasoning of domestic courts. A tallying approach also risks obscuring important assumptions about the relative quality of domestic legal systems, with

particular note that the thresholds are context-sensitive and 'that the number and distribution of States taking part in the relevant practice (like the number of instances of practice)' 'should include those that had an opportunity or possibility of applying the alleged rule' (paras 2–3).

15 See further Section 3.3.3. See also Anthea Roberts, 'Comparative international law? The role of national courts in creating and enforcing international law' (2011) 60 ICLQ 57–92 at 61–64 (highlighting the roles domestic courts play in both CIL formation and the enforcement of public international law); Tzanakopoulos, 'Domestic courts in international law', 145–54.

16 *North Sea Continental Shelf* at pp. 44–46. See further notes 14–15 and accompanying text.

17 For an early analysis of domestic court decisions as CIL data points, see Hersch Lauterpacht, 'Decisions of municipal courts as a source of international law' (1929) 10 BYBIL 65–96. See also Benedetto Conforti, *International Law and the Role of Domestic Legal Systems* (Leiden: Martinus Nijhoff, 1993), p. 79; Committee on the Formation of Customary (General) International Law, 'Statement of principles applicable to the formation of general customary international law', Sixty-Ninth Conference of the International Law Association, London, 2000, principle 9; ILC, 'Draft conclusions', conclusion 13; André Nollkaemper, *National Courts and the International Rule of Law* (Oxford: Oxford University Press, 2011), pp. 267–71.

18 Petersen, for instance, disputes that the ICJ adopts a 'tallying approach', instead stressing that the Court's limited use of domestic court judgments in its reasoning, as well as institutional constraints which require the Court to actively portray impartiality, makes it hard to find such an approach in its practice (see Niels Petersen, 'The International Court of Justice and the judicial politics of identifying customary international law' (2017) 28 EJIL 357–85). And Talmon argues that the Court adopts a practice of mere assertion (see Stefan Talmon, 'Determining customary international law: The ICJ's methodology between induction, deduction and assertion' (2015) 26 EJIL 417–43). Other commentators argue that the 'numbers game' is a simplistic attempt to create an objective and material method to establish the existence of a CIL norm; for instance, see László Blutman, 'Conceptual confusion and methodological deficiencies: Some ways that theories on customary international law fail' (2014) 25 EJIL 529–52 at 543–44, and Andrew T. Guzman and Jerome Hsiang, 'Some ways that theories on customary international law fail: A reply to László Blutman' (2014) 25 EJIL 553–59.

failures to consider a relevant cross-section or diversity of practice raising concerns about reverse engineering of judgments[19] and cultural bias.[20]

3.2.2 *Judicial Borrowing*

In cases where the subject matter of a dispute before an IDS body and a domestic court overlaps or is substantially the same, international courts and treaty-monitoring bodies may engage with decisions of domestic courts substantively by way of 'borrowing' judicial reasoning in the interpretation or application of international law. There are certain domestic decisions, bearing on international norms, which help move the international law discussion along.[21] For example, the reasoning of the UK House of Lords in *Pinochet*[22] has been widely relied on by domestic courts and IDS bodies alike.[23] This kind of borrowing engages substantively with domestic court decisions, not as

[19] As Justice Scalia infamously noted, selectively treating judgments when determining the existence of a CIL norm raises eyebrows as to a 'result-oriented approach', whereby it appears to an outsider that the court is using its CIL-tallying exercise with a specific end already in mind and that some kind of evidential manipulation has taken place: Antonin Scalia and Stephen Breyer, 'The relevance of foreign legal materials in U.S. constitutional cases: A conversation between Justice Antonin Scalia and Justice Stephen Breyer' (2005) 3 IJCL 519–41 at 530.

[20] Given the languages in which international courts and tribunals tend to operate, they will often focus on the case law of Western States. Anthea Roberts, *Is International Law International?* (Oxford: Oxford University Press, 2017), pp. 166–67, makes this argument in respect of the countries whose domestic court decisions are most often referenced in public international law textbooks and casebooks.

[21] See Kanetake, 'Interfaces between the national and international rule of law', 29. Making this point in the context of the ECtHR, Judge Bratza explains that the Court has 'been particularly respectful' of UK decisions taken under the Human Rights Act 1998 due to their 'very high quality', in some instances engaging in a form of judicial borrowing by relying heavily on domestic court reasoning; Nicolas Bratza, 'The relationship between the UK courts and Strasbourg' (2011) 5 EHRLR 505–12 at 507–8. By way of example, see *Pretty* v. *The United Kingdom*, App No. 2346/02 (ECtHR, 29 April 2002) at para. 30, where the ECtHR borrowed the reasoning of the UK appellate courts on the legality of assisted suicide, following the same jurisprudential roadmap of ECtHR and domestic UK jurisprudence, before confirming that the existence of positive rights does not necessarily grant the equivalent inverse rights.

[22] *R.* v. *Bow Street Stipendiary Magistrate and Others, Ex Parte Pinochet Ugarte (Amnesty International and Others Intervening) (No. 3)* [1999] UKHL 17, [1999] 2 All ER 97.

[23] Distinguished in *Al-Adsani* v. *The United Kingdom*, App. No. 35763/97 (ECtHR, 21 November 2011) at paras 60–61, 65. This judgment, in the words of the Court, 'incorporated [the *Pinochet* case] into its case-law in this sphere'; see *Demir and Baykara* v. *Turkey*, App. No. 34503/97 (ECtHR, 12 November 2008) at para. 73. Further, see Philippa Webb, '*House of Lords, Judgment, R v Bow Street Metropolitan Stipendiary Magistrate, Ex Parte Pinochet Ugarte (Amnesty International Intervening) (No 3)*, 1999', in Jill Barrett and Jean-Pierre Gauci (eds.), *British Contributions to International Law, 1915–2015* (Leiden: Brill Nijhoff, 2019), pp. 145–66.

precedents or data points but as sources of legal reasoning. With increasingly complicated questions of international law coming before domestic courts, and the sophistication of some domestic courts in their engagement with these questions, there may well be increasing opportunity for judicial borrowing in this sense.

At least in respect of inter-State disputes, and given the limited number of languages in which so many IDS bodies operate, such borrowing may, of course, prove problematic: thoroughly reasoned judicial decisions in languages that are accessible to members of IDS bodies are features of a particular subset of States. And the charge of Western-centric approaches to international law has certainly been raised in this context.[24] In practice, there may be more scope for such judicial borrowing, and it may be less problematic on these counts, in regional systems like the ECtHR, where the domestic court decisions of member States are more accessible and easily relied on.

3.3 INTERNATIONAL DISPUTE INVOLVING A STATE PARTY'S OWN JUDICIAL DECISION(S) OR LEGAL FRAMEWORK

In a CIL analysis or judicial borrowing by IDS bodies, the domestic court's decision is simply part of the broader legal landscape which might inform the settlement of an international dispute. The IDS body engages with the domestic court decision as a relevant fact, or as a source of inspiration for legal reasoning, but not as part of the subject matter of the dispute. In cases where a State's domestic legal framework or conduct (including in respect of judicial proceedings) is itself the source, or subject matter, of the international dispute, different elements of a domestic court's decision touching on these may invite more or less engagement by IDS bodies. The degree of deference or intrusiveness of this engagement sits along a spectrum – identified in Sections 3.3.1 and 3.3.2 (in which we see the most deference) through to Sections 3.3.3 and 3.3.4 (in which the nature of the international legal obligations at stake, and the mandate of the IDS body, may require a higher level of intrusion and less deference).

There are broader distinctions that inform, and are reflected in, the analysis below. For instance, a distinction might be drawn between 'pure' domestic law and domestic law which gives effect to international law or to which international law otherwise applies. 'Pure' domestic law is perhaps an increasingly rare creature – law which has been adopted or exists within the domestic

[24] For a sustained critique, see B. S. Chimni, 'Customary international law: A third world perspective' (2018) 112 AJIL 1–46.

realm with no direct or indirect influence from international law. International law which requires States to adapt their domestic legal landscape to meet international standards and which imposes primary obligations against which the conduct or outputs of State organs (executive, legislative, or judicial) might be evaluated is increasingly subject to the jurisdiction of both domestic courts and IDS bodies. This distinction is important for present purposes. With 'pure' domestic law, where relevant to an international dispute, we can expect to see a great deal of deference from IDS bodies.[25] This will evidently not be the case in respect of domestic law or State conduct which gives effect to international law, or which is otherwise governed by international law, particularly where a domestic court's decision in respect of such domestic law or State conduct forms the basis of the legal claim before an IDS body.

This said, IDS bodies do not formally sit in a hierarchical relationship with their domestic counterparts, and the sovereign equality and plurality of State parties to a particular dispute settlement system will often (even if not always or consistently) invite some measure of respect for the autonomy of domestic legal systems, as reflected in the analysis below.

3.3.1 *Factual Determinations by a Domestic Court*

It will rarely be the case that IDS bodies addressing law which imposes horizontal obligations as between States have an opportunity to engage with factual determinations made by domestic courts during domestic proceedings. Factual determinations by domestic courts in the course of proceedings bearing on either domestic law which gives effect to international law, or on State conduct to which international law otherwise applies, however, do come before international courts and tribunals and treaty-monitoring bodies. And in these cases, the degree of IDS scrutiny of purely factual determinations by domestic courts is, in general, limited,[26] with IDS bodies simply accepting the

[25] This is reminiscent of the 'domaine réservé', in that the constituent instruments of international organisations reserve certain matters for the domestic domain; see Antonios Tzanakopoulos, 'The right to be free from economic coercion' (2015) 4 CJICL 616–33 at 620, and the citations within. See also Heike Krieger, 'Populist governments and international law', KFG Working Paper Series No. 29, February 2019, https://publishup.uni-potsdam.de/opus4-ubp/frontdoor/deliver/index/docId/42686/file/kfg_wp29.pdf (accessed 25 June 2022), pp. 15–18, 23–24; Michael N. Schmitt, 'Autonomous cyber capabilities and the international law of sovereignty and intervention' (2020) 96 Int Law Stud 549–76 at 559–62.

[26] A distinction should be drawn here between facts which have been adjudicated on by domestic courts and facts which emerge after domestic remedies have been exhausted and while the dispute is before an IDS body. For example, in respect of the IACtHR, only facts which have

domestic court's findings. If IDS bodies were to regularly adopt some form of appellate role (revisiting and revising determinations of fact made by domestic courts), this would raise serious concerns regarding consistency, efficiency and judicial economy, institutional competence, and victims' and witnesses' rights. In respect of consistency, uniformity of decisions on factual issues supports a consistent application of the law, or at least the best chance of developing or clarifying the law insofar as the dispute before an IDS body and domestic court decisions are based on the same understanding of the facts. In respect of judicial economy, it would generally be seen as an unnecessary duplication of work, costing a large amount of time and resources for an international court to make a factual determination *de novo*, not to mention the more general institutional (in)competence of IDS bodies which are not resourced in a way that facilitates fact-finding on a necessary scale. Finally, reviewing and revising factual determinations in IDS bodies following a final decision by domestic courts would pose a burden on victims and witnesses, which, in light of the other issues addressed above, is certainly not justified.

Here it may be useful to draw a distinction between a domestic court's determination or conclusion on the factual matrix underlying the dispute before it, and the process by which it made such a determination or came to such a conclusion. While the general practice of IDS bodies is to accept findings of fact at face value for the reasons identified above, there is certainly no similar justification for such deference in respect of domestic courts' factual assessments – which is to say the process of fact-finding. Indeed, any such deference could prevent the IDS body from engaging substantively with the alleged breach – in particular where the primary obligation imposes

been the subject of prior determination by the Inter-American Commission on Human Rights (the Commission) can be considered by the IACtHR (Art 35, IACtHR, 'Rules of Procedure of the Inter-American Court of Human Rights, approved by the Court during its LXXXV Regular Period of Sessions, held from November 16 to 28, 2009', www.corteidh.or.cr/reglamento.cfm?lang=en (accessed 25 June 2022)). This said, in cases involving systematic breaches of human rights in respect of many victims, it is not uncommon for facts in respect of victims that were not identified or referred to by the Commission to come to light after the Commission's report is delivered, and to be referenced in pleadings before the IACtHR. The IACtHR has determined that it can consider these 'new' facts if and to the extent that they are related to the facts described in the Commission's merits report and to the evidence provided to the IACtHR, taking into account also the magnitude of the violation (see, e.g., *Case of the Hacienda Brasil Verde Workers* v. *Brazil*, Judgment, IACtHR Series C No. 318 (20 October 2016) at para. 45). In such cases, an IDS body which makes determinations in respect of the 'new' fact is not acting as an appellate court in respect of domestic proceedings, but is rather fulfilling its function and engaging fully with the dispute before it. Such engagement does not raise the concerns regarding consistency, efficiency and judicial economy, institutional competence, and victims' and witnesses' rights identified below.

standards against which a judicial process (including in its fact-finding) might be evaluated. For instance, in the human rights context, the IDS or treaty-monitoring bodies adjudicating on the right to a fair trial will often be required to assess the adequacy of the domestic trial process to determine if the right has been violated. This may certainly require an assessment of the domestic court's decision-making process, including its fact-finding methodology and any substantive conclusions it has reached.

By way of example, the ECtHR's approach to its treatment of the factual determinations of domestic courts is articulated in its fourth instance doctrine and the exceptions thereto. The fourth instance doctrine is that the ECtHR will only address factual or legal errors made by a domestic court to the extent that these infringe on Convention rights.[27] The doctrine has been described as 'a brake on the Court's interpretations of the Convention by ensuring it bears in mind the constitutional limits on its competence'.[28] But the fourth instance doctrine does not absolutely insulate factual determinations by domestic courts from any scrutiny, because while 'it is not [the Court's] function to deal with errors of fact or law allegedly committed by a national court', the Court will do so 'in so far as [these] may infringe rights and freedoms protected by the Convention'.[29] This said, the threshold for interference in factual determinations by domestic courts is high, with the Court giving effect to the fourth instance doctrine unless the judicial process was 'manifestly unreasonable or in any other way arbitrary'.[30] 'As long as the resulting decision is based on a full and thorough evaluation of the relevant factors ... it will escape the scrutiny of the Court.'[31] As an arbitrary process for determining facts would itself form part of the breach of (for instance) access to justice rights, the ECtHR effectively limits its review of the domestic factual determination process to that which is necessary to adjudicate on fundamental rights violations arising therefrom. In so doing, the Court balances the

[27] For more information, see Jonas Christoffersen, *Fair Balance: Proportionality, Subsidiarity and Primarity in the European Convention on Human Rights* (Leiden: Martinus Nijhoff, 2009), pp. 257–76.

[28] Maija Dahlberg, '"It is not its task to act as a Court of Fourth Instance": The case of the European Court of Human Rights' (2014) 7 Eur J Leg Stud 84–118 at 91. The Court explains, in *Baumann* v. *Austria*, App. No. 76809/01 (ECtHR, 7 October 2004) at para. 49, that 'it is the domestic courts which are best placed for assessing the credibility of witnesses and the relevance of evidence to the issues in the case'.

[29] *Tomić and Others* v. *Montenegro*, App. Nos 18650/09, 18676/09, 18679/09, 38855/09, 38859/09, 38883/09, 39589/09, 39592/09, 65365/09, and 7316/10 (ECtHR, 17 April 2012) at para. 62.

[30] *Ebanks* v. *The United Kingdom*, App. No. 36822/06 (ECtHR, 26 January 2010) at para. 74.

[31] *Lalmahomed* v. *The Netherlands*, App. No. 26036/08 (ECtHR, 22 February 2011) at para. 37.

concerns highlighted above (in respect of consistency, efficiency and judicial economy, institutional competence, and victims' and witnesses' rights) against its broader human rights protection mandate. The inter-American system of human rights protection has also operated on the basis of a fourth instance doctrine,[32] but its approach to 'conventionality control', which imposes an obligation on domestic judges to uphold the American Convention on Human Rights,[33] creates greater scope for interference in the domestic legal proceedings of member States than we see in the European system. This can in part be explained by socio-legal factors explored further in Section 3.4.

3.3.2 *Interpretation and Application of Domestic Law by a Domestic Court*

Drawing a clear line between purely domestic law and domestic law which gives effect to international law is not necessarily straightforward. This is not least because States may not fully or adequately implement relevant primary obligations under international law which are designed to sound in or shape their domestic legal systems – such that there may be domestic law which is co-extensive with or related to international law, without in fact giving effect thereto. As a result, the characterisation of law as purely domestic or in some sense international (derived, inspired, co-extensive, or related) happens along a spectrum. There is, nevertheless, some domestic law which is at least principally domestic. For instance, domestic law which allocates regulatory authority to different branches or levels of government might be characterised as principally domestic. And in respect of such purely or principally domestic law, international courts and tribunals treat the pronouncements of their domestic counterparts as they do factual determinations. By way of a particularly clear example, in *Certain Questions of Mutual Assistance in Criminal Matters*, the ICJ accepted the Paris Court of Appeal's decision on relevant competences under French law, simply noting that 'is not for this Court

[32] See, e.g., *Clifton Wright* v. *Jamaica*, Case No. 9260 (Inter-American Commission on Human Rights, 1988) at para. 5 (in which the Commission held that, in instances where irregularities of domestic judicial proceedings result in 'manifest violations' of due process or other rights protected by the Convention, it may intrude further into the domestic court's fact-based decision-making process); *Genie Lacayo* v. *Nicaragua*, Judgment, IACtHR Series C No. 45 (13 September 1997) at para. 94. See further Mónica Pinto, 'National and international courts – Deference or disdain?' (2008) 30 Loy LA Int'l & Comp L Rev. 247–73; Álvaro Paúl, 'The Inter-American Commission on Human Rights' initial review of petitions, its backlog, and the principle of subsidiarity' (2016) 49 Geo Wash Int'l L Rev 19–52 at 37–38.

[33] *Almonacid Arellano* v. *Chile*, Judgment, IACtHR Series C No. 154 (26 September 2006) at para. 124. See further Mac-Gregor, 'Conventionality control', 93.

to do other than accept the findings of the Paris Court of Appeal on this point'.[34]

Human rights courts and treaty-monitoring bodies take a similar approach as the ICJ. The ECtHR does so through its fourth instance doctrine (as referenced in Section 3.3.1), under which the Court stresses that it is primarily for the national courts to interpret and assess compliance with domestic law.[35] The Human Rights Committee (responsible for monitoring the implementation of the ICCPR[36] by State parties) also applies its own form of the fourth instance doctrine. Barring an absence of good faith, the Committee will not review whether the national court has properly interpreted or applied national law.[37] Deference to decisions by domestic courts in such cases, however, will not preclude courts and human rights treaty–monitoring bodies from addressing errors of law by national courts insofar as these may infringe rights and freedoms protected by the relevant human rights convention.[38]

[34] *Certain Questions of Mutual Assistance in Criminal Matters (Djibouti* v. *France)* (Judgment) [2008] ICJ Rep. 177 at para. 146. There is the related question of the relationship between IDS bodies and domestic constitutional courts. See further the commentary surrounding the dialogue between the Italian Constitutional Court and the ICJ in *Germany* v. *Italy*, for instance. Karin Oellers-Frahm, 'A never-ending story: The International Court of Justice – the Italian Constitutional Court – Italian tribunals and the question of immunity' (2016) 76 ZaöRV 193–202; and Massimo Lando, 'Intimations of unconstitutionality: The supremacy of international law and Judgment 238/2014 of the Italian Constitutional Court' (2015) 78 MLR 1028–41. In the ECtHR context, see, for instance, Jeffrey Kahn, 'The relationship between the European Court of Human Rights and the Constitutional Court of the Russian Federation: Conflicting conceptions of sovereignty in Strasbourg and St Petersburg' (2019) 30 EJIL 933–59.

[35] See *Perez* v. *France*, App. No. 47287/99 (ECtHR, 12 February 2004) at para. 82. This said, distinguishing between substantive review of a domestic court's decision on the interpretation or application of its domestic law, a review of a domestic court's decision-making process, and a review of the domestic court's appreciation of the correct balance between competing interests in the human rights context (which is subject to the ECtHR's 'margin of appreciation' doctrine addressed further in Section 3.4) is not always straightforward. See, e.g., the Dissenting Opinion of Judges Kjølbro, Poláčková, Koskelo, and Nordén in *Strand Lobben and Others* v. *Norway*, App. No. 37283/13 (ECtHR, 10 September 2019) at paras 15–17.

[36] International Covenant on Civil and Political Rights, New York, 16 December 1966, in force 23 March 1976, 999 UNTS 171 (the ICCPR).

[37] See *Hertzberg et al* v. *Finland* (1985) Selected Decisions of the Human Rights Committee 124 at para. 9.2, qualifying domestic decisions on domestic law as a 'matter of fact' unless they are not *bona fide*.

[38] See, e.g., *Perez v. France*, para. 82. See further Dahlberg, 'It is not its task to act as a Court of Fourth Instance', 85.

3.3.3 A Domestic Court's Interpretation and Application of Domestic Law Which Gives Effect to or Is Otherwise Governed by International Law

As noted above, there is a growing body of international law which obliges States to adopt certain regulatory and legislative frameworks domestically (many with a view to substantive and procedural protection of rights, the suppression of international or transnational crime, and the achievement of other important policy aims) or to engage or refrain from engaging in certain conduct vis-à-vis persons and property subject to a State's jurisdiction, providing standards against which the conduct of States (executive, legislative, and judicial) can be measured. When domestic law or State conduct which gives effect to or is otherwise governed by international law first comes before domestic courts and subsequently IDS bodies, IDS bodies do not rely on doctrines of deference as discussed in Sections 3.3.1 and 3.3.2. Instead, to decide the international law question before them, they may need to engage substantively with the 'correctness' of the domestic court's analysis of domestic law or the evaluation of State conduct from the perspective of relevant international law.

When the domestic court's interpretation or application of a domestic legal framework is in keeping with the interpretation or application of the 'source' international law which domestic law does (or ought to) give effect to, there will simply be no breach of the international obligation. This is, of course, one of the rationales for admissibility criteria, most notably the exhaustion of local remedies requirement (discussed further in Section 3.3.4), as this affords the domestic legal system multiple opportunities to get their interpretation and application of domestic law 'right' from an international law perspective.[39] By adjudicating on the merits only when the domestic legal system has had multiple opportunities to reach the 'correct' interpretation and application (insofar as international law is concerned), the international court has effectively balanced its mandate with the need to respect the autonomy of domestic legal systems. Indeed, when national courts interpret and apply domestic law which gives effect to or is otherwise governed by international

[39] See Silvia D'Ascoli and Kathrin Maria Scherr, 'The role of prior exhaustion of local remedies in the international law doctrine and its application in the specific context of human rights protection', European University Institute Working Papers – Law 2007/02, https://cadmus.eui.eu/bitstream/handle/1814/6701/LAW_2007_02.pdf (accessed 25 June 2022), p. 11. The authors also illustrate this in reference to the exceptions to the exhaustion of the local remedies rule before human rights courts (pp. 13–15).

law correctly, 'they prevent a controversy from reaching the international level, which strengthens the subsidiary nature of the international legal order'.[40]

On the other hand, assuming domestic remedies have been exhausted, IDS bodies will, of course, have occasion to review a domestic court's interpretation or application of domestic law which either gives effect to international law or to which international law otherwise applies. The finding of a breach of international law will be based either on a failure to properly implement the international obligation in domestic law (which failure domestic courts give effect to) or on an 'international law' error by the domestic court (e.g. a discrepancy between the domestic court's interpretation or application of the 'source' international law which domestic law gives effect to and the IDS body's own interpretation and application of that 'source' international law).[41] Such a treatment of domestic court decisions is evidently more intrusive than the approach discussed in Section 3.3.2. But it bears noting that the IDS body's enquiry is in respect of compliance with the 'source' international law as it applies on the international plane.[42] Any review of the correctness of a domestic court's interpretation or application of international law as implemented or given effect to within the domestic legal system is incidental. The precise nature and content of the international legal norm at issue before the IDS body and the degree to which that international norm has been given effect within the domestic legal sphere will evidently affect the degree of engagement with the domestic court's decision. Although not conclusive when trying to make sense of an international court's treatment of a domestic court's decision, as discussed further in Section 3.4.2, these factors nonetheless play a significant role.

[40] Mac-Gregor, 'What do we mean when we talk about judicial dialogue?' 94.

[41] E.g., in *Naït-Liman* v. *Switzerland*, App. No 51357/07 (ECtHR, 15 March 2018) at paras 103–11, the ECtHR analysed the domestic court's interpretation of domestic law in light of both the ECHR and the Torture Convention to ascertain whether, and in what manner, victims of torture had a right to obtain compensation (Convention against Torture and Other Cruel, Inhuman or Degrading Treatment or Punishment, New York, 10 December 1984, in force 26 June 1987, 1465 UNTS 85 (the Torture Convention)). For an overview of the ECtHR's treatment of the UK courts' decisions in this manner, see Alice Donald, Jane Gordon, and Philip Leach, *The UK and the European Court of Human Rights. Equality and Human Rights Commission Research Report* 83 (Manchester: Equality and Human Rights Commission, 2012), pp. 125–34 and cases cited therein.

[42] Bratza, 'Relationship between UK courts and Strasbourg', 506–8.

3.3.4 *Domestic Judicial Decisions Which Are the Subject of the International Dispute*

The exhaustion of domestic (or local) remedies rule has a systemic effect on the relationship between domestic and international courts. This is due to its role as an admissibility rule applicable to international disputes bearing on law which imposes an obligation on States in respect of persons (natural and legal) subject to their jurisdiction. The domestic legal process in such cases is not only an essential element of the admissibility calculus; it can equally be a feature of the internationally wrongful act which forms the substance of the international dispute (for instance, in respect of access to justice claims). Where the domestic legal process is purely relevant to admissibility, an international court's engagement with that process (including decisions taken by domestic courts) will often be formal – which is to say a verification that the dispute was fully vetted by competent domestic authorities with a view to finally settle the dispute. In such cases, the domestic court process is treated as a potentially relevant 'fact'. This said, an exhaustion of domestic remedies analysis is not strictly a box-ticking exercise – particularly in cases where a dispute was not, or could not be, fully vetted by competent domestic authorities. In such cases, the international court, tribunal, or treaty-monitoring body may need to consider the effectiveness of the relevant domestic legal process, and whether dispute resolution was genuinely available to the applicant.[43] This will very naturally put the IDS body in the position of judging a domestic legal process, including a judicial one.[44]

Where domestic remedies were formally effective and have been exhausted, but the domestic court's decision is nevertheless an element of the internationally wrongful act,[45] the international court or tribunal

[43] See ILC, 'Draft articles on diplomatic protection, with commentaries', in *Yearbook of the International Law Commission, 2006, Volume II, Part Two: Report of the Commission to the General Assembly on the Work of Its Fifty-Eighth Session* (New York: UN, 2006), 26, Part 3. See further D'Ascoli and Scherr, 'Role of prior exhaustion of local remedies'. See also Martin Dietrich Brauch, 'Exhaustion of local remedies in international investment law', IISD Best Practices Series, January 2017, www.iisd.org/system/files/publications/best-practices-exhaustion-local-remedies-law-investment-en.pdf (accessed 25 June 2022), pp. 2–7, 12–14, 18–21; Takele Soboka Bulto, 'Exception as norm: The local remedies rule in the context of socio-economic rights in the African human rights system' (2012) 16 Int'l J Hum Rts 555–76.

[44] E.g., see *Velasquez Rodriguez* v. *Honduras*, IACtHR Series C No. 4 (29 July 1988) at 291, 304–9.

[45] This would be the case in respect of a breach of substantive rights which are not protected and upheld in genuinely held domestic proceedings, resulting in international proceedings relating to both the substantive breach and the breach of the independent right to a remedy for the substantive breach.

will be required to assess the 'correctness' of the domestic court's decision. This will be insofar as it must determine for itself whether there has been a substantive breach (as discussed in Section 3.3.3). Any claim related to access to justice flows from the domestic court's determination on substance (which is to say: if the applicant's claim of a substantive breach is upheld by the IDS body, there will be an associated breach of the right of access to justice).[46]

While factual determinations and interpretations and applications of purely domestic law invite deference by IDS bodies, there is no such deference on display when the domestic court's decision forms the basis of the legal claim on the international stage. In such cases, it is not uncommon to see IDS bodies, primarily human rights courts, telling domestic courts what to do when ordering remedies for violations (e.g. of the right to a fair trial). The ECtHR, for instance, has concluded that in such instances the 'most appropriate remedy would be to reconsider the applicant's appeal',[47] while both the Human Rights Committee and the Committee against Torture make recommendations that the respondent State investigate and punish and, to a certain extent, also supervise the implementation of their judgments.[48] The IACtHR has in some cases gone much further, 'ordering, specifying, monitoring, and guiding national criminal prosecutions',[49] perhaps reflecting some of the socio-legal context of the birth of the inter-American system of human rights discussed further in Section 3.4.

[46] On this point, see Jean-Paul Costa, 'The relationship between the European Court of Human Rights and the national courts' (2013) 3 EHRLR 264–74. In the human rights context, and to a lesser extent before the ICJ when it is addressing individual rights, the result is that Judge Lauterpacht's pronouncement in *Norwegian Loans* (*Case of Certain Norwegian Loans (France v. Norway)* (Preliminary Measures) [1957] ICJ Rep. 9 at 33) that the exhaustion of local remedies cannot bring an otherwise domestic dispute onto the international stage is no longer correct.

[47] *Jovanović* v. *Serbia*, App. No. 32299/08 (ECtHR, 2 October 2012) at para. 59.

[48] Contrast Ineke Boerefijn, 'Towards a strong system of supervision: The Human Rights Committee's role in reforming the reporting procedure under Article 40 of the Covenant on Civil and Political Rights' (1995) 17 Hum Rts Q 766–93, and Makau wa Matua, 'Looking past the Human Rights Committee: An argument for de-marginalizing enforcement' (1998) 4 Buff Hum Rts L Rev 211–60. See also Ronagh McQuigg, 'How effective is the United Nations Committee against Torture?' (2011) 22 EJIL 813–28.

[49] See Kanetake, 'Interfaces between the national and international rule of law', 23. See further Alexandra Huneeus, 'International criminal law by other means: The quasi-criminal jurisdiction of the human rights courts' (2013) 107 AJIL 1–44.

3.4 FACTORS WHICH AFFECT THE NATURE AND DEGREE OF ENGAGEMENT WITH DOMESTIC DECISIONS

Taking account of the spectrum of deference to domestic court decisions by the IDS bodies mapped out in Sections 3.2 and 3.3, this section will look at some of the factors which may influence the depth and nature of an IDS body's engagement with the decisions of domestic courts, bearing in mind that these do not operate in a vacuum and both influence and overlap with each other. Evidently, these factors will be more relevant where there is substantive engagement with the decisions of domestic courts, as opposed to, for instance, cases in which a great deal of deference is the practice of IDS bodies (in respect of factual determinations and interpretation of purely or principally domestic law, as discussed in Sections 3.3.1 and 3.3.2, respectively).

3.4.1 *Conception of the Judicial Function in IDS*

Much has been written on the 'judicial function' in IDS,[50] including, of course, in Professor Merrills' seminal work.[51] Broadly, the institutional framework of a particular IDS body, the basis of its adjudicative powers and limitations of its jurisdiction (including whether it is consent-based or inherent in participation in the relevant legal regime), the normative framework being applied, and the nature of the disputants (including whether it is a body to which only States have access, a forum for the vindication of individual rights to which individuals have direct access, or a mixture of both) might all have their impact on the nature of the judicial function. In this section, we want to make a rather brief point which hangs on two distinct (but, in practice, overlapping and complementary) conceptions of the judicial function. In contentious cases in particular, IDS bodies may be formally restricted to

[50] By way of examples, see Hersch Lauterpacht, *The Function of Law in the International Community*, rev. ed. (Oxford: Oxford University Press, 1933/2011), ch. III; Philip Allott, 'The International Court and the voice of justice', in Vaughan Lowe and Malgosia Fitzmaurice (eds.), *Fifty Years of the International Court of Justice: Essays in Honour of Sir Robert Jennings* (Cambridge: Cambridge University Press, 1996), pp. 17, 23; Yuval Shany, 'No longer a weak department of power? Reflections on the emergence of a new international judiciary' (2009) 20 EJIL 73–91; Gleider I. Hernández, *The International Court of Justice and the Judicial Function* (Oxford: Oxford University Press, 2014).

[51] See, e.g., Professor Merrills' discussion of the ICJ's function in John G. Merrills, *International Dispute Settlement*, 6th ed. (Cambridge: Cambridge University Press, 2017), pp. 15–177.

dispute settlement – applying the law to facts put before the court in a claim expressed in terms of the applicable legal framework(s).[52] To say so, however, shouldn't obscure that IDS bodies – whether implicitly or more boldly in some cases – can also play a systemic or constitutional role, in particular in respect of the development of law.[53] The balance between dispute settlement and a more systemic function is, of course, an institutional question, but it is also one on which different judges in the same IDS body may have different views, and in fact one that may, in some circumstances, be affected by the circumstances of the case at hand.[54]

The point for present purposes is that this balance, and the views of the members of an IDS body in respect of the judicial function, can be expected to affect the degree and nature of engagement of that IDS body with the decisions of domestic courts. The more an IDS body conceptualises of its judicial function as limited to dispute settlement (and the shyer it is about any more systemic role), the more it will confine itself to the pleadings and circumstances of the parties, or a 'tallying' approach discussed in Section 3.2.1.

[52] See, e.g., the Statute of the International Court of Justice, San Francisco, 26 June 1945, in force 24 October 1945, 33 UNTS 993, Arts 36 and 38(1). Contrast this with Protocol No. 11 to the Convention for the Protection of Human Rights and Fundamental Freedoms Restructuring the Control Machinery Established Thereby, Strasbourg, 11 May 1994, in force 1 November 1998, 2061 UNTS 12, 3 ETS 155, Art 35(2)(b), which excludes from admissibility any case that is 'substantially the same as a matter that has already been examined by the Court', emphasising in some respects the ECtHR's constitutional role in human rights protection amongst member States at the expense of its dispute settlement and reparations functions.

[53] For one of the more compelling arguments to this effect in respect of the ICJ, see Hernández, *International Court of Justice*, 90–91. See further Christian J. Tams and James Sloan (eds.), *The Development of International Law by the International Court of Justice* (Oxford: Oxford University Press, 2013). Then president of the ICJ, HE Judge Rosalyn Higgins, implicitly recognised the challenge in conceptualising the judicial function purely in dispute settlement terms (and ignoring the more systemic function that IDS bodies may need to fulfil) when she observed that the ICJ's decisions 'must continue to provide that core of predictability that distinguishes law from politics' while being 'responsive to the legitimate needs and aspirations of the international community', and that 'in carefully balancing continuity and change, the Court will remain the lighthouse beacon in our ever-expanding system of international law'. ICJ, 'Press Release No. 2006/15', 12 April 2006, www.icj-cij.org/public/files/press-releases/0/000-20060412-PRE-01-00-EN.pdf (accessed 25 June 2022).

[54] See, e.g., Judge Simma's separate opinion in *Oil Platforms* (p. 325), in which he characterises the court's fulfilment of 'its duty' as inappropriately restrained, with particular regard for the nature of the norm at issue (the prohibition on the use of force), in respect of which he asserts the 'Court ought to take every opportunity to secure that the voice of the law of the Charter rise above the current cacophony' (p. 328).

3.4.2 *The Nature of the Legal Norms at Issue in the International Dispute*

Here we simply note that the extent to which a binding primary norm has or has not been given effect to in a domestic legal system, and the nature of that norm[55] (at issue in some form in domestic proceedings and subsequently before an IDS body), will evidently influence the depth and nature of any IDS engagement with the domestic court's decision. A complete matrix, which plots the different categories of primary obligations and their manifestations in domestic legal systems and processes as against the nature of IDS engagement and the degree of deference IDS bodies pay to the decisions of their domestic counterparts in respect thereof, is beyond the scope of a book chapter, but may be of interest to aspiring doctoral students. This said, an example will help to flesh out the point that the nature of the primary norm influences not only the domestic court's assessment of that norm's role in the domestic legal system, but also an international court's or tribunal's analysis or review of domestic court's decisions related thereto.

For instance, the primary rules which confer the rights on individuals (which States are obliged to give effect to in their domestic legal systems through the general obligation to 'secure' or 'respect and ensure' such rights)[56] can take many different forms. In some cases, such primary rules impose negative obligations on States which prohibit (absolutely or in defined circumstances) certain conduct vis-à-vis natural or legal persons.[57] These negative obligations may come before a State's domestic courts to the extent that they have been given some effect in that State's legal system. In relevant cases, the domestic court will have to incorporate multiple elements into its judicial analysis, including the scope of the prohibition (for instance, whether it applies extraterritorially), the precise content of the prohibition, and whether the facts alleged are in breach of the prohibition in question.

Unless international treaty law is directly effective in that State's domestic legal system,[58] or the norm in question is a directly effective CIL

55 See note 2.

56 See, e.g., Art 1 of the European Convention on Human Rights, Rome, 4 November 1950, in force 3 September 1953, 213 UNTS 222 (the ECHR); Art 2(1) of the ICCPR.

57 E.g., Art 3 of the ECHR absolutely prohibits torture or inhuman or degrading treatment or punishment.

58 The most familiar example of directly effective treaty law is, of course, the EU law. See note 3. See further Morten Rasmussen, 'Revolutionising European law: A history of the *Van Gen den Loos* judgment' (2014) 12 Int J Const Law 136–36. Direct effect of treaty law otherwise depends on the domestic legal system and whether an international treaty is self-executing. See further John H. Jackson, 'Status of treaties in domestic legal systems: A policy analysis' (1992)

rule[59] which gives rise to a domestic cause of action, the domestic court will be interpreting and determining the scope of the domestic law which gives effect to the primary rule of international law, before then applying that domestic law to the facts as determined. Depending on applicable interpretive rules, and as part of its interpretation and application of the domestic law which gives effect to international law, the domestic court may have recourse to the jurisprudence of IDS bodies[60] and to relevant commentary[61] which give their own, sometimes conflicting, interpretations of the relevant law.

As noted in Section 3.3.3, the nature of IDS engagement with the domestic court's decision in such cases will necessarily be more intrusive – in some broad sense measuring the correctness of the interpretation and application as against the 'source' international law at issue before the IDS body.[62] The IDS

86 AJIL 310–40; David Sloss, 'The domestication of international human rights: Non-self-executing declarations and human rights treaties' (1999) 24 Yale J Int'l L 129–221.

59 As translated into the domestic legal system. See O'Keefe, 'Doctrine of incorporation revisited'.

60 E.g., in *R.* v. *Secretary of State for the Home Department, Ex Parte Mullen* [2004] UKHL 18, the UK House of Lords considered Human Rights Committee (HRC) jurisprudence on the Art 14(6) ICCPR's right to compensation for wrongful conviction to inform the interpretation of the domestic incorporating law (s. 133 of the Criminal Justice Act 1988, paras 9–11). In *Hutchinson* v. *Newbury Magistrates Court* (2000) ILR 499 at 505–6, the England and Wales Divisional Court analysed in detail the ICJ's *Threat or Use of Nuclear Weapons Advisory Opinion* (*Legality of the Threat or Use of Nuclear Weapons* (Advisory Opinion) [1996] ICJ Rep. 226) in determining whether the UK's development of Trident nuclear warheads amounted to a breach of CIL.

61 E.g., see the discussion in *Benkharbouche* v. *Secretary of State for Foreign and Commonwealth Affairs* [2017] UKSC 62 at paras 25–29 of the ECtHR's treatment of the ILC, 'Draft articles on jurisdictional immunities of states and their property, with commentaries', in *Yearbook of the International Law Commission. 1991, Volume II, Part Two: Report of the Commission to the General Assembly on the Work of Its Forty-Third Session* (New York: UN, 1999). The International Committee of the Red Cross (ICRC) is often relied upon by domestic courts examining questions of international humanitarian law when this has a nexus to applicable domestic law: see *R.* v. *Gul* [2012] EWCA Crim 280 at paras 38–41 (on combatant immunity) and paras 44–49 (on CIL relating to terrorist designations during non-international armed conflicts). In *Gul*, the Court of Appeal then read the domestic law in light of the ICRC's elucidation of these international law norms: see paras 50–60.

62 Evidently, the jurisdiction of the IDS body and the nature of the judicial function (as referenced in Section 3.4.1) will equally be relevant, underscoring that the factors set out in this section do not operate in isolation from each other. By way of example, the ICJ – in cases bearing on individual rights – also behaves more 'intrusively' in respect of decisions by domestic courts in human rights cases. Despite the historical approach that domestic court decisions are treated as part of the essential factual matrix before the court (see *Certain German Interests in Polish Upper Silesia (Germany* v. *Poland)* [1926] PCIJ Rep. Series A No. 7 at 10), we have seen greater scrutiny into the decision-making process of domestic courts in cases such as *LaGrand (Germany v. United States of America)* (Judgment) [2001] ICJ Rep. 466 and *Avena and Other Mexican Nationals (Mexico v. United States of America* (Judgment) [2004] ICJ Rep. 12 (in which individuals had legal rights protected by international law, whether given effect to

body may also have cause to review whether the facts as determined by the domestic court (which determinations will attract a fair amount of deference unless the process of fact-finding was in breach of relevant rights)[63] are in breach of the primary rule of international law. Indeed, in such cases, the IDS body may well go further, being prescriptive in respect of the domestic judicial process.[64]

Alternatively, primary rules which confer rights on individuals may take the form of broad aims which are expressly subject to competing policy priorities and/or resource limitations,[65] to be given effect to through relevant legislative frameworks.[66] The competing policy priorities and resource issues will be as determined within the domestic legal system. To the extent that IDS bodies assess compliance with these primary rules and have occasion to consider the decisions of a domestic court in relation thereto, the nature of any 'review' is necessarily different from that in respect of negative obligations (and

in domestic law or not). For a close analysis, see Nollkaemper, 'Role of domestic courts', 321. More recently, the ICJ in *Jadhav* set tangible limits for any future domestic judgment and legal proceedings to comply with Pakistan's international obligations, albeit not to the extent requested by India. *Jadhav Case (India* v. *Pakistan)* (Judgment) [2019] ICJ Rep. 418 at para. 146. See also Yuval Shany, 'Toward a general margin of appreciation doctrine in international law?' (2005) 16 EJIL 907–40 at 938–39, in which the author applies this distinction to scrutinise the ICJ's reasoning in *Legal Consequences of the Construction of a Wall in the Occupied Palestinian Territory* (Advisory Opinion) [2004] ICJ Rep. 136.

63 See Sections 3.3.1 and 3.3.2.

64 See note 48.

65 For instance, under the ICCPR and the International Covenant on Economic, Social, and Cultural Rights, New York, 16 December 1966, in force 3 January 1976, 993 UNTS 3 (the ICESCR), many of the qualified rights have been held to be subject to domestic policy and resource limitations. See generally Amrei Müller, 'Limitations to and derogations from economic, social and cultural rights' (2009) 9 HRLRev 557–601. For instance, Art 18(3) of the ICCPR permits limitations on the freedom to manifest religion or belief if these are proscribed by law, applied only for an ICCPR-linked purpose, and are proportionate to this aim (UN Human Rights Committee, 'General Comment No. 22: Article 18 (Freedom of thought, conscience or religion)' (30 July 1993) UN Doc. CCPR/C/21/Rev.1/Add.4, para. 8): see Gehan Gunatilleke, 'Criteria and constraints: The Human Rights Committee's test on limiting the freedom of religion or belief' (2020) 15 Relig Hum Rights 20–38 at 23–36, wherein the author distinguished between a 'flexible' (more deferential to national policy and resource constraints) and a 'rigorous' test taken by the HRC in assessing limitations on such rights.

66 E.g., Art 2(1) of the ICESCR, which states that 'each State Party to the present Covenant undertakes to take steps, individually and through international assistance and co-operation, especially economic and technical, to the maximum of its available resources, with a view to achieving progressively the full realization of the rights recognized in the present Covenant by all appropriate means, including particularly the adoption of legislative measures'. See further Rolf Künnermann, 'A coherent approach to human rights' (1995) 17 Hum Rts Q 323–42.

particularly those which are absolute) outlined above and subject to significantly more deference and respect for the autonomy of domestic legal systems.[67]

By way of contrast, we might consider a dispute before an IDS body in respect of binding primary rules which the respondent State has failed to effectively implement within their domestic legal system. Any domestic court's decision which touches on the subject matter of the international law dispute is likely to be treated as fact (as discussed in Sections 3.3.1 and 3.3.2), with any divergence from international norms evidencing an omission, rather than a positive conduct to be evaluated against international law standards.[68] Similarly, where an IDS body is engaging with domestic court's decisions by way of a CIL analysis or in determining the existence of a consensus (discussed further in Section 3.4.3), the engagement is more superficial. While the point hangs on the nature of the legal norm at stake in the dispute, this is also a different lens through which to consider the conception of the judicial function.

3.4.3 *The Socio-Legal Context within Which the IDS Body Operates*

In an international legal system premised on the principles of sovereign equality and State consent, it is inevitable that the nature of engagement of IDS bodies with domestic court's judgments will be influenced by a range of socio-legal factors. We consider two in particular: the perceived legitimacy of an IDS body, and the degree of 'consensus' that can be found among member States of the IDS body on social, cultural, legal, and other values.[69]

[67] See note 62 and the examples cited therein.

[68] This will also occur when the domestic dispute is decided on a distinct legal point from the content and nature of the primary obligation. See, for instance, the discussion on ECtHR and HRC proceedings in *Legal Consequences of the Separation of the Chagos Archipelago from Mauritius in 1965* (Advisory Opinion) [2019] ICJ Rep. 95 at paras 113–31, and the omission of domestic analysis from the ICJ's assessment.

[69] There are, of course, additional factors to consider, some of which could be described as controversial. For instance, the developed nature or 'quality' of member States' legal systems in respect for the rule of law is a factor that appears to influence international courts' treatment of domestic judicial decisions. This factor is implicit in the history and development of a particular dispute settlement body's approach to domestic court decisions, which impacts the extent to which IDS bodies feel compelled to engage in a substantive review of domestic court decisions and the degree to which they must impose a strict harmonising standard of human rights protection or can respect a margin of appreciation. See Jorge Contesse, 'Contestation and deference in the inter-American human rights system' (2016) 79 LCP 123–45 at Section III; Huneeus, 'International criminal law by other means', 5.

3.4.3.1 Perceived Legitimacy of an IDS Body

The perceived legitimacy of an IDS body will in some measure be influenced by whether there is a gap (and how big it is) between State parties' conception of the judicial function and jurisdiction of the IDS body, and the judicial function and jurisdiction the IDS body allows itself. Our question here is whether these perceptions of legitimacy affect, or should affect, an IDS body's treatment of or engagement with domestic court's decisions.[70]

This is a question particularly worth asking in the current climate where consent-based jurisdiction is coupled with the nationalist (or perhaps populist) 'turn towards' withdrawal from the IDS.[71] Together, they highlight an important constraint under which international courts, tribunals, and treaty-monitoring bodies operate. The IDS bodies (and indeed the international rules–based system which in part depends on the availability, integrity, and robustness of independent and impartial dispute settlement) cannot afford to alienate State parties. Lauterpacht made this point some moons ago: an 'international court which yields conspicuously to the urge to modify the existing law – even if such action can be brought within the four corners of a major legal principle – may bring about a drastic curtailment of its activity. Governments may refuse to submit disputes to it or to renew obligations of compulsory judicial settlement already in existence'.[72] In the current climate, the chilling effect this threat has on the IDS is (worryingly) perhaps ever more present.

Hence why some scope for judicial deference – whether with a formal legal basis such as the margin of appreciation before the ECtHR, or more informally – can be a useful means of accounting for concerns governments may have about the degree to which an IDS body intrudes in domestic decision-making. The ECtHR's doctrine of 'margin of appreciation', for instance, recognises and, in some sense, gives legal effect to the pluralism and diversity of ECHR member States, and is particularly relevant in respect of cases

[70] See generally Petersen, 'International Court of Justice', 364–66.

[71] See generally Campbell McLachlan, 'The assault on international adjudication and the limits of withdrawal' (2019) 68 ICLQ 499–537. See further Øyvind Stiansen and Erik Voeten, 'Backlash and judicial restraint: Evidence from the European Court of Human Rights' (2020) 64 Int Stud Q 770–84; Wayne Sandholtz, Yining Bei, and Kayla Caldwell, 'Backlash and international human rights courts: Crisis, accountability, and opportunity', in Alison Brysk and Michael Stohl (eds.), *Contracting Human Rights: Crisis, Accountability, and Opportunity* (Cheltenham: Edward Elgar, 2018), pp. 159–78.

[72] Hersch Lauterpacht, *The Development of International Law by the International Court* (London: Stevens, 1958), p. 76.

bearing on rights which can be limited in pursuit of important and often competing policy objectives and values which may vary across member States (such as the right to privacy and the right to freedom of religion).[73] Effectively, the doctrine allows for different (even opposite) outcomes in respect of such cases to account for the different balances and priorities which States might seek to achieve in their domestic frameworks.[74] The ECtHR frames the underlying socio-legal facts addressed by the margin of appreciation thusly: 'Europe is marked by a great diversity between the States of which it is composed, particularly in the sphere of cultural and historical development', giving rise to a 'duty' to respect State parties' decisions in these matters provided they did not give rise to a rights violation.[75]

Follesdal has argued, in respect of the IACtHR, that although not presently implemented as part of its jurisprudence, a deferential application of the margin of appreciation (along similar lines to that of the ECtHR) would help aid some of the more political ailments the system suffers, primarily the lack of political will in following binding decisions.[76] The inter-American system is more intrusive in its approach to domestic judicial processes than is the ECtHR on the basis of its doctrine of conventionality control.[77] Perhaps Follesdal might be understood to be suggesting that less intrusive engagement with the processes and decisions of domestic courts by the IACtHR (in the form of a margin of appreciation) could increase its overall effectiveness of human rights protection, even accounting for the negative impact which might result from somewhat lighter-touch scrutiny.[78]

[73] See discussion in note 65.

[74] See Angelika Nussberger, *The European Court of Human Rights* (Oxford: Oxford University Press, 2020), p. 89.

[75] *Lautsi and Others* v. *Italy*, App. No.30814/06 (ECtHR, 18 March 2011) at para. 69.

[76] Andreas Follesdal, 'Exporting the margin of appreciation: Lessons for the Inter-American Court of Human Rights' (2017) 15 Int J Const Law 359–71 at 361–62.

[77] See note 33. While there are undoubtedly a range of factors which might account for this difference, it has been suggested that the socio-legal contexts within which these two regional human rights systems were born is relevant. In particular, the IACtHR was, from its outset, confronted by an overwhelming number of states in which systematic State-sponsored human rights violations were occurring without accountability. See Contesse, 'Contestation and deference in the inter-American human rights system', Section III; Huneeus, 'International criminal law by other means', 5. As a result, the IACtHR and the Commission arguably had less room to defer to domestic judicial decisions arrived at within the context of systems which were perpetrating systemic human rights breaches with impunity.

[78] Shany articulates the balance required in his approach to subsidiarity: IDS bodies must maintain their external legitimacy by intruding in domestic court decisions less readily while at the same time fulfilling their mandates: 'Toward a general margin of appreciation doctrine', 912–14.

3.4.3.2 *Social and Cultural Values and Degree of 'Consensus' among Member States*

This subsection looks at the extent to which certain values are shared among the member States of a particular IDS system, and the impact any such value 'consensus' may have on the IDS body's engagement with domestic court's decisions. This factor is particularly relevant in the context of regional human rights systems and has infiltrated the European system of human rights protection in respect of its exercise of the margin of appreciation,[79] but also has practical implications for global human rights systems which seek to assert universal conceptions of human rights at the risk of aforementioned claims of 'Western bias' or 'human rights imperialism'.

While the universalism of human rights might pull in the direction of harmonisation (calling for a robust review of domestic courts' decisions when they implicate rights protection and uniformity in relevant standards applied), doctrines like the margin of appreciation pull in the opposite direction, in part respecting the expectations of State parties in regard to the judicial function and jurisdiction noted above.[80] Part of the way the ECtHR navigates this tension is through reliance on the consensus of member States on a particular social or cultural value, thus decreasing the margin of appreciation that States (and domestic courts) are afforded in defining their own values and the nature of the balances against which human rights protection will be measured.[81] The absence of consensus, on the other hand, justifies judicial deference to democratic legitimacy and a State's (and its domestic courts') own balances in respect of human rights.[82] As a result, the degree and nature of the ECtHR's engagement with and review of domestic decisions will in part depend on the socio-legal context of member States (as a collective) at the time of the

79 See note 6.

80 Marisa Iglesias Vila, 'Subsidiarity, margin of appreciation and international adjudication within a cooperative conception of human rights' (2017) 15 Int J Const Law 393–413, engages with the relationship between the legitimacy of the ECtHR and subsidiarity and the margin of appreciation as articulated in Protocol 15.

81 'Consensus' in the ECtHR's jurisprudence need not be understood as a vehicle for imposing 'harmonisation'. Instead, 'consensus' can be understood as looking more broadly at the minimum standards that are shared by the member States, such as the 'common heritage of political traditions, ideals, freedom and the rule of law' as found in the ECHR Preamble. In such situations, the domestic court, if it fails to reflect a 'consensus' in its judgment, is in essence violating its own legal, social, and cultural values.

82 Kanetake, 'Interfaces between the national and international rule of law', 5; Dean Spielmann, 'Whither the margin of appreciation?' (2014) 67 CLP 49–65 at 53. See further Eyal Benvenisti, 'Margin of appreciation, consensus, and universal standards' (1999) 31 Int'l L & Politics 843–54.

relevant dispute. And this may well, of course, change over time, because 'consensus' is not static but dynamic.[83] But in circumstances in which there is a lack of consensus, Arnardóttir describes the ECtHR's practice as almost creating a 'rebuttable presumption' in favour of domestic court compliance with ECHR principles, reflecting the more traditional subsidiary approach to domestic courts' judgments.[84]

While the ECtHR gives itself permission to be more intrusive or robust in its review of domestic court's decisions in the case of consensus, such intrusiveness very evidently raises the spectre of a gap between member States' conception of judicial functions and limitations on the Court's jurisdiction and the practices of the Court (addressed in Section 3.4.1). Additionally, due to the large number of judges that sit on ECtHR panels (and their differing cultural, social and legal educations, and lived experiences), it is likely that judges hold varied opinions on the sorts of contentious issues in respect of which the existence of a consensus is interrogated. It is therefore not surprising that the threshold for finding a 'consensus' is generally a high one.[85]

[83] For example (as Judge Spielmann notes), the degree of protection afforded by Art 8's right to respect for private and family life to same-sex couples changed within Council of Europe member States to the extent that, in 2001, there was no 'consensus' (*Mata Estevez* v. *Spain*, App. No 56501/00 (ECtHR, 10 May 2001)), but in 2010 the ECtHR held that there was no margin of appreciation for State conduct and that same-sex couples could not have their Art 8 right limited in ways that would not apply to heterosexual relationships based on a European-wide consensus (*Schalk and Kopf* v. *Austria*, App. No. 30141/04 (ECtHR, 24 June 2010)). Spielmann, 'Whither the margin of appreciation?' 55.

[84] Oddný Mjöll Arnardóttir, '*Res interpretata*, *erga omnes* effect and the role of the margin of appreciation in giving domestic effect to the judgments of the European Court of Human Rights' (2017) 28 EJIL 819–43 at 829–34, 843.

[85] Nikos Vogiatzis, 'The relationship between European consensus, the margin of appreciation and the legitimacy of the Strasbourg Court' (2019) 25 EPL 445–80. This is additionally due to the role of 'consensus' in checking an expansive role for the evolutive interpretation of the ECHR; see Kanstantin Dzehtsiarou, 'European consensus and the evolutive interpretation of the European Convention on Human Rights' (2011) 12 Ger Law J 1730–45. In the case of *Animal Defenders International* v. *The United Kingdom*, App. No. 48876/08 (ECtHR, 22 April 2013), both the Joint Dissenting Opinion of Judges Ziemele, Sajó, Kalaydjieva, Vučinić, and De Gaetano in its entirety, and the Dissenting Opinion of Judge Tulkens, joined by Judges Spielmann and Laffranque, at paras 9–17, disagreed on the issue of 'consensus', concluding that minimum standards should be imposed on regulations limiting political advertising across member States, particularly considering the contrasting judgment of the Court in *VgT Verein gegen Tierfabriken* v. *Switzerland*, App. No. 24699/94 (ECtHR, 28 June 2001). By contrast, the Concurring Opinion of Judge Bratza, at paras 14–15, and the majority judgment at para. 123 indicate that there was no such 'consensus'. Further, see Thomas Kleinlein, 'Consensus and contestability: The ECtHR and the combined potential of European consensus and procedural rationality control' (2017) 28 EJIL 871–93.

By contrast, the IACtHR has not adopted a margin of appreciation. Instead, one of the initial aims of the Court was to build a degree of common practice or 'consensus' on human rights norms among the member States,[86] in part explaining the Court's more robust relationship with domestic courts' decision-making process – which, in the words of Judge Mac-Gregor, amounts to a 'vertical dialogue'.[87]

3.4.4 *Quality of the Domestic Court's Engagement with 'Source' International Law*

One further factor which may affect the nature and degree of an IDS body's engagement with domestic court's decisions – interplaying and overlapping with the socio-legal factors outlined above – is the quality of the domestic court's assessment, interpretation, and application of international law norms and principles.

In assessing the relationship between the ECtHR and domestic courts, Judge Mahoney noted: 'In practice, the closer the analysis of the national courts reflects the European Convention and its case law, the more likely the finding will be that the national courts have remained within the domestic margin of appreciation.'[88] By way of example, Mahoney further explains that aligning closely with Strasbourg when granting domestic remedies grants the reward of greater deference when it comes to the substantive aspect of subsidiarity.[89]

The suggestion is almost that national courts can insulate themselves from intrusive scrutiny, or at least invite a wide margin of appreciation or deference, and less intrusion,[90] if they speak Strasbourg's language. Arnardóttir notes that this could lead to differing approaches to the margin of appreciation in

[86] Mac-Gregor, 'What do we mean when we talk about judicial dialogue?' 108, 116, 119–20. The HRC likewise does not utilise a doctrine of subsidiarity on the grounds that there is no 'consensus' among ICCPR State parties; however, it takes the opposite approach to the IACtHR and does not impose common standards. This would likely not be possible due to the global mandate of the HRC and the cultural plurality of such States. Further, see McGoldrick, 'Defence of the margin of appreciation', 42–53.

[87] Mac-Gregor, 'What do we mean when we talk about judicial dialogue?' 109. For instance, in the *Villagran-Morales* judgment, the IACtHR authorised their own factual assessment as a result of the inadequacy of the domestic court's process. *Case of the 'Street Children' (Villagran-Morales et al.)* v. *Guatemala*, Merits, IACtHR Series C No. 63 (19 November 1999) at para. 68.

[88] Mahoney, 'Relationship between Strasbourg Court and national courts', 571.

[89] Ibid.

[90] See Bratza, 'Relationship between UK courts and Strasbourg', 507.

otherwise similar cases involving different State parties[91] – problematic in terms of the potential for human rights treaties to at least provide a minimum common denominator of protection. Nevertheless, mutual recognition, respect, and a willingness to engage in judicial dialogue (or at least domestic court judicial receptivity) undoubtedly have their role to play in IDS bodies' treatment of domestic court's judgments. In the words of Lord Kerr, there is a 'conscientious mutual striving to fulfil the common aim of providing for the societies we serve the civilised human rights standards to which we all aspire'[92] – respect can be a two-way street.

3.5 CONCLUSION

Comprehensively mapping the role of domestic courts in IDS generally is a rather big challenge. This chapter, in exploring this terrain, has instead singled out two different aspects to this question for analysis: the first (in Sections 3.2 and 3.3) explored the opportunities for IDS bodies to engage with the decisions of domestic courts. In Section 3.2, we mapped the role that domestic court decisions play in international law, both in the formal and classical sense of providing CIL 'data points' for determination by an IDS body and, more infrequently, with their reasoning being borrowed by an international decision-maker. While such IDS engagement with the decisions of domestic courts tends to invite less controversy insofar as the disputing/respondent States are concerned (in that they are not intrusive in domestic legal processes), they do raise systemic concerns regarding the development of international law more broadly, and the pluralism of sources taken into account as inspiration for, and in the identification of, international law.

In Section 3.3 we situated the opportunities for engagement (triggered by the domestic legal framework or court decision being in issue before the IDS body) along a spectrum of deference to greater intrusion. What is clear is that the more the normative framework of international law penetrates domestic legal systems, the greater the substantive engagement by IDS bodies with domestic court decisions bearing on that international law. And to the extent that the domestic court's interpretation or application of the 'source' international law might give rise to responsibility, the less room there is for

91 Arnardóttir, '*Res interpretata, erga omnes*', 829.

92 Lord Kerr, 'The need for dialogue between national courts and the European Court of Human Rights', in Spyridon Flogaitis, Tom Zwart, and Julie Fraser (eds.), *The European Court of Human Rights and Its Discontents: Turning Criticism into Strength* (Cheltenham: Edward Elgar, 2013), pp. 104–15.

deference by the IDS body to its domestic counterparts. This said, the degrees of deference or intrusion by the IDS bodies to domestic court decisions are driven by a multiplicity of factors, of which the nature of the international legal norm at stake in domestic proceedings is but one. The second aspect of the role of domestic courts in the IDS (which we explored in Section 3.4) is therefore some of the other factors which might shape the nature of an IDS body's engagement with decisions by domestic courts. These are significantly more relevant as we travel along the spectrum of deference to intrusion and raise difficult issues regarding whether there is, or should be, an objective understanding of what it looks like for IDS bodies to fulfil their mandates robustly and without hesitation, or whether that understanding needs to be shaped in some way by the expectations of sovereign States in submitting themselves to IDS (account taken of the systemic consequences of too great a disconnect between those expectations and the practice of the IDS body in meeting its mandate). And in confronting these issues, IDS bodies are naturally informed by their own socio-legal contexts and those of their member States – highlighting that we are indeed here confronted with a mosaic of IDS.

4

Binding Advisory Opinions

MASSIMO LANDO

4.1 REASSESSING THE ROLE OF ADVISORY OPINIONS IN INTER-STATE DISPUTE SETTLEMENT

The preface to John Merrills' last own edition of his classic *International Dispute Settlement* declared that 'the aim . . . is to examine the techniques and institutions available to states for the peaceful settlement of disputes, taking full account of recent developments'.[1] In the section on advisory opinions, found in the first of two chapters dedicated to the International Court of Justice (ICJ or Court), Merrills wrote that 'the details and functioning of the advisory jurisdiction are outside the scope of this work'.[2] Given the stated aim of his work, Merrills appeared to hold the view that advisory opinions are not among those mechanisms that States may use peacefully to settle their disputes.

Merrills' statement on advisory jurisdiction is not without justification. Advisory opinions are non-binding decisions conveying an international court's or tribunal's legal advice to a requesting organ.[3] Not all international courts and tribunals can exercise advisory jurisdiction, but only those on which States have conferred that kind of jurisdiction pursuant to their

[1] John G. Merrills, *International Dispute Settlement*, 6th ed. (Cambridge: Cambridge University Press, 2017), p. ix.

[2] Ibid., 142. A seventh edition of *International Dispute Settlement* has been published since Merrills' passing, edited by Eric De Brabandere. This latest edition takes the same position as Merrills' last edition, although it does refer to the 2019 *Chagos* advisory opinion and the Special Chamber's judgment in *Mauritius/Maldives*. See Eric De Brabandere, *Merrills' International Dispute Settlement*, 7th ed. (Cambridge: Cambridge University Press, 2022), pp. 218–21, 274–75.

[3] *Interpretation of Peace Treaties with Bulgaria, Hungary and Romania* (Advisory Opinion) (First Phase) [1950] ICJ Rep. 65 at 71; *Request for Advisory Opinion Submitted by the Sub-Regional Fisheries Commission* (Advisory Opinion) [2015] ITLOS Rep. 4 at para. 76.

constituent instruments. States conferred advisory jurisdiction on, among others, the ICJ,[4] the Seabed Disputes Chamber of the International Tribunal for the Law of the Sea (ITLOS),[5] the Inter-American Court of Human Rights (IACtHR),[6] and the European Court of Human Rights (ECtHR).[7] Arbitral tribunals, including in investor–State dispute settlement, typically have no advisory jurisdiction. ITLOS has found also to have advisory jurisdiction as a full tribunal, although commentators have argued that ITLOS' reasoning in support of that finding is problematic.[8] Furthermore, advisory opinions are a relatively young feature of international judicial institutions. Distinct from the long-established contentious jurisdiction of such institutions, the beginnings of which can be traced back centuries, advisory jurisdiction was first conferred on the Permanent Court of International Justice (PCIJ) in 1922.[9]

Merrills' view presumably reflects the ICJ's traditional position under which, as a matter of its discretion not to render the opinions requested,[10] the Court would decline to render an advisory opinion when 'to give a reply would have the effect of circumventing the principle that a State is not obliged to allow its disputes to be submitted to judicial settlement without its consent'.[11] The Court's position, originating from the PCIJ's 1923 decision in *Status of Eastern Carelia*,[12] in principle entails that advisory opinions cannot

4 Art 92 of the Charter of the United Nations, San Francisco, 26 June 1945, in force 24 October 1945, 1 UNTS 16; Art 65 of the Statute of the International Court of Justice, San Francisco, 26 June 1945, in force 24 October 1945, 33 UNTS 993.

5 Art 191 of the United Nations Convention on the Law of the Sea, Montego Bay, 10 December 1982, in force 16 November 1994, 1833 UNTS 397.

6 Art 64 of the American Convention on Human Rights, San José, 22 November 1969, in force 18 July 1978, 1144 UNTS 143.

7 Art 47 of the Convention for the Protection of Human Rights and Fundamental Freedoms, Rome, 4 November 1950, in force 3 September 1953, 213 UNTS 221.

8 Massimo Lando, 'The advisory jurisdiction of the International Tribunal for the Law of the Sea: Comments on the *Request for an Advisory Opinion Submitted by the Sub-Regional Fisheries Commission*' (2016) 29 LJIL 441–61; Michael A. Becker, '*Request for an Advisory Opinion Submitted by the Sub-Regional Fisheries Commission*' (2015) 109 AJIL 851–58; Tom Ruys and Anemoon Soete, '"Creeping" advisory jurisdiction of international courts and tribunals? The case of the International Tribunal for the Law of the Sea' (2016) 29 LJIL 155–76.

9 Hugh Thirlway, *The International Court of Justice* (Oxford: Oxford University Press, 2016), p. 61.

10 Pierre d'Argent, 'Article 65', in Andreas Zimmermann et al. (eds.), *The Statute of the International Court of Justice: A Commentary*, 3rd ed. (Oxford: Oxford University Press, 2019), pp. 1783, 1803; Malcom N. Shaw, *Rosenne's Law and Practice of the International Court, 1920–2015*, 5th ed., 4 vols (Leiden: Brill, 2015), vol. II, p. 1000.

11 *Western Sahara* (Advisory Opinion) [1975] ICJ Rep. 12 at para. 33.

12 *Status of Eastern Carelia*, PCIJ Rep. Series B No. 5 at 28–29.

be the means to settle inter-State bilateral disputes.[13] However, Merrills' view can seem puzzling. Article 14 of the Covenant of the League of Nations stated that, beyond having jurisdiction to decide disputes between States, the PCIJ 'may also give an advisory opinion upon any dispute or question referred to it by the Council or by the Assembly [of the League]'. Merrills himself also wrote that 'even advisory opinions which do not relate to legal disputes between states in the strict sense are usually concerned directly or indirectly with matters of inter-State controversy'.[14] Moreover, in its most recent advisory opinions, the ICJ has effectively touched on issues arising in the context of inter-State disputes, although certain relevant States had not accepted the Court's contentious jurisdiction in relation to the disputes to which they were parties and to which the Court's opinions related.[15]

The latest development that calls for reassessing Merrills' view on advisory opinions only took place on 28 January 2021. On that day, the Special Chamber of ITLOS constituted to hear the *Maldives/Mauritius* maritime delimitation case delivered its judgment on the preliminary objections raised by the Maldives. The Maldives argued that 'the Special Chamber has no jurisdiction to determine the disputed issue of sovereignty over the Chagos Archipelago, which it would necessarily have to do if it were to determine Mauritius' claims in these proceedings'.[16] The Special Chamber adopted the ICJ's finding, made in the 2019 *Chagos* advisory opinion, that the continued administration of the Chagos Archipelago by the UK was unlawful,[17] finding that 'Mauritius' sovereignty over the Chagos Archipelago can be inferred from the ICJ's determinations'.[18]

The Special Chamber's judgment seems likely to entail significant consequences. The Special Chamber's distinction between the 'binding character' and 'authoritative nature' of the ICJ's advisory opinions opens the debate concerning the legal effects of judicial determinations in the advisory

[13] The only exception to the applicability of the *Eastern Carelia* doctrine would be when both States agree to the court giving an advisory opinion directly addressing the main point of a dispute between them. However, this scenario has never taken place in any request for an advisory opinion in which the *Eastern Carelia* doctrine was invoked.

[14] Merrills, *International Dispute Settlement*, 142.

[15] *Legal Consequences of the Construction of a Wall in the Occupied Palestinian Territory* (Advisory Opinion) [2004] ICJ Rep. 136; *Legal Consequences of the Separation of the Chagos Archipelago from Mauritius in 1965* (Advisory Opinion) [2019] ICJ Rep. 95.

[16] *Delimitation of the Maritime Boundary between Mauritius and Maldives in the Indian Ocean (Mauritius/Maldives)* (Preliminary Objections) Judgment of 28 January 2021, para. 79.

[17] *Chagos* (Advisory Opinion), paras 177–82.

[18] *Mauritius/Maldives* (Judgment), paras 242–46.

context.[19] The judgment also calls into question the *Eastern Carelia* doctrine and *Monetary Gold* principle insofar as they are intended to protect the principle of consent to third-party settlement of disputes. In addition, the Special Chamber's reasoning is likely to impact the legitimacy of the exercise of advisory jurisdiction.

This chapter aims to evaluate the Special Chamber's judgment and discuss its implications for the possible use of advisory opinions as a means of dispute settlement in the future. Section 4.2 outlines the reasoning in the ICJ's *Chagos* advisory opinion, as the background to the judgment of 28 January 2021, and the Special Chamber's reasoning in that judgment. Section 4.3 discusses the implications of the Special Chamber's judgment. Section 4.4 concludes.

4.2 THE *CHAGOS* ADVISORY OPINION AND THE SPECIAL CHAMBER'S JUDGMENT

Mauritius' claim to maritime delimitation before the Special Chamber depended on whether it could be considered to have sovereignty over Chagos. Without the maritime entitlements generated by Chagos, Mauritius would have had no maritime entitlements overlapping with those of the Maldives.[20] In deciding whether Mauritius had sovereignty over Chagos, the Special Chamber built on the ICJ's determinations in the 2019 advisory opinion on the decolonisation of Mauritius. Thus, the Special Chamber's reasoning should be understood in the context of the ICJ's advisory opinion.

4.2.1 *The Chagos Territorial Dispute and the ICJ's Advisory Opinion*

Mauritius transitioned from the status of a UK colony to an independent State in 1968. The process culminating with independence had started in the early 1960s, when the UK had begun to establish institutions of self-government in Mauritius, with a view eventually to end its colonial status.[21] A significant event in this process was the passing by the UK of an Order in Council

[19] Ibid., para. 203. This chapter does not discuss the instance of ICJ advisory opinions made binding by virtue of legal provisions in the statute of certain administrative tribunals constituted within the UN framework. See Tullio Treves, *Diritto Internazionale: Problemi Fondamentali* (Milano: Giuffrè, 2005), p. 626.

[20] Overlapping maritime entitlements are a necessary precondition to delimitation. See *Maritime Delimitation in the Black Sea (Romania* v. *Ukraine)* (Judgment) [2009] ICJ Rep. 61 at para. 77.

[21] *Chagos* (Advisory Opinion), paras 98–112.

separating the Chagos Archipelago from the rest of the colony of Mauritius to create a new administrative subdivision called the British Indian Ocean Territory (BIOT). The BIOT comprised the Chagos Archipelago, which the UK had administered as part of Mauritius from 1814, when France had ceded Mauritius to the UK, to its separation from Mauritius in 1965. Following the separation of Chagos, the UK leased the island of Diego Garcia to the United States to build a US military facility on it, consistent with the intentions expressed by both States in a series of talks that started in 1964.[22] To prepare the archipelago for the installation of the US military facility, between 1967 and 1973 the UK deported the entire local Chagossian community, which forcibly relocated mainly to the island of Mauritius and the UK itself.[23]

Starting in 1975, certain members of the deported Chagossian community issued proceedings in English courts against the UK government in relation to their forcible removal from Chagos.[24] Certain of these cases led to an application to the ECtHR against the UK for alleged breaches of Articles 3, 6, 8, and 13 of the European Convention on Human Rights (ECHR), as well as Article 1 of Protocol 1 to the Convention. In its 2012 judgment, the European Court found the application to be inadmissible because, by accepting compensation as a result of domestic court proceedings, the applicants had effectively renounced bringing a claim for breaches of the ECHR.[25] In addition, in 2011 Mauritius filed a request for arbitration against the UK for alleged breaches of the United Nations Convention on the Law of the Sea (UNCLOS). Mauritius claimed that the marine protected area created by the UK around the Chagos Archipelago was unlawful. Mauritius' first submission was that the UK was not the 'coastal State' within the meaning of Article 56 of UNCLOS. In its 2015 award, the arbitral tribunal found that Mauritius' first submission concerned a dispute 'properly characterized as relating to land

[22] Ibid., paras 94–97.

[23] Ibid., para. 43.

[24] *Chagos Islanders* v. *Attorney-General and BIOT Commissioner* [2003] EWHC 2222 (QB); *R (Bancoult)* v. *Secretary of State for Foreign and Commonwealth Affairs and Another (No. 1)* [2000] EWHC 413 (Admin); *R (Bancoult)* v. *Secretary of State for Foreign and Commonwealth Affairs (No. 2)* [2008] UKHL 61; *R (Bancoult)* v. *Secretary of State for Foreign and Commonwealth Affairs (No. 3)* [2018] UKSC 3. Since the ICJ rendered its 2019 advisory opinion, the Court of Appeal dismissed the appeal against the High Court's decision to reject a judicial review claim to quash the UK government's decision not to support the resettlement of the Chagossians to the Chagos Archipelago. See *R (Hoareau and Bancoult)* v. *Secretary of State for Foreign and Commonwealth Affairs* [2020] EWCA Civ 1010.

[25] *Chagos Islanders* v. *United Kingdom*, App. no. 35622/04 (ECHR, 11 December 2012).

sovereignty over the Chagos Archipelago'.[26] Because territorial disputes did not concern the 'interpretation or application of [UNCLOS]',[27] the tribunal held that it lacked jurisdiction to decide on Mauritius' first submission.[28]

The request to the ICJ for an advisory opinion on Chagos was another attempt by Mauritius to obtain a judicial pronouncement concerning its territorial dispute with the UK. In 2017, two years after the *Chagos Marine Protected Area* award, the UN General Assembly requested the ICJ to render an advisory opinion on whether the decolonisation of Mauritius had been lawfully completed in 1968 and on the legal consequences of the UK's continued administration of Chagos.[29] The General Assembly's questions did not expressly touch on territorial sovereignty. Nevertheless, the ICJ's possible reply that the decolonisation of Mauritius had not been lawfully completed in 1968 would have implied that Mauritius was the lawful sovereign over Chagos. The Court thus could have pronounced on the main point of the Chagos territorial dispute indirectly by exercising its advisory function.

One of Mauritius' main obstacles in the advisory proceedings was to show that the Court did not have to decline to render the opinion requested although the UK had not consented to the third-party settlement of the Chagos territorial dispute. The issue was whether the *Eastern Carelia* doctrine could have justified not rendering the opinion as a matter of discretion. The ICJ stated that 'the General Assembly has not sought the Court's opinion to resolve a territorial dispute between two States . . . the purpose of the request is for the General Assembly to receive the Court's assistance so that it may be guided in the discharge of its functions relating to the decolonization of Mauritius'.[30] According to the ICJ, 'the issues raised by the request are located in the broader frame of reference of decolonization, including the General Assembly's role therein, from which those issues are inseparable'.[31] Accordingly, the Court decided that the absence of the UK's consent to

26 *Chagos Marine Protected Area Arbitration (Mauritius* v. *United Kingdom)*, Award of 18 March 2015, 31 RIAA 359 at para. 212.

27 Art 288 of UNCLOS.

28 *Chagos Marine Protected Area* (Award), paras 213–21.

29 UNGA, 'Request for an advisory opinion of the International Court of Justice on the legal consequences of the separation of the Chagos Archipelago from Mauritius in 1965: Resolution', UN GAOR, 71st Session Supp. No. 49 (22 June 2017) UN Doc. A/RES/71/292.

30 *Chagos* (Advisory Opinion), para. 86.

31 Ibid., para. 88.

third-party settlement was not a compelling reason to decline to give the opinion requested.[32]

To advise on whether the decolonisation of Mauritius had been lawfully completed in 1968, the Court first established that self-determination was a right under customary international law at the relevant time.[33] The ICJ also established that the UK, as the administering power, had an obligation to 'respect the territorial integrity of that country [Mauritius], including the Chagos Archipelago'.[34] On these bases, the Court concluded that 'the process of decolonization of Mauritius was not lawfully completed when Mauritius acceded to independence in 1968'.[35] As to the UK's continued administration of Chagos, the Court found it to be an internationally wrongful act entailing the UK's international responsibility[36] and, consequently, stated that 'the United Kingdom is under an obligation to bring an end to its administration of the Chagos Archipelago as rapidly as possible'.[37] The Court added that, because self-determination entails obligations *erga omnes*, third States 'must co-operate with the United Nations to complete the decolonization of Mauritius'.[38]

Judge Donoghue dissented from the Court's decision. In her dissenting opinion, she took issue with the Court's approach to discretion. In her view, the Court should have declined to give the opinion requested because a pronouncement on the Chagos territorial dispute was a necessary implication of the finding that the UK's continued administration of Chagos was unlawful.[39] Not entirely surprisingly, Judge Donoghue's dissenting opinion predicted the approach that the Special Chamber would have taken in its judgment of 28 January 2021.

4.2.2 *The Special Chamber's Judgment of 28 January 2021*

Originally, Mauritius had not instituted proceedings against the Maldives at ITLOS. On 18 June 2019, a mere few months after the ICJ's advisory opinion,

32 Ibid., paras 90–91. Participant States had argued that there were other grounds for the court to decline to give the opinion requested, distinct and additional to the absence of the UK's consent to third-party settlement. See also paras 69–82.

33 Ibid., paras 144–62.

34 Ibid., para. 173.

35 Ibid., para. 174.

36 Ibid., para. 177.

37 Ibid., para. 178.

38 Ibid., para. 182.

39 Ibid., especially para. 22 (Dissenting Opinion Donoghue).

Mauritius instituted arbitral proceedings against the Maldives pursuant to Annex VII of UNCLOS. The parties subsequently transferred the proceedings to ITLOS by virtue of a special agreement that provided for the formation of an *ad hoc* chamber to preside over the case.[40]

The Maldives objected to the Special Chamber's jurisdiction and the admissibility of Mauritius' claim. The first and second preliminary objections related to the impact of the territorial dispute over Chagos on the proceedings before the Special Chamber. The Maldives' first objection, based on the *Monetary Gold* principle,[41] was that 'the United Kingdom is an indispensable third party to the present proceedings, and, as the United Kingdom is not a party to these proceedings, the Special Chamber does not have jurisdiction over the alleged dispute'.[42] The Maldives' second objection was that 'the Special Chamber has no jurisdiction to determine the disputed issue of sovereignty over the Chagos Archipelago, which it would necessarily have to do if it were to determine Mauritius' claims'.[43] As both these objections were premised on the existence of a territorial dispute over Chagos between Mauritius and the UK, the Special Chamber examined them together.[44]

The Special Chamber set out to establish whether there was an extant dispute concerning sovereignty over Chagos, which the parties had agreed would fall outside the Special Chamber's jurisdiction pursuant to Article 288 of UNCLOS.[45] First, the Special Chamber found the *Chagos Marine Protected Area* award to have 'some relevance' to determining the legal status of Chagos, at least inasmuch as it indicated that there was a territorial dispute over Chagos.[46] Second, the Special Chamber considered the ICJ's 2019 advisory opinion. In that regard, Mauritius had contended that 'there can be no doubt that the issue of sovereignty over the Chagos Archipelago has been disposed of by the Court in its Advisory Opinion, the conclusions of which carry legal consequences for all UN Member States and international institutions'.[47] Conversely, the Maldives had argued that the Chagos territorial

40 *Mauritius/Maldives* (Judgment), paras 1–2.

41 *Monetary Gold Removed from Rome in 1943 (Italy* v. *France, United Kingdom and United States of America)* (Preliminary Question) [1954] ICJ Rep. 19.

42 *Mauritius/Maldives* (Judgment), para. 79. The *Monetary Gold* principle is traditionally seen as a matter of admissibility, but the Maldives raised it as an objection to the Special Chamber's jurisdiction. See Zachary Mollengarden and Noam Zamir, 'The *Monetary Gold* principle: Back to basics' (2021) 115 AJIL 41–77.

43 *Mauritius/Maldives* (Judgment), para. 79.

44 Ibid., para. 100.

45 Ibid., para. 111.

46 Ibid., para. 139.

47 Ibid., para. 142.

dispute had not been settled by the Court's advisory opinion for three main reasons: the General Assembly had not asked the ICJ to advise on that dispute; the settlement of that dispute was not a necessary implication of the ICJ's advisory opinion; and, in any case, that advisory opinion was not binding.[48] The Special Chamber addressed these arguments in turn.

First, on the scope of the General Assembly's questions, the Special Chamber stated that

> the pronouncement that the General Assembly did not submit to the ICJ a bilateral dispute over sovereignty does not necessarily carry with it the inference that the advisory opinion therefore has no relevance or implication for the issue of sovereignty. Given the close relationship between decolonization and sovereignty, such inference is far from evident.[49]

The Special Chamber repeated the sacrosanctity of the principle of consent to binding third-party settlement, but, in an apparently contradictory comment that suggests idiosyncrasy, added that the principle of consent 'does not mean that the advisory opinion could not entail implications for the disputed issue of sovereignty'.[50] Going a step further, the Special Chamber stated that the ICJ's advisory opinion has 'unmistakable implications for the United Kingdom's claim to sovereignty over the Chagos Archipelago': the UK's claim 'is contrary to the determinations made by the ICJ that the detachment of the Chagos Archipelago was unlawful and that the United Kingdom's continued administration of the Chagos Archipelago constitutes an unlawful act of a continuing character',[51] and the determination that the UK, as the administering power, was obligated to preserve Mauritius' territorial integrity 'can be interpreted as suggesting Mauritius' sovereignty over the Chagos Archipelago'.[52]

Second, concerning the implications of the ICJ's advisory opinions for sovereignty over Chagos, the Special Chamber built on the view that 'decolonization and territorial sovereignty are closely interrelated'[53] while recognising that the extent to which 'decolonization may implicate territorial sovereignty depends on the particular circumstances of each case'.[54] Without setting out the particular circumstances of the *Chagos* case, the Special Chamber simply proceeded to state that 'the decolonization and

48 Ibid., para. 141.
49 Ibid., para. 166.
50 Ibid., para. 168.
51 Ibid., para. 173.
52 Ibid., para. 174.
53 Ibid., para. 188.
54 Ibid.

sovereignty of Mauritius, including the Chagos Archipelago, are inseparably related'.[55] The bases of this finding were the *Chagos Marine Protected Area* award's acknowledgement that Mauritius and the UK disputed sovereignty over Chagos, and the ICJ's determination, in the 2019 advisory opinion, that the issues raised in the opinion were located in the broader frame of reference to decolonisation.[56]

Third, concerning the legal effects of the ICJ's advisory opinion, the Special Chamber stated that, while an advisory opinion 'cannot be considered legally binding',[57] it 'entails an authoritative statement of international law on the questions with which it deals'.[58] The Special Chamber drew a crucial distinction between the 'binding character' and 'authoritative nature' of ICJ's advisory opinions: although those opinions do not formally create obligations for States, judicial determinations in the advisory context 'carry no less weight and authority than those in judgments because they are made with the same rigour and scrutiny by the "principal judicial organ" of the United Nations with competence in matters of international law'.[59] The Special Chamber concluded, in general, that 'determinations made by the ICJ in an advisory opinion cannot be disregarded simply because the advisory opinion is not binding',[60] and, in particular, that the ICJ's determinations on sovereignty over Chagos 'do have legal effect'.[61]

The result of the Special Chamber's analysis was that the Maldives' argument as to the existence of a territorial dispute concerning Chagos was unconvincing[62] and that 'Mauritius' sovereignty over the Chagos Archipelago can be inferred from the ICJ's determinations'.[63] The Special Chamber thus concluded that the UK was not an indispensable party under the *Monetary Gold* principle and that Mauritius 'can be regarded as the coastal State in respect of the Chagos Archipelago', therefore rejecting the first and second preliminary objections of the Maldives.[64]

55 Ibid., para. 189.
56 Ibid.
57 Ibid., para. 202.
58 Ibid.
59 Ibid., para. 203.
60 Ibid., para. 205.
61 Ibid.
62 Ibid., para. 245. Before making this final determination, the Special Chamber also addressed the parties' arguments concerning other matters not directly related to the ICJ's advisory opinion. See also ibid., paras. 207–44.
63 Ibid., para. 246.
64 Ibid., paras 247–51.

4.3 SIGNIFICANCE OF THE *MAURITIUS/MALDIVES* JUDGMENT

The Special Chamber's reasoning on the *Chagos* advisory opinion will conceivably have significant implications for the exercise of advisory jurisdiction by international courts and tribunals. These implications concern the legal effect of advisory opinions, the circumvention of the principle of consent to third-party settlement, and the legitimacy of the advisory function.

4.3.1 *Legal Effect of Advisory Opinions*

The traditional position is that, as a matter of positive international law, advisory opinions are not binding.[65] The Special Chamber in *Mauritius/Maldives* recognised this aspect in relation to the advisory opinions of the ICJ.[66] Nevertheless, to confine oneself simply to the black letter law would be at the expense of a much more nuanced picture of the legal effects of advisory opinions. Even before the *Mauritius/Maldives* case, writers had acknowledged that advisory opinions entail certain legal consequences despite the lack of binding character.[67] The Special Chamber's judgment has given new impetus to the analysis of those consequences.

The distinction drawn by the Special Chamber between the 'binding character' and 'authoritative nature' of ICJ's advisory opinions should give one pause for reflection. The Special Chamber did not explain exactly what it meant by either notion. 'Binding character' likely refers to the formal quality of a judicial decision as an instrument creating international obligations on the State parties to the relevant case. This formal quality stems from the States' acceptance, by way of treaty, of an international judicial organ's power to issue decisions that may impose international obligations on them. For instance, in relation to the ICJ's contentious jurisdiction, the binding character of

65 *Interpretation of Peace Treaties* (Advisory Opinion), p. 71; *Fisheries Commission* (Advisory Opinion), para. 76; *Reports of the Inter-American Commission on Human Rights (Art 51 American Convention on Human Rights)*, Advisory Opinion OC-15/97, IACtHR Series A No. 15 (14 November 1997) at para. 26; ECtHR, *Advisory Opinions Concerning the Recognition in Domestic Law of a Legal Parent–Child Relationship between a Child Born through a Gestational Surrogacy Arrangement Abroad and the Intended Mother*, Request No. P16–2018-001 (Advisory Opinion of 10 April 2019) at para. 34.

66 *Mauritius/Maldives* (Judgment), para. 202.

67 Thirlway, *International Court of Justice*, 139–42; Gleider I. Hernández, *The International Court of Justice and the Judicial Function* (Oxford: Oxford University Press, 2014), pp. 76–78; Jo M. Pasqualucci, *The Practice and Procedure of the Inter-American Court of Human Rights*, 2nd ed. (New York: Cambridge University Press, 2012), pp. 77–80.

judgments derives from the conventional rules under Article 94(1) of the UN Charter and Article 59 of the Court's Statute.[68]

To the contrary, 'authoritative nature' appears to be a much-less-defined concept, but one that it is necessary to understand in order to grasp the implications of the *Mauritius/Maldives* judgment. The main problem with this concept is that the Special Chamber failed to articulate a standard to establish the degree of 'authoritative nature', or 'authoritativeness', of the judicial determinations of international courts and tribunals. Theoretically, 'authoritative nature' could be linked to ideas of court authority, legitimacy, and effectiveness in the exercise of the judicial function. Whether a judicial decision is 'authoritative' would therefore depend on an international judicial organ's 'right to rule' as well as on factors concerning the input and output legitimacy of the exercise of the judicial function by that organ.[69] Yet, understanding 'authoritative nature' primarily or even only by reference to scholarly theories on court authority is unlikely to represent that concept as one capable of real-world application. While conceptions of authority may be useful to understand certain normative and sociological aspects of the judicial function, they are unlikely to be of great interest to States, the main concern of which is whether or not they are bound by an international obligation stemming from a judicial decision.

To unpack the meaning of 'authoritative nature' in respect of advisory opinions, the appropriate point of departure is the Special Chamber's articulation of that concept in the *Mauritius/Maldives* judgment. The Special Chamber conceived of 'authoritative nature' as relating to the 'weight and authority' of judicial determinations, but also seemed to understand it in the advisory context by means of comparing it to 'authoritative nature' in contentious cases. The Special Chamber implied that decisions in contentious cases have maximum authority. Conversely, the 'authoritative nature' of advisory pronouncements could be represented by a sliding scale, the highest point of which coincides with the 'authoritative nature' of decisions in contentious cases. 'Authoritative nature' in the advisory context is thus defined not in absolute terms but relative to the 'authoritative nature' of decisions in the

[68] Art 94(1) of the Charter stated that 'each Member of the United Nations undertakes to comply with the decision of the International Court of Justice in any case to which it is a party'. Art 59 of the ICJ's Statute provides that 'the decision of the Court has no binding force except between the parties and in respect of that particular case'.

[69] These issues are discussed in more detail in Section 4.3.3.

contentious context. This implicit understanding of 'authoritative nature' by the Special Chamber seems problematic for a number of reasons.

Defining 'authoritative nature' by reference to the 'weight and authority' of a judicial organ's determinations is circular. The Special Chamber might as well not have spilt any ink on defining that concept. Moreover, the question arises as to how one can assess the 'weight and authority' of judicial determinations. One way of doing so would be to consider whether judicial decisions are binding on States, the idea being that, if binding, judicial decisions would be endowed with a high degree of authority. This consideration would do no more than fall back on the concept of 'binding character', which the Special Chamber sought to distinguish from the notion of 'authoritative nature'. Perhaps aware of this problem, the Special Chamber linked its understanding of 'weight and authority' to the level of 'rigour and scrutiny' with which judicial organs reach their determinations. In the Special Chamber's view, this level is the same whether one considered the contentious or advisory context.

What exactly one should understand 'rigour and scrutiny' to mean is as unclear as the understanding one should have of 'weight and authority'. The level of 'rigour and scrutiny' could be understood as an attribute of judicial determinations, which suggests that it may be evaluated by reference to whether international courts and tribunals follow their established procedures to reach their conclusions of law and fact. For example, these procedures include the presence or absence of adversarial process, the manner of gathering evidence, and the burden and standard of proof. Following the Special Chamber's line of reasoning, these procedures should be implemented similarly for advisory opinions to carry the same 'weight and authority' as judgments in the contentious context. However, international courts and tribunals do not implement these procedures in the same way in both contexts.

In contentious cases, the constituent instruments and rules of procedure show that both States and courts and tribunals themselves have a preference for adversarial proceedings.[70] The adversarial model is characterised by direct confrontations between the parties that take place in the written and oral submissions, which aims at ensuring that the relevant judicial organ is able to test the arguments of all parties with a view to reaching a truth in its

[70] On the ICJ, see Robert Jennings, Rosalyn Higgins, and Peter Tomka, 'General introduction', in Andreas Zimmermann et al. (eds.), *The Statute of the International Court of Justice: A Commentary*, 3rd ed. (Oxford: Oxford University Press, 2019), pp. 3, 17.

decision.[71] The adversarial model requires the parties to exchange pleadings to both identify the areas of agreement and refute the opposing party's contentions with which they disagree. Under this modus operandi, the parties are given the chance first to present their case and then to reply to the other party's arguments.[72] Advisory proceedings are not adversarial. Formally, there are no parties in advisory proceedings, but simply participants.[73] Substantively, the procedure in advisory cases does not aim to allow parties to identify areas of agreement and disagreement using successive rounds of written and oral argument. While the ICJ usually allows each participant to file one written statement and one document containing written comments on the written statements, in the oral arguments each participant takes the floor only once.[74] Furthermore, the purpose of written and oral pleadings in advisory cases is not to 'establish the truth' in an inter-State dispute but to assist the Court to provide the best possible advice in relation to the questions raised by the requesting organ.

The absence of parties in advisory proceedings affects matters of proof. Lack of parties entails lack of claims, which also means that the Court does not weigh evidence to reach its conclusions.[75] The only measure available to the Court in cases of limited information available concerning the subject matter of the request is to exercise its discretion not to render the opinion requested.[76] In this sense, there are no burden and standard of proof in advisory proceedings, which extends to the Court's evaluation of whether judicial propriety requires not giving the opinions requested.[77] It follows that

[71] Most scholarly literature on the features of the adversarial model focuses on international criminal tribunals. For instance, see Fabricio Guariglia, '"Admission" v. "submission" of evidence at the International Criminal Court' (2018) 16 JICJ 315–39; William A. Schabas, 'International criminal courts', in Cesare Romano, Karen J. Alter, and Yuval Shany (eds.), *The Oxford Handbook of International Adjudication* (Oxford: Oxford University Press, 2014), pp. 205, 218–19.

[72] E.g., see the provisions concerning the written and oral submissions in the ICJ's Statute (Arts 43–54) and Rules of Procedure (Arts 44–72).

[73] Markus Benzing, 'Evidentiary issues', in Andreas Zimmermann et al. (eds.), *The Statute of the International Court of Justice: A Commentary*, 3rd ed. (Oxford: Oxford University Press, 2019), pp. 1373, 1412. Art 68 of the ICJ's Statute states that 'in the exercise of its advisory functions the Court shall further be guided by the provisions of the present Statute which apply in contentious cases to the extent to which it recognizes them to be applicable', but this provision does not mean that advisory cases follow the same adversarial model as contentious cases.

[74] For instance, see verbatim records of *Chagos* (Advisory Opinion), CR 2018/20, 25–27; *Wall* (Advisory Opinion), CR 2004/1, 16–17.

[75] Robert Kolb, *The Elgar Companion to the International Court of Justice* (Cheltenham: Edward Elgar, 2014), p. 237.

[76] Thirlway, *International Court of Justice*, 115–16.

[77] Benzing, 'Evidentiary Issues', 1412.

one may not rely on the Court's approach to matters of proof to evaluate the 'rigour and scrutiny', and thus the 'weight and authority', of its judicial determinations in advisory opinions.

The question arises as to whether there is any method to evaluate the 'authoritative nature' of the ICJ's advisory opinions. One could look at the jurisprudence of other international courts and tribunals trying to find indications of how to assess the legal effects of advisory opinions, but that search would not be fruitful. The ICJ has not elaborated on the legal effects of its opinions, and neither has ITLOS or its Seabed Disputes Chamber in the exercise of advisory jurisdiction. In a 1997 opinion, the IACtHR stated that 'while an advisory opinion of the Court does not have the binding character of a judgment in a contentious case, it does have undeniable legal effects'.[78] Yet, the IACtHR did not comment on those 'undeniable legal effects' or on how they can be evaluated. The pragmatic, and perhaps disappointing, reality appears to be that the legal effects of advisory opinions, including but not limited to their 'authoritative nature', cannot be determined a priori. The influence of advisory opinions on the development of international law or the resolution of inter-State controversies should fall to be assessed depending on whether States and international organisations have acted on, and consistent with, the judicial determinations in those opinions.

In the specific case of *Mauritius/Maldives*, the Special Chamber assessed the legal effects of the ICJ's 2019 opinion on two grounds: first, the logical implication of the determination that the UK's continued administration of Chagos was unlawful; second, the passing by the General Assembly of Resolution 73/295 demanding that the UK 'withdraw its colonial administration from the Chagos Archipelago unconditionally within a period of no more than six months'.[79] Only the latter is an action by States or international organisations subsequent to the delivery of the Court's opinion, but whether a single General Assembly resolution is sufficient to evaluate the effects of the ICJ's opinion seems doubtful, also considering the non-binding character of that resolution.[80] It appears beyond dispute that the UK has an obligation to respect the Mauritian people's right to self-determination, which, as an obligation *erga omnes*, may warrant restatement by the representative organ of the international community of States. Whether the General Assembly's

[78] *Reports of the Inter-American Commission* (Advisory Opinion), para. 26.

[79] UNGA, 'Advisory opinion of the International Court of Justice on the legal consequences of the separation of the Chagos Archipelago from Mauritius in 1965: Resolution' UN GAOR, 73rd Session Supp. No. 49 (24 May 2019) UN Doc. A/RES/73/295, para. 3.

[80] Art 10 of the UN Charter.

restatement adds anything to the obligation itself, and thus to the effects of the advisory opinion which ascertained that obligation's existence, remains doubtful. The Special Chamber's reasoning could have been more convincing if it had built on additional material showing States and international organisations adopting a course of action or expressing a view on sovereignty over Chagos consistent with those stated in Resolution 73/295.

4.3.2 *Circumvention of Consent to Binding Third-Party Settlement*

The Special Chamber's judgment in *Mauritius/Maldives* raises questions concerning the principle of consent to binding third-party settlement: first, the impact of the judgment on the *Eastern Carelia* doctrine; second, its implications for the *Monetary Gold* principle.

4.3.2.1 Eastern Carelia *Doctrine*

The *Eastern Carelia* doctrine relates to the discretion that the ICJ and ITLOS have not to render advisory opinions if there are compelling reasons not to do so.[81] Under established jurisprudence, one of these compelling reasons is that to render an advisory opinion would amount to deciding the main point of a dispute in relation to which a State has not consented to binding third-party settlement. The Court has consistently upheld this doctrine since its 1950 advisory opinion in *Interpretation of Peace Treaties*,[82] although the PCIJ, which had originally rendered the *Eastern Carelia* decision, has never referred to it for that same proposition and has never refused to render an advisory opinion on that basis.[83]

The doctrine was one of the most contentious issues in the *Chagos* advisory proceedings.[84] The ICJ's decision not to decline to render the *Chagos* opinion, as Judge Donoghue argued that the Court should have done, can be criticised on the ground that the advisory opinion did not touch on the territorial dispute only formally, while in practice determining that the

[81] *Accordance with International Law of the Unilateral Declaration of Independence in Respect of Kosovo* (Advisory Opinion) [2010] ICJ Rep. 403 at para. 30; *Fisheries Commission* (Advisory Opinion), paras 70–79.

[82] *Interpretation of Peace Treaties* (Advisory Opinion), p. 71.

[83] A full-scale treatment of the *Eastern Carelia* doctrine is beyond the scope of this chapter, in which the remarks will be limited to commenting on the possible effects of the *Mauritius/Maldives* decision on the doctrine.

[84] See Section 4.2.1.

decolonisation of Mauritius had not been lawfully completed in 1968 necessarily implied that Mauritius was sovereign over Chagos.[85]

One could take the view that there is nothing extraordinary in the ICJ's approach, as *Chagos* was not the first time that the Court had made statements concerning pending disputes in advisory proceedings without the consent of one of the States involved. The problem rather seems to be that *Mauritius/Maldives* has shown the limits of the ICJ's 'broader framework' approach, discussed below, by exposing that approach as an empty one.

The criticism of the ICJ's approach has become all the more compelling following the *Mauritius/Maldives* judgment. By finding that 'Mauritius' sovereignty over the Chagos Archipelago can be inferred from the ICJ's determinations',[86] the Special Chamber took a non-binding statement made by the ICJ in an advisory capacity and adopted it as its own in a binding judgment made in a contentious setting. Because of the principle of *res judicata*, the Special Chamber's judgment only binds Mauritius and the Maldives, at least in theory.[87] In practice, the consequences of judicial decisions go beyond the State parties to the relevant case. Writing in a judicial capacity, Sir Robert Jennings stated that 'it would be unrealistic even in consideration of strict legal principle, to suppose that the effects of a judgment are … wholly confined by Article 59 [i.e. the provision on *res judicata* in the ICJ's Statute]'.[88] Sir Robert Jennings based his view on the general obligation under Article 94 of the UN Charter that UN member States have to comply with the ICJ's decision.[89] A comparable obligation exists pursuant to Article 296 of UNCLOS, which is drafted similarly to Article 94 of the UN Charter. States also seem likely to regard a judicial statement made by way of binding judgment in a contentious case as, using the Special Chamber's words, carrying great 'weight and authority' and which they should thus respect.

Limiting oneself to noting that the *Mauritius/Maldives* judgment only binds the parties to that case would overlook the wider consequences of the Special Chamber's decision. States that may have been on the fence as to

85 See Ksenia Polonskaya, 'International Court of Justice: The role of consent in the context of judicial propriety deconstructed in light of *Chagos Archipelago*' (2019) 18 LPICT 189–218; Giuseppe Puma, 'Preliminary questions in the ICJ Advisory Opinion on the Legal Consequences of the Separation of the Chagos Archipelago from Mauritius in 1965' (2019) 79 ZaöRV 841–80.

86 *Mauritius/Maldives* (Judgment), para. 246.

87 Art 33 of ITLOS's Statute (in Annex VI of UNCLOS).

88 *Continental Shelf (Libya/Malta)* (Application by Italy for Permission to Intervene) [1984] ICJ Rep. 3 at para. 28 (Dissenting Opinion Jennings).

89 On its text, Art 94 requires compliance with the ICJ's judgment only by State parties to a case, not by the wider UN membership.

whether to follow the ICJ's advisory pronouncement on sovereignty over Chagos might now decide to do so, based on the Special Chamber's judgment.[90] The higher the number of States adhering to the ICJ's pronouncement, the higher the likelihood that the UK might relinquish control over Chagos because of diplomatic pressure. If this were to take place, the UK would comply with an advisory opinion which effectively decided a dispute to which it was a party and in respect of which it had not consented to binding third-party settlement. The *Eastern Carelia* doctrine therefore would be deprived of practical significance. Circumventing the doctrine and the principle of consent that it purports to protect would thus become relatively easy: all an aggrieved State should do is to file a contentious case with an international court or tribunal other than the ICJ and argue for it to follow the Special Chamber's approach in *Mauritius/Maldives*. This approach is premised on obtaining an advisory opinion from the ICJ, which would remain a more cumbersome task to accomplish than filing an application instituting contentious proceedings.

The *Mauritius/Maldives* judgment also calls for the Court to rethink its approach in applying the *Eastern Carelia* doctrine. The Court decided not to decline to render the *Chagos* opinion on the basis of the *Eastern Carelia* doctrine because 'the issues raised by the request [were] located in the broader frame of reference of decolonization'.[91] The Court upheld its 'broader framework' approach already applied in the *Western Sahara* and *Wall* advisory opinions,[92] according to which the Court will not decline to give an advisory opinion on the basis of *Eastern Carelia* doctrine where the questions raised in the request are located within a broader frame of reference within which the requesting organ discharges duties under the UN Charter. In her *Chagos* dissenting opinion, Judge Donoghue wrote that 'surely any bilateral dispute that attracts sufficient support in the General Assembly so as to lead that organ to request an advisory opinion could be described as falling within a "broader frame of reference"'.[93] Her criticism of the 'broader framework' approach appeared convincing already at the time when the Court delivered its *Chagos* opinion, but the *Mauritius/Maldives* judgment makes it even more persuasive. To be fair to the ICJ, one should recognise that the possibility of a *Mauritius/Maldives*-like situation may not have been concrete when the Court first developed its 'broader framework' approach in *Western Sahara*,

[90] The author is unaware of any express statements in this sense.

[91] *Chagos* (Advisory Opinion), para. 88.

[92] *Western Sahara* (Advisory Opinion), para. 38; *Wall* (Advisory Opinion), para. 49.

[93] *Chagos* (Advisory Opinion), para. 20 (Dissenting Opinion Donoghue).

or perhaps even when the Court rendered its *Chagos* opinion. However, *Mauritius/Maldives* shows that the Court's 'broader framework' approach cannot prevent the principle of consent from being circumvented where another judicial organ is requested to grapple with the legal effects of an advisory opinion touching on the main point of a pending bilateral dispute, although only by implication.

The *Eastern Carelia* doctrine's loss of significance, especially exposed by the *Chagos* opinion and *Mauritius/Maldives* judgment, does not mean that advisory opinions that circumvent the principle of consent are to be considered as binding. If the *Eastern Carelia* doctrine had never existed, advisory opinions would have no stronger binding character than they do, at least as a matter of positive law. Yet, limiting the significance of that doctrine would likely suggest that advisory pronouncements could be regarded as intended directly to facilitate the settlement of inter-State disputes. Overcoming the *Eastern Carelia* doctrine thus could mean endowing advisory opinions with not only persuasive but even quasi-binding character. If they were considered quasi-binding, advisory opinions would occupy a middle ground between dispute settlement by binding third-party processes and dispute settlement by means not involving binding third-party decisions. This possibility would raise the question of the precise legal effects of advisory opinions, which, as stated above, currently remain rather unclear. Related problems would be the lack of an express obligation to comply with advisory opinions and the likely inconsistency between the quasi-binding character of such opinions and the ICJ's established view that they are not binding.

4.3.2.2 Monetary Gold *Principle*

Consent to binding third-party settlement is also relevant with respect to the *Monetary Gold* principle, on which the Maldives had based its first preliminary objection. Under that principle, an international judicial organ may not render a decision when the legal interests of a State not before it, and which thus has not consented to binding third-party settlement in its own respect, 'would form the very subject-matter of the decision'.[94] In *Certain Phosphate Lands in Nauru* and *East Timor*, the ICJ restricted the scope of the *Monetary Gold* principle by stating that it could only apply when the determination on a third State's legal interests was both a temporal and a logical prerequisite to

[94] *Monetary Gold* (Preliminary Question), p. 32.

resolving the case between the States before it.[95] The ITLOS adopted this reading of the *Monetary Gold* principle in its 2016 judgment in *M/V 'Norstar'*.[96] On the basis of these decisions, a commentator has argued that objections based on the *Monetary Gold* principle can only succeed in exceptional circumstances.[97]

In *Mauritius/Maldives*, the Special Chamber further limited the scope of that principle, lending support to the view that the *Monetary Gold* principle only applies in exceptional circumstances. Different from the ICJ's *Monetary Gold* jurisprudence, the Special Chamber in *Mauritius/Maldives* focused on whether the UK had a 'sufficient' legal interest, stemming from its claim to sovereignty over Chagos, which could have formed 'the very subject-matter' of the Special Chamber's decision.[98] Based on its finding that 'Mauritius' sovereignty over the Chagos Archipelago can be inferred from the ICJ's determinations',[99] the Special Chamber concluded that

> whatever interests the United Kingdom may still have with respect to the Chagos Archipelago, they would not render the United Kingdom a State with *sufficient legal interests*, let alone an indispensable third party, that would be affected by the delimitation of the maritime boundary around the Chagos Archipelago.[100]

After referring to the 'sufficiency' of the UK's legal interest, the Special Chamber found that, on the basis of the *Chagos* advisory opinion, 'it is inconceivable that the United Kingdom ... can have *any legal interest* in permanently disposing of maritime zones around the Chagos Archipelago by delimitation'.[101] The Special Chamber commented on 'sufficient legal interests' in the abstract while finding that, in the facts of the case, the UK lacked 'any legal interest' capable of justifying the application of the *Monetary Gold* principle. The Special Chamber's judgment thus introduced a 'sufficient

95 *Certain Phosphate Lands in Nauru (Nauru* v. *Australia)* (Preliminary Objections) [1992] ICJ Rep. 240 at para. 55; *East Timor (Portugal* v. *Australia)* (Judgment) [1995] ICJ Rep. 90 at paras 31–33. See Mollengarden and Zamir, 'The *Monetary Gold* principle', 51, 54.

96 *M/V 'Norstar' Case (Panama* v. *Italy)* (Preliminary Objections) [2016] ITLOS Rep. 44 at paras 172–73.

97 Filippo Fontanelli, 'Reflections on the indispensable party principle in the wake of the judgment on preliminary objections in the Norstar case' (2017) 100 Rivista di Diritto Internazionale 112–32 at 112, 131.

98 *Mauritius/Maldives* (Judgment), paras 97–99.

99 Ibid., para. 246.

100 Ibid., para. 247 (emphasis added).

101 Ibid.

legal interest' requirement into the *Monetary Gold* principle, previously unknown in the jurisprudence.

The introduction of this 'sufficient legal interest' requirement seems to turn the application of the *Monetary Gold* principle into a two-stage process. First, international courts and tribunals would have to assess whether the third State's legal interest is 'sufficient'; second, they would have to decide whether that 'sufficient legal interest' forms 'the very subject-matter of the decision'. It is in the second stage that the jurisprudence before *Mauritius/Maldives* would be relevant. Conceivably, if the Special Chamber had not developed the *Monetary Gold* principle into a two-stage test, its finding on the Maldives' first preliminary objection could have been different. There appears to be little doubt that the UK's legal interests concerning sovereignty over Chagos would have formed 'the very subject-matter' of the Special Chamber's decision on maritime delimitation between Mauritius and the Maldives. It was the Special Chamber's inquiry into the 'sufficiency' of the UK's legal interests that justified the decision to reject the Maldives' first preliminary objection.

Owing to its focus on the existence of a 'sufficient legal interest', the first stage seems related to standing, which would be consistent with the understanding of the *Monetary Gold* principle as one concerning the absence of indispensable third parties. There would be no question of applying the *Monetary Gold* principle unless the relevant third State had standing to bring a case concerning the 'very subject-matter of the decision'. Therefore, one could see the Special Chamber's judgment as being less than a novelty, because it simply spelt out a requirement already implicit in the *Monetary Gold* principle. At the same time, that judgment may have further implications. The 'sufficient legal interest' requirement appears likely to generate controversy in future cases in which the *Monetary Gold* principle may be at issue. The key question would be to determine what it would take for a legal interest to be 'sufficient'. In cases similar to *Certain Phosphate Lands in Nauru* and *East Timor*, in which a third State's international responsibility is the legal interest at stake, there should be hardly any doubt as to 'sufficiency'. To the contrary, the Special Chamber seemed to consider that, in cases in which a third State's legal interest stems from a disputed territorial claim, the 'sufficiency' of that interest is less clear-cut and depends on the strength of that third State's claim in international law.

The implicit distinction made by the Special Chamber in relation to the 'sufficiency' of a third State's legal interest is not necessarily problematic. Yet, problems may arise, and have arisen in *Mauritius/Maldives*, depending on the basis on which an international judicial organ relies to assess the strength of, for example, a disputed territorial claim. No problems would exist if that basis were a judicial decision in a contentious case concerning sovereignty over the disputed territory. Less clear would be the situation where that basis is a treaty concerning title over the disputed territory.[102] If that basis is a non-binding advisory opinion, as in *Mauritius/Maldives*, doubts could justifiably arise as to whether the reasoning regarding the 'sufficiency' of a third State's legal interest stands on solid ground. This difficulty may be inherent in the elusiveness of the Special Chamber's 'sufficiency' standard. Future judicial decisions should clarify the means by which States should seek to show whether the legal interest of a third State is 'sufficient' enough (or sufficiently 'sufficient', as it were) to justify applying the *Monetary Gold* principle.

The *Monetary Gold* principle is not applicable in the advisory context, but by refusing to apply that principle in *Mauritius/Maldives*, the Special Chamber used it to confer a binding effect on the judicial determinations of the ICJ's 2019 advisory opinion. Isolating the 'sufficient legal interest' requirement allowed the Special Chamber to give an effective binding character to the *Chagos* advisory opinion. The *Mauritius/Maldives* judgment shows that legal principles applicable in the contentious context can be instruments to enhance the binding character of judicial determinations in advisory opinions.

4.3.3 *Legitimacy Implications*

The *Mauritius/Maldives* judgment raises questions of legitimacy concerning both the exercise of contentious jurisdiction by the Special Chamber and the exercise of the advisory function. These two aspects are interrelated because, taking stock of the possibility that judicial determinations in advisory opinions may be adopted into binding judicial decisions, a legitimate exercise of advisory jurisdiction in future cases seems also to depend on whether the Special Chamber's decision to adopt such judicial determinations into its binding judgment was itself legitimate. An exhaustive analysis into the legitimacy of the advisory function is beyond the scope of this chapter, which only focuses on making some comments circumscribed to the implications of the Special Chamber's judgment.

[102] Several contentious cases on sovereignty arose out of agreements concerning title to territory, which shows that treaties attributing title to territory are not always incontrovertible evidence that a State's sovereignty claim over a certain territory is well founded. See *Sovereignty over Pedra Branca/Pulau Batu Puteh, Middle Rocks and South Ledge (Malaysia/Singapore)* (Judgment) [2008] ICJ Rep. 12; *Frontier Dispute (Burkina Faso/Niger)* (Judgment) [2013] ICJ Rep. 44.

Legitimacy is a multifaceted notion. In its most basic sense, legitimacy can be understood as the right to rule.[103] Legitimacy can be subdivided into its normative component, which is the right of an institution to rule according to predefined standards, and its sociological component, which is the perception or belief by the relevant constituency that an institution has the right to rule. Normative and sociological legitimacy inform one another.[104] Legitimacy also can be distinguished into input and output legitimacy: the former relates to whether an institution has exercised its right to rule in accordance with predefined procedures;[105] the latter relates to whether an institution, by its operation, achieves the concerns of its constituency.[106] The input/output distinction shares similarities with the normative/sociological distinction. Sociological and output legitimacy also are linked to issues of effectiveness, understood as the capacity of an international judicial organ to meet the goals set by its constituency.[107]

Legitimacy is audience-relative, which means that an institution's exercise of its right to rule must be assessed in the context of that institution's relevant constituency.[108] For the exercise of advisory jurisdiction by the ICJ, the relevant constituency is made of the community of States represented in the requesting organs. In respect of other international judicial organs, the relevant constituency likely is limited to the State parties to the constituent

103 John Tasioulas, 'The legitimacy of international law', in Samantha Besson and John Tasioulas (eds.), *The Philosophy of International Law* (Oxford: Oxford University Press, 2010), pp. 97–100.

104 Harlan Grant Cohen et al., 'Legitimacy and international courts: A framework', in Harlan Grant Cohen et al. (eds.), *Legitimacy and International Courts* (Cambridge: Cambridge University Press, 2018), pp. 1, 4; Karen J. Alter, Laurence R. Helfer, and Mikael Rask Madsen, 'International court authority in a complex world', in Karen J. Alter, Laurence R. Helfer, and Mikael Rask Madsen (eds.), *International Court Authority* (Oxford: Oxford University Press, 2018), pp. 3, 7–11.

105 Rüdiger Wolfrum, 'Legitimacy of international law from a legal perspective: Some introductory considerations', in Rüdiger Wolfrum and Volker Röben (eds.), *Legitimacy in International Law* (Berlin: Springer, 2008), pp. 1, 6.

106 Tomer Broude, 'The legitimacy of the ICJ's advisory competence in the shadow of the *Wall*' (2005) 38 Israel L Rev 189–210 at 189, 194, 206.

107 Yuval Shany, 'Stronger together? Legitimacy and effectiveness of international courts as mutually reinforcing or undermining notions', in Harlan Grant Cohen et al. (eds.), *Legitimacy and International Courts* (Cambridge: Cambridge University Press, 2018), pp. 354, 363–70. See also Laurence R. Helfer, 'The effectiveness of international adjudicators', in Cesare Romano, Karen J. Alter, and Yuval Shany (eds.), *The Oxford Handbook of International Adjudication* (Oxford: Oxford University Press, 2014), pp. 464–81.

108 Andrei Marmor, 'Authority of international courts: Scope, power, and legitimacy', in Karen J. Alter, Laurence R. Helfer, and Mikael Rask Madsen (eds.), *International Court Authority* (Oxford: Oxford University Press, 2018), pp. 374, 378.

instruments of those judicial organs: ITLOS' constituency would be co-extensive with the UNCLOS State parties, while the IACtHR's constituency would be made, at a minimum, of the member States of the Organization of American States. In the contentious context, the relevant constituency of an international court or tribunal could seem to be limited only to the parties to a particular case, but this would be a mistaken view. Because States other than the parties may have legal interests concerning the subject matter of a case, those States should be part of the constituency relevant to assess the legitimacy of the exercise of contentious jurisdiction by the international court or tribunal concerned.

The *Mauritius/Maldives* judgment appears not to raise problems of input legitimacy, because the Special Chamber made its judgment following the established procedures under ITLOS' Statute and Rules of Procedure. Questions arise in relation to output legitimacy and effectiveness of the Special Chamber's exercise of contentious jurisdiction. Such questions stem from doubts as to the cogency of the Special Chamber's reasoning concerning the Maldives' first and second preliminary objections. First, the Special Chamber failed to articulate a workable standard for evaluating the 'authoritative nature' of judicial determinations in advisory opinions.[109] The absence of convincing reasoning in this regard led the Special Chamber to establish a vague standard, detrimental to legal certainty and predictability.[110] This lack of certainty and predictability can adversely affect the legitimacy of the *Mauritius/Maldives* judgment because it appears unsuitable to limit the arbitrary power that international courts and tribunals could exercise, in future cases, to appreciate the 'authoritative nature' of judicial determinations in the advisory context.[111] Lack of certainty and predictability is owed to the lack of clarity in Special Chamber's decisions, which in itself could negatively affect legitimacy.[112]

Second, the Special Chamber's reasoning seems to circumvent the principle of consent, which the *Monetary Gold* principle aims to protect.[113] In contentious cases, consent legitimates the exercise of the judicial function because it is the basis of the *potestas decidendi* of international courts and

[109] See Section 4.3.1.

[110] Thomas M. Franck, *Fairness in International Law and Institutions* (Oxford: Oxford University Press, 1998), p. 39.

[111] Tasioulas, 'Legitimacy of international law', 115–16.

[112] Tullio Treves, 'Aspects of legitimacy of decisions of international courts and tribunals', in Rüdiger Wolfrum and Volker Röben (eds.), *Legitimacy in International Law* (Berlin: Springer, 2008), pp. 169, 172.

[113] See Section 4.3.2.2.

tribunals.[114] In the context of the *Monetary Gold* principle, consent does not confer input legitimacy because consent to third-party settlement may have been validly given by the State parties to the dispute in which a *Monetary Gold*-type objection arises. Consistency with the *Monetary Gold* principle can be an index of output legitimacy, insofar as that principle is intended to meet the concerns of third States having legal interests relating to a case that they should be subject to binding third-party settlement without their consent. The isolation by the Special Chamber of a new 'sufficient legal interest' requirement as part of the *Monetary Gold* principle and the consequential limitation of the scope of that principle could signal that, far from meeting the concerns of its constituency, the Special Chamber has gone in the opposite direction.

Third, the likelihood of compliance with the Special Chamber's judgments, on both preliminary objections and merits, could also have legitimacy consequences.[115] One could expect the parties, and especially Mauritius, to comply readily with the judgments of the Special Chamber. In fact, the parties would be under an express legal obligation to comply pursuant to Article 296 of UNCLOS. Compliance with the judgment on the merits, the implementation of which will require positive action on the part of Mauritius and the Maldives, appears difficult without the UK's cooperation in the form of ending its administration of Chagos. Although there are convincing legal grounds for the UK to end its administration of Chagos, as the Special Chamber stated in its judgment on preliminary objections, its persistent refusal to do so could undermine the legitimacy of the Special Chamber's final judgment delimiting the maritime boundary between Mauritius and the Maldives.

Doubts exist as to the legitimacy of the Special Chamber's exercise of its judicial function in *Mauritius/Maldives*. The question is how these doubts may affect the legitimacy of the exercise of advisory jurisdiction, especially by the ICJ. So long as advisory opinions are rendered in accordance with the applicable procedural rules, there should be no question concerning the input

[114] Yuval Shany, *Assessing the Effectiveness of International Courts* (Oxford: Oxford University Press, 2014), p. 151.

[115] Questions of compliance have been suggested to influence, to varying degrees, the legitimacy of international law institutions. See Allen Buchanan, 'The legitimacy of international law', in Samantha Besson and John Tasioulas (eds.), *The Philosophy of International Law* (Oxford: Oxford University Press, 2010), pp. 79, 85; Alexandra Huneeus, 'Compliance with judgments and decisions', in Cesare Romano, Karen J. Alter, and Yuval Shany (eds.), *The Oxford Handbook of International Adjudication* (Oxford: Oxford University Press, 2014), pp. 437, 453; Alter et al., 'International court authority', 11–12; Shany, *Effectiveness of International Courts*, 155–56.

legitimacy of the exercise of advisory jurisdiction. Input legitimacy is linked to the principle of consent to third-party settlement, which in advisory cases relates to the *Eastern Carelia* doctrine. In principle, consent seems not to raise problems of input legitimacy, because States have already given their consent to the exercise of advisory jurisdiction in the constituent instruments of the international courts and tribunals concerned.[116] There is no room for *ad hoc* consent in respect of the exercise of the advisory function, also considering the non-binding character of advisory opinions.[117]

The problem with the *Eastern Carelia* doctrine arises rather as a matter of output legitimacy. The ICJ's unconvincing treatment of the doctrine in the *Chagos* advisory opinion could be said to have deprived it of practical significance, which calls into question the cogency of the Court's reasoning. Furthermore, the Court's 'broader framework' approach is so ill-defined as to appear arbitrary, which undermines the certainty and predictability of the exercise of advisory jurisdiction.

The *Mauritius/Maldives* judgment raises issues of legitimacy of the advisory function indirectly. The Special Chamber's adoption of judicial determinations in an advisory opinion could adversely affect not the input or output legitimacy of the exercise of advisory jurisdiction, but the initial legitimacy capital of the relevant international judicial organ. An international judicial organ's initial legitimacy capital depends, inter alia, on the source of that organ's power to issue judicial decisions.[118] This aspect appears to relate also to the scope of that power, which, in the case of advisory opinions, is one to render non-binding legal advice to the requesting organs. Decisions by international courts and tribunals to adopt non-binding advisory pronouncements into their binding contentious judgments risk broadening the power that States conferred on them.

However, international courts and tribunals could offset the conceivably adverse effects of the *Mauritius/Maldives* judgment for the legitimacy of the exercise of their advisory jurisdiction. For example, the ICJ could develop its 'broader framework' approach from an open-textured standard into one that limits the arbitrariness of the Court's decisions on whether to decline to render an advisory opinion pursuant to the *Eastern Carelia* doctrine. Alternatively, international courts and tribunals could, in future contentious cases, decide not to follow the Special Chamber's approach in *Mauritius/Maldives*. It is not

[116] One may justifiably have doubts in relation to the advisory jurisdiction of ITLOS as a full tribunal. See note 8.

[117] *Interpretation of Peace Treaties* (Advisory Opinion), p. 71.

[118] Shany, *Effectiveness of International Courts*, 145–46.

implausible that the Special Chamber's approach was determined by the peculiar circumstances of the case before it relating to the long-standing territorial dispute over Chagos. On this basis, international judicial organs hearing contentious cases that may require adopting judicial determinations made in advisory opinions could distinguish such cases from *Mauritius/Maldives*, thus justifying departing from the Special Chamber's approach.

The legitimacy implications of *Mauritius/Maldives* go beyond the impact of the Special Chamber's judgment on the exercise of advisory jurisdiction. The constituency relevant to evaluating whether the exercise of the advisory function is legitimate may have other concerns, which likely affect the legitimacy of that exercise. Among these, one could include the swift decolonisation of territories currently still under colonial administration. There appears to be little doubt that, in relation to this concern, the Special Chamber's judgment should be considered to have a high degree of output legitimacy. Nonetheless, one cannot be sure that addressing this paramount concern of the community of States can offset entirely the other legitimacy problems raised by the *Mauritius/Maldives* judgment. Plausibly, the Special Chamber was under some pressure to align with the ICJ's findings in *Chagos*. If the Special Chamber had distanced itself from those findings, it could have adversely affected the legitimacy of the ICJ's advisory opinion and, as a consequence, the States' follow-up action in the General Assembly. Deviating from the ICJ's findings might have created a *Tadić*-like scenario, where two different international tribunals are seen to reach opposite findings on comparable issues.[119] Such a scenario would have been detrimental to the perception, by a variety of stakeholders, of how the ICJ and the Special Chamber had exercised their judicial function. Inconsistent judicial decisions do not promote resorting to international dispute settlement, especially at the current time of open challenges to multilateral institutions and processes.[120]

4.4 NEW DIRECTIONS IN INTER-STATE DISPUTE SETTLEMENT

The Special Chamber's judgment in *Mauritius/Maldives* may seem problematic because of its reasoning, which leaves open a number of questions and

[119] In its 2007 judgment in *Bosnian Genocide*, the ICJ clarified that the 'overall control' test set out in *Tadić* did not govern the attribution to a state of conduct of non-State actors, but applied to determining whether an armed conflict was international or non-international. See *Application of the Convention on the Prevention and Punishment of the Crime of Genocide (Bosnia and Herzegovina* v. *Serbia and Montenegro)* (Merits) [2007] ICJ Rep. 43 at paras 403–7.

[120] James Crawford, 'The current political discourse concerning international law' (2018) 81 MLR 1–22; Harlan Grant Cohen, 'Multilateralism's life cycle' (2018) 112 AJIL 47–66.

potential implications. First, the Special Chamber did not succeed in articulating a persuasive standard to evaluate the 'authoritative nature' of judicial determinations in advisory opinions, which one should understand as the prerequisite for adopting such determinations in a contentious judgment. Second, the Special Chamber's decision calls into question the existence of the *Eastern Carelia* doctrine. That doctrine has lost much of its significance as a result of the *Chagos* and other opinions, and even more so by the Special Chamber's decision to adopt the ICJ's opinion in order to determine that Mauritius had sovereignty over Chagos. Third, the Special Chamber's judgment developed the *Monetary Gold* principle into a two-stage test, adding a 'sufficient legal interest' requirement which did not seem to exist prior to *Mauritius/Maldives*. This additional requirement restricts the scope of the principle, on which applicant States in future contentious cases will likely capitalise. Fourth, the Special Chamber's judgment has conceivable adverse effects for the legitimacy of the exercise of advisory jurisdiction.

Despite these potential problems, the *Mauritius/Maldives* judgment may be the start of a new chapter in the history of the advisory function of international courts and tribunals. The Special Chamber's adoption of advisory pronouncements for the purpose of deciding a contentious case could presage the use of advisory opinions to settle inter-State disputes through the medium of contentious cases on matters collateral to the issues on which those advisory opinions touched. Conversely, it seems also possible that the *Mauritius/Maldives* judgment could generate backlash from States dissatisfied with the Special Chamber's approach that blurs the distinction, not always neat anyway, between contentious and advisory cases. This backlash could show itself in the form of stronger opposition to future requests for advisory opinions, which could potentially stifle the resort to advisory opinions itself.

If John Merrills could oversee his own new edition of *International Dispute Settlement*, the *Mauritius/Maldives* judgment may be the reason for revisiting his decision not to cover advisory opinions. The Special Chamber's judgment at least would give Merrills a reason to consider inserting some new comments on its potential implications. After 28 January 2021, the settlement of inter-State disputes by way of advisory opinion should no longer be seen as an eventuality, but instead as a reality.[121]

[121] On reimagining advisory opinions as instruments of dispute settlement, see Massimo Lando, 'Advisory Opinions of the International Court of Justice in respect of disputes' (2023) 61 Columbia J Transn L 67–132.

PART II

Effectiveness, Authority, and Legitimacy of the Current System of International Dispute Settlement and Possible Reforms

5

Navigating Choppy Waters

UNCLOS Dispute Settlement Coming of Age?

RICHARD COLLINS

5.1 INTRODUCTION: ON 'CONSTITUTIONS', 'CEMENT', AND OTHER METAPHORS

It might now seem somewhat trite, unhelpfully ambiguous even, to describe the 1982 United Nations Convention on the Law of the Sea (UNCLOS) as a 'constitution' for the oceans.[1] Undoubtedly, its conclusion following a long period of negotiation represented a phenomenal achievement: the result was unprecedented in scale, scope, and ambition. Even if the 'constitutional' moniker might mischaracterise this achievement, this 'public' framing of UNCLOS has clear explanatory merit: its broad, quasi-universal reach and its attempt to deal with 'practically every aspect of the uses and resources of the seas and the oceans'[2] set it apart from a simple contractual bargain between States. There were clearly many compromises required to reconcile the competing interests of, for example, coastal and flag States, developed and developing worlds, and so on, but the result was a regime that puts the parties in a very different position, subject to innovative and far-reaching institutional mechanisms. Most significant, though, is how UNCLOS looks beyond its own text, functioning as an umbrella framework for the incorporation of a range of marine regulatory standards and, thereby, opening up to and interacting with other areas of international law.

[1] See Tommy T. B. Koh, 'A constitution for the oceans', www.un.org/Depts/los/convention_agreements/texts/koh_english.pdf (accessed 1 June 2022). For a fuller consideration of this framing, see Shirley V. Scott, 'The LOS Convention as a constitutional regime for the oceans', in Alex G. Oude Elferink (ed.), *Stability and Change in the Law of the Sea: The Role of the LOS Convention* (Leiden: Brill, 2005), pp. 9–38.

[2] Koh, 'Constitution for the oceans'.

It is unsurprising therefore that there were considerable expectations for the dispute settlement provisions included in Part XV[3] of the Convention. The Convention imposes a binding obligation on States to settle disputes amicably whilst relying on mandated judicial settlement as a last measure. This mechanism was thought important to protect the integrity of the 'constitutional' settlement whilst also helping to flesh out many of UNCLOS' more nuanced and tricky provisions. Indeed, the system was supposed to be, in the words of the first president of the Third UN Conference on the Law of the Sea, 'the pivot upon which the delicate equilibrium of the compromise must be balanced'.[4] Beyond the resolution of particular disputes, therefore, judges and arbitrators have been tasked with adding clarity to areas of (strategic) ambiguity and giving meaning to key provisions, particularly newly created rights, entitlements, and permitted uses of the reconfigured maritime zones. As Boyle concluded, 'binding compulsory dispute settlement becomes the cement which should hold the whole structure together and guarantee its continued acceptability and endurance for all parties'.[5]

These metaphors and framings place a good deal of responsibility on the shoulders of judges and arbitrators, who must navigate tricky terrain, affording a certain deference to the strategic interests of States whilst attempting to give a persuasive response to questions that were left ambiguous and unresolved (sometimes deliberately so) in order to achieve a compromise between those interests. Perhaps for this reason, the system of dispute settlement was initially greeted with some caution and scepticism. Too full of deferential caveats and qualifications, many early commentaries saw the system as neutered from its birth; with only a handful of cases brought initially and hesitancy from tribunals to assume jurisdiction,[6] early practice seemed to bear out this narrative.[7] In particular, the dearth of cases brought before the newly created

3 And in Part XI on the role of the ITLOS Seabed Disputes Chamber.

4 A/CONF.62/WP.9/Add.1 (1976), para. 6, contained in UN Office for Ocean Affairs and the Law of the Sea, *Compilation of the Official Records of the Third United Nations Conference on the Law of the Sea, 1973–1982*, 17 vols (New York: UN, 2004), vol. 3, p. 122.

5 Alan E. Boyle, 'Dispute settlement and the Law of the Sea Convention: Problems of fragmentation and jurisdiction' (1997) 46 ICLQ 37–54 at 38.

6 See further Section 5.4.

7 Some argued that strategic interests and jurisdictional limitations would cause States to bypass UNCLOS dispute settlement in many instances. See, e.g., Natalie Klein, *Dispute Settlement in the UN Convention on the Law of the Sea* (Cambridge: Cambridge University Press, 2005). Others, like Churchill, are more sanguine and were unsurprised by the relative paucity of cases initially brought through a relatively new system. See Robin Churchill, 'Trends in dispute settlement in the law of the sea: Towards the increasing availability of compulsory means', in Duncan French, Matthew Saul, and Nigel D. White (eds.), *International Law and Dispute Settlement: New Problems and Techniques* (Oxford: Hart, 2011), pp. 148–49.

International Tribunal for the Law of the Sea (ITLOS)[8] even caused some to question the merit of its existence.[9]

More recently, however, we are witnessing the system finally creak into action, with a growing number and broadening diversity of cases brought, including increasingly before ITLOS as well.[10] However, this awakening of the system now provokes its own set of concerns. Recent cases have raised diverse, often controversial, issues – including questions of sovereignty,[11] human rights,[12] the use of force,[13] and sovereign immunities[14] – many of which seem to be expanding the jurisdictional reach of UNCLOS courts and tribunals. Whilst some overlap between subject matters is inevitable, there is concern that the system may be being used opportunistically to advance States' strategic interests to the detriment of the coherence of UNCLOS overall: a reckless judicial activism that threatens the delicate balance put in place.[15] Is the system thus being 'gamed' for more particular ends and, thereby, jeopardising the international rule of law? Or are these cases,

8 Over the first fifteen years (approx.) of its existence, aside from provisional measures rulings and requests for prompt release of vessels, the tribunal heard and ruled upon only one substantive case: *M/V 'Saiga' (No. 2) (Saint Vincent and the Grenadines* v. *Guinea)* (Judgment of 1 July 1999) ITLOS Reports 1999, p. 10. See further discussion in Dapo Akande, 'The Hamburg Tribunal heats up? Is ITLOS now in business?', *EJIL: Talk!*, 15 September 2010, www.ejiltalk.org/the-hamburg-tribunal-heats-up-is-itlos-now-in-business (accessed 1 June 2022).

9 See, e.g., Jillaine Seymour, 'The International Tribunal for the Law of the Sea: A great mistake?' (2006) 13 Indiana J Glob Leg Stud 1–35.

10 Although, whilst there has been a steadier flow of substantive disputes brought before ITLOS, Annex VII arbitration still accounts for the bulk of cases brought under the Convention.

11 *Chagos Marine Protected Area Arbitration (Mauritius* v. *United Kingdom)* (Final Award of 18 March 2015) PCA Case No. 2011-03; *South China Sea Arbitration (Philippines* v. *China)* (Award on Merits of 12 July 2016) PCA Case No. 2013-19. Also with the sovereignty issue at its heart is the pending case: *Dispute Concerning Coastal State Rights in the Black Sea, Sea of Azov, and Kerch Strait (Ukraine* v. *The Russian Federation)* PCA Case No. 2017-06.

12 *The Arctic Sunrise Arbitration (Kingdom of the Netherlands* v. *The Russian Federation)* (Award on Merits of 14 August 2015) PCA Case No. 2014-02.

13 This was at issue already in the *M/V 'Saiga' (No. 2)* case, but more recently a similar scenario arose in *M/V 'Virginia G' (Panama* v. *Guinea-Bissau)* (Judgment of 14 April 2014) ITLOS Reports 2014, p. 4.

14 *The 'Enrica Lexie' Incident (The Italian Republic* v. *The Republic of India)* (Award of 21 May 2020) PCA Case No. 2015-28.

15 See inter alia Stefan Talmon, 'The Chagos Marine Protected Area Arbitration: The expansion of the jurisdiction of UNCLOS Part XV courts and tribunals' (2016) 65 ICLQ 927–51; Peter Tzeng, 'Jurisdiction and applicable law under UNCLOS' (2016) 126 Yale LJ 242–60; Natalie Klein, 'The vicissitudes of dispute settlement under the Law of the Sea Convention' (2017) 32 Int J Mar Coast Law 332–63.

especially the 'David v. Goliath'-style challenges from weaker States, a sign of the rule of law in action?[16]

Of course, these conflicting intuitions might just reveal something about the tensions in the very idea of an international rule of law.[17] To risk one final metaphor, as the system wades into choppy waters, we can, I believe, more readily see signs of its maturity, both in terms of the realisation of judicial accountability and the working out of the appropriate bounds of its adjudicative reach. There is a tendency in the literature to simplistically caution against judicial overreach or to frame its jurisdictional limits through a dichotomous struggle between judicial effectiveness and the principle of consent. I believe that this kind of framing is wrong-headed and unhelpful. Those two pressures are encapsulated in the delicate compromise of Part XV and – as I will briefly outline towards the end of the chapter – reflect conflicting rule-of-law urges institutionalised at the international level. If we are to better adjudge the appropriate bounds of law of the sea adjudication, we should look to this value itself, where necessary submissions to judicial oversight are tempered by the requirement for legal reasoning which is coherent, consistent, transparent, predictable, non-arbitrary, and so on.[18] Before I can return to this point, I must first give a brief overview of the dispute settlement system (Section 5.2), before setting out its evolving practice since the Convention came into force (Section 5.3), which has now begun to prompt the noted concerns surrounding 'creeping jurisdiction' (considered in different ways in Sections 5.4 and 5.5).

5.2 A BRIEF APPRAISAL OF UNCLOS DISPUTE SETTLEMENT

Like the Convention overall, the system of dispute settlement included within UNCLOS was initially met with some fanfare. Writing after its conclusion,

[16] See Douglas Guilfoyle, 'Governing the oceans and dispute resolution: An evolving legal order?', in Danielle Ireland-Piper and Leon Wolff (eds.), *Global Governance and Regulation: Order and Disorder in the 21st Century* (Abingdon: Routledge, 2018), pp. 173–91; and, more extensively, Douglas Guilfoyle, 'The rule of law and maritime security: Understanding lawfare in the South China Sea' (2019) 95 Int Aff 999–1017.

[17] I discuss these different uses of rule-of-law discourse in international law in Richard Collins, 'Two idea(l)s of the international rule of law' (2019) 8 Glob Const 191–226.

[18] Whilst the rule of law is a notoriously contested notion (see Collins, 'Two idea(l)s'), in this chapter I embrace an essentially 'Fullerian' approach, stressing a standard of 'legality' as a commitment to a certain kind of social ordering which is tempered by standards of publicity, prospectivity, intelligibility, consistency, practicability, stability, and congruence in legal reasoning. See Lon L. Fuller, *The Morality of Law* (New Haven, CT: Yale University Press, 1964).

though still several years prior to UNCLOS' entry into force,[19] one commentator described it as 'the most sophisticated and detailed system for international dispute settlement ever drafted'.[20] Some years later, another claimed that it represented 'probably the most important development in the settlement of international disputes since the adoption of the UN Charter and the Statute of the International Court of Justice'.[21] These grand claims are perhaps less related to the inclusion of a compulsory mechanism per se – indeed, by this point, compromissory clauses in multilateral regimes were far from remarkable[22] – and much more to do with the Convention's ambitious reach and the complexity and innovations of the mechanism put in place for this purpose. For example, one of its more striking features falls entirely outside of Part XV, with the unprecedented jurisdiction bestowed upon the ITLOS Seabed Disputes Chamber under Part XI. The Chamber not only has power to give advisory opinions in relation to all activities occurring on the deep seabed ('The Area'),[23] but also has a broad binding jurisdiction over all State parties, contractors, and natural and legal persons engaged in relevant activities.[24] Furthermore, Part XV itself contains a distinctive procedure for the prompt release of vessels that grants a compulsory jurisdiction to ITLOS,[25] which feels more akin to an administrative judicial review procedure at the national level.[26]

[19] It entered into force on 16 November 1994, twelve months after Guyana became the sixtieth State to ratify the Convention (in accordance with Art 308).

[20] John E. Noyes, 'Compulsory third-party adjudication and the 1982 United Nations Convention on the Law of the Sea' (1989) 4 Conn J Int'l L 675–96 at 675.

[21] Boyle, 'Dispute settlement and the LOS Convention', p. 37.

[22] In this light, Churchill describes the UNCLOS scheme as essentially 'a compromissory clause of a fairly traditional kind'. Churchill, 'Trends in dispute settlement', p. 144. See further Robin Churchill, 'The general dispute settlement system of the UN Convention on the Law of the Sea: Overview, context, and use' (2017) 48 Ocean Dev & Int'l L 216–38 at 217–18, 221. Indeed, by the time of the Convention's entry into force, a significant number of multilateral treaties included a dispute resolution mechanism. In a quantitative analysis of such mechanisms in 236 major multilateral treaties, Laidlaw and Kang found that most such treaties (75 per cent) contained a dispute settlement mechanism, with the majority of those (79 per cent) providing for compulsory referral to third-party settlement. See Anais Kedgley Laidlaw and Shaun Kang, 'The dispute settlement mechanisms in major multilateral treaties', NUS Law Working Paper Series 2018/028, October 2018, https://law.nus.edu.sg/wp-content/uploads/2020/04/028_2018_CIL02.pdf (accessed 2 June 2022).

[23] Art 191 of UNCLOS.

[24] Art 187 of UNCLOS. See further Richard Collins and Duncan French, 'A guardian of universal interest or increasingly out of its depth? The International Seabed Authority turns 25' (2020) 17 IOLR 633–63 at 651–53.

[25] Art 292 of UNCLOS.

[26] Seline Trevisanut, 'The exercise of administrative functions by ITLOS: A comment on prompt release case-law', in Nerina Boschiero et al. (eds.), *International Courts and the Development of*

My focus here, however, is the main system of dispute settlement in Part XV, which itself includes some distinctive quirks and innovations, though, importantly, several clear limitations also. Broadly, this system imposes an obligation to settle disputes peacefully whilst providing for mandatory judicial settlement in the last measure, though also offering significant flexibility in terms of choice of forum. This stress on party autonomy was a product of the need to reach consensus within the UNCLOS negotiations. As was well described by John Merrills himself, different factions emerged with some supporting referral to the International Court of Justice (ICJ), others the creation of an entirely new tribunal, and others still opting for general or specialist arbitration. The resulting system ended up reconciling these different perspectives by incorporating each as a possible option for State parties.[27] As we shall see, however, this was not the only concession granted to ensure consensus.

The Part XV system operates by way of a tripartite structure. Section 1 sets out the broad obligation to settle disputes peacefully, though it leaves flexibility as to the choice of means. As noted by both Oxman[28] and Churchill,[29] Section 1 does little more than reiterate States' existing obligations under the UN Charter to settle disputes peacefully, and the means listed – negotiation, mediation, conciliation, and so on – reflect the traditional diplomatic and judicial forms included in Article 33(1) of the UN Charter. Nevertheless, it does set out certain procedural limitations, including that priority will be given to agreements in place between parties to settle disputes amicably, unless there is a failure to reach settlement (Article 281), or to relevant other treaties providing for binding determinations between the parties (Article 282). Furthermore, Article 284 provides a distinct conciliation procedure (detailed in Annex V), though this procedure remains entirely dependent upon State

International Law: Essays in Honour of Professor Tullio R. Treves (The Hague: TMC Asser, 2013), pp. 309–21.

27 John G. Merrills, *International Dispute Settlement*, 6th ed. (Cambridge: Cambridge University Press, 2017), p. 170.

28 Bernard H. Oxman, 'Courts and tribunals: The ICJ, ITLOS, and arbitral tribunals', in Donald R. Rothwell et al. (eds.), *The Oxford Handbook of the Law of the Sea* (Oxford: Oxford University Press, 2015), p. 396. The general obligation to settle disputes peacefully (Art 279) refers back to the UN Charter obligation to similar effect (Art 2(3) of the Charter), which in turn points forward to Art 33 of the Charter, which references 'negotiation, enquiry, mediation, conciliation, arbitration, judicial settlement, resort to regional agencies or arrangements, or other peaceful means of [the parties'] own choice'.

29 See Robin Churchill, '"Compulsory" dispute settlement under the United Nations Convention on the Law of the Sea: How has it operated? Pt. 1', *PluriCourts Blog*, 9 June 2016, www.jus.uio.no/pluricourts/english/blog/guests/2016-06-09-churchill-unclos-pt-1.html (accessed 2 June 2022).

agreement and has been used so far in only one case.[30] Another clear duty that exists prior to engaging judicial means is the obligation to exchange views under Article 283.[31]

Although the above are clear legal limitations on jurisdiction in theory, as I will show below, in practice these provisions rarely act to preclude jurisdiction outright. In principle, however, it is only when failing to reach any settlement through Section 1 – and there exists, under Article 286, a 'dispute concerning the interpretation or application of [the] Convention' – that binding judicial settlement will kick in under Section 2.[32] Article 286 (read with Article 288) thus places an important material limitation on jurisdiction – again, more on this later – but when its terms are met, States then have a choice of means of compulsory settlement. This includes the newly created ITLOS, the ICJ, arbitration (as detailed in Annex VII), or special arbitration (a discrete procedure which allows inclusion of various non-judicial expertise, as set out in Annex VIII).[33] Article 287 provides that when 'signing, ratifying or acceding to [the] Convention or at any time thereafter, a State shall be free to choose, by means of a written declaration, one or more' of these means as their preferred forum. It further provides that where there is no declaration in place, or where there is a difference between parties in terms of preferred forum, Annex VII arbitration will be the default forum. Despite this choice, it is important to highlight the enhanced role granted to ITLOS, which not only has the aforementioned power over prompt release claims but also acts as a default forum for provisional measures pending the establishment of an Annex VII tribunal.[34]

Finally, in Section 3, a somewhat complex array of exceptions and voluntary opt-outs are detailed, though these exceptions themselves give rise to further exceptions.[35] Under Article 297, disputes 'with regard to the exercise by a coastal State of its sovereign rights or jurisdiction' over a number of areas, especially rights of navigation and preservation of the marine environment, will generally be admissible except that coastal States are not obliged to accept disputes brought in relation to their discretionary powers in the exclusive

30 See *Timor Sea Conciliation (Timor-Leste* v. *Australia)* PCA Case No. 2016-10.

31 Art 283 of UNCLOS.

32 Art 286 of UNCLOS.

33 The Convention (under Annex XIII, Art 2(1)) requires that a special list of experts is drawn up and maintained in the following fields: (1) fisheries, (2) protection and preservation of the marine environment, (3) marine scientific research, and (4) navigation, including pollution from vessels and by dumping.

34 Art 290(5) of UNCLOS.

35 For a useful summation in this respect, see Guilfoyle, 'Governing the oceans', pp. 176–77.

economic zone (EEZ) over marine scientific research or fisheries.[36] Under Article 298, States also have the freedom to declare that they do not accept jurisdiction in relation to disputes arising over maritime boundaries or historic bays and titles, though States must instead accept submission to conciliation; disputes concerning military activities or law enforcement related to the exercise of sovereign rights or jurisdiction over the activities excluded under Article 297, above; and disputes in relation to which the Security Council is exercising its authority under the UN Charter. Finally, under Article 299, State parties that are able to avail of any of these exceptions may nonetheless submit such disputes by agreement to settlement procedures under Section 2. The overall working of this system of inclusion and exception is somewhat complex and perhaps best summed up by Guilfoyle: *'Everything is in, until it's out, unless it is brought in again'*.[37]

5.3 PART XV IN PRACTICE: FROM QUIET INFANCY TO DIFFICULT TEENAGE YEARS

Perhaps because of the quite complex, somewhat deferential model put in place, early reflections on the outlook for the dispute settlement mechanism were quite pessimistic or cautious in tone. It seemed likely, for many, that Part XV would be underutilised and, when it was used, its provisions cautiously interpreted.[38] In an early assessment, former ICJ president Shigeru Oda saw the impact of the various exceptions as essentially blunting the 'compulsory' aspects of the procedure.[39] Likewise, Boyle predicted that the more contentious of cases were likely to be settled outside of the system through more consensual means, thus largely perpetuating the pre-UNCLOS status quo.[40] He foresaw that creative legal engineering might be required in order to 'size' disputes to fit the UNCLOS model.[41] Furthermore, the flexibility in choice of forum also, he believed, risked the 'fragmentation' of the system.[42]

[36] Though in these cases compulsory conciliation procedures may come into play.

[37] Guilfoyle, 'Governing the oceans', p. 176 (emphasis added).

[38] Douglas Guilfoyle, 'The South China Sea Award: How should we read the UN Convention on the Law of the Sea?' (2018) 8 Asian JIL 51–63 at 53–54.

[39] See Shigeru Oda, 'Some reflections on the dispute settlement clauses in the United Nations Convention on the Law of the Sea', in Jerzy Makarczyk (ed.), *Essays in International Law in Honour of Judge Manfred Lachs* (The Hague: Martinus Nijhoff, 1984), p. 655.

[40] See Boyle, 'Dispute settlement and the LOS Convention', pp. 46–47, 54.

[41] Ibid., pp. 39, pp. 41–47.

[42] Ibid., pp. 39–41.

How have these predictions played out in practice? Boyle seems to have been quite astute in predicting that a certain 'salami-slicing'[43] of disputes would be required to make cases fit the UNCLOS mould – a point to which I return in Section 5.5. At least initially, the predicted hesitancy to engage dispute settlement seemed also foresightful. In total, just seven cases were brought under Part XV during its first fifteen years of functioning. It is difficult to take the total number of cases as a measure of the scheme's performance, given, particularly, that the occurrence of peaceful resolution would be a clearer sign of success, albeit one that is difficult to measure. However, Churchill speculates that the minimal take-up stemmed at least partially from the perceived narrowness of UNCLOS' jurisdictional reach.[44] Writing in 2014, similarly, Klein suggested that in numerous instances States had preferred to bypass UNCLOS dispute settlement, either because it was not in their strategic interest to bring an action, or because its jurisdictional limitations necessarily limited access.[45]

In other respects, however, it seems that the system has not entirely functioned as anticipated – or indeed feared. First, the risk of fragmentation appears not to have substantially materialised, with a degree of substantive coherence between cases evident,[46] and a relatively small pool of judges meaning a certain institutional overlap also.[47] Second, despite significant differences during negotiations surrounding the choice of forum, only a limited number of States initially made declarations under Article 287,[48] which has meant that the majority of cases have gone to Annex VII arbitration.[49] Furthermore, a significant number of law-of-the-sea cases (especially maritime delimitation disputes) have continued to be brought to the ICJ outside of the Part XV framework. Given that ITLOS was created as a free-to-use mechanism largely at the behest of developing States' mistrustful of the

[43] Ibid., p. 39.

[44] Churchill, 'General dispute settlement system', p. 226.

[45] See Natalie Klein, 'The effectiveness of the UNCLOS dispute settlement regime: Reaching for the stars?' (2014) 108 ASIL Proc 359–64.

[46] Alan Boyle, 'UNCLOS dispute settlement and the uses and abuses of Part XV' (2014) 47 Revue Belge de Droit 182–204 at 182, 199–200.

[47] Churchill, 'General dispute settlement system', p. 224.

[48] There has been a small increase in recent years, but as of 1 November 2021, only fifty-three such declarations have been made. For detail, see ITLOS, 'Declarations made by States parties under Article 287', www.itlos.org/en/main/jurisdiction/declarations-of-states-parties/declarations-made-by-states-parties-under-article-287 (accessed 2 June 2022).

[49] For a useful analysis up to the end of 2016, see Churchill, 'General dispute settlement system', p. 223.

ICJ, the limited number of cases heard (on the merits at least)[50] by the tribunal during its first two decades of operation might appear a cause for concern.[51] At the same time, however, given its 'untried and untested' nature, it is perhaps unsurprising that there would be a slow take-up initially,[52] and it is notable that in a number of Annex VII arbitrations the parties have decided to transfer the dispute to ITLOS.[53] In relation to provisional measures rulings and specialist prompt release procedures, also, the ease of access to ITLOS proved popular initially.[54] Third, and finally, the types of dispute brought under Part XV have also not quite panned out as anticipated. From the literature, three motivating factors behind the inclusion of Part XV emerge: protection of the traditional freedoms of flag States against potential jurisdictional overreach from coastal States; securing weaker coastal States' acquired rights against incursions by more powerful States; and, more broadly, the clarification or fleshing out of certain controversial or compromise provisions in the text.[55] Until relatively recently, as Churchill notes, a good proportion of cases (approximately two-thirds) have concerned vessel detention (especially prompt release requests) and more traditional maritime boundary disputes (despite the option to exclude the latter under Article 298). Examples that fit precisely into the above categories, however, are rather more limited.[56] Certainly, there have been few if any cases of the first type. We are now perhaps witnessing more of the second – 'David v. Goliath'-type scenarios, though with some of these cases, as we will see in Section 5.5, a doubt persists over whether these are properly categorised as law-of-the-sea disputes.[57] Within this framing, one interesting though still relatively underutilised aspect

[50] Indeed, until the decision in *Bangladesh* v. *Myanmar* in 2012, the tribunal had concluded only one case on the merits: *M/V 'Saiga' (No. 2)* in 1999.

[51] Churchill, 'General dispute settlement system', p. 220.

[52] Akande, 'Hamburg Tribunal'.

[53] This has included the aforementioned *Bangladesh* v. *Myanmar* case: *Dispute Concerning Delimitation of the Maritime Boundary in the Bay of Bengal (Bangladesh* v. *Myanmar)* (Judgment of 14 March 2012) ITLOS Reports 2012, p. 4 (transferred to ITLOS 2009); the *M/V 'Virginia G'* case (transferred to ITLOS 2011); and *Dispute Concerning Delimitation of the Maritime Boundary between Ghana and Côte d'Ivoire in the Atlantic Ocean (Ghana* v. *Côte d'Ivoire)* ITLOS Reports 2015 (transferred to ITLOS Special Chamber 2014).

[54] Of the twenty-nine completed cases (decided or withdrawn), nine have been prompt-release claims (though, interestingly, all nine were brought before 2007) and eight have been *solely* provisional measures rulings.

[55] In their assessments of the operation of the Convention, both Churchill and Klein roughly categorise cases in this way, though Klein subsumes the first two categories together under a balancing of interests. See, respectively, Churchill, 'General dispute settlement system', p. 218, and Klein, 'Effectiveness of UNCLOS dispute settlement', p. 360.

[56] Churchill, 'General dispute settlement system', p. 228.

[57] Ibid.

of Part XV has been the requirement of conciliation as a fallback provision under Article 298, which in the recent *Timor Sea Conciliation* provided a valuable means of overcoming differences, and notable power imbalances, in securing agreement on a maritime boundary delimitation between Australia and Timor-Leste.[58] Finally, the *M/V 'Saiga'*[59] and *M/V 'Virginia G'*[60] cases are perhaps the clearest examples of disputes in the third category (here clarifying rights and obligations with regard to the EEZ), and parts of *South China Sea* (especially around maritime entitlements) also fit this mould,[61] as do aspects of the two ITLOS advisory opinions given to date.[62]

Nevertheless, it is really over the last decade where the concern for the 'unexpected' has really resonated, with UNCLOS tribunals using the system in a way that may 'overreach the confines of Part XV'.[63] Already in 2014, Boyle warned against an overly expansive approach to jurisdiction, which might threaten to undermine the principle of consent underlying interstate dispute settlement, risking 'unpredictability' and 'incoherence' in the system.[64] Even if one disagrees with the framing, it is perhaps hard to fault his foresight, considering the growing number and complexity of cases brought over the following years. Accusations of a 'creeping expansion of jurisdiction' became common,[65] potentially threatening the goodwill of States who had consented to the Convention's careful compromise.[66] These concerns have arisen in two main areas: first, the ease with which Section 1's procedural requirements are

58 *Timor Sea Conciliation (Timor-Leste v. Australia)* (Report and Recommendations of the Compulsory Conciliation Commission of 9 May 2018) PCA Case No. 2016-10. For commentary on the importance of this conciliation in the scheme of UNCLOS dispute settlement, see S. Jayakumar, 'Compulsory dispute settlement and conciliation under UNCLOS', in Hao Duy Phan et al. (eds.), *The Timor-Leste/Australia Conciliation: A Victory for UNCLOS and Peaceful Settlement of Disputes* (Singapore: World Scientific, 2019), pp. 1–30.

59 The *M/V 'Saiga'* case.

60 The *M/V 'Virginia G'* case.

61 The *South China Sea Arbitration*.

62 This includes the perhaps surprising assumption of jurisdiction in *Request for Advisory Opinion Submitted by the Sub-regional Fisheries Commission* (Advisory Opinion of 2 April 2015) ITLOS Reports 2015, p. 4 (re: coastal and flag obligations surrounding IUU fishing), and the so far only Seabed Disputes Chamber case, *Responsibilities and Obligations of States Sponsoring Persons and Entities with Respect to Activities in the Area* (Advisory Opinion of 1 February 2011), ITLOS Reports 2011, p. 10, which clarified environmental obligations of sponsoring States and contractors in 'The Area'.

63 Klein, 'Effectiveness of UNCLOS dispute settlement', p. 364.

64 Boyle, 'UNCLOS dispute settlement', p. 203.

65 Talmon, 'Chagos Marine Protected Area Arbitration', p. 950.

66 Kate Parlett, 'Beyond the four corners of the convention: Expanding the scope of jurisdiction of Law of the Sea tribunals' (2017) 48 Ocean Dev & Int'l L 284–99.

bypassed in practice; and second, the perhaps more fundamental question of whether many of the cases being brought are even properly characterised as law-of-the-sea disputes. I will look at the first issue in Section 5.4 and the broader, and potentially more troubling, subject matter question in Section 5.5, before offering some concluding thoughts on the veracity of these claims.

5.4 OVERCOMING PROCEDURAL HURDLES AND DIVING INTO CHOPPY WATERS

To recall, under Article 286, it is only where Section 1's terms have been exhausted that a dispute should advance to compulsory settlement under Section 2. Initially, cases brought under Part XV seemed to take quite a cautious approach in this regard, arguably reinforcing the narrow reading given by inter alia Klein, above.[67] This was especially the case in the *Southern Bluefin Tuna*[68] and, to some degree, *MOX Plant* cases.[69] In the former case, in fact, in finding that the tribunal lacked jurisdiction on the basis of a prior agreement between the parties (under Article 281),[70] the tribunal glibly commented that 'UNCLOS falls significantly short of establishing a truly comprehensive regime of compulsory jurisdiction entailing binding decisions'.[71] Whether or not it was correct in this assessment, or indeed on the main finding on jurisdiction, its ruling has attracted significant criticism,[72] and later cases appear to have moved away from its restrictive reading of Article 281 and, indeed, the narrow picture painted of UNCLOS dispute settlement.[73]

Article 281 played a critical part in China's disavowal of jurisdiction in the *South China Sea* case. Although refusing to take part in proceedings, in its

[67] Klein, *Dispute Settlement*, pp. 35–43.

[68] *Southern Bluefin Tuna (New Zealand* v. *Japan, Australia* v. *Japan)* (Jurisdiction and Admissibility, Award of 4 August 2000) (2000) 23 RIAA 45.

[69] *MOX Plant Case (Ireland* v. *United Kingdom)* PCA Case No. 2002-01.

[70] Art 16 of the Convention for the Conservation of Southern Bluefin Tuna, Canberra, 10 May 1993, in force 20 May 1994, 1819 UNTS 359.

[71] *Southern Bluefin Tuna*, para. 62. This is a common view in the literature. See, e.g., Rosemary Rayfuse, 'The future of compulsory dispute settlement under the Law of the Sea' (2005) 36 Vic Univ Wellingt Law Rev 683–712 at 702, who argues that Part XV of UNCLOS is 'neither as comprehensive nor as compulsory as its proponents suggest'.

[72] See inter alia Igor V. Karaman, *Dispute Resolution in the Law of the Sea* (Leiden: Martinus Nijhoff, 2012), pp. 259–61; Alan Boyle, 'The Southern Bluefin Tuna Arbitration' (2001) 50 ICLQ 447–52.

[73] For discussion, see Klein, 'Vicissitudes of dispute settlement', pp. 336–37, and further Natalie Klein, 'Expansions and restrictions in the UNCLOS dispute settlement regime: Lessons from recent decisions' (2016) 15 Chinese JIL 403–15 at 405–6.

position paper, China argued, following *Southern Bluefin Tuna*, that the joint China–ASEAN Declaration on the Conduct of Parties in the South China Sea constituted an agreement under the terms of Article 281.[74] In its award on jurisdiction and admissibility, the Annex VII tribunal found that only express language would suffice to exclude compulsory jurisdiction under Article 281 (and Article 282 also).[75] Furthermore, where alternative means of settlement have been exhausted, it claimed that any such agreement would need to expressly preclude further recourse to Part XV procedures to absolutely displace jurisdiction.[76] Finding essentially that *Southern Bluefin Tuna* was wrongly decided, the tribunal argued that Article 281 had to be read in the context of the Convention as a whole:

> Requiring express exclusion for Article 281 is ... consistent with the overall object and purpose of the Convention as a comprehensive agreement. The drafters of the Convention recalled that 'the system for the settlement of disputes must form an integral part and an essential element of the Convention'. ... In these circumstances it is difficult to accept that the Parties may remove a pivotal part of the Convention without clearly expressing an intention to do so.[77]

As suggested above, a similarly limited reading seems to be apparent for Article 282 also. Although the tribunal in *MOX Plant* eventually took a quite deferential approach in suspending proceedings between the parties, as the European Court of Justice was also engaged in ruling on the dispute,[78] like ITLOS in its provisional measures ruling beforehand,[79] the tribunal gave a restricted reading to Article 282,[80] essentially endorsing a kind of 'parallelism' between the parties' obligations under UNCLOS and those arising under other relevant treaties.[81] This reasoning was followed in *South China Sea*, where the tribunal noted, first, that only an agreement involving a compulsory

74 *South China Sea Arbitration (Philippines* v. *China)* (Award on Jurisdiction and Admissibility of 29 October 2015) PCA Case No. 2013-19 at para. 204.

75 Ibid., paras 221–29.

76 Ibid., para. 224.

77 Ibid., para. 225.

78 Which eventually led to the termination of proceedings under the Convention. See *MOX Plant Case (Ireland* v. *United Kingdom)* (Order No. 6 of 6 June 2008) PCA Case No. 2002-01.

79 *MOX Plant Case (Ireland* v. *United Kingdom)* (Provisional Measures, Order of 3 December 2001) ITLOS Reports 2001, p. 95 at paras 50–51.

80 See *MOX Plant Case (Ireland* v. *United Kingdom)* (Order No. 3 of 24 June 2003) PCA Case No. 2002-01 at paras 18–22.

81 For discussion, see Karaman, *Dispute Resolution*, pp. 123–26, as well as Nigel Bankes, 'Precluding the applicability of section 2 of Part XV of the Law of the Sea Convention' (2017) 48 Ocean Dev & Int'l L 239–68 at 243–44.

and binding procedure would act to displace jurisdiction under Part XV, Section 2,[82] and, second, that a mere overlap in subject matter was insufficient to displace jurisdiction: 'Parallel regimes remain parallel regimes'.[83]

The unwillingness of tribunals to preclude their own jurisdiction under the terms of Section 1 has been equally evident in relation to Article 283 (duty to exchange views). As Bankes attests, UNCLOS courts and tribunals have 'not been very demanding as to the nature of such an exchange and have found that Article 283 is easily satisfied'.[84] Although respondent States have frequently alleged a failure to adequately exchange views prior to a dispute, to date this argument has never been accepted as a means to deny jurisdiction in practice.[85] This obligation was given a good deal of consideration in the *Chagos MPA* case, which ultimately seems to make clear that the kind of views exchanged do not need to invoke the substance of the dispute, only the procedure by which it might be addressed.[86] This position was adopted also in *South China Sea*, which further confirmed that an exchange does not require an agreement,[87] as well as in the provisional measures award in *Arctic Sunrise*, which seemed to accept a one-sided diplomatic note as sufficient to satisfy the terms of Article 283.[88] As such, it is hard to disagree with Talmon, who views it as 'highly unlikely that the provision will ever act as a procedural bar to … compulsory dispute settlement'.[89]

5.5 FINDING ITS FEET OR OVERSTEPPING THE MARK? DETERMINING THE SUBJECT MATTER OF UNCLOS DISPUTES

From the preceding analysis it is apparent that there has been a tendency to 'read down' the procedural obligations in Section 1 to remove fetters to jurisdiction.[90] More alarming, perhaps, are broader concerns that UNCLOS courts and tribunals are essentially expanding their jurisdiction by hearing and

82 *South China Sea* (Jurisdiction/Admissibility), at para. 291.
83 Ibid., para. 285.
84 Bankes, 'Applicability of section 2', p. 259. Similarly, Naldi and Magliveras find that this obligation is not 'unduly burdensome'. Gino Naldi and Konstantinos Magliveras, 'Jurisdictional aspects of dispute settlement under the UN Convention on the Law of the Sea: Some recent developments' (2018) 16 NZYIL 207–40 at 226.
85 Ibid., and Karaman, *Dispute Resolution*, p. 126.
86 *Chagos MPA* (Final Award), para. 378.
87 *South China Sea* (Jurisdiction/Admissibility), paras 333, 342–43.
88 *The 'Arctic Sunrise' Case (Kingdom of the Netherlands* v. *Russian Federation)*, Provisional Measures (Order of 22 November 2013), ITLOS Reports 2013, p. 230 at paras 151–53.
89 Talmon, 'Chagos Marine Protected Area Arbitration', p. 932.
90 Ibid., pp. 930, 948.

ruling on matters that more rightfully fall outside of UNCLOS altogether. Underlying this concern are the terms of the main compromissory clause in UNCLOS, Article 286, which, in tandem with Article 288, focuses jurisdiction *rationae materiae* on 'any dispute concerning the interpretation or application of this Convention'. In addition, although not strictly a provision on jurisdiction as such, Article 293(1) defines the applicable law to be taken into account as UNCLOS as well as 'other rules of international law not incompatible with [UNCLOS]'. Whilst the issue of subject matter jurisdiction and applicable law thus feed into each other, technically the two issues should be kept conceptually and chronologically distinct. It is 'only after an international court has found itself competent ... [that it] may ... consider the applicable law to resolve the dispute'.[91]

At the heart of recent jurisdictional concerns, then, is the extent to which UNCLOS courts and tribunals can concern themselves with, apply, or ultimately rule upon the principles of law which technically fall outside of the Convention. Reading these provisions together certainly invites ambiguity in this respect. The beginnings of an answer might start with the useful distinction given by Marotti between references to 'secondary', systemic rules – the law of treaties, the law of international responsibility, and so on – which are applied by most international courts without controversy, and references to other substantive, 'primary' rules of international law, which could well be more problematic.[92] Breaking this second category down further, a court might apply other primary rules as interpretative aids to give full effect to law-of-the-sea provisions, which may also often pass without controversy (especially given the broad, umbrella nature of UNCLOS). However, in certain cases – for example, where the rules on 'hot pursuit' or the arrest of ships are interpreted in accordance with the law on the use of force[93] – there may well be an accusation that Article 293(1) is actually allowing a tribunal to expand its jurisdiction by essentially *ruling* on extraneous questions.[94] A further, perhaps more troubling way in which other rules enter into consideration,

91 Fabian Simon Eichberger, 'Give a court an inch and it will take a yard? The exercise of jurisdiction over incidental issues' (2021) 81 ZaöRV 235–64 at 243.

92 Loris Marotti, 'A satisfactory answer? The Enrica Lexie Award and the jurisdiction over incidental questions' (2020) 30 Ital YB Int'l L 191–208 at 196–97.

93 See, e.g., *M/V 'Saiga' (No. 2)*, para. 155.

94 An accusation that has been levelled at the judgment in *M/V 'Saiga' (No. 2)*, ibid., which seemed to go beyond considering the law on the use of force, but making a substantive determination of an unlawful use of force. See Tzeng, 'Jurisdiction and applicable law', pp. 243–44, and Loris Marotti, 'Between consent and effectiveness: Incidental determinations and the expansion of the jurisdiction of UNCLOS tribunals', in Angela Del Vecchio and Roberto Virzo (eds.), *Interpretations of the United Nations Convention on the Law of the Sea by*

though, is as so-called incidental or ancillary issues that arise as part of broader, multifaceted disputes. The concern here, increasingly, is that the incidental issue is actually the 'real' issue at the heart of the dispute.[95] It is in these cases that Boyle's predictions about careful formulation of disputes, or 'salami-slicing' the dispute to fit, seem to have most resonance.

Here, three recent cases warrant further attention. The first is the *Chagos MPA* case,[96] which was mentioned briefly above in relation to its treatment of Article 283. It centred on the UK's declaration of a marine protected area (MPA) around the Chagos archipelago, which it administers as the British Indian Ocean Territory. Prior to Mauritius gaining independence in 1968, Mauritian authorities had concluded an agreement with the UK which gave their consent to the separation of Chagos, in the form of the 1965 'Lancaster House Undertakings' (LHU). The undertakings included promises that the UK would, inter alia, return the archipelago to Mauritius when no longer needed for defence purposes, continue to secure local fishing rights in the surrounding waters, and preserve Mauritian rights to any discovered natural resources. Following the declaration of the MPA, over which it had been only minimally consulted, Mauritius commenced arbitration proceedings under Part XV, arguing four grounds:[97]

1. that the UK was not the coastal State entitled to declare an MPA;
2. that within the LHU, the UK had made certain commitments to Mauritius as the 'coastal State' (as understood in UNCLOS);
3. that the LHU also gave Mauritius rights in oil and mineral resources such that the UK could not frustrate its submission to the UN Commission on the Limits of the Continental Shelf (CLCS); and
4. that the UK's declaration of the MPA undermined Mauritius' fishing and related rights as granted under the LHU and guaranteed by UNCLOS as well as the 1995 Fish Stocks Agreement.[98]

The tribunal found – narrowly, by just three votes to two – that it lacked jurisdiction to hear Mauritius' first submission (which it understood as really

International Courts and Tribunals (Cham: Springer, 2019), pp. 386–88, who identifies at least four candidate cases where jurisdiction has been expanded in this way.

95 Marotti, 'A satisfactory answer?' p. 201.

96 *Chagos MPA* (Final Award).

97 Ibid., para. 158.

98 Agreement for the Implementation of the Provisions of the United Nations Convention on the Law of the Sea of 10 December 1982 Relating to the Conservation and Management of Straddling Fish Stocks and Highly Migratory Fish Stocks, New York, 4 August 1995, in force 11 December 2001, 2167 UNTS 88.

being a determination of sovereignty)[99] and therefore also the second claim which was essentially predicated on the first.[100] The third submission was deemed to not be in dispute by the time of the hearing, given that the UK had agreed to co-operate with Mauritius in a submission to the CLCS.[101] However, it unanimously decided that it did have jurisdiction to hear Mauritius' final submission[102] and, on that basis, found that in declaring the MPA, the UK had breached obligations arising under Articles 2(3), 56(2), and 194(4) of UNCLOS, as it had failed to pay sufficient regard to Mauritius' rights under the LHU.[103]

This narrow victory for Mauritius was surprising to some commentators, who thought that the case should have been entirely dismissed as a disguised sovereignty dispute,[104] or that, to the extent that fisheries rights were implicated, it would be excluded anyway under Article 297.[105] However, by framing the dispute as one, at least partly, related to environmental obligations (and with it due regard for the rights of others), and from reading Article 297 as a jurisdiction affirming provision for such disputes, the tribunal was able to bring the fourth submission back in for review.[106] More worrying for some, however, was the way in which this ruling was framed and constructed. Rather than the applicable law provision in Article 293(1), the tribunal used the more specific references to 'other rules of international law' in Article 2(3) of UNCLOS (rights in territorial waters), the 'due regard' provisions in Article 56(2) (concerning the EEZ), and the 'unjustifiable interference' reference in Article 194(4) (protection of the marine environment), to uphold Mauritius' rights arising under the LHU. Whilst it claimed it could only have regard to the rules of general international law and not specific obligations under the LHU, those obligations were nonetheless held to bind the UK on the basis of its good faith obligation under general international law.[107] As Parlett argues, what appears to be a restrictive interpretation of those provisions actually significantly expands the tribunal's scope of jurisdiction in practice.[108] Talmon, also, is particularly critical of the decision, arguing that the terms

[99] *Chagos MPA* (Final Award), para. 212.
[100] Ibid., paras 229–30.
[101] Ibid., paras 349–50.
[102] Ibid., paras 304, 323.
[103] Ibid., paras 536, 541.
[104] See, e.g., Klein, 'Effectiveness of UNCLOS dispute settlement', pp. 361–62.
[105] Guilfoyle, 'Governing the oceans'.
[106] See the very thorough (and very critical) overview of Talmon, 'Chagos Marine Protected Area Arbitration', in this regard.
[107] Ibid., paras 517, 520.
[108] Parlett, 'Beyond the four corners', p. 295.

of the LHU were essentially smuggled back into UNLCOS 'through the back door of a balancing exercise'.[109]

Although the tribunal refused to countenance review of the broader sovereignty question under the first two submissions, Nguyen also points to a number of problems in the reasoning deployed by the majority verdict.[110] Whilst not ruling out categorically 'that in some instances a minor issue of territorial sovereignty could indeed be ancillary to a dispute concerning the interpretation or application of the Convention',[111] the majority saw the sovereignty question as the main issue at stake in this instance, centrally implicated in the question of coastal State rights. However, their reasoning on this point is far from convincing. The ruling explicitly refers to the ICJ's contention in the *Fisheries Jurisdiction* case that the determination of the character of a dispute requires it to follow how the applicants themselves structure their claims,[112] and endorses the reasoning in the *Nuclear Tests* decision,[113] where the ICJ argued that it must seek to isolate the 'real issue in the case and to identify the object of the claim'.[114] Putting aside for now how appropriate these authorities are as determinants of subject matter jurisdiction – I will come back to this shortly – the more immediate problem is that they are not really applied in a convincing way. Instead, the majority claim they must 'evaluate where the relative weight of the dispute lies',[115] which – as Nguyen suggests, echoing the concerns of the dissenting judges in the minority[116] – essentially sidelines how Mauritius actually presented its own claim and thereby undermines the precedents cited as justification.[117] Instead, its actual determination is based on a somewhat vague and overly subjective weighting which, as we shall see, has been unconvincingly applied in later cases also.[118]

These concerns soon resurfaced, in fact, in the *South China Sea* case. The background to this dispute is by now well known, but the immediate legal

[109] Talmon, 'Chagos Marine Protected Area Arbitration', p. 940.

[110] Lan Ngoc Nguyen, 'The Chagos Marine Protected Area Arbitration: Has the scope of LOSC compulsory jurisdiction been clarified?' (2016) 31 Int J Mar Coast Law 120–43 at 124–35.

[111] *Chagos MPA* (Final Award), para. 221.

[112] *Fisheries Jurisdiction Case (Spain* v. *Canada)* (Judgment) [1998] ICJ Rep. 432 at para. 30.

[113] *Nuclear Tests (New Zealand* v. *France)* (Judgment) [1974] ICJ Rep. 457 at para. 30.

[114] *Chagos MPA* (Final Award), para. 208.

[115] Ibid., para. 211.

[116] *Chagos Marine Protected Area Arbitration (Mauritius* v. *United Kingdom)* (Dissenting and Concurring Opinion of Judges Kateka and Wolfrum of 18 March 2015) PCA Case No. 2011-03.

[117] Nguyen, 'Chagos Marine Protected Area Arbitration', pp. 130–32.

[118] See, e.g., Talmon, 'Chagos Marine Protected Area Arbitration'.

dispute arose as a response from the Philippines to China's *note verbale* sent to the UN Secretary-General in 2009, in which it claimed 'indisputable sovereignty over the islands in the South China Sea and the adjacent waters' and which included the now infamous 'nine-dash' line map.[119] The Philippines initiated arbitration in 2013, arguing a number of grounds including inter alia that China's maritime claims, based alternatively on 'historic rights' or the 'nine-dash line', were not permitted under UNCLOS and that many geographical features considered (fully entitled) 'islands' by China were either 'rocks' (as defined under Article 121(3)) or 'low-tide elevations' (as defined under Article 13), and thereby attracted no or fewer maritime entitlements. Importantly, the Philippines also stressed that it was not asking the tribunal to rule on territorial sovereignty, nor to delimit overlapping maritime boundaries. China refused to participate in proceedings, but published a position paper in 2014 in which it argued firmly against jurisdiction inter alia because it felt that the actual subject matter of the dispute concerned territorial sovereignty over the various maritime features and therefore, like *Chagos*, fell outside of the ambit of Part XV.[120]

The tribunal eventually upheld the vast majority of the Philippines' claims. At the jurisdiction and admissibility stage, it accepted that no determination of sovereignty was needed to rule on the claims put forward[121] and in doing so endorsed and followed the balancing exercise set out in *Chagos MPA*.[122] However, as Eichberger notes, in differentiating the dispute it also seems to further qualify that test, reasoning that the incidental issue – the determination of sovereignty – should not form a 'condition' of ruling on the merits of the claim, meaning that, if sovereignty is incidentally or implicitly determined as a 'consequence' of a ruling, it does not mean that the dispute is focused on that question.[123] This reorientation of cause and effect is deeply problematic for Klein, who argues that the Philippines position, as endorsed by the tribunal, artificially transforms the subject matter of the broader dispute, thus running 'against the fundamental nature of maritime space' and the oft-

[119] People's Republic of China, UN Doc. CML/17/2019, 7 May 2019, www.un.org/depts/los/clcs_new/submissions_files/mysvnm33_09/chn_2009re_mys_vnm_e.pdf (accessed 2 June 2022).

[120] People's Republic of China, 'Position Paper of the Government of the People's Republic of China on the Matter of Jurisdiction in the South China Sea Arbitration Initiated by the Republic of the Philippines', 7 December 2014, www.fmprc.gov.cn/nanhai/eng/snhwtlcwj_1/201606/t20160602_8527277.htm (accessed 2 June 2022).

[121] *South China Sea* (Jurisdiction/Admissibility), para. 153.

[122] Ibid., para. 150, citing the *Nuclear Tests* case.

[123] Eichberger, 'Give a court an inch', pp. 256–57.

reiterated principle that 'land dominates the sea' under international law.[124] In Klein's view, such a 'blinkered examination' of law-of-the-sea arguments thus 'has the potential to expand what disputes are resolved within the compulsory procedures of the LOSC dispute settlement regime'.[125] Furthermore, taking account of China's reservations under Article 298 with regard to maritime boundary disputes, the tribunal's findings on unlawful Chinese actions in the Philippines' EEZ were hardly capable of determination – as the tribunal acknowledged at the jurisdiction stage[126] – without making a determination on maritime entitlements (such as to thereby neutralise China's territorial claims).[127]

Whether or not one fully agrees with Klein's criticism, the inconsistencies in and unconvincing aspects of the tribunal's reasoning, like *Chagos*, add to a sense of uncertainty surrounding the proper bounds of UNCLOS jurisdiction. These concerns have not been assuaged in the recent *Enrica Lexie* award.[128] The case concerned a long-running legal and diplomatic dispute between Italy and India. It followed the fatal shooting of two Indian fisherman on board the vessel *St Antony* by two Italian marines deployed as a vessel protection detachment on board the Italian-flagged *Enrica Lexie*. The incident took place within India's EEZ, and the *Enrica Lexie* was later intercepted by the Indian authorities approximately sixty nautical miles from its shoreline and ordered to port in Kochi, where the two marines were subsequently arrested and criminal proceedings commenced. Annex VII tribunal proceedings were initiated, however, following disagreement over applicable jurisdiction and the claimed immunity of the Italian marines. I have commented elsewhere on the somewhat troubling reading of high seas jurisdiction in the case,[129] but of concern here is the tribunal's claimed jurisdiction over the incidental immunity question. India had asserted that this was in fact the core of the dispute which should accordingly be declared inadmissible.[130] In response, the tribunal followed both *South China Sea* and *Chagos MPA* in declaring that it had

[124] Klein, 'Vicissitudes of dispute settlement', p. 346, citing inter alia *North Sea Continental Shelf (Federal Republic of Germany* v. *Denmark; Federal Republic of Germany* v. *Netherlands)* (Judgment) [1969] ICJ Rep. 3 at pp. 51–52.

[125] Ibid., p. 349.

[126] *South China Sea* (Jurisdiction/Admissibility), para. 157.

[127] Klein, 'Vicissitudes of dispute settlement', p. 355, referencing *South China Sea*, ibid.

[128] *Enrica Lexie* (Award).

[129] See Richard Collins, 'Outlaw Oceans' and 'Lawless Seas'? Revisiting the high seas regime under (and after) UNCLOS 1982', *forthcoming* in K. Siig, F. Billing, and B. Feldtmann (eds.), *UNCLOS as a System of Regulation: An Exploratory and Methodological Study* (Abingdon: Routledge, 2023).

[130] *Enrica Lexie* (Award), para. 226.

to isolate the 'real issue' in the case in order to properly 'identify the object of the claim'.[131] On this basis, however, it positioned the immunity issue as central to the jurisdictional dispute, thereby implicating a number of provisions under UNCLOS,[132] such that the case could be said to centrally concern 'the interpretation or application of the Convention'.[133]

Beyond the somewhat ambiguous nature of the balancing exercise deployed in this and the earlier cases, Lando and Oral point to a more fundamental problem with this line of reasoning.[134] The tribunal's method, although seemingly consistent with the two earlier cases, is nonetheless out of line with established international precedents for the determination of subject matter jurisdiction, especially the reasoning deployed by the ICJ in the *Oil Platforms* case.[135] In that case, the ICJ claimed the task was simply one of determining 'whether the violations of the [treaty in question] do or do not fall within the provisions of [that treaty] and whether, as a consequence, the dispute is one which the Court has jurisdiction *ratione materiae* to entertain'.[136] This approach has also been endorsed by ITLOS in both the *M/V 'Louisa'*[137] and *M/V 'Norstar'*[138] cases. At the same time, the test actually adopted by the Annex VII tribunals is one that does not relate at all to the question of subject matter jurisdiction.[139] Indeed, the characterisation questions in *Nuclear Tests* and *Fisheries Jurisdiction* were concerned solely with the resolution of specific substantive issues in each case, not the question of the court's jurisdiction.[140] As such, not only is the 'characterisation' approach unsupported by appropriate authority, but, as argued by Harris, there is also no compelling reason of principle to adopt it specifically in UNCLOS cases either.[141]

131 Ibid., para. 231.
132 Ibid., para. 243.
133 Ibid., para. 245.
134 Massimo Lando and Nilüfer Oral, 'Jurisdictional challenges and institutional novelties: Procedural developments in law of the sea dispute settlement in 2020' (2021) 20 LPICT 191–221 at 213–18.
135 *Oil Platforms (Islamic Republic of Iran* v. *United States of America)* (Preliminary Objections, Judgment) [1996] ICJ Rep. 13.
136 Ibid., para. 16.
137 *M/V 'Louisa' Case (Saint Vincent and the Grenadines* v. *Spain)* (Judgment of 28 May 2013) ITLOS Reports 2013, p. 4 at para. 99.
138 *M/V 'Norstar' Case (Panama* v. *Italy)* (Preliminary Objections, Judgment of 4 November 2016) ITLOS Reports 2016, p. 44 at para. 110.
139 Lando and Oral, 'Jurisdictional challenges', p. 214.
140 Callista Harris, 'Claims with an ulterior purpose: Characterising disputes concerning the "interpretation or application" of a treaty' (2019) 18 LPICT 279–99 at 291–92.
141 Ibid., p. 296.

Of perhaps broader concern in the *Enrica Lexie* case was the applicable law question, that is, whether the tribunal could appropriately rule on the immunity issue. The tribunal considered the argument that similar *renvoi* provisions to those in *Chagos MPA* allowed it to import the immunity issue, though dismissed this argument as the prosecution (and thus the claim of immunity) did not occur in the territorial sea or EEZ, but was commenced inshore.[142] Nevertheless, it did determine that it was necessary to rule on the issue as incidental to the broader jurisdictional dispute: 'While the Convention may not provide a basis for entertaining an independent immunity claim under general international law, the arbitral tribunal's competence extends to the determination of the issue of immunity of the Marines that *necessarily arises* as an incidental question in the application of the Convention.'[143] The problem with this reasoning appears to be the logic behind it. Whilst immunity might be *necessarily implicated*, that is not the same thing as saying that a *ruling on immunity is necessary* to determine the dispute. Accordingly, the tribunal's conclusion has been met with fierce criticism, especially from two dissenting judges in the case.[144] Lando and Oral also highlight how this finding seemingly departs from *Chagos*,[145] ignoring the necessity to ask whether the immunity question formed simply an 'integral part' of its determination of the broader jurisdictional dispute.[146] In that sense, not only did the tribunal just assume necessity, but it failed to engage the kind of weighting or balancing exercise advocated in the earlier cases.[147]

Taken together, then, the reasoning deployed in all three cases seems only to prompt rather than resolve questions as to the appropriate jurisdictional reach of Annex VII courts and tribunals. Still, it is too easy, and I think unhelpful, to respond to these concerns, as has been somewhat common, by simply advocating more judicial restraint,[148] or perhaps calling for a rebalancing of a concern for judicial effectiveness and the fundamental principle of consent.[149] For instance, Eichberger suggests that judges might be more consistent by deploying a two-pronged approach to the implicated issue

[142] *Enrica Lexie* (Award), para. 798.

[143] Ibid., para. 809.

[144] *Enrica Lexie* (Concurring and Dissenting Opinion – Dr Sreenivasa Rao Pemmaraju of 21 May 2020) and (Dissenting Opinion – Judge Patrick Robinson of 21 May 2020) PCA Case No. 2015-28.

[145] Lando and Oral, 'Jurisdictional challenges', p. 217, referencing *Chagos MPA* (Final Award), para. 220.

[146] *Enrica Lexie* (Award), para. 808.

[147] Eichberger, 'Give a court an inch', pp. 248–49.

[148] See, e.g., Klein, 'Vicissitudes of dispute settlement', pp. 361–63.

[149] Naldi and Magliveras, 'Jurisdictional aspects', p. 240.

question: first, a test of necessity (whether the resolution of the issue is needed in order to rule on the underlying law-of-the-sea issue), and second, a judgment on the weight of the issue being put forward for review: essentially, the more contentious it is in the dispute between the parties, the less likely they have implicitly consented to its resolution.[150] As Marotti suggests, however, judgments of seriousness are no less subjective or vague than other forms of weighting.[151]

Overall, it is hard not to feel that these kinds of exercises are just unhelpful distractions from the jurisdictional test that is actually required from UNCLOS courts and tribunals – as attested by Lando and Oral, as well as Harris, above – who must simply assess the arguments as formulated by the parties themselves to judge whether they are essentially concerned with interpreting and applying the Convention. To be sure, there will be no certainty and automaticity to the outcome of any such test. As noted by Guilfoyle, the negotiating history of the Convention reveals that few issues are clearly and centrally matters of interpretation and application of the Convention.[152] However, this does not absolve judges and arbitrators from the exercise of judgment on that question. Calls for deference or further balancing, particularly between consent and judicial effectiveness, are, I believe, entirely misplaced. Article 286, and the broader scheme of Part XV overall, already contains within it a consensual mandate and an attempt at balancing these concerns.[153] The rule of law necessarily calls for the exercise of jurisdiction, *and thus reasoned judgment from appointed decision-makers*, unless there are compelling and convincing reasons to decline to do so. However, it is by the standards of that very same principle that we can most appropriately determine the persuasiveness, cogency, coherence, and so on of those reasons. As I have argued elsewhere,[154] the international rule of law has an intrinsic instrumental value as a means by which we call for the restraint of the exercise of arbitrary public power, yet it also has a non-instrumental value in requiring that we do so in a way that accords with the principle of 'legality'. On this basis, we can thus see more clearly where the issue lies in cases such as *Enrica Lexie*, where the desire to assume jurisdiction and do justice to the dispute comes at the price of a coherent and ultimately persuasive application of the law: it tips the balance towards ends at the expense of means.

[150] Eichberger, 'Give a court an inch', p. 255.
[151] Marotti, 'A satisfactory answer?' pp. 205–6.
[152] Guilfoyle, 'Governing the oceans'.
[153] James Harrison, 'Defining disputes and characterizing claims: Subject-matter jurisdiction in Law of the Sea Convention litigation' (2017) 48 Ocean Dev & Int'l L 269–83 at 269.
[154] Collins, 'Two idea(l)s'.

5.6 CONCLUSION

Because of, and not despite, the fact that these cases have raised these concerns, one can see signs that UNCLOS dispute settlement is indeed coming of age. To be clear, there is much to be critical of in the cases just reviewed, but it is, I believe, a good thing that 'ITLOS and Annex VII Arbitral Tribunals are not reluctant to be pioneers in answering unprecedented and controversial questions of law'.[155] As noted right at the start of this chapter, if there was an intrinsic importance to dispute settlement in the overall 'constitutional' settlement of UNCLOS, it was not just to do justice between the parties, but to give effect, meaning, and application to matters that were left partially unsaid, unresolved, or else otherwise ambiguous. As John Merrills would have gladly endorsed, courts and tribunals tasked with jurisdiction under the Convention were always going to play a role in creatively developing the law in a 'living instrument' such as UNCLOS.[156] They cannot and should not absolve themselves of their responsibility in this respect. The rule of law demands this from them. However, that same value also calls for reasoned, principled, coherent, and consistent reasoning and justification, and the likely future success of the system will surely depend on courts' and tribunals' performance in this regard. Certainly, there will be occasions where it is right for tribunals to reject jurisdiction where the system is clearly being 'gamed' for strategic advantage but, as we have seen, the system as constructed invites States to size disputes to fit in order to bring their actions to resolution. This is no naïve call for judicial restraint, then, especially not at a time when many powerful States seem increasingly inclined to seek to undermine the legitimacy of international dispute settlement.[157] It is, however, a recognition that the best way to advance dispute settlement's contribution to international social ordering is by adhering to the kinds of standards and principles that will ultimately buttress its authority and support its longevity to fulfil the task assigned to it.[158]

[155] Lan Ngoc Nguyen, 'The UNCLOS dispute settlement system: What role can it play in resolving maritime disputes in Asia?' (2018) 8 Asian JIL 91–115 at 110.

[156] See, e.g., John Merrills, 'The place of international litigation in international law', in Natalie Klein (ed.), *Litigating International Law Disputes: Weighing the Options* (Cambridge: Cambridge University Press, 2014), p. 15.

[157] Campbell McLachlan, 'The assault on international adjudication and the limits of withdrawal' (2019) 68 ICLQ 499–537.

[158] In other words, it must function as 'a device which gives formal and institutional expression to the influence of reasoned argument in human affairs'. See Lon L. Fuller and Kenneth I. Winston, 'The forms and limits of adjudication' (1978) 92 Harv L Rev 353–409 at 366.

6

Legitimacy in Settlement of Disputes in International Environmental Law: From Classical to Non-compliance Procedures

MALGOSIA FITZMAURICE

6.1 INTRODUCTION

This chapter presents the question of legitimacy relating to the settlement of environmental disputes. It also deals with the issue of classical settlement of environmental disputes and the fairly new and still evolving phenomenon of so-called non-compliance procedures (NCPs), which are an element of the legal structure of Multilateral Environmental Agreements (MEAs). These procedures do not belong to *sensu stricto* settlement of disputes, but their object and purpose is to deal with non-compliance by the parties to MEAs, which is determined by the Conferences of the Parties/Meetings of the Parties (COPs/MOPs). The problem of legitimacy in the settlement of disputes and NCPs is closely connected with the general question of consent to be bound in the law of treaties. Its relevance is particularly evident in the case of NCPs. As will be explained, the question has arisen about the extent of consent by State parties to MEAs in cases of the determination of non-compliance by COPs/MOPs. It can be mentioned that COPs/MOPs are also, to a certain extent, empowered to fill in the gaps in MEAs through their law-making activities, which is an equally contentious issue triggering the legitimacy debate (exceeding, however, the framework of this chapter).

6.2 PEACEFUL SETTLEMENT OF ENVIRONMENTAL DISPUTES AND THEIR LEGITIMACY

The judicial settlement of environmental disputes has mostly been focused on the International Court of Justice (ICJ) and the International Tribunal for the Law of the Sea (ITLOS). It may be said that there have been certain environmental considerations in the jurisprudence of the World Trade Organization, but essentially analysed from the point of view of a limitation to the liberalisation of trade.[1] The European Court of Human Rights (ECtHR) dealt with a number of cases where environmental harm was interfering with private and family lives (Article 8 of the European Convention on Human Rights) and endangered the right to life (Article 2 of the Convention). However, the limitations imposed on invoking such a harm in cases essentially involving breaches of human rights, as well as the firm statement of the court that the right to a clean environment does not exist in the catalogue of the rights protected by the Convention, strictly narrow the jurisdiction of the European Court as a forum for the settlement of environmental disputes.[2] There has been some support in the literature for the view that environmental disputes are amenable to judicial settlement partly due to 'hardening' of the fabric of international environmental law.[3] This view is not entirely shared by the author of this chapter. The existing jurisprudence of international courts and tribunals admittedly has relied to some extent on the principles of international environmental law and, in some instances, even clarified and developed them. It is, however, an uncontested fact that international courts and tribunals (in particular the ICJ) prefer to invoke well-tested principles of

[1] See, e.g., WTO, 'DS26: European communities – Measures concerning meat and meat products (hormones), AB-1997-4, Report', www.wto.org/english/tratop_e/dispu_e/hormab.pdf (accessed 11 October 2020); WTO, 'DS291: European communities – Measures affecting the approval and marketing of biotech products', www.wto.org/english/tratop_e/dispu_e/cases_e/ds291_e.htm (accessed 11 October 2020).

[2] Tim Stephens, *International Courts and Environmental Protection* (Cambridge: Cambridge University Press, 2009); Tim Stephens, 'The settlement of disputes in international environmental law', in Shawkat Alamet et al. (eds.), *Routledge Handbook of International Environmental Law* (London: Routledge, 2013), p. 175; Tim Stephens, 'International environmental disputes: To sue or not to sue?', in Natalie Klein (ed.), *Litigating International Law Disputes: Weighing the Options* (Cambridge: Cambridge University Press, 2014), p. 284; Alan Boyle and James Harrison, 'Judicial settlement of international environmental disputes', (2013) 4 J Int Disput Settl 245–76 at 245; James Harrison, 'Reflections on the role of international courts and tribunals in the settlement of environmental disputes and the development of international environmental law' (2013) 29 JEL 501–14 at 501; James Harrison, 'Significant international environmental law cases: 2017–18' (2018) 30 J Environ Law 527–41; Alan Boyle, 'Environmental dispute settlement', in *Max Planck Encyclopedia of International Law* (Oxford: Oxford University Press, 2012), vol. 3, p. 561; Stewart Bruce, 'The project for an international environmental court', in Christian Tomuschat et al. (eds.), *Conciliation in International Law* (Leiden: Brill/Nijhoff, 2016), p. 133; Malgosia Fitzmaurice, 'The International Court of Justice and international environmental law', in Christian Tams and James Sloane (eds.), *The Development of International Law by the International Court of Justice* (Oxford: Oxford University Press, 2013), p. 353; Duncan French, 'Environmental dispute settlement: The first (hesitant) signs of spring?' (2006) 19 Hague YB Int'l L 3–32 at 3; Yoshifumi Tanaka, *The Peaceful Settlement of International Disputes* (Cambridge: Cambridge University Press, 2018), p. 65.

[3] Stephens, 'Settlements of disputes', pp. 175–76.

general international law; and attempts to venture into the realm of pure international environmental law are often subject to severe criticism. Such an example is the judgment on compensation for environmental damage in the *Nicaragua/Costa Rica* cases in which the ICJ made some important pronouncements, but the court has not entirely grasped the particularities of international environmental law.[4] It was stated that 'overall, the judgment demonstrates that the law on this topic may not be completely settled and there is plenty to argue about in future cases'.[5] The court was much more comfortable in relying on the classical *Chorzow Factory* jurisprudence and applying it to international environmental law according to which a responsible State has to 'wipe out all consequences of a wrongful act'.[6] Such an approach to a specialist area of international law is understandable in view of the ICJ being a general court of international law and therefore approaching non-classical fields of international law through the lens of general international law principles, and due to the fact that the cases before the ICJ constitute a nexus of general international law and international environmental law. The present author would like to reiterate, however, that this is not to say that the court has not made several very significant pronouncements concerning, for example, environmental impact assessments in the *Pulp Mills* case[7] and in the above-mentioned 2015 *Nicaragua/Costa Rica* cases.[8] However, the expanding realm of international environmental law requires

4 *Certain Activities Carried Out by Nicaragua in the Border Area (Costa Rica* v. *Nicaragua)* (Compensation, Judgment) [2018] ICJ Rep. 1.

5 Harrison, 'Significant cases', pp. 530–31. See also critical comments by Diane Desierto, 'Environmental damages, environmental reparations, and the right to a healthy environment: The ICJ Compensation Judgment in *Costa Rica v. Nicaragua* and the IACtHR Advisory Opinion on marine protection for the Greater Caribbean', *EJIL: Talk!*, 14 February 2018, www.ejiltalk.org/environmental-damages-environmental-reparations-and-the-right-to-a-healthy-environment-the-icj-compensation-judgment-in-costa-rica-v-nicaragua-and-the-iacthr-advisory-opinion-on-marine-protection (accessed 11 October 2020).

6 *Case Concerning the Factory at Chorzow (Germany* v. *Poland)* (Merits) [1928] PCIJ Rep. Series A No. 9 at 47.

7 *Pulp Mills on the River Uruguay (Argentina* v. *Uruguay)* [2010] ICJ Rep. 14. The court declared that an EIA is required 'where there is a risk that the proposed industrial activity may have a significant adverse impact in a transboundary context, in particular, on a shared resource' (para. 204) and that 'the Court also considers that an environmental impact assessment must be conducted prior to the implementation of a project. Moreover, once operations have started and, where necessary, throughout the life of the project, continuous monitoring of its effects on the environment shall be undertaken' (para. 205). The court also stated that a conduct of the EIA is a requirement of customary international law.

8 *Certain Activities Carried Out by Nicaragua in the Border Area (Costa Rica* v. *Nicaragua) and Construction of a Road in Costa Rica along the San Juan River (Nicaragua* v. *Costa Rica)* [2015] ICJ Rep. 665.

more in-depth specialist studies and analyses, which cannot be expected from a general court of international law.[9] At this juncture, the *Whaling in Antarctic* case may be recalled. This case was an example of the court tackling technical issues, but not all judges were convinced of the appropriateness of such an approach. Judge Yusuf (the president of the court) stated:

> It is a pity that instead of such a legal assessment, the Court has engaged in an evaluation of the design and implementation of the programme and their reasonableness in relation to its objectives, a task that normally falls within the competence of the Scientific Committee of the IWC, which is scheduled to undertake an overall review of the JARPA II programme in 2014.[10]

However, there are views that regard the generality of the ICJ as an asset in adjudicating all kinds of disputes, including environmental. Bruce, for example, asserts that 'the ICJ with its unlimited competence over international law matters, is the most obvious forum to hear environmental disputes'.[11] However, he admits that the 1993 ICJ Chamber of Environmental Matters was never used and closed permanently in 2006.[12] That would prove the point that the ICJ's role is to remain the general court of law, dealing with environmental law as one of the fields of international law, but not to be expected to develop it in a systematic and in-depth manner. It was argued persuasively that the difficulties of adjudging environmental disputes are the definitional problem of what constitutes such a dispute and the search for finding an adequate jurisdictional basis.[13] One of the most widely submitted and obvious arguments is that the majority of environmental disputes involve many other legal issues apart from environmental law,[14] of which the best example is the *Gabčikovo-Nagymaros* case, where the legal questions concerning the environment, the law of treaties, and the law of State responsibility are linked together in a Gordian knot.[15]

9 See critique of the judgment in Diane Desierto, 'Evidence but not empiricism? Environmental impact assessments at the International Court of Justice in *Certain Activities Carried Out by Nicaragua in the Border Area (Costa Rica v. Nicaragua) and Construction of a Road in Costa Rica along the San Juan River* (*Nicaragua v. Costa Rica*)', *EJIL: Talk!*, 26 February 2016, www.ejiltalk.org/evidence-but-not-empiricism-environmental-impact-assessments-at-the-international-court-of-justice-in-certain-activities-carried-out-by-nicaragua-in-the-border-area-costa-rica-v-nicaragua-and-con (accessed 11 October 2020).

10 *Whaling in the Antarctic (Australia* v. *Japan: New Zealand Intervening)* [2014] ICJ Rep. 226, Dissenting Opinion of Judge Yusuf at 404, para. 61.

11 Bruce, 'International environmental court', p. 137.

12 Ibid.

13 Boyle and Harrison, 'Judicial settlement', pp. 247–50, 250–55.

14 Ibid., p. 249.

15 *Gabčikovo-Nagymaros Project (Hungary v. Slovakia)* [1997] ICJ Rep 7.

It may be suggested, however, that more specialist courts and tribunals whose areas of adjudication are somewhat akin to international environmental law have contributed in a more significant way to the development of this field. Such an example may be given in relation to the jurisprudence of the ITLOS that has crystallised certain fundamental principles of international environmental law, in particular the Seabed Disputes Chamber of the ITLOS *Advisory Opinion on the Responsibilities of States with Respect to Seabed Mining* under Part XI of the 1982 United Nations Convention on the Law of the Sea (UNCLOS).[16] In this Advisory Opinion, the court has further developed the notions of the precautionary principle, the environmental impact assessment, due diligence, and the ensuing responsibilities of States in relation to these principles.

International arbitration practice has contributed, to a certain extent, to the development and consolidation of the principles of international environmental law. The *Trail Smelter* arbitration[17] has, it may be said, originated international environmental law. The *Iron Rhine* arbitration[18] and the *South China Sea* arbitration[19] have evolved, to a certain extent, the underlying principles of environmental law, such as sustainable development and the precautionary principle, the due diligence principle, and the principles of protection of marine species. However, overall there are very few examples of such arbitrations, and accordingly their input in the evolution of international environmental law is not particularly significant.

Finally, diplomatic means of settlement of disputes must be mentioned. Negotiations appear to be the means of settlement of disputes to which States have resource most frequently. Negotiations can be conducted at different stages, including the stage when the dispute has not been fully crystallised, as a means of avoiding it.[20] Mediation, conciliation, and good offices are less popular means. MEAs often include an obligation to consult (also a part of the composite obligation of environmental impact assessment), which is considered by some authors to be coterminous with negotiations.[21] However, in some of the agreements, 'consultation' is listed as a separate form

[16] *Responsibilities and Obligations of States Sponsoring Persons and Entities with Respect to Activities in the Area* (Advisory Opinion of 1 February 2011) ITLOS Reports 2011, p. 10.

[17] *Trail Smelter Case (United States* v. *Canada)* (1952) 3 RIAA 1905.

[18] *Iron Rhine Arbitration (Belgium* v. *Netherlands)* PCA Case No. 2003-2.

[19] *South China Sea Arbitration (Philippines* v. *China)* PCA Case No. 2013-19.

[20] Natalie Klein, 'Settlement of international environmental law disputes', in Malgosia Fitzmaurice et al. (eds.), *Research Handbook of International Environmental Law* (Cheltenham: Edward Elgar, 2010), p. 383.

[21] Stephens, 'Settlements of disputes', p. 181.

from negotiation, thus indicating that these institutions are not the same.[22] The example of the Non-navigational Uses Convention indicates that consultations are treated as a first step, and if they fail, negotiations should start. It may be noted that 'consultations' as a means for peaceful settlement of disputes are not included in Article 33 of the UN Charter. The classical case, where consultations were accorded an important role, is the *Lac Lanoux Case* arbitration.[23]

MEAs, in relation to the clauses on settlement of disputes, adopt a so-called integrated approach which combines both diplomatic means, such as negotiation/consultation, mediation/good offices, and conciliation (non-binding), and legal means, such as arbitration or judicial settlement (binding), depending on the common agreement of the parties to the dispute to submit it to a relevant organisation. Such an example is Article 11 of the Vienna Convention on the Protection of the Ozone Layer setting up the mechanisms of settlement of disputes.[24]

[22] E.g., Art 17 of the Convention on Non-navigational Uses of International Watercourses, New York, 21 May 1997, in force 17 August 2014, UNGA Res. 51/229 states as follows: 'Consultations and Negotiations Concerning Planned Measures'.

[23] *Lac Lanoux Case (France* v. *Spain)* (1957) 12 RIAA 285.

[24] Vienna Convention on the Protection of the Ozone Layer, Vienna, 22 March 1985, in force 22 September 1988 1513 UNTS 323; (1987) 26 ILM 152, Art 11:

'1. In the event of a dispute between Parties concerning the interpretation or application of this Convention, the parties concerned shall seek solution by negotiation.

2. If the parties concerned cannot reach agreement by negotiation, they may jointly seek the good offices of, or request mediation by, a third party.

3. When ratifying, accepting, approving or acceding to this Convention, or at any time thereafter, a State or regional economic integration organization may declare in writing to the Depositary that for a dispute not resolved in accordance with paragraph 1 or paragraph 2 above, it accepts one or both of the following means of dispute settlement as compulsory:

(a) Arbitration in accordance with procedures to be adopted by the Conference of the Parties at its first ordinary meeting;

(b) Submission of the dispute to the International Court of Justice.

4. If the parties have not, in accordance with paragraph 3 above, accepted the same or any procedure, the dispute shall be submitted to conciliation in accordance with paragraph 5 below unless the parties otherwise agree.

5. A conciliation commission shall be created upon the request of one of the parties to the dispute. The commission shall be composed of an equal number of members appointed by each party concerned and a chairman chosen jointly by the members appointed by each party. The commission shall render a final and recommendatory award, which the parties shall consider in good faith.

6. The provisions of this Article shall apply with respect to any protocol except as provided in the protocol concerned.'

The same mechanism is applicable to the Montreal Protocol on Substances That Deplete the Ozone Layer, Montreal, 16 September 1987, in force 1 January 1989, 1522 UNTS 3.

There have been some contentious issues in international arbitral proceedings concerning their legality. These issues surfaced in the *South China Sea* arbitration, which was initiated on the basis of Article 287 of and Annex VII to the UNCLOS. The Chinese scholars have emphasised the initiation of arbitral proceedings against China by the Philippines in relation to matters which, they argued, were excluded from the compulsory jurisdiction of the arbitral tribunal by China, thus breaching the principle of consent.[25] Such questions of legality are rare, and the majority of arbitral proceedings in environmental matters, such as the *Trail Smelter* and *Lac Lanoux* arbitrations, which were both based on special agreements, have not resulted in challenges to legality.

This section indicates that classical mechanisms of dispute settlement do not pose any questions of legitimacy. They are all based on the consent of parties to the dispute according to classical international law. The settlement-of-disputes clauses included in MEAs indicate that States favour 'soft' diplomatic means (non-binding), and that States can have recourse to legal (binding) means only on the basis of a special declaration. Such an example is the above-mentioned 1997 Convention on Non-navigational Uses of International Watercourses.[26] The consent of States, which is necessary for submitting a dispute to be resolved by a binding decision, is clear evidence

[25] Chinese Society of International Law, 'The South China Sea Arbitration Awards: A critical study' (2018) 17 Chin J Int Law 207–748 at 249.

[26] Art 33 of the Convention on Non-navigational Uses of International Watercourses:
'Settlement of Disputes

1. In the event of a dispute between two or more parties concerning the interpretation or application of the present Convention, the parties concerned shall, in the absence of an applicable agreement between them, seek a settlement of the dispute by peaceful means in accordance with the following provisions.

2. If the parties concerned cannot reach agreement by negotiation requested by one of them, they may jointly seek the good offices of, or request mediation or conciliation by, a third party, or make use, as appropriate, of any joint watercourse institutions that may have been established by them or agree to submit the dispute to arbitration or to the International Court of Justice.

3. Subject to the operation of paragraph 10, if after six months from the time of the request for negotiations referred to in paragraph 2, the parties concerned have not been able to settle their dispute through negotiation or any other means referred to in paragraph 2, the dispute shall be submitted, at the request of any of the parties to the dispute, to impartial fact-finding in accordance with paragraphs 4 to 9, unless the parties otherwise agree.

4. A Fact-finding Commission shall be established, composed of one member nominated by each party concerned and in addition a member not having the nationality of any of the parties concerned chosen by the nominated members who shall serve as Chairman.

5. If the members nominated by the parties are unable to agree on a Chairman within three months of the request for the establishment of the Commission, any party concerned may request the Secretary-General of the United Nations to appoint the Chairman who shall not

that States exercise total control over classical means of settlement of environmental disputes. Regrettably, legal (binding) mechanisms of dispute resolution in MEAs were never used. Thus far, environmental disputes have been brought before international courts and tribunals on the basis of different mechanisms than those included in MEAs.

Yet, the protection of the environment requires a multilateral action from States which have a common interest in its preservation. Therefore, the classical bilateralism of international disputes is not suitable in environmental disputes. In this respect, the case which merits mentioning is the *Whaling in the Antarctic* case. This case was brought before the ICJ by Australia (New Zealand intervening) on behalf of all parties to the International Convention for the Regulation of Whaling (*erga omnes parties*),[27] reflecting Article 48(1)(a) of the ILC Articles on the Responsibility of States for Internationally Wrongful Acts (ARSIWA), which refer to obligations owed to a group of States. However, it may be doubted that there will be many more similar cases brought on this

have the nationality of any of the parties to the dispute or of any riparian State of the watercourse concerned. If one of the parties fails to nominate a member within three months of the initial request pursuant to paragraph 3, any other party concerned may request the Secretary-General of the United Nations to appoint a person who shall not have the nationality of any of the parties to the dispute or of any riparian State of the watercourse concerned. The person so appointed shall constitute a single-member Commission . . .

10. When ratifying, accepting, approving or acceding to the present Convention, or at any time thereafter, a party which is not a regional economic integration organization may declare in a written instrument submitted to the depositary that, in respect of any dispute not resolved in accordance with paragraph 2, it recognizes as compulsory ipso facto, and without special agreement in relation to any party accepting the same obligation:

(a) Submission of the dispute to the International Court of Justice; and/or

(b) Arbitration by an arbitral tribunal established and operating, unless the parties to the dispute otherwise agreed, in accordance with the procedure laid down.'

27 A classical case in this respect is *Questions Relating to the Obligation to Prosecute or Extradite (Belgium v. Senegal)* [2012] ICJ Rep. 422, where the court said: 'The States parties to the Convention have a common interest to ensure, in view of their shared values, that acts of torture are prevented and that, if they occur, their authors do not enjoy impunity. The obligations of a State party to conduct a preliminary inquiry into the facts and to submit the case to its competent authorities for prosecution are triggered by the presence of the alleged offender in its territory, regardless of the nationality of the offender or the victims, or of the place where the alleged offences occurred. All the other States parties have a common interest in compliance with these obligations by the State in whose territory the alleged offender is present. That common interest implies that the obligations in question are owed by any State party to all the other States parties to the Convention. All the States parties "have a legal interest" in the protection of the rights involved (*Barcelona Traction, Light and Power Company, Limited*, Judgment, I.C.J. Reports 1970, p. 32, para. 33). These obligations may be defined as "obligations *erga omnes partes*" in the sense that each State party has an interest in compliance with them in any given case' (para. 68).

basis because the *Whaling in the Antarctic* case has already proved to be controversial regarding its jurisdictional aspect.[28]

6.3 CONFERENCES (MEETINGS) OF THE PARTIES AND THEIR LEGITIMACY

This section of the chapter deals with an intriguing phenomenon, namely the role of COPs and MOPs[29] in relation to treaties which have established them[30] and their international law-making function. There is a sizeable body of literature on this subject, but there is no particular consent regarding the legal basis of their functions and the normative content of their decisions. The legitimacy of their law-making (or perhaps *quasi* law-making) character is also much debated.[31] There is a plethora of bodies established by various multilateral treaties, whose functions go beyond just managing the treaty regime. It may be said, however, that it was the advent of MEAs, in particular, which initiated a very fertile legal (if inconclusive) discourse on the nature of their functions. The phenomenon of COPs is relatively recent. MEAs were

28 Hironobu Sakai, 'After *Whaling in the Antarctic* judgment: Its lessons and prospects from a Japanese perspective', in Malgosia Fitzmaurice and Dai Tamada (eds.), *Whaling in the Antarctic: Significance and Implications of the ICJ Judgment* (Leiden: Brill/Nijhoff, 2015), p. 308.

29 The Conferences of the Parties and Meetings of the Parties will be referred to in this chapter under one name of Conferences of the Parties.

30 In this chapter, the terminology used will be 'Conference of the Parties' to cover also the 'Meeting of the Parties', as their functions and legal problems involved are coterminous.

31 See, e.g., Jutta Brunnée, 'COPing with consent: Law-making under multilateral environmental agreements' (2002) 15 LJIL 1–52, 16; Alan E. Boyle, 'Saving the world? Implementation and enforcement of international environmental law through international institutions' (1991) 3 JEL 229–45 at 229, 235; Robin R. Churchill and Geir Ulfstein, 'Autonomous institutional arrangements in multilateral environmental agreements: A little-noticed phenomenon in international law' (2000) 94 AJIL 623–59 at 623, 636–42; Annecoos Wiersema, 'The new international law-makers? Conferences of the Parties to multilateral environmental agreements' (2009) 31 Mich J Intl L 231–87 at 231; T. Gehring, 'Treaty-making and treaty evolution', in Daniel Bodansky, Jutta Brunnee, and Ellen Hey (eds.), *The Oxford Handbook of International Environmental Law* (Oxford: Oxford University Press, 2007), pp. 467–97; Malgosia Fitzmaurice, 'Compliance with multilateral environmental agreements' (2009) 21 Natl Law Sch India Rev 1–38 at 1; Daniel Costelloe and Malgosia Fitzmaurice, 'Lawmaking by treaty: Conclusion of treaties and evolution of treaty regimes in practice', in Catherine M. Brölmann and Yannick Radi (eds.), *Research Handbook on the Theory and Practice of International Lawmaking* (Cheltenham: Edward Elgar, 2016), p. 111; Lukasz Gruszczynski, 'Tobacco and international trade: Recent activities of the FCTC Conference of the Parties' (2015) 49 J World Trade 665–84 at 665; Aurélie Tardieu, 'Les conférences des états parties' (2011) 57 Annuaire Français de Droit International 111–43 at 111.

established after the 1972 Stockholm Conference on the Human Environment. COPs were created to make the managing of MEAs more efficient and flexible, in contrast to previous very bureaucratic arrangements. Early MEAs exemplify the development of the functions of COPs. Their functions have evolved from the basic COP with limited powers such as the Ramsar Convention on Wetlands of International Importance. The original Article 6 of the Convention provided that the COP would 'as the necessity arises, convene Conferences on the Conservation of Wetlands and Waterfowl'. It also stated that the COP had an advisory character. This Article was amended in 1986 to create a Conference of the Contracting Parties to be tasked with the oversight and promotion of the implementation of the Convention. The reference to the advisory character of the Convention was deleted.

The 1972 London Convention on the Prevention of Marine Pollution by Dumping created a body (the Consultative Meeting of State Parties) that enjoyed more powers than the Ramsar Convention. This body, however, lacked any express authority to establish subsidiary bodies and had limited powers of supervision. The term 'Conference of the Parties' was first used in the 1973 Convention on International Trade in Endangered Species of Wild Fauna and Flora (CITES).

The powers of COPs vary, and there is no one standard common to all COPs. Camenzuli has observed one common trend, however: their powers are expanding, including, at present, in law-making. She has identified the following general powers: setting priorities and reviewing the implementation of the Convention, based on the reports submitted by governments; consolidating and analysing information from governments, NGOs, and individuals to make recommendations to the parties on the implementation of the Convention; making decisions necessary for promoting the effectiveness of the Convention; revising the Convention when necessary; and acting as a forum for discussing matters of importance.[32] As a rule, the powers of COPs are set out in a treaty. However, certain treaties are open-ended regarding the extent of the powers of COPs. For example, the London Convention provides that the COP is 'to consider any additional action that may be required' (Article XIV(4)(f)). The 1979 Convention on Long-Range Transboundary Air Pollution (CLRTAP)

[32] Louise Kathleen Camenzuli, 'The development of international environmental law at the Multilateral Environmental Agreements' Conference of the Parties and its validity', IUCN, 2007, www2.ecolex.org/server2neu.php/libcat/docs/LI/MON-085461.pdf (accessed 11 October 2020). See also Sebastian Rioseco, 'Conferences of the Parties Beyond International Environmental Law: How COPs Influence the Content and Implementation of their Parent Treaties' (2023) 36 LJIL 699–719.

provides that the COP can 'fulfil such other functions as may be appropriate under the provisions . . . of the Convention' (Article 10(2)(c)).[33] The Framework Convention on Climate Change (UNFCCC) states that the COP is to 'exercise such other functions as are required for the achievement of the objective of the Convention' (Article 7(2)).[34] The functions of COPs concern both external and internal matters of managing the Convention.[35]

Several functions of COPs can be identified in which they develop international law. They are the following: (1) the powers of decision on the amendment and modification of the convention and the adoption of new protocols, (2) decision-making and resolution powers, (3) supervisory powers, (4) interpretative powers, and (5) powers in respect of the establishment of non-compliance mechanisms.[36] As observed previously, there is no uniform and consistent approach to the legal nature of COPs in the legal debate. The most prevalent is that they are of a hybrid character, positioned between issue-specific diplomatic conferences and the permanent plenary bodies of international organisations, and that they exercise their functions at the interface of the law of treaties and the law of international organisations.[37] This is a very wide approach, lacking a more specific and detailed definition. Nolte, in his seminal work, *Treaties and Subsequent Practice*, stated that they are situated somewhere in-between a diplomatic conference and an international organisation.[38] They constitute useful *fora* for State parties to evolve treaty regimes and to co-operate. They are treaty bodies in the sense they are created based on treaties; they are not to be equated, however, with bodies which comprise independent experts or bodies with a limited membership.[39]

The extensive functions of MEAs are exemplary of the growing area of so-called creative legal engineering.[40] The powers of the organs based on MEAs, particularly COPs, gave rise to varying views as to the nature of the convention organs or bodies concerned in making decisions. They can be seen as free-standing entities, involving institutional arrangements or structures independent from the parties, an autonomous character, to a certain extent, with their

33 Convention on Long-Range Transboundary Air Pollution, Geneva, 13 November 1979, in force 16 March 1983, 1302 UNTS 217.

34 The United Nations Framework Convention on Climate Change, New York, 9 May 1992, in force 21 March 1994, 1771 UNTS 107, (1992) 31 ILM 849.

35 Camenzuli, 'Development of international environmental law', p. 7.

36 Ibid., p. 8.

37 E.g., Brunnée, 'COPing with consent'.

38 Georg Nolte, 'Subsequent agreements and subsequent practice of States outside of judicial and quasi-judicial proceedings', in Georg Nolte (ed.), *Treaties and Subsequent Practice* (Oxford: Oxford University Press, 2013), p. 365.

39 Ibid.

40 Rene Lefeber, 'Creative legal engineering' (2004) 13 LJIL 1–9.

own law-making or rule-making powers, or, at least, powers to generate or alter obligations of the parties between themselves and to formulate or operate mechanisms, such as compliance mechanisms, within the treaty regime which may have binding effects on the parties. Churchill and Ulfstein call such institutions 'autonomous institutional arrangements' (AIA).[41] COPs can also be seen as no more than a form of diplomatic conferences providing a continuous, or at least regular, context within which decisions can more readily be made than through the calling of *ad hoc* diplomatic conferences. In fact, it is submitted that COPs and MOPs may partake of either character, depending on both the substantive nature of what is discussed and on whether their decisions will require subsequent validation to become binding on the parties or not.

6.3.1 *Non-compliance Procedures*

This section deals with so-called non-compliance procedures, which concern measures directed at the parties to MEAs in cases of non-compliance with the treaty provisions or the decisions of COPs. NCPs can be deemed quasi-legal, because they – with the possible exception of the non-compliance mechanism under the Kyoto Protocol – do not result in 'absolutely' binding decisions from which States cannot escape. However, it may be mentioned that decisions of COPs on non-compliance carry a great weight, and although formally non-binding, they have proven to be a very effective mechanism of bringing States to compliance. Moreover, through compliance procedures, COPs exercise powers that shape the obligations of State parties to MEAs. The question that may be asked concerning compliance procedures in relation to law-making is whether they 'make' law for the parties to MEAs. Since the establishment of an NCP under the Montreal Protocol on Substances That Deplete the Ozone Layer in 1992, it has been common practice by State parties to MEAs to create treaty bodies, called 'Compliance Committees' or 'Implementation Committees', with the functions of determining a State party's compliance with its international obligations and reporting non-compliance to the COPs. NCPs are usually established on the basis of so-called enabling clauses in MEAs, which provide for the establishment of such a procedure by a decision of the COPs. An example of this is found in Article 8 of the Montreal Protocol.[42] However, in a few cases, such NPCs were established without

[41] Churchill and Ulfstein, 'Autonomous institutional arrangements'.

[42] Art 8: 'The Parties, at their first meeting, shall consider and approve procedures and institutional mechanisms for determining non-compliance with the provisions of this Protocol and for treatment of Parties found to be in non-compliance.'

authorisation. Such an example is the NCP in the Basel Convention on Transboundary Movement of Hazardous Wastes.

It may be observed that the functions that non-compliance bodies are based on are a composite notion of compliance comprising monitoring, verification, and national reporting, which are of fundamental importance for the functioning of MEAs. There are several examples of MEAs setting up such mechanisms. Monitoring is a system set up by COPs, and this task is entrusted either to a non-compliance body or to a secretariat, as in the case of the CLRTAP. Under the CLRTAP regime, the Implementation Committee is responsible for the monitoring of the parties' reporting obligations as well as their obligations to reduce emissions under the various protocols. Based on resolutions, the CITES' COP has established mechanisms designed to improve compliance, such as the 'Review of Significant Trade' procedure originally introduced to monitor trade in Appendix II species. This procedure was established to identify difficulties experienced by national scientific authorities in their determination as to whether continued trade in a species would be detrimental to that species' survival. Non-compliance with the recommendations of the Animals or Plants Committee may result in the Standing Committee taking appropriate action, which may include a possible suspension of trade between parties and the range State in non-compliance.

NCPs were designed to respond to a breach of environmental obligations in the multilateral, not bilateral, context, which are capable of accommodating community interests in a truly satisfactory manner. Environmental obligations, in particular relating to global issues, are not reciprocal in nature. Therefore, the classical procedures of dispute settlement as envisaged by Article 33 of the UN Charter, bilateral in nature, are not suitable for addressing non-compliance within a multilateral context and remedying non-compliance relating to global issues such as climate change, protection of biodiversity, or the ozone layer. There are alternative explanations as to why NCPs are more suited to deal with non-compliance than traditional dispute settlement procedures. It may be that States prefer NCPs, because they exercise more control over the whole process and its results than over third-party mechanisms such as the judicial or arbitral procedures. These procedures have less stringent effects; the decisions of non-compliance bodies are not final in the form of *res judicata* and are less intrusive. NCPs are based on an approach favouring prevention, which better suits the general trend in international environmental law of rather relying on such means as reporting or verification processes than on procedures of dispute settlement.

The character of NCPs is well defined by the NCP of the Basel Convention. In its mandate it is stated as follows:

> The objective of the mechanism is to assist Parties to comply with their obligations under the Convention and to facilitate, promote, monitor and aim to secure the implementation of and compliance with the obligations under the Convention.[43]

The nature of mechanism is described in the following terms:

> The mechanism shall be non-confrontational, transparent, cost-effective and preventive in nature, simple, flexible, non-binding and oriented in the direction of helping parties to implement the provisions of the Basel Convention. It will pay particular attention to the special needs of developing countries and countries with economies in transition, and is intended to promote cooperation between all Parties. The mechanism should complement work performed by other Convention bodies and by the Basel Convention Regional Centres.[44]

The first classical NCP was established under the 1987 Montreal Protocol on Substances That Deplete the Ozone Layer to the 1985 Vienna Convention on the Protection of the Ozone Layer. At present almost all MEAs have established NCPs. Although NCPs share certain common features, they are designed to reflect the character of the MEA on the basis of which they are established. For example, in the Aarhus Convention, which is a hybrid human right and environmental treaty, civil society play a major role in submitting cases to the Compliance Committee.

The main features of the NCP of the Montreal Protocol are its facilitative character and transparency. In addition, the NCP under the Montreal Protocol follows the requirements of due process: notification, right to fair hearing, and impartiality. It may be observed that although the NCP is not a judicial procedure, certain of its characteristics – such as the right to fair hearing, according to paragraph 10 of the NCP – accord to the party potentially in non-compliance the right to participate in the consideration by the committee of that submission. The party in alleged NCPs is not allowed to participate in the elaboration and adoption of recommendations concerning its own compliance (paragraph 11 of the NCP). Three organs are involved in the NCP: the Implementation Committee, the Secretariat, and the COP. The main function of the Secretariat regarding non-compliance is to receive the reports of parties concerning non-compliance and submit them to the

[43] Conference of the Parties to the Basel Convention, 'Report on the control of transboundary movements of hazardous wastes and their disposal', Sixth Meeting, Geneva (9–13 December 2002) UNEP/CHW.6/40 at Decision VI/12.

[44] Ibid.

Implementation Committee. The Secretariat may also ascertain non-compliance on the basis of the reports of the parties and inform the Implementation Committee (paragraphs 1, 2, 4 of the NCP). The main task of the Implementation Committee is to act in an advisory capacity to the COP. It must be stressed that the final decision of non-compliance rests with the COP.

The Implementation Committee is composed of ten representatives of the parties and is elected by the COP for a term of two years, based on equitable geographical representation (paragraph 5 of the NCP). The COP is the highest body, representing all parties. It has the powers to adopt a decision on non-compliance and to decide what measure will be applied in the event of non-compliance (see below). The NCP may be triggered either by the Secretariat, or by any party (parties) concerned about non-compliance or potential non-compliance of another party (paragraph 1 of the NCP), or by the party in non-compliance itself (paragraph 4 of the NCP). The NCP includes several procedural safeguards for a party under this procedure. A party which is not a member of the Implementation Committee and is identified as being potentially in non-compliance or has itself made such a submission shall be entitled to participate in the meetings of the Implementation Committee when it considers its non-compliance (paragraph 10 of the NCP). The NCP is also based on confidentiality, that is, the parties and the Implementation Committee involved in deliberations protect the confidentiality of information they receive (paragraph 15 of the NCP). Exceptionally, only the Kyoto Protocol allowed its Compliance Committee to make all decisions without the participation of the COP. Decisions of both branches of the Compliance Committee (Facilitative and Enforcement) are final (there is a limited possibility of an appeal from a decision of the Enforcement Branch to the COP). The question was raised whether, in particular, any Enforcement Branch's decision of a punitive nature could be regarded as legally binding. The consequences of non-compliance were very onerous when a State party had failed to comply with its emissions reduction target under the Kyoto Protocol. The Enforcement Branch was empowered to deduct a number of tonnes equal to 1.3 times the amount in tonnes of excess emissions from that State party's assigned amount in a second commitment period. Article 18 of the Kyoto Protocol stipulates that NCPs 'entailing binding consequences shall be adopted by means of an amendment to this Protocol'. It may be thus argued that in the absence of such a formal amendment, future decisions by the Enforcement Branch lack legitimacy.

The very controversial nature of NCPs under the Kyoto Protocol has resulted in its exclusion from the regime of the Paris Agreement. Therein an NCP is based on Article 15(1) and (2), which is an enabling clause. The task of the Non-compliance Committee is only facilitative. Article 15 states that the committee is expected to enhance the effective functioning of the Paris Agreement by encouraging parties to implement it.[45]

The committee is a standing expert body with a mandate to address situations related to the performance of individual parties. The complex procedure under the Paris Agreement is described as follows:

> The language of Article 15 makes clear that this is not an 'enforcement' mechanism, but rather that it is to be 'facilitative in nature'. A mechanism that is facilitative in nature would only take measures to encourage means by which the Party itself can enhance its implementation and compliance including through capacity-building and by ensuring the provision of support to developing country Parties, while assessing compliance of developed country Parties in mitigation, adaptation and provision of support in accordance with relevant provisions of the Paris Agreement, and would not be to punish a Party for failing to comply and implement its obligations. The Committee is therefore not intended to be a quasi-judicial or adjudicative body of any kind, but rather is meant to facilitate implementation and promote compliance by Parties in a cooperative manner.[46]

The set of classical measures adopted in the case of non-compliance is exemplified by the Montreal Protocol: (1) appropriate assistance, including for reporting of data, technical assistance, financial assistance, information transfer, and training; (2) issuing cautions; (3) suspension, in accordance with applicable international law, of the operation of specific rights and privileges under the protocol, subject to time limits, including those concerning rationalisation, production, consumption, trade, technology, financial mechanisms, and institutional arrangements.

[45] Art 15 of the Paris Agreement, Paris, 12 December 2015, in force 4 November 2016, UN Doc. FCCC/CP/2015/L.9/Rev/1:

'1. A mechanism to facilitate implementation of and promote compliance with the provisions of this Agreement is hereby established.

2. The mechanism referred to in paragraph 1 of this Article shall consist of a committee that shall be expert-based and facilitative in nature and function in a manner that is transparent, non-adversarial and non-punitive. The committee shall pay particular attention to the respective national capabilities and circumstances of Parties.'

[46] Like-Minded Developing Countries Group, 'LMDC submission on modalities and procedures for the effective operation of the Article 15 committee to facilitate implementation and promote compliance', UNFCCC, https://unfccc.int/sites/default/files/lmdc_submission_on_art_15_implementation_and_compliance_mechanism__30_sep_2017_-_final.pdf (accessed 14 October 2020) at 4.

As we can see from the Paris Agreement's NCP regime, harsh measures of suspension have been abandoned. Therefore, there is a marked evolution in recent NCPs, departing from the 'classical' regimes based on harsh measures.

It may be added that the International Law Commission in its Guideline 11 in the Articles on Protection of the Atmosphere has included a provision on non-compliance, which follows the patterns set out in other MEAs.[47] However, it is worth noting that the Special Rapporteur (Murase) explained that he 'favoured cooperative compliance mechanisms, meant to give assistance to a non-compliant party, over punitive or enforcement mechanisms, which were based on the responsibility of States and intended to place penalties on the non-compliant party'.[48]

6.4 LEGITIMACY OF COPS' DECISIONS

Although much has been written about the legitimacy of international environmental law and the far-reaching functions of COPs, an elaborate analysis of these theories is outside the scope of this chapter.[49]

However, in the view of the author of this chapter, two such theories evidence the complexity of capturing the legitimacy of acts of COPs, that is,

[47] ILC, Seventieth Session, New York (30 April–1 June 2018) and Geneva (2 July–10 August 2018) A/CN.4/L.909:

'Guideline 11 Compliance:

1. States are required to abide with their obligations under international law relating to the protection of the atmosphere from atmospheric pollution and atmospheric degradation in good faith, including through compliance with the rules and procedures in the relevant agreements to which they are parties.

2. To achieve compliance, facilitative or enforcement procedures may be used, as appropriate, in accordance with the relevant agreements:

(a) facilitative procedures may include providing assistance to States, in cases of non-compliance, in a transparent, non-adversarial and non-punitive manner to ensure that the States concerned comply with their obligations under international law, taking into account their capabilities and special conditions;

(b) enforcement procedures may include issuing a caution of non-compliance, termination of rights and privileges under the relevant agreements, and other forms of enforcement measures.'

[48] Ibid.

[49] See on this extensively, Zerrin Savaşan, 'Legitimacy questions of non-compliance procedures: Examples from Kyoto and Montreal Protocols', in Christina Voigt (ed.), *International Judicial Practice on the Environment: Questions of Legitimacy* (Cambridge: Cambridge University Press, 2019), p. 364.

the theory of fairness of Thomas Franck[50] and the interactional theory of Lon Fuller.[51]

Bodansky, commenting on legitimacy in the context of international environmental law, expressed the view that although environmental law had developed 'through a consensual rather than an authoritative process', the phenomenon of authority plays an ancillary role.[52] This statement also holds true in relation to the issue of legitimacy in the case of COPs, due to their – at times – authoritarian functions and activities, influencing the behaviour of States. As explained earlier in this chapter, such authoritarian functions revolve around the content of certain vague general principles, even of fundamental importance for the State parties (such as the fleshing out of flexible mechanisms in the Kyoto Protocol) and for setting out procedures of the most significant importance for States (impacting on their behaviour, such as non-compliance mechanisms).

The question of legitimacy of actions and functions of COPs has taken a central place in discussions relating to the role of COPs. As stated by Bernstein:

> Legality is potentially violated when a treaty body, group of experts such as scientists empowered by a treaty ... or even a representative body of state delegates, makes a decision that appears to go beyond the mandate given to them by the statute to which states consented.[53]

The question of legitimacy can be analysed from the point of view of fairness, a theme that was elaborated on by Professor Thomas Franck. A full account of the author's theory exceeds the purpose of this chapter. However, it is worthwhile to remind oneself of the main tenets of his theory in order to pose the question whether far-reaching obligations of States beyond their consent fall within the concept of legitimacy, understood as fairness. It was emphasised by Franck that the key factor of legitimacy is fairness, which accommodates a popular belief that a system of rules, in order for it to be fair, must be firmly rooted in a framework of formal requirements about how the rules are made,

[50] Thomas Franck, *Fairness in International Law and Institutions* (Oxford: Oxford University Press, 1995).

[51] Jutta Brunnée and Stephen Toope, 'International law and constructivism: Elements of an interactional theory of international law' (2000) 39 Colum J Transnat'l L 19–74 at 49–53.

[52] Daniel Bodansky, 'The legitimacy of international governance: A coming challenge for international environmental law' (1999) 93 AJIL 596–624 at 604.

[53] Steven Bernstein, 'Legitimacy in a global environmental governance' (2005) 1 JILIR 139–66 at 153–54.

interpreted, and applied.[54] The belief that a rule is legitimate reinforces the perception of its fairness and contributes to compliance. Fairness, as he says, is the only formula which will command respect of the law and ensure compliance.[55] The attributes of legitimacy are symbolic validation, determinacy, adherence, and coherence. The first – determinacy – is defined by Franck as 'the ability of a text to convey a clear message. To appear transparent in the sense that can see through the language of law to its essential meaning'.[56]

The perceived legitimacy of a rule also relies on the generality (coherence) of principles the rules apply. The belief of illegitimacy is rooted in the rule's lack of generality, that is, its applicability only to one instance. Such rules are, as Franck observes, 'unprincipled' and 'lack coherence'.[57] The rule is coherent

> when its application treats cases alike and when the rule relates in a principled fashion to other rules in the same system. Constancy requires that a rule, whatever its content, be applied uniformly in every 'similar' or 'applicable' instance.[58]

COPs amend/modify MEAs by fleshing out certain of their fundamental provisions and formulate general, coherent, and well-determined new rules, which are applicable in a repeated fashion in the practice of State parties, as was evidenced in cases of the CITES and the Kyoto Protocol. The same reasoning applies to NCPs. Although each non-compliance case is different and analysed separately by COPs, the rules of procedure and the measures to be adopted in cases of non-compliance are set out and made applicable to all cases. Again, it may be said, the test of fairness is fulfilled by decisions adopted by COPs in the event of non-compliance. Therefore, legitimacy perceived as fairness characterises COPs' decisions.

There are also attempts by theorists to explain the question of legitimacy of COPs' decisions based on the 'interactional theory' of Lon Fuller, transposed into the field of international environmental law by Jutta Brunnée and Stephen Toope.[59] This theory of 'internal morality' is based on the avoidance of contradiction, generality, and congruence with underlying rules. Fuller's 'internal morality' is associated with the essential processes by which law is

[54] Franck, *Fairness in International Law,* p. 25 et seq.
[55] Ibid., p. 13.
[56] Ibid., p. 30
[57] Ibid., p. 38.
[58] Ibid., p. 43.
[59] Brunnée and Toope, 'International law', pp. 49–53; Brunnée, 'COPing with consent', p. 15.

created, interpreted, and administered.[60] In this theory, legitimacy is based on cooperation and interaction between actors (the governing and the governed) rooted within the social practice and conventions they created, within the context of norms and institutions they established.[61] Legitimacy is based on a 'thick' acceptance of the need for emerging norms, which is 'promoted by reference to past practice, contemporary aspirations and the deployment of reasoning by analogy'.[62]

The interactional perspective is not based on formal 'bindingness' and thus abandons the division between soft and hard law. The differentiation between legal and non-legal norms is effected through internal characteristics, which entail distinctive legal legitimacy and persuasiveness, requiring that rules be compatible with one another and reasonable, that official action be congruent with known rules, and that rules be transparent and relatively predictable. The degree to which these requirements are met defines the legitimacy of the norms or legal system 'and their power to promote adherence'.[63]

Brunnée describes the working of this theory as follows:

> States (and other international actors), through their interaction, influence the scope and content of international norms and institutions. In turn, these norms and institutions furnish the context within which interaction takes place and shape the identities of the actors themselves. In other words, in this continuous process, actors come to understand themselves and their interests in light of their interaction with others and in light of the norms that frame the interaction. International law is generated as patterns of social practice emerge and increasingly influential mutual expectations and shared understandings of actors evolve.[64]

Brunnée explains that, due to its characteristics, the interactional theory (without the formal division between binding and non-binding norms) depicts in a more accurate way the role of COPs as legislators, as 'in an interactional account, legislation, whether at the national or international level, is never unidirectional imposition of authority'.[65] COPs' legislating process, according to this theory, is engaged in a broader collective process, congruent with the

60 Jutta Brunnée and Stephen Toope, *Legitimacy and Legality in International Law: An Interactional Account* (Cambridge: Cambridge University Pres, 2010), p. 56.
61 Ibid.
62 Ibid., p. 66.
63 Brunnée, 'COPing with consent', p. 36.
64 Ibid., p. 34.
65 Ibid., p. 38.

expectations of society, and meets internal requirements. In this theory of law-making, State consent plays a secondary role:

> States may be most likely to agree to make law 'enforceable' when it has become binding in the interactional sense. Alternatively, states may be most likely to insist on formal consent where there is an insufficient foundation of shared understandings (such as when a protocol or an amendment on new substances or control measures has to be negotiated). In this context, the requirement of formal consent may in fact provide a protective mechanism that facilitates effective interactive processes by enabling states to participate, at least in principle, as equals.[66]

Brunnée analyses the question of legitimacy within the context of COPs through the prism of interactional theory. Law-makers, such as COPs, should keep the various legitimacy criteria in constant reference; the rules will gain more legitimacy (be more persuasive and influential) when there is stronger adherence to the criteria, with the participation of all actors.[67]

The question of legitimacy can also be analysed through the lens of simple consent, which, of course, is anything but simple. However, as Bowman opined, legitimacy is itself often a prerequisite to efficacy in international affairs, and the great virtue of collective decision-making through treaty institutions is that it has the capacity for continuous self-legitimation through its inherently inclusive and consensual nature. Of course, what counts as 'consent' for legal purposes depends very much upon the circumstances, and it is clear that simply forgoing the chance to object may often be sufficient. Accordingly, mere acquiescence can serve as an extremely powerful vector for legitimating change in international legal relationships, but at the very least this will require the conferral of a formal opportunity to dissent, which regular plenary meetings obviously provide.[68]

Savaşan, in order to clarify the question of legitimacy of NCPs, refers to the legal basis of their establishment, that is, whether an enabling clause in the primary treaty was the basis of the NCP, or whether they were established without such a clause. According to her, the problem of legitimacy only arises in the absence of such a clause and if the COP's decision establishes a 'hard' NCP whose outcomes are binding and have effects in the sense of creating obligations beyond the agreement (i.e. new obligations or amending existing

[66] Ibid.

[67] Ibid., p. 46.

[68] Michael J. Bowman, 'Beyond the "keystone" COPs: The ecology of international governance in conservation treaty regimes', in Malgosia Fitzmaurice and Duncan French (eds.), *International Law and Governance* (Leiden: Brill/Nijhoff, 2013), p. 27.

ones).[69] Such an approach would eliminate from objectionable NCPs a new generation of 'soft' NCPs (which do not include far-reaching measures in relation to a non-compliant State), as was represented by the NCP in the Paris Agreement.

Savaşan is of the view that procedural safeguards protect legitimacy, such as a preliminary phase of a prior consultation between the parties concerned, due process, and transparency of proceedings. However, as Savaşan has also observed, the concept of legitimacy is very complicated and complex, consisting of diverse elements. Thus, diversity related to this issue of legitimacy commands further examination and empirical studies 'on the distinctive characteristics of different institutions and to develop legitimacy perspective for each one of these'.[70] Currently there is a great variety of such mechanisms which require case-by-case study of their legitimacy[71] based on theory and practice. Therefore, legitimacy in relation to NCPs and the role of COPs is still very much an unresolved question, awaiting further studies.

This short section is meant to be illustrative of the complex question of the legitimacy of the decisions of COPs. The author of this chapter does not presume that there is one theory which would 'legitimise' – in a persuasive and acceptable fashion – COPs' functions. However, the quest for justification evidences the dilemma faced by States. Such functions of COPs reformulate the notion of consent as classically established, therefore resulting in attempts at legitimatisation.

6.5 CONCLUSION

Classical settlement of environmental disputes, which are based on the methods included in Article 33 of the UN Charter, do not generate issues of legitimacy. They are well-tested methods, and the use of diplomatic and legal means of settlement of environmental disputes has had a long tradition. The legal (judicial and arbitral) settlement of environmental disputes has rarely been challenged, and decisions adopted under these proceedings have contributed to a certain degree to the development of international environmental law, frequently in the context of general international law. However, the inherent bilateralism of these mechanisms for the settlement of disputes is

69 Savaşan, 'Legitimacy questions', pp. 377, 389.
70 Ibid.
71 Ibid.

not best suited to serve the protection of the environment, which is a common concern of humankind.[72]

Questions regarding the legitimacy of COPs' decisions should not detract from the general issue of their usefulness in protecting the environment. In the view of the author, the multilateral system on which they are based makes them much better suited than the classical mechanisms of dispute settlement predicated upon bilateralism. They indeed serve a common interest of States in the protection of environment. It may be added that NCPs, which at present are based on assistance rather than stricter measures in cases of non-compliance, are also better equipped to fulfil environmental aims than adversarial mechanisms.

Therefore, questions relating to the legitimacy of decisions of COPs in matters of non-compliance are not as current as they were in the past, where the preferable system was that of a 'hard' regime with far-reaching consequences for non-compliance. A more modern trend, as exemplified by the NCP in the Paris Agreement and by the approach of the ILC Special Rapporteur Murase, is focused on co-operative efforts, thus eliminating, to a certain degree, the legitimacy issue. Therefore, taking into account the new approaches and trends in NCPs, the question of their legitimacy may well be a concern of the past.

72 See, e.g., the Preamble of the UNFCCC, which states as follows: 'The Parties to this Convention, acknowledging that change in the Earth's climate and its adverse effects are a common concern of humankind.'

7

The Role and Legitimacy of International Human Rights Mechanisms of Dispute Settlement

SIR MALCOLM D. EVANS

7.1 INTRODUCTION

That there might be some dissonance between the views of the multifarious bodies engaged in the interpretation and application of international legal instruments is hardly a surprise. Indeed, it is to be expected. Such disagreement helps pinpoint controversy and, through its reconciliation, helps advance understanding of the scope of relevant legal obligations at issue. It is equally commonplace that the International Court of Justice (ICJ) can pass judgment upon the interpretation and application of any legal instrument either by virtue of its general jurisdiction, when applicable, under Article 36(1) of the ICJ Statute, or by virtue of any compromissory clause that a particular legal instrument may contain. This may be so even when that other instrument sets up its own systems for resolving disputes between parties. Some years ago, concerns about divergent interpretations by different bodies of the same obligations prompted the 'fragmentation' debate, reminding international lawyers that such fragmentation was little more than an inevitable by-product of the current configuration of the international system instead of an existential crisis.[1] Yet there *is* something bordering on the existential about the manner in which the ICJ appears to be

[1] In 2000 the International Law Commission (ILC) added the topic of 'Risks ensuing from the fragmentation of international law' to its programme of work, which led to the seminal report for the ILC by Martti Koskenniemi (ILC, 'Fragmentation of international law: Difficulties arising from the diversification and expansion of international law. Report of the Study Group of the International Law Commission' (13 April 2006) UN Doc. A/CN.4/L.682). Of the considerable literature on the subject, works of particular relevance to the themes addressed in this chapter include Philippa Webb, *International Judicial Integration and Fragmentation* (Oxford: Oxford University Press, 2013) and Mads Andenas and Eirik Bjorge (eds.), *A Farewell to Fragmentation: Reassertion and Convergence in International Law* (Cambridge: Cambridge University Press, 2015).

engaging with the work of the UN Committee on the Elimination of Racial Discrimination (CERD Committee) at the moment, and vice versa.

Following this introduction, Section 7.2 of this chapter considers several issues which have arisen as a result of State parties seeking to use compromissory clauses to bring cases before the ICJ, particularly in relation to the Convention for the Elimination of All Forms of Racial Discrimination (CERD). Arguably, one of the consequences of the court's approach has been the first ever use of the 'inter-State communication' procedure in Article 11 of the CERD. This has opened a series of difficult questions concerning the relationship between the work of the ICJ and of the CERD, which are explored in Section 7.3. As they largely focus on procedural issues, these questions can only be understood in the light of the nature of the CERD Article 11 process, which is considered in Section 7.4. Section 7.5 turns to the manner in which the court has engaged with the work of the UN human rights treaty bodies, and in particular the CERD Committee, whilst Section 7.6 explores what appears to be a growing disjuncture between the approaches of the CERD Committee and the ICJ to each other's work, its consequences, and legitimacy. Section 7.7 offers some concluding reflections.

7.2 THE UN HUMAN RIGHTS TREATIES, COMPROMISSORY CLAUSES, AND THE ICJ

There are currently ten UN human rights treaty bodies, established by nine conventions and one optional protocol,[2] and, in somewhat different ways, they

[2] The Committee on the Elimination of Racial Discrimination (CERD Committee) was established by the International Convention on the Elimination of All Forms of Racial Discrimination, New York, 21 December 1965, in force 4 January 1969, 660 UNTS 195 (CERD). The CERD Committee held its first session in January 1970. The Human Rights Committee (HRC) was established by the International Covenant on Civil and Political Rights (ICCPR), New York, 16 December 1966, in force 23 March 1976, 999 UNTS 171. The HRC met for the first time in March 1977. The Committee on the Elimination of Discrimination against Women (CEDAW) was established by the Convention on the Elimination of All Forms of Discrimination against Women, New York, 18 December 1979, in force 3 September 1981, 1249 UNTS 13. The CEDAW met for the first time in October 1982. The Committee against Torture (CAT) was established by the United Nations Convention against Torture and Other Cruel, Inhuman, and Degrading Treatment or Punishment (UNCAT), New York, 10 December 1984, in force 26 June 1987, 1465 UNTS 85. The CAT met for the first time in April 1988. The Committee on the Rights of the Child (CRC) was established by the Convention on the Rights of the Child, New York, 20 November 1989, in force 2 September 1990, 1577 UNTS 3. The CRC met for the first time in September 1991. The United Nations Economic and Social Council (ECOSOC) had originally been tasked with overseeing the reporting procedures provided for in the International Covenant on Economic, Social, and Cultural Rights (ICESCR), New York, 16 December 1966, in force 3 January

are all tasked with what is generally described as 'monitoring compliance' by States with the substantive obligations they contain.[3] Many (but by no means all) of the substantive obligations found within the UN human rights treaties bind all States as a matter of customary international law[4] and so may be considered by the ICJ on that basis in cases where it has jurisdiction on other grounds.[5] Obviously, this can include cases involving State parties to a particular human rights treaty and thus potentially resulting in the ICJ determining whether a State has, or has not, acted in conformity with its legal obligations under that treaty, as well as determining what those legal obligations entail. The *Diallo* case in 2010 was of this nature: the ICJ was able to exercise jurisdiction on the basis of Article 36(2) of its Statute and concluded that the Democratic Republic of the Congo (DRC) had breached various Articles of both the International Covenant on Civil and Political Rights and of the African Charter on Human and Peoples' Rights.[6] This is all the more likely to happen in respect of the five UN human rights treaties which contain compromissory clauses permitting a State party to bring a case against another

1976, 993 UNTS 3. The Committee on Economic, Social, and Cultural Rights (CESCR) first met in March 1987. The Committee on Migrant Workers (CMW) was established by the International Convention on the Protection of the Rights of All Migrant Workers and Members of their Families, New York, 18 December 1990, in force 1 July 2003, 2220 UNTS 3. The CMW met for the first time in March 2004. The Subcommittee for Prevention of Torture (SPT) was established by the Optional Protocol to the Convention against Torture and Other Cruel, Inhuman, and Degrading Treatment or Punishment, New York, 18 December 2002, in force 22 June 2006, 2375 UNTS 237. The SPT met for the first time in February 2007. The Committee on the Rights of Persons with Disabilities (CRPD) was established by the Convention on the Rights of Persons with Disabilities, New York, 13 December 2006, in force 3 May 2008, 2515 UNTS 3. The CRPD met for the first time in February 2009. The Committee on Enforced Disappearances (CED) was established by the International Convention for the Protection of All Persons from Enforced Disappearances, New York, 20 December 2006, in force 23 December 2010, 2716 UNTS 3. The CED met for the first time in November 2011. It is appreciated that the abbreviations for the names of the committees and the conventions are largely identical, but the context in which they are used should allow for their differentiation.

3 For a recent examination of the work of each of the treaty bodies framed against the background of their 'monitoring' role, see Frédéric Mégret and Philip Alston, *The United Nations and Human Rights*, 2nd ed. (Oxford: Oxford University Press, 2020), part III.

4 See William A. Schabas, *The Customary International Law of Human Rights* (Oxford: Oxford University Press, 2021). For an earlier influential exploration of this subject, see Theodor Meron, *Human Rights and Humanitarian Norms as Customary Law* (Oxford: Clarendon Press, 1989).

5 For an insightful overview of the engagement of the ICJ with human rights issues, see Bruno Simma, 'The International Court of Justice', in Frédéric Mégret and Philip Alston (eds.), *The United Nations and Human Rights*, 2nd ed. (Oxford: Oxford University Press, 2020), p. 152.

6 *Ahmadou Sadio Diallo (Republic of Guinea* v. *Democratic Republic of the Congo)* (Merits, Judgment) [2010] ICJ Rep. 639.

before the ICJ, provided certain prerequisites have been fulfilled, three of which have so far been considered by the court.

In the *Armed Activities* case, the DRC unsuccessfully sought to bring claims against Rwanda based on a swathe of compromissory clauses in various treaties, including Article 30(1) of the UNCAT and Article 29(1) of the CEDAW. These are identical and provide that:

> 1. Any dispute between two or more States Parties concerning the interpretation or application of this Convention which cannot be settled through negotiation shall, at the request of one of them, be submitted to arbitration. If within six months from the date of the request for arbitration the Parties are unable to agree on the organization of the arbitration, any one of those Parties may refer the dispute to the International Court of Justice by request in conformity with the Statute of the Court.

The court swiftly concluded that Article 30(1) of the UNCAT was inapplicable as Rwanda was not a party to the Convention at the time of the application.[7] It also concluded that the essential prerequisites of its having jurisdiction under Article 29(1) of CEDAW had not been met, in that the DRC had sought to neither negotiate with Rwanda nor submit its dispute concerning the Convention to arbitration as that Article requires,[8] these being cumulative requirements.[9]

Article 30(1) of the UNCAT was used to ground the jurisdiction of the ICJ in the *Habré* case (2012), brought by Belgium against Senegal. This was the first case in which a compromissory clause in one of the UN human rights treaties was used successfully. Belgium was able to do so since, unlike the situation in the *Armed Activities* case, there had been both unsuccessful negotiations between the parties and an unsuccessful attempt by Belgium to submit the dispute to arbitration, and so the requirements of Article 30(1) had been met.[10] The court went on to find that Senegal had been in breach of its

7 *Armed Activities on the Territory of the Congo (New Application: 2002) (Democratic Republic of the Congo* v. *Rwanda)* (Jurisdiction and Admissibility, Judgment) [2002] ICJ Rep. 6 at para. 16. Rwanda subsequently acceded to the UNCAT on 15 December 2008.

8 Ibid., paras 92–93.

9 Ibid., para. 87, as had been argued by Rwanda (see para. 81).

10 *Questions Relating to the Obligation to Prosecute or Extradite (Belgium* v. *Senegal)* (Judgment) [2012] ICJ Rep. 442 at para. 63. This also meant that the court did not have to determine the thornier question of whether it also had jurisdiction based on declarations made by the parties in accordance with Art 36(2), which was strongly contested by Senegal. Belgium became a party to the UNCAT in July 1999. Proceedings against Habré were commenced in Belgium in 1999. Belgium had been engaging with Senegal on matters relating to his prosecution since 2001, and it issued an international arrest warrant in 2005, the rejection of which ultimately precipitated the case before the ICJ. See generally Sharon Weill, Kim Thuy Seelinger, and

obligations under Article 7 of the UNCAT due to its failure to investigate and submit allegations of torture to its prosecuting authorities against Hissène Habré, the former president of Chad, despite his having been living in Senegal since 1991 and Senegal having been bound by the UNCAT since its entry into force in June 1987.

In the *Armed Activities* case, the DRC had also attempted to ground jurisdiction on Article 22 of the CERD, but this failed because, when acceding to the Convention, Rwanda had entered a reservation in relation to that Article,[11] the validity of which was upheld by the court.[12] As a result, the terms of that Article were not considered in any detail in the court's judgment. However, this took centre stage in the case concerning the *Application of the International Convention on the Elimination of All Forms of Racial Discrimination* brought by Georgia against the Russian Federation.

Article 22 of the CERD provides that

> any dispute between two or more States Parties with respect to the interpretation or application of this Convention, which is not settled by negotiation or by the procedures expressly provided for in this Convention, shall, at the request of any of the parties to the dispute, be referred to the International Court of Justice for decision, unless the disputants agree to another mode of settlement.

In its 2001 judgment, the court determined that there was a 'dispute' between the parties concerning the interpretation and application of the Convention.[13] However, the court also took the view that the dispute had

Kerstin Bree Carlson (eds.), *The President on Trial: Prosecuting Hissène Habré* (Oxford: Oxford University Press, 2020).

[11] The reservation provides in straightforward language that 'the Rwandese Republic does not consider itself as bound by article 22 of the Convention'; see *Armed Activities on the Territory of the Congo*, para. 74. The CERD in Art 29(2) and the UNCAT in Art 30(2) expressly provide that 'each State Party may at the time of signature or ratification of the present Convention or accession thereto declare that it does not consider itself bound by paragraph 1 of this article. The other States Parties shall not be bound by that paragraph with respect to any State Party which has made such a reservation'.

[12] *Armed Activities on the Territory of the Congo*, para. 79.

[13] *Application of the International Convention on the Elimination of All Forms of Racial Discrimination (Georgia v. Russian Federation)* (Preliminary Objections, Judgments) [2001] ICJ Rep. 70 at para. 113, not uncontroversial, given that the court felt that the dispute only emerged in the period of 9–12 August 2008, with the proceedings being instituted by Georgia on 12 August itself. Some have gone further and doubted whether the 'dispute' was really about obligations under the CERD at all. See, e.g., Phoebe Okowa, 'The International Court of Justice and the Georgia/Russia dispute' (2011) 11 HRL Rev 739–57. Bruno Simma, writing extrajudicially, has accepted that whilst the CERD was engaged by the dispute between the two States, it was 'as far from constituting a "pure" human rights case as one could get, because

not yet been the subject of negotiations between the parties, and so the conditions of its having jurisdiction under Article 22 had not been met.[14]

The court's judgment did, however, leave open a very important question: if there *had* been negotiations, would it *also* have been necessary for Georgia to have availed itself of the 'procedures expressly provided for' by the Convention to resolve disputes between parties before the court could exercise jurisdiction under Article 22 (this being understood as a reference to the 'inter-State communication' procedure provided for in Articles 11–13 of CERD[15])? In other words, did the use of the word 'or' in the subclause mean that these were alternatives, or was it necessary for both to have been undertaken before the court could exercise jurisdiction based on Article 22? As it was accepted that no attempt had been made to use the procedures provided for in the CERD, once the court decided that no negotiations had taken place, it was clear that it could not exercise jurisdiction, and so it did not have to decide this question.[16]

It is important to remember that, of the three human rights treaty compromissory clauses so far considered by the ICJ, the need to have recourse to the inter-State procedure only arises in relation to CERD, since the others do not make reference to the 'procedures expressly provided for' in the convention in question.[17] The differences between these compromissory clauses in some ways reflect crucial differences in the inter-State communication procedures provided for in the conventions themselves. The 'inter-State' procedure set out in Articles 11–13 of the CERD is, uniquely among the UN human rights treaties, 'compulsory' and automatically applicable to all State parties. The

if there was ever an instance of ICJ litigation presenting all the features of a legal *Nebenkreigsschauplatz*, in the sense of a legal side-show in a much wider political conflict, this was the one'. See Simma, 'The ICJ', p. 162. There have, of course, since been others.

14 *Application of the CERD (Georgia* v. *Russia)*, para. 184. Logically, a non-cumulative approach would suggest that it would be sufficient if one of the parties had triggered the inter-State procedure without seeking to 'negotiate'. However, since that procedure commences with a period for negotiation (see Arts 11(1) and (2)) between the parties and only progresses further if they are unsuccessful, there will always have to be some form of negotiation if the court is ever to have jurisdiction.

15 Ibid., para. 149.

16 In ibid., para. 133, the court said it was 'leaving aside the question of whether the two modes of peaceful resolution are alternative or cumulative', and in para. 183 it concluded that it was unnecessary to return to it.

17 Art 92 of the Convention on Migrant Workers is also identical to that found in the CEDAW and UNCAT. However, and somewhat oddly, Art 42 of the International Convention for the Protection of All Persons from Enforced Disappearance, which is otherwise also identical to them, includes such a reference too, providing that disputes 'which cannot be settled through negotiation or by the procedures expressly provided for in this Convention shall, at the request of one of them, be submitted to arbitration'.

inter-State procedure in Article 21 of the UNCAT, however, is 'voluntary', in that it is only applicable to those States which have made a declaration accepting it,[18] and there is no equivalent inter-State procedure within the CEDAW at all. It might, then, be thought that this explains these differences between the compromissory clauses, since it might seem strange to provide for the use of a procedure which might either be inapplicable or, in the case of CEDAW, non-existent.

It is, however, unwise to read too much into this: the reason why the compromissory clauses in the later treaties are different from that in the CERD was not because they lacked a compulsory inter-State mechanism, but because of a desire to expressly provide State parties with the opportunity to 'opt out' of the compromissory clause altogether if they so wished. A model which provided for this was to be found in Article 14 of the 1971 Convention on Unlawful Acts against the Safety of Civil Aviation (the Montreal Convention).[19] This was replicated as Article 29(2) of the CEDAW and Article 30(2) of the UNCAT, and indeed as Article 92(2) of the CMW and Article 42(2) of the CED.[20] Thus, the only UN human rights treaty with a compromissory clause which refers to the use of a compulsory inter-State procedure is the CERD. As a result, whilst determining the relationship between the compromissory clause and the inter-State procedure is very important as regards cases concerning the CERD, doing so has little real direct relevance for the other UN human rights treaties. The indirect significance may, however, be considerable.

7.3 INTER-STATE COMMUNICATIONS BEFORE THE CERD

For the most of fifty years, the best that could be said about the inter-State procedures provided for in the UN human rights treaties was that their potential was untried. Or, to put it rather less kindly, they had never been used, and many – possibly most – commentators tended to assume it was unlikely that they ever would be.[21] This changed abruptly in the spring of 2018 when, on 8 March, Qatar submitted two communications against the

[18] UNCAT, Art 21(1). At the time of writing only sixty-two of the 171 State parties to the UNCAT have made such a declaration.

[19] See, e.g., Manfred Nowak, Mortiz Binz, and Giuliana Monina, *The United Nations Convention against Torture and Its Optional Protocol: A Commentary*, 2nd ed. (Oxford: Oxford University Press, 2019), p. 684.

[20] For the text of CEDAW Art 29(2), see n. 11.

[21] Many more recent general works barely mention the inter-State procedures of the UN human rights treaty bodies at all, including those written by UN 'insiders'. See, e.g., Jane Connors and

UAE and against Saudi Arabia under the Article 11 procedure of the CERD. This was shortly followed by the State of Palestine, on 23 April 2018, submitting a communication against Israel.[22] However, the communications brought by Qatar were suspended at the request of the parties following the Al Ula Agreement of 5 January 2021 and subsequently terminated in accordance with the provisions of that agreement in January 2022 and January 2023.[23] The communication brought by the State of Palestine, however, remains under consideration by the CERD Committee, having been declared admissible on 30 April 2021.[24]

It is not difficult to discern a potential motivation for Qatar bringing the communication against the UAE under the CERD's inter-State procedure: it was still unclear whether it was necessary to have utilised the CERD's inter-State procedure in relation to a dispute before the ICJ could exercise jurisdiction over that dispute under the compromissory clause. In May 2018, the CERD Committee formally transmitted the communications to the respondent States and requested that they respond within three months, as required by the Article 11 procedure.[25]

Shortly afterwards, on 11 June 2018 and some three months after it had submitted its communication under the CERD, Qatar instituted proceedings against the UAE before the ICJ in the case concerning the *Application of the International Convention on the Elimination of Racial Discrimination* (here-

Markus Schmidt, 'United Nations', in Daniel Moeckli, Sangeeta Shah, and Sandesh Sivakumaran (eds.), *International Human Rights Law*, 2nd ed. (Oxford: Oxford University Press, 2014), p. 381, which laconically mentions them in three lines (this being before the communications to the CERD in 2018); Neuman, a former member of the HRC, when considering its 'principal activities', does not mention it at all (Gerald L. Neuman, 'Giving meaning and effect to human rights: the contributions of Human Rights Committee members', in Daniel Moeckli, Helen Keller, and Corina Heri (eds.), *The Human Rights Covenants at 50* (Oxford: Oxford University Press, 2018), p. 31).

22 See OHCHR, 'CERD information note on inter-State communications', 30 August 2018, www.ohchr.org/en/press-releases/2018/09/cerd-information-note-inter-state-communications (accessed 1 July 2022).

23 See the decisions issued by the CERD Committee on 19 January 2022 (OHCHR, 'Decision of the *ad hoc* Conciliation Commission on the termination concerning the interstate communication *Qatar* v. *the Kingdom of Saudi Arabia*'), and on 26 January 2023 ('Decision of the *ad hoc* Conciliation Commission on the termination of the proceedings concerning the interstate communication Qatar v. the United Arab Emirates'). https://www.ohchr.org/en/treaty-bodies/cerd/inter-state-communications (accessed 18 August 2023).

24 CERD Committee, *Decision on the Admissibility of the Inter-State Communication Submitted by the State of Palestine against Israel* (30 April 2021) UN Doc. CERD/C/103/R.6. This is considered further in Section 7.5.

25 See OHCHR, 'CERD information note'.

after *Qatar* v. *UAE*) with jurisdiction grounded in Article 22 and made a request for the indication of provisional measures. For the first time, the court had the opportunity to consider whether it could exercise jurisdiction over a claim where the inter-State process within a UN human rights treaty had been initiated. The position regarding Saudi Arabia was very different from that of the UAE since, like Rwanda in the *Armed Activities* case,[26] it had made a declaration excluding the application of Article 22 at the time of its accession to the CERD in September 1997. As a result, no case could be taken to the ICJ, and the communication under the CERD procedure was the only option available.

This, however, was not the only case concerning the CERD then before the ICJ. In 2017 Ukraine had invoked Article 22 of CERD as providing a basis of jurisdiction when initiating proceedings against the Russian Federation for a range of alleged violations in the case concerning the *Application of the International Convention on the Suppression of International Terrorism and of the International Convention on the Elimination of All Forms of Racial Discrimination* (hereafter *Ukraine* v. *Russia*). In its order of 19 April 2017, the court observed that it was unnecessary for it to resolve the question left open in *Georgia* v. *Russia* of whether the procedures provided for in Article 22 were alternative or cumulative when determining whether it had prima facie jurisdiction to make an award of provisional measures. It simply observed that 'the fact that Ukraine did not bring the matter before the CERD Committee does not prevent the Court from concluding that it does have *prima facie* jurisdiction'.[27] It was, then, hardly surprising that the court took a similar approach in its order of 23 July 2018 when granting provisional measures in *Qatar* v. *UAE*.[28]

The question of whether these procedures were alternative or cumulative was finally settled by the court in its order of 8 November 2019 concerning the preliminary objections of Russia to the court's exercising jurisdiction in *Ukraine* v. *Russia*, when it concluded that 'Article 22 of CERD imposes alternative preconditions to the Court's jurisdiction'.[29] As a result, and

[26] See n. 11. Rwanda removed its declaration concerning CERD Art 22 in December 2008.

[27] *Application of the International Convention on the Suppression of International Terrorism and of the International Convention on the Elimination of All Forms of Racial Discrimination (Ukraine* v. *Russian Federation)* (Provisional Measures, Order) [2017] ICJ Rep. 104 at para. 60.

[28] *Application of the International Convention on the Elimination of All Forms of Racial Discrimination (Qatar* v. *United Arab Emirates)* (Provisional Measures, Order) [2018] ICJ Rep. 406 at paras 39–40.

[29] *Application of the International Convention on the Suppression of International Terrorism and of the International Convention on the Elimination of All Forms of Racial Discrimination*

although the question had figured heavily in the written pleadings of the parties,[30] by the time of the oral hearings in *Qatar* v. *UAE* in August 2020, Qatar was able simply to refer to the court's admissibility decision in *Ukraine* v. *Russia* case in conclusive support of its position.[31]

Just over a year later, Armenia became the next State to bring a case before the ICJ concerning the interpretation and application of the CERD, against Azerbaijan. In its application of 16 September 2021, Armenia briefly noted that 'the Parties have been unable to settle this dispute through negotiations or by the procedures expressly provided for in the CERD'. This was not entirely true since Armenia had not made an inter-State communication to the CERD, but, as it correctly pointed out, 'the Court has held that the language of Article 22 "imposes alternative preconditions to the Court's jurisdiction", such that a State seeking to refer a dispute under the CERD to the Court need only satisfy one of the two preconditions. In the present case, the negotiation precondition has been satisfied'.[32] A week later, Azerbaijan brought a similar case against Armenia based on Article 22, and it did not even mention the issue in its application when discussing seisin.[33] It too had not brought an inter-State communication under the CERD procedures. It seems that matter has been resolved and is no longer even worth raising.

However, in the *Qatar* v. *UAE* case, Qatar had brought a communication before the CERD Committee, and as a result there was a danger that Qatar might be hoist on its own petard: having initiated the process before the CERD (in what the UAE claimed was merely a 'tick-box' process in order to be seen to be fulfilling a potential precondition for the exercise of jurisdiction[34]), might it be necessary for the ICJ to allow that process to run its course before it could consider the case? This argument was advanced by the UAE during the oral hearings before the court, but was challenged by Qatar, which claimed that 'all [Article 22] says is that if the dispute is not settled by

(Ukraine v. *Russian Federation)* (Preliminary Objections, Judgment) [2019] ICJ Rep. 558 at para. 113.

30 See, e.g., *Qatar* v. *UAE* (Qatar, Memorial), paras 3.115–57 and (UAE, Counter-memorial), p. 92.

31 *Qatar* v. *UAE* (Oral Pleadings, 2 September 2020, CR 2020/7), p. 18 (Mr Al-Khulaifi, para. 25) and p. 50 (Mr Martin, paras 4 ff).

32 ICJ, *Application Instituting Proceedings and Application for Provisional Measures (Republic of Armenia* v. *Republic of Azerbaijan*), vol. I, 16 September 2021, www.icj-cij.org/public/files/case-related/180/180-20210916-APP-01-00-EN.pdf (accessed 1 July 2022), para. 17.

33 ICJ, *Application Instituting Proceedings, Republic of Azerbaijan* v. *Republic of Armenia*, 23 September 2021, www.icj-cij.org/public/files/case-related/181/181-20210923-APP-01-00-EN.pdf (accessed 1 July 2022), paras 24–26.

34 *Qatar* v. *UAE* (UAE, Counter-memorial), p. 92.

negotiation or by recourse to the CERD procedures, an applicant State may go to Court. There is nothing about this language that even hints in the direction of an implicit bar on parallel proceedings.'[35]

This is a somewhat disingenuous argument, since parallel proceedings are one thing (and might give rise to an issue of admissibility),[36] and preconditions to jurisdiction are quite another. If, as seems clear, the court assumed that adopting the cumulative approach would mean that negotiations would have failed to resolve the dispute before the CERD procedures could be initiated,[37] why should it not also mean that the procedure initiated under the CERD also had to fail to do so before the ICJ could be seized of the dispute if the procedures were alternatives? Indeed, in *Ukraine* v. *Russia*, the very reason that the court felt that – for the purposes of Article 22 – negotiations and the inter-State procedure were to be considered as alternatives and not cumulative prerequisites was that, given the nature of the Article 11 process, they amounted to more or less the same thing: the court said that '"negotiation" and the "procedures expressly provided for in [the] Convention" are two means to achieve the same objective, namely to settle a dispute by agreement'.[38] It was for this reason that the court took the view that[39]

> should negotiation and the CERD Committee procedure be considered cumulative, States would have to try to negotiate an agreed solution to their dispute and, after negotiation has not been successful, take the matter before the CERD Committee for further negotiation, again in order to reach an agreed solution . . . . It would not be reasonable to require States parties which have already failed to reach an agreed settlement through negotiations to engage in an additional set of negotiations in accordance with the modalities set out in Articles 11 to 13 of CERD.

Against this background, it is not obvious why – if a State has chosen to structure its search for a negotiated solution through the procedures of the CERD, and if those procedures are still ongoing – the court should treat them

35 *Qatar* v. *UAE* (Oral Pleadings, 2 September 2020, CR 2020/7), p. 55 (Mr Martin, para. 22).

36 On this point, see Chapter 2 in this volume.

37 *Ukraine* v. *Russia* (Preliminary Objections, Judgment), para. 110, where it says: 'It follows that should negotiation and the CERD Committee procedure be considered cumulative, States would have to try to negotiate an agreed solution to their dispute and, *after negotiation has not been successful*, take the matter before the CERD Committee for further negotiation, again in order to reach an agreed solution' (emphasis added).

38 Ibid.

39 Ibid.

as if they have already failed to produce one. The argument against parallel proceedings seems persuasive.

As it turned out, none of this mattered since, in February 2021, the court ultimately concluded in *Qatar* v. *UAE* that it did not have jurisdiction anyway, because the subject matter of the dispute did not fall within the scope of the Convention,[40] something that the CERD Committee might not necessarily agree with and which will be considered further below. It is, however, notable that the court made no reference to its statements in *Ukraine* v. *Russia* concerning the nature of the CERD's inter-State process, nor did it make any comment on the suggestion that the CERD process would need to run its course (or had to have failed) before the court could assume jurisdiction under Article 22. This, therefore, remains an open question.

As a result, the 'new dawn' for the use of the inter-State procedure under the CERD might be very short-lived. One does not have to be overly cynical to wonder whether Qatar's use of the Article 11 procedure was simply intended to 'head off at the pass' any objection to the ICJ assuming jurisdiction based on the compromissory clause, given that the question of whether the use of the procedure was a prerequisite for its having jurisdiction under Article 22 of the CERD was still an open question at the time the case was brought. Moreover, it was already clear from the provisional measures award in *Ukraine* v. *Russia* that doing so would not stand in the way of such an award being made, and so it proved.

It is, then, known that the use of the Article 11 inter-State procedure is not a prerequisite, but it is still *not known* whether, if initiated, it is necessary to allow that process to run its course before the court can exercise jurisdiction under Article 22. As a result, it is very difficult to see why a State contemplating recourse to the ICJ under the compromissory clause would now choose to bring such a claim before the CERD, and, as has been seen, the most recent States to bring cases before the ICJ on the basis of the compromissory clause – Armenia and Azerbaijan – have not done so.[41] This suggests that States are only likely to do so if they genuinely believe it would help resolve a dispute which they may have with another State concerning matters falling within the scope of the CERD – and the lack of any such cases for nearly fifty years might suggest that not many do.

[40] ICJ, *Application of the International Convention on the Elimination of All Forms of Racial Discrimination (Qatar* v. *United Arab Emirates)* (Preliminary Objections, Judgment), 4 February 2021, www.icj-cij.org/public/files/case-related/172/172-20210204-JUD-01-00-EN.pdf (accessed 1 July 2022), para. 114.

[41] See nn. 32 and 33.

Nevertheless, there are a significant number of States in respect of whom the Article 11 inter-State procedure may still be the only available option. There are currently some twenty-five States which have made declarations excluding the operation of Article 22. As has been seen, Rwanda was one such State, and this prevented the DRC from bringing a claim before the court on that basis.[42] Saudi Arabia is another, which may explain why Qatar has not sought to lodge proceedings against it, as it has against the UAE. Yet another State which has not made such a declaration is Israel.[43] This may again explain why Palestine initiated a case before the CERD under the Article 11 procedure rather than initiating proceedings before the ICJ based on Article 22; it may not have had any better alternative.[44]

Alongside these procedural points, there are more positive and powerful reasons why a State might choose the CERD inter-State procedure, now that it has become better known and better understood. The chief attraction may be the nature of the procedure itself and the manner in which it has now come to be understood by the CERD. As a result, it may well be that now the genie is out of the 'inter-State procedure' bottle, it will not so easily be put back in.

7.4 THE NATURE OF THE CERD ARTICLE 11 PROCESS

By November 2019, when the ICJ decided in *Ukraine* v. *Russia* that the requirements of Article 22 were alternative rather than cumulative, the CERD Committee had itself already come to the same conclusion, although it is not entirely clear why it felt it necessary to do so. As has been said, in May 2018 the CERD Committee referred the communications received in March 2018 to the UAE and Saudi Arabia. Under the terms of Article 11(1): 'Within three months, the receiving state shall submit to the Committee written explanations or statements clarifying the matter and the remedy, if any, that may have been taken by that State.' If this does not produce a satisfactory outcome, Article 11(2) then provides that 'within six months after the receipt by the receiving state of the initial communication, either State shall have the right to refer the matter again to the Committee by notifying the

[42] See n. 11.

[43] Its declaration provides that 'the State of Israel does not consider itself bound by the provisions of article 22 of the said Convention'; see https://treaties.un.org.

[44] Other States with declarations excluding the obligation in Art 22 are Afghanistan, Bahrain, China, Cuba, Egypt, Equatorial Guinea, India, Indonesia, Iraq, Kuwait, Lebanon, Libya, Madagascar, Morocco, Mozambique, Nepal, Singapore, Syria, Thailand, Turkey, USA, Vietnam, and Yemen. A further ten countries have now removed similar declarations which they had made at the time of their ratification or accession.

Committee and also the other state'. Qatar did so in respect of the UAE on 29 October 2018, thus triggering the next stage of the process.

The CERD Committee received submissions concerning its jurisdiction and the admissibility of both cases and gave its decisions on 27 August 2019.[45] The UAE argued, inter alia, that the case should be inadmissible as a result of there being 'parallel proceedings', arguing that by taking its case before the ICJ, Qatar had both created a situation of *lis pendens* and 'made its choice' as to how it wished to proceed.[46] It argued that the process was, in essence, linear: first, a State needed to action the Article 11 process and only after having done so could it turn to the ICJ under Article 22. The suggestion was that once Qatar had made its application to the ICJ, there could be no 'going back' to the inter-State procedure under Article 11, and so the communication should be considered inadmissible by the CERD Committee.

If there was a real concern that the possibility of parallel proceedings might render the communication inadmissible before the CERD Committee, then the easiest way to address this might have been for the CERD Committee to have taken the view that the ICJ should only have jurisdiction under Article 22 if the inter-State process in Article 11 had in fact been utilised. That approach would avoid the possibility completely. However, the CERD Committee decided otherwise, and, pre-empting by some months the decision of the ICJ in November 2019 in the *Ukraine* v. *Russia* case on this key question, it decided that 'the word "or" between "by negotiation" and "by the procedures expressly provided for in this Convention" in Article 22 of the Convention clearly indicates that the States parties may choose between the alternatives proposed by that provision'.[47]

The logic of this finding was that the ICJ should be able to consider the dispute as well as, and potentially at the same time as, the CERD Committee itself. This was a prudent, and arguably inevitable, conclusion. If the CERD Committee had taken a different view, this would have meant that the ICJ should not have been able to exercise jurisdiction under Article 22, at least as

45 See CERD Committee, *Decision on the Jurisdiction of the Inter-State Communication Submitted by Qatar against the United Arab Emirates* (27 August 2019) UN Doc. CERD/C/99/3; CERD Committee, *Decision on the Admissibility of the Inter-State Communication Submitted by Qatar against the United Arab Emirates* (27 August 2010) UN Doc. CERD/C/99/4; CERD Committee, *Decision on the Jurisdiction of the Inter-State Communication Submitted by Qatar against Saudi Arabia* (27 August 2019) UN Doc. CERD/C/99/5; CERD Committee, *Decision on the Admissibility of the Inter-State Communication Submitted by Qatar against Saudi Arabia* (27 August 2010) UN Doc. CERD/C/99/6.

46 *Decision on Admissibility*, *Qatar* v. *UAE*, CERD/C/99/4, paras 18–21.

47 Ibid., para. 49.

far as the CERD Committee was concerned. But the ICJ had not yet decided this point – and what if the ICJ thought otherwise? There was no good reason to suppose that the ICJ would defer to the views of the CERD Committee regarding the interpretation of Article 22 and the extent of its own jurisdiction. At the same time it is not entirely obvious why the CERD Committee thought it necessary to comment on this question at all. It was not relevant to the question of its own jurisdiction, and all that it did was confirm that parallel proceedings were a possibility. It would only have been necessary for the CERD Committee to arrive at a conclusion on this question were it to believe that parallel proceedings before the ICJ might, in fact, render the case inadmissible as far as the CERD Committee was concerned.

However, reaching such a conclusion would fail to recognise the different purposes of Articles 11 and 22. Article 22 is about seizing the ICJ of a dispute concerning the interpretation and application of the Convention. Article 11 (1) is very different: it permits a State to bring a communication 'if it considers that another state is not giving effect to the provisions of this Convention'. In other words, the 'threshold' for initiating the inter-State procedure under Article 11 is very different: unlike Article 22, it does not necessarily require that there be a 'dispute' as such when the process is initiated *at all.*[48] What is required is that the applicant State believes that there *might be* a dispute, and the first stage of the process, as set out in Article 11(1), is very much geared towards confirming whether this is, in fact, the case. It is only if there is a dispute, and if that dispute is not otherwise resolved by the parties, that the procedure progresses to the next stage.

Moreover, should it progress, the procedure to be followed barely qualifies as a 'dispute settlement mechanism' at all. According to that procedure, the dispute is to be referred to an *ad hoc* Conciliation Commission, established in accordance with Article 12 of the CERD, the role of which is to produce a report which the State parties involved are free to either accept or reject. Whilst the process is overseen by the chair of the CERD Committee, the CERD Committee itself is not involved in the substantive aspects of that process *as a committee* at all. Under Article 12(1)(a):

> The Chairman shall appoint an ad hoc Conciliation Commission ... comprising five persons who may or may not be members of the Committee. The Members of the Commissions shall be appointed with the unanimous consent of the parties to the dispute, and its good offices shall be made

[48] On the existence of an international dispute, see Chapter 1 in this volume.

available to the States concerned with a view to an amicable settlement of the matter on the basis of respect for this Convention.

If there is no agreement between the parties concerning the composition of the commission within three months, the Committee is to elect the remaining members from amongst its own members,[49] but they are to serve in a personal capacity.[50] Against this background, it is easy to understand why the ICJ in *Ukraine* v. *Russia* felt able to conclude that[51]

> the references to the 'amicable solution' of the dispute and to the States' communication of acceptance of the Conciliation Commission's recommendations indicate, in the Court's view, that the objective of the CERD Committee procedure is for the States concerned to reach an agreed settlement of their dispute .... In the view of the Court, the context of Article 22 rather indicates that it would not be reasonable to require States parties which have already failed to reach an agreed settlement through negotiations to engage in an additional set of negotiations in accordance with the modalities set out in Articles 11 to 13 of CERD.

What is less easy to understand is why the CERD Committee felt the need, a few months beforehand, to go considerably further and say that[52]

> the Committee, an expert monitoring body entitled to adopt non-binding recommendations is not convinced that a principle of *lis pendens* or *electa una via* is applicable which should rule out proceedings concerning the same matter by a judicial body entitled to adopt a legally binding judgment.

Such a remarkably self-effacing statement is probably unprecedented in the history of the UN human rights treaty system which over the years has gone out of its way to press for its having quasi-judicial credentials.[53] It is difficult to

[49] CERD, Art 12(1)(b).

[50] Ibid., Art 12(2).

[51] *Ukraine* v. *Russia* (Preliminary Objections, Judgment), paras 109–10.

[52] *Decision on Admissibility, Qatar* v. *UAE*, CERD/C/99/4, para. 49.

[53] In its General Comment No. 33 ('The obligations of State parties under the Optional Protocol to the International Covenant on Civil and Political Rights' (5 November 2008) UN Doc. CCPR/C/GC/33), the HRC expressly says that 'while the function of the Human Rights Committee in considering individual communications is not, as such, that of a judicial body, the views issued by the Committee under the Optional Protocol exhibit some important characteristics of a judicial decision. They are arrived at in a judicial spirit.' See, e.g., Ludovic Hennebel, 'The Human Rights Committee', in Frédéric Mégret and Philip Alston (eds.), *The United Nations and Human Rights*, 2nd ed. (Oxford: Oxford University Press, 2020), p. 355, who stresses the importance of recognising the committee's quasi-judicial function, since it is 'the closest thing to a "universal human rights court"'. He refers to the oft-used expression that whilst it is not a court, 'it acts in a "judicial spirit"'. See also Andrew Byrnes, 'The Committee

avoid the conclusion that the CERD Committee – perhaps unwittingly, and in a well-meaning attempt to both distance itself from the ICJ whilst preserving its capacity to persevere with its Articles 11–13 inter-State process – has thrown several 'babies out with the bath water'. At the very least, such a comment tends to legitimise a 'parting of the ways' between the work of the human rights treaty bodies and adjudicative bodies established under other mechanisms – a trend which arguably has been long in the making and which, in its subsequent admissibility decision in the third of its Article 11 cases, *Palestine* v. *Israel*,[54] the CERD Committee seems to have made a manifest reality.

7.5 THE WORK OF THE UN HUMAN RIGHTS TREATY BODIES AND THE ICJ

It cannot really be said that the ICJ has visibly accorded a great deal of weight to the work of the UN human rights treaty bodies in its judgments. Historically the court was reluctant to draw on the work of other courts and tribunals directly, though its practice in this regard has changed significantly over time. In the early phases of that transition, it had on several occasions referenced the work of various UN human rights treaty bodies when this was supportive of the approach the court was planning to take on other grounds.[55] However, in the first case in which it set out its approach to their work in more generic terms, the *Diallo* case in 2010, it sent out some mixed messages. The court was called on to determine whether the arrest and expulsion of Mr Diallo had been in breach of Article 13 of the ICCPR and, having set out its interpretation of that Article, noted that it was 'fully corroborated by the jurisprudence of the Human Rights Committee established by the Covenant to ensure compliance with that instrument by the States parties'.[56] This reflected its approach in previous cases. However, it then noted that the HRC had 'built up a considerable body of interpretative case law' and expressed the view that[57]

against Torture', in Frédéric Mégret and Philip Alston (eds.), *The United Nations and Human Rights*, 2nd ed. (Oxford: Oxford University Press, 2020), p. 499, who emphasises the quasi-judicial formulation of the decisions of the CAT.

54 See CERD Committee, *Decision on the Committee's Jurisdiction Regarding the Inter-State Communication Submitted by the State of Palestine v. Israel* (12 December 2019) Part I (UN Doc. CERD/D/100/3), Part II (UN Doc. CERD/D/100/4), and Part III (UN Doc. CERD/D/100/5), considered further below.

55 E.g., *Legal Consequences of the Construction of a Wall in the Occupied Palestinian Territory* (Advisory Opinion) [2004] ICJ Rep. 136, paras 109 and 136.

56 *Ahmadou Sadio Diallo*, para. 66. It also quoted the work of the European Court of Human Rights, the Inter-American Court of Human Rights, and the African Commission on Human and Peoples' Rights in support of its views (paras 66–68).

57 Ibid.

> although the Court is in no way obliged, in the exercise of its judicial functions, to model its own interpretation of the Covenant on that of the Committee, it believes that it should ascribe great weight to the interpretation adopted by this independent body that was established specifically to supervise the application of that treaty.

The reason given for this was[58]

> to achieve the necessary clarity and the essential consistency of international law, as well as legal security, to which both the individuals with guaranteed rights and the States obliged to comply with treaty obligations are entitled.

As this makes clear, whilst the court was willing to place 'great weight' on the approaches taken by the treaty bodies to the interpretation of the conventions, it did not feel itself to be constrained by them. Indeed, in the *Diallo* case, Judge Greenwood and Judge Keith believed the court to have gone further than the HRC in its interpretation of Article 13 of the ICCPR.[59]

Shortly afterwards, in the *Habré* case (2012), the court made a somewhat caustic reference to the 2006 decision of the CAT in *Guengueng et al.* v. *Senegal*,[60] which dealt with substantially the same issue: the failure of Senegal to fulfil its obligations under the UNCAT regarding the prosecution or extradition of Habré as regards acts of torture committed in Chad by his agents whilst he was president. The ICJ was making a fairly obvious point that treaty obligations under the UNCAT are not retrospective, and it is difficult to see why it thought it necessary to criticise the CAT for not having directly addressed this in its decision, when it was wholly unnecessary for it to have done so. More significant for the current purposes, the court said nothing about the general relevance of the work of the CAT for its own consideration of the question; indeed, but for this critical aside, the ICJ fails to even acknowledge that in 2006 the Committee had decided that Senegal 'has violated Article 5, paragraph 2, and Article 7 of the Convention'[61] some six years before the ICJ itself came to the same conclusion as regards Article 7.[62]

58 Ibid.

59 *Ahmadou Sadio Diallo*, Declaration of Judges Keith and Greenwood, paras 11–13. See also Eirik Bjorge, 'Case concerning Ahmadou Sadio Diallo' (2011) 105 AJIL 534–40.

60 The Court observed that 'when the Committee considered Mr. Habré's situation, the question of the temporal scope of the obligations contained in the Convention was not raised, nor did the Committee itself address that question'. *Questions Relating to the Obligation to Prosecute or Extradite* (Judgment), para. 101, referencing CAT, *Guengueng et al.* v. Senegal (19 May 2006) UN Doc. CAT/C/36/D/181/2001.

61 *Guengueng et al.* v. *Senegal*, para. 9.11.

62 *Questions Relating to the Obligation to Prosecute or Extradite* (Judgment), para. 112(5).

The court also found Senegal to be in violation of Article 6(2) due to its failure to have made preliminary inquiries into the facts of the case. This finding was really only possible because – following the decision of the CAT in 2006 that Senegal was in breach of its obligations under Article 5(2) of the UNCAT by not having legislation granting its courts universal jurisdiction in respect of acts of torture – Senegal in 2007 enacted the relevant legislation.[63] The court recognised this, made reference to domestic decisions to this effect in the case brought by Guengueng in 2001, and noted that 'the fact that the required legislation had been adopted only in 2007 necessarily affected Senegal's implementation of the obligations imposed on it by Article 6, paragraph 2, and Article 7, paragraph 1, of the Convention'.[64] The failure of the ICJ to even mention in passing the 2006 decision of the CAT on this very point, which helped precipitate the legislation in question, is quite remarkable – and hardly speaks to the work of the human rights treaty bodies being accorded much respect, let alone 'weight', despite ritual incantations to the contrary.

The 2021 decision of the ICJ in *Qatar* v. *UAE* takes this to an altogether different level. It is axiomatic that a court can only hear a case if its jurisdiction embraces the subject matter of the dispute – jurisdiction *ratione materiae*. Thus, in a case brought under the compromissory clause in the CERD, there must be an alleged breach of the CERD before the court can proceed to the merits. The essence of the cases brought by Qatar before both the CERD Committee and the ICJ concerned a series of measures which it claimed were discriminatory against Qataris.[65] The UAE objected, both before the CERD Committee and the ICJ, that the measures in question did not raise any issues under the CERD since, for the purposes of the Convention, racial discrimination was defined in Article 1 as meaning 'any distinction, exclusion, restriction or preference based on race, colour, descent, or national or ethnic origin'. Discrimination based on 'nationality' alone was not, it argued, addressed by the Convention, and so neither body exercised jurisdiction *ratione materiae*.[66]

63 See generally Lutz Oette, 'Universal and extraterritorial jurisdiction for torture', in Malcolm D. Evans and Jens Modvig (eds.), *Research Handbook on Torture: Legal and Medical Perspectives on Prohibition and Prevention* (Cheltenham: Edward Elgar, 2020), p. 357.

64 *Questions Relating to the Obligation to Prosecute or Extradite* (Judgment), paras 112, 77.

65 The core of the issue lay in the statement issued by the UAE on 5 June 2017, which Qatar characterised as an 'expulsion order' and 'travel ban', in which the UAE took action aimed at 'preventing Qatari nationals from entering the UAE or crossing its point of entry, giving Qatari residents and visitors in the UAE 14 days to leave the country for precautionary security reasons. The UAE nationals are likewise banned from traveling to or staying in Qatar or transiting through its territories.' See *Qatar* v. *UAE* (Preliminary Objections, Judgment), para. 26.

66 Perhaps the clearest and pithiest summary of this is to be found in *Decision on Jurisdiction, Qatar* v. *UAE*, CERD/C/99/3, para. 36, which sums up the Qatari argument on this as being

This debate has a long lineage, which is beyond the scope of this chapter to review. Basically, it comes down to whether nationality is to be understood as a transient status and, as such, is to be differentiated from the enduring characteristics of race, colour, descent, or national or ethnic origin, which are to be understood as immutable. This is then reflected in the confused interplay between Article 1(2) of the CERD, which provides that 'the Convention shall not apply to distinctions, exclusions, restrictions or preferences made by a State Party to this Convention between citizens and non-citizens', and Article 1(3) of the CERD, which provides that 'nothing in this Convention may be interpreted as affecting in any way the legal provisions of States Parties concerning nationality, citizenship or naturalization, provided that such provisions do not discriminate against any particular nationality'. For some, this suggests that discrimination on grounds of current nationality, rather than on grounds of national origin, is not addressed by the CERD at all. For others, it means that whilst such distinctions are indeed permissible in favour of citizens as against non-citizens generally, they cannot be targeted against a *particular* nationality.[67] Whatever view one takes of this debate, it is clear that it goes to the very heart of the meaning and scope of the application of CERD – a classic case of 'interpretation and application' of a convention if ever there was one.

It was the ICJ which first had to address this issue when, in July 2018, it considered whether to make an award of provisional measures.[68] Perhaps unsurprisingly, the court thought it 'need not decide at this stage of the proceedings . . . . Which of these divergent interpretations of the Convention is the correct one', it being sufficient that they evidenced the existence of a dispute concerning the CERD.[69] This tied into the related question of whether the measures adopted by the UAE did in fact target Qataris rather than all non-nationals, and, given that it appeared that they did, the court was able to

'the communication only refers to differentiated treatment based on nationality, a matter falling wholly outside the scope of the Convention'.

67 The difficulties posed by this are reflected by Patrick Thornberry, 'The Committee for the Elimination of Racial Discrimination', in Frédéric Mégret and Philip Alston (eds.), *The United Nations and Human Rights*, 2nd ed. (Oxford: Oxford University Press, 2020), p. 329, who notes that whilst 'the provisions are not unambiguous', the text appears 'narrow' when compared to 'the canon of international human rights' and that 'in practice, CERD has endeavoured to transcend any such limitations'. Loosely translated, this seems to suggest that the CERD does indeed try to go somewhat beyond the strict confines of the text.

68 *Qatar* v. *UAE* (Provisional Measures, Order), p. 406; the position of the UAE on this question is set out at para. 24.

69 Ibid., paras 29 and 41.

conclude that 'at least some of the rights asserted by Qatar ... are plausible',[70] thus justifying an award of provisional measures.

This, however, provoked a trenchant joint declaration by Judges Tomka, Gaja, and Gevorgian who entertained no doubts that 'when the Convention considers "national origin" as one of the prohibited bases for discrimination, it does not refer to nationality. In our view, the two terms are not identical and should not be understood as synonymous'.[71] They thought the reason 'easily explained', arguing:[72]

> Should CERD be considered as covering also discrimination based on nationality, the Convention would be a far-reaching instrument, that contains a clause providing that, with regard to a wide array of civil rights that are protected under the CERD, all foreigners must be treated by the host State in the same way as nationals of the State who enjoy the most favourable treatment.

As a result, they felt the dispute did not fall, even on a prima facie basis, within the scope of the CERD, and the rights invoked were simply 'not plausible'.[73]

They were not alone in their doubts. Judge Crawford identified this as a 'legal difficulty' facing Qatar, but one he felt he need not resolve[74] since, on the facts as he read them, provisional measures were not justified on other grounds.[75] Judge Salam, however, had no such reservations. He said: 'I am convinced that the Court does not have prima facie jurisdiction *ratione materiae* .... It is clear from Article 1 of the CERD that this Convention applies to "any distinction, exclusion, restriction or preference based on race, colour, descent, or national or ethnic origin". There is, however, no mention of discrimination on the basis of "nationality", the object of the Applicant's complaints.'[76] Noting also that this was a question which the court had not previously faced, he thought 'the distinction between "nationality" and "national origin" should not ... admit of any confusion'.[77]

Where, then, had this 'confusion' come from? Although he does not say so, it is implicit that it comes from the interpretive work of the CERD

70 Ibid., para. 54.

71 Ibid., Joint Declaration of Judges Tomka, Gaja, and Gevorgian, para. 4.

72 Ibid.

73 Ibid., para. 7.

74 Ibid., Dissenting Opinion of Judge Crawford, paras 1 and 17. He left the question ajar by observing that the collective expulsion of persons of a certain nationality 'is not *apparently* covered by the CERD' (para. 1, emphasis added).

75 These being that there was neither a risk of irreparable prejudice nor urgency (ibid., para. 18).

76 Ibid., Dissenting Opinion of Judge Salam, para. 2.

77 Ibid., para. 5.

Committee, in particular its General Recommendation No. 30, which concerns discrimination against non-citizens.[78] In their declaration, Judges Tomka, Gaja, and Gevorian are careful to point out that in this recommendation the CERD Committee did *not* equate nationality and national origin. Rather, it 'identified certain conditions for the prohibition of discrimination that are specific to nationality and immigration and do not apply when the bases of discrimination listed in Article 1, paragraph 1, are in question'.[79] In other words, the CERD Committee has, in their view, extended the definition of racial discrimination beyond that provided for in the text of the Convention. As they put it, 'it would be difficult to give weight to this view of the CERD Committee since it gives no reason for its interpretation'.[80]

Judge Salam went further, however, challenging the relevance of the CERD Committee's opinion altogether, saying:[81]

> I would further note that, regardless of the 'great weight' that should be ascribed to the work of an 'independent body' such as the CERD Committee (see *Ahmadou Sadio Diallo (Republic of Guinea v. Democratic Republic of the Congo), Merits, Judgment, I.C.J. Reports 2010 (II)*, p. 664, para. 66), the fact remains that the recommendations of that Committee cannot be considered to be an expression of a subsequent practice of the parties to CERD (in the sense of Article 31, paragraph 3 (b), of the 1969 Vienna Convention on the Law of Treaties).

For all its robustness, this puts the issue in stark relief: whilst it may be one thing to accord 'great weight' to the work of a UN human rights treaty body, can this lead to potentially extending the scope of the treaty in the manner of General Recommendation No. 30? Was this merely interpreting the CERD, or was it tantamount to the establishment of a new set of obligations not sanctioned by the text?

In August 2019 the CERD Committee itself considered the question and, perhaps unsurprisingly, followed the approach it set out in its General Recommendation. Importantly, however, the Committee seems to have conceded that its approach does indeed go beyond the text of the Convention and, in effect, stakes out new ground by affirming that 'differential treatment

78 CERD Committee, 'General Recommendation No. 30: Discrimination against non-citizens', 1 October 2002, www.refworld.org/publisher,CERD,GENERAL,,45139e084,0.html (accessed 1 July 2022).

79 *Qatar* v. *UAE* (Provisional Measures, Order), Joint Declaration of Judges Tomka, Gaja, and Gevorgian, para. 5.

80 Ibid.

81 Ibid., Dissenting Opinion of Judge Salam, para. 8.

based on citizenship or immigration status will constitute discrimination if the criteria for such differentiation, judged in the light of the objectives and purposes of the Convention, are not applied pursuant to a legitimate aim, and are not proportional to the achievement of this aim'.[82] Alluding to the claim that there is no basis for this in the Convention, the Committee says that 'it is in the light of this constant practice' that it exercises competence *ratione materiae* when confronted with differences of treatment based on nationality and that 'it considers itself competent' to consider whether such differences have a legitimate aim, are proportionate, and 'do not result in a denial of fundamental human rights of non-citizens'.[83] In short, the reason why it is acceptable for the CERD Committee to say this is because it says so.

How 'great' is the weight to be put on such opinions of the CERD Committee? 'Not a lot' appears to be the answer given by the ICJ in its judgment in February 2021. As has been seen, the court concluded that there was no jurisdiction *ratione materiae* over the subject matter of the dispute. Approaching the question initially on the basis of Article 31 of the Vienna Convention on the Law of Treaties, it accepted that 'nationality is a legal attribute which is within the discretionary power of the State and can change during a person's lifetime', whereas 'national origin', like race, colour, and descent, are all 'characteristics that are inherent at birth'.[84] It almost inevitably flows from this that the court would consider the 'ordinary meaning' of nationality as 'not encompassing current nationality';[85] that Article 1(2) and (3) 'does not prevent States parties from adopting measures that restrict the right of non-citizens to enter a State and their right to reside there ... on the basis of their current nationality';[86] that the aim of the Convention was to eliminate all forms of racial discrimination 'on the basis of real or perceived characteristics as of their origin, namely at birth',[87] meaning that 'the term "national origin" ... in accordance with its ordinary meaning, read in its

[82] *Decision on Admissibility*, *Qatar* v. *UAE*, CERD/C/99/4, para. 59, quoting CERD Committee, 'General Recommendation No. 30', point 4.

[83] Ibid., para. 63.

[84] *Qatar* v. *UAE* (Preliminary Objections, Judgment), para. 81. This, of course, is a highly contentious assertion. See, e.g., Diane Desierto who notes the failure of the court to consider the argument that race is a social construct, rather than an immutable fact. See Diane Desierto, 'A study in contrasting jurisdictional methodologies: The International Court of Justice's February 2021 judgments in *Iran* v. *USA* and *Qatar* v. *UAE*', *EJIL: Talk!*, 15 February 2021, www.ejiltalk.org/a-study-in-contrasting-jurisdictional-methodologies-the-international-court-of-justices-february-2021-judgments-in-iran-v-usa-and-qatar-v-uae/ (accessed 1 July 2022).

[85] *Qatar* v. *UAE* (Preliminary Objections, Judgment), para. 83.

[86] Ibid.

[87] Ibid., para. 86 – again, a contentious assertion, and the addition of 'as at birth' particularly so.

context and in the light and purpose of the Convention, does not encompass current nationality'.[88] It finds support for its interpretation in the *travaux preparatoires*,[89] but then finds it necessary to turn to the practice of the CERD Committee which, as has been seen, had taken a very different approach.

Qatar, entirely predictably, had asked the court to place 'great weight' on the CERD Committee's 2019 determination that the case was admissible, it being the 'guardian of the Convention'.[90] The court declined to do so. It acknowledged that 'it has taken into account the practices of committees established under the human rights conventions',[91] going on to describe the CERD Committee as being 'a body of independent experts established specifically to supervise the application of CERD'.[92] This notably fails to acknowledge its having any role in relation to the interpretation of the Convention. The court then notes that the CERD Committee had relied on its own General Recommendation when declaring Qatar's communication admissible.[93] It then said, in a paragraph that demands to be quoted in full, that[94]

> the Court recalls that in its Judgment on the merits in the *Diallo* case, to which reference is made in paragraph 77 above, it indicated that it should 'ascribe great weight' to the interpretation of the International Covenant on Civil and Political Rights – which it was called upon to apply in that case – adopted by the Human Rights Committee (*Ahmadou Sadio Diallo (Republic of Guinea* v. *Democratic Republic of the Congo), Merits, Judgment, I.C.J. Reports* 2010 *(II)*, p. 664, para. 66). In this regard, it also affirmed, however, that it was 'in no way obliged, in the exercise of its judicial functions, to model its own interpretation of the Covenant on that of the Committee' *(ibid.)*. In the present case concerning the interpretation of CERD, the Court has carefully considered the position taken by the CERD Committee, which is specified in paragraph 100 above, on the issue of discrimination based on nationality. By applying, as it is required to do (see paragraph 75 above), the relevant customary rules on treaty interpretation, it came to the conclusion indicated in paragraph 88 above, on the basis of the reasons set out above.

This is a very clear assertion of the court's belief in its primacy. The best that can be said of this from the point of view of the CERD Committee is that,

88 Ibid., para. 87.
89 Ibid., paras 88–97.
90 Ibid., para. 99.
91 Ibid., para. 77.
92 Ibid., para 100.
93 Ibid.
94 Ibid., para. 101.

whilst it amounts to a resounding rejection of the legitimacy of its interpretation of the Convention, it holds open the prospect of weight being given to its application of the Convention should its interpretation accord with that of the court. This, however, is perhaps an overly benign reading of a passage, the ordinary and natural meaning of which is that the court will place great weight on the work of the Committee when it agrees with what it has done, but will place no weight on it whatsoever when it does not.

7.6 'HUMAN RIGHTS FIRST'?

Against this background, the words of the CERD Committee in its 2019 admissibility decision concerning parallel proceedings appear to be prescient, if not clairvoyant. To recall its words when responding to the question of whether the existence of parallel proceedings should render the application inadmissible, it said 'the Committee, as an expert monitoring body entitled to adopt non-binding recommendations is not convinced that a principle of *lis pendens* or *electa una via* is applicable which should rule out proceedings concerning the same matter by a judicial body entitled to adopt a legally binding judgment'.[95] Rather than an act of self-abnegation in the face of the majesty of the court, this now appears in an altogether different light.

In so saying, the CERD Committee, in effect, chooses to embrace a different path. It accepts that its General Recommendations may not be binding on State parties as a matter of law – but it has never said that they were, nor have the other UN human rights treaty bodies said as much as regards their own General Comments.[96] The question of whether the work of the expert treaty bodies amounts to 'subsequent practice' for the purposes of the Vienna Convention as raised by Judge Salam was always something of a red herring too: it is only 'practice which establishes the agreement of the parties regarding its interpretation' that can have an effect as such,[97] and it is

[95] *Decision on Admissibility*, *Qatar* v. *UAE*, CERD/C/99/4, para. 49.

[96] The HRC understands its General Comments as representing a form of 'codification' of its experience and practice and an authoritative guide to its understanding of the Convention. See, e.g., Neuman, 'Giving meaning and effect to human rights', p. 35, who says that 'General Comments guide States and the HRC's own conduct in drafting concluding observations and Views. Nonetheless, the HRC may further develop its jurisprudence without first amending or replacing an older General Comment.' As this makes clear, they are not seen as 'binding' on the HRC itself, let alone on anyone else. As such, and as the ICJ has observed (n. 54), they are entitled to great weight, but not undue deference.

[97] Vienna Convention on the Law of Treaties, Vienna, 23 May 1969, in force 27 January 1980, 1155 UNTS 331; (1969) 8 ILM 679, Art 31(3)(b). This was made very clear by the ILC ('Draft conclusions on subsequent agreements and subsequent practice in relation to the

not the role of the treaty body experts to broker this. Indeed, the very text of the CERD suggests otherwise.[98] Their role is to bring their expertise to the conduct of their mandated functions as set out in their respective treaties. The normative force to be accorded to that work is, ultimately, a matter for others to determine, but the potential response by others to their work ought not to be a source of constraint.[99] Such an approach places 'clear water' between their work and that of the court, or of any other judicial process or body.

At a procedural level, this means the CERD Committee need not concern itself with whether the ICJ is, or is not, considering the matter which is also before it: whether the ICJ believes the CERD Committee's consideration of that matter affects its own jurisdiction or admissibility is up to it to decide, and the effects of its decision are limited to its effects upon itself and the integrity of its own procedures. There was a good reason for this. In June 2019, before the CERD Committee had made its decision, the ICJ considered a request made by the UAE for an award of provisional measures, including that 'Qatar immediately withdraw its Communication submitted to the CERD Committee … against the UAE and take all necessary measures to terminate consideration thereof by the CERD Committee'.[100] In other words, the UAE was asking the ICJ to seek to put an end to the case before the CERD Committee, arguing that this was necessary to 'protect its rights to "procedural fairness, to an equal opportunity to present its case and to proper administration of justice" … [and] that it has a right not to be compelled to defend itself in parallel proceedings before the Court of the CERD Committee'.[101]

interpretation of treaties', in *Yearbook of the International Law Commission. 2018, Volume II, Part Two: Report of the Commission to the General Assembly on the Work of Its Seventieth Session*) (New York: UN, 2018). Conclusion 13 rather dismissively addresses the 'pronouncements of expert treaty bodies', underlining that how States might respond in the light of what treaty bodies say – rather than what the treaty bodies themselves have said – which might qualify as subsequent practice.

98 See CERD, Art 9(2), which says that the CERD Committee, when reporting its General Recommendations to the UN General Assembly shall do so 'with comments, if any, from States Parties', thus suggesting that State parties are indeed free to have views concerning the positions adopted by the Committee in its General Recommendations and which can hardly therefore claim to be definitive.

99 Though arguably it might be a cause for restraint.

100 *Application of the International Convention on the Elimination of All Forms of Racial Discrimination (Qatar* v. *United Arab Emirates)* (Provisional Measures, Order) [2019] ICJ Rep. 361 at para. 7.

101 Ibid., para. 19.

Although the ICJ gave a short shrift to this, considering that it 'does not concern a plausible right under the CERD',[102] it also said that this concerned the 'interpretation of the compromissory clause in Article 22 of CERD *and the permissibility of proceedings before the CERD Committee when the Court is seised of the same matter*'.[103] This was unexpected, and suggests that if the court were to determine that, under Article 22, negotiations and the inter-State process were alternatives rather than cumulative, it might also consider it impermissible for a State to continue with the Article 11 process. The court's use of language here betrays a failure to appreciate the nature of the inter-State process which, as has been seen, is really a stepped process of facilitated negotiation and conciliation and hardly aptly described as 'proceedings before the CERD Committee'. Be that as it may, it is not difficult to see why the CERD Committee might have feared that the 'rug could be pulled from under its feet' in this way or, at the very least, that this might give a respondent State plausible grounds from refusing to engage with the CERD process were the ICJ to be seized of the matter.

This, perhaps, goes some way to explain the observation of the CERD Committee in its decision on admissibility the following month, in which (as shown above) the UAE argued that the CERD Committee should declare the communication inadmissible because of Qatar having also taken its claim to the ICJ. In response the Committee noted that 'the ICJ could ... suspend its proceedings until the Committee renders its final conclusions concerning the communication submitted by Qatar'.[104] However, suspecting that it did not think this was very likely, and seemingly addressing the arguments of the UAE before the ICJ as much as those made before itself, the Committee said:[105]

> The Committee fails to see how the existence of 'parallel proceedings' would entail the risk of compromising the fairness of the procedure and the equality of arms between the parties, since both parties have equal procedural rights before the two bodies. This is the more so when the term 'parallel' applies

[102] Ibid., para. 25.

[103] Ibid. (emphasis added).

[104] *Decision on Admissibility*, *Qatar* v. *UAE*, CERD/C/99/4, para. 51. This was reportage of the suggestion in the dissent by *ad hoc* Judge Cot. This too is somewhat misleading, as the Art 11 process does not include an opportunity for the Committee to make 'final conclusions' on the communication, although, doubtless, in practice a means of doing so would arise. Arguably there is also a degree of mischief-making: the CERD Committee rather unnecessarily pointed out that *ad hoc* Judge Cot was appointed by the UAE, the clear implication being that this might be why he thought the ICJ might wish to delay its consideration of Qatar's application, even if correctly seized.

[105] Ibid., para. 51.

essentially to the concurrent time at which the two proceedings are being held when the purport and scope of the decision called for in those two proceedings are dissimilar.

Once again, the emphasis here is on the differences, rather than the similarities, between the processes of the court and the CERD Committee, with 'parallel proceedings' having been recast as 'dissimilar processes' taking place at the same time – and, indeed, the section heading in the decision refers to 'concurrent' (rather than 'parallel') proceedings.[106]

It therefore appears that the CERD Committee has chosen to emphasise its distinctiveness and has used this to 'insulate' itself from potential limitations on its work in terms both of procedural issues and substantive interpretation: if the ICJ considers itself free to hear a case which is also being considered under the CERD process, then it is free to do so, but this has no implications for the CERD Committee's ability to consider the same matter given that the 'purport and scope' of the decisions are 'dissimilar'. Similarly, if the CERD Committee believes that the dictates of its mandate require it to offer up and act in accordance with approaches to the substantive obligations set out in the Convention which do not necessarily accord with the views of the ICJ and of others, then it is free to do so. It is against this background that the jurisdictional decision of the CERD Committee in *Palestine* v. *Israel* needs to be viewed.

The legal complexities of this case hardly need rehearsing. Israel has been a State party to the CERD since 1979, and the State of Palestine since 2014. On 23 April 2018, Palestine submitted a communication against Israel, alleging various breaches of the Convention in the Occupied Palestinian Territories (OPT), which was transmitted to Israel by the Committee in accordance with the Article 11(1) procedure in May 2018.[107] Shortly before it did so, however, Israel raised with the CERD Committee the fact that it had objected to Palestine acceding to the Convention, that it did not consider it to be in a treaty relationship with Palestine, and that therefore the inter-State communication procedure was inapplicable between themselves.[108]

Following a series of exchanges which failed to resolve any of these questions, either procedural or substantive, Palestine referred the matter back to the CERD Committee in November 2018, in accordance with Article 11(2)

[106] See ibid., section IVB, headed 'On the existence of concurrent proceedings'.

[107] The full procedural details and positions of Palestine and Israel are set out in CERD Committee, *Decision on the Committee's Jurisdiction*, Part I (CERD/D/100/3) and Part II (CERD/D/100/4).

[108] CERD Committee, *Decision on the Committee's Jurisdiction*, Part I (CERD/D/100/3), paras 4.1–12.

of the procedure, which the Committee continued to progress. In January 2019, Israel reiterated its position that there were no treaty relations between 'Israel and the Palestinian entity', and that this went to the very question of whether Article 11 was applicable.[109] Long and complex arguments on a broad range of issues were offered by both Israel and Palestine in support of their positions concerning the applicability of the treaty to their mutual relations, in response to which the CERD Committee sought advice from the UN Office of Legal Affairs (the OLA), which was received in July 2019.[110] That advice, according to the CERD Committee itself, was categoric: 'A State party to the Convention is able, through a unilateral statement, to prevent the creation of obligations and rights under the Convention between itself and another specific State party' and that 'the statement made by Israel precludes the Committee from examining the inter-state communication submitted by the State of Palestine'.[111]

The Committee accepted that it was necessary to consider whether it had 'jurisdiction to deal with the inter-state communication by the State of Palestine against Israel',[112] and, although it did not say it in so many words, it accepted the general proposition, set out by the OLA, that State parties to multilateral treaties can exclude relations with entities they do not recognise.[113] It added, however, that 'the Committee considers ... that particular treaty regimes, due to their particular character, may depart from those general principles'[114] – and depart from them the Committee did, quite spectacularly so.

The Committee drew on the long-established and widely accepted idea that human rights treaties are not merely a series of reciprocal obligations and that the object and purpose of such treaties are to further 'the common good'.[115] It also pointed to the Convention being based on 'super common values' and established 'a body responsible for supervising the implementation by the State parties of the obligations contained therein' and, as such, 'constitute a special category of treaties, to which certain rules of treaty law are not applicable'.[116] Perhaps, with the intention of not implicating all other human

[109] Ibid., paras 9.1–3.
[110] CERD Committee, *Decision on the Committee's Jurisdiction*, Part III (CERD/D/100/5), paras 2.1–2.
[111] Ibid., para. 2.3.
[112] Ibid., paras 3.1–4.
[113] Ibid., para. 3.13.
[114] Ibid.
[115] Ibid., paras 3.25 and 3.32–33.
[116] Ibid., para. 3.34.

rights treaty bodies in its approach, the CERD Committee drew attention to 'the particular character of the Convention within the category of human rights treaties', racial discrimination being 'the first violation of human rights to be taken care of by the international community, just after the international crime of genocide'.[117]

There is much to contest in both this and in the ever onward and upward spiral of elevating prose that follows, but to do so would miss the point. The point is encapsulated in the committee's finding:[118]

> Within the category of human rights treaties, the Convention is of a particular character, taking into account that racial discrimination has been universally recognised as a scourge which must be combated by all available and pragmatic means, as a matter of the highest priority for the international community as a whole, without consideration to bilateral issues between States parties.

If one takes such an approach, obviously there is jurisdiction – when could there not be? Five members appended an individual opinion, suggesting that 'a body set up by a treaty to monitor the treaty obligations of States should itself respect the rules of treaty law', and pointing out that the committee's decision, in effect, flew in the face of the International Law Commission (ILC), the Vienna Convention on the Law of Treaties, the jurisprudence of the ICJ, and, of course, the opinion of the OLA on this question.[119] However, whilst it is difficult to fault the legal analysis on which the separate opinion is based, the entire point of the CERD Committee's approach is to move beyond legal analysis and act in a manner which, it believes, is more 'practical, constructive and effective'.[120]

Against this background it is hardly surprising that the Committee subsequently affirmed that the communication was also admissible, despite the argument that there had been a failure to exhaust local remedies.[121] Palestine argued – quite correctly – that the need to exhaust local remedies was inapplicable to challenges concerning generalised policies and practices.[122]

[117] Ibid., para. 3.35.

[118] Ibid., para. 3.50(e).

[119] See ibid., Annex, Individual Opinion of the following Committee members: Marc Bossuyt, Rita Izak-Nyiaye, Keiko Ko, Yanduan Li, and Maria Teresa Verdugo Morena (Dissenting), para. 1, and throughout.

[120] CERD Committee, *Decision on the Committee's Jurisdiction*, Part III (CERD/D/100/5), para. 3.52(f).

[121] CERD Committee, *Decision on the Admissibility of the Inter-State Communication Submitted by the State of Palestine against Israel* (30 April 2021) UN Doc. CERD/C/103/R.6.

[122] Ibid., paras 19, 63.

The CERD Committee agreed, whilst pointing out that the mere assertion that practices and policies were of a generalised nature was not sufficient to set aside the requirement: there had to be prima facie evidence of this.[123] Happily for the Committee, it felt able to find such evidence easily enough, in its own expressions of concern and its own recommendations in its own concluding observations.[124] Once again the CERD Committee felt no compunction to draw on anyone other than itself in order to be 'satisfied' that the prima facie threshold had been meet. One might conclude that the Committee is somewhat prone to being 'self-satisfied'.

Whether the CERD Committee really is acting in a manner which is 'practical, constructive and effective' to address the issues raised by Palestine remains to be seen, and much depends on what those terms are taken to mean in this context. More generally, however, both the jurisdiction and admissibility decisions in *Palestine* v. *Israel* reflect and reinforce the approaches taken by the CERD Committee in the *Qatar* v. *UAE* communication in response to the orders and judgments of the ICJ relating to the CERD, in which the Committee's role as a 'champion' of the superior values encapsulated in the human rights ideal takes centre stage, transcending the formalism of judicial fora.

7.7 CONCLUSION

It seems undeniable that one of the consequences of the activation of the inter-State communication procedure under Article 11 of the CERD is that there has been a prising apart of the work of that treaty body from that of the court. This started with what might best be described as a procedural tussle, in which the CERD strove – arguably unnecessarily – to ensure it retained jurisdictional competence to consider the cases brought before it. Following the court's 2021 judgment in *Qatar* v. *UAE*, however, there is a real question to be asked concerning who is to be the ultimate arbiter of the legal obligations contained in the human rights conventions.[125]

[123] Ibid., para. 63.

[124] Ibid., para. 64.

[125] See Patrick Thornberry, 'The Committee for the Elimination of Racial Discrimination', p. 321, who thinks the CERD Committee's decisions in favour of Qatar might encourage other States to use the procedure. For reasons given above, however, it is unlikely that those contemplating recourse to the ICJ are likely to find this an attractive option, unless they feel that the approach of the CERD Committee to the substance of the communication is likely to be more favourable. The result is in fact more likely to encourage 'forum shopping' based on the perceptions of the likelihood of favourable outcomes.

This is not just a question for the CERD. As we know, obligations in other human rights treaties have been examined by the ICJ in the past, and this is likely to become more, rather than less, common. Although human rights issues frequently arise before other judicial and arbitral fora, consideration by the ICJ is different in that, at least in relation to those treaties which have a compromissory clause, the ICJ is expressly empowered to determine questions concerning their interpretation and application in the cases and between the parties which come before it. This puts the ICJ on a potential collision course with the work of the treaty bodies, and its 2021 judgment is a road crash of some considerable magnitude.

Juxtaposing the CERD Committee's decisions in *Palestine* v. *Israel* with that of the ICJ's in *Qatar* v. *UAE* leaves the impression of two bodies with little regard for each other's work – and certainly does not suggest that the other's work is to be accorded 'great weight'. The ICJ has, in effect, redefined the boundaries of the CERD for the CERD Committee. Should the CERD Committee choose to follow the path it has taken of late, it will simply rise above this provocation and continue in its work, possibly troubled but fundamentally unmoved.

It is important to remember that the nature of the work of the UN human rights treaty bodies has always been something of a 'contested space'. State parties frequently challenge the approaches taken by the treaty bodies, not only when appearing before them but also in political and other fora. The ILC and others have also treated with some scepticism some of the more innovative ideas which they have spawned, some of which have gained great traction over time, whilst others have not.[126] Tensions are not crises. As remarked in the introduction, disputes over the interpretation and application of treaties, and of legal obligations more generally, are both inevitable and a proper means of advancing an understanding of the law.

[126] The most well-known example concerns the effect of impermissible reservations to human rights treaties, set out by the HRC, 'General Comment No. 24: Issues relating to reservations made upon ratification or accession to the Covenant or the Optional Protocols thereto, or in relation to declarations under Article 41 of the Covenant' (4 November 1994) UN Doc. CCPR/C/21/Rev.1/Add.6, which was not endorsed by the ILC in its 'Guide to practice on reservations to treaties', in *Yearbook of the International Law Commission. 2011, Volume II, Part Two: Report of the Commission to the General Assembly on the Work of Its Sixty-Third Session* (New York: UN, 2011). For an overview, see Ineta Ziemele and Lasma Liede, 'Reservations to human rights treaties: From Draft Guideline 3.1.12 to Guideline 3.1.5.6' (2013) 24 EJIL 1135–52. For an interesting analysis of how Universal Periodic Review is increasingly being used to address the problem of impermissible reservations, see Frederick Cowell, 'Reservations to human rights treaties in recommendations from the universal periodic review: An emerging practice?' (2021) 25 Int'l J Hum Rts 274–94.

Despite the rather overblown rhetoric of the CERD Committee in its *Palestine* v. *Israel* jurisdiction decision, there is some truth in its argument that the function of the treaty bodies is not necessarily limited by the more traditional boundaries of international law.[127] Whilst some of the mechanisms at their disposal utilise the 'tools' of dispute settlement and may from time to time have the effect of 'resolving international disputes', this does not mean that they are to be seen as a means of international dispute settlement or, at least, not primarily as such. Other tools at their disposal are not of this nature at all, such as the system of periodic reporting, which is primarily about offering challenge and bringing about change.[128] As the CERD Committee rightly observes, 'the obligations which States owe under articles 11–13 of the Convention on the one hand and article 9 [the Reporting obligation] on the other, are of the same family, with the common purpose of ensuring the effective prohibition of racial discrimination'.[129] Viewed from this perspective, the mechanisms deployed by the treaty bodies have their own logic and legitimacy. Against this background, whether their work is to be accorded 'great weight' by the ICJ is, ultimately, fascinating, but somewhat beside the point.

The real question is whether the work of the treaty bodies contributes effectively to their central task of ensuring that States comply with their human rights obligations; and helping to settle disputes between States concerning compliance is arguably something of an unnecessary and unhelpful distraction. This does not mean that treaty bodies ought to ride roughshod over the terrain of international law, of which they are a creation. It does, however, mean that their enterprise when seeking to devise effective ways of securing such compliance in complex practical settings should be treated with respect and reflection, and certainly not met with dismissive rejection by those tasked with other functions. The treaty bodies work at the intersection of law, politics, ethics, and morality. It is to be expected that the precise strictures of law may not always meet the exigencies of the occasion, and human rights bodies which fail to respond to the broader dictates of what they see and hear are ones that fail to live up to the demands of that broader calling.

[127] Cf. Simma, 'The ICJ', p. 175, who at times leans in this direction when suggesting that the ICJ should exercise some caution so that the 'acquis' of specialist human rights bodies is not 'levelled by the participation in the discourse of a generalist court like the ICJ'.

[128] See, e.g., Neuman, 'Giving meaning and effect to human rights', p. 33.

[129] CERD Committee, *Decision on the Committee's Jurisdiction*, Part III (CERD/D/100/5), para. 3.43.

8

Settlement of Water-Related Disputes in International Law

MARIA A. GWYNN

8.1 INTRODUCTION

States have a right to freely exploit natural wealth and resources.[1] The basis on which natural resources are allocated among States and the right to utilise them rests on the principle of territorial sovereignty. The UN General Assembly Resolution 1803/62 on 'Permanent sovereignty over natural resources' reinforced this by declaring 'the right of peoples and nations to permanent sovereignty over their natural wealth and resources must be exercised in the interest of their national development and of the wellbeing of the people of the state concerned'.[2] Water is a vital natural resource, and, pursuant to the principle of territorial sovereignty, when a natural resource is completely captured and secured within a State's territory, then the State with jurisdiction over it has full sovereignty over the resource. A slightly different situation arises when the resource spans through the territory of more than one State, making it a *shared* natural resource. When there are shared or transboundary natural resources, a State's sovereignty is limited. States are compelled to co-operate by taking into account each other's interests and utilise or exploit their shared resource in a reasonable and equitable manner. This is referred to as the cornerstone principle of the utilisation of international watercourses.[3] It applies to all international watercourses, including transboundary rivers, lakes, and aquifers.

1 UNGA, 'Right to exploit freely natural wealth and resources' (21 December 1952) UN Doc. A/RES/626(VII).

2 UNGA, 'Permanent sovereignty over natural resources' (14 December 1962) UN Doc. A/RES/1803(XVII); see also UNGA, 'Permanent sovereignty over natural resources' (25 November 1966) UN Doc. A/RES/2158(XXI).

3 See Stephen C. McCaffrey, *The Law of International Watercourses*, 2nd ed. (Oxford: Oxford University Press, 2007); see also definition and interpretation in Alistair Rieu-Clarke,

However, because States have different interests in the utilisation of shared or transboundary water resources, disputes may arise when two or more States do not reach a satisfactory agreement on how to utilise their shared natural resources. Disputes can arise due to many factors, such as the water supply not being sufficient, pollution, or over the competitive and multiple uses of the water. Also, the nature of disputes can vary; sometimes they concern a technical issue, and sometimes a legal one.[4] This is why international water law spells out substantive obligations for the uses of international watercourses (equitable and reasonable utilisation and participation; no significant harm) as well as procedural obligations (exchange of data and information, and consultations). The management of resources pursuant to these obligations can be crucial for the settlement of disputes.[5] In the area of international water law, States have an obligation to settle their disputes in a peaceful manner.[6]

The UN Charter establishes that 'the parties to any dispute, the continuance of which is likely to endanger the maintenance of international peace and security, shall, first, seek a solution by negotiation, enquiry, mediation, conciliation, arbitration, judicial settlement, resort to regional agencies or arrangements, or other peaceful means of their own choice'.[7]

These mechanisms to settle disputes can be included in an existing agreement or agreed upon *ad hoc* after a dispute has emerged. Today, there is a myriad of agreements governing transboundary water resources, and some of the mechanisms of dispute settlement are mentioned in almost all of them.

What makes the settlement of water-related disputes more particular is that most treaties or agreements concerning the utilisation of international watercourses establish a joint or international commission. In most cases, the commission has a key role in the settlement of disputes. Furthermore, in regions like South America or Southern Africa, the complementary nature of different agreements that pertain to water resources has opened a way for creating a regional mechanism to resolve disputes. In some cases, the regional mechanism for settling disputes is formalised, as we shall see with the example

Ruby Moynihan, and Bjorn Oliver Magsig, *UN Watercourses Convention User Guide* (Dundee: IHP-HELP Center for Water Law, Science and Policy, 2012).

4 For example, a technical dispute could arise from the form or periodicity of data exchange, whereas a legal one could arise from finding the right balance for the uses of watercourses among riparians.

5 For further information about substantive and procedural obligations of international watercourses, see McCaffrey, *The Law of International Watercourses.*

6 Charter of the United Nations, San Francisco, 26 June 1945, in force 24 October 1945, 1 UNTS 16, Art 2(3).

7 Ibid., Art 33(1).

of the SADC Treaty; in other cases, it operates de facto to prevent or resolve the dispute, as we shall see with the South American experience.

When we consider both the utilisation and protection of shared or transboundary resources, States' borders are, to an extent, relativised. When States accept that their practices must embrace the sustainability of the resource for the sake of the natural resource and for future generations that will continue to rely on the resource, cooperation is important. Striking the right balance by taking all interests into account is critical, as we shall see with the State practice from South America.

The chapter considers dispute settlement provisions by looking first at the global conventions concerning international watercourses in Sections 8.2 and 8.3, and then at some regional agreements and related practices in Asia, Africa, Europe, and South America in Sections 8.4 to 8.7. This will enable us to assess the extent to which the recommended provisions of the global conventions have been implemented and in what way they differ from other processes. A comparative assessment in Section 8.8 will provide us with an overview of how the different dispute resolution mechanisms for international watercourses can integrate or complement each other to become tools for the States' main purpose of settling their water disputes peacefully. Section 8.9 provides a summary of the prevailing mechanisms for the settlement of international watercourses disputes and Section 8.10 concludes.

8.2 THE GLOBAL CONVENTION: THE 1997 UN WATERCOURSES CONVENTION

The Non-navigational Uses of International Watercourses Convention was adopted by the UN General Assembly on 21 May 1997, and entered into force in 2014.[8] The Convention defines 'watercourse' to include both surface waters and groundwaters. It is set forth as a framework convention, leaving the parties the option to complement it further with other agreements. This Convention came about through the study of customary international law, a task entrusted to the International Law Commission by the UN General

[8] Convention on the Law of the Non-navigational Uses of International Watercourses, New York, 21 May 1997, in force 17 August 2014, 2999 UNTS 77; see also Salman M. A. Salman, 'Entry into force of the UN Watercourses Convention: Why should it matter?' (2014) 31 Int J Water Resour Dev 4–16; Salman M. A. Salman, 'The Helsinki Rules, the UN Watercourses Convention and the Berlin Rules: Perspectives on international water law' (2007) 23 Int J Water Resour Dev 625–40; Stephen C. McCaffrey and Mpazi Sinjela, 'The 1997 United Nations Convention on International Watercourses' (1998) 92 AJIL 97–107.

Assembly.[9] The Convention sets out the core principles of international water law, namely, substantive obligations, such as the reasonable and equitable utilisation and participation, the obligation not to cause harm, and the obligation to co-operate; and procedural obligations, such as notification and consultation. Its provisions are codifications of customary international law, and international courts and tribunals have used them in the settlement of disputes over international watercourses.[10] Commenting on the relevance of the Convention, Salman points out: 'Shared water resources are no longer the only major area without a treaty regulating their uses, sharing, management and protection. For the first time in history, international watercourses are now regulated by a global framework Convention that aims at promoting their optimal and sustainable utilization for present and future generations.'[11]

The participation referred to in the cornerstone principle[12] 'includes both the right to utilize the watercourse and the duty to cooperate in the protection and development thereof'.[13] McCaffrey argues that equitable participation involves an affirmative obligation to co-operate,[14] meaning that 'States sharing an international watercourse have an affirmative obligation to cooperate in its protection and development and implicitly in its management in order to achieve and maintain a regime of equitable utilization and protection of the water course'.[15]

But what do we understand by reasonable and equitable utilisation? According to Birnie, Boyle, and Redgwell, 'reasonable' utilisation is understood as 'while as a last resort it may enable states to argue that pollution or the exploitation of natural resources are illegal if so excessive that the interests of other states are disproportionately affected, it is not a substitute for other, more concrete rules limiting the right of states to pollute or requiring sustainable use

9 By 1994 the work on the study on international watercourses was completed by the International Law Commission. See UNGA, 'Draft articles on the law of the non-navigational uses of international watercourses' (9 December 1994) UN Doc. A/RES/49/52.

10 For the latest cases, see *Case Concerning the Gabčíkovo-Nagymaros Project (Hungary* v. *Slovakia)* (Judgment) [1997] ICJ Rep. 7; *Case Concerning Pulp Mills on the River Uruguay (Argentina* v. *Uruguay)* (Judgment) [2010] ICJ Rep. 14.

11 Salman, 'Entry into force of the UN Watercourses Convention', pp. 11–12.

12 UN Watercourses Convention, Art 5.

13 Ibid., Art 5(2).

14 Stephen C. McCaffrey, 'The contribution of the UN convention on the law of the non-navigational uses of international watercourses' (2001) 314 Int J Glob Environ Issues 250–63.

15 Stephen C. McCaffrey, 'International watercourses: The UN Convention on Non-Navigational Uses of International Watercourses', UN Audiovisual Library of International Law, 30 June 2008, https://legal.un.org/avl/ls/McCaffrey_IW.html (accessed 12 November 2020).

of resources'.[16] On the other hand, 'equitable' utilisation is understood as a situation which requires a balance of interests and consideration of all factors. Article 6 of the Convention states that these factors include (1) geographic, hydrographic, hydrological, climatic, ecological, and other factors of natural character; (2) the social and economic needs of the watercourse States concerned; (3) the population dependent on the watercourse in the watercourse State; (4) the effects of the uses of watercourses in one watercourse State on other watercourse States; (5) existing and potential uses of the watercourse; (6) conservation, protection, development, and economy of the water resources of the watercourse and the cost of measures taken to that effect; and (7) the availability of alternatives, of comparable value, to a particular planned or existing use.[17]

Article 6 further recommends that countries should enter into consultations, if the need arises, as a form of cooperation. It also notes that all factors should be taken into account when reaching a conclusion on the equitable and reasonable uses of watercourses, which dispenses with any form of hierarchy between factors. However, it is important to note that the Convention states that in the event of a conflict between uses of an international watercourse, it shall be resolved with reference to the articles pertaining to equitable and reasonable utilisation and the obligation to not cause significant harm. However, the Convention also states that special regard shall be given to the requirements of vital human needs.[18] In light of the above, it becomes evident that a State's sovereignty is limited, and States are compelled to co-operate by taking into account each other's interests and to utilise or exploit their shared resource in a reasonable and equitable manner. And it is particularly important to note that the provisions of Articles 5 and 6 of the Convention reinforce the principle of reasonable and equitable utilisation, and not that of sovereignty, when international watercourses are concerned.

The obligation not to cause significant harm, the so-called no harm rule, is another important substantive provision in the UN Watercourses Convention.[19] It is sometimes argued that the principle of equitable and reasonable utilisation is in tension with the no harm rule, and that upstream countries favour the first, while downstream countries tend to favour the latter.

[16] Patricia W. Birnie, Alan E. Boyle, and Catherine Redgwell, *International Law and the Environment* (Oxford: Oxford University Press, 2009), p. 201.

[17] UN Watercourses Convention, Art 6. McCaffrey also pointed out that the list of factors is non-exhaustive. Stephen C. McCaffrey, *The Law of International Watercourses: Non-navigational Uses* (Oxford: Oxford University Press, 2001).

[18] UN Watercourses Convention, Art 10.2.

[19] Ibid., Art 7.

However, as Salman argues, this tension derives from a misunderstanding that only lower stream countries will face harm; in fact, harmful effects can go both ways. For example, developments in the downstream State can affect the upstream State.[20] Thus, it is better to interpret the two principles as complementing each other, rather than competing with each other.[21]

Regarding some procedural rules of the Convention, they require the regular exchange of data and information as well as notification and consultation of other riparian States when planning measures with possible significant adverse effects. During consultations following a notification, disputes might arise, but consultations are still part of the procedural rules of the utilisation of international watercourses, and thus they should not be confused with the negotiation stage of a dispute settlement mechanism, which is normally triggered by an existing dispute.[22] Attached to the procedural obligations is the general obligation to co-operate with the creation of joint bodies or commissions, this being a good way to enforce said provisions. That said, how well parties will co-operate depends on trust, which in turn is based on a good understanding of the principles contained in the Convention.

Dispute settlement is addressed in Part VI of the Convention. Part VI establishes a non-discrimination provision in granting access to judicial or other procedures to those who suffered harm (Article 32), and restates that parties shall seek the resolution of their disputes by peaceful means

[20] Examples include the development of a dam that can block navigation or affect fish migration. Salman states that 'it is much less obvious, and generally not recognized, that the upstream riparians can be harmed by the potential foreclosure of their future use of water caused by the prior use and the claiming of rights by downstream riparians. For example, a poor upstream country could be precluded from developing the water resources of an international waterway tomorrow if a richer downstream riparian, without consultation or notification, develops it today'. Salman M. A. Salman, 'The United Nations Watercourses Convention ten years later: Why has its entry into force proven difficult?' (2007) 32 Water Int 1–15 at 9.

[21] McCaffrey, *The Law of International Watercourses: Non-navigational Uses*; McCaffrey, *The Law of International Watercourses*. However, Art 7(2) of the Convention also states that countries must 'take all appropriate measures, having due regard for the provisions of articles 5 and 6, in consultation with the affected State, to eliminate or mitigate such harm and, where appropriate, to discuss the question of compensation'. According to Salman, the result of analysing these provisions is that 'the prevailing view is that the convention has, like the Helsinki Rules, subordinated the obligation not to cause significant harm to the principle of equitable and reasonable utilization'. This is because Art 7 of the Convention establishes that even when there is significant harm to another watercourse State, the State that causes it is required to take all appropriate measures, in consultation with the affected State, to eliminate or mitigate such harm and to discuss compensation. See Salman, 'The Helsinki Rules', p. 633.

[22] Maria A. Gwynn, *Adapting Watercourse Agreements to Developments in International Law* (Leiden: Brill, 2019). See also the different categorisation of questions, differences, and disputes in the Indus Water Treaty mentioned in s. 8.4.2.

(Article 33). The international rapporteur on the Law of the Non-navigational Uses of International Watercourses, Stephen McCaffrey, has long stressed that resorting to private remedies to avoid disputes and the proper settlement of disputes are two important aspects of the law of international watercourses.[23] As we shall see, both aspects are contained in the UN Watercourses Convention. The dispute settlement provisions of the UN Watercourses Convention encourage the parties to first aim to reach a solution to their disputes through diplomatic means and non-binding procedures, but it also offers binding mechanisms.

8.2.1 *Non-binding Mechanisms: Negotiation and Other Means*

The UN Watercourses Convention first mentions negotiation as a mechanism to settle disputes. However, if a dispute is not resolved through negotiation, then other mechanisms are available to the parties. Namely, the Convention establishes that the parties may jointly seek the good offices of a third party, or request mediation or conciliation by a third party. Furthermore, the Convention also recommends the use of joint watercourses institutions that may have been established between the parties to resolve disputes.

Negotiations, or any of the other means, however, can be unpredictable and take a very long time. McCaffrey points out that

> negotiations should be conducted in the way described in the Lake Lanoux arbitration and in the decisions of the International Court of Justice, which has said that the parties 'are under an obligation so to conduct themselves that the negotiations are meaningful, which will not be the case when either of them insists upon its own position without contemplating any modification of it'.[24]

Aiming at the parties reaching a solution, the Convention establishes a time limit. It determines that if, after six months from the date of request for negotiations, the dispute is not settled by negotiation or other means, then, at the request of one of the parties, the dispute becomes subject to impartial fact-finding.

Although there are not many examples in which the Convention per se was applied to invoke negotiations or fact-finding, its recommendations, such as the utilisation of joint institutions to settle disputes, have become

[23] Stephen C. McCaffrey, *Sixth Report on the Law on Non-navigational Uses of International Watercourses* (Geneva: UN, 1990), pp. 57–80.

[24] McCaffrey, *The Law of International Watercourses: Non-navigational Uses*, p. 515.

part of a common State practice. In fact, if we refer to the table in Section 8.7, we see how many treaties and agreements concerning international watercourses have created joint watercourses institutions. These joint institutions constitute a first stage for negotiations among the parties to discuss many of the issues concerning the international watercourses and can prevent disputes from arising between riparian countries. For example, in South America, the Itaipu Governing Council, a joint body created by the Itaipu Treaty between Brazil and Paraguay, and composed of Brazilian and Paraguayan nationals, considers many of the issues concerning the binational Entity Itaipu, its hydropower production, and issues concerning the international river Paraná, including the monitoring of its sediments, flow of water, droughts, the ecosystem and environmental actions, and their respective impacts on energy production. These issues are dealt with first by the Board of Directors, then the Governing Council, and, only if controversy persists, the riparian States would be involved, as discussed further in Sections 8.6 and 8.7.

The use of joint institutions is important. It keeps the dispute out of politics and can help in preventing disputes from arising by addressing particular problems through technical means and by preventing States from taking actions that can potentially cause harm to other States.

8.2.2 *Fact-Finding*

The UN Watercourses Convention establishes a detailed fact-finding procedure. It starts with the procedure to form a fact-finding commission. For this, each party nominates one member, and the two appointed members nominate a third member to act as chairman, who must not have the nationality of any of the parties. When no appointment is made by either of the parties, the UN Secretary-General has the power to appoint the members. Accordingly, all members of the commission are permitted to have access for inspection in each State's respective territory, and the final decision of the commission is taken by majority vote. The commission drafts a report with recommendations for the parties, which must consider it in good faith. This mechanism is not binding. Even if the commission recommends a solution, it is still up to the parties to decide whether to adopt it.

An example analogous to the fact-finding procedure described in the Convention is the utilisation of a neutral expert under the Indus Water Treaty. This was in relation to the Baglihar dam project, in which Pakistan had concerns regarding water flows if India were to carry out the dam project. The World Bank nominated a neutral expert, who was asked to investigate the different positions of the countries regarding the project.[25] See Section 8.3 for further details about the dispute settlement mechanism of the Indus Water Treaty.

8.2.3 *Binding Mechanisms: Arbitration and/or the International Court of Justice*

The Convention allows parties to agree to submit their disputes to arbitration or to the International Court of Justice (ICJ). Parties may agree – in advance or once the dispute arises – to resolve their disputes by recourse to either of these two mechanisms. The parties then become subject to the arbitral award or judgment of the ICJ, respectively.

For example, just four months after the UN Watercourses Convention was adopted, the ICJ dealt with the 1997 *Gabčíkovo-Nagymaros Project case* between Hungary and Czechoslovakia (Slovakia).[26] The ICJ explicitly referred to the Convention in its judgment.[27] The application of the principle of equitable and reasonable uses of international rivers was considered by the Court, and in the said case, the ICJ noted that the Danube was a shared international watercourse and an international boundary river to which the principle of equality between riparian States applied. Therefore, the ICJ argued, any unilateral action of one country to divert its waters deprived the other country of a right to a reasonable and equitable share of the uses of the watercourse. The Court found that both parties had violated the treaty with their actions, and that both had the duty to compensate each other for these violations and to co-operate further in the development of their shared watercourse.[28]

Another case in which the ICJ referred to the Convention was the *Pulp Mills* Case of 2010. It concerned a dispute between Argentina and Uruguay over activities on the river Uruguay, a boundary river between the two countries.[29] The Court found that Uruguay had breached its procedural obligations (notification and consultation) but had adhered to its obligation of due diligence. It also found that Uruguay had not breached the substantive

[25] Muhammed Siyad A. C., 'Indus Water Treaty and Balihar Project: Relevance of international watercourse law' (2005) 40 Economic & Political Weekly 3145–54.

[26] With respect to this case before the ICJ, the special agreement between Hungary and Slovakia specified that the Slovak Republic was the successor State of Czech and Slovak Federal Republic.

[27] *Case Concerning the Gabčíkovo-Nagymaros Project* (Judgment).

[28] See Gwynn, *Adapting Watercourse Agreements*, p. 66.

[29] *Case Concerning Pulp Mills* (Judgment).

obligations regarding the protection and preservation of the environment because it had provided an environmental impact assessment.[30]

However, there are other disputes in which the status of whether the watercourse is international or not is questioned. In such a situation, the submission of the controversy to the ICJ might also be helpful for the parties. In fact, currently there is a case pending at the ICJ about the status and use of the waters of the Silala – a dispute between Chile and Bolivia – in which the court is asked to decide whether the water of the Silala is an international watercourse and, if so, whether Chile and Bolivia are entitled to the reasonable and equitable utilisation of said waters.[31]

8.3 THE 1992 UNECE WATER CONVENTION

Initially developed as a regional agreement for Europe, the United Nations Economic Commission for Europe (UNECE) drafted the Convention on the Protection and Use of Transboundary Watercourses and International Lakes in 1992.[32] In 2003 the provisions of the Convention restricting it to the regional members were amended. This amendment entered into force in 2013, and since then, it has been allowing any other State members to become a contracting party to the Convention.[33]

The UNECE Water Convention establishes a duty to co-operate, hold consultations, exchange information, and establish joint bodies, all of which are obligations for the parties of the Convention. As mentioned before, all these obligations are instrumental to avoid or mitigate disputes. The UNECE Water Convention's institutional framework allows for meetings of the parties, which create neutral platforms for dialogue among the parties. This forum allows parties to build trust, discuss cooperation opportunities, or resolve any conflict in an amicable way at an early stage. However, one of the main

30 See Gwynn, *Adapting Watercourse Agreements*, p. 71.

31 *Dispute over the Status and Use of the Waters of the Silala (Chile* v. *Bolivia)* (ICJ pending). See ICJ, 'Press release no. 2016/16: Chile institutes proceedings against Bolivia with regard to a dispute concerning the status and use of the waters of the Silala', 6 June 2016, www.icj-cij.org/public/files/case-related/162/19018.pdf (accessed 30 July 2022).

32 Convention on the Protection and Use of Transboundary Watercourses and International Lakes, Helsinki, 17 March 1992, in force 6 October 1996, 1936 UNTS 269. The Convention was adopted by the senior advisers to the Economic Commission for Europe Government on Environmental and Water Problems at their resumed fifth session held at Helsinki from 17 to 18 March 1992. It has forty-two parties, out of which twenty-six countries have ratified it.

33 UNECE, 'Amendments to Articles 25 and 26 of the Convention on the Protection and Use of Transboundary Watercourses and International Lakes' (12 January 2004) UN Doc. ECE/MP.WAT/14, in force 6 February 2013.

differences between the 1992 UNECE Water Convention and the 1997 UN Watercourses Convention is precisely in the details on dispute settlement.[34]

The UNECE Water Convention, Article 22(1), establishes that the parties shall seek a solution by negotiation or by any other means of dispute settlement acceptable to the parties to the dispute. In Article 22(2), it creates an 'opt in' formula for arbitration or adjudication at the ICJ as a *compulsory* dispute settlement mechanism. When either arbitration or submission to the ICJ is chosen, then the submission of the dispute to the ICJ has precedence. The UNECE Water Convention contains an Annex IV detailing the rules and procedure of arbitration.

Furthermore, the creation of an Implementation Committee under the framework of the UNECE Water Convention is very useful for avoiding or mitigating disputes. The parties to the Convention adopted Decision VI/1 in 2012 to facilitate, promote, and safeguard the implementation and application of, and compliance with, the Convention.[35] Per said decision, parties can consider requesting advice from the Implementation Committee, which can be self-submissions or party-to-party submissions, and it also offers the parties the possibility of undertaking a committee initiative. The members of the committee are lawyers and technical experts specialising in water issues whose advice can aid the parties in mitigating or avoiding disputes.

Today, both the 1997 and 1992 Conventions can be very useful for States and are considered as frameworks designed to complement the information for State practices regarding international watercourses.[36]

[34] Odili summarises the differences and characteristics between the substantive and procedural rules of the two legal instruments, and though they can complement each other, there are some crucial differences, for instance, in the definition of criteria for factors to be taken into account for the equitable uses, which are not present in the UNECE Water Convention, or the lack of detail for the settlement of international disputes. Nwamaka Chigozie Odili, *Shared Water Resources in West Africa* (Leiden: Brill, 2018), p. 27.

[35] UNECE, 'Decision VI/1 on support to implementation and compliance' (adopted at MOP-6, Rome, 28–30 November 2012) UN Doc. ECE/MP.WAT/37/Add.2.

[36] There were other instruments that were updated. For instance, the International Law Association worked to update the Helsinki Rules (ILA, *Helsinki Rules on the Uses of the Waters of International Rivers* (London: International Law Association, 1967)) by establishing the Berlin Rules in 2004 (ILA, 'The Berlin Rules on Water Resources', 2004, www.internationalwaterlaw.org/documents/intldocs/ILA/ILA_Berlin_Rules-2004.pdf (accessed 30 July 2022)). These do not have the same status as the UN Watercourses Convention, in that they are not binding. The Berlin Rules remark on the obligation to manage the shared watercourse in an equitable and reasonable manner. The 2001 Draft Articles on Prevention of Transboundary Harm (ILC, 'Draft articles on prevention of transboundary harm from hazardous activities, with commentaries', in *Yearbook of the International Law Commission. 2001, Volume II, Part Two: Report of the Commission to the General Assembly on the Work of Its Fifty-Third Session* (New York: UN, 2008)) noted that the consideration of different factors

In Sections 8.4 to 8.7, we shall look at some regional agreements concerning international watercourses and focus on their international dispute settlement provisions. We shall see how many of the recommended provisions from the global conventions are implemented and in which way they differ. This will enable us to draw some more general conclusions on dispute settlement mechanisms in international water law.

8.4 ASIA

In Asia, the Tibetan Plateau is the origin of three important rivers: the Salween River that extends through China, Myanmar, and Thailand, on the one hand; and the rivers Yangtze and Mekong that extend through Cambodia, China, Laos, Myanmar, Thailand, and Vietnam, on the other hand. The Salween River is the only international river in Asia that has no dams or industrial projects in it, making it the last free-flowing international river on the continent. Though the Yangtze River holds today's biggest dam in the world, it belongs exclusively to China. Accordingly, it is regarding the uses of the Mekong River which have gathered efforts of international cooperation, resulting in an agreement which is also relevant for settling disputes.[37]

8.4.1 *The 1995 Mekong Agreement*

This agreement was signed between Cambodia, Laos, Thailand, and Vietnam.[38] China and Myanmar, also States that are part of the Mekong river basin, have not signed the agreement; they are considered 'dialogue partners' under the Mekong Agreement. The importance of this agreement is that it created the Mekong River Commission, which has an important role to play in the settlement of disputes. The agreement establishes that the commission

involves an equitable balance of the States' interests; the Berlin Rules also mention a balancing process between the equitable and reasonable use principle and that of no harm to be worked out in each case individually. See ILA, *Report of the Seventy First Conference, Berlin* (London: International Law Association, 2004), p. 362, in Salman, 'The Helsinki Rules', p. 637; 2001 Draft Articles, Art 10, commentary (2). With regard to the international co-operation and administration of international watercourses, the Berlin Rules do not depart from the Helsinki Rules or the UN Watercourses Convention. As the preceding legal instruments, they establish an exchange of information, notification of planned projects, or activities and consultations. Berlin Rules, Arts 56, 57, and 58.

37 Aaron T. Wolf (ed.), *The Atlas of International Freshwater Agreements* (Nairobi: United Nations Environment Programme, 2002).

38 Agreement on the Co-operation for the Sustainable Development of the Mekong River Basin, Chiang Rai, signed and entered into force on 5 April 1995, 2069 UNTS 3.

shall first make every effort to resolve the issue (Article 34). As for the following stages, it establishes that when the commission is unable to resolve a dispute, the dispute shall be referred to the States for resolution by negotiation through diplomatic channels. Article 35 of the agreement establishes that in said cases, the States may use mediation as a means to resolve the dispute. Though mediation involves the use of a third party, and thus recommendations are given to the parties to help them settle their dispute, the 1995 Mekong Agreement does not expressly mention any binding mechanism to resolve disputes.

8.4.2 *The 1960 Indus Water Treaty*

Another agreement in Asia, which also established a commission, is the 1960 Indus Water Treaty. This treaty was signed between India and Pakistan, and it creates a Permanent Indus Commission, composed of a representative from each State.[39] Regarding dispute settlement, the treaty is very particular as it distinguishes between 'questions', 'differences', and 'disputes'.

'Questions' relate to the interpretation or application of the treaty, or to the existence of any fact which might constitute a breach; these questions are handled by the Commission. The treaty contains a list of twenty-three questions that form part of its Annex F.

'Differences', on the other hand, are questions that are to be resolved by a neutral expert.

Finally, 'disputes' are those questions not referred to in any of the listed questions (I–XXIII) in Annex F of the treaty, and for those the neutral expert of the previous stage informs the commission that the difference should be treated as a dispute.

When the issue has been categorised as a 'dispute', it is reported to the two governments. The governments can negotiate or agree to use mediation to settle the dispute. Pursuant to Article 9 of the treaty, a Court of Arbitration is also allowed upon the agreement of the parties, especially after an unfruitful negotiation or mediation.

Another important aspect of this treaty is that the World Bank is a signatory. Its role is limited to circumstances in which either 'differences' or 'disputes'

[39] Indus Waters Treaty 1960 between the Government of India, the Government of Pakistan, and the International Bank for Reconstruction and Development, Karachi, 19 September 1960, in force 12 January 1961, 419 UNTS 125.

arise by appointing people to fulfil certain roles when requested by either or both of the parties.

8.4.3 *The 1992 Almaty Agreement (Aral Sea Basin)*

This agreement is another example of how States settle watercourses disputes in Asia, signed between the Republic of Kazakhstan, the Kyrgyz Republic, the Republic of Tajikistan, Turkmenistan, and the Republic of Uzbekistan.[40] This agreement also establishes an Interstate Commission for Water Coordination 'to deal with the issues related to regulation, rational use, and protection of water resources'.[41] This Commission is composed of the heads of water agencies, and pursuant to this agreement, when a dispute arises, the heads of national water agencies of the respective countries shall settle the dispute. The agreement also establishes that, when necessary, these agencies shall settle disputes with the involvement of a third party.[42]

8.5 AFRICA

Africa is a continent rich in water basins that are shared between two or more countries. The uses of the majority of these basins are regulated by a treaty between the countries that share them.[43] Below we discuss some agreements concerning international rivers that bring about a variety of mechanisms to resolve disputes in this region.

8.5.1 *The 1986 Treaty on the Lesotho Highlands Water Project*

This treaty was signed by the Kingdom of Lesotho and the Republic of South Africa.[44] The treaty concerns the international Senqu/Orange River. It created specific authorities in each country and a commission to implement the provisions of the treaty. For the Kingdom of Lesotho, the Lesotho Highlands Development Authority (LHDA) 'shall have the responsibility for the

40 Agreement between the Republic of Kazakhstan, the Kyrgyz Republic, the Republic of Tajikistan, Turkmenistan, and the Republic of Uzbekistan on Co-operation in the Field of Joint Management on Utilisation and Protection of Water Resources from Inter-State Sources, Almaty, signed and entered into force on 18 February 1992 (http://cawater-info.net/library/eng/agreement.pdf (accessed 18 January 2020)). Hereinafter referred to as 'Almaty Agreement'.

41 Almaty Agreement, Art 7.

42 Ibid., Art 13.

43 Wolf, *Atlas of International Freshwater Agreements*, p. 27.

44 Treaty on the Lesotho Highlands Water Project between the Government of the Kingdom of Lesotho and the Government of the Republic of South Africa, Maseru, 24 October 1986, in force 24 October 1986, 1462 UNTS 24808.

implementation, operation and maintenance of that part of the Project situated in the Kingdom of Lesotho, in accordance with the provisions of this Treaty and shall be vested with all powers necessary for the discharge of such responsibilities'.[45] For the Republic of South Africa, the Trans-Caledon Tunnel Authority (TCTA) 'shall have the responsibility for the implementation, operation and maintenance of that part of the project in the Republic of South Africa, in accordance with the provisions of this Treaty, and shall be vested with all powers necessary for the discharge of such responsibilities'.[46]

As a way of overseeing both the LHDA and TCTA, the treaty also creates a Joint Permanent Technical Commission, which is composed of two delegations, one from each party. The treaty establishes that each party shall nominate three representatives constituting its delegation, as well as an alternate for each of the nominated representatives residing in Maseru. Each delegation shall alternately nominate a chairman for meetings of the Joint Permanent Technical Commission.[47]

With regard to the mechanisms of dispute settlement in this treaty, the Joint Permanent Technical Commission plays a key role.[48] As per the dispute settlement clause, when a dispute arises, the parties, the LHDA, or the TCTA, respectively, may request the Joint Permanent Technical Commission to conduct an investigation, which in turn may recommend the proper action to be taken at the end of its investigation.[49] However, if the dispute persists, and on the basis of the investigation report, the Joint Permanent Technical Commission can call for more formal procedures, namely the submission of the dispute to the two governments for resolution through negotiations. Failing the settlement of the dispute by negotiation, the parties shall proceed to arbitration, whose decision is final and binding.[50]

8.5.2 *The Treaty of the South African Development Community and the 2000 Revised Protocol on Shared Watercourses of the Southern African Development Community*

The Treaty of the South African Development Community (SADC) was adopted in 1992. The member parties are Angola, Botswana, Comoros,

[45] Treaty on the Lesotho Highlands Water Project, Art 7.
[46] Ibid., Art 8(1).
[47] Ibid., Art 9(1).
[48] The Joint Permanent Technical Commission can give advice and make recommendations and has audit powers over both the LHDA and the TCTA. Ibid., Arts 9(8)–(10).
[49] Treaty on the Lesotho Highlands Water Project, Art 16(4).
[50] Ibid., Art 16.

Democratic Republic of Congo, Eswatini, Lesotho, Madagascar, Malawi, Mauritius, Mozambique, Namibia, Seychelles, South Africa, United Republic of Tanzania, Zambia, and Zimbabwe.[51] The SADC Treaty, in Article 4, establishes as one of its principles the peaceful settlement of disputes.

In 2000, the member States agreed on a Revised Protocol on Shared Watercourses that adopted many of the provisions of the UN Watercourses Convention.[52] Regarding the settlement of disputes, the Revised Protocol in Article 7 establishes that State parties shall strive to resolve all disputes amicably.

The particularity of this agreement is the utilisation of its own regional tribunal, one that was created by the SADC Treaty, to resolve arising disputes. Thus, the 2000 Revised Protocol states that disputes that are not settled amicably shall be referred to the tribunal created by the SADC Treaty. The tribunal has the power to issue advisory opinions and decisions. In the case of the latter, they are binding.[53] The Protocol further states that if a dispute arises between the SADC and a State party, a request shall be made for an advisory opinion, which, though not binding, can carry a lot of weight when States try to settle the dispute brought before them.

8.5.3 *The 2005 Zamcom Agreement*

This agreement was signed by the Republic of Angola, Republic of Botswana, Republic of Malawi, Republic of Mozambique, Republic of Namibia, United Republic of Tanzania, Republic of Zambia, and Republic of Zimbabwe to establish a commission to protect the sustainable use of the Zambezi watercourse. This agreement established the Zamcom Commission.[54]

The Zamcom Commission is given the status of an international organisation and is composed of the Council of Ministers (which in turn is composed

[51] Treaty of the South African Development Community (SADC Treaty), Windhoek, 17 August 1992, in force 30 September 1993 (consolidated text as amended can be viewed at www.sadc.int/sites/default/files/2021-08/Consolidated_Text_of_the_SADC_Treaty_-_scanned_21_October_2015.pdf (accessed 30 July 2022)).

[52] Revised Protocol on Shared Watercourses of the South African Development Community, Windhoek, 7 August 2000, in force 22 September 2003 (available at www.sadc.int/sites/default/files/2021-08/Revised_Protocol_on_Shared_Watercourses_-_2000_-_English.pdf (accessed 30 July 2022)).

[53] SADC Treaty, Art 16.

[54] Agreement on the Establishment of the Zambezi Watercourse Commission, Kasane, 13 July 2004, in force 19 June 2011 (available at www.zambezicommission.org/sites/default/files/clusters_pdfs/ZAMCOM%20agreement.pdf (accessed 18 July 2021)).

of a delegate of the government of each State), a Technical Committee, and a Secretariat.

The dispute settlement clause of this agreement establishes that disputes shall be resolved by consultations and negotiations. At all times, the Council of Ministers may make recommendations to the parties, with a view to arrive at an amicable settlement. However, according to Article 21 of the agreement, unless the parties agree otherwise, if the dispute is not settled, it may be brought before the tribunal established in the SADC Treaty adopted in 1992 (see above). The dispute settlement clause of the agreement also allows for the use of the SADC Tribunal in case of a dispute between the Commission and a member State. Pursuant to the agreement, the Council of Ministers may request the SADC tribunal to give an advisory opinion, whose costs are borne by the commission.[55]

In this region, both the Protocol and the Zamcom Agreement are examples of treaties implementing a formalised regional mechanism to settle disputes by having treaties that include the submission of eventual water-related disputes to a regional tribunal, such as the one established by the SADC Treaty.

8.5.4 *The 2010 Agreement on the Nile River Basin Co-operative Framework*

The Nile Basin Initiative was created in 1999 by ten countries to provide a forum to discuss the sustainable management and development of the Nile's water resources.[56] In 2010, this initiative developed the Co-operative Framework Agreement, outlining the principles and rights for the management and development of the Nile basin's water resources and establishing a permanent Nile River Basin Commission to facilitate the agreement's implementation.[57] The agreement is not yet in force. It needs to be ratified by six countries to enter into force. It has so far been ratified by Ethiopia, Rwanda, and Tanzania; Uganda, Burundi, and Kenya have signed it, and Egypt and Sudan have rejected it. However, this agreement is worth mentioning as it contains a detailed clause on dispute settlement.

Article 34 reinforces the obligation to settle disputes by peaceful means, including negotiation, good offices, mediation, conciliation, and the use of

[55] Ibid., Art 22.

[56] Nile Basin Initiative Agreement, Entebbe, 22 February 1999, agreed by ten Nile basin countries: Burundi, DR Congo, Egypt, Ethiopia, Kenya, Rwanda, South Sudan, The Sudan, Tanzania, and Uganda; Eritrea as an observer.

[57] Agreement on the Nile River Basin Cooperative Framework, Sharm el Sheikh, 13 April 2010, not yet in force (https://nilebasin.org/images/docs/CFA%20-%20English%20%20FrenchVersion.pdf (accessed 8 August 2022)).

the Nile River Basin Commission or another third party to settle disputes. The agreement also gives the member States the choice of either using a fact-finding commission or, by agreement, submitting the dispute to arbitration or the ICJ.

8.6 EUROPE

Like other regions, Europe has several instruments but also specific European Union legislation to govern its different river basins. Below are some examples of watercourse agreements in Europe and their dispute settlement provisions.

8.6.1 *The 1994 Danube River Protection Convention*

The Convention was signed by Austria, Bulgaria, Croatia, Slovenia, Hungary, Moldova, Romania, the Czech Republic, Slovakia, and Ukraine.[58] It promotes cooperation among all States for a sustainable and equitable use of the Danube River as well as reduction of pollution and control of hazardous substances reaching its waters.

The Convention establishes an International Commission for the Protection of the Danube River, which participates in the settlement of disputes.[59] This is similar to the practices of many States in other regions of the world. In this regard, Article 24 of the Convention details the dispute settlement mechanisms and establishes the following: to begin with, parties shall resolve disputes by negotiation with the assistance of the International Commission. If the dispute is not resolved within the twelve months following the notification to the International Commission, then the parties must submit the dispute for a compulsory decision to either arbitration in accordance with the rules of its Annex, or to the ICJ.

The same clause establishes that parties must accept both or either of the means offered to resolve the dispute. When accepting both, the ICJ takes precedence; when accepting only one, arbitration shall be the mechanism to resolve the dispute.

8.6.2 *The 2002 Sava Agreement*

This framework agreement on the Sava river basin was signed by Bosnia and Herzegovina, the Republic of Croatia, the Republic of Slovenia, and the

[58] Convention on Co-operation for the Protection and Sustainable Use of the Danube River, Sofia, 29 June 1994, in force 22 October 1998 (www.icpdr.org/main/resources/danube-river-protection-convention (accessed 18 January 2021)).

[59] Ibid., Art 18.

Federal Republic of Yugoslavia.[60] The agreement covers both navigation and non-navigational utilisation of the Sava River. The Sava river basin is part of the Danube basin. The agreement establishes the main obligation to cooperate among parties and with national and international organisations. It also contains the main substantive and procedural obligations established in the 1997 UN Watercourses Convention, namely, the reasonable and equitable use of the resource and not to cause significant harm, including transboundary harm. Regarding the procedural obligations, it mentions the exchange of data and information, though it stays silent on consultations.

Part IV of the agreement details the cooperation mechanisms. The agreement creates the Sava River Basin Commission with international legal capacity. It also establishes the Meeting of the Parties which takes place once every two years and reviews the implementation based on the reports of the commission.

As for dispute settlement, once a dispute arises, the parties shall first seek a solution by negotiation. The parties may jointly seek good services, mediation, or conciliation from a third party, or they may agree to refer the dispute to arbitration or to the ICJ.

The international dispute settlement clause also states that if, within six months of submitting a request, the parties do not resolve their dispute by negotiation, good services, mediation, or conciliation, any party concerned may request that an independent fact-finding expert committee be established.[61]

8.6.3 *The 1999 Rhine Convention*

This Convention was signed by France, Germany, Luxembourg, the Netherlands, Switzerland, and the European Community.[62] It established the International Commission for the Protection of the Rhine composed of delegates from each country. The commission has legal capacity, and is in charge of implementing the Convention. The role of the commission in the settlement of disputes is not expressly mentioned in the Convention; however, similar to other commissions established by conventions, the commission does

60 Framework Agreement on the Sava River Basin, Kranjska Gora, 13 December 2002, in force 29 December 2004, 2366 UNTS 479.

61 Ibid., Art 22.

62 Convention on the Protection of the River Rhine, Berne, 12 April 1999, in force 1 January 2003, L289 European Union Treaties Office 31.

maintain an important role in providing a forum for dialogue that serves the purpose of mitigating or avoiding disputes among the parties.

Regarding the settlement of disputes, the contracting parties shall first strive to settle their dispute by negotiation or any other form of dispute settlement mechanism that the parties choose. If the dispute is not settled in such a way, then arbitration is established under the rules of procedure set forth in the annex of the Convention.[63]

8.7 SOUTH AMERICA

8.7.1 1969 *La Plata Basin Treaty*

This treaty was signed by Argentina, Bolivia, Brazil, Paraguay, and Uruguay in 1969.[64] It came about to put an end to regional conflicts concerning the use of the international river Paraná between Brazil, Paraguay, and Argentina over the location of the Itaipu dam project.[65] Thus, all countries bordering the La Plata basin, namely, Argentina, Bolivia, Brazil, Paraguay, and Uruguay, met to discuss a treaty with the objective of 'promoting the harmonious development and physical integration of the basin, in areas of direct or potential influence'.[66] The treaty included the aims of the institutionalisation of the water basin, rational use of water resources, and its equitable exploitation.

The La Plata Basin Treaty created two important institutions to this effect, namely the Intergovernmental Coordinating Committee (CIC) in 1969 and, much later, in 1992, the Hydroway Intergovernmental Committee (CIH). The latter is concerned only with navigational uses of the Paraguay and Paraná Rivers.

The treaty has no clause on dispute settlement. However, in practice, the provisions of this treaty, together with other subsequent regional agreements, have been used by the States to amicably prevent and settle disputes, which we shall discuss below.

8.7.2 *The 1973 Itaipu Treaty*

The Itaipu Treaty was signed by Brazil and Paraguay to use the international river Paraná for the production of hydroelectric energy. This treaty established

63 Ibid., Art. 16.

64 Cuenca del Plata Treaty, Brasilia, 23 April 1969, in force 14 August 1970 (www.oas.org/dsd/plata/legalf.htm (accessed 18 October 2020)).

65 For further details on the conflict, see Gwynn, *Adapting Watercourse Agreements*, pp. 10–18.

66 OAS, 'Cuenca del Plata' (documents), www.oas.org/dsd/plata/legalf.htm (accessed 14 June 2020).

a binational entity, also called Itaipu. This binational entity is slightly different from other joint or international commissions implemented by international watercourse conventions in that the binational entity has two main shareholders, namely the respective national electricity companies of the two countries.[67] The treaty contains the by-laws of this entity and allows it to operate as an international corporation, though remaining non-profit.[68] The established Itaipu Entity, however, maintains the representatives of the two countries in its overall structure. It is governed by a Governing Council, composed of six members appointed by each State that have a voice and a vote. The two general directors of the respective countries, and a representative of foreign affairs, also from each country, attend the council meetings and have a voice but no vote. The foreign affairs representative of each country was included in the Council specifically to handle the cases of expropriation when constructing the dam and for the purpose of dispute settlement.[69] For executive matters, the Itaipu Entity has a Board of Directors, also composed of six representatives by each State, each with different specialisations, such as juridical, administrative, coordination (also in charge of environmental issues), technical, and finance, and with a General Director of each country to coordinate the directors' executive activities. Main decisions of the Board of Directors must be submitted to the Governing Council for final approval. The treaty and subsequent regulations thereof define the different levels of competence for deciding issues concerning the administration of the Itaipu Entity.

Annex A (the Statute of the Itaipu Entity) states that any cases (disputes) that are not foreseen in the statute, and that cannot be resolved by the Governing Council, shall be settled by the two governments, with approval of the two countries' electricity companies (the shareholders). In this case, the provision in the statute demands to use internal mechanisms – the Board of Directors and the Governing Council – before submitting the dispute to the two governments.

67 While the Paraguayan National Electricity Company (ANDE) remains State-owned, the Brazilian Electricity Company (ELETROBRAS) became partly privatised in the 2000s. To date, due to full privatisation plans of ELETROBRAS, the Brazilian Nuclear and Binational Energy Holding Company (ENBpar) will be taking over ELETROBRAS' position at the Itaipu entity. See Gwynn, *Adapting Watercourse Agreements*, p. 31.

68 Treaty between Brazil and Paraguay Concerning the Hydroelectric Utilisation of the Water Resources of the Paraná River Owned in Condominium by the Two Countries, from and including the Salto Grande de Sete Quedas or Salto del Guairâ, to the Mouth of the Iguassu River, Brasilia, 26 April 1973, in force 13 August 1973 (923 UNTS 13164) (Itaipu Treaty), Annex C, IV.1, establishes that the total income of the entity shall be equal to its costs.

69 Ibid., Note Verbale No. 6 dated 26 April 1973.

However, once a dispute is at the governmental level, the dispute settlement clause of the treaty only refers to negotiations as a means to resolve disputes among the two States, with no indication of arbitration or another third-party impartial body.

8.7.3 *1979 Tripartite Agreement*

This agreement came about to ease the concerns of Argentina over the Itaipu project. It was signed by Argentina, Brazil, and Paraguay for the uses of hydropower deriving from the Paraná River.[70] The Tripartite Agreement expressly mentions the 1969 Plata Basin Treaty in its preamble and the two bilateral dam projects on the Paraná River – Brazil–Paraguay (Itaipu) and Argentina–Paraguay (Yacyreta).[71] Both projects are mentioned in the 1979 Tripartite Agreement as cases of successful cooperation pursuant to the implementation of the La Plata Basin Treaty.[72] The Tripartite Agreement established what would count as acceptable changes in water levels, as well as environmental protections and water quality standards. To monitor compliance, the agreement established a mechanism for the three countries to exchange information on hydrological conditions. It contains no express provision on dispute settlement. It is worth mentioning that this Tripartite Agreement in itself avoided further disputes between the three contracting parties over the uses of the Paraná River.

8.7.4 *The 2018 Guarani Aquifer Agreement*

This agreement was signed by Argentina, Brazil, Paraguay, and Uruguay and entered into force in 2020.[73] The Guarani aquifer is part of the La Plata basin and is transboundary on all mentioned States' territories. These States have expressly included a provision on the maintenance of their sovereignty over the respective portion of the aquifer in their territories while at the same time

[70] Acuerdo Tripartito Referente al Aprovechamiento hidroeléctrico del río Paraná, Note Verbale No. 16 dated 19 October 1979 (Tri-Partite Agreement). For English translation, see Argentina, Brazil, Paraguay: Agreement on Paraná River Projects, President Stroessner City, Paraguay, signed and entered into force on 19 October 1979, 19 ILM 615.

[71] The Treaty of Yacyreta between the Republic of Paraguay and the Argentine Republic, Asunción, 3 December 1973, in force 27 March 1974 (1380 UNTS 23141), was signed the same year as the Itaipu Treaty.

[72] Tri-Partite Agreement, para. 2.

[73] Agreement on the Guarani Aquifer between Argentina, Brazil, Paraguay, and Uruguay, San Juan, 2 August 2010, in force 26 November 2020 (www.internationalwaterlaw.org/documents/regionaldocs/Guarani_Aquifer_Agreement-English.pdf (accessed 31 July 2022)).

maintaining that they will do so according to international law,[74] which in fact determines the limited sovereignty over shared natural resources, such as the Guarani aquifer. The agreement thus aligns with the provisions of the 1997 UN Watercourses Convention. The Guarani Aquifer Agreement also created a Commission formed by representatives of each country, mainly to coordinate any activities relating to the aquifer. The Commission does not have a legal capacity.

Regarding dispute settlement, the States have decided that disputes shall be settled by direct negotiations, notifying the established commission of such negotiations. If the dispute persists, then the parties can request recommendations from the Commission, which must issue its recommendations within sixty days.[75] If the recommendations are not fruitful, then the parties can submit the dispute to arbitration. The agreement establishes that the arbitration procedure shall be established by a different protocol which has yet to be decided among the parties.

8.8 COMPARISON OF INTERNATIONAL WATERCOURSES DISPUTE SETTLEMENT PROVISIONS IN DIFFERENT GLOBAL AND REGIONAL AGREEMENTS

From the global and regional agreements provided as examples to illustrate the different ways in which States, in their treaty practices, settle their disputes, we can reach some interesting conclusions.

When comparing the different agreements regarding watercourses, we can see that the global conventions have very detailed dispute settlement provisions. By contrast, the regional and bilateral treaties mention only some of the mechanisms contained in the global conventions, often with less specification. Of the examined watercourses agreements, only the Agreement on the Nile River Basin Co-operative Framework and the 2002 Sava Agreement contain almost all the mechanisms recommended in the global conventions.

Most regional and bilateral agreements concerning the utilisation of international watercourses do establish an international institution or commission. This body typically has a key role in settling disputes before submitting the disputes to States, and it provides a platform for dialogue for States to resolve disputes. Pursuant to some agreements, these commissions can act to

74 Ibid., Art 2.

75 Ibid., Art 17.

Settlement of International Watercourses Disputes in Different Global and Regional Agreements										
	Settlement of Disputes by Commission Created by Treaty	State-to-State Settlement of Disputes								
Treaty		Negotiations	Other Means	Good Offices	Mediation	Conciliation	Joint Institutions	Fact-Finding	Arbitration	ICJ
UN 1997		X	X	X	X	X	X	X	X	X
UNECE 1992		X	X						X	X
Asia										
The 1995 Mekong Agreement	Mekong River Commission	X			X		(ex ante)			
The 1960 Indus Water Treaty	Permanent Indus Commission Questions: by Commission Differences: by neutral expert Disputes: next stages submitted to States	X			X		(ex ante)		X	
The 1992 Almaty Agreement (Aral Sea basin)	Interstate Commission for Water Coordination						Heads of national water agencies, which are members of the commission		X (involvement of third party)	
Africa										
The 1986 Treaty on the Lesotho Highlands Water Project	Joint Permanent Technical Commission	X					(ex ante)		X	

The 2000 Revised Protocol on Shared Watercourses of the Sothern African Development Community							Regional tribunal			
The 2005 Zamcom Agreement	Zamcom Commission	X and consultations					Regional tribunal			
Agreement on the Nile River Basin Co-operative Framework	Nile River Basin Commission	X	X	X	X			X	X	X
Europe										
The 1994 Danube River Protection Convention	International Commission for the Protection of the Danube River	X							X	X
The 2002 Sava Agreement	Sava River Basin Commission	X	X	X	X	X		X	X	X
The 1999 Rhine Convention	International Commission for the Protection of the Rhine	X	X						X	

(continued)

(continued)

Settlement of International Watercourses Disputes in Different Global and Regional Agreements										
	Settlement of Disputes by Commission Created by Treaty	State-to-State Settlement of Disputes								
Treaty		Negotiations	Other Means	Good Offices	Mediation	Conciliation	Joint Institutions	Fact-Finding	Arbitration	ICJ
South America										
1969 La Plata Basin Treaty	Intergovernmental Coordinating Committee									
1973 Itaipu Treaty	Governing Council	X					(ex ante)			
1979 Tripartite Agreement										
2018 Guarani Aquifer Agreement	Guarani Aquifer Agreement Commission	X							X	

coordinate investigations (Lesotho Treaty), provide recommendations or advice to the parties (Lesotho Treaty, Zamcom Agreement), or to engage in procedural steps to internally settle disputes (Indus Treaty, Itaipu Treaty). For certain agreements, when submitting a dispute to the States, the notification of the dispute to the commission has a procedural value as it determines the time frame for following subsequent stages of the mechanism to settle disputes (Guarani Aquifer Agreement, Danube River Protection Convention). Pursuant to other agreements, even at the moment of submitting the disputes to States, the respective institution participates in assisting all parties throughout the dispute settlement process (Danube River Protection Convention).

We have also seen in the reviewed watercourses agreements that most provide for the possibility of a third-party neutral arbitration, or the use of a regional tribunal to resolve disputes. In the case of the Indus Treaty, the World Bank is also a party to the treaty and can assist with the settlement of disputes. However, the utilisation of a neutral third party or arbitration for the settlement of disputes is not included in some of the mentioned watercourses agreements of South America. In fact, in South America, two very important watercourses agreements contain no dispute settlement provisions at all (the La Plata Basin Treaty and the Tripartite Agreement).

These particularities could have arisen from the time when the treaties were concluded, which was before the time of the global conventions. The global conventions and their detailed mechanisms can be useful for States which just need to consent to settle their dispute with one of the recommended mechanisms.

Cooperation in matters of transboundary water resources and the peaceful settlement of disputes go hand in hand. In the case of the Nile River, for example, the construction of the Grand Ethiopian Renaissance Dam has increased tensions between Ethiopia and Egypt despite an existing Cooperative Framework Agreement that details almost all the mechanisms of dispute resolution recommended by the 1997 UN Watercourses Convention.[76] Tension among riparians concerning the uses of international rivers has also arisen in South America due to the extreme weather (droughts) conditions recently affecting the region and especially the water flow of international rivers. The reaction of the riparians was, however, different from

76 Biniam Bedasso and Maria A. Gwynn, 'How to share a river', Project Syndicate, 8 September 2020 (www.project-syndicate.org/commentary/egypt-ethiopia-dispute-blue-nile-dam-by-biniam-bedasso-and-maria-a-gwynn-2020-09 (accessed 11 August 2022)).

that of the riparians of the Nile. In the early months of 2020, extreme drought had severely reduced the Paraná River's water flow, and all three riparians – Argentina, Brazil, and Paraguay – were affected and had to drastically limit their use of the river. As noted above, the international river Paraná has dams that depend on water for hydropower production. Facing low water flow, a natural operation of dams is to retain some water in their reservoir. Upstream countries like Brazil retained some of the water in their upper stream dams' reservoirs, but this contributed to reducing Argentina's water supply and made it difficult for landlocked Paraguay to navigate the river, which is essential for its agricultural export industry. Following a request of the Ministry of Foreign Affairs of Paraguay to the binational entity Itaipu (Brazil–Paraguay) to release more water from the Itaipu reservoir to increase downstream flow of the river, an intergovernmental technical committee was formed from representatives of the riparian States and key institutions to enable more exchange of information and hydrological data. This, together with the treaties mentioned herein and international law establishing reasonable and equitable uses of any international river, was crucial for the Governing Council of the Itaipu Entity's decision to grant the request.[77] As a result, just enough water from the reservoir was released to ease the drought's effects for downstream countries, without compromising energy production and thereby helping the water flow levels of the Paraná River. Thus, several uses could be balanced among all riparians.

This example of current State practice in the region of South America shows that, although there is no independent arbitration body in place in any of their agreements concerning the uses of the international river Paraná, the complementarity of the different treaties and of international law, coupled with States' willingness to co-operate with one another, enabled the riparians to negotiate and resolve their disputes amicably and according to the principles contained in the 1997 UN Watercourses Convention.

Indeed, when judging a watercourse dispute, the ICJ stated that a 'treaty is not static, and is open to adapt to emerging norms of international law'.[78] Current practices show that international cooperation is needed, and nothing prevents States from aligning to the traditional forms of dispute settlement

[77] Ibid.; Maria A. Gwynn, 'South America and the living principle of equitable and reasonable uses of international watercourses', Water Science Policy, 27 March 2021 (https://watersciencepolicy.com/article/south-america-and-the-living-principle-of-equitable-and-reasonable-uses-of-international-watercourses-6670d6d28a2c?language=English (accessed 11 August 2022)).

[78] *Case Concerning the Gabčíkovo-Nagymaros Project* (Judgment), para. 112, pp. 64–65.

mechanisms even when their regional agreements do not expressly contain dispute settlement provisions.

8.9 PREVAILING MECHANISMS FOR INTERNATIONAL WATERCOURSE DISPUTES

In the preceding sections, we discussed different international watercourses agreements in different regions of the world. The 1997 UN Watercourses Convention, which codified State practice in the area, continues to be an important tool to prevent disputes from arising and provides recommendations to States on the mechanisms of dispute settlement, specifically those arising when using international watercourses.

Most watercourses agreements have in common express provisions on substantive obligations, such as reasonable and equitable utilisation and the obligation not to cause harm; procedural obligations, such as exchange of data, notification, and consultation; and the establishment of joint or international commissions. All of these can help the riparians in their relationship during their utilisation of the international watercourse and prevent disputes from arising.

As for the substantive obligations such as reasonable and equitable utilisation and the obligation not to cause harm, these can help the parties reach a balance in the multiple uses of international watercourses. It is often the case that there are multiple uses deriving from international watercourses, for example, water consumption, energy production, navigation, and so on. It is with the application of these core principles, coupled with the guidance of the Convention regarding which factors are to be taken into consideration to achieve equitable and reasonable utilisation, that parties are enabled to reach a balance between keeping the multiple uses of the international watercourse while at the same time accounting for all riparian interests and needs.

Equally important, and also connected to the aim of balancing the multiple uses of an international watercourse, are the procedural obligations such as the exchange of data, notification, and consultation. It is of paramount importance to have the results of the technical work pertaining to the particular uses on the ground. For example, in the use of an international watercourse for hydropower production, a dam must collect and register multiple types of data ranging from climate, hydrology, variation of water flows in upper and downstream areas, and environmental impacts including that of climate change. It is important not only to collect and gather this data but also to share it with other riparians and key institutions in the sector in order to overcome common challenges that riparians face, such as extreme droughts. The exchange of data and notification of any relevant aspect to all parties concerned can provide an early opportunity to the parties to reach and mitigate any adverse impact affecting their utilisation of the international watercourse. Thus, diligent compliance with the procedural obligations can also be a way of preventing disputes from arising. We have seen how this was successfully implemented with the interactions of all key actors when facing the drought in South America.

One way in which the dispute settlement mechanisms of international watercourses agreements often differ from the standard dispute settlement mechanisms in other areas is the establishment of joint or international commissions or councils and their role in settling disputes before involving the States. For the utilisation of international watercourses, firstly, it is reasonable to have a joint or international commission because of the very nature of the relationship, that is, the need to manage the diverse issues of interests between two or more States that share an international watercourse. Secondly, a joint or international commission also provides a forum to the parties to discuss and resolve issues that would otherwise have to be handled by the States through diplomatic means.

While the bilateral agreements create these joint institutions, global conventions, such as the UNECE Water Convention, also establish such multilateral forums for the parties. Having joint or international institutions in this area has the advantage of facilitating dialogue and at the same time promoting the implementation of, and compliance with, the provisions of the agreements. Thus, providing technical assistance, building capacity, or sharing knowledge to support the joint institutions also remain important.

The advantages of settling disputes before reaching a government level are manifold, but in this area in particular, two points should be highlighted. Firstly, earlier stages in the process and institutions involved therein will already gather data and allow for technical reports concerning the natural resource and the expert information on any of the uses thereof. This is why these stages, though not binding to the parties, have often helped resolve a conflict before it became an international dispute. Even if a dispute reaches the respective governments, technical data will already be available to them. Secondly, settling a dispute before reaching the government level can help in not making the matter of the dispute a political issue.

Despite the above, a dispute can persist and eventually reach the respective governments. When this happens, the negotiation stage is very important. States can enter into negotiations in order to find a compromise. Nonetheless, as mentioned in the 1899 Hague Convention for the Pacific Settlement of International Disputes, one of the earliest conventions on dispute settlement, arbitration is 'the most effective, and at the same time the most equitable means of settling disputes *which diplomacy has failed to settle*'.[79]

Thus, if negotiations fail, adjudication through arbitration or an impartial third body is also recommended by most international watercourses agreements. Having other mechanisms when negotiations fail, such as conciliation, mediation, or arbitration, is an advantage in the face of typical asymmetric levels of interdependence between States. As seen in some of the examples, a non-governmental third party can also sign an international watercourse treaty. The World Bank, for example, signed the Indus Water Treaty not only for funding purposes but also to partake in the dispute settlement mechanism. Furthermore, as a last resort, we have seen how crucial the ICJ is for States to settle their disputes. After the decisions of the ICJ in cases concerning an international watercourse (*Gabčíkovo-Nagymaros Project* and *Pulp Mills*), the States resumed the utilisation of their shared international watercourses and continued to carry out their respective projects, in alignment with the decision. Today both projects have been completed and provide economic and social benefits to the respective countries and regions.

8.10 CONCLUSION

Utilising the processes set out in international watercourse treaties to resolve disputes reinforces the international requirement to settle disputes peacefully and the requirement to exhaust all remedies internal to the treaty prior to bringing the matter to international processes external to the treaty.

The preceding discussion has demonstrated that there are important features of dispute settlement which are particular to international watercourse disputes, such as the role that joint or international commissions play in mitigating or settling disputes. The collection and exchange of technical data, either through these commissions or through independent neutral experts appointed by said institutions, enable the parties to reach a balanced solution based on the technical data by also taking into account the interests of all parties. Also, having such commissions can promote dialogue, provide solutions for local implementation, and help maintain and keep the enforcement of the provisions in check.

The crucial role of international cooperation should also be highlighted. As we have seen, the substantive and procedural obligations in this area, including equitable and reasonable utilisation, no harm, exchange of data,

[79] Convention for the Pacific Settlement of International Disputes, The Hague, 29 July 1899, in force 4 September 1900, (1899) 187 CTS 410, Art 16. My emphasis.

notifications and consultations, and negotiations, can all procure benefits that member countries can share, but all of these rest upon the good faith of the parties to take each other's interests into account and make compromises. In the end, the most critical concern is the optimisation of the management and utilisation of the natural resources – especially those as vital as watercourses – that are shared among countries.

An optimal management and utilisation following the principles of international law encompasses the use of water resources in a way that promotes the very concept of sustainable development while at the same time maintaining them for the benefit of our future generations.

9

Coherence, Consistency, and the Reform of Investment Treaty Arbitration

ERIC DE BRABANDERE

9.1 INTRODUCTION

Debates regarding (and in fact prompting) the reform of investment arbitration have been and are permeated with statements that the current investor–State dispute settlement system (ISDS) is deficient in terms of 'predictability and interpretative consistency of case law' and hence requires reform in order, amongst others, to remedy that deficiency.[1] The investment court system (ICS) proposed by the European Commission (EC) of the European Union (EU) has, amongst others, as objective to provide a 'public justice' dispute settlement mechanism, including an appellate tribunal 'where consistency of judicial decisions is ensured'.[2]

That there is a certain inconsistency between certain arbitral awards in investment arbitration is beyond doubt. The question, however, is not necessarily whether there is (some) inconsistency, but rather whether this is inherently problematic and whether the reform proposals, such as the replacement of arbitration by a standing court or tribunal, will provide an answer to the inconsistency of arbitral awards.

In this chapter I explore these questions and offer some reflections also on the broader context in which the discussion needs to be situated. I consider that the consistency debate cannot and should not be isolated from the

[1] European Commission, 'Multilateral reform of investment dispute resolution, accompanying the document "Recommendation for a council decision authorising the opening of negotiations for a convention establishing a multilateral court for the settlement of investment disputes"', Doc. Nr. COM(2017) 493 final', https://ec.europa.eu/transparency/regdoc/rep/10102/2017/EN/SWD-2017-302-F1-EN-MAIN-PART-1.PDF (accessed 10 June 2021).

[2] Art 2(d)(xv) of the European Parliament, 'Resolution containing the European Parliament's recommendations to the European Commission on the negotiations for the Transatlantic Trade and Investment Partnership (TTIP)' (8 July 2015) A8–0175/2015.

broader questions of the coherence of international law, the determinacy of legal norms, and the role of judges or arbitrators in the interpretation of these norms. Thus, what is at stake here is not necessarily how to reconcile conflicting arbitral awards (or how to avoid this in the first place), but rather the question of content determination of international investment law. This in turn is linked to questions such as the (in)determinacy of international (investment) law, the interpretation of investment law norms, and the legal reasoning of international investment tribunals.

The place of international investment law in the international legal system is also an important aspect of the debate, as the search for coherence and consistency in international investment law and arbitration is, in parts, the modern-day version of the fragmentation debate that existed in international law more than a decade ago,[3] but on the micro or internal level of international investment law. It is beyond doubt that international investment treaties, like international law instruments, operate under the broader umbrella of general international legal norms relating, for example, to the interpretation of treaties, to the sources of international legal obligation, and to State responsibility.[4]

I will first proceed with an analysis of the concepts of coherence and consistency, in the broader framework of public international law (Section 9.2), to then focus on the question of the determinacy and determination of international investment law norms (Section 9.3). In Section 9.2, I will also discuss the roles and functions of arbitral tribunals and the importance of arbitral awards in international investment law. In Section 9.3, I will discuss the inconsistencies that have been detected in the arbitral awards and analyse whether this should or can be perceived as problematic (Section 9.4). Finally, I will sketch the contours of the reform proposals and discuss the likely impact of these reforms – chiefly the creation of a standing tribunal or court – on the coherence and consistency debate (Section 9.5). This chapter is not concerned generally with the specific features of the proposed 'multilateral investment court' (MIC) or other alternatives. Rather, it explores the link between the proposed reforms and the 'coherence' and 'consistency' of decision-making in investment arbitration.

3 International Law Commission, 'Fragmentation of international law: Difficulties arising from the diversification and expansion of international law. Report of the Study Group of the International Law Commission' (13 April 2006) UN Doc. A/CN.4/L.682.

4 See generally Eric De Brabandere, *Investment Treaty Arbitration as Public International Law: Procedural Aspects and Implications* (Cambridge: Cambridge University Press, 2014).

9.2 COHERENCE, CONSISTENCY, AND DETERMINACY IN INTERNATIONAL LAW

The coherence of international law has long been a subject of discussion, and I do not intend here to settle the question of whether international law is or should be coherent. Because this chapter zooms in on consistency more than on coherence, I will instead, in this section, map the debate to better situate the discussion on consistency in the specific context of investment law and arbitration. Also, because both coherence and consistency are often discussed in conjunction,[5] each must be clearly delineated.

9.2.1 *The Coherence of International (Investment) Law*

What constitutes 'coherence' has been answered and conceptualised in different ways, and various meanings – normative or not – have been ascribed to the notion. Yet, there are some common features to all proposed definitions of 'coherence'. These common features are well captured by Claus Kress' definition: 'An idea or theory is coherent if it hangs or fits together, if its parts are mutually supportive, if it is intelligible, if it flows from or expresses a single unified viewpoint.'[6] To this normative proposition, others have added methodological aspects, which relate in essence to the question of how legal reasoning can be considered 'coherent'.[7] Coherence thus generally implies some form of internal 'logic' of a legal system in the sense that there is a positive connection between the various elements of a legal system which unites these.[8]

Aside from the question of whether there would be an obligation to 'aim for coherence',[9] a good starting point for a discussion of the question of whether

5 See, amongst others, Christoph Schreuer, 'Coherence and consistency in international investment law', in Roberto Echandi and Pierre Sauvé (eds.), *Prospects in International Investment Law and Policy: World Trade Forum* (Cambridge: Cambridge University Press, 2013), pp. 391–402.

6 Claus Kress, 'Coherence', in Dennis Patterson (ed.), *A Companion to Philosophy of Law and Legal Theory*, 2nd ed. (Chichester: Wiley-Blackwell, 2010), p. 521.

7 See, e.g., Robert Alexy and Aleksander Peczenik, 'The concept of coherence and its significance for discourse rationality' (1990) 3 Ratio Juris 130–47.

8 Schreuer, 'Coherence and consistency', p. 391. See also Christophe Hillion, 'Tous pour un, un pour tous! Coherence in the external relations of the European Union', in Marise Cremona (ed.), *Developments in EU External Relations Law. Collected Courses of the Academy of European Law* (Oxford: Oxford University Press, 2008), pp. 13–14.

9 See Nele Matz-Lück, 'Harmonization, systemic integration, and "mutual supportiveness" as conflict-solution techniques: Different modes of interpretation as a challenge to negative effects of fragmentation' (2006) 17 FYBIL 39–54 at 46. See also Nele Matz-Lück, 'Norm

international investment law is coherent is to link the question of coherence to the doctrine of sources in legal systems. The coherence in civil law systems flows chiefly from the unity of the sources, which were originally (and mostly still are) written sources – that is, legislation.[10] This idea gained prominence after the French Revolution and strong adherence to Rousseau's *Du Contrat Social*, which gave rise to the idea of the primacy of the law as adopted by a legislative body.[11] This in turn implies an inexistent or limited law-making role for courts and tribunals in domestic legal systems which in theory apply, but do not make, law. The absence of a rule of precedent in civil law systems is a consequence of these premises, and when cases are cited, this is done for their 'actual holdings' as supporting authority rather than because they *are* the law.[12] In common law systems, it has been argued that the prohibition of *non liquet* has been a driving force behind the granting of a certain need for judges to fill in gaps in the existing law.[13] Moreover, others add that the absence of codification of existing law, in contrast with civil law systems, also has been a reason for the emergence of the doctrine of *stare decisis* in common law systems.[14] It is not the place here to retrace the origins of the role of decisions – and of courts more generally – in common law and civil law systems.[15] The important point is that in common law systems, cases are cited because they are binding law, and binding precedents in turn ensure the coherence of the law.

This difference between civil and common law systems also explains the difference between *stare decisis* and *jurisprudence constante*. Both ensure overall coherence (and a certain form of consistency), but the underlying *rationale* in both systems differs fundamentally.[16] The precise reasons for why a distinction exists between legal systems which adhere to the *stare decisis* or to

interpretation across international regimes: Competences and legitimacy', in Margaret Young (ed.), *Regime Interaction in International Law: Facing Fragmentation* (Cambridge: Cambridge University Press, 2012), pp. 201–34.

10 Maurice Adams, '"Law is as I've told you before". Over de zwaartekrachtwerking van rechterlijke uitspraken in België' (1997) 1 Tijdschrift voor Privaat Recht 1383–88 at 1331.

11 Ibid.

12 For a discussion, see Lawrence Solan, 'Precedent in statutory interpretation' (2015–16) 94 NCLRev 1165–234 at 1125–26.

13 Christian Autexier, '5es Journées juridiques franco-allemandes (Lübeck, 13-16 juin 1984)' (1984) 36 Revue internationale de droit comparé 839–52 at 844.

14 Adams, 'Law is as I've told you before', 1383–88; and John Hanna, 'The role of precedent in judicial decision' (1957) 2 Vill L Rev 367–84 at 377.

15 See, e.g., Martin Shapiro, *Courts: A Comparative and Political Analysis* (Chicago: University of Chicago Press, 1981), chs 2 and 3.

16 See generally David Baragwanath, 'The interpretative challenges of international adjudication across the common law/civil law divide' (2014) 3 CJICL 450–88.

the *jurisprudence constante* practice are multiple. Some authors have explained the distinction by referring to the different roles of the judiciary in general, pointing out that the judicial function in civil law systems focuses on the *interpretation* of laws and statutes, as opposed to common law systems.[17] In civil law systems, the idea (simply put) that a judge interprets the law – but does not make the law – prevails. This is essentially a question of difference in method and methodology.[18] A second reason might be the codification movement which occurred in mostly European civil law systems and the existence of the Roman law tradition in these States compared to common law countries. While this may have been true originally,[19] others have pointed out that, over time, this difference has resulted in a difference not only in judicial activity but also in legal professional education, which in turn affects and perpetuates the methodology of judges.[20]

Transposed to the international legal system, some scholars argue that coherence is an absolute necessity for international law, or any legal system more generally, since it ensures a form of certainty.[21] Others in turn deny any value to the notion, viewing international law instead as an argumentative practice or a language.[22] The discussion is in essence a question of degree; on both extremes, one finds the view either that a system can be considered coherent only when there is an alignment of (most of) its rules (including the subsystem, 'branches', 'fields', and self-contained regimes), or that, by its very nature, international law lacks any internal cohesion or logic, and hence coherence.

Somewhere in between those two lines of thought, some authors have argued that 'in principle, a certain degree of coherence of the international legal system exists and is beneficial for constructing public international law . . . Several fundamental elements of a coherent international legal system exist despite further specialization.'[23] This 'middle road' approach can probably best be aligned to the link made above between the coherence of legal systems and the doctrine of sources. Sir Christopher Greenwood, for example, considers that irrespective of the diversity of or within international law, the

[17] Autexier, '5es Journées', p. 844.

[18] Hanna, 'Role of precedent', p. 376.

[19] See Adams, 'Law is as I've told you before', pp. 1383–88, and ibid.

[20] Hanna, 'Role of precedent', p. 376.

[21] See, amongst others, Dirk Pulkowski, *The Law and Politics of International Regime Conflict* (Oxford: Oxford University Press, 2014), 251 ff.

[22] See notably Martti Koskenniemi, 'Law, teleology, and international relations: An essay in counterdisciplinarity' (2011) 26 Int Relat 3–34 at 19–20.

[23] Matz-Lück, 'Norm interpretation', p. 208.

sources of international law provide a certain unity or coherence. He argues that 'customary international law is a coherent body of rules and principles applicable to all States', and, as regards international treaties, the principles of treaty interpretation codified in the 1969 Vienna Convention on the Law of Treaties include rules concerning the need to take into account other rules applicable between the parties as well as rules concerning the relation between treaties and other norms of international law.[24] This perspective conforms to the account of Yuval Shany, according to whom a legal system comprises at least the following components: a set of elements, arranged in an order, which is 'characterized by the interaction between the different element' and 'possessing a certain degree of unity or cohesion'.[25] Shany argues that, applying this definition to international law, 'one might reasonably deduce ... that the norms of international law can be viewed as a system of norms according to the dominant legal theories'.[26] Subsystems or regimes within international law, to the extent they can be linked to international law, are, according to Shany, part of a bigger whole, in particular as they resort to norms that originate in general international law.[27]

If one looks at the question of whether international investment law *is* coherent, one could therefore argue that international investment law indeed is coherent, as it forms part of international law, which is in turn a coherent legal system from the perspective of the sources or the secondary norms of international law. But, of course, this entire perspective hinges on the hypothesis that general international law is a coherent system of law and that international investment law is part of that system.[28]

Other accounts of the systemic nature of international investment law are not necessarily excluding the general perspective that within international law, international investment law operates as a sub-regime or field. While I do not intend here to offer an exhaustive account of all approaches to the systemic nature of international investment law, I will briefly expand on some approaches to the field which offer specific perspectives on the formation and evolution of norms in this specific area and, to that extent, may also shed some light on the consistency and coherence debate.

24 Christopher Greenwood, 'Unity and diversity in international law', in Mads Andenas and Eirik Bjorge (eds.), *A Farewell to Fragmentation: Reassertion and Convergence in International Law* (Cambridge: Cambridge University Press, 2015), pp. 40–43.

25 Yuval Shany, *The Competing Jurisdictions of International Courts and Tribunals* (Oxford: Oxford University Press, 2003), p. 83.

26 Ibid., p. 93.

27 Ibid., p. 99.

28 As I have argued in De Brabandere, *Investment Treaty Arbitration*.

As Stephan Schill has explained, two main perspectives, or 'ordering paradigms', of international investment law exist: bilateralism and multilateralism. A third perspective (multilateralisation), which he endorses, lies somewhat in between the former two as it situates bilateralism and bilateral treaty-making into a broader (multilateral) 'overarching conceptual framework' which is created by the entirety of the bilateral law and practice.[29] These different 'ordering paradigms' influence how one views international investment law. A bilateral approach in essence would counter the perspective of international investment law as a system in and of itself, while multilateralism in turn would stress the commonalities of international investment law obtained through the few multilateral treaties that exist, notably the ICSID Convention and sectoral or regional investment treaties.[30] The existence, despite the reality of the essential bilateral nature of international investment treaties, of common principles in these treaties, however, would depict a multilateralised regime or system.[31] Schill approaches the question from the perspective of 'ordering paradigms' in order to *analyse* international investment law and to answer the question of whether international investment law is 'a regime or field at all' or merely 'an unconnected patchwork of episodes of treaty-making and dispute settlement without inter-linkages in an overarching structure'.[32] Schill, endorsing the multilateralisation approach, does not consider international investment law as a system in and of itself – it remains a '(sub-)system of international law'.[33]

Another account, offered by Joost Pauwelyn, attempts to understand how international investment law has emerged, changed, and evolved over time and how it 'operates as a largely self-organizing, decentralized system made up of many interacting components'.[34] Drawing from biology, Pauwelyn has characterised international investment law as a 'complex adaptive system' based on three identified features of international investment law: 'decentralized composition, organic emergence and highly contested but dynamic stability'.[35] He argues that international investment law is best understood as

[29] Stephan W. Schill, 'Ordering paradigms in international investment law: Bilateralism-multilateralism-multilateralization', in Zachary Douglas, Joost Pauwelyn, and Jorge E. Viñuales (eds.), *The Foundations of International Investment Law: Bringing Theory into Practice* (Oxford: Oxford University Press, 2014), p. 113.

[30] Ibid., p. 114.

[31] Ibid., p. 115.

[32] Ibid., p. 109

[33] Ibid., p. 127.

[34] Joost Pauwelyn, 'At the edge of chaos? Foreign investment law as a complex adaptive system, how it emerged and how it can be reformed' (2014) 29 ICSID Rev/FILJ 372–418 at 372.

[35] Ibid., pp. 374–75, 377 ff.

a system of 'dispersed interactions between many agents, institutions and instruments', characterised by 'collective behaviour', as evidenced, amongst others, by 'evolution, diffusion and cross-fertilization between an intertwined network of FCN treaties, BITs and FTA', 'social networks of a limited number of repeat-appointed arbitrators deeply influencing the ongoing development of FIL and providing a certain level of coherence to the system', and 'limited rules of precedent across *ad hoc* tribunals notwithstanding the absence of a formal rule of stare decisis'.[36] Pauwelyn argues that international investment law, hence, cannot be analysed by reference to 'whether it is, for example, more like commercial arbitration, public international law or public or administrative law', but rather through international investment law's 'constituent components, its myriad sources and actors, and how they interact and have interacted over time'.[37]

As such, Pauwelyn does not necessarily conclude that international investment law is a 'system' in the legal sense. Rather, his ambition is to offer an alternative account of the criticism of international investment law as a 'deeply pathological regime riddled with birth defects in need of drastically greater coherence and structure'.[38] While he accepts that international investment law 'distinguishes itself from other regimes, like the World Trade Organisation (WTO) or the Kyoto Protocol, with much higher levels of centralization', he argues that it does possess 'a deep underlying coherence that provides minimal structure and continuity'.[39] Indeed, and this conclusion does not, as such, differ much from the account of Yuval Shany, 'a high degree of formal centralization and global control are not indispensable for a regime to emerge and thrive'.[40] Pauwelyn thus readily admits that international investment law has a minimal, yet sufficient, level of coherence necessary to be considered as a system under his theory.

While these are not the only approaches to international investment law, Schill and Pauwelyn accept that international investment law is a subsystem or subfield within international law, which offers some level of coherence. Schill, however, does so only to the extent that one views international investment law through a 'multilateralisation' lens; to that extent, it does seemingly depart from the approaches adopted by Greenwood (and Shany), which have stressed the coherence of international investment law through

[36] Ibid., pp. 374–75, 384.
[37] Ibid., pp. 374–75.
[38] Ibid., p. 376.
[39] Ibid.
[40] Ibid., pp. 374–75.

the application of the general rules of international law despite the bilateral nature of the field. In any event, for the purposes of this chapter, I adopt the proposition that international investment law essentially is a part of public international law and qualifies either as a subsystem, subfield, or sub-regime within international law. The existence of a field-specific system or mechanism of dispute settlement does not in and of itself run counter to this perspective.[41]

9.2.2 *Consistency and Determinacy in International Investment Law*

Consistency implies that similar situations be treated in an identical or analogous way. Identical disputes should result in similar outcomes. Consistency may form part of the idea that a legal system is 'coherent' or internally 'logical', but it operates on a different level. Consistency is, in comparison to 'coherence', perhaps more practical and measurable in nature, or at least more observable.

Consistency relates closely to the (in)determinacy of international investment law, and it is on that aspect that I will focus here. Indeed, the determination of the content of international investment law, and notably the mandate of arbitral tribunals in determining that content, is an important aspect of the 'consistency' debate in that the question can be asked, firstly, whether international investment law has a determined content and, secondly, whether arbitral tribunals, in deciding disputes under international investment treaties, have an obligation or should strive to ensure a 'consistent' application of similarly formulated norms to similar situations.

These questions are of particular relevance to international investment law and arbitration – perhaps more so than for general international law. The scattered nature of the norms constituting the investment law 'system', and the *ad hoc* nature of the interpreters of those norms (investment tribunals), is directly linked to the question of whether it is acceptable at all that one norm is interpreted and its content determined differently – and therefore

[41] As Dupuy noted in relation to the multiplication of international courts and tribunals: 'The establishment of new jurisdictions and systems of control improves efficiency by helping in the implementation of obligations and by generating a more refined and precise system of interpretation of norms . . . The growing number of international jurisdictions and international institutions of control should be seen, from a technical point of view at least, as a decisive step in the evolution of the international legal system as it develops a real judicial function.' ('The danger of fragmentation or unification of the international legal system and the International Court of Justice' (1999) 31 NYU J Int'l L & Pol 791–807 at 795–96).

inconsistently – by different arbitral tribunals.[42] This point links directly to the broader question of the (in)determinacy of international law, the interpretation of international legal norms, and the legal reasoning of international courts and tribunals. Hence, before looking at the indeterminacy of international investment law, in particular, and the role of arbitral tribunals in this debate, it is necessary to first discuss the ongoing debate on the indeterminacy of international law in general.

The indeterminacy of international law hinges on the idea that international law norms and rules cannot be identified with certainty.[43] Indeterminacy can be subdivided into several categories depending, amongst others, on whether it is linked to linguistic or structural issues.[44] If we leave aside the structural perspectives on the (radical) (in)determinacy of international (investment) law, the point can be made that international investment law, and international law in general, has a certain indeterminacy in the sense that one can interpret one single norm in different ways.[45] This has famously been posited by Hans Kelsen, who admitted and accepted that the interpretation of a norm could lead to different solutions, as norms do not necessarily have one meaning:

> The law to be applied constitutes only a frame within which several applications are possible, whereby every act is legal that stays within the frame.
>
> If 'interpretation' is understood as cognitive ascertainment of the meaning of the object that is to be interpreted, then the result of a legal interpretation can only be the ascertainment of the frame which the law that is to be interpreted

[42] See for a discussion Jürgen Kurtz, 'Building legitimacy through interpretation in investor-state arbitration: On consistency, coherence and the identification of applicable law', in Zachary Douglas, Joost Pauwelyn, and Jorge Viñuales (eds.), *The Foundations of International Investment Law: Bringing Theory into Practice* (Oxford: Oxford University Press, 2014), pp. 257–95. See also Giovanni Zarra, 'Orderliness and coherence in international investment law and arbitration: An analysis through the lens of state of necessity' (2017) 34 J Int'l Arb 653–78.

[43] Cameron A. Miles, 'Indeterminacy', in Jean d'Aspremont and Sahib Singh (eds.), *Concepts for International Law: Contributions to Disciplinary Thought* (Cheltenham: Edward Elgar, 2019), p. 447.

[44] Ibid., pp. 105–16.

[45] To put this question also into the perspective of the 'coherence' debate, it has been argued that the fact that 'another interpretation or another argument can always be found does not necessarily jeopardise the coherence of law'. See Andrea Bianchi, 'Textual interpretation and (international) law reading: The myth of (in)determinacy and the genealogy of meaning', in Pieter Bekker, Rudolf Dolzer, and Michael Waibel (eds.), *Making Transnational Law Work in the Global Economy: Essays in Honour of Detlev Vagts* (Cambridge: Cambridge University Press, 2010), p. 50.

> represents, and thereby the cognition of several possibilities within the frame. The interpretation of a statute, therefore, need not necessarily lead to a single decision as the only correct one, but possibly to several, which are all of equal value, though only one of them in the action of the law-applying organ (especially the court) becomes positive law.[46]

To consider international law as radically indeterminate, in the sense that any meaning can be attributed to any norm, is contestable. Norms have at least a core or minimal understanding for international lawyers, but this (minimal or core) understanding does not, of course, in and of itself guarantee consistency in the interpretation and application of norms. The situation in international investment law is exacerbated by the fact that the most important set of norms governing foreign investment are international treaties, most often a bilateral investment treaty (BIT). Many, but certainly not all, States have developed 'model' investment treaties, and considering that the majority of the provisions on the protection of foreign investment are present in all modern BITs, there is a certain uniformity both in the content and structure of BITs.[47] However, the precise terms of BITs vary according to the specific needs of the negotiating States. Hence two very similarly phrased BIT provisions may or may not have a similar meaning and operation. The main consequence of the diversity in treaties and signatory States is that the norms included in such treaties are not consistent in their formulation,[48] or that, even if similar formulations may be used, the parties to the treaties containing such formulations are not identical. Different treaty parties may intend an identically worded provision to have different meanings.

This is where the role of arbitral tribunals comes into play, since, in practice, investment tribunals are the main interpreters of international investment norms. This brings us to the role of courts and tribunals in determining the content and the question of whether, once the content has been determined, this precludes any contrary finding on that point.

46 Hans Kelsen, *Pure Theory of Law* (translation from the 2nd German ed. by Max Knight) (Clark, NJ: The Lawbook Exchange, 2009), p. 351. See also Jörg Kammerhofer, *Uncertainty in International Law: A Kelsenian Perspective* (London: Routledge, 2011), p. 105.

47 See for the claim that international law is 'multilateralising' despite the majority of treaties being bilateral, Stephan W. Schill, *The Multilateralization of International Investment Law* (Cambridge: Cambridge University Press, 2010).

48 It is not the purpose here to engage in the various formulations used in treaty practice. For a discussion of the most used standards of treatment, see August Reinisch (ed.), *Standards of Investment Protection* (Oxford: Oxford University Press, 2008).

9.3 CONSISTENCY, DETERMINACY, AND THE ROLE OF ARBITRAL TRIBUNALS

Whether judicial and arbitral decisions are a source of law, and thus binding upon international courts and tribunals, is a relatively easy question to answer, but nevertheless proves to be a controversial one when considering the practice of international courts and tribunals. Judicial decisions are explicitly mentioned in Article 38 of the Statute of the International Court of Justice (ICJ) 'as subsidiary means for the determination of rules of law'. The exception in respect of judicial decisions is the *inter partes* effect of a binding judicial or arbitral decision which in itself implies that the decision is a formal source of legal obligation applicable between the parties to the dispute.[49] Despite the theoretical premise that judicial and arbitral decisions are merely a subsidiary source of the law, previous judicial and arbitral decisions play a very important role in arbitral decision-making.

9.3.1 *The De Facto Importance of Precedent(s) in International Investment Law*

The fundamental principle that there is no binding precedent in international investment arbitration is reflected in Article 53(1) of the ICSID Convention, which provides that the award rendered by the arbitral tribunal is binding upon the parties, thus implicitly excluding any precedential value to awards rendered under the ICSID Convention. The arbitral tribunal in SGS v. *The Philippines* did raise doubts as to whether the wording of Article 53(1) of the ICSID Convention can be read as implying the absence of any precedential value to arbitral awards:

> The ICSID Convention provides only that awards rendered under it are 'binding on the parties' (Article 53(1)), a provision which might be regarded as directed to the *res judicata* effect of awards rather than their impact as precedents in later cases.[50]

At the same time, the tribunal in that case confirmed that 'there is no doctrine of precedent in international law, if by precedent is meant a rule of the binding effect of a single decision'.[51]

[49] Paul Reuter, *Droit International Public* (Paris : Presses Universitaires de France, 1958), p. 85.

[50] *SGS Société Générale de Surveillance S.A. v. Republic of the Philippines* (Decision on Jurisdiction of 29 January 2004) ICSID ARB/02/6 (Swiss Confederation/Republic of the Philippines BIT) at para. 97 (footnotes omitted).

[51] Ibid. (footnotes omitted).

That arbitral decisions are not a source of law, and are not binding upon States generally or on future tribunals, was well explained by the tribunal in *Methanex* v. *United States of America*, in which, confronted with an argument raised by the claimant that allowing *amicus curiae* briefs might set a precedent, the tribunal argued:

> This Tribunal can set no legal precedent, in general or at all. It has no power to determine for other arbitration tribunals how to interpret Article 15(1); and in later arbitrations, there may be other circumstances leading that tribunal to exercise its discretion differently. For each arbitration, the decision must be made by its tribunal in the particular circumstances of that arbitration only.[52]

Despite the relative clarity of the principle that arbitrators are not bound by previously decided cases, the practice of investment tribunals shows that they very often rely upon previous awards of both investment tribunals and other international courts and tribunals, as evidenced by several empirical analyses.[53]

There are several reasons why this is the case. Indeed, that investment tribunals cite prior decisions is, as such, not problematic and forms part of the legal reasoning of arbitral tribunals. Even if judicial and arbitral decisions are not a formal source of law, the fact that several tribunals have developed a consistent line of reasoning can add authority in the broad sense to the tribunal's own reasoning. First of all, arbitral decisions are important material sources of law.[54] They give guidance on how a certain treaty provision or other legal rules have been interpreted and applied by arbitral tribunals, and arbitral decisions thus form an important part of the parties' and their counsel's task to convince the tribunal of their argument.[55] Secondly, situating a decision or reasoning within the existing interpretations by other tribunals in prior decisions can add to the overall perceived legitimacy of the decision. The idea that previous case law functions as a source of inspiration, and of authority, in the broad sense interconnects with the idea that judges and arbitrators should consider authorities invoked by the parties to the dispute. As noted by the tribunal in *Glamis*: 'In terms of its case-specific mandate, a tribunal should

52 *Methanex Corporation* v. *the United States of America* (Decision of the Tribunal on Petitions from Third Persons to Intervene as 'Amici Curiae' of 15 January 2001) UNCITRAL at para. 51.

53 See, e.g., Jefferey P. Commission, 'Precedent in investment treaty arbitration: A citation analysis of a developing jurisprudence' (2007) 24 J Int'l Arb 129–58; and Ole Kristian Fauchal, 'The legal reasoning of ICSID tribunals: An empirical analysis' (2008) 19 EJIL 301–64.

54 Barton Legum, 'The definitions of "precedent" in international arbitration', in Yas Banifatemi (ed.), *Precedent in International Arbitration* (Huntington: Juris, 2008), pp. 8–9.

55 Emmanuel Gaillard, 'Foreword', in Yas Banifatemi (ed.), *Precedent in International Arbitration* (Huntington: Juris, 2008), p. 2.

decide the matter before it on the basis of the authorities submitted to it, and to the degree that the parties to the dispute do not raise what the tribunal regards to be a particularly relevant authority, the tribunal should bring such an authority to the attention of the parties and provide them an opportunity to comment.'[56] Similar considerations have also been made in relation to decisions on challenges of arbitrators.[57]

A different question which crosses the line between treating precedents as a material or subsidiary source and as a formal source is when tribunals rely on precedents without any other argumentation, or when tribunals consider it necessary to follow a developed *jurisprudence constante*.

9.3.2 Precedents and *Jurisprudence Constante*

For certain scholars, the absence of a binding precedent in international investment law would undermine the consistency within the field[58] and the need for legal predictability in international business transactions.[59] Some tribunals thus have argued that tribunals have a duty to contribute to the harmonisation of international investment law. The idea is that the development of a *jurisprudence constante* is necessary 'to foster consistency', especially in those areas of the law which are not yet well developed.[60] This idea has been explicitly adopted by certain arbitral tribunals. In *Saipem* v. *Bangladesh*, for example, the tribunal, although adhering to the principle that 'it is not bound by previous decisions'[61] noted:

> It must pay due consideration to earlier decisions of international tribunals. It believes that, subject to compelling contrary grounds, it has a duty to adopt

[56] *Glamis Gold, Ltd.* v. *United States* (Final Award of 8 June 2009) NAFTA (UNCITRAL) at para. 8 (footnote omitted). See also *El Paso Energy International Company* v. *Argentine Republic* (Decision on Jurisdiction of 27 April 2006) ICSID ARB/03/15 at para. 39. See also *Pan American Energy LLC and BP Argentina Exploration Company v. Argentine Republic* (Decision on Preliminary Objections of 27 July 2006) ICSID ARB/03/13 (US/Argentina BIT) at para. 42; and *BP America Production Co. and Others v. Argentine Republic* (Decision on Preliminary Objections of 27 July 2006) ICSID ARB/04/8 (US/Argentina BIT) at para. 42.

[57] *Vattenfall AB and Others* v. *Federal Republic of Germany* (Recommendation on the Proposal to Disqualify the Tribunal of 4 March 2019) ICSID ARB/12/12 at para. 42.

[58] Ian Laird and Rebecca Askew, 'Finality versus consistency: Does investor-State arbitration need an appellate system?' (2005) 7 J App Prac & Process 285–302.

[59] Frank Spoorenberg and Jorge E. Viñuales, 'Conflicting decisions in international arbitration' (2009) 8 Law Pract Int Court Trib 91–113 at 92.

[60] Gabrielle Kaufmann-Kohler, 'Arbitral precedent: Dream, necessity or excuse?' (2007) 23 Arb Int'l 357–78 at 377.

[61] *Saipem* v. *People's Republic of Bangladesh* (Award of 30 June 2009) ICSID ARB/05/7 at para. 90.

> solutions established in a series of consistent cases. It also believes that, subject to the specifics of a given treaty and of the circumstances of the actual case, it has a duty to seek to contribute to the harmonious development of investment law and thereby to meet the legitimate expectations of the community of States and investors towards certainty of the rule of law.[62]

The 'need' to develop or contribute to the development of a *jurisprudence constante*, or to adhere to a 'settled jurisprudence', is a relatively recent phenomenon, which started a little over a decade ago in conjunction with the rise in the number of investment arbitrations and hence the rise in or risk of inconsistent decisions. One can easily understand why certain consistency in the outcome of arbitral decisions would be beneficial to the development of international investment law. In the long run, references to previous awards can indeed enhance legal certainty within the system of international investment law. This idea has been reflected in certain arbitral decisions, such as the decision of the tribunal in *ADC* v. *Hungary*, which noted that 'cautious reliance on certain principles developed in a number of those cases, as persuasive authority, may advance the body of law, which in turn may serve predictability in the interest of both investors and host States'.[63] However, *jurisprudence constante*, as is visible from the quote of the tribunal in *Saipem* v. *Bangladesh*, often boils down to treating a 'settled jurisprudence' as (the correct interpretation of) the applicable law.[64] The 'duty to adopt solutions established in a series of consistent cases' is nothing but a 'duty' to follow a series of precedents, unless there is a 'compelling reason' not to.

The application of *jurisprudence constante* in investment arbitration, however, is based on a different conception than that operates in most civil law systems. *Jurisprudence constante* is often used or referred to in civil law systems to denote a series of cases on similar issues which form a uniform and

62 Ibid., para. 90. See also *M.C.I. Power Group L.C. and New Turbine Inc.* v. *Republic of Ecuador* (Decision on Annulment of 19 October 2009) ICSID ARB/03/6 at para. 25; and *Víctor Pey Casado and President Allende Foundation* v. *Republic of Chile* (Award of 8 May 2008) ICSID ARB/98/2 at para. 119 for other examples of similar language. See for a similar but perhaps more nuanced understanding of *jurisprudence constante*: *Electrabel S.A.* v. *Republic of Hungary* (Decision on Jurisdiction, Applicable Law and Liability of 30 November 2012) ICSID ARB/07/19 at para. 4.15.

63 *ADC Affiliate Limited and ADC & ADMC Management Limited* v. *Republic of Hungary* (Award of 2 October 2006) ICSID ARB/03/16 at para. 293.

64 Thomas Wälde, 'Confidential awards as precedent in arbitration: Dynamics and implication of award publication', in Yas Banifatemi (ed.), *Precedent in International Arbitration* (Huntington: Juris, 2008), p. 115.

consistent interpretation or application of a certain rule.[65] In that sense, the value of previous case law resides in the de facto recognition of a certain 'persuasive authority'.[66] The Supreme Court of Louisiana, which follows in part the civil law legal system, noted that 'the chief distinction between *stare decisis* and *jurisprudence constante* is that a single case affords sufficient foundation for *stare decisis*, while a series of adjudicated cases, all in accord, form the basis for *jurisprudence constante*'.[67] However, *jurisprudence constante* only functions as a 'persuasive authority'.[68]

In other civil systems, the principle that a series of consistent cases have a persuasive force, rather than any form of obligatory force, has also been confirmed.[69] In several civil law systems, a reference in the decisions of (mostly) supreme courts to certain *jurisprudence constante* is made to showcase that the court or tribunal intends not to deviate from that consistent line of *its own* previous decisions. In Belgium, the *Cour de cassation* will *itself* not deviate from its own consistent case law unless there are 'serious reasons' to do so.[70] References to *jurisprudence constante* are therefore part of the argument of the court or tribunal and usually imply no *obligation or duty* to follow this:[71] 'L'efficacité du précédent n'est pas celle de la loi, son autorité n'est qu'une autorité de fait'.[72] Put differently,

> civil law courts are expected to take past decisions into account when there is a sufficient level of consistency in case law. Generally speaking, when

65 See generally Robert L. Henry, 'Jurisprudence constante and stare decisis contrasted' (1929) 15 ABAJ 11–13; and Vincy Fon and Francesco Parisi, 'Judicial precedents in civil law systems: A dynamic analysis' (2006) 26 Int Rev Law Econ 519–35.

66 Albert Tate Jr, 'Techniques of judicial interpretation in Louisiana' (1962) 22 La L Rev 727–55 at 743.

67 *Willis-Knighton Medical Center* v. *Caddo-Shreveport Sales and Use Tax Commission* 903 So. 2d 1071 (La. 2005) at n. 17. See also Richard D. Moreno, '*Scott* v. *Corkern*: Of precedent, jurisprudence constante, and the relationship between Louisiana commercial laws and Louisiana pledge jurisprudence' (1995) 10 Tul Eur & Civ LF 31–60 at 31.

68 Ibid., p. 62.

69 For a discussion in Italy, see Nicolette Perlo, 'La cour constitutionnelle italienne et ses résistances à la globalisation de la protection des droits fondame ntaux: un 'barrage contre le Pacifiq ue'?' (2013) 95 Rev Fr Dr Const 717–34 at 723.

70 Alfons De Vreese, 'De taak van het Hof van Cassatie' (1967) 4 Tijdschrift voor Privaatrecht 567–97 at 567 ff.

71 See, e.g., Cour de Cassation, France, 'Chambre sociale, du 24 janvier 2001, 98-45.055, Inédit', www.legifrance.gouv.fr/juri/id/JURITEXT000007424333 (accessed 24 June 2022), stating 'qu'il est de jurisprudence constante (Cassation, 12 janvier 1989, Chambre sociale, bulletin 16) que la reconnaissance de la qualification de cadre ne dépend pas seulement de la sticte application de la convertion collective comme l'a fait la cour, mais de l'application des engagements contractuels'.

72 Autexier, '5es Journées', p. 842.

uniform case law develops, courts treat precedents as a source of 'soft' law, taking them into account when reaching a decision.[73]

At the level of international courts and tribunals, this understanding of *jurisprudence constante* bears similarities with the principle – often recalled by the ICJ – that while prior decisions are in no way binding on the Court, 'it will not depart from its settled jurisprudence unless it finds very particular reasons to do so'.[74] *Jurisprudence constante* hence is a *consistency in practice* and does not amount to treating previous cases as a binding authority as such.[75] For example, in the event of *revirement de jurisprudence*[76] – a reversal of an established *jurisprudence constante* – a court or tribunal is in no way obliged to justify this reversal.[77]

Finally, it is important to point out that *jurisprudence constante* operates in centralised or hierarchical legal systems whereby a 'supreme court', which would be at the top of the pyramid of civil courts and tribunals, decides cases, which are then followed by the 'lower' courts. In such cases, moreover, courts are not *obligated* to follow the decisions of higher courts, with the exception perhaps of the court to which the case is remanded after cassation.[78]

9.4 THE 'CONSISTENCY PROBLEM' IN INVESTMENT ARBITRATION

The increased use of international arbitration to settle disputes between foreign investors and States over the past decades has resulted in an amorphous set of arbitral awards. On occasion, this did involve tribunals determining similar cases, or interpreting similar norms, in a divergent manner.[79] There are numerous examples of such inconsistent decisions,[80] and it is not the

[73] Fon and Parisi, 'Judicial precedents', p. 519.

[74] See, e.g., *Application of the Convention on the Prevention and Punishment of the Crime of Genocide (Croatia* v. *Serbia)* (Preliminary Objections, Judgment) [2008] ICJ Rep. 412 at para. 53.

[75] Arthur L. Goodhart, 'Precedent in English and continental law' (1934) 50 LQR 40–65 at 42–43.

[76] See generally Isabelle Rorive, *Le revirement de jurisprudence: Etude de droit anglais et de droit belge* (Brussels: Bruylant, 2003).

[77] René David and John E. C. Brierly, *Major Legal Systems in the World Today* (London: Stevens, 1985), p. 136.

[78] De Vreese, 'Hof van Cassatie', pp. 569 ff.

[79] Emmanuel Gaillard, 'The representations of international arbitration' (2010) 1 JIDS 271–81 at 274.

[80] See for a discussion Teresa Cheng, 'The search for order within chaos in the evolution of ISDS' (2020) 35 ICSID Rev 1–19; Greenwood, 'Unity and diversity', pp. 40–43, 54.

purpose here to discuss these in an exhaustive manner. I will confine myself to a couple of illustrative examples.

9.4.1 *Inconsistent Decisions in International Investment Law*

Before engaging in a discussion of inconsistent decisions, it is important to first categorise the inconsistencies and divergences. The starting point here is the definition of consistency stated above, which implies that similar situations be treated in an identical or analogous way. Disputes arising out of identical or similar situations and which require the application of identical legal norms should then ideally result in the same final outcome. In light of this, one therefore needs to distinguish decisions where the applicable law or norms are similar but not identical from those where the applicable law or norms are identical and the factual circumstances are similar, if not identical.

When the applicable law or norms are similar but not identical, there is, in fact, no genuine conflict between decisions which give different interpretations to these similar norms. As Jurgen Kurtz has noted, 'a critical difference in the textual construction of a given treaty obligation, for instance, would offer a justifiable basis for an alternative approach to that adopted by earlier tribunals ruling on a similar but not identical norm'.[81] This, in fact, would conform to the bilateral nature of the current regulation of international investment law and hence result in a preservation of the 'carefully negotiated variances in BIT provisions between different states'.[82]

In practice, tribunals have 'departed' from previous cases, and hence avoided a 'conflict' in outcome, by emphasising the differences in the law applicable to the dispute, despite the overall similar 'genus' of the norm in question. The tribunal in *Salini*, for example, noted in respect of the 'umbrella clause' that 'Article 2(4) of the BIT between Italy and Jordan is couched in terms that are appreciably different from the provisions applied in the arbitral decisions and awards cited by the Parties'.[83] Arbitral tribunals also have differentiated between the *facts* underlying a previous dispute and the *facts* underlying the dispute under consideration in order to justify a 'departure' from previous cases.[84]

[81] Kurtz, 'Building legitimacy', p. 274.
[82] Ibid.
[83] *Salini Costruttori S.p.A. and Italstrade S.p.A.* v. *Jordan* (Decision on Jurisdiction of 9 November 2004) ICSID ARB/02/13 at para. 126.
[84] See *Sempra Energy International* v. *Argentine Republic* (Award of 28 September 2007) ICSID ARB/02/16 at para. 346.

Other examples are the decisions of the arbitral tribunals in *SGS* v. *The Philippines* and *SGS* v. *Pakistan*,[85] both of which concerned the application of 'umbrella clauses'. The tribunals had to apply different treaties and differently formulated clauses yet of a similar genus, despite Switzerland being a signatory State to both treaties. Both tribunals arrived at different interpretations of the umbrella clauses in both treaties, and the tribunal in *SGS* v. *The Philippines* explained in respect of the value of the decision of the tribunal in *SGS* v. *Pakistan* that

> although different tribunals constituted under the ICSID system should in general seek to act consistently with each other, in the end it must be for each tribunal to exercise its competence in accordance with the applicable law, which will by definition be different for each BIT and each Respondent State.[86]

In such cases, there is technically no conflict or inconsistency since both outcomes can rationally be justified on a distinction in law or, in fact, between the two cases. Non-identical cases need not produce identical outcomes.

The second type of inconsistency, which in fact constitutes a genuine conflicting outcome, occurs when the *same* treaty is at stake. In such cases, the deviation between two arbitral awards is more difficult to explain rationally. Inconsistency can cover both *ratio decidendi* and the final outcome of the decision, but it might not be as problematic in a situation where *ratio decidendi* in two decisions would be inconsistent, while the final outcome would not be affected, as compared to a situation where this affects the final outcome. Certain contradictory decisions have been rendered in relation to the exact same investment treaty, that is, a single provision in a treaty with identical State parties.[87] This situation occurred, for example, in *BG Group* v. *Argentina* and *National Grid* v. *Argentina*, which concerned the interpretation of the 'full protection and security' (FPS) standard in the UK–Argentina BIT. In *BG Group* v. *Argentina*, the tribunal interpreted the FPS standards as applicable only to situations where the physical integrity of the investor or investment is compromised, thereby excluding the extension of the scope of application of the clause to cover also a certain legal stability requirement.[88]

85 *SGS Société Générale de Surveillance S.A.* v. *Islamic Republic of Pakistan* (Decision of 6 August 2003) ICSID Case No. ARB 01/13; *SGS Société Générale de Surveillance S.A.* v. *Republic of the Philippines* (Decision on Jurisdiction of 29 January 2004) ICSID Case No. ARB/02/6.

86 *SGS* v. *The Philippines* (Decision on Jurisdiction), para. 97 (footnotes omitted).

87 For a discussion, see Greenwood, 'Unity and diversity', pp. 40–43, 53–54.

88 *BG Group Plc.* v. *The Republic of Argentina* (Final Award of 24 December 2007) UNCITRAL at paras 324 ff.

In *National Grid* v. *Argentina*, the tribunal interpreted the same provision as not 'inherently limited to protection and security of physical assets'.[89]

The situation can also occur when the applicable norms are not related to the investment treaty but are norms of general international law. Two interesting decisions in this respect are *Ampal* v. *Egypt*[90] and *Unión Fenosa Gas, S.A.* v. *Egypt*,[91] which relate to similar circumstances yet were decided according to different applicable investment treaties. Both disputes required the application of general international law norms relating to the attribution of the conduct of the same Egyptian entities (the Egyptian General Petroleum Corporation (EGPC) and the Egyptian Natural Gas Holding Company (EGAS)).

The tribunal in *Ampal* v. *Egypt* accepted that EGPC is 'an Egyptian State organ', without however explaining whether it considers EGPC to be a *de jure* or *de facto* organ, or providing much information as to the general criteria to be met in order for a State-owned enterprise to be considered an organ of the State.[92] The tribunal in *Unión Fenosa Gas, S.A.* v. *Egypt* decided the case more than a year after the decision in *Ampal* v. *Egypt*[93] and departed from the latter's findings in several respects, including on this precise point. The tribunal concluded, contrary to that in *Ampal* v. *Egypt*: '[The] EGPC is not considered to be an organ of the State under Egyptian law; and that it instead enjoys a separate legal personality under Egyptian law. The fact that it is wholly owned by the State is of no material consequence.'[94]

The tribunal in *Unión Fenosa Gas* further explained its departure from the decision in *Ampal*. It argued that the reasons cited by the tribunal in *Ampal* v. *Egypt* 'do … not explain why these factors show that EGPC is part of the structure of the State so as to deny its autonomous existence'.[95] The interpretations of Article 4 of the ILC[96] in both cases clearly are in conflict, and the tribunal in *Unión Fenosa Gas* has acknowledged as much.

89 *National Grid plc* v. *The Argentine Republic* (Award of 3 November 2008) UNCITRAL at paras 187 ff.

90 *Ampal* v. *Egypt* (Decision on Liability and Heads of Loss of 21 February 2017) ICSID ARB/12/11.

91 *Unión Fenosa Gas, S.A.* v. *Arab Republic of Egypt* (Award of 31 August 2018) ICSID ARB/14/4.

92 *Ampal* v. *Egypt* (Decision on Liability), para. 138.

93 *Unión Fenosa Gas* (Award), paras 9.115–16.

94 Ibid., para. 9.97.

95 Ibid., para. 9.109.

96 International Law Commission, 'Draft Articles on the Responsibility of States for Internationally Wrongful Acts', in *Yearbook of the International Law Commission* (2001), vol. 2 (part 2).

Why do conflicting awards exist? In relation to the first category of 'conflicts' in which the applicable law or norms are similar but not identical, States might not necessarily have intended for international investment law to be interpreted in a uniform way. That is, there is not and cannot be a presumption that the State parties to one treaty intended a provision which is similar or even identical to a treaty concluded with two different States to have precisely the same meaning as the provision in the latter treaty. As Greenwood explains:

> Each treaty is an agreement in its own right and . . . the words used have to be interpreted in the light of the context, object and purpose and, where appropriate, drafting history of that treaty. To approach each BIT in that light is to respect a diversity that is the product of the specific wills of the parties to each BIT; it is quite wrong to treat the language of BITs simply as 'boilerplate' texts which must necessarily be given a single, unified meaning.[97]

Absent a uniform set of norms, consistency is difficult to achieve. The view from the WTO appellate body that previous reports of either panels or the appellate body itself 'should be taken into account where they are relevant to any dispute'[98] only works in a regime or system whereby the substantive law to the applied is the same.[99]

On the second type of conflicting or inconsistent decisions, I agree with Kurtz that the case for consistency should be 'carefully confined to [that] particular and defined subset of arbitral disputes'.[100] It is also on this specific type of conflict that the UNICTRAL Working Group III has decided to focus its attention.[101] However, investment treaty arbitration is a decentralised *ad hoc* legal system of dispute settlement, which means that even in relation to identical facts and/or norms, consistency cannot be guaranteed, even if this is considered desirable or rational. The very fact that States have chosen to establish a horizontal system of *ad hoc* arbitration with no appellate mechanism by necessary implication results in a system whereby each arbitral tribunal assesses the case without any obligation to consider or apply previous case law. As the tribunal in *SGS* v. *The Philippines* noted, 'there is no hierarchy of

97 Greenwood, 'Unity and diversity', pp. 40–43, 53.
98 WTO, 'US – Shrimp (Article 21.5 – Malaysia). Report of the appellate body' (22 October 2001) WT/DS58/AB/RW at paras 107–9.
99 See also Kurtz, 'Building legitimacy', pp. 270–71.
100 Ibid., p. 271.
101 UNCITRAL, 'Possible reform of investor-State dispute settlement (ISDS): Consistency and related matters. Note by the Secretariat' (28 August 2018) UN Doc. A/CN.9/WG.III/WP.150, para. 7.

international tribunals, and even if there were, there is no good reason for allowing the first tribunal in time to resolve issues for all later tribunals'.[102] International arbitration is substantially different from permanent international courts and tribunals, mainly because an international arbitral tribunal is created only to settle one specific dispute between two parties and so its composition differs from one case to another. I do not intend here to say that consistency is guaranteed, or that there is a requirement of consistency in proceedings before permanent international courts and tribunals. As I have explained elsewhere, there are similar considerations underlying the use of prior decisions and *jurisprudence constante* before the ICJ, for example.[103] However, compared to an *ad hoc* system of adjudication, at least the *expectation* of consistency is fundamentally different in the case of international courts and tribunals because of their permanent and unitary nature. Although one could perhaps ideally expect arbitral tribunals to decide similar issues in the same way if the applicable law is identical, the fact that it is an *ad hoc* tribunal, instead of a standing body, weakens the expectation of 'consistency' and also the purported existence of a 'duty' to follow a consistent line of cases. There is, so to speak, no interconnection between the various investment tribunals which operate independently from each other, besides the similarity in the object of the dispute and the various sets of procedural rules.

9.4.2 *Are Inconsistent Decisions a Problem?*

In general, inconsistency in decisions can only be perceived as a problem if one views consistency as a prerequisite for, or a fundamental characteristic of, a legal system to be considered as such; consistency then is a value in and of itself which needs to be pursued. As shown in Section 9.1, it can readily be admitted that international investment law is a subsystem, subfield, or subregime within international law. International investment law, moreover, has at least a minimal form of coherence. The question here, however, is whether conflicting or inconsistent decisions within international investment law are problematic – that is, do they impact the coherence of the international investment law, and if not, how can they be rationalised.

First of all, inconsistent decisions in and of themselves do not affect the systemic nature or coherence of a field or regime, and hence conflicting or

[102] *SGS* v. *The Philippines* (Decision on Jurisdiction), para. 97 (footnotes omitted).

[103] Eric De Brabandere, 'The use of precedent and external case law by the International Court of Justice and the International Tribunal for the Law of the Sea' (2016) 15 Law Pract Int Court Trib 24–55.

inconsistent decisions are not necessarily a problem per se.[104] More important than the inconsistencies in decisions themselves, Schill, for example, views the engagement of arbitral tribunals with precedents and inconsistent prior decisions as depicting the perspective of a multilateral or multilateralised investment law framework.[105] On the specific question of consistency, Schill notes that the choice of 'ordering paradigm' influences the roles of arbitral tribunals – bilateralism would stress the pure dispute settlement function of arbitral tribunals; multilateralism and multilateralisation, in turn, view international investment tribunals as serving a broader goal, that is, the 'preservation and further development of the entire system of investment protection'.[106] Multilateralism and multilateralisation, as approaches to the field, also view inconsistent decisions as problematic as they could compromise the predictability and stability of the 'treaty-overarching structure'.[107] Bilateralism as an approach would partly be based on the reality of inconsistent decisions and the fragmented or bilateral nature of international investment law.[108] The extensive reliance on precedent, in turn, according to Schill, would militate for the existence of the middle road between bilateralism and multilateralism in that it de facto results in a 'uniform and treaty-overarching' system of international investment law.[109]

Even under the bilateral approach discussed by Schill, which would result in 'an unconnected patchwork of episodes of treaty-making and dispute settlement without inter-linkages in an overarching structure',[110] one cannot necessarily consider that the mere existence of inconsistent decisions defeats the coherence of the field. Some argue that the practice of engagement with other decisions *in itself* shows a connection between the various tribunals; other scholars have pointed to coherence achieved by the reasoning employed by arbitral tribunals, more than to the specific outcome.[111] This in turn matches the perspective of Greenwood discussed above. At the same time, some authors have considered that consistency is in fact fundamentally desirable and necessary,[112] but simultaneously concede that inconsistency in

[104] Cf. Pauwelyn, 'At the edge of chaos?', p. 384.
[105] Schill, 'Ordering paradigms', pp. 127–28.
[106] Ibid., p. 113.
[107] Ibid.
[108] Ibid., p. 114.
[109] Ibid., p. 125.
[110] Ibid., p. 109
[111] Kurtz, 'Building legitimacy', p. 274.
[112] Katharina Diel-Gligor, *Towards Consistency in International Investment Jurisprudence* (Leiden: Brill Nijhoff, 2017), p. 120.

decisions is a 'constructive element of a self-regulating mechanism', and that the engagement of arbitral tribunals with precedents, by providing substantiated arguments on why prior cases are followed or not, ensures a sufficient level of coherence.[113]

In any event, as Greenwood also noted, inconsistency in decisions is not a phenomenon restricted to investment arbitration and has existed in domestic legal systems which are not composed of bilateral treaty norms in essence. Greenwood, for instance, points to the fact that the French *Conseil d'état* and the French *Cour de Cassation* held different views on the issue of the supremacy of European Community law over French law.[114] Other examples are the historical opposing views of the Belgian Constitutional Court and the Belgian *Cour de Cassation* on several issues[115] and the divergent decisions of the Belgian *Cour de Cassation* and the Belgian *Conseil d'état* on the conditions for the direct application of international law in the domestic legal order.[116] On the international level, there are also several decisions by different international courts and tribunals which cannot be reconciled with each other.[117] Inconsistencies within a single legal system, therefore, are not exceptional, have always existed, and have not caused legal systems to 'collapse as a result'.[118]

All that this explains is that consistency is not an absolute or indispensable characteristic of legal systems. Inconsistency is not necessarily a fundamental problem in investment law and arbitration. Inconsistent decisions are perfectly plausible within a coherent legal system, notably because they can in and of themselves be 'in coherence' with general international law or international investment law norms.[119]

While the existence of inconsistencies does not run counter to the idea that a certain field of law can be a system of itself, or part of a broader legal system, the avoidance (or absence) of inconsistent decisions undoubtedly has certain value, because it does increase legal certainty. It has indeed been noted on occasion that consistent decisions are a fundamental aspect of the rule of law,

113 Ibid., p. 155.
114 Greenwood, 'Unity and diversity', pp. 40–43, 54.
115 See generally Floris Parrein, 'It is not lonely enough at the top: De tegenstellingen tussen het Hof van Cassatie en het Arbitragehof' (2005–6) 42 Jura Falconis 285–330.
116 Eric De Brabandere and Anne Lagerwall, 'Le conflit entre le droit belge et le droit international: un conflit dont les multiples formes sont abordées par les juges sous différents angles' (2012) 2 Rev Belge Droit Int'l 399–423.
117 See, amongst others, Philippa Webb, *International Judicial Integration and Fragmentation* (Oxford: Oxford University Press, 2013); Rosalyn Higgins, 'The ICJ, the ECJ, and the integrity of international law' (2003) 52 ICLQ 1–20.
118 Greenwood, 'Unity and diversity', pp. 40–43, 54.
119 See also Kurtz, 'Building legitimacy', pp. 270 ff.

at least when one confines the inconsistencies to the understanding of situations where the rules are identical and the facts similar or identical. Kurtz has argued that even 'the thinnest conception of rule of law in any legal system' would militate in favour of like cases to be treated alike.[120]

In the context of the UNCITRAL Working Group III discussions on the reform of investment arbitration, the need for certainty and predictability also has been highlighted.[121] This need has, moreover, been considered important not only in relation to States in order 'to understand whether their actions, such as possible future legislative or regulatory activities, might breach their obligations' but also in relation to foreign investors to allow them 'to assess whether certain treatment was in accordance with treaty obligations'.[122]

But the ideal of legal certainty is not the equivalent of an overarching value which needs to be pursued, nor does this transform a practice into an overarching objective for legal systems. The advantage that legal certainty is enhanced by consistent decisions can easily be conceded, but it is different from considering that all decisions *should* be consistent, or, in the negative, that inconsistent decisions are a fundamental problem. Even in the context of the Working Group III discussions, it was agreed that

> seeking to achieve consistency should not be to the detriment of the correctness of decisions, and that predictability and correctness should be the objective rather than uniformity. Indeed, the Working Group considered that consistency and coherence were not objectives in themselves and that caution should be taken in trying to achieve uniform interpretation of provisions across the wide range of investment treaties, considering that the underlying investment treaty regime itself was not uniform.[123]

Moreover, putting consistency as an overarching ambition does, in fact, tell us how consistency should be achieved.

9.5 REFORMING OF INVESTMENT TREATY ARBITRATION AND THE SPECTRE OF INCONSISTENCY

The UNCITRAL has in 2017 entrusted its Working Group III to work on the 'possible reform of investor–State dispute settlement (ISDS)'.[124] At that time,

[120] Ibid., p. 271.
[121] See in general UNCITRAL, 'Possible reform of ISDS'.
[122] Ibid., para. 28.
[123] Ibid., para. 8.
[124] UNCITRAL, 'Report of the United Nations Commission on International Trade Law', UN GAOR, 72nd Session Supp. No. 17 (2017) UN Doc. A/72/17, paras 263, 264.

the precise topics for 'reform' were rather broadly formulated and concerned, amongst others, 'inconsistency', 'lengthy duration and extensive cost', 'lack of transparency', and 'lack of an early dismissal mechanism'.[125] Over time, the list of 'concerns' and areas of 'possible reform' have gradually expanded and been further detailed. In October 2019 the list of current and potential topics[126] included, amongst others, 'diversity among arbitrators', 'third-party funding', 'exhaustion of local remedies', 'regulatory chill', and 'reflective loss'. The topics identified for possible 'reform' thus encompass a wide range of procedural or quasi-procedural issues which occur in investor–State arbitration and have over time also shifted to substantive investment law questions.

Specifically in relation to consistency and coherence, the 2017 report of UNCITRAL Working Group III notes 'the importance of ensuring a coherent and consistent ISDS regime', and that 'inconsistency and lack of coherence, on the other hand, could negatively affect the reliability, effectiveness and predictability of the ISDS regime and, in the longer term, its credibility and legitimacy'.[127] The same report mentions that 'consistency [is] a crucial element of the rule of law and would contribute to the development of investment law'; although it was also noted that 'consistency and coherence were not objectives in themselves and extreme caution should be taken in trying to achieve uniform interpretation of provisions across the wide range of investment treaties'.[128]

In parallel and conjunction, the EU is urging to replace investor–State arbitration with an 'international investment court'. In May 2015, in light of the public consultation organised on the Transatlantic Trade and Investment Partnership (TTIP), the EC presented a concept paper titled 'Investment in TTIP and beyond – The path for reform: Enhancing the right to regulate and moving from current *ad hoc* arbitration towards an investment court'. The paper set out a two-step approach to reforming the current *ad hoc* ISDS. The first step was the inclusion of an institutionalised court system (i.e. ICS) for resolving investment disputes to apply in each future EU-level trade and

[125] UNCTRAL, 'Working Group III (Investor-State Dispute Settlement Reform). Possible reform of investor-State dispute settlement (ISDS). Note by the Secretariat' (18 September 2017) UN Doc. A/CN.9/WG.III/WP.142, para. 20.

[126] UNCITRAL, 'Working Group III (Investor-State Dispute Settlement Reform). Possible reform of investor-State dispute settlement (ISDS). Note by the Secretariat' (30 July 2019) UN Doc. A/CN.9/WG.III/WP.166, para. 5 et seq. See also UNCITRAL, 'Presentation of reform options', https://uncitral.un.org/en/reformoptions (accessed 24 June 2022).

[127] UNCITRAL, 'Report of Working Group III (Investor-State Dispute Settlement Reform) on the work of its thirty-fourth session' (26 February 2018) UN Doc. A/CN.9/930/Add.1/Rev.1, para. 11.

[128] Ibid.

investment agreement. The EU also has inserted bilateral ICS in recently negotiated international investment agreements, including those with Canada, Mexico, Singapore, and Vietnam; the agreements also include provisions anticipating the transition from the bilateral ICS to a permanent MIC.[129]

The second step is that the EU should in parallel work towards the establishment of an international investment court and appellate mechanism with tenured adjudicators. This court would aim to replace all the bilateral ICS included in the EU's trade and investment agreements. It would also provide the EU, EU member States, and partner countries with the possibility to replace the ISDS provisions featuring in their existing investment agreements with access to the MIC.[130]

An important aspect of the ICS was the creation of an appellate mechanism to 'review awards as regards errors of law and manifest errors in the assessment of facts (this would include an incorrect factual treatment of domestic law as interpreted by domestic courts), ensure consistency in the interpretation of TTIP and increase legitimacy both on substance and through institutional design by strengthening independence, impartiality and predictability'.[131] The ICS proposed by the EC has as objective, amongst others, to provide a 'public justice' dispute settlement mechanism, including an appellate tribunal 'where consistency of judicial decisions is ensured'.[132]. The need for a reform, in light of the lack of consistency, amongst others, was further mentioned during the public consultation regarding the Comprehensive Economic and Trade Agreement (CETA) in 2017. The EC outlined the problems affecting the ISDS system: 'Other concerns relate to the current ISDS system's deficiency in predictability and interpretative consistency of case-law, lack of possibility of review of decisions, lack of transparency and costs of the proceedings.'[133]

These 'concerns' are considered by the EC to be highly problematic. The EC considers that there is no coordination between the various tribunals, and

[129] See European Commission, 'Trade: European Court of Justice confirms compatibility of investment court system with EU treaties', press release, 30 April 2019, https://ec.europa.eu/commission/presscorner/detail/en/IP_19_2334 (accessed 10 June 2021).

[130] European Commission, 'Investment in TTIP and beyond – The path for reform: Enhancing the right to regulate and moving from current *ad hoc* arbitration towards an investment court', May 2015, http://trade.ec.europa.eu/doclib/docs/2015/may/tradoc_153408.PDF (accessed 10 June 2021).

[131] Ibid., p. 9.

[132] Art 2(d)(xv) of European Parliament, 'Resolution on the negotiations for the TTIP'.

[133] European Commission, 'Multilateral reform'.

> there is no compelling incentive or requirement for the different tribunals to, when interpreting standards in a given treaty, be informed by past interpretations of those standards in the same or other agreements where it may be very similarly if not identically worded. ISDS arbitrators have therefore no mandate or incentive (for example through being reversed by an appeal mechanism) to build a coherent body of investment case law.[134]

Aside from the questionable point that adjudicators should have a mandate to develop a coherent body of law,[135] there is a conviction that the only way to achieve consistency, and hence avoid conflicting outcomes, is through an overhaul of the dispute settlement system and a replacement of arbitration by a standing international court coupled to an appellate mechanism.[136] Both the tribunal of first instance and the appeals tribunal would be staffed by tenured adjudicators. The purpose of this new framework would be to bring efficiency through increased consistency and predictability of case law.

The creation of a multilateral (and universal) investment court is the subject of a process that started in late 2017 under the auspices of UNCITRAL Working Group III. As part of its reform options, the Working Group has outlined the option of creating a standing first instance and appeal investment court, with full-time judges to address, amongst others, the lack of consistency and predictability.[137]

An interesting point, however, in the discussion regarding the reformation of ISDS is that the EC readily acknowledges that consistency and predictability cannot and will not be remedied by the inclusion of the ICS in bilateral treaties:

> The ICS addresses the issue of a lack of consistency and predictability of case-law in relation to substantive standards contained in a given agreement, given that standards will be interpreted by a permanent body even if in different disputes. However, the same or very similar substantive rules across agreements will continue to be interpreted by different bodies without any incentive to be informed by previous decisions. In these cases, the risk of disparate interpretation of the same or very similar substantive rules remains.[138]

[134] Ibid., p. 12.

[135] See on this Armin von Bogdandy and Ingo Venzke, *In Whose Name? A Public Law Theory of International Adjudication* (Oxford: Oxford University Press, 2014).

[136] 'Option 5', ibid., pp. 29 ff.

[137] UNCTRAL, 'Working Group III (Investor-State Dispute Settlement Reform). Possible reform of investor-State dispute settlement (ISDS). Appellate and multilateral court mechanisms. Note by the Secretariat' (29 November 2019) UN Doc. A/CN.9/WG.III/WP.185.

[138] European Commission, 'Multilateral reform', p. 16.

> The inherently bilateral nature of ICS implies that predictability and consistency of case-law, where applicable, will be limited, i.e., within the limits of each ICS.[139]

Hence what was identified as a core problem of the current system will, in fact, not be remedied at this stage. And this is not surprising considering the discussion in the previous sections: the differences in interpretation are an inevitable by-product of the bilateral nature of investment treaties and treaty language and the bilateral nature of the dispute settlement system mandated to interpret these provisions. The EC acknowledges the difference in treaty language and the need to take account of this, but cautions that there is indeed a core minimum understanding of norms irrespective of different formulations and/or differences in treaty parties:

> Although the provisions on these standards are not worded in exactly the same way across agreements (there are differences, for example, to the standard US approach), the basic function of the standards is the same across agreements. Indeed, the fact that a majority of these treaties are bilateral and their provisions must be read in light of each agreement's context and negotiating parties' intention, does not mean that there is no margin for a significant degree of consistency to be achieved across agreements. An interpretation of a key standard, for example national treatment, can form the core of an interpretation of that standard as included in multiple agreements which is then adjusted, as appropriate, to take account of variations in drafting or context of other agreements which use similar or identical terms.[140]

This assessment, while framed as a criticism of the lack of consistency in decision-making by arbitral tribunals, is not so much at variance with what I have stated in Sections 9.1 and 9.2. As I have noted, norms have a core or minimal understanding for international lawyers, but this (minimal or core) understanding does not, of course, in and of itself guarantee consistency in the interpretation and application of norms when there are indeed variances in the use of terminology across different treaties.

In general, the creation of a 'court-like' system, including an appellate mechanism, will enhance a consistent interpretation of the investment treaty for which the mechanism was set up. In doing so, the mechanism is likely to introduce and subsequently rely on system-internal precedents, in respect of both the standards contained in the applicable treaty and the applicable

[139] Ibid., p. 17.
[140] Ibid.

(secondary) norms of general international law. However, the ICS is unlikely to generate a form of consistency throughout the various investment treaties and in respect of the provisions they contain, to which the EU is a party. This is mainly so because the proposed ICS is, at this stage, conceived as a treaty-specific body.

This leaves us to briefly touch upon the question of whether a multilateral court will manage to achieve what the ICS, as the EC has conceded, will or might not achieve. Beyond doubt, consistency and predictability are easier to achieve within one single adjudicatory system. Consistency, moreover, may be in conformity with the expectations that actors before the Court have, namely that like cases will be treated alike.[141] A consistent body of case law may thus serve the need for predictability for States wishing to bring cases before a multilateral court or tribunal. One needs to be mindful, however, of the fact that even the ICJ has in the past deviated from its own case law.[142] The plausibility of the rights asserted by a party requesting provisions measures, for instance, was added by the court only recently and which first explicitly appeared in the *Belgium* v. *Senegal* case in 2009.[143]

The new mechanism is likely to introduce and subsequently rely on system-internal precedents. Especially in the early stages of a new court or tribunal, judges are required to 'lay the foundations', which implies, amongst others, settling the rules of procedure.[144] While there will be no prior cases to rely upon in the early stages of the investment court, it is likely that support will be found in the decisions of other courts and tribunals and international arbitral awards, especially since the procedural rules might not be dissimilar. Over time, courts and tribunals tend to replace the use of external cases with their own prior decisions, as we have seen in respect of the International Tribunal for the Law of the Sea, which has extensively relied on cases decided by the ICJ on questions of procedure and substance in the first years of its functioning, then gradually replacing these references with those to its own case law.[145]

[141] Armin von Bogdandy and Ingo Venzke, 'The spell of precedents: Lawmaking by international courts and tribunals', in Cesare Romano, Karen Alter, and Yuval Shany (eds.), *The Oxford Handbook of International Adjudication* (Oxford: Oxford University Press, 2014), p. 509.

[142] See De Brabandere, 'Use of precedent', pp. 24–55.

[143] *Questions Relating to the Obligation to Prosecute or Extradite (Belgium* v. *Senegal)* (Order on Provisional Measures) [2009] ICJ Rep 139 at p. 151, paras 57–60.

[144] Daniel Terris, Cesare P. Romano, and Leigh Swigart, *The International Judge: An Introduction to the Men and Women Who Decide the World's Cases* (Oxford: Oxford University Press, 2007), p. 109.

[145] See De Brabandere, 'Use of precedent', pp. 24–55.

But here also one cannot so easily equate the ICJ with a possible future MIC, as the ICJ, in contrast to the MIC, is not mandated to settle (investment) disputes based on bilateral (investment) treaties which have no similar wording. In other words, unless the single adjudicator is combined with a single treaty, it cannot necessarily be expected that a standing body will interpret two different provisions – even with an identical core understanding – in the same manner, let alone maintain this over time, as the composition of the court or tribunal changes. An individual judge's view on a particular case matters: 'International courts are collegial bodies. Decisions are taken by the majority. But, at the same time, courts are composed of remarkable individuals with well-developed ideas and awareness of their own value, and, very often, price.'[146]

9.6 CONCLUSION: 'IF DRAWING RULES TIGHTLY CANNOT ALONE MAKE THE LAW SECURE, IT WILL OFTEN BE A NECESSARY FIRST STEP IN MAKING IT LESS INSECURE'[147]

As discussed in Section 9.1, coherence implies some form of internal 'logic' of a legal system. This is a broad concept that may encapsulate certain aspects of consistency, but is clearly altogether different and more systemic in nature. Whether or not one views a legal system as coherent, or how one views the need for a legal system to be coherent, depends very much on the theoretical perspectives of the nature of a legal system or regime and is a question of degrees rather than one of affirmation or negation. Applying it to a specific context of investment law and arbitration, I have argued that a 'middle road' perspective might be to consider that international investment law forms part of general international law, which is a coherent legal system from the perspective of the sources or secondary norms of international law.

Coherence, I have argued, differs from consistency, which implies that similar situations are treated in an identical or analogous way. Consistency, indeed, may imply that the application of norms should be non-conflicting (i.e. similar situations should be dealt with in similar ways in terms of the application of law). I have argued that the current investment law, with its lack of uniformity in terms of substantive law, and the *ad hoc* method of dispute settlement cannot and should not be expected to achieve absolute consistency in outcome. Even notions such as *jurisprudence constante* are of limited avail

146 Terris et al., *International Judge*, p. 123.

147 John Merrills, *Anatomy of International Law*, 2nd ed. (London: Sweet & Maxwell, 1981), p. 101.

in that respect. *Jurisprudence constante* simply indicates that a series of cases have decided a certain point of law in a particular manner,[148] and that because of the existence of this sequence of cases, they constitute 'persuasive authority'. It does not imply that a judge or arbitrator has a specific obligation to decide the case in the same sense as the 'established' *jurisprudence constante*.

I have also argued that consistency in arbitral decisions is not necessarily an overarching objective which needs to be pursued in and of itself in the international legal system, and that inconsistency, especially in relation to one single investment treaty, is not necessarily a fundamental problem. Inconsistent decisions are perfectly plausible within a coherent legal system, notably because they can in and of themselves be 'in coherence' with the general international law or international investment law norms. Expecting absolute consistency in arbitral awards, moreover, runs counter to the very nature of international (investment) law which, as noted, has certain indeterminacy in the sense that one can interpret one single norm in different ways, aside from the core understanding of the norm.

But it is precisely this point, linked to the determination of the content of international investment law, which has been at the forefront of recent debates, criticism, and ensuing (and ongoing) attempts at reforming investment law and arbitration. The main argument I have developed in this respect is that, in general, the creation of a 'court-like' system, including an appellate mechanism in general, will *enhance* but probably not guarantee a consistent interpretation of the investment treaty for which the mechanism was set up. In doing so, the mechanism is likely to introduce and subsequently rely on system-internal precedents. However, as it now stands, the ICS is unlikely to generate a form of consistency throughout the various investment treaties to which the EU is a party. This is mainly so because the proposed ICS is conceived as a treaty-specific body.

More fundamentally, I have conceded that consistency in the interpretation of identical disputes is an ideal one can readily expect, notably since it ensures predictability and legal certainty. The question then is how this can be achieved. Instead of focusing only on the role of arbitral tribunals, other options can also be explored. Indeed, if the end goal is consistency, as UNCITRAL's Working Group III has mentioned, States can redefine and reformulate the specific contents of investment treaties. States have on several occasions reacted to investment arbitration jurisprudence by altering treaty

148 Catherine Kessedjian, 'To give or not to give precedential value to investment arbitration awards', in Catherine A. Rogers and Roger P. Alford (eds.), *The Future of Investment Arbitration* (Oxford: Oxford University Press, 2009), p. 49.

provisions in existing or post-decision investment treaties or in procedural rules. Alongside the attempts to reform international investment law, the past years have seen a gradual recalibration of investment treaties by the States themselves, targeting most notably the substantive standards contained in these treaties, but also procedural issues.[149]

Certainty can be achieved indeed by treaty (re)drafting. However, treaty (re) drafting is unlikely to eradicate inconsistencies in general. While the norms of international investment law carry certain indeterminacy, a careful drafting of these norms – in particular through the addition of language that confirms the inclusion or exclusion of a possible meaning that can be given to that norm – is likely to curtail the interpretation of that norm in accordance with the intention of the parties to the treaty. A similar objective can be achieved by States by issuing authoritative interpretations of the text. While this has on occasion been done by States to show their discontent with a certain interpretation given by arbitral tribunals,[150] States have also explicitly included this possibility in their investment treaties.[151] In this way, the predominance given to one single interpretation, which would elevate the decision above the text, and the role of arbitral tribunals above the States, can be avoided. This has, in fact, been skilfully argued by Professor Merrills in his 1981 book *Anatomy of International Law*:

> Of course, effectiveness in law is not guaranteed by drafting, however skillful.[152] . . . But if drawing rules tightly cannot alone make the law secure, it will often be a necessary first step in making it less insecure.[153]

[149] See Eric De Brabandere, '(Re)calibration, standard-setting and the shaping of investment law and arbitration' (2018) 59 BCLRev 2607–34.

[150] See Eleni Methymaki and Antonios Tzanakopoulos, 'Masters of puppets? Reassertion of control through joint investment treaty interpretation', in Andreas Kulick (ed.), *Reassertion of Control over the Investment Treaty Regime* (Cambridge: Cambridge University Press, 2016), pp. 155–81.

[151] See, e.g., Art 24(4) of the 2019 Dutch Model BIT: UNCTAD, 'Netherlands Model Investment Agreement', 22 March 2019, https://investmentpolicy.unctad.org/international-investment-agreements/treaty-files/5832/download (accessed 28 December 2021).

[152] Merrills, *Anatomy of International Law*, p. 91.

[153] Ibid., p. 101.

10

The WTO DSU 2.0

How Can We Go Back to the Future?

ARIS GEORGOPOULOS AND PETROS C. MAVROIDIS

10.1 INTRODUCTION

The stalemate in multilateral trade negotiations under the auspices of the World Trade Organization (WTO) in combination with the deadlock of the WTO dispute settlement system creates a potent mix. As things stand, it seems quite unlikely that the WTO will go back to 'business as usual' anytime soon, notwithstanding the more co-operative attitude of the Biden administration. With this as a given, solving the dispute settlement deadlock remains a top priority.

Although there seems to be a commitment among WTO parties to work collectively towards resolving the stalemate, it is not yet clear *how* their resolution will be translated into meaningful action. Yet, the existence of such commitment, even without a specified roadmap, is not necessarily a curse and could even prove to be a blessing.

In this chapter, we explain how this opportunity could be used to design a viable dispute resolution regime at the WTO. In particular, we put forward concrete proposals for the establishment of a new WTO court and explain why we believe such a course of action has realistic chances of breaking the current impasse.

In order to elucidate the rationale behind our proposal of a new court, we first present and assess the reasons which allegedly led to the current impasse in Section 10.2. We do this through the lenses of two theoretical models, namely the veto players theory, and Hirschman's 'exit, voice, and loyalty' model which, if employed jointly, can capture the essence and the hidden dynamics of the current impasse. These theoretical perspectives also enable us to appreciate the ability to elicit change to overcome the current impasse by identifying, on the one hand, the existing systemic disincentives that nurture the intransigence of key actors, and by highlighting, on the other hand, the possible incentives which in turn could nudge the relevant actors to alter their current position. In the same section, we contextualise the current impasse, which, in our view, reflects wider geopolitical concerns.

We then explain in Section 10.3 why the identity of WTO judges matters, and we go on to elucidate in Section 10.4 the importance (added value) of having a functioning dispute settlement system at times when the wider operation of the WTO (substantive negotiations) has become sluggish and needs to be revived by drawing from the experience of another international ecosystem that promotes trade and integration, albeit via a markedly different degree of intensity, namely the EU. In Section 10.5, we present our own ideal WTO court, expanding on the work already initiated by Hoekman and Mavroidis. In Section 10.6, we explain the reasons why, in our opinion, our proposal can address the current impasse and why it is viable. Section 10.7 recaps our key points.

10.2 SETTING THE SCENE OF ANALYSIS: THE WAY WE WERE(?)

Between 1989 and the end of 2020, the WTO was an anomaly in international relations: its DSU (Dispute Settlement Understanding), the agreement administering dispute adjudication, continued the practice already established at the WTO Montreal Ministerial Conference (1989) to always submit disputes to an impartial judge, irrespective of the willingness of the respondent to do so. This practice came to be known as 'negative consensus', an awkward term for sure, and was, as per Hudec's[1] perceptive account, the consequence of General Agreement on Tariffs and Trade's (GATT) successful handling of trade disputes over the years.

This is the case no more.[2] The WTO appellate body (the second instance court in the DSU architecture) has in effect ceased to exist, and its demise has cast doubt on the wisdom to 'empanel' disputes in the first place, since 'appeals to the void' are (have been) possible. These are appeals launched by parties *despite the absence* of the appellate body, which could bring the final decision regarding a dispute into a never-ending judicial/procedural limbo, since, pursuant to Article 16.4 of the DSU, 'the report by the panel would not be considered for adoption by the dispute settlement body (DSB)

1 Robert E. Hudec, *Enforcing International Trade Law: The Evolution of the Modern GATT Legal System* (Oxford: Butterworth, 1993).

2 In 2018 the US blocked the appointment of new appellate body members with the immediate consequence of rendering the latter de facto non-functional due to the applicable quorum rules. The US position on this score has so far remained the same, even under the Biden administration.

until after completion of the appeal' (emphasis added). Without a functioning appellate body, the appeal *cannot be completed*, and therefore the panel report cannot be adopted by the DSB. Yet, enforcement is a quintessential element of the WTO regime: why sign the agreement in the first place if enforcement is not on the cards?

Under the current circumstances, some WTO members have had recourse to ingenious measures aiming to avoid the negative effects of non-enforcement. However, the MPIA (Multi-party Interim Agreement),[3] an attempt to provide an interim appeals board spearheaded by the European Union and China, failed in persuading the WTO membership, whereas *ad hoc* agreements to forego appeals are scarce. The consequence has been a dramatic drop in the volume of adjudicated disputes. Hoekman, Mavroidis, and Saluste[4] report that the WTO adjudicated approximately twenty-four disputes per year between 1995 and 2019, if by 'disputes' we understand a submission requesting consultations. The numbers for 2020, 2021, and 2022, the three years without the appellate body, are five, nine, and seven, respectively. This is a far cry from an average of over twenty submitted disputes per year during the first twenty years of the WTO.[5]

There is no point in providing a detailed historical account of how we ended up where we are. It is pertinent, though, to highlight the significance of overcoming the stalemate of the DSU as a condition for enabling the WTO to

3 It is interesting to note the key characteristics of the MPIA by reference to the wider system. In this regard it is observed that the MPIA exhibits some similarities as well as some differences to the *plurilateral* agreements administered by the WTO. On the one hand, it is similar because it allows those willing WTO members to proceed with forms of cooperation/agreement which will remain under the auspices and the wider system of the WTO without securing the support and participation of the whole membership. On the other hand, as opposed to the existing plurilateral agreements, the mission of the MPIA is *provisional* and connected with a key aspect of the *multilateral* framework: it is in place until the functioning of the main dispute settlement system is restored. Think of it as the smaller reserve wheel, used in case of a flat tyre: it replaces the normal wheel, but not permanently; it simply facilitates the drive to the garage. This is what Art 25 of GATT and the MPIA do: they provide for an *ad hoc*/interim arbitration mechanism. This is quite different from plurilateral agreements such as the Government Procurement Agreement. Why? Because plurilateral agreements are topic-specific and include new or higher levels of commitment for participating members. The MPIA is different in the sense that, from a substantive perspective, the applicable rules of the agreement are those of the multilateral dispute settlement system (the MPIA does not create new substantive commitments).

4 Bernard M. Hoekman, Petros C. Mavroidis, and Maarja Saluste, 'Informing WTO reform: Dispute settlement performance, 1995–2020' (2021) 55 J World Trade 1–50.

5 WTO, 'Chronological list of disputes cases', www.wto.org/english/tratop_e/dispu_e/dispu_status_e.htm (accessed 9 December 2022).

solve the more fundamental impasse connected with the multilateral trade negotiations within the WTO.

Granted, the demise of the appellate body and the ensuing crisis that afflicted the WTO judiciary are the consequence of the hostile attitude adopted by the Trump administration, but as Fiorini et al.[6] have shown through their survey, some key aspects of Trump's criticism are shared by others. Where the US and the rest of the WTO membership parted company is the manner in which their concerns were addressed.

10.2.1 *Contextualising the Dispute Settlement Deadlock*

Understanding the reasons behind the stalemate and the importance of its resolution requires a contextual analysis. Such contextualisation will enable us to assess the relevance of the proposals we present in Section 10.5 and why we believe they may lead some key stakeholders to consider changing their current position. That said, we first need to clearly articulate our point of departure, which is the purpose of the WTO dispute settlement adjudication.

10.2.2 *What Does the WTO Dispute Settlement Adjudication Purport to Achieve?*

The GATT/WTO is no co-ordination game. Players will not align their interests in such a manner that there will be no negative spillovers from each other's actions. Political economy-motivated litigation is to be expected (let us call it 'bad faith' disputes), as, in democracies at least, serving the (national) private sector's interests might yield considerable rewards to the government. But the GATT/WTO is also an 'obligationally' incomplete contract. Horn, Maggi, and Staiger[7] have explained that, since all instruments in equilibrium affect trade (at least potentially and/or indirectly), negotiators face diminishing returns when moving from generic language (e.g. public health protection) to disaggregated language (e.g. the EU legislation on food additives). Consequently, they stop at the generic information level, and judges might be called on to provide the missing information (does the EU legislation amount to the protection of public health, for instance?). Let us use the term 'good faith' disputes for this type of litigation.

6 Matteo Fiorini et al., 'WTO dispute settlement and the appellate body crisis: Insider perceptions and members' revealed preferences' (2020) 54 J World Trade 667–98.

7 Henrik Horn, Giovanni Maggi, and Robert W. Staiger, 'Trade agreements as endogenously incomplete contracts' (2010) 100 Am Econ Rev. 394–419.

In practice, it might on occasion be quite difficult to distinguish between the two. Whether a dispute is 'good faith' or 'bad faith' is, after all, a question of private information. Unavoidably thus, the legislator (and not just the WTO legislator) will treat all of them as disputes. The DSU, like many regimes, must operate inevitably as a system organising dispute adjudication without distinguishing between good faith and bad faith disputes. Remedies do not differentiate between the two categories. Thus, the underlying presumption is that all challenged behaviour is not bad faith behaviour.

The allocation of the burden of proof follows this logic. The complainant always carries the burden to produce evidence to establish a prima facie case.

In this constellation, the WTO judge is an agent, not a principal (lawmaker), by virtue of Article 3.2 of the DSU.

The DSU embeds an ordinal preference for finding a solution which is mutually acceptable to the parties, and which is consistent with the covered agreements. A solution can occur even before a panel has been established, but nothing stops the litigating parties from continuing to consult thereafter. If a settlement proves impossible, the first objective of the dispute settlement mechanism is to secure the withdrawal of the measures concerned. Compensation (in practice, always in the form of tariff retaliation) should be resorted to only if the immediate withdrawal of the measure is impracticable and as a temporary measure, pending the withdrawal of the measure. Parties might voluntarily offer compensation, but if compensation is either not offered or not accepted at all, then the injured party may request authorisation to adopt self-help measures. Unlike other areas of international law, *it is not unilateral self-help* measures. The WTO judge will decide what amount of retaliation is appropriate.

Practice under the DSU is thus called to serve the objectives as explained above: settlement, before withdrawal, before retaliation.

10.2.3 *Should One Stay, or Should One Go?*

The current stalemate invites a brief reminder of the dynamics within the DSU system. What are the parties' possible courses of action when the dispute settlement system is seemingly not fully responsive to their preferences or concerns? A useful tool to facilitate such examination is Hirschman's[8] 'exit, voice, and loyalty' theoretical model which, in the context of WTO dynamics,

8 Albert O. Hirschman, *Exit, Voice and Loyalty: Responses to Decline of Firms, Organizations and States* (Cambridge: Harvard University Press, 1970).

has been used by Pauwelyn[9] and more recently by Paine,[10] together with the 'veto players' theoretical model introduced by Tsebelis.[11] Although these two theoretical models are independent in principle, their parallel deployment in this case enables us to better understand the decisions which led to the current WTO dispute settlement stalemate.

According to Hirschman's 'exit, voice, and loyalty' argument, members of an organisation who are dissatisfied with its performance or operation would consider the option of exiting when the exit (and re-entry) costs are either low or when these costs are offset by the gains of being outside the organisation. A relevant example would be the US approach to United Nations Educational, Scientific and Cultural Organisation (UNESCO) membership. The US, a founding member of UNESCO, exited the organisation in 1984, rejoined in 2003, and withdrew again in 2018. However, when the exit and re-entry costs are high, members would consider using processes and opportunities within the organisation to voice their concerns and make their dissatisfaction apparent. Depending on the capacity, ability, and/or willingness of the organisation to accommodate them in a way that creates the impression that their voices are heard and that they have an input in reshaping or reforming the organisation or its direction of travel, the loyalty of the particular State to the organisation can be strengthened, or weakened, accordingly.

In the case of the WTO, the reasons why the exit option is perceived to be costly is self-evident: WTO exit entails the loss of all membership benefits, such as preferential treatment in a wide array of trade areas and, more critically, the difficulty of replicating such a system of advantages outside the WTO.

Moving now to Tsebelis' 'veto player' model, members of a system (which could be an individual actor or a number of actors acting collectively) become veto players when their consent is necessary for a systemic change (procedural or substantive) to occur.

Looking at the WTO, we observe that regarding substantive commitments and disciplines, there is clearly a veto player system in place in the sense that changes in the disciplines require the consensus of members. By contrast, the WTO's dispute settlement system – and this is one of the peculiarities of the WTO architecture – is based on the abovementioned 'negative consensus'

9 Joost Pauwelyn, 'The transformation of world trade' (2005) 104 Mich L Rev 1–54.

10 Joshua Paine, 'The WTO's dispute settlement body as a voice mechanism' (2019) 20 J World Invest Trade 820–61.

11 George Tsebelis, *Veto Players: How Political Institutions Work* (Princeton, NJ: Princeton University Press, 2002).

according to which dispute proceedings commence even if the respondent does not acquiesce, unless there is consensus among the other members *against* the introduction of the dispute. In other words, the respondent does not enjoy a veto player status. Nevertheless, there is still an element of consensus in the process governing the periodic appointment of new appellate body members. At that point, for a member dissatisfied with the operation of the organisation where the exit option is associated with high exit and re-entry costs, there is an opportunity to voice their concerns by using a part of the organisation's internal process where they hold a veto player position. And this is precisely what the US did with the appellate body: its decision can be viewed as a loud 'voice' manifestation, which illustrates the point.

Having provided a theoretical explanation of the current stalemate, in the next section we will explain the importance of having an adjudicative body composed of judges, whereas in Section 10.5, we will revert to the EU to consider the lessons drawn from having a functioning dispute resolution system at times when substantive negotiations in the same organisation lose momentum. This discussion will provide the background to our proposal discussed in Sections 10.6 and 10.7.

10.2.4 *The Geopolitical Parameter: Are We Facing a New Thucydides' Trap?*

As previously mentioned, having an understanding of the wider geopolitical contest is of paramount importance in order to properly understand the subject of our examination, namely the WTO dispute resolution impasse.

Allison[12] provides a comprehensive historical account of transitions from one superpower to the next. History points to no case where hegemony was exercised collectively. Kindleberger (1986) and Keohane (1984) have explained why it is in the interest of the 'hegemon' to invest in the stability of the world system, whereas Tucker (2022), in a recent provocative statement, presented the first design of how power could be exercised collectively.[13] But this is the world of tomorrow, hopefully. For now, Pax Americana, the successor to Pax Britannica, is waning, and the question is whether we are on the cusp of Pax Sinica. This geopolitical volatility has also affected the workings of the WTO. The US is effectively asking whether and, if so, under

[12] Graham Allison, *Destined for War: Can America and China Escape Thucydides's Trap?* (New York: Houghton Mifflin Harcourt, 2017).

[13] Charles P. Kindleberger, *The World in Depression 1929–1939* (Berkeley: University of California Press, 1986); Robert O. Keohane, *After Hegemony, Cooperation and Discord in the World Political Economy* (Princeton, NJ: Princeton University Press, 1984); Paul Tucker, *Global Conflict* (Princeton, NJ: Princeton University Press, 2022).

what conditions trading with China can (continue to) take place. Its attitude regarding WTO dispute adjudication is, in substantial part, motivated by its ongoing antagonism with China.

The current legislative framework is inadequate to deal with modern challenges. Take the WTO Agreement on Subsidies and Countervailing Measures, which rests on the presumption that national and corporate links coincide (Article 1). But this is non-sensical, as a substantial part of trade is channelled through GVCs (global value chains). China through its OBOR (One Belt One Road) has been subsidising its branches around the world running little risk of retaliation. And we do live a return to industrial policy as the various Chips Acts[14] adopted around the world show. Add to that the fact that industrial policy is routinely justified on national security grounds, the justiciability of which is highly contested by the US (and a few minor players). Is this really the moment for a strong WTO judiciary and a weak legislative (hampered by the consensus rule, which operates as veto). Barfield (2001) warned about this risk, as did Jackson (2000).[15] The risk materialised a few years later. The US, quite unhappy with the outcomes in a few disputes that it had litigated with China, hardened its stance towards the WTO judiciary.[16] But the reason for doing so run deeper.

10.3 WHO WILL BE APPOINTED JUDGE, MATTERS

> 'Well Sir, goodbye. Do justice!' He turned quite sharply and he said: 'Come here. Come here.' I answered: 'Oh I know, I know.' He replied: 'That is not my job. My job is to play the game according to the rules.'[17]

This is a dialogue between Oliver Wendell Holmes, who responds to the nudge of Learned Hand, two giant personalities in US legal history and legal thinking in general, as reproduced by Dilliard. The reputed jurists understood

[14] The term refers to national legal instruments aimed at boosting domestic production capacity in technologically important areas such as semiconductors.

[15] Claude Barfield, *Free Trade, Sovereignty, Democracy: The Future of the World Trade Organization* (Washington, DC: American Enterprise Institute, 2001); John H. Jackson, *The Role and Effectiveness of the WTO Dispute Settlement System* (Washington, DC: Brookings Trade Forum, Brookings Institution, 2000), pp. 179–219.

[16] Petros C. Mavroidis and André Sapir, *China and the WTO, Why Multilateralism Still Matters* (Princeton, NJ: Princeton University Press, 2021).

[17] Irving Dilliard, *The Spirit of Liberty: Papers and Addresses of Learned Hand*, 3rd ed. (New York: Alfred A. Knopf, 1974), p. 307. See also the excellent analysis of Michael Herz ('"Do justice!" Variations of a thrice-told tale' (1996) 82 Va L Rev 111–61) of this dialogue, the variations of the story that different storytellers have provided us with, and what these variations entail.

their role as agents, leaving the role of principals to the US lawmakers. The institutional design of the DSU took a leaf from this story.

10.3.1 *WTO Judges Are Agents*

The DSU understands that panellists and appellate body members are agents who cannot undo the balance of rights and obligations agreed by the principals, the WTO members. According to Article 3.2 of the DSU:

> The dispute settlement system of the WTO is a central element in providing security and predictability to the multilateral trading system. The Members recognise that it serves to preserve the rights and obligations of Members under the covered agreements, and to clarify the existing provisions of those agreements in accordance with customary rules of interpretation of public international law. Recommendations and rulings of the DSB cannot add to or diminish the rights and obligations provided in the covered agreements.

In various other provisions, the DSU provides that the agents (judges) must be independent and competent. We subscribe to all of this. The problem, though, is that independence, impartiality, and competence are standards, not rules. Policing ex ante and ex post is necessary to ensure that judges do adjudicate behind a 'veil of ignorance'. But the DSU process is largely based on self-disclosure, which is not always a guarantee for DSU-consistent behaviour. Why would any agent, in this case WTO judges, submit self-incriminating information, which could be private (and, thus, difficult to discover)?[18] While this may be true also in other contexts (including judicial ones), the nature of the DSU,[19] combined with the nature of the WTO legal framework as incomplete contract[20] par excellence, means that the standards of impartiality, competence, and consistency become even more important and that any diversion is less tolerable.

Yet, a critical issue is the policing of the behaviour of WTO judges: have they really behaved as agents? To appreciate this point, we need to digress into the mode of interpreting the WTO agreements, the 'customary rules of

[18] We offered examples of cases where the membership has questioned the impartiality of appointed adjudicators see Petros C. Mavroidis, *The WTO Dispute Settlement System: How, Why and Where?* (Cheltenham: Edward Elgar, 2022).

[19] As mentioned above under Section 10.2.2, according to the DSU, the WTO judge decides both the legality and the amount of retaliatory action.

[20] Incomplete contracts are agreements which do not cover all contingencies and aspects in great detail, leaving scope for more negotiations between the parties to the agreement to develop the agreement and resolve/concretise these grey areas.

interpretation' according to the wording of Article 3.2 of the DSU. This is critical because the substantive provisions of the WTO agreements are usually expressed as 'standards', and not as 'rules', which leaves WTO adjudicators with a substantial margin of discretion.[21]

10.3.2 *Agents in a Non-enviable Position*

The explicit reference to 'customary rules' in Article 3.2 of the DSU, and hence the Vienna Convention on the Law of Treaties (VCLT), could be seen as departure from earlier GATT practice when GATT panels were routinely criticised for behaving as if the GATT was a self-contained regime.[22]

As mentioned earlier, the WTO contract is filled with 'standards', which makes it an 'obligationally' incomplete contract. In contrast, in a complete contract, disputes would have been motivated by bad faith because a complete contract would have been regulatorily complete and clear. Feasible contracts, though, are incomplete, as is evident in WTO agreements – contracts dealing with trade integration. All policies affect directly or indirectly, actually or potentially international trade. This explains to a large part, as per the authoritative account of Baldwin,[23] why behind-the-border policies were not identified and were all lumped together under one heading in Article III of the GATT. Contracts (like the GATT/WTO Agreement) are gradually completed, mostly through experience, as elements beyond legislative foresight risk giving rise to disputes.

In the early GATT days, institutional details about dispute settlement did not matter much. The GATT was a relational contract, namely a contract whose operation and effects were based on a relationship of trust. This was facilitated by the fact that early GATT was a contract among like-minded countries. In relational contracts, incompleteness is less of a problem. Good faith permeated the relations between players and substituted the missing

[21] Louis Kaplow, 'Rules versus standards: An economic analysis' (1992) 42 Duke LJ 557–629, provides a very elegant discussion of this distinction.

[22] We have offered an empirical account of WTO practice to make the point that WTO 'openness' to the rest of international law and relations is incoherent (and not linear). Furthermore, in the overwhelming majority of cases, WTO panels have referred to non-WTO law to support conclusions they had already reached while confined within the four corners of the WTO legal regime. See Petros C. Mavroidis, *The Sources of WTO Law and Their Interpretation: Is the New OK, OK?* (Cheltenham: Edward Elgar, 2022).

[23] Robert E. Baldwin, *Non-tariff Distortions of International Trade* (Washington, DC: Brookings Institution, 1970).

words. Disputes were also settled regularly, as Hudec[24] and Daswani, Santana, and Volkai[25] have highlighted.

But things changed as membership changed. As GATT membership expanded, they were all becoming increasingly aware that the presumption of 'good faith' was a shaky basis to fill the gaps for various reasons, ranging from the lack of common perceptions to the lack of common history.[26] In other words, widened membership meant that the 'same wavelength' engagement with the rules by all parties was not a given anymore.

Furthermore, new members did not have property rights over the old regime, and they wanted to have their say in the shaping of the new agreements. The new agreements continued to be incomplete for the reasons already explained, but also because the increasing heterogeneity of the members rendered consensus elusive. The result was that, unlike the GATT, the WTO Agreement is no relational contract, and incompleteness now comes at an additional cost. One cannot rely on good faith as much as before to resolve disputes.

An example will highlight this point. In the 1950s, Germany had been violating its obligations with respect to duties that it had agreed to impose on cereal starch and potato flour. The Benelux countries complained. During the panel proceedings, Germany made the following offer:

> The German delegation, while pointing out that the German Government was not in a position to modify the customs tariff without approval by Parliament and that the delegation was not therefore prepared to indicate a date for the reduction of the tariff rates, agreed to *request the Federal Government to propose to Parliament, within three months* after the end of the Ninth Session of the GATT, to grant the following tariff concessions.[27]

This does not look like an undertaking by Germany to implement its obligations. And yet, the Benelux countries agreed and accepted the offer. The Benelux countries and Germany had, of course, co-operated in different fora over the years, and a level of trust had developed between them. Would the Benelux countries have accepted similar promises from countries with which they did not share as much as they did with Germany? For the Benelux countries and Germany (as with many of the initial GATT members),

[24] Hudec, *Enforcing International Trade Law*.

[25] Arti-Gobind Daswani, Roy Santana, and Janos Volkai, *GATT Disputes 1948–1995: Dispute Settlement Procedures* (Geneva: WTO, 2018).

[26] Or even absence of consolidated levels of mutual trust due to historical reasons.

[27] WTO, 'German import duties on starch and potato flour' (7 February 1955) GATT Doc. W.9/178, para. 5 (emphasis added).

GATT was a relational contract whose operation and effects were based on a relationship of trust. For them, what had explicitly been included in the contract was just an outline of their overall agreement. There were additional implicit terms and an implicit understanding regarding the operation of the GATT, which determined their behaviour as well as their relations.

Although the heterogeneity of GATT membership was welcome because it helped transform the GATT into a global organisation, it also meant that all members no longer shared the implicit terms and understandings.

This is as far as the GATT is concerned. Reverting now to the VCLT, it lays down the methods of interpretation without explaining their relative importance. As rightly pointed out by the ILC Fragmentation Report : 'It is in fact hard to think of any approach to interpretation that would be excluded from articles 31 and 32 [VCLT].'[28] As a result, textualists will criticise contextualists; both will be criticised by originalists and modernists, and so on and so forth.

Although this is true for other international regimes where the VCLT's interpretation tools apply, in the case of the WTO and the DSU, an added complication is the even more incomplete nature of the WTO Agreement combined with the structure of the WTO settlement system, which is not designed in a way to promote an institutional alignment or instil an *esprit de corps* among WTO judges, leading to consistent (judicial) outcomes.

To give an example, two different appellate body formations have reached divergent conclusions regarding the understanding of the same terms by applying the VCLT. The appellate body, dealing with the passing of subsidies, within two years and without explanation, totally reversed its case law to the effect that auctioning price exhausts previously bestowed benefits while employing the same VCLT interpretative canon.[29]

All this shows that WTO adjudicators are asked to interpret one incomplete contract (the WTO Agreement) through another incomplete contract (the VCLT). This is no walk in the park.

And then there is the institutional design. The framers of the DSU had spent most of their negotiating capital in bringing about the provisional agreement reached during the Montreal Ministerial Conference (1988), namely, to transform multilateral adjudication from de facto into de jure compulsory third-party adjudication. This is exactly what the negative

[28] ILC, 'Fragmentation of international law: Difficulties arising from the diversification and expansion of international law – Report of the Study Group of the International Law Commission' (13 April 2006) UN Doc. A/CN.4/L.682 and Add.1, para. 427.

[29] See Mavroidis, *Sources of WTO Law*.

consensus amounted to. Citing archival record, we argued elsewhere[30] that the DSU framers largely based their negotiations on the premise that 'if it works, don't change it'. Several contributions in the comprehensive account that Marceau[31] put together, and especially that of Steger,[32] have underlined that even key institutions like the appellate body were an afterthought.

New challenges piled on in the first twenty-five years of WTO DSU experience: does the current regime of prospective remedies serve the interests of the weaker trading nations? What should be the role of compliance panels? Where to draw the line between compliance panels and arbitrators operating under Article 22.6 of the DSU? What should be the role of the Secretariat, an area where Pauwelyn and Pelc[33] have been quite vocal? There is a lengthy list of complaints, worries, and interrogations, some of which found its way into the inconclusive DSU review.[34]

10.4 THE IMPORTANCE OF HAVING A FUNCTIONING DSB DURING PERIODS OF NEGOTIATION INERTIA: LESSONS FOR THE WTO/DSU FROM THE EU EXPERIENCE

It is important to remember that the DSU stalemate inhabits the environment of a wider WTO legislative crisis, which is really the elephant in the room. The WTO has added only one new multilateral agreement to its arsenal since the Uruguay round package: the ATF (Agreement on Trade Facilitation). In the meantime, we witness a proliferation of FTAs (free trade areas) mushrooming and occupying the trade agenda.[35] This was probably to be expected, as it is behind-the-border policies that segment markets nowadays. To address

30 Petros C. Mavroidis, 'Mind over matter', in Kyle Bagwell and Robert W. Staiger (eds.), *Handbook on Commercial Policy* (Amsterdam: Elsevier, 2016), pp. 333–78.

31 Gabrielle Marceau (ed.), *A History of Law and Lawyers in the GATT/WTO* (Geneva: WTO, 2015).

32 Debra P. Steger, 'The founding of the appellate body', in Gabrielle Marceau (ed.), *A History of Law and Lawyers in the GATT/WTO* (Geneva: WTO, 2015), pp. 447–65.

33 Joost Pauwelyn and Krzysztof Pelc, 'Who writes the rulings of the World Trade Organization? A critical assessment of the role of the Secretariat in WTO dispute settlement', *SSRN*, 2019, https://ssrn.com/abstract=3458872 (accessed 9 December 2022).

34 See McDougall's excellent account of the content of the discussions: 'The crisis in WTO dispute settlement: Fixing birth defects to restore balance' (2018) 52 J World Trade 867–96.

35 See the excellent World Bank 'twin' studies: Claudia Hofmann, Alberto Osnago, and Michele Ruta, 'Horizontal depth: A new database on the content of preferential trade agreements. Policy Research Working Paper No. WPS 7981', *World Bank Group*, 2017, http://hdl.handle.net/10986/26148 (accessed 9 December 2022); Aaditya Mattoo, Nadia Rocha, and Michele Ruta (eds.), *Handbook of Deep Trade Agreements* (Washington, DC: World Bank Group, 2020).

them, like-mindedness is a key ingredient, but the widening of WTO membership and the deepening of obligations appear to amount increasingly to a zero-sum game.

Although we do not equate the DSU stalemate resolution with the end of the wider WTO legislative crisis, the boost that the resolution of the appellate body stalemate would provide to the process of substantive WTO negotiations is apparent and acknowledged in the highest echelons.[36]

With this in mind, we argue that there are few cases which highlight the importance of having a functioning dispute resolution system during periods of loss of momentum in (trade) negotiations other than the EU experience during the years which followed France's 'empty chair' practice in the mid-1960s.

Looking at that experience could provide useful lessons for the WTO if one does not lose sight of the inherent differences that characterise the two systems. During this period where decision-making at the Council of the EU (then the European Economic Community) was at best sluggish, a substitute for maintaining some sort of momentum emerged. In the case of the EU, it was the Court of Justice of the European Union (CJEU) that maintained the momentum of integration with a series of important judgments which directly affected the European integration's direction of travel.[37] Likewise, one may argue, in the WTO, the stalemate of trade negotiations left a similar space to be filled by the organ entrusted with the job of resolving disputes within the multilateral trade system. However, this is where the similarities end.

The principals of the EU and of the WTO system had envisaged different roles for their dispute settlement bodies. In the case of the EU, the role of the CJEU is not merely to settle disputes among the principals (one might argue, in fact, that this aspect is not even the most significant one). In addition, the CJEU functions as the ultimate arbitrator for the interpretation of EU law in the context of cases that emerge in disputes which arise before national courts through the mechanism of a preliminary reference embedded in

36 See statement of DDG Ellard, highlighting the 'existential' need to resolve the stalemate for some members and, one may argue, for the entire WTO system (WTO, 'DDG Ellard stresses need to maintain WTO momentum, importance of dispute settlement reform', 6 December 2021, www.wto.org/english/news_e/news21_e/ddgae_06dec21_e.htm (accessed 9 December 2022)).

37 E.g., case 8/74, *Procureur du Roi* v. *Dassonville* [1974] ECR 837; case 11/70, *Internationale Handelsgesellschaft mbH* v. *Einfuhr- und Vorratsstelle für Getreide und Futtermittel* [1970] ECR 114; case 120/78, *Rewe-Zentral AG* v. *Bundesmonopolverwaltung für Branntwein* [1979] ECR 649.

Article 267 of the Treaty on the Functioning of the European Union. This is the essence of the *Van Gend & Loos* and *Costa* v. *ENEL* judgments, the cases which established the instrumental concepts – for the purposes of the EU integration process – of *direct effect* and *primacy* of EU law, respectively.[38]

Therefore, although the idea of the role of the judge as an agent who does not challenge the balance agreed to by the principals is a description which could depict, on paper at least, the role of the CJEU in the EU system, there is one key difference: the CJEU assumed the role of an 'active, assertive' agent who is focused not always on the actual rule but rather on the overall incentives, aims, and objectives stated by the principals, and used them to reshape the rules.

It is true that such a role is not an invention of the CJEU; it is mentioned in the treaties, but the vigour, eagerness, and assertiveness in the exercise of its role, at least so far, were not always predetermined in terms of extent and intensity. For example, there is nothing predetermined in the *Van Gend & Loos*,[39] *Cassis de Dijon*,[40] and *Costa* v. *ENEL*[41] cases in the sense that they involve a *choice* of legal narrative scenario by the CJEU – a choice which was not obvious at the time, at least as far as the balance of the rules agreed by the principals was concerned or, to be more precise, as far as the principals' understanding of the balance of the rules they have agreed upon.

Contrary to the EU paradigm, the multilateral system established by the WTO never had ambitions comparable to those of the European experiment. This was clear by the design of the system itself, and its dispute settlement system in particular. In other words, the WTO system *was designed not* as a 'new legal order of international law', to borrow from the language of *Van Gend & Loos*, but rather as a system 'which merely creates mutual obligations between the contracting states'.[42] Likewise, the DSU was not conceived as an institution 'endowed with sovereign rights' and tasked with the role of overseeing a legal system which created rights and obligations not only for its signatory States but also for the natural and legal persons in or connected with those signatory States.

[38] Case 26/62, *NV Algemene Transport- en Expeditie Onderneming van Gend & Loos* v. *Netherlands Inland Revenue Administration* [1963] ECR 1; case 6/64, *Flaminio Costa* v. *ENEL* [1964] ECR 585.

[39] Case 26/62, *NV Algemene Transport- en Expeditie Onderneming van Gend & Loos* v. *Netherlands Inland Revenue Administration* [1963] ECR 1.

[40] Case 120/78, *Rewe-Zentral AG* v. *Bundesmonopolverwaltung für Branntwein* [1979] ECR 42.

[41] Case 6/64, *Flaminio Costa* v. *ENEL* [1964] ECR 585.

[42] *Algemene Transport- en Expeditie Onderneming*, 11.

Moreover, in the examination of the ways in which the CJEU operationalised its role as agent, one needs to recall that in the EU dispute settlement system, the CJEU sits at the apex of a pyramid of enforcement which has as its base and foundation the national judge who functions as the first tier of EU judges for protecting the EU law rights of private and legal bodies. This is true for most of the cases that reach the CJEU, which use the preliminary reference pathway from national courts. This architecture means that the CJEU *does not decide* the cases that arrive before it through the preliminary reference route. The CJEU interprets the rules, and a decision on the dispute is then carried out by the referring court. This means that the CJEU may interpret the EU rules in a particular way that appears to be assertive in the knowledge that the actual application of the rule, including any margin of adaptation (e.g. the decision as to which national measures comply with the principle of proportionality and which do not in a specific case), is taken by the national judge.[43]

The DSU system, on the other hand, does not enjoy this embedded margin because its decisions are 'final' on a specific dispute.

This brings us to a discussion of the specific lessons than can be learnt from the European experience.

The first useful lesson regarding the dispute settlement system design is that when it comes to disputes between member States and/or disputes between EU institutions and member States (inter-State/inter-institutional disputes), the dispute settlement system follows the *one-instance judicial format*: the CJEU is the only and final arbitrator. The two-tier instance format exists for disputes which arise in the context of challenges brought against EU acts by the so-called category of non-privileged applicants (natural and legal persons, only when they have a legal standing), and it involves an application to the General Court (GE) (first instance) and an appeal on matters of law against the decision of the GE to the CJEU (second instance). As this two-tier format relates to actions by natural or legal persons, we think it does not provide a desirable template for the inter-State disputes, which is the nature of the dispute settlement system at the WTO (at the current juncture of the WTO system at least).

[43] See, e.g., case 333/14, *Scotch Whiskey Association and Others* v. *Lord Advocate and The Advocate General for Scotland* [2015] ECR 845, where the CJEU prima facie adopted a strict application of the rules pointing to the illegality of the national measure under scrutiny subject to the application of the test of proportionality by the national judge, and the national judge found in that case that the measure was in fact proportionate, therefore compatible with EU law.

But even if we focus on the institutional design that governs only the inter-State/inter-institutional dispute resolution in the EU (namely the one-instance court paradigm), what is the relevance of the EU experience for the WTO DSU stalemate? After all, during the period of sluggish EU integration, the CJEU adopted a judicial activist stance that made up for and offset, to a degree, the legislative inaction.

We argue that the *opposite* approach should be taken with the resurrection of the DSU. In other words, the revived DSU should apply the agreed rules of the game, within the prescribed time limits, highlighting the cases where lacunae exist, thus passing the ball to a member State's court, as will be analysed in Section 10.6, instead of adopting a 'judicial activist' approach which compensates for the 'legislative inaction'. Such a 'judicial activist' approach, by which the CJEU in effect makes an integration choice, which the member States then either have to live with or legislate upon to ditch or amend it, can be sustained by the design and telos of the EU system, but not by the design and telos of the WTO.

In the WTO case, the term 'less is more', for the judicial practice to find solid grounding and meaning can have positive effects for restarting substantive negotiations.

That said, the fixing of the adjudicative stalemate in the WTO is a prerequisite for continuing the discussion of the substantive rules and disciplines in the WTO. The comparison with EU experience during the years of legislative inaction does not imply the replication of *what* the CJEU *did* during that period, because the direction of travel between the EU and the WTO were, and still is, different. In the case of the EU, a functioning court led the way towards a pre-agreed pathway and an ever closer Union.

The WTO, however, does not contain any such pre-agreed, ever-closer ambitions; however, it still has a (more modest in comparison to the EU) pre-agreed direction of travel that now desperately needs the shoulders of a functioning adjudicative arm to carry the increasingly damaging weight of inaction. Sometimes 'jumpstarts' require a strong push forward (that was the role played by the CJEU during the years of legislative inaction), whereas at other times, *jettisoning unnecessary* payload/weight is the recommended course of action. It is the latter we envisage in our proposals for the DSU WTO, as we will explain in Section 10.6.

10.5 WHERE ARE WE NOW, AND WHERE SHOULD WE GO FROM HERE

As we have discussed, the proximate cause for the demise of the appellate body that threw WTO dispute adjudication into disarray was the attitude of

President Trump and his refusal to appoint appellate body members. But the ultimate cause lies beyond such a whimsical reaction. The DSU review has been ongoing for over twenty years, and a last-gasp effort by the former head of the WTO, Roberto Azevedo, to save the regime has proven futile.[44]

With MPIA and *ad hoc* agreements to forego appeals proving to be, so far at least, an imperfect substitute for the appellate body, the resuscitation of this organ was entertained during the Twelfth WTO Ministerial Conference (the MC12) which was held between 12 and 17 June 2022 at the WTO headquarters in Geneva, Switzerland. Against predictions, MC12 evidenced an in-principle agreement to work together to reform the WTO.

However, discussions so far have failed to both address the root causes of the legislative crisis and resolve the crisis of the judiciary. There is, nevertheless, an intention to work together to address the dispute resolution stalemate.[45]

In what follows, we put forward concrete proposals regarding the future design of WTO adjudication in the hope that we can contribute in a meaningful and timely fashion to the debate about the resolution of the WTO stalemate and invite reflection by relevant decision-makers.

10.5.1 *The New WTO Court*

In our opinion, the key features of the new WTO court should be the following:[46]

- Permanent panellists (to guarantee independence from nominating parties as well as from the Secretariat) are needed.
- Panellists should be genuine experts and not necessarily lawyers, as expertise in international economics could come in handy for the resolution of disputes and the proper understanding of concepts like 'causality', 'like products', 'removing effects of subsidies', 'constructing the counterfactual under Article 22.6', and so on. This variety of experience will become even more relevant and important the further international trade moves into the digital age, requiring the panellists to understand the

44 Mavroidis, *WTO Dispute Settlement System*. See the relevant discussion in ch. 1.

45 See, e.g., WTO, 'MC12 outcome document' (22 June 2022) WTO Doc. WT/MIN(22)/24, para. 4, which reads: 'We acknowledge the challenges and concerns with respect to the dispute settlement system including those related to the Appellate Body, recognize the importance and urgency of addressing those challenges and concerns, and commit to conduct discussions with the view to having a fully and well-functioning dispute settlement system accessible to all Members by 2024.'

46 For a more complete discussion of this proposal, see Mavroidis, *WTO Dispute Settlement System*.

impact of modern technologies and the emerging national and international frameworks and standards which regulate them.

- Effective mechanisms should be in place to ensure (to the extent possible) that independence and impartiality are observed, and competence is ensured.
- Long-term appointment (e.g. six to eight years) which is non-renewable will further enhance independence from those nominating.
- Panellists should appoint their own clerks (so the Secretariat staff are not caught in the middle between advising the membership and having to act upon their advice when disputes arrive); although such differentiation in labour distribution might lead to some degree of loss regarding the ability/flexibility of the Secretariat to blur the edges, it will provide gains in the field of procedural and institutional clarity, which are needed at present.
- The WTO court should meet in plenum to discuss specific disputes, but also in chambers with specialised knowledge in various fields of WTO law. Chambers will leave important decisions for the plenum.

Although there is no room for an appellate body in our DSU 2.0, there are two features of the appellate body that should be maintained. First, within the one-instance regime of dispute settlement, we believe it makes sense to introduce precedent-based judgments.[47] Second, we believe the WTO judiciary should be hermetically insulated from the rest of the WTO. We will explain this immediately.

The appellate body, as explained by the chair of the Uruguay round's negotiating group that gave birth to the DSU,[48] was *not* supposed to provide a second look into all panel decisions. It was intended to intervene only occasionally to quash doubts about the proper understanding of the terms of substantive WTO agreements. The appellate body, of course, accomplished more than that. It contributed to the further *depoliticisation* of dispute adjudication in the multilateral trading system. Its legacy will be served through the establishment of a court with permanent judges, but insisting on reinstating the appellate body sounds like the sunk cost fallacy. It is a divisive issue, which can only increase existing divisions. If WTO members can agree on a depoliticised adjudication regime and manage to preserve the precedent-setting

[47] On the contemporary use of precedent in WTO case law, see the thorough analysis of James Bacchus and Simon Lester, 'The rule of precedent and the role of the appellate body' (2020) 54 J World Trade 183–98.

[48] ACWL, 'Interview with Ambassador Lacarte-Muró', www.acwl.ch/interview-with-ambassador-julio-lacarte-muro (accessed 9 December 2022).

function as we suggest, why spend negotiating capital on resurrecting the appellate body? What matters is not one- or two-instance adjudication. What matters is depoliticised dispute adjudication. The appellate body stalemate has been *erroneously* regarded as a *battle for the soul* of the multilateral trade system, leading to counterproductive simplifications which categorise all those who raise concerns about the current state of affairs surrounding the dispute settlement system as opponents of multilateralism. Our proposal instead focuses on the root cause of the issue, not the rhetoric around the issue.

10.5.1.1 A One-Instance Court

The membership should consider appointing a pool of fifteen judges. This is an old idea[49] that the EU launched but did not insist upon. Variations of this idea (e.g. permanent chairs and *ad hoc* panellists) have been floating around as well. No matter what the angle is, institutional guarantees of independence and impartiality, expertise, incentive to invest in acquiring additional knowledge, and appointing permanent panellists represent a net improvement on the current regime.

The court could be divided into chambers of three and five members and adjudicate disputes accordingly, using the value of a dispute (the requested sum) as benchmark for submission to one of the chambers. Chambers could also be allocated specific subject matter areas, and the expertise of the members of the chambers should reflect those subject matter areas.

In this regard, two to four members must have demonstrable expertise in GATS and TRIPS. The appointed judges do not have to be exclusively lawyers. Trade economists and/or experts in international trade policy should be welcome as well. Economics expertise will also be essential for clerks. Many of the issues the panel routinely deal with (e.g. non-discrimination, causality, quantification of damage) require counterfactual analysis, an area where legal expertise has little to offer. Moreover, expertise in emerging modern technologies, digital platforms, and ecosystems bound to affect international trade would be of increased importance, especially in the performance of counterfactual analysis. The plenum will be the precedent-setter, and chambers will be established with a mandate to adjudicate the submitted

49 There are dozens of accounts on the idea to bring in permanent panellists. For a discussion of all that matters on this score, see William J. Davey, 'The WTO and rules-based dispute settlement: Historical evolution, operational success and future challenges' (2014) 17 J Int'l Econ L 679–700.

disputes. A plenum of fifteen could be requested to intervene and discuss the following issues exclusively:

- confirming the *non liquet* status of questions/issues raised by one of the parties;
- novel issues;
- issues where chambers have reached irreconcilable outcomes.

These three categories relate to the establishment or clarification of important rules and principles defining the WTO system. Given the proposed one-instance structure, it is logical that the resolution of such cutting-edge issues should benefit from the brain power, expertise, and wisdom of the plenum. We will explain them in turn in what follows.

10.5.1.2 *Confirming/Pronouncing* Non Liquet

Non liquet is Latin for 'it is not clear'. Think of the treatment of *amicus curiae* in WTO practice. In DS61,[50] an NGO had submitted a letter to the panel. The panel dutifully refused to entertain it, claiming that it did not have the mandate to do so. The appellate body rejected the panel's approach and instead came up with a halfway house, where *amici* can submit, but panels are not obliged to take their views into account.[51]

What happened next? An extraordinary meeting of the WTO Council was called where all participants, except the US, voiced their disagreement with the ruling. The EU and Canada offered some mild support to the US view. The appellate body had clearly moved into an area which had not been explicitly addressed in the DSU and ruled on the conditions under which *amicus* briefs should be entertained by WTO panels, instead of sending the issue back to the membership. Has this approach been vindicated in practice? Far from it.

[50] WTO, *United States – Import Prohibition of Certain Shrimp and Shrimp Products*, WT/DS58/AB/R (12 October 1998).

[51] Howse ('Membership and its privileges: The WTO, civil society, and the amicus brief controversy' (2003) 9 ELJ 496–510) mounted a valiant effort and defended this position much better than the appellate body itself had done in its report. But the appellate body position cannot be right. For if it were right, some source of international law (customary? general principles?) will always serve to dictate a particular outcome, when contractual language is silent. But international law does not pre-exist the volition of its actors. It follows it. It exists as long as the stakeholders see gains from cooperation. Unless, of course, someone believes in natural law. But then, proponents must carry the associated (formidable) burden to prove their case.

There is no agreed procedure on submissions of *amicus* briefs across cases. As a result, over time, *amicus* submissions have dwindled, and it is questionable if they have had any influence at all. When considering that this would have been a powerful instrument that could have raised the level of awareness of WTO panels about societal sensitivities, it may have been better for the appellate body to simply refer the case back to the membership and ask for clear guidance on the treatment of *amicus curiae* briefs.

Pronouncing a *non liquet* thus offers at least two advantages:

- the institutional equilibrium of the WTO ecosystem (the balance of rights and obligations) is maintained; and
- from a policy perspective, the membership, armed with the information that an issue that has been debated before a panel has not been (adequately) regulated, will reflect on the need to intervene through legislative means and address the observed gap.

Such a process would create a powerful dynamic, namely a declaration that functions as a 'nudge' to the membership to fill the gap.

The ICJ (International Court of Justice), being a court of general jurisdiction, is opposed, in principle at least, to *non liquet*. It can rule on any issue of international law and is used to having recourse to the general principles of law to resolve disputes when the letter of law does not provide it with enough guidance. Likewise, the use of general principles to fill gaps is par excellence the modus operandi of the CJEU as a court of general jurisdiction of the EU legal order.

Weil,[52] siding with Lauterpacht,[53] has suggested that the reason why *non liquet* was not declared in contentious proceedings is simply because of the common belief that litigation must be brought to an end (*ut sit finis litium*), irrespective of whether law is 'complete' or not: when parties submit voluntarily to a judge, they do so in order to settle their dispute. *Non liquet* frustrates the will of the parties to end their dispute, and therefore academics have argued against it (and courts have discarded its existence).

Weil[54] continues by saying that the aforementioned reasons which support the refutation of *non liquet*, in fact, constitute proof that international law is

[52] Prosper Weil, '"The court cannot conclude definitively . . .": *non liquet* revisited' (1998) 36 Colum J Transnat'l L 109–19.

[53] Hersch Lauterpacht, 'Some observations on the prohibition of "non liquet" and the completeness of the law', in Frederik M. van Asbeck (ed.), *Symbolae Verzijl: Préséntés au Prof. J.H.W. Verzijl, à l'Occasion de son LXXième Anniversaire* (The Hague: Martinus Nijhoff, 1958), pp. 196–221.

[54] Weil, 'The court cannot conclude definitively . . .'.

riddled with gaps: why would recourse to general principles be necessary if there were no gaps in the first place? And if all that is not prohibited were permitted, how to manage the potential conflicts resulting from the exercise of unbridled national sovereignty? Recourse to general principles as an autonomous source of law will always lead to the demise of *non liquet*, especially since, as Lauterpacht[55] notes, the completeness of law is a general principle in and of itself. It thus becomes a self-fulfilling prophecy: if (international) law is complete, how could there ever be an instance of *non liquet*?[56]

Contract completeness has occupied the minds of not only international lawyers but also contract theorists and international economists. Antràs,[57] building on the seminal contribution by Grossman and Hart, has adequately explained why, in practice, trade agreements, like the WTO Agreement, cannot specify what is to be done in every possible future contingency. Horn, Maggi, and Staiger[58] have added an interesting dimension, namely that incompleteness is also due to the fact that negotiators face diminishing returns. This is the case because not all instruments (policies) affect trade in the same manner, and it is only reasonable that negotiators focus on those that affect trade the most. When shifting to instruments that exert less impact on trade, the outcome is not the same, even though the effort to negotiate could be the same. Recourse to aggregate language (vagueness) is a way to mitigate these problems (lumping all behind-the-border instruments under one heading, for example). But this is the best one can hope for, and, of course, there is an associated cost inherent in this approach: an agent (usually a judge) asked to pronounce on an eventual dispute will have to disaggregate the language while enjoying substantial discretion when doing so. The risk for error increases, as it is sometimes unclear what policies fall under a heading expressed in aggregate language. To provide an illustration: one can easily show why the freedom of establishment of foreign investors can affect the sale of their traded goods. Does this mean that WTO members must observe the principle of most favoured nation when entering into bilateral investment treaties? The conventional wisdom suggests a response in the negative. But it is not the text of Article III.4 of GATT that makes this point clear. It is State practice. The contract per se is hardly clear on this issue.

55 Lauterpacht, 'Some observations'.

56 Compare Rosalyn Higgins, *Problems and Process: International Law and How We Use It* (Oxford: Clarendon Press, 1994).

57 Pol Antràs, 'Grossman-Hart (1986) goes global: Incomplete contracts, property rights, and the international organization of production' (2014) 30 J L Econ & Org 118–75.

58 Horn et al., 'Trade agreements'.

Since the WTO contract is incomplete, should the WTO 'judge' (panels and the appellate body) complete it, when necessary? This brings us straight into the discussion of institutional balance in the WTO. While the WTO contract does assign the power to amend and interpret the covered agreements to the membership, it does not address the interplay between the legislative and the judicial function, other than in what is covered in Article 3.2 of the DSU.

There is not one single instance where WTO panels have pronounced a *non liquet*. And yet, there are three reasons why the claim for *non liquet* pronouncement in the WTO seems well founded:

- WTO members are entrusted with the exclusive competence to adopt authentic interpretations of the Agreement Establishing the WTO (Article IX.2). This demonstrates that the role envisaged for the WTO court is to apply the agreed rules. The settlement of disputes is the corollary of such application. This is a clear distinction from other jurisdictions – for instance, the EU institutional framework where the authoritative interpretation of the agreed rules lies with the CJEU. The DSU design lacks such delegation from the principals.
- WTO panels cannot undo the balance of rights and obligations as struck by the principals (WTO members); that is, they can neither add to the obligations assumed nor diminish the rights conferred (Article 3.2 of DSU).
- Finally, the WTO practice reveals that recourse to the general principles of law is not an independent source of law, but a mitigating factor which could usefully point to the correct interpretation of the WTO sources of law, which is the Agreement Establishing the WTO and its various Annexes. WTO panels have never adjudicated disputes using 'equity' as the legal benchmark for pronouncing on alleged inconsistencies.

Let us use an analogy to illustrate this point: let us consider the WTO and the EU as two distinct concert halls. Let us imagine now the principals/States as the trustees of these halls but, more importantly, as the composers of the musical pieces (the agreements) that will be played in the two halls. In our analogy, the courts are the musicians who play the musical pieces. In the case of the EU concert hall, the composers entrusted the musicians with a wide scope for interpreting the musical pieces. The musicians can change the rhythm, add 'staccatos' and 'rests', fill in gaps in the musical pieces, and even add some lines in order to achieve the desired and pre-agreed overall musical effect (ever closer Union). By contrast, the design of the WTO hall does not envisage such wide powers of interpretation for the musicians, let alone the power to add lines in the musical piece, because the overall instruction to the musicians is to 'play just the music you were given'.

Furthermore, there is a precedent of *non liquet* in GATT/WTO jurisprudence. In 1952, the GATT panel on Belgian Family Allowances[59] faced a challenge against a Belgian measure that imposed a tax only on imported goods originating from countries which had not implemented a system of family allowances comparable to one Belgium itself had implemented. This dispute raised the issue of how much of its behind-the-border regime a GATT member can apply to imports.

The panel report reads like a *non liquet*. Only the words *non liquet* are missing from the first sentence:

> 8. The Panel felt that the legal issues involved in the complaint under consideration are such that *it would be difficult for the CONTRACTING PARTIES to arrive at a very definite ruling*. On the other hand, it was of the opinion that the Belgian legislation on family allowances was not only inconsistent with the provisions of Article I (and possibly with those of Article III, paragraph 2), but was based on a concept which was difficult to reconcile with the spirit of the General Agreement and that the CONTRACTING PARTIES should note with satisfaction the statements made at the Sixth and Seventh Sessions by the Belgian representatives and should recommend to the Belgian Government to expedite the consideration and the adoption of the necessary measures, consistent with the General Agreement, including a possible amendment of the Belgian legislation, to remove the discrimination complained of, and to refer to the CONTRACTING PARTIES not later than the first day of the Eighth Session.[60]

The panel thus refrained from providing a definitive ruling. It observed the inconsistency of the challenged measure with the spirit of the GATT, its likely inconsistency with Article III.2 of GATT (which constituted the heart of the complaint against Belgium), and left it at that. This is a classic case of *non liquet*.

The point we are making here is that there is a precedent of *non liquet* in the WTO/GATT jurisprudence. The mechanism we are proposing is to support this approach by providing a specific institutional pathway in the dispute settlement system: such matters will go to the plenum to be decided. This will ensure that *non liquet* would not be a distant or hypothetical

[59] WTO, 'GATT panel report, *Belgian Family Allowances*, G/32' (7 November 1952) GATT BISD 1S/59.

[60] Ibid., para. 8 (emphasis added).

prospect, an outlier, in the modus operandi of the dispute settlement system, but a possible outcome which now has its proper institutional outlet, the plenum.

A pronouncement of *non liquet* is anyway in consonant with Article 3.2 of the DSU and hence warranted from a legitimacy perspective. It is also warranted from an effectiveness perspective if the *amicus* saga serves as an illustration. Through their patchwork solution in DS61, the appellate body judges deprived the membership of the opportunity to reflect on the necessity to step in and 'complete' the contract by adding, for example, a paragraph in Article 13 of the DSU that would explain under what conditions *amici* could file before WTO panels. Had the appellate body done just that in DS61, maybe the saga of filing *amicus* to the WTO would have been a happier story. As things stand, there is absolutely no basis to think that *amici* briefs have had any influence in the shaping of WTO case law.

10.5.1.3 Novel Issues

What constitutes a novel issue could be a matter of agreement, as it could be a case of disagreement between disputing parties. Furthermore, the WTO court could agree or disagree with such a view. Let us go back to 1995. The first GATS or TRIPS or SPS (Sanitary and Phyto-sanitary Measures) dispute – to provide but a few illustrations – by definition dealt with novel issues. None of these agreements existed before the advent of the WTO. But what about disputes under Article III of GATT (National Treatment)? Should GATT 1994 be considered a distinct instrument from the original GATT, with the consequent firewall between the two? The appellate body established an umbilical cord between the two instruments when holding that the adopted GATT panel reports were part of the GATT *acquis* that it would consider. And what about *obiter dicta* – remarks in passing which are not necessary to resolve a dispute – by GATT panels? What if an issue discussed in an *obiter dictum* in 1991 becomes a claim before a panel in 1996? Is it a novel issue, or not? All this is to state that disputes can legitimately arise regarding the novelty of an issue.

Why do we suggest that novel issues should, preferably, go to the plenum? Largely because we would like to see the record set straight, from the beginning. Granted, conflicting jurisprudence can contribute to innovation, but at the cost of uncertainty regarding transaction costs (is interpretation A or interpretation B the correct one?). For this reason, we want to reserve the role of precedent-setter for the plenum. It should be clarified at this point that we do not envisage this precedent-setting as manifestation of law-making by the court. On the contrary, we understand the decision on novel issues as part of rule interpretation within the confines of the agreement. If such interpretation is not possible, we revert to the *non liquet* scenario. The important issue is that the decision as to the distinction between a novel issue and *non liquet* will be taken by the same and well-equipped institutional mechanism, the plenum, thus ensuring consistency.

This brings us to the discussion regarding *stare decisis* (stand by things decided) and how we understand the term. The DSU does not address this issue. Still, the DSU does make some room for precedent-based judgments. Article 17.6 reads: 'An appeal shall be limited to issues of law covered in the panel report and legal interpretations developed by the panel.' Issues of law, by definition, cut across cases. What was requested from the appellate body was effectively to explain how the law should be understood, irrespective of facts-intensive idiosyncratic elements. The appellate body waited for some time before providing its own understanding on how it viewed its institutional role, in light of the mandate the DSU had provided it with.

In DS344, *US – Stainless Steel (Mexico)*, it revisited all prior case law and held that it expected panels to follow its prior rulings dealing with the same issue.[61]

In addition, in *Japan – Alcoholic Beverages II*, the appellate body found that

> adopted panel reports are an important part of the GATT acquis. They are often considered by subsequent panels. They create legitimate expectations among WTO Members, and, therefore, should be taken into account where they are relevant to any dispute.[62]

The reference to 'legitimate expectations' is important. This reference highlights a fundamental shortcoming of the system: an incomplete contract, such as the WTO, not benefiting from the opportunities for clarifying the nuances of the undertaken obligations, *or* one that creates the space for 'mixed messages' due to an *inconsistent application* of the rules, undermines legal certainty even more.

[61] See, in particular, WTO, *US – Stainless Steel (Mexico), Report of the Appellate Body*, WT/DS344/AB/R (20 May 2008), §158: 'It is well settled that Appellate Body reports are not binding, except with respect to resolving the particular dispute between the parties. This, however, does not mean that subsequent panels are free to disregard the legal interpretations and the ratio decidendi contained in previous Appellate Body reports that have been adopted by the DSB.'

[62] WTO, *Japan – Taxes on Alcoholic Beverages II, Report of the Appellate Body*, WT/DS8/AB/R, WT/DS8/AB/R, WT/DS11/AB/R (4 October 1996), p. 14.

It also shows that precedent-based decisions were thus not only appropriate but expected from panels as well. In large part, panels respected such precedents set by the appellate body, but with some notable outliers, with zeroing[63] being the most prominent one. It could also be argued that the appellate body followed its precedents by and large, but by tailoring the ambit of its decisions, it has eviscerated the scope of precedent to an extent.

We emphasise the importance of precedent because, ultimately, legal rulings and judicial awards aim to provide some certainty about transaction costs. Conflicting case law undoes that. And yet, as already stated, competition across jurisdictions may yield gains from innovation. How can we maximise gains from innovation without reducing innovation costs? Usually, this is done by assigning one court with the jurisdiction to apply and interpret the law and thus reap the benefits from innovation. This will be an informed court, a court that has good knowledge of the way in which issues are being debated and resolved in lower jurisdictions. It will also be a court that maintains the right to change its mind when new theories appear. It must be stressed here that our view is not about following precedent for the sake of following precedent. At the end of the day, precedents matter precisely because of the force of their reasoning, and not because of their cult-like features.[64]

In short, our argument is that, within the confines of the powers transferred to the WTO, the new DSU should assign to the plenum the power to deviate from precedent.

In *Spector Motor Service Inc.* v. *Walsh*,[65] Judge Learned Hand explained in the most pertinent terms why lower courts should refrain from acting as precedent-setters:

> It is always embarrassing for a lower court to say whether the time has come to disregard decisions of a higher court, not yet explicitly overruled, because they parallel others in which the higher court has expressed a contrary view. I agree that one should not wait for formal retraction in the face of changes plainly foreshadowed; the higher court may not entertain an appeal in the case before the lower court, or the parties may not choose to appeal. In either event the actual decision will be one which the judges do not believe to be

63 Zeroing is the methodology used by the US to calculate anti-dumping charges against foreign goods. The methodology is controversial because it arguably leads to higher anti-dumping duties.

64 The US complained about the use of 'precedent' by WTO courts. This was quite paradoxical, as the US legal system is based on precedent. It is more likely that the US was unhappy, not with the overall use of precedent but with the fact that, in the name of precedent, WTO panels would not undo the prior (hostile to the US position) appellate body rulings on zeroing.

65 *Spector Motor Service Inc.* v. *Walsh* 139 F. 2d 809 (2d Cir. 1944).

> that which the higher court would make. But nothing has yet appeared which satisfies me that the case at bar is of that kind; and, as I have said, I can see no good reason for making any distinction between one kind of federal activity and another. The way out is in quite another direction and includes both. Nor is it desirable for a lower court to embrace the exhilarating opportunity of anticipating a doctrine which may be in the womb of time, but whose birth is distant; on the contrary I conceive that the measure of its duty is to divine, as best it can, what would be the event of an appeal in the case before it.

It is precisely the same reasoning that justifies why chambers should leave it to the plenum to decide cases where a change in case law is warranted.

10.5.1.4 Irreconcilable Case Law

As we contemplate a court-based dispute settlement mechanism for the WTO with plenum and various chambers, the latter might be dealing with overlapping issues. One cannot thus exclude the possibility of conflicting views resulting in irreconcilable case law. In the WTO case law, it is not only on zeroing where we observe divergent positions; in fact, conflicting case laws regarding the most foundational obligations exist.

Already in the GATT era, the panels on *US – Taxes on Automobiles* and *Japan – Taxes on Alcoholic Beverages I* had reached antithetical understandings of the term 'like products'. In the WTO years, the appellate body resolved the conflict only in name: while rejecting the aims-and-effects test (espoused by the panel report on *US – Taxes on Automobiles*) in DS8,[66] a few years later in DS135,[67] it fitted regulatory concerns under the guise of unproven consumer preferences under the 'marketplace test'.

A clearer conflict exists with respect to the understanding of the term 'less favourable treatment': the appellate body reports on DS169,[68] DS302,[69] and DS401[70] are simply irreconcilable. The highest WTO judicial organ first stated that disparate effects suffice to qualify the challenged measures as less

[66] WTO, *Japan – Taxes on Alcoholic Beverages II.*

[67] WTO, *European Communities – Measures Affecting Asbestos and Asbestos-Containing Products*, WT/DS135/AB/R (12 March 2001).

[68] WTO, *Korea – Measures Affecting Imports of Fresh, Chilled and Frozen Beef*, WT/DS169/AB/R (11 December 2000).

[69] WTO, *Dominican Republic – Measures Affecting the Importation and Internal Sale of Cigarettes*, WT/DS302/AB/R (25 April 2005).

[70] WTO, *European Communities – Measures Prohibiting the Importation and Marketing of Seal Products*, DS401/AB/R (22 May 2014).

favourable treatment. It then held the opposite view, to the effect that treatment is not less favourable if disparate effects are justified by a regulatory rationale, which is unrelated to the origin of goods. And later it reverted to the issue only to caution all of us that we had misunderstood it. As a result, when subsequently it decided to return to a 'disparate effects full stop' test, it did so without deviating at all from prior case law.[71]

The apex of inconsistencies is the case law on 'pass through' of subsidies. Recall briefly that, following a decade-long conflicting case law, in DS316,[72] the three members of the appellate body read past the decisions in irreconcilable ways and then worked together to resolve the dispute before them (which involved, inter alia, the analysis of pass-through).[73]

There are also instances where case law is not internally incoherent but is, on its face, irreconcilable with the rationale of the law itself. This demonstrates a lack of understanding of the parameters which justify government intervention or regulation when there is divergence between the preferences of the consumers and the 'private' information – namely information not shared with the consumers or disregarded by the latter – held by the government which leads it to take regulatory action. How, for example, the appellate body overlooked in DS381[74] the impact of conformity assessment on the likeness of goods traded is hard to understand. If WTO members can lawfully assess the conformity of imported goods with domestic regulatory requirements, how can consumer preferences matter? Do regulatory requirements not exist precisely because States' and consumers' preferences were at variance?

Decisions which are irreconcilable either with case law or with the rationale of the law itself create uncertainty about the status of law and, of course, reduce the confidence of the WTO membership in the judiciary. In similar cases, the plenum should intervene and settle the issue one way or the other.

Such cases also demonstrate that the set of skills that WTO judges ought to possess go beyond the safeguarding of doctrinal consistency. This reinforces our argument about the need to ensure that the body of WTO judges must be composed of genuine experts (not necessarily lawyers) to ensure not only the

71 We discussed all this case law in detail in Petros C. Mavroidis, *The Regulation of International Trade*, vol. 1 (Cambridge: MIT Press, 2016), pp. 374 et seq. and 383 et seq.

72 WTO, *European Communities and Certain Member States – Measures Affecting Trade in Large Civil Aircraft*, WT/DS316/AB/R (18 May 2011).

73 In Petros C. Mavroidis, *The Regulation of International Trade*, vol. 2 (Cambridge: MIT Press, 2016), pp. 223 et seq., we provide a detailed discussion, quoting from the appellate body report.

74 WTO, *United States – Measures Concerning the Importation, Marketing and Sale of Tuna and Tuna Products*, WT/DS381/AB/R (16 May 2012).

doctrinal consistency of case law but also the coherence of case law with the internal rationale of the relevant rules. The plenum would be an appropriate forum where all the wealth and variety of the WTO court's expertise can be deployed, thus limiting the probability of the emergence of problematic judgments.

10.5.1.5 No More Excessive Compartmentalisation

The DSU sacrificed the efficiency and speedy resolution of disputes on the altar of third-party adjudication. The natural question to ask is whether there is a genuine trade-off between third-party adjudication and the speedy resolution of disputes.

Let us start with the wedge that the framers of the DSU drove between compliance panels and arbitration under Article 22.6 of the DSU. The only reason why the two processes have been compartmentalised is that compliance panel reports are appealable. One might wonder whether this makes any sense, as the DSU framers also decided against the possibility to appeal arbitral awards under Article 22.6 with no explanation at all. What if a finding that a measure is inconsistent with the WTO Agreement included a recommendation to withdraw the challenged measure anyway, as per Article 3.7 of the DSU? Would we need a compliance panel then? Withdrawing an illegal measure is, after all, the only good faith measure of implementing a decision. Keeping an illegal measure in place amounts to persisting illegality. And, of course, replacing it with another measure is tantamount to adopting a new measure.

Faced with such situations, panels stepped in and expanded their mandate by reviewing the consistency of all sorts of measures that have a 'nexus' (a very elastic term) with the measures challenged in the original proceedings. By not recommending the obvious statutory remedy, for example, withdrawal of the challenged measure, they opened a Pandora's box.

And what has the world trading community come to realise when the box was opened? What has the WTO membership found in there? Not much in terms of resolving the aforementioned problem, which could be characterised as 'delete and replace by an equally illegal measure'. First, there are serious doubts whether compliance panels, as they now stand, have contributed to the implementation of the findings of the original panels/appellate body, the holy grail of WTO dispute settlement. In large part, this is the case because they responded to the rather difficult question, 'Is what X did enough?' The difficulty of answering such a question is that it relies on the deciphering of a web of often cryptic rulings in panel/appellate body reports pronouncing the illegality of challenged measures.

We argue that the emphasis should be on reviewing whether 'X has withdrawn the illegal measure'. After all, is not withdrawal the objective of dispute settlement, as per the wording of Article 3.7 of the DSU? When withdrawal has not been recommended, human ingenuity can lead interested agents to all sorts of variations of withdrawal-like implementing measures. And it can also lead compliance panels to (very) complicated evaluations.

Second, the data provided by Hoekman, Mavroidis, and Saluste[75] show that compliance panels take a long time, an awfully long time sometimes. Consequently, the entire process is time-burdened. In principle, though, there is no need for this stage at all. Indeed, compliance proceedings are not replicated in other jurisdictions. Usually, either withdrawal is recommended or even more drastic suggestions are put forward. In short, the DSU could have been designed to serve compulsory third-party adjudication with no excessive compartmentalisation. As things stand, the same people decide whether:

- the complaint should be upheld (step 1);
- the respondent needs time to implement, and, if so, how much (step 2);
- the respondent has complied in the agreed time (step 3);
- and, if not, what the level of countermeasures should be (step 4).

With this in mind, the following observations are pertinent: first, it is clearly not necessary to count three-and-a-half years, roughly, between the first and the last step. Secondly, it is not obvious what other information is required for the panel to decide on steps 2–4 in addition to the information it possess already to decide step 1. Why can the original panel not, considering the current DSU objectives, recommend withdrawal within a reasonable time already at stage 1? If it does not happen, then the question should be, what the remedies in case of non-compliance should be?

At the moment of issuing its decision, the WTO court can also calculate the amount of retaliation in cases of non-compliance during the proscribed period. The WTO court should offer the respondent the choice between paying a lump-sum compensation (calculated based on trade effects, to avoid issues with sequential enforcement) or realigning its tariff protection.

10.5.1.6 Deadlines

Requesting panels to complete their work in six – and exceptionally nine – months is asking too much. Consistently, panels miss the statutory deadline,

[75] Hoekman et al., 'Informing WTO reform'.

irrespective of whether they act as original or compliance panels or even as arbitrator under Article 22.6. Arbitral tribunals dealing with comparable issues take as much or even longer than the time the panels de facto need to complete the process. DSU deadlines should be revised upwards.

Some might demur that, by doing so, a lengthy process will become even lengthier. But the trading community can economise a lot through the amendments we have suggested above (e.g. a one-instance body and no artificial compartmentalisation of the process). The WTO court should be given between twelve and fifteen months to adjudicate disputes, allowing it to extend when warranted.

10.6 HOW DO THE PROPOSALS SQUARE WITH THE 'EXIT, VOICE, AND LOYALTY' PARADIGM?

Arguably, the reformed court would constitute a reshaping of the current arrangements because of strong 'voice' manifestations, such as the appellate body stalemate. This means that the proposal is consistent with the 'voice' paradigm. But how does it square with the 'exit, voice, loyalty' equilibrium? Arguably the proposal does two things.

First, it shelters the judicial function from the implications of political signalling that members would, without a doubt, continue to attempt in the political arm of the dispute settlement system within the operation of the DSB. As Paine[76] argues, the DSB makes a significant contribution to the implementation and operationalisation of recommendations and rulings. Although its role appears uneventful due to the system of reverse consensus on the basis of which it functions, it plays another important role: that of a 'voice mechanism' where States can express their concerns and thus potentially diffuse some tensions. This, he argues, can have a legitimising effect on WTO adjudication, but can also undermine judicial independence due to the signals that member States may send to panels[77] at the panel formation stage regarding a dispute. It is at this point that our proposed WTO court would shelter the judicial function of the DSU.

Second, that sheltering is accompanied by a more modest circumscription of the realm of the sheltered adjudicative body, which does not create risks for a loss of control from the members, or, to be more precise, it softens the perception of such risk on the part of member States, given that the risk of loss of control is embedded in the third-party adjudication based on accepted

[76] Paine, 'WTO's dispute settlement body'.
[77] Ibid., p. 826.

commitments. If this is correct, then we may see a reduction of the members' need to resort to the use of the DSU as a 'voice' forum. The mechanism of identifying gaps at plenary and alerting the membership of such gaps is intended to play that role. Thus, the proposals appear to strengthen and support the 'voice' mechanisms of the WTO by the *renvoi* of 'jurisdictional boundary hot potatoes' to the membership. To use the musical analogy again, the essence of the proposed solution vis-à-vis the grey zone issues is for the musicians (the plenum) to ask the composers (membership) to decide if they want to add new lines to the musical score (the applicable rules).

10.6.1 *Uptake of Proposals*

Having presented the proposals and contextualised their likely impact within the WTO habitat, we need to address the elephant in the room regarding the likelihood of the proposals' uptake: why would the membership and those members who have used the DSU as a mechanism to 'voice' their dissatisfaction – for example, the US – accept the proposed new system if they were not happy with the appellate body?

We believe that one reason is the clarity and arguably faster resolution of disputes facilitated by the one-instance adjudication. Another reason is that the quality of appointed judges will lead to more consistent application of the rules. We argue that the solution we propose has the potential of addressing, for example, the US reservation formulated against the workings of the appellate body. If one looks at the reservation expressed by various quarters on the US side, the problem is not with the idea of a third party (the court) having a decisive impact on matters which touch upon US trade policy per se. It is with the third party transitioning from 'agent' to 'principal by stealth'. The conclusion of the *US Trade Representative 2020 Report* is indicative:

> By holding itself out as an ersatz 'Supreme Court of International Trade' that creates 'WTO law', the Appellate Body has diminished the stature of dispute panellists and diminished the impact of the WTO agreements as written.[78]

It is true that the US is against the 'precedential' effect of appellate body decisions, but we argued that this reservation is predicated on the appellate body or any other adjudicating body going beyond the text and filling the gaps or engaging in 'common law' modus operandi. By contrast, what we propose is

78 United States Trade Representative, 'Report on the appellate body of the World Trade Organization', February 2020, https://ustr.gov/sites/default/files/Report_on_the_Appellate_Body_of_the_World_Trade_Organization.pdf (accessed 9 December 2022), p. 120.

a body which functions on clear instructions, among others, to raise the flag of *lacunae legis* – not to step in and fill the gap – and be more flexible regarding precedent. We do not know if this would convince the US to drop their reservations towards the 'precedential' impact of the court's decisions immediately. We think, nevertheless, that it would make such softening of stance more palatable and less 'costly' given the potential yield of bringing the WTO dispute settlement system back on track and possibly helping substantive WTO negotiations to jumpstart.

10.7 CONCLUDING REMARKS

The WTO will have to address its legislative crisis against a background where consensus voting as practised in the WTO looks increasingly like the exercise of veto power. Even if the current crisis has been addressed, it simply cannot be that the WTO will continue to adjudicate disputes regarding agreements concluded in the past century. These agreements reflect today's concerns only in small part.

Solving the crisis of the judiciary is the necessary, but not sufficient, condition for solving the wider legislative crisis at the WTO. It is the necessary first step towards rekindling cooperation at the trade front. The negotiating partners should not miss this opportunity. The heterogeneity of the membership suggests that a lowering of expectations is probably warranted. One should recall in this respect that the upcoming negotiation of the DSU post-MC12 will be the first where China would express its views on dispute adjudication. So far China has participated in the DSU review, of course, but the mandate of MC12 requests WTO members to reach tangible outcomes by 2024.

What matters is to keep the key element of the current DSU intact. It should continue to be depoliticised. Judges should fulfil their role in an appropriate fashion, namely, behave like agents who comprehend the limits of their mandate. Reshuffling the court along the lines that we suggest will not only facilitate negotiation but also maintain the precious depoliticised nature of WTO adjudication while contributing to the fast resolution of disputes with a court which possesses the necessary expertise and skills to discharge its entrusted duty in an independent, diligent, and efficient manner.

11

The Security Council and Impartiality in the Peaceful Settlement of Disputes

NIGEL D. WHITE

11.1 WHY IMPARTIALITY?

Writing in 1944, Hans Kelsen argued that it was essential to replace the political bias in the League of Nations' settlement system, stating that the only legitimate system of collective security would be one based on the enforcement of international law where the executive would enforce the judicial pronouncements of an international court. He was adamant that the judgment as to whether the law had been broken by any parties to a dispute had to be removed from States and be placed in an independent judicial body.[1] The establishment of such an independent and impartial judicial dispute settlement mechanism would help move the international legal system from one of primary rules enforced by methods of self-help towards a union of primary and secondary rules (including the rules of adjudication) subsequently envisaged by Hart.[2]

However, although the UN Charter recognised the International Court of Justice (ICJ) as the 'principal judicial organ' of the UN,[3] and the Court does perform an important role in the peaceful settlement of disputes between States,[4] it was not a radical departure from the Permanent Court of

[1] Hans Kelsen, *Peace through Law* (Chapel Hill: University of North Carolina, 1944), pp. 13, 49, 67.

[2] H. L. A. Hart, *The Concept of Law* (Oxford: Clarendon, 1961), p. 94.

[3] Charter of the United Nations, San Francisco, 26 June 1945, in force 24 October 1945, 1 UNTS 16, Art 92. See generally Mohamed Sameh M. Amr, *The Role of the International Court of Justice as the Principal Judicial Organ of the United Nations* (The Hague: Kluwer, 2003).

[4] John G. Merrills, *International Dispute Settlement*, 6th ed. (Cambridge: Cambridge University Press, 2017), pp. 171–76. But see Richard A. Falk, 'On identifying and solving the problem of compliance with international law' (1964) 58 ASIL Proc 1–9 at 2.

International Justice which operated under the League system.[5] Instead, the drafters of the Charter placed greater emphasis on the role of the executive (the Security Council) in the peaceful settlement of disputes. This returns us to the presumption underlying Kelsen's proposition, namely that the independent and impartial application of the law to such disputes will be difficult to achieve in such a political organ. Following this line of thinking, instead of authoritative judgments and impartial decisions based on law, the role of law in the Council is mainly reduced to the adversarial legal arguments of the disputant States and their allies on the Security Council. Falk distinguishes adversarial arguments from impartial judgments in the following terms: 'In domestic society we have no problem in distinguishing the argument of counsel from the judgment of the court; the former is understood as adversary, the latter as impartial. In international society the absence of generally competent adjudicating institutions makes it very difficult to move beyond the adversary level of discourse.'[6]

Under this conception, the settlement of disputes based on international law can only be achieved through the Security Council if the member States have no national interests in the dispute – to enable them to remain above the fray and exercise impartiality in shaping a collective response, moreover, one based on law. If those conditions do not exist, the result will either be inaction due to a lack of consensus or veto, or decisions based on political compromises about how to achieve international peace and security.

Falk discusses the structure of international society and the role of law in general terms:

> We associate the intervention of law in human affairs with the role of the third-party decision-maker who is entrusted with the task of sorting out adversary contentions. International society as it is decentralized often successfully works out the content of reasonableness through action and inaction of adversary parties, provided the issues at stake are not vital to national security or national honour. In the context of force, however, the differential of power between adversaries of unequal strength influences their degree of flexibility in responding to counterclaims; the differences between the results of adversary interaction and of impartial third-party judgment are likely to be pronounced. The substitution of law for force in any social order involves,

5 Manley O. Hudson, 'The succession of the International Court of Justice to the Permanent Court of International Justice' (1957) 51 AJIL 569–73.

6 Richard A. Falk, 'New approaches to the study of international law' (1967) 61 AJIL 477–95 at 477–78.

> then, the gradual replacement of the ideology of self-help by that of third-party judgment.[7]

Falk recognises that in a decentralised international society, impartiality in the absolute sense of the decision-maker being indifferent to the adversarial arguments of the parties, applying objectively verifiable rules to resolve the dispute,[8] is rarely achievable. Even the ICJ allows judges from the disputant States not to recuse themselves from the case.[9] Falk argues that the 'absence of centralized procedures of interpretation and implementation in international society' means that 'the effectiveness of a decision' depends 'largely on voluntary patterns of compliance', which in turn is dependent on the 'persuasiveness' and 'authoritativeness' of the decision.[10] To be persuasive and authoritative, the decision-maker has to recognise that international law has problems of indeterminacy, and, therefore, account must be taken 'of value diversities, as well as value convergencies' in reaching or recommending the terms of settlement.[11] The Charter stipulates that disputes should be settled peacefully in accordance with international law *and justice*, in recognition that, certainly in complex disputes, law by itself is often not enough. However, this flexibility in dispute settlement does not mean that impartiality is not possible, or at least it is a standard by which the authoritativeness and persuasiveness of the decision are to be measured. Impartiality in dispute settlement can be seen as a standard or principle that is to be aimed for but not always achieved. The failure to be impartial, either wholly or in part, does not necessarily signify that the judgment of the decision-maker will not be accepted by the disputants, but it will mean that its authoritativeness, particularly in the longer term, will be in doubt. Lack of impartiality is likely to mean that a settlement will not be founded on law but on more transient political factors, which not only are detrimental to the lasting worth of the settlement but also undermine the development of the rule of law and the benefits of certainty and predictability that it brings to international relations.

This chapter tests the assumption that impartial law-based dispute settlement by the Security Council is neither achievable because of its political

7 Richard A. Falk, *Legal Order in a Violent World* (Princeton, NJ: Princeton University Press, 1968), p. 270.

8 See Higgins' review of Falk's work in Rosalyn Higgins, 'Policy and impartiality: The uneasy relationship in international law' (1969) 23 Int'l Org 914–31 at 930–31.

9 Statute of the International Court of Justice, San Francisco, 26 June 1945, in force 24 October 1945, 33 UNTS 993, Art 31.

10 Richard A. Falk, 'On treaty interpretation and the New Haven approach: Achievements and prospects' (1968) 8 Va J Int'l L 323–55 at 326–27.

11 Ibid.

nature, nor required by the UN Charter. It considers the functions and powers of the Security Council as the UN organ with a 'primary responsibility for the maintenance of international peace and security',[12] with powers granted regarding the peaceful or 'pacific settlement of disputes' under Chapter VI of the UN Charter. However, although the focus of the analysis is on Chapter VI of the Charter, the Council's coercive powers to take 'action with respect' to threats or breaches of the peace under Chapter VII must be considered. The UN Charter promises both coercive action and impartial dispute settlement when it declares that the UN's first purpose is:

> To maintain international peace and security, and to that end: to take effective collective measures for the prevention and removal of threats to the peace, and for the suppression of acts of aggression or other breaches of the peace, and to bring about by peaceful means, and in conformity with the principles of justice and international law, adjustment or settlement of international disputes or situations which might lead to a breach of the peace.[13]

A textual interpretation of this key provision signifies that peaceful settlement efforts of the UN should be in conformity with 'the principles of justice and international law', while collective measures are not so clearly confined. Following this line, a decision by the Security Council to take action under Chapter VII can create its own international laws, at least in relation to the specific situation deemed to be a threat to the peace.[14] The Security Council can thus both apply international law under Chapter VI and make international law under Chapter VII. However, having both sets of powers (of peaceful dispute settlement and of enforcement) at its disposal has led to the blurring of the two and to the Council exercising its range of powers in a discretionary, selective, and partial way. This descent towards arbitrariness has been fuelled by the expansion of the Council's peaceful dispute settlement and peacekeeping functions from inter-State to intra-State disputes and situations.

It may be expected that placing peaceful dispute settlement in the hands of a political – as opposed to a legal – organ is bound to lead to a subjective and partial approach to dispute resolution. There are in effect two barriers to

[12] UN Charter, Art 24(1).

[13] Ibid., Art 1(1).

[14] Ibid., Art 25. As to whether the Security Council has a more general legislative competence, see the debates surrounding the adoption of Resolution 1373 in 2001 (UNSC Res 1373 (28 September 2001) UN Doc. S/RES/1373); e.g., Luis Miquel Hinojosa Martinez, 'The legislative role of the Security Council in its fight against terrorism: Legal, political and practical limits' (2008) 57 ICLQ 333–59.

achieving impartiality: an internal one, caused by the Security Council as a political institution dominated by the permanent members, and an external one, as to which rules, norms, and values should be applied – those of law, justice, peace, and security, or simply those dictated by the national interests of the members of the Council. Despite these substantial barriers, there is certainly an expectation of objectivity and impartiality created by the provisions of the Charter.[15] In addition to Article 1(1) cited above, the Preamble of the Charter expresses a determination 'to establish conditions under which justice and respect for the obligations arising from treaties and other sources of international law can be maintained'. In addition to legal expectations, there are also legitimacy expectations in that international organisations can only expect to 'build up enough authority to be successful' peace-brokers if they are seen as 'impartial agents'.[16]

This chapter analyses the provisions of the Charter and practices of the Security Council in the field of peaceful dispute settlement, as well as looks for evidence of impartiality in both inter-State and intra-State disputes and assesses the influence of peacekeeping mandated by the Council upon impartiality. This analysis will show that the concept of impartiality in peaceful dispute settlement has largely disappeared and asks, in the conclusion, whether it is possible and desirable to (re)turn to impartiality.

11.2 THE PACIFIC SETTLEMENT OF DISPUTES UNDER CHAPTER VI

Despite the promise of peaceful dispute settlement in accordance with international law found in the Preamble and Article 1(1) of the UN Charter, as well as Article 2(3) and the provisions of Chapter VI, the lack of impartiality in practice is traceable to the institutional design of the Security Council. That body is accorded a key role in peaceful dispute settlement under Chapter VI, thereby giving each of the permanent members ultimate control over this function. However, the empowerment of the Council with both recommendatory and coercive competence under Chapter VII has led to the conceptual and practical conflation of peaceful dispute settlement with peace enforcement. This is exemplified by the transition of peacekeeping from consensual operations designed to impartially support peaceful dispute settlement by the

[15] See the step-by-step schemata of the Charter procedure for peaceful settlement in Hans Kelsen, *The Law of the United Nations* (New York: Praeger, 1950), pp. 381–87.

[16] Bob Reinalda and Bertjan Verbeek, 'Policy autonomy of international organizations', in Richard Collins and Nigel D. White (eds.), *International Organizations and the Idea of Autonomy: Institutional Independence in the International Legal Order* (London: Routledge, 2011), p. 94.

parties towards coercive operations designed to secure settlement outcomes decided by the Council.

When considered in isolation, the provisions of the UN Charter on peaceful dispute settlement hold a false promise of objective, impartial peaceful settlement of disputes in accordance with international law. Chapter VI reinforces this promise when detailing the obligation that member States have accepted in Article 2(3) of the Charter to 'settle their international disputes by peaceful means in such a manner that international peace and security, and justice, are not endangered'. The reference to 'justice' harks back to Article 1 (1)'s reference to the 'principles of justice and international law' and the Preamble's promise 'to establish conditions under which justice and respect for the obligations arising from treaties and other sources of international law can be maintained'.[17]

The opening provision of Chapter VI, Article 33(1), requires States that are parties 'to any dispute, the continuation of which is likely to endanger the maintenance of international peace and security' to, first of all, seek a solution using the traditional forms of peaceful dispute settlement: negotiation, enquiry, mediation, conciliation, arbitration, judicial settlement, or resorting to regional organisations. Thereby, Chapter VI is demonstrably based on traditional forms of diplomacy and settlement.[18] Article 33(2) brings the Council to the equation by requiring it, where necessary, to call upon the parties to settle their disputes by such means. Thereafter, Chapter VI contains what have often been termed the Security Council's 'quasi-judicial' powers to investigate disputes that are likely to endanger international peace and security (Article 34); recommend procedures or methods of adjustment to the disputants, including reference to the ICJ, in the case of 'legal disputes' (Article 36); or recommend terms of settlement to them (Article 37).[19] By tying the obligation to settle disputes placed on States to the powers of the Security Council, the idea was that the Council would, as a third party, help the parties towards a settlement agreement after they had tried and failed to sort out their dispute themselves, although in practice the Council has not necessarily waited for this to happen.[20]

[17] See Kelsen, *Law of the UN*, p. 18, for a discussion of the potential differences between 'justice' and 'international law'.

[18] See generally Merrills, *International Dispute Settlement*; Leland M. Goodrich, 'Pacific settlement of disputes' (1945) 39 Am Polit Sci Rev 956–70.

[19] Kelsen, *Law of the UN*, p. 372.

[20] Christian Tomuschat, 'Article 33', in Bruno Simma et al. (eds.), *The Charter of the United Nations: A Commentary*, 3rd ed. (Oxford: Oxford University Press, 2012), p. 1072.

Although international law is not expressly posited as the basis of peaceful dispute settlement in any of these provisions, except for 'legal disputes' which should 'as a general rule be referred by the parties' to the ICJ,[21] the purposes and principles of the Charter referencing peaceful dispute settlement (Articles 1(1) and 2(3) and the Preamble) make it clear that peaceful dispute settlement should be undertaken in accordance with the principles of justice and international law. These foundational and underpinning Charter provisions require that settlement efforts by the Council (or other UN organs such as the General Assembly and the Secretariat) be framed by the norms of justice and international law and, consequently, be undertaken in an impartial manner in order to achieve settlement in accordance with those norms. As indicated in Section 11.1, impartiality is inherent in the notion of settlement by a third party in accordance with international law and justice: the third party must evaluate both sides' adversarial legal arguments in order to make an independent and objective judgment, decision, or recommendation based on the application of international law and justice.

11.3 SOME EARLY EVIDENCE OF OBJECTIVITY AND IMPARTIALITY

There is some early evidence of the willingness of the Security Council to undertake impartial peaceful dispute settlement in the crises that emerged in the immediate shadow of the Second World War, including the Iranian,[22] Greek,[23] and Spanish questions. However, the focus of the Council was more on the correct application of the internal law of the UN Charter, rather than the application of external rules and principles of international law. In these crises, the provisions of Chapter VI were discussed in the Security Council as were the 'triggers' that would unlock the Council's powers under Chapters VI or VII. The practice indicated that before any substantive resolutions addressing an issue of peace and security could be adopted, the Security Council had to determine whether it was a situation or dispute 'likely to endanger international peace and security' (Articles 33 and 34) and so appropriate for

[21] UN Charter, Art 36(3).

[22] UNSC Res 5 (8 May 1946) UN Doc. S/RES/5, in which the Security Council resolved to 'defer further proceedings on the Iranian matter in order that the Government of Iran may have time in which to ascertain ... whether all USSR troops have been withdrawn from the whole of Iran'. The USSR was absent from the Council at the adoption of the Resolution.

[23] UNSC Res 15 (19 December 1946) UN Doc. S/RES/15, in which the Security Council established a Commission of Investigation under Art 34 of the Charter to 'ascertain the facts relating to the alleged border violations' along borders between Greece, on the one hand, and Albania, Bulgaria, and Yugoslavia, on the other.

Chapter VI recommendations, or whether it was a 'threat to the peace, breach of the peace, or act of aggression' (Article 39) requiring recommendations for settlement or action under Chapter VII.

That these trigger terms are imprecise is shown by the fact that the original Dumbarton Oaks proposals for the UN Charter had provided for a link between Chapters VI and VII of the Charter. The proposals had a provision at the beginning of Chapter VII that empowered the Council to find a threat to the maintenance of international peace and security if the procedures in Article 33(1) had failed, or if recommendations made under Article 36(1) were ignored.[24] In other words, the scale or nature of the security situation might not have changed to signify a move into Chapter VII – rather, it may simply have been the case that the Council had failed to help settle it peacefully under Chapter VI. This provision was removed not because it muddied the distinction between a danger to peace under Chapter VI and a threat to the peace under Chapter VII, but because it might have fettered the Council's power to make those determinations.[25] So even though the concepts of danger and threat have no determinate meaning, they are treated as preconditions before the Security Council can act under either Chapter VI or VII.

The purported need for a formal determination under Chapter VI or VII on the nature of the security situation was demonstrated by the Security Council's response to the 'Spanish Question' in 1946. The Council adopted a Resolution establishing a subcommittee to determine whether the existence and activities of the Franco regime in Spain endangered international peace and security.[26] The subcommittee reported that the situation did not 'justify direct executive action by the Security Council itself under Chapter VII which deals with various types of enforcement action which Members are obligated to take at the direction of the Security Council'.[27] It was of 'international concern' but not yet a 'threat to the peace' within Article 39.[28] There was a 'potential menace to international peace' and, therefore, a situation that is likely to endanger international peace within the meaning of Article 34 of

[24] UN, *Documents of the United Nations Conference on International Organization (UNCIO)* (New York: UN, 1945–54), vol. 3, p. 13.

[25] Ruth B. Russell and Jeannette E. Muther, *A History of the United Nations Charter* (Washington, DC: Brookings, 1958), pp. 669–70.

[26] UNSC Res 4 (29 April 1946) UN Doc. S/RES/4.

[27] UNSC, 'Report of the sub-committee on the Spanish question' (1 June 1946) UN Doc. S/75, paras 16 and 22.

[28] Ibid., paras 3 and 22.

Chapter VI.[29] Accordingly, it was held that the 'situation in Spain thus falls to be dealt with by the Security Council under Chapter VI of the Charter, which covers measures of peaceful settlement and adjustment'.[30]

Although the Security Council was unable to agree on a resolution under Chapter VI that would have led to settlement or agreement, the General Assembly did recommend the withdrawal of ambassadors from Spain,[31] and Spain remained outside the UN until 1955. Yet, at the same time, no agreement was made in the UN on how to address the problems posed to peace by the last remaining fascist regime in Europe, and one brought to power with the aid and assistance of fascist Germany and Italy.[32] The sub-committee's report made it clear that Spain was a menace to neighbouring States – France having closed its border in 1946 – and to its own population: 'The Franco regime continues to practice those methods of persecution of political opponents and police supervision over its people which are characteristic of Fascist regimes and which are inconsistent with the principles of the United Nations concerning the respect for human rights and for the fundamental freedoms.'[33] The subcommittee's report opens the prospect of settlement based on the principles of human rights, but the Council could not progress beyond narrow jurisdictional issues raised by the Charter to explore the international legal basis for settlement of the situation as required by Chapter VI. Once it has decided that Chapter VI was the appropriate framework for tackling the Spanish question, the Council's attention should have turned to the applicable principles of international law and justice. Overt concern for the internal situation in Spain was an early sign of the Council's competence over intra-State situations and conflicts, but that did not lead to a development of law-based methods to settle such disputes.

Debates about the relationship between Chapter VI and VII were also evident in the Security Council's close involvement in helping to achieve peaceful dispute settlement in Indonesia,[34] an example of an armed struggle for independence from colonial rule (in that case, from the Netherlands). Indeed, as Kelsen points out, the initial debate over Indonesia was concerned

[29] Ibid., para. 30(a).

[30] Ibid., para. 27.

[31] UNGA, 'Relations of members of the United Nations with Spain' (12 December 1946) UN Doc. A/RES/39(I).

[32] UNSC, 'Report of the sub-committee on the Spanish question', para. 6(a).

[33] Ibid., para. 7.

[34] UNSC Res 27 (1 August 1947) UN Doc. S/RES/27; UNSC Res 30 (25 August 1947) UN Doc. S/RES/30; UNSC Res 31 (25 August 1947) UN Doc. S/RES/31; UNSC Res 36 (1 November 1947) UN Doc. S/RES/36; UNSC Res 67 (28 January 1949) UN Doc. S/RES/67.

with whether this should be settled within the framework of Chapter VII on the basis that the situation constituted a threat to, or breach of, the peace under Article 39, bearing in mind that Article 39 does not necessarily mean that enforcement action will be taken but allows for making recommendations or decisions imposing coercive measures.[35] Political pressures concerning the premature use of Chapter VII, and the unwillingness of some members to even suggest that the Council might 'decide' on the future status of Indonesia,[36] led to the removal of implied determinations under Article 39 in Security Council Resolutions on Indonesia. This left the Council to operate under Chapter VI and to guide the parties towards peace settlement, culminating in the adoption of Resolution 67 on 28 January 1949. In this Resolution, the Council invoked its primary responsibility for peace and security and built on the expressed desires of both parties in the Linggadjati and Renville Agreements – facilitated with the aid of the Council's Committee of Good Offices for Indonesia – to establish a federal, independent, and sovereign Indonesia.[37] The Council recommended the establishment of an interim federal government, elections to an Indonesian constituent assembly, and the transfer of sovereignty to Indonesia, all within a specified timetable and supported by a UN Commission for Indonesia.[38] Following these developments, Indonesia achieved independence from the Netherlands in December 1949.

In the Indonesian situation, the Council acted as an impartial peace-broker, in effect treating the situation as a dispute between two equals, even though it involved a colonial State and one of its colonies. Although Kelsen conservatively states that a 'civil war which takes place within a state Member of the United Nations is certainly not an international dispute within the meaning of Article 2, paragraph 3', the Security Council disregarded the arguments of the Netherlands to that effect and treated Indonesia as a separate State.[39] The approach to Indonesia highlighted the Council going beyond narrow issues of Charter law to act as an impartial peace-broker helping a colonised State

35 Kelsen, *Law of the UN*, pp. 438–43.

36 See statement by Belgium in UNSC, 'Official records, 4th year: 417th meeting, 11 March 1949, Lake Success, New York' (11 March 1949) UN Doc. S/PV/417, p. 9: 'With regard to the settlement of the substance of the question, the Council can only make recommendations, and it could not be otherwise. To acknowledge the Council's right to decide on the liberation of the peoples of Indonesia, or of any other people, would be the equivalent of granting it the authority to settle the fate of a territory.'

37 UNSC Res 67 (28 January 1949) UN Doc. S/RES/67.

38 Ibid., paras 3–4.

39 Kelsen, *Law of the UN*, p. 365.

achieve external self-determination, thereby bringing about a settlement of the situation based on the principles of international law and justice. However, the situation also showed the potential limitations of that role – that is, for it to be triggered, the dispute has to be of an inter-State character or to be construed as such. As Section 11.6 will make clear, one of the problems faced by the Council in brokering and supporting modern peace agreements concerning only one State is in identifying what principles to apply and whether one of those is impartiality between the parties.

11.4 THE BROKEN PROMISE OF IMPARTIALITY

The crucial importance of ensuring the impartiality of the Security Council as a third-party peacemaker, armed with several 'quasi-judicial' powers under Chapter VI,[40] is reflected in the only substantive limitation on the veto accorded to each of the five permanent members in Article 27(3) of the Charter. In the case of non-procedural matters, Article 27(3) requires the affirmative vote of nine members of the Council, including the concurring votes of all the permanent members, provided that in decisions under Chapter VI 'a party to a dispute shall abstain from voting'.[41] Jenks clearly links this obligation to abstain to the quasi-judicial function of the Security Council, when he wrote in 1945 that 'parties to a dispute are to abstain from voting while the Council is discharging its quasi-judicial function of promoting pacific settlement as distinguished from its political function of action for the maintenance of peace and security'.[42] Accordingly, any member of the Security Council which is a party to a dispute before the Council shall abstain from voting and, in the case of a permanent member, abstain from vetoing a Resolution proposed under Chapter VI. As Wortley states, this aspect of Article 27 contains a basic principle of natural justice that 'a party to a dispute shall not be a judge of its own cause and shall abstain from voting'.[43]

In 1945 the four sponsoring powers at the San Francisco conference issued a joint statement on voting procedures in the Security Council, which introduced the idea of a 'chain of events' as an explanation of why the veto should extend beyond Chapter VII Resolutions to Chapter VI. However, even though this would allow for the encroachment of the Council's political

40 Ibid., p. 372.

41 UN Charter, Art 27(3).

42 Clarence Wilfred Jenks, 'Some constitutional problems of international organizations' (1945) 22 BYBIL 11–72 at 39.

43 Ben A. Wortley, 'The veto and the security provisions of the UN Charter' (1946) 23 BYBIL 95–111 at 102.

function into its quasi-judicial one, the statement recognised that there remained an obligation to abstain if a permanent member was a party to a dispute:

> Decisions and actions by the Security Council may well have major political consequences and may even initiate a chain of events which might, in the end, require the Council under its responsibilities to invoke measures of enforcement ... This chain of events begins when the Council decides to make an investigation, or determines that the time has come to call upon states to settle their differences, or makes recommendations to the parties. It is to such decisions and actions that unanimity of the permanent members applies, with the important proviso ... for abstention from voting by parties to a dispute.[44]

Although this statement preserves the obligation to abstain and, therefore, supports the principle of impartiality in dispute settlement, the problem under Chapter VI is in identifying the parties to a dispute, which should trigger the obligation to abstain if any of the disputants are members of the Council. This issue arose early in the practice of the Security Council in 1946, when it was about to vote on the presence of British troops in Greece. The Netherlands asked whether the parties, in this case the UK, should vote in this matter. The President declared that the Council had 'not declared the matter to be a dispute, and at such time as the Council declares any situation to be a question of dispute, it in that way brings into operation Article 27 of the Charter'.[45] It is very unlikely that a permanent member who might be seen as a party to a dispute will allow such a determination unless it is in their interests to do so. This same thinking undermines the whole of Chapter VI, at least where a permanent member is involved in a dispute. Under Article 33(2), for example, the Council is empowered to call upon the parties to settle their dispute by peaceful means. If a permanent member is alleged to be a party to the dispute, it may either veto any such call and, in so doing, deny that it is a party, or claim that there is a 'situation' that endangers peace and not a 'dispute' between defined parties.[46] Thus, a permanent member can block Security Council involvement under Chapter VI even though objectively it is

[44] UN, *Documents of UNCIO*, vol. 11, p. 714.

[45] Loraine Sievers and Sam Daws, *The Procedure of the UN Security Council*, 4th ed. (Oxford: Oxford University Press, 2014), p. 341.

[46] Wortley, 'Veto and security provisions', pp. 99, 104. Also 100 where he explains that the difference between a 'dispute' and a 'situation' 'would appear to be that there are *defined parties* to a dispute, whereas a situation does not necessarily present itself as an issue between defined states'.

a party to a dispute, in the absence of mechanisms to prevent this or challenge the exercise of the veto in these circumstances.

If, under Article 35, a State brings a dispute to the attention of the Security Council and names a permanent member as one of the disputants, or if, under Article 99, the Secretary-General uses their power to bring to the attention of the Security Council a 'matter' which may threaten international peace and security and, in so doing, identifies the matter as a dispute involving a permanent member, could the permanent member still ignore its obligation to abstain and use its veto? There remains a problem of how that veto could be challenged, for example, by the remainder of the Security Council agreeing that there is a dispute involving a permanent member and that its negative vote is invalid, or that it should be treated somehow as an abstention. Despite Kelsen's statement that a negative vote cast in these circumstances is illegal and 'must not be counted',[47] practice does not support any sustained challenge to the veto, although there have been limited criticisms in the Security Council chamber over the misuse of the veto.[48] Sievers and Daws review member State practice and conclude:

> The Security Council has developed no consistent practice with respect to when the restrictions of Article 27(3) should apply, either for permanent or non-permanent members. In fact, while abstention under the conditions set out by Article 27(3) is considered *obligatory*, in practice, when a Council member has abstained in that context, the decision to do has actually been *voluntary* on the part of that member, rather than imposed by the Council.[49]

Zimmermann's review of practice is even more damning, demonstrating that it is the Security Council 'that not only decides whether a dispute has arisen but also, ultimately, who the parties to the dispute are'.[50] Thus, each permanent member has the power of veto over the issues of whether there is a dispute and who the parties to it are. It must not be forgotten that it is not just practice but the design of the Security Council as well that has driven this, and that, in these matters at least, it is impossible to draw a clear line between the Security Council as a corporate actor and the powers and privileges of each permanent

[47] Kelsen, *Law of the UN*, p. 264.

[48] Wortley, 'Veto and security provisions', p. 104, on early practice.

[49] Sievers and Daws, *Procedure of the UNSC*, p. 350. An example of a voluntary abstention (or, more accurately in this case, non-participation in the vote) is that of the UK on a Chapter VI Resolution referring the dispute between the UK and Albania over incidents in the Corfu Channel to the International Court of Justice under Art 36(3) – UNSC Res 22 (9 April 1947) UN Doc. S/RES/22.

[50] Andreas Zimmerman, 'Article 27', in Bruno Simma et al. (eds.), *The Charter of the United Nations: A Commentary*, 3rd ed. (Oxford: Oxford University Press, 2012), p. 925.

member. Design and practice have effectively allowed each permanent member a veto over the proposed resolutions purporting to tackle disputes in which it is a party (or situations in which it is involved), and, furthermore, this blocking effect has been extended to cover the client countries of each permanent member.[51] Together these represent a series of moves away from the idea of the Security Council as an impartial third party when it exercises its quasi-judicial powers under Chapter VI.

Initiatives to curtail the exercise of the veto, such as a proposed code of conduct, are aimed at establishing a form of non-binding convention creating an expectation that permanent members would refrain from the use of the veto to prevent appropriate action to address core crimes under Chapter VII.[52] The focus on increasing Chapter VII measures reflects the misconception that has been present since the inception of the UN Charter in 1945, namely that the Security Council should be an organ of action, when its constitutional makeup with the veto at its heart inevitably meant that its basic function was to be a facilitator for diplomacy and peaceful dispute settlement.[53] However, the pervasive and unrestricted use of the veto to thwart resolutions under both Chapters VI and VII signifies that the Council is neither an organ of action nor an impartial peace-broker, at least in a predictable, sustained, and coherent sense.

The Covenant of the League of Nations was in some ways more effective in removing a member State from voting on matters in which it was involved. Under Article 15, member States agreed to submit disputes to the Council of the League, which 'shall endeavour to effect a settlement of the dispute'. If unsuccessful in this endeavour, the Council was required to produce a report, either unanimously or by majority vote, containing a statement of the facts of the dispute and 'the recommendations which are deemed just and proper in regard thereto'. Article 15(6) stated that if the report was agreed unanimously by the members of the Council 'other than the Representatives of one or more of the parties to the dispute, the Members of the League agree that they will not go to war with any party to the dispute which complies with the recommendations of the report'. These are significant departures from the basic principle of unanimity found in Article 5 of the Covenant, and they maintained the impartiality of the Council of the League by disregarding the votes

[51] Wortley, 'Veto and security provisions', p. 105.

[52] UNGA and UNSC, 'Code of conduct regarding Security Council action against genocide, crimes against humanity or war crimes' (14 December 2015) UN Doc. A/70/621-S/2015/978.

[53] Inis L. Claude Jr, 'The Security Council', in Evan Luard (ed.), *The Evolution of International Organizations* (London: Thames and Hudson, 1966), p. 68.

of disputants. In other words, in the Council of the League, a great power was unable to block the adoption of a Resolution which purported to address it as a party to a dispute.

According to McNair, the report generated under Article 15(6), 'which when adopted unanimously (excluding the disputing parties)', should have 'definite legal consequences', illustrated by the dispute between Italy and Abyssinia when sanctions were ultimately imposed by States on Italy despite its opposition.[54] It must be remembered that Italy was one of the great powers in the League's Council. In effect, the League could act in dispute settlement and enforcement (through sanctions or military action) without being stopped by the negative vote of a great power. This may appear to be a counterintuitive conclusion when considering that the League is often characterised as being hindered by the requirements of unanimity in contrast to majority voting in the UN. However, the conclusion that the principle of natural justice – whereby a party to a dispute should not be able to vote on any organisational initiative to settle that dispute – was more effectively upheld in the League than in the UN is a result of the increased centralisation engineered by the drafters of the UN Charter, and also because of the more legalistic approach of the Covenant when compared to the UN Charter.[55] The centralised and politicised approach of the Charter meant that the Security Council amassed significant collective powers, but the exercise of those powers had to be approved by each and every permanent member. While this might be expected to be the case when the Council is exercising its 'political' executive function under Chapter VII, it seriously undermines the Council as an impartial actor performing its 'quasi-judicial' function under Chapter VI.[56] The League appeared institutionally weak and hobbled by the requirements of unanimity, which seemingly gave every State a veto. But this was not the case as the Council of the League could disregard the negative vote of any State deemed to be a party to the dispute. The weaknesses of the League lay elsewhere.[57]

11.5 INTER-STATE AND INTRA-STATE DISPUTE SETTLEMENT

The powers granted to the Security Council under Chapter VI are firmly based on the traditional paradigm that international disputes are those that occur between States, and further that the applicable rules of international law

54 Arnold D. McNair, 'Collective security' (1936) 17 BYBIL 150–64 at 155.
55 J. L. Brierly, 'The Covenant and the Charter' (1946) 23 BYBIL 83–94.
56 Jenks, 'Some constitutional problems', p. 39.
57 Nigel D. White, 'From Covenant to Charter: A legacy squandered?' (2020) 22 Int Community Law Rev 310–30.

to such disputes revolve around conceptions of State sovereignty, political independence, and territorial integrity. There was also evidence in early and later Security Council practice of support for the application of the principle of external self-determination in the achievement of independence for territories under colonial or similar rule. In these cases, the Security Council was prepared to treat the situation as being equivalent to an inter-State dispute, thereby stretching the inter-State paradigm. The Security Council demonstrated that it could exercise its powers of peaceful dispute settlement in an impartial way that accords with such basic axioms of international law in the struggle for Indonesian independence, discussed in Section 11.3. Indeed, the situation in Indonesia in the late 1940s demonstrated that the Council could be innovative within the inter-State paradigm when it approached the issue as a dispute or situation involving two States, namely the colonial State and the emerging post-colonial State, one enabling settlement that resulted in the achievement of independence for the Indonesian people.

Within this extended inter-State dispute paradigm, Security Council practice has inevitably been uneven, so that when the interests of the permanent members have more directly been engaged, impartiality is significantly eroded. Resolution 242, adopted following the Six-Day War of 1967 when Israel captured large tracts of territory in pre-emptive military operations against its Arab neighbours, appears to be an impartial attempt to bring peace to the Middle East.[58] Resolution 242 appeared to be built upon respect for the fundamental principles of international law – the non-use of force, territorial integrity, and sovereignty. However, the desire to keep Israel engaged with the peace process meant that law played a secondary role to the politics of peace, since the Resolution did not make it clear that Israel should withdraw from 'all' the occupied territories, an interpretation Israel has followed to this day. Moreover, by solely focusing on the inter-State aspects of the situation, the Resolution ignores the Palestinian right to self-determination, even though this right has been subsequently recognised by other organs in the UN system.[59] The Security Council has failed to stretch its understanding of the inter-State paradigm to cover the dispute between Israel and an emerging State of Palestine. While often cited as the basis for a peace agreement in the Middle East,[60] Resolution 242 is arguably too flawed to carry that weight.

58 UNSC Res 242 (22 November 1967) UN Doc. S/RES/242. Adopted unanimously.

59 See, e.g., UNGA, 'Question of Palestine' (10 November 1975) UN Doc. A/RES/3236 (XXIX).

60 See, e.g., the Preamble to the Israeli–Palestinian Interim Agreement on the West Bank and the Gaza Strip, Washington, DC, 28 September 1995, which states, in part, 'that the aim of the Israeli-Palestinian negotiations within the current Middle East peace process is, amongst other things, to establish a Palestinian Interim Self-Government Authority . . . for a transitional

Nevertheless, when the political context allowed, the Security Council has been able to settle colonial and post-colonial conflicts in an impartial manner following axioms of international law. For instance, in relation to South Africa's occupation of Namibia, the Security Council exercised quasi-judicial settlement powers over a long period. In 1969, the Council decided 'that the continued occupation of the Territory of Namibia by the South African authorities constitutes an aggressive encroachment on the authority of the United Nations, a violation of the territorial integrity and a denial of the political sovereignty of the peoples of Namibia'.[61] In 1978, the Council reaffirmed 'the legal responsibility of the United Nations over Namibia' and approved the Secretary-General's proposal for the settlement of the Namibia situation, involving the withdrawal of South Africa's illegal administration from Namibia, the transfer of power to the people of Namibia with the assistance of a UN Transition Assistance Group (UNTAG), and the early independence of Namibia through free elections under the supervision and control of the UN.[62] UNTAG was not deployed until 1989,[63] marking the beginning of the implementation of this plan and leading to Namibia's independence.

UNTAG was deployed at the cusp of a transition in the practice of the Security Council from addressing the legacies of colonialism by supporting the external self-determination of peoples struggling for independence (e.g. in Indonesia, Rhodesia, and Namibia), towards its post–Cold War concern with supporting peace settlements and processes aimed at achieving internal self-determination in already independent States fractured by intra-State conflict. At this point, it appears that the inter-State dispute settlement paradigm was not extended any further. Although the Council became extensively involved in these situations, the normative framework of Chapter VI did not appear to play a significant constraining role in this regard, and, further, the wider normative framework of international law was a disputed one, revolving around the contested concept of democracy. As will be seen in Section 11.6, the matter has been intimately linked to the development of

period not exceeding five years . . . leading to a permanent settlement based on Security Council Resolutions 242 and 338'. UNSC Res 338 (22 October 1973) UN Doc. S/RES/338 was adopted during the 1973 conflict in the Middle East, simply called for a cease-fire and for the implementation of Resolution 242, and decided that negotiations shall start 'aimed at establishing a just and durable peace in the Middle East' (para. 3).

61 UNSC Res 269 (12 August 1969) UN Doc. S/RES/269. France, the US, and the UK abstained.

62 UNSC Res 435 (29 September 1978) UN Doc. S/RES/435. Soviet Union abstained.

63 UNSC Res 632 (16 February 1989) UN Doc. S/RES/632. Adopted unanimously.

peacekeeping, operating in the murky waters of implied powers and the space between Chapters VI and VII, underpinned somewhat shakily by the UN's move towards supporting the emergence of democratic States as a way of achieving internal self-determination.[64]

Irrespective of this significant development in UN practice regarding the settlement of intra-State conflicts, there has been little attempt to bring it within the framework of Chapter VI. In other words, there has been a failure to modernise dispute settlement to include intra-State as well as inter-State disputes. Indeed, there has been little normative development of peaceful settlement for inter-State disputes beyond a reiteration of the core obligations on States and the powers of the Security Council and General Assembly in a number of Assembly resolutions, including the Declaration on Friendly Relations of 1970 and the Manila Declaration of 1982.[65] A strengthening of the normative framework might have improved both the legitimacy and the effectiveness of peaceful dispute settlement, especially by developing the nexus between the obligations of States, the methods of peaceful dispute settlement, and the powers of the Council. The repackaging of peaceful dispute settlement as 'peacemaking' has made little difference normatively. 'Peacemaking' was defined by the UN Secretary-General Boutros Boutros-Ghali in 'An Agenda for Peace' (1992) as 'action to bring hostile parties to agreement, essentially through such peaceful means as those foreseen in Chapter VI of the Charter of the United Nations'.[66] The Office of Legal Affairs' *Handbook on the Peaceful Settlement of Disputes* (1992) is primarily confined to the methods and mechanisms available to States and, therefore, provides flesh on the bare bones of the methods listed in Article 33. The *Handbook* is stated to have been 'prepared in strict conformity with the Charter of the United Nations; being descriptive in nature and not a legal instrument'. Further, it is confined to disputes between States, excluding any internal disputes.[67] Peaceful dispute settlement between States seems to have remained firmly rooted in the traditional concepts of international law, such as sovereign equality, consent, and agreement embodied in Chapter VI of the

[64] Thomas M. Franck, 'The emerging right to democratic governance' (1992) 86 AJIL 46–91.

[65] UNGA, 'Declaration on principles of international law concerning friendly relations and co-operation among states in accordance with the Charter of the United Nations' (24 October 1970) UN Doc. A/RES/2625(XXV); 'Manila declaration on the peaceful settlement of international disputes' (30 November 1982) UN Doc. A/RES/37/10, para. II.4.

[66] UN Secretary-General, 'An agenda for peace' (17 June 1992) UN Doc. A/47/277, para. 20.

[67] OLA, *Handbook on the Peaceful Settlement of Disputes between States* (New York: UN, 1992), p. 1, adopted pursuant to UNGA Res 39/79 (13 December 1984) UN Doc. A/RES/39/79 and UNGA Res 39/88 (13 December 1984) UN Doc. A/RES/39/88.

UN Charter.[68] Peaceful dispute settlement within States is underdeveloped and contested, both normatively and in practice.

The post–Cold War era has been characterised by the efforts to unlock the peace enforcement powers of the Security Council under Chapter VII, rather than improving the UN's record of peaceful dispute settlement under Chapter VI: leading examples can be found in *An Agenda for Peace* (1992), the *High Level Panel Report* of 2004, and the *World Summit Outcome Document* of 2005.[69] These documents recognised the reality being faced by the UN with threats caused by civil wars, but they failed to produce concrete recommendations as to how to bring the parties to such conflicts to a peaceful solution. Chapter VI is predicated on disputes between States being the subject of recommendatory powers of the Security Council, and although the provisions of Chapter VI can be used by way of analogy to end civil wars and other violent or potentially violent intra-State disputes and conflicts, there is a need to develop a set of impartially exercised peaceful dispute settlement powers for intra-State conflicts based on the principles of international law and justice.

The lack of preparation by the UN for intra-State conflicts, often involving outside States, as has been occurring in Syria for over a decade, is encapsulated in a 2014 Resolution in which the Security Council recognised that 'some of the tools in Chapter VI . . . which can be used for conflict prevention, have not been fully utilized', but it simply listed the methods that States should use under Article 33, rather than asserting and developing the powers of the Security Council regarding peaceful dispute settlement.[70]

It remains the case that peaceful dispute settlement is modelled on settling disputes between States, and not settling disputes within States where the government is normally the only recognised international actor. There are exceptions in international law – for example, when an armed group represents a people fighting for self-determination, but that is narrowly confined to colonial and similar situations and does not extend to a people struggling to overthrow an undemocratic regime.[71] Thus, the main problems of

68 Nigel D. White, 'The Security Council, peace-making and peace settlement: Between executive and pragmatic', in Marc Weller, Mark Retter, and Andrea Varga (eds.), *International Law and Peace Settlements* (Cambridge: Cambridge University Press, 2021), p. 237.

69 UN Secretary-General, 'Agenda for peace', para. 20; UN Secretary-General, 'A more secure world: Our shared responsibility – Report of the High-Level Panel on Threats, Challenges and Changes' (2 December 2004) UN Doc. A/59/565, para. 84; UNGA, '2005 world summit outcome' (24 October 2005) UN Doc. A/RES/60/1, paras 73–76.

70 UNSC Res 2171 (21 August 2014) UN Doc. S/RES/2171.

71 James Crawford, *Brownlie's Principles of Public International Law*, 8th ed. (Oxford: Oxford University Press, 2012), pp. 646–47.

peacemaking in Syria are the lack of legal parity between the parties to the conflict and the dependency of any effective peacemaking on the Security Council or the agreement of that body to any settlement proposal, along with the practical mixture of these two issues with permanent members intervening on both sides of the conflict. How can the Security Council be an impartial third party when Russia, the US, the UK, and France, each holding a veto, are parties to a conflict(s) raging inside Syria?

There have been numerous resolutions addressing aspects of the conflict in Syria, including demands for a ceasefire,[72] but it was not until December 2015 that the Council moved towards a more impartial and comprehensive approach. In Resolution 2254, the Security Council set out a framework for settlement in Syria, involving UN-mediated political talks, a national ceasefire, and a two-year period to achieve a political transition.[73] In a March 2017 press statement, in furtherance of this Resolution 2254, the Security Council supported the Secretary-General's Special Envoy's efforts to facilitate a lasting political settlement of the Syrian crisis 'through an inclusive and Syrian-led political process that meets the legitimate aspirations of the Syrian people', and welcomed the reopening of talks in Geneva while reaffirming a commitment to the sovereignty, independence, unity, and territorial integrity of Syria.[74] The adoption of Resolution 2254 and the continuing yet faltering attempts to implement it[75] provide some glimmer of hope for the people of Syria.[76] The need for a peace agreement on Syria involving the parties, their backers, and other guaranteeing States and organisations, based on respect for

[72] UNSC Res 2268 (26 February 2016) UN Doc. S/RES/2268; UNSC Res 2401 (24 February 2018) UN Doc. S/RES/2401.

[73] UNSC Res 2254 (18 December 2015) UN Doc. S/RES/2254.

[74] UN Doc. SC/2749 (2017).

[75] UN Doc. S/RES/2236 (2016), welcoming mediation by Turkey and Russia. Russia, Turkey, and Iran sponsored the 'Astana' talks, involving the Syrian government and an opposition delegation, starting in January 2017, and said to be within the framework of Resolution 2254. In December 2018 the Security Council adopted a Resolution in which it reiterated 'that the situation will continue to deteriorate further in the absence of a political solution to the Syrian conflict and *recalls* its demand for the full and immediate implementation of Resolution 2254 (2015) to facilitate a Syrian-led and Syrian-owned political transition, in accordance with the Geneva Communiqué as set forth in the ISSG Statements, in order to end the conflict in Syria and *stresses* again that the Syrian people will decide the future of Syria' – UNSC Res 2449 (13 December 2018) UN Doc. S/RES/2449.

[76] But see recent Security Council Resolutions which have focused solely on the humanitarian situation in Syria: UNSC Res 2504 (10 January 2020) UN Doc. S/RES/2504; UNSC Res 2533 (11 July 2020) UN Doc. S/RES/2533; UNSC Res 2585 (9 July 2021) UN Doc. S/RES/2585.

both the sovereignty of Syria and the human rights of its people, remains all too apparent.[77]

11.6 PEACEKEEPING AND THE SETTLEMENT OF INTRA-STATE DISPUTES

Conceived in 1956, peacekeeping was a measure aimed at securing a ceasefire and withdrawal of troops from a conflict zone as a prequel to efforts to settle the underlying dispute. It was consistent with the UN acting as an impartial actor, promoting peaceful dispute settlement within the parameters of basic principles of international law, reflected in Article 2, paragraphs 1, 4, and 7 of the UN Charter, namely sovereignty, non-intervention, and non-aggression. Peacekeeping was based on the consent of the host State(s), and even though it appeared to constitute military intervention, its respect for sovereignty was reflected in the neutrality of such a force between States. Peacekeeping also provided breathing space for the disputing States to settle their dispute peacefully, exemplified by the withdrawal of British and French forces from Suez in 1956, and the eventual agreement in 1979 of Israel to withdraw from Egyptian territory in the Sinai.

The fact that the UN General Assembly mandated the original force (UNEF I) is no coincidence,[78] in that its functions reflected the views of the non-aligned majority of member States as well as the traditional principles of international law that gave such States protection from intervention. The ICJ recognised the constitutionality of the Assembly exercising its subsidiary powers in peace and security under Articles 11 and 14 of the UN Charter to mandate peacekeeping forces at the request of the States concerned, and the Court found that such forces did not impinge upon the exclusive mandatory enforcement powers of the Security Council.[79] However, peacekeeping subsequently crossed into the domain of the Security Council as part of its primary responsibility for peace and security under Article 24 of the UN Charter. This has led to the possibility of a more coercive version of peacekeeping empowered, in whole or in part, under Chapter VII of the UN

[77] See the Geneva Peace Talks of 2014, 2016, and 2017 – Robert S. Ford, 'Keeping out of Syria: The least bad option' (2017) 96(6) Foreign Aff 16–22 at 18; Anon., 'Talks to draft Syria's Constitution to resume on October 18', *Al Jazeera*, 28 September 2021, www.aljazeera.com/news/2021/9/28/syria-constitution-talks-to-resume-october-18-in-geneva-un (accessed 29 October 2021).

[78] UNGA Ress 998–1101 (November 1956) UN Docs A/RES/998–1001.

[79] *Certain Expenses of the United Nations* (Advisory Opinion) [1962] ICJ Rep. 151 at pp. 163–64, 177.

Charter. It also led to the possibility of the Security Council combining peacekeeping with peaceful dispute settlement, which had the potential to erode the image of the UN peacekeeping force as an impartial actor facilitating, but not imposing, peaceful solutions.

Peacekeeping facilitated the creation of peaceful conditions between the parties, enabling the pursuit of settlement based on equality and impartiality. This meant that it was normal for peaceful dispute settlement efforts to be kept separate from peacekeeping in inter-State disputes such as Suez in 1956, and even in intra-State disputes where clear ceasefire lines could be patrolled as in Cyprus in 1964, when a peacekeeping force was mandated by the Security Council. In that dispute, the Security Council recommended that:

> The Secretary-General designate, in agreement with the Government of Cyprus and the Governments of Greece, Turkey and the United Kingdom, a mediator, who shall use his best endeavours with the representatives of the communities and also with the aforesaid four Governments, for the purpose of promoting a peaceful solution and an agreed settlement of the problem confronting Cyprus, in accordance with the Charter of the United Nations, having in mind the well-being of the people of Cyprus as a whole and the preservation of international peace and security.[80]

The Council was acting as an impartial promotor of peaceful dispute settlement by encouraging the parties towards agreement by means of mediation utilising its powers under Article 33(2). Peacekeeping in this guise is clearly created within the confines of Chapter VI as an appropriate procedure or method of adjustment under Article 36(1). The Council was careful not to impose a solution to the Cyprus problem, but this might lead to protracted and inconclusive settlement efforts as borne out by subsequent events. However, the Congo crisis of the early 1960s saw the Security Council's deployment of a more forceful form of peacekeeping by mandating a force to achieve a solution based on preventing the break-up of the country.[81] The Council's array of powers, of peaceful dispute settlement and peace enforcement, signifies that it can take a range of approaches to settlement. At one end of the spectrum, settlement is left to the parties with impartial guidance from the Council, while at the other end, a solution can be imposed with the danger of erosion to the Council's impartiality.

80 UNSC Res 186 (4 March 1964) UN Doc. S/RES/186, para. 7.

81 UNSC Res 161 (21 February 1961) UN Doc. S/RES/161; UNSC Res 169 (24 November 1961) UN Doc. S/RES/169.

The aftermath of the Cold War provided a brief period of creative peaceful dispute settlement due to the massive shift in geopolitics. This took the form of UN-supported elections within broader peace operations, producing some successes to bring an end to internationalised civil conflicts in Central America, Cambodia, and Africa,[82] as well as some failures.[83] This was not, as it turns out, the end of history[84] or the emergence of a right to democracy[85] but a brief opportunity for the UN to fill the space vacated by the global confrontation between the superpowers. Although sponsoring elections proved to be too superficial a solution for an enduring settlement in several situations, peacekeeping forces in this period respected the principles of impartiality, consent, and limited use of force in that their aim was to support the peace settlement agreed to by the parties to the intra-State conflict. However, in a number of instances, the peacekeeping force became embroiled in supporting the elected government in establishing its authority over a State fractured by the civil war.[86] This was recognised in the UN's Capstone document on peacekeeping: 'In order to generate revenue and provide basic services to the population, the State must be able to exert control over its territory', and UN peacekeeping operations 'may support the restoration and extension of State authority by creating an enabling environment, providing political leadership or coordinating the efforts of other actors'.[87]

Gilder identifies a deepening of peacekeeping support for establishing State authority through the development by the Security Council of 'stabilisation' mandates, which not only include 'robust posture' and 'active patrolling within their terms' but also witness 'increased logistical capabilities from Western military hardware, the encroachment of a counterterrorism rhetoric,

[82] See, e.g., Joachim A. Koops, 'United Nations Observer Group in Central America (ONUCA)', in Joachim A. Koops, Norrie MacQueen, and Paul D. Williams (eds.), *The Oxford Handbook of United Nations Peacekeeping Operations* (Oxford: Oxford University Press, 2015), p. 306.

[83] See, e.g., Caroline Guyot and Alex Vines, 'United Nations Angola Verification Missions II and III (UNAVEM II and III)', in Joachim A. Koops, Norrie MacQueen, and Paul D. Williams (eds.), *The Oxford Handbook of United Nations Peacekeeping Operations* (Oxford: Oxford University Press, 2015), p. 338.

[84] Francis Fukuyama, *The End of History and the Last Man* (London: Penguin, 1993).

[85] Thomas M. Franck, 'Legitimacy and the democratic entitlement', in Gregory H. Fox and Brad R. Roth (eds.), *Democratic Governance and International Law* (Cambridge: Cambridge University Press, 2000), p. 25.

[86] See, e.g., Alan Doss, 'United Nations Organization Mission in the Democratic Republic of the Congo (MONUC)', in Joachim A. Koops, Norrie MacQueen, and Paul D. Williams (eds.), *The Oxford Handbook of United Nations Peacekeeping Operations* (Oxford: Oxford University Press, 2015), p. 656.

[87] UNDKPO, 'United Nations peacekeeping operations: Principles and guidelines', 2008, www.un.org/ruleoflaw/files/Capstone_Doctrine_ENG.pdf (accessed 8 July 2022), pp. 27–28.

operations alongside host State forces, and an emphasis on (re)establishing the rule of law',[88] citing missions in the DR Congo, Mali, and the Central African Republic. In the case of the UN Multidimensional Integrated Stabilisation Mission in Mali (MINUSMA), for example, 'the mission has contingents of forces from Western countries and sophisticated military hardware including short range drones, and attack and transport helicopters'.[89] According to the Secretary-General, MINUSMA has attempted to 'progressively dominate areas adjacent to population centres' in order to 'prevent incursion by criminals and terrorist groups',[90] and the Security Council has called on MINUSMA to engage in direct operations against asymmetric threats while claiming continued allegiance to the principles of peacekeeping.[91] Despite this claim, the principles of peacekeeping – of impartiality and of the limited use of force, which are based on the basic principles of international law – have been reinterpreted to allow for proactive force in support of the government. As Gilder states: 'The position of the UN as an impartial actor becomes tenuous when the mandates of MINUSCA [UN Multidimensional Stabilisation Mission in the Central African Republic] and MINUSMA expressly call for the missions to assist with the extension of state authority, assist with the redeployment of host state forces, and to conduct joint operations and share intelligence.'[92] Furthermore, stabilisation involves 'peacebuilding in the power vacuum left behind after displacing armed groups' and is based on the peacekeeping mission establishing the rule of law by helping the host State rebuild its criminal justice system.[93] It may also entail peacekeepers using force as an exceptional and temporary measure to maintain law and order and to fight impunity.[94]

The desire to achieve an enduring peace in an intra-State situation has led to the Security Council blurring its Chapter VI and VII powers in mandating peacekeeping forces, effectively placing itself on the side of the government so that it is neither an impartial actor nor is the peacekeeping force. The settlement of intra-State disputes remains skewed towards the government, meaning that impartiality is understood as the impartial defence of the peace

[88] Alexander Gilder, 'The effect of "stabilization" in the mandates and practice of UN peace operations' (2019) 66 NILR 47–73 at 47.

[89] Ibid., p. 51.

[90] UNSC, 'Report of the Secretary-General on the situation in Mali' (9 June 2014) UN Doc. S/2014/403, para. 66.

[91] UNSC Res 2295 (29 June 2016) UN Doc. S/RES/2295.

[92] Gilder, 'Effect of "stabilization"', p. 64.

[93] Ibid.

[94] See, e.g., UNSC Res 2149 (10 April 2014) UN Doc. S/RES/2149 re MINUSCA.

process, rather than impartiality between the parties. Having said that, given that the UN-sponsored peace agreements are based on the understandings of international law, including 'democratic access to power (including minority rights where relevant), with a human rights framework including measures such as bills of rights, constitutional courts, human rights commissions, reforms of policing and criminal justice, and mechanisms to address past human rights violations',[95] it could be argued that the focus of impartiality has been shifted – or at least would shift in time – from impartiality between the parties to a dispute to the impartial upholding of agreements based on international law. According to the UN's Capstone doctrine on peacekeeping: 'The need for even-handedness towards the parties should not become an excuse for inaction in the face of behavior that clearly works against the peace process. Just as a good referee is impartial, but will penalize infractions, so a peacekeeping operation should not condone actions by the parties that violate the undertakings of the peace process or the international norms and principles that a United Nations peacekeeping operation upholds.'[96] Despite this declaration of impartiality between the parties, in practice, forceful measures by peacekeeping forces are taken against non-State armed groups and not against the government. Indeed, in the *Expenses* case, the ICJ was of the opinion that forceful action against the government would change the nature of the military intervention from peacekeeping to peace enforcement.[97] Although the peace process leads to a government born out of elections supervised and legitimated by the UN according to the peace agreement, the peace operation is then committed to supporting that government even though it might either be ineffective or become corrupt or unrepresentative; moreover, peace is seen as being achievable through force as opposed to ongoing peaceful dispute settlement efforts to ensure that the peace agreement is implemented in a sustainable and representative way.

11.7 CONCLUSION: A (RE)TURN TO IMPARTIALITY?

In its role as a key actor in peaceful settlement of disputes, the Security Council has moved a long way from the premises underlying Chapter VI, namely that it should be an impartial third party objectively utilising the principles of international law to recommend peaceful dispute settlement

95 Christine Bell, *Peace Agreements and Human Rights* (Oxford: Oxford University Press, 2000), p. 1.

96 UNDKPO, 'UN peacekeeping operations', p. 33.

97 *Certain Expenses of the United Nations* (Advisory Opinion), p. 177.

and to help implement peace agreements. Some of its practices evidenced such an understanding of its powers, both in identifying disputes or situations that should be dealt with under Chapter VI and in extending its practice on inter-State dispute settlement to situations of decolonisation. The Council demonstrated that it could act as an impartial third party, treating disputants equally, promoting settlement based on international law, supported, where possible, by traditional and wholly impartial peacekeeping forces.

However, impartiality can only be assured if any member of the Security Council, including a permanent member who is a party to a dispute, respects its obligation to abstain from voting against a Chapter VI proposal. This obligation should be triggered: if a dispute and the disputants have been identified by the parties or the Security Council under Article 33; or if an investigation commissioned by the Security Council under Article 34 identifies a dispute and the disputants; or if the Secretary-General identifies a dispute and the disputants using implied fact-finding powers under Article 99. In order to prevent a permanent member from blocking any of the above steps at an early stage, the Security Council needs to develop the provisions of Chapter VI to ensure that an investigation under Article 34 should be the norm, and that the investigation's findings regarding the dispute and the disputants will trigger the obligation to abstain. The Covenant of the League of Nations is illuminating in this regard.

If a permanent member is identified as a party to a dispute but persists in exercising its veto to block Chapter VI Resolutions, then, as in the League system, its vote should be ignored because the veto is being exercised unconstitutionally.[98] This would amount to developing an understanding of the veto found in the advisory opinion of the ICJ in 1948, when it made it clear that there were definite Charter limitations upon its exercise in the case of membership applications under Article 4 of the Charter; otherwise, this 'would lead to conferring upon Members an indefinite and practically unlimited power of discretion'.[99] The same argument must apply to the issue of abstention under Chapter VI proposals where replacing the obligation to abstain under Article 27(3) with a practice of voluntary abstention has conferred on permanent members such an 'unlimited power of discretion'. The implementation of the obligation to abstain contained in Article 27(3) would not necessarily address the problem of a permanent member exercising its veto to protect a client State, which is a party to a dispute, but it would wrest the

[98] Kelsen, *Law of the UN*, p. 264.

[99] *Conditions of Admission of a State to Membership in the United Nations* (Advisory Opinion) [1948] ICJ Rep. 57 at p. 63.

current complete control of the Council's agenda away from each permanent member. Chapter VI Resolutions would be possible in a dispute where, for example, the forces of a permanent member were involved given that it must be seen as a 'party' in those circumstances.

A law-making resolution along the lines of the Assembly's Declaration of Friendly Relations of 1970 needs to be adopted by the General Assembly establishing a normative framework for the peaceful settlement of intra-State disputes and situations. This declaration could contain the principles of international law and justice upon which peaceful dispute settlement is to be achieved involving the normative development of 'peace' and 'security' to reflect the sub-norms of international law, including territorial integrity, political independence, self-determination, and human rights (core civil-political and socio-economic rights) with positive commitments to gender and racial equality. This should be combined with a clear recognition that all the internal parties to the dispute or conflict have an equal right of participation in the peace process, subject to certain qualifying criteria based on a combination of control and willingness to respect the rule of law, including accountability for past abuses.

The creation of a peacekeeping force to assist the parties to implement any peace agreement should be premised on the basis of the consent of all the parties and implemented impartially between the parties, rather than the current trend towards impartiality in the implementation of the mandate and restricting consent to the government, no matter if interim, ineffectual, or corrupt. Peacekeeping forces cannot impose peace. Peacekeepers' use of force should again be restricted to self-defence, including the defence of unarmed civilians. This would require the re-evaluation and resetting of the principles of peacekeeping. It would amount to a rediscovery of the origins of peacekeeping not only in Chapter VI but also, more broadly, in the fundamental idea of the UN as an impartial third party operating within the framework of the Charter and the broader international legal order to help achieve peaceful settlement of disputes based on international law and justice.

12

International Criminal Law and the Peaceful Settlement of International Disputes

Grand Aspirations and Minimal Impact

JAMES MEHIGAN

12.1 INTRODUCTION

The establishment of a permanent international criminal court in 1998 to try serious international crimes was a great achievement for those hoping to end impunity for the greatest atrocities. The International Criminal Court (ICC) now sits at the top of the complex pyramid of national, international, and 'hybrid' courts that try those accused of violating international criminal law (ICL). It can no longer be guaranteed that those in positions of political or military power can commit atrocity crimes with impunity. As a result of this long development of laws and processes, there are many commentators who see ICL as a mechanism for the resolution of international disputes because it, inter alia, aids post-conflict reconciliation, records history, enables fact-finding, and engenders a sense of justice for victims.[1] Such claims are appealing, but they are not generally backed by evidence of impact. This chapter asks if ICL is really a mechanism for resolving international disputes. It makes three points about ICL and its relationship with the settlement of 'international disputes'.

The first is that we need to understand ICL as a form of retributive justice used as part of a broader collection of tools applied by the international community to international disputes involving allegations of international crimes. In ICL, retribution is uppermost in the legal framework and professional thinking of those involved. Any sense of reconciliation, reintegration, or reconstruction is a secondary outcome, almost a side-effect of the retributive process. This is so because of the way the major tribunals of ICL were

[1] See, e.g., Kenneth Anderson, 'The rise of international criminal law: Intended and unintended consequences' (2009) 20 EJIL 331–58; Bartlomiej Krzan, 'International Criminal Court facing the peace vs. justice dilemma' (2016) 2 Intern Comp Jurisprud 81–88; and Frédéric Mégret, 'International criminal justice as a peace project' (2018) 29 EJIL 835–58.

established and because of the professional cultures of those working within the tribunals.

The second important consideration is that conflicts differ hugely from each other. This makes it difficult to generalise about how ICL can contribute to the settlement of international disputes. The nature of conflict has changed significantly in the decades since Nuremberg. Most international crimes now take place in the context of disputes not between States themselves but between non-State armed groups (albeit often those who may be acting as proxies for States).[2] These disputes are not necessarily 'international disputes' in the sense of being based on a conflict between nation States with clashing national interests. They may be international in character, but played out by interests free from or oppositional to the State in which they operate. Furthermore, some of the core crimes of ICL can be committed entirely domestically, without any infringement on the interests of another State. This variety in the ways in which conflicts are conducted makes it extremely difficult to say conclusively what impact ICL has on the eventual settlement of the conflict. It is even harder to draw conclusions that would be generalisable on a greater scale.

Thirdly, ICL draws upon the principles of both international and criminal law. Its overall aim is to contribute to international peace and security, and it seeks to do this using the theories of punishment that are well developed in criminal courts on the national level. These factors make it clear that ICL can, almost by definition and because of its peculiar nature, only have a limited impact on the resolution of international disputes. Even this limited impact should not be overstated.

To understand this lack of impact, this chapter looks, first, at the international and criminal law aims of ICL. These are set out in the founding documents of ICL's various international and hybrid tribunals. Not every tribunal is established for ostensibly identical reasons, but the aims are principally the promotion of international security and world peace, and the punishment of crimes whose seriousness has piqued the conscience of the international community.

In Section 12.3, these aims are compared to the impact of ICL in practice. Just how effective is it at achieving these aims? The part looks at three areas which may help assess if ICL is effective in its own terms: whether there is any evidence that ICL deters international crimes; what we can learn from the

2 Thomas S. Szayna et al., 'What are the trends in armed conflicts, and what do they mean for US defense policy?' *RAND Corporation*, 2017, www.rand.org/content/dam/rand/pubs/research_reports/RR1900/RR1904/RAND_RR1904.pdf (accessed 13 September 2022).

criminalisation of aggression; and what the experience in the Former Yugoslavia can tell us about the role of ICL in post-conflict reconciliation. In all three areas, the evidence does not support more than a minimal impact from ICL.

In my opinion, ICL must be seen for what it is in practice: a criminal law process. By taking this pragmatic approach to ICL, it is easier to avoid the grand and unrealistic claims made for it and take it for what it is: a mechanism for retributive justice. ICL can only ever make a minimal contribution to the resolution of disputes between nation States because its purpose is something else: punishment of criminal offenders. If this causes any resolution of an international dispute, it is almost certainly a by-product of the criminal process rather than an example of an effective international criminal justice system.

12.2 WHAT DOES ICL SET OUT TO DO?

As ICL is a body of law that combines international and criminal legal principles, it is fair to say that the aims of ICL can be found to have both criminal and international law aspects. The criminal law aspect has aims which would be recognisable to a domestic criminal lawyer, such as retribution, deterrence, rehabilitation, incapacitation, reparation, and the application of procedural justice. The international aspect also brings with it further aims such as post-conflict reconciliation, recording history, fact-finding, and engendering a sense of justice for victims. Some of these aims can be found in the charters or judgments of the tribunals. Others derive from the statements of academic commentators and civil society groups. In any event, these aims are disparate and potentially contradictory. It is worth unpicking them in a little detail to try to understand which of these aims helps with the peaceful settlement of international disputes.

International as well as criminal law aims can be seen, for instance, in the Preamble to the Rome Statute,[3] in the Security Council Resolutions that established the *ad hoc* criminal tribunals for Rwanda and the Former Yugoslavia, as well as in the statutes of hybrid tribunals such as the Special Court for Sierra Leone (SCSL) and the Extraordinary Chambers in the Courts of Cambodia (ECCC).[4]

[3] Rome Statute of the International Criminal Court, Rome, 17 July 1998, in force 1 July 2002, 2187 UNTS 3, Preamble.

[4] Gerhard Werle and Aziz Epik, 'Theories of punishment and sentencing decisions of the International Criminal Court', in Florian Jessberger and Julia Geneuss (eds.), *Why Punish Perpetrators of Mass Atrocities?* (Cambridge: Cambridge University Press, 2020), pp. 323–52.

The criminal law aims are clearly set out in the documents that led to the foundation of the Nuremberg and Tokyo Tribunals (and can be seen in the founding documents of the later tribunals). The Potsdam Declaration which defined terms for Japanese surrender and led to the establishment of the Tokyo Tribunal made it clear: 'We do not intend that the Japanese shall be enslaved as a race or destroyed as a nation, but stern justice shall be meted out to all war criminals, including those who have visited cruelties upon our prisoners.'[5] Similarly, the first preambular paragraph of the London Agreement for the establishment of the Nuremberg Tribunal also refers to the Allied 'intention that war criminals shall be brought to justice'.[6] Both of these declarations of intent demonstrate a retributive aim consistent with notions of criminal justice and individual punishment. They set out the tribunals' aims to punish offenders, but do not make any explicit claims around other criminal law aims such as deterrence, denunciation, or special prevention.

While such criminal law aims continued to be expressed in later instruments establishing international criminal courts and tribunals, these were accompanied by a series of international aims coalescing around broad aspirations about peace, security, and reconciliation.

The first of the *ad hoc* tribunals – the International Criminal Tribunal for the Former Yugoslavia (ICTY) – is the creation of a Security Council Resolution.[7] The Resolution makes it clear that the Tribunal is being established in the hope that it will end the criminality arising out of the conflict. The Tribunal was expected to do this by imposing criminal sanction, and this can be seen in the Resolution's opening paragraphs:

> Determining that this situation constitutes a threat to international peace and security,
>
> Determined to put an end to such crimes and to take effective measures to bring to justice the persons who are responsible for them,
>
> Convinced that in the particular circumstances of the former Yugoslavia the establishment of an international tribunal would enable this aim to be achieved and would contribute to the restoration and maintenance of peace.[8]

A notable thing from the quoted paragraph is its similarity to a paragraph in the Security Council Resolution establishing the International Criminal Tribunal

[5] Proclamation Defining Terms for Japanese Surrender, Potsdam, 26 July 1945 (Department of State Bulletin, XIII(318), 29 July 1945), para. 10.

[6] Agreement for the Prosecution and Punishment of the Major War Criminals of the European Axis, London, 8 August 1945, in force 8 August 1945, 82 UNTS 280, Preamble.

[7] UNSC Res 808 (22 February 1993) UN Doc. S/RES/808 (1993).

[8] Ibid.

for Rwanda (ICTR).[9] As is well known, both Resolutions state that their respective situations amount to 'a threat to international peace and security', as the latter is necessary to justify intervention under Chapter VII of the UN Charter. A 'simple' commission of a mass atrocity is not enough to justify the Security Council to intervene in line with its role as set out in the UN Charter.

It is also of note that the Security Council is 'convinced' that penal interventions will contribute to the aims of ending such crimes, bringing to justice those responsible for them, and 'contribut[ing] to the restoration and maintenance of peace'.[10] In the case of the ICTR, the Security Council goes further, saying that it believes an international tribunal can contribute to not only ending violations but also ensuring effective redress and contributing to 'national reconciliation and the restoration and maintenance of peace'.[11] The text of the Resolution reveals the broad aspirations of its authors:

> Determining that this situation continues to constitute a threat to international peace and security,
>
> Determined to put an end to such crimes and to take effective measures to bring to justice the persons who are responsible for them,
>
> Convinced that in the particular circumstances of Rwanda, the prosecution of persons responsible for serious violations of international humanitarian law would enable this aim to be achieved and would contribute to the process of national reconciliation and to the restoration and maintenance of peace,
>
> Believing that the establishment of an international tribunal for the prosecution of persons responsible for genocide and the other above-mentioned violations of international humanitarian law will contribute to ensuring that such violations are halted and effectively redressed.[12]

These broad aspirations for the ICTR were largely repeated in the Security Council's Resolution that led to the treaty establishing the SCSL. Although it formulates the aims of the SCSL in slightly different language, those aims again coalesce around punishing those responsible, contributing to national reconciliation, and the maintenance of peace:

> Reaffirming the importance of compliance with international humanitarian law, and reaffirming further that persons who commit or authorize serious violations of international humanitarian law are individually responsible and accountable for those violations and that the international community will

9 UNSC Res 955 (8 November 1994) UN Doc. S/RES/955 (1994).
10 UNSC Res 808 (1993).
11 UNSC Res 955 (1994).
12 Ibid.

> exert every effort to bring those responsible to justice in accordance with international standards of justice, fairness and due process of law,
>
> Recognizing that, in the particular circumstances of Sierra Leone, a credible system of justice and accountability for the very serious crimes committed there would end impunity and would contribute to the process of national reconciliation and to the restoration and maintenance of peace …
>
> Recognizing further the desire of the Government of Sierra Leone for assistance from the United Nations in establishing a strong and credible court that will meet the objectives of bringing justice and ensuring lasting peace,[13]

These aims (reconciliation, world peace, and the pursuit of criminal or retributive justice, broadly speaking) are again present in the Resolution which requested the UN Secretary General to conclude an agreement with Cambodia to establish a hybrid tribunal within the courts of Cambodia (the ECCC). It contains a language that makes a causal link between prosecuting individuals, national reconciliation, and stability of the State:

> Recognizing the legitimate concern of the Government and the people of Cambodia in the pursuit of justice and national reconciliation, stability, peace and security,
>
> Recognizing also that the accountability of individual perpetrators of grave human rights violations is one of the central elements of any effective remedy for victims of human rights violations and a key factor in ensuring a fair and equitable justice system and, ultimately, reconciliation and stability within a State.[14]

Perhaps, then, these aims of ICL are most succinctly put in the Preamble of the Rome Statute which established the ICC. The Preamble sets out that the ICC (and, by extension, ICL) aspires to protect the 'peace, security and well-being of the world'.[15] World peace and international security are the core values underpinning the United Nations itself and can be found in the UN Charter.[16] The inclusion of the concept of 'well-being of the world' in the Preamble appears to add little to these already developed concepts.[17] It transpires that the founding

[13] UNSC Res 1315 (14 August 2000) UN Doc. S/RES/1315 (2000).

[14] UNGA, 'Resolution adopted by the General Assembly [on the report of the Third Committee (A/57/556/Add.2 and Corr.1-3)] Khmer Rouge trials' (27 February 2003) UN Doc. A/RES/57/228.

[15] Rome Statute, Preamble.

[16] See, e.g., Charter of the United Nations, San Francisco, 26 June 1945, in force 24 October 1945, 1 UNTS 16, Art 1(1).

[17] Gerhard Werle and Florian Jessberger, *Principles of International Criminal Law*, 4th ed. (Oxford: Oxford University Press, 2020), p. 38.

documents of these tribunals indicate that the international community think that they can play a role in establishing peace and security. In other words, the instruments that have been deployed in the last half century to implement ICL have been given a function beyond just securing justice by punishing individuals; they are also to secure peace and security among States.

The historical record of the use of this peace-making aspiration begs the question whether this peace-making function is real, or whether it was simply a rhetorical justification to enable the setting up of the tribunals. It is one thing for the sponsors of the Security Council Resolutions to say that a breach of peace was necessary to set up the tribunals, but how realistic was the expectation that a criminal tribunal would help resolve that breach?

It is interesting that the ICTY's first judgment – the *Tadic* jurisdiction decision in October 1995 – considered whether the establishment of an international tribunal was an appropriate measure under Chapter VII of the UN Charter. The Tribunal has found that it had been lawfully established and dismissed the defendant's argument as follows:

> The third argument is directed against the discretionary power of the Security Council in evaluating the appropriateness of the chosen measure and its effectiveness in achieving its objective, the restoration of peace.
>
> Article 39 leaves the choice of means and their evaluation to the Security Council, which enjoys wide discretionary powers in this regard; and it could not have been otherwise, as such a choice involves political evaluation of highly complex and dynamic situations.
>
> It would be a total misconception of what are the criteria of legality and validity in law to test the legality of such measures ex post facto by their success or failure to achieve their ends (in the present case, the restoration of peace in the former Yugoslavia, in quest of which the establishment of the International Tribunal is but one of many measures adopted by the Security Council).[18]

The ICTY itself is implicitly accepting that it can conduct its processes of retributive justice, but it cannot know with certainty whether there is any positive impact on the resolution of the international dispute at the heart of the conflict. Nor can it know if this is its task, as a criminal court, to begin with. That question is too complex for a criminal court, and one best answered on a political or diplomatic level.

The aims of establishing and maintaining peace in the context of internationalised atrocities require in some way the settlement of disputes at the

[18] *Prosecutor* v. *Tadic* (Decision on Interlocutory Motion on Jurisdiction) ICTY-94-1 (2 October 1995) at paras 39–40.

heart of those conflicts from which the atrocities arose. These disputes may not be, or indeed are unlikely to be, settled to the satisfaction of all parties, but if there is peace at the end of conflict, then the dispute may be said to be, in some way, 'settled'.

At its simplest, this settlement may be what Galtung calls 'negative peace' – that is to say, the absence of war.[19] However, a more sophisticated form of peace, sometimes referred to as 'positive peace',[20] in which parties to the conflict become increasingly reconciled, can also be seen to be an aspiration of ICL. This deeper form of settlement of the underlying dispute is clearly an aspiration set out in the founding documents of the ICTR, the SCSL, and the ECCC. It is also often referred to by commentators on ICL,[21] and it is this deeper form of 'positive peace' that is referred to in the Rome Statute's Preamble. Whether the criminal law process is the best way to achieve that peace raises the questions of how ICL's criminal law aims are operationalised.

Once an international criminal tribunal (whether *ad hoc*, hybrid, or permanent) is established, its tools of the trade become that of a criminal court. A criminal court can indict, try, convict, and sentence those accused of crimes within its jurisdiction. It is by using these processes that an international criminal tribunal seeks to advance those aims of peace, security, and reconciliation. There are two steps to this process that are considered here: the trial process (and its procedural fairness), and the sentencing after conviction.

The first of these steps is relevant to this chapter because in some ways the credibility of the entire ICL project rests on the perceived fairness of the investigations and hearings themselves. If such hearings are considered unfair or loaded in favour of conviction, the entire ICL enterprise is undermined. Procedural fairness is therefore an essential component of the work of the tribunals. The process therefore has a significant emphasis on testing the evidence presented by the prosecutor.

One disadvantage of this emphasis is that there is limited space for victim participation in the process. The ICC has tried to ameliorate this by giving victims the right to representation.[22] However, it is fair to say that their precise role in the Court's procedures remains unclear.[23]

19 Johan Galtung, *Theories of Peace: A Synthetic Approach to Peace Thinking* (Oslo: International Peace Research Institute, 1967).

20 Patricia M. Shields, 'Limits of negative peace, faces of positive peace' (2017) 47 Parameters 5–12.

21 E.g., Janine Clark, 'From negative to positive peace: The case of Bosnia and Hercegovina' (2009) 8 J Hum Rights 360–84; Mirjan Damaška, 'What is the point of international criminal justice?' (2008) 83 Chi-Kent L Rev 329–65.

22 ICC, *Rules of Procedure and Evidence*, 2nd ed. (The Hague: ICC, 2013), Rules 89–93.

23 Rianne Letschert, 'International criminal proceedings: An adequate tool for victims' justice?', in Kinga Tibori-Szabó and Megan Hirst (eds.), *Victim Participation in International Criminal Justice: Practitioners' Guide* (The Hague: TMC Asser Press, 2017), pp. 467–72.

Moreover, to strengthen its perceived fairness, the criminal process should in principle have a strong set of protections for defendants. They should be considered innocent until proven guilty.[24] The burden of proof should be on the prosecutor to prove to the criminal standard ('beyond a reasonable doubt') that the defendants committed the international crimes which they are accused of.[25] The advantages of this high standard are at least two-fold. The first is that once these procedural hurdles are properly passed, the international community and those affected by the offence can be reasonably sure that the conviction is safe.

The second great advantage of this process is that it should, if properly applied, reduce the risk of miscarriages of justice. This point is almost never considered in discussions about ICL. Very few, if any, civil society reports critique the procedural issues which may increase the risk of miscarriages of justice in ICL. However, these risks are very real. The closeness of the prosecutor's office and the judiciary in international criminal justice has been noted as far back as the Nuremberg Tribunal.[26] Disclosure, the heart of a fair trial process, is often critiqued by defence lawyers as unsatisfactory.[27] Similarly, legal aid for defendants (and victims) continues to be unsatisfactory and the basis of a potential imbalance in the 'equality of arms' upon which the common law fair trial relies.[28]

Notwithstanding these criticisms, the trial process and its fundamental fairness is at the heart of the purpose and values of ICL. This form of procedural justice is central to the legitimacy of international criminal justice. However voluminous the evidence or heinous the crime may be, the legitimacy of the conviction comes from the independence, thoroughness, and fairness of the trial process. It is upon this foundation that the retributive justice that ICL contributes to the international legal order can be built.

24 Rome Statute, Art 66(1).

25 Ibid., Art 66(2).

26 Geoffrey Robertson, *Crimes against Humanity: The Struggle for Global Justice* (London: Allen Lane, 1999).

27 Michael G. Karnavas, 'Gathering evidence in international criminal trials: The view of the defence lawyer', in Michael Bohlander (ed.), *International Criminal Justice: A Critical Analysis of Institutions and Procedures* (Berlin: Cameron May, 2007), pp. 75–152; Rupert Skilbeck, 'Ensuring effective defence in hybrid tribunals' (2010) Rev Quebec Droit Int'l 91–108.

28 See, e.g., IBA, 'IBA comments on "Concept paper: Review of the International Criminal Court legal aid system"', 9 June 2017, www.ibanet.org/document?id=IBA-LAS-Comments-Paper-9-June-2017 (accessed 15 September 2022); ICCBA, 'ICCBA response on the legal aid issue', 24 April 2017, www.coalitionfortheicc.org/sites/default/files/cicc_documents/1._concept_paper_-_comments_-_final_1-id-637d0e55-77e4-43be-d52a-53dfe11a3e49.pdf (accessed 15 September 2022).

Once there is a foundation of fair procedures, it is possible to justify sentencing offenders in line with the traditional aims of criminal justice. This can be seen in the sentencing judgments at the tribunals. As the tribunals have gone about their work, they have made statements in their judgements about how they view the traditional aims of criminal punishment when played out in an international context. This is particularly true of the ICTY which has mostly stated that the preferred philosophies of punishment in that tribunal are retribution and deterrence with some reference to incapacitation, rehabilitation, and other purposes.[29] Although the ICC's jurisprudence on sentencing is still in its infancy, the theories of punishment that appear to be most prevalent are retribution, deterrence, rehabilitation, and denunciation.[30] These are worth considering briefly here before their contribution to international dispute settlement can be discussed.

Retribution is perhaps the easiest theory to understand and see in operation. It is in essence the infliction of pain upon somebody who is guilty of an offence, either as an act of vengeance or as a form of 'just deserts'. At the end of a trial that ends in conviction, experienced judges are able to measure the harm and culpability of the offending party before applying a proportionate prison sentence. Criminal courts are reasonably good at this balancing exercise, and the international tribunals have developed a body of sentencing law that reflects the experience of imposing punishment for international crimes.[31]

The second theory of punishment that is relied upon by the tribunals (see, e.g., the jurisprudence of the ICTY and the ICC)[32] is deterrence. This is the idea that by imposing a penalty on an offender, they will be deterred from offending again in the future. Furthermore, advocates of deterrence hope that the imposition of criminal penalties will create an environment in which those who have the capacity to breach ICL would decide not to, on the basis that they did not wish to be punished.

Whereas retribution relates to the crime itself and is therefore considered a 'deontological' form of punishment, imposing punishment based on deterrence need not be related to the harms of the crime itself, nor the culpability of the individual offender. To that extent, it is more of a 'teleological' theory of punishment. The overarching purpose of deterring future breaches of ICL justifies the sentence regardless of the harm. In principle, deterrent sentencing

29 Robert Cryer, Håkan Friman, Darryl Robinson, and Elizabeth Wilmshurst, *An Introduction to International Criminal Law and Procedure* (Cambridge: Cambridge University Press), pp. 23–24.

30 Werle and Epik, 'Theories of punishment', p. 352, refer to denunciation as 'positive general prevention'.

31 See ibid. for a discussion of the developing sentencing jurisprudence at the ICC.

32 Ibid.

could involve very harsh sentences for even very minor breaches of ICL. The international criminal tribunals have (rightly, it is submitted) strayed away from this draconian approach to deterrence. They have maintained an approach that places proportionality at the centre of their sentencing.[33] The tribunals aspire to deterring international crime, but the evidence, as discussed in the next section, does not demonstrate a great deterrent effect from ICL sentencing.

Alongside deterrence, crime can also be prevented through punishment in processes that theorists have described as internalising values rather than fear of punishment.[34] This process of denunciation (also known as positive general prevention,[35] or the communicative, educative, or expressive theory of punishment[36]) is thought to work by imposing criminal penalties in order to define and reinforce social norms, or international norms in the case of ICL. This educative function was expressly referred to in the *Kordić and Čerkez* decision of the ICTY, where the Court stated that sentencing conveyed the messaging that international humanitarian law rules must be obeyed in all circumstances.[37] Whether or not the statement is received, the process of denunciation is important for the statement-maker, in this case the international community through its criminal tribunals.

Two other theories of punishment, which are occasionally raised in ICL, are incapacitation and rehabilitation.[38] Incapacitation is a controversial justification for punishment. This is because it involves detaining somebody for what they might do rather than what they have done. Cryer et al. point to the concept's use at the Tokyo Tribunal and in the context of refuting the value of amnesties.[39] It is a sentencing philosophy rarely used to justify sentences in ICL. Indeed, in the case of *Krnojelac*,[40] the ICTY Trial Chamber held that the incapacitation of the dangerous was of little significance in the context of the ICTY. Rehabilitation, on the other hand, does appear in the jurisprudence of the tribunals in relation to lower-level offenders. A good example of this is

33 Joseph W. Doherty and Richard H. Steinberg, 'Punishment and policy in international criminal sentencing: an empirical study' (2016) 110 AJIL 49–81.

34 Werle and Epik, 'Theories of punishment', pp. 329–30.

35 Elena Maculan and Alicia Gil, 'The rationale and purposes of criminal law and punishment in transitional contexts' (2020) 40 OJLS 132–57 at 147–51.

36 Richard S. Frase, 'Punishment purposes' (2005) 58 Stan L Rev 67–83.

37 *Prosecutor* v. *Kordić and Čerkez* (Judgment) ICTY-95-14/2-A (17 December 2004) at para. 1080-1.

38 Karim A. A. Khan and Rodney Dixon, *Archbold: International Criminal Courts. Practice, Procedure and Evidence* (London: Sweet and Maxwell, 2009), para. 18.42.

39 Cryer et al., *An Introduction to International Criminal Law and Procedure*, p. 28.

40 *Prosecutor* v. *Milorad Krnojelac* (Judgment) ICTY-97-25-T (15 March 2002) at para. 505.

the *Erdemović* case at the ICTY. In that case, the Tribunal decided that the relatively young offender, who had participated in the Srebrenica massacre under duress, could potentially rehabilitate and should be given a second chance.[41] Given the seriousness of the offences that come before the tribunals and their mandate to try those who are most involved in them, cases like this are unusual in ICL.

Although the Rome Statute does not specifically provide for these foregoing theories of punishment, it does expressly provide for reparatory justice.[42] The Statute establishes a Trust Fund for Victims,[43] which works with the Court to provide reparations for the crimes that come within its jurisdiction. This was an innovative development for the ICC.[44] If it were properly supported financially and politically, it may be something that could conceivably make a genuine contribution to the establishment of stable peace and reconciliation in countries facing post-conflict transition.

All these aims need to be carefully considered when asking what ICL can contribute to the peaceful settlement of international disputes. Criminal courts are outstanding at retribution. However, criminal punishment, particularly when it takes the form of imprisonment, struggles to justify itself empirically against the aspirations of deterrence and rehabilitation. This extensive list of legal aims, both international and criminal in nature, begs the question, 'how effective is ICL at achieving its objectives?' If it is ineffective at meeting certain criminal aims, does that undermine its capacity to contribute to the settlement of international disputes and further the aims of peace and security? It is to this question of effectiveness that the chapter now turns.

12.3 MEASURING ICL AGAINST ITS STATED AIMS

Although criminal courts are good at retribution, punishing individuals in the abstract is unlikely to impact the settlement of international disputes unless it is in some way connected to a teleological purpose of sentencing.

As discussed above, incapacitation and rehabilitation are rarely used. Reparatory justice at the ICC (in the form of the Trust Fund for Victims) is

[41] *Prosecutor* v. *Dražen Erdemović* (Sentencing Judgment) ICTY-96-22-T*bis* (5 March 1998) at para. 16.

[42] Rome Statute, Art 75.

[43] Ibid., Art 79.

[44] Anne Dutton and Fionnuala Ní Aoláin, 'Between reparations and repair: Assessing the work of the ICC Trust Fund for Victims under its assistance mandate' (2019) 19 Chic J Int Law 490–547.

in its infancy and so chronically underfunded as to make it a minor factor in ICL's impact on international disputes. This means that the main theories of punishment that go towards encouraging peaceful settlement of international disputes are deterrence and denunciation.

This part of the chapter looks at the evidence in support of deterrence in the international context. In so doing, the section also briefly looks at the crime of aggression. This supreme international crime goes to the heart of the international community's values of international peace and security. It is argued that, in its current formulation, the crime of aggression may have a denunciatory effect, but it is unlikely to be a deterrent to those who wish to prosecute an aggressive war. Finally, this part goes on to draw upon the experiences from the Former Yugoslavia to get a sense of how much ICL can contribute to post-conflict reconciliation. It is possible that even if ICL is successful in its criminal law aims, and this is not a given, it can simultaneously fail at attaining its international law aims. In the Former Yugoslavia, it is clear that the ICTY has individualised guilt well, but the evidence suggests that the purported reconciliatory benefits of ICL have not materialised. These benefits are much more intricately linked with the settlement of international disputes than the benefits from criminal punishments such as deterrence or denunciation.

12.3.1 *Deterrence*

It is easy to be sceptical about the deterrent capacity of criminal justice. Many Western democracies have political systems which generate punitive policies to achieve so-called law-and-order or crime reduction policy goals. The evidence to support deterrence as a benefit of such approaches is scant. In a review of the literature, Wright has found some support for the contention that certainty of punishment may deter crime, but that severity of punishment had little or no impact.[45] Such an effect is likely to be even weaker when applied in an international context.[46] Only a small number of people are ever prosecuted for international crimes. While sentences may be considered severe at times, punishment is by no means certain. International criminal trials are relatively rare and very slow. The separation between the imposition of punishment and the criminal act is often both temporally and geographically enormous. This

[45] Valerie Wright, 'Deterrence in criminal justice: Evaluating certainty vs. severity of punishment', *Sentencing Project*, 19 November 2010, www.sentencingproject.org/wp-content/uploads/2016/01/Deterrence-in-Criminal-Justice.pdf (accessed 15 September 2022).

[46] Marieke de Hoon, 'The future of the International Criminal Court: On critique, legalism and strengthening the ICC's legitimacy' (2017) 17 Int Crim Law Rev 591–614 at 601.

contributes to undermining the deterrent effect of ICL on those potential perpetrators for whom The Hague is, at most, a distant abstraction.

Notwithstanding this dearth of evidence in support of the principle of deterrence, it has long had a phenomenal political and 'common sense' attraction to it.[47] In the field of international criminal justice, mirroring the view of scholars of domestic criminal justice,[48] there is significant scepticism as to whether ICL has any deterrent value at all.[49]

A decision-maker considering whether to commit an atrocity crime in 2023 could have that decision-making process come under scrutiny in The Hague in a way which was inconceivable when the Berlin Wall collapsed. That risk, of course, is reduced if the decision-maker is a functionary of a State that is not a State party to the Rome Statute and has a veto on Security Council references, such as Russia, China, or the US. It may also be similarly reduced for functionaries of their client States, such as Syria, Myanmar, or Israel.

Yet, notwithstanding this developed legal architecture, there is a notable absence of evidence that there is a deterrent value to ICL.[50] If deterrence is to have any meaning, it must be based on the idea of a rational actor making cost–benefit analyses. These analyses may change significantly due to the immediate pressures of conflict. Balancing the perceived costs of not committing an international crime versus the costs of committing it, including perhaps the costs of facing justice at a future date, a political or military operative may decide that maintaining their position of power (or other military goal) far outweighs the risk of prosecution.

Buitelaar, taking a criminological approach to the question, reaches similar conclusions.[51] Although his finding is that the possibilities for a deterrent effect from the existence of the ICC are slim, he does offer a more hopeful perspective that the ICC can 'contribute to the prevention of atrocities by focusing on the long-term, transformative process that can lead to the internalization of norms and the creation of self-regulating communities'.[52] Buitelaar

[47] John Pratt, *Penal Populism* (New York: Routledge, 2007).

[48] Stanley Cohen, 'The revenge of the null hypothesis: Evaluating crime control policies' (1997) 8 Crit Criminol 21–25; Karol Lucken, 'Still asking "what works": A punishment question for the ages or an aging punishment question?' (2021) 1 Histories 53–68.

[49] Dawn L. Rothe and Victoria E. Collins, 'The International Criminal Court: A pipe dream to end impunity?' (2013) 13 Int Crim Law Rev 191–210; Tom Buitelaar, 'The ICC and the prevention of atrocities: Criminological perspectives', *Hague Institute of Global Justice*, April 2015, https://thehagueinstituteforglobaljustice.org/wp-content/uploads/2015/10/The_ICC_and_The_Prevention_of_Atrocities.pdf (accessed 15 September 2022).

[50] Rothe and Collins, 'The ICC'.

[51] Buitelaar, 'ICC and the prevention of atrocities'.

[52] Ibid., p. 14.

is therefore pinning his deterrent hopes not on the specific deterrence of changing the calculus of a rational actor considering whether to commit a core crime but on the educational value of denouncing an atrocity crime.

That aspiration, one which recognises international criminal justice as part of a larger, lengthy, and committed process of peace-building, is perhaps more realistic than the aims of specifically deterring those in a position to commit atrocity crimes.

To draw again from the analogy with municipal criminal justice, it is clear that the problems that cause crimes in a municipal setting are rarely, if ever, fixed by criminal justice responses alone. So, why would we expect this type of approach to work for international crimes? The answer is probably that we should not expect ICL alone to fix the problems of atrocity crimes. We should accept ICL for what it is – a system of retributive (and perhaps reparatory) justice – and place it within a wider set of measures in developing post-conflict reconciliation.

12.3.2 *Denunciation of Aggression*

One criminal aim which may be a by-product of the efforts to deter international crimes is the process of denunciating particular acts by marking them out as criminal. This section looks at how that may operate in relation to the crime of aggression. The crime of aggression, perhaps more than any other act prohibited by ICL, is the quintessential example of a crime inextricably linked with an international dispute. Its definition requires that the State for which the defendant works has itself committed an internationally wrongful act.[53] It should be an area in which ICL makes a difference to international dispute settlement because the prosecution of the crime subjects that dispute to a form of adjudication. Yet, as will be discussed below, the circumscribed definition and jurisdictional requirements of the crime of aggression create many challenges. They make aggression more a definition of behaviour that the international community wishes to denounce than a crime for which we can expect a deterrent effect arising out of trial and punishment.

The concept of aggression itself was envisaged in the UN Charter[54] and formed part of the indictments at the Nuremberg and Tokyo Tribunals. However, it took longer to become an indictable offence before the major

[53] Dapo Akande and Antonios Tzanakopoulos, 'The crime of aggression in the ICC and State responsibility' (2017) 58 Harv Int'l LJ 33–36.

[54] Art 39 of the UN Charter directs the Security Council to 'determine the existence of any threat to peace, breach of the peace, or act of aggression' and to decide what measures are appropriate to ensure the restoration of international peace and security.

international criminal tribunals after the Cold War. The UN General Assembly made an effort to define aggression in 1974.[55] This definition, building on the Charter, did not define individual criminal liability. Instead, the 1974 definition deals with the State act of aggression. Notwithstanding the existence of this definition, the drafting process for the Rome Statute failed to develop an agreeable definition for the crime of aggression, and this was put off until the first conference reviewing the Statute in Kampala in 2010.[56] It was at Kampala that the current definition was established.[57] Yet, even at this point, it took a further seven years to gather the requisite thirty ratifications required for the crime of aggression to finally become the fourth 'core crime' of the ICC[58] on 15 December 2017.

Legislating against aggression includes the criminalisation of certain acts of planning and preparation of a State's aggressive military action.[59] In theory, at least, a leader preparing to go to war could be prosecuted before the act of aggression took place, thus leading to the prevention of an aggressive act. This theoretical prospect of a prosecution before a war begins is highly unlikely to occur in practice. However, it is a possible way in which ICL could resolve a nascent international dispute.

Putting this theoretical contribution aside, the important point about the crime of aggression for ICL is that it goes to the act of warmongering, a source or cause of many great harms and disputes. For example, the prohibition on war crimes is the criminalisation of a specific conduct rather than the war itself. If war crimes are the criminalisation of breaches of *jus in bello*, the crime of aggression is the criminalisation of *jus ad bellum* breaches. Aggression is an overarching super-crime of the core crimes. As the Nuremberg Tribunal noted almost eight decades ago, aggression 'contains within itself the accumulated evil of the whole' and this makes it the 'supreme international crime'.[60]

55 UNGA, 'Definition of aggression' (14 December 1974) UN Doc. A/RES/3314(XXIX).

56 Dapo Akande and Antonios Tzanakopoulos, 'Treaty law and ICC jurisdiction over the crime of aggression' (2018) 29 EJIL 939–59.

57 Institute for International Peace and Security Law, *Handbook on the Ratification and Implementation of the Kampala Amendments on the Crime of Aggression to the Rome Statute of the ICC*, 3rd ed. (Cologne: Institute for International Peace and Security Law, 2019).

58 Coalition for the International Criminal Court, 'Historic activation of crime of aggression at International Criminal Court', 15 December 2017, www.coalitionfortheicc.org/news/20171215/historic-activation-jurisdiction-crime-aggression-international-criminal-court (accessed 16 September 2022).

59 Rome Statute, Art 8*bis*(1).

60 IMT, *The Trial of German Major War Criminals. Proceedings of the International Military Tribunal Sitting at Nuremberg, Germany, Part 22* (London: His Majesty's Stationery Office, 1946), Judgment of 1 October 1946 at 13, cited in Kevin Jon Heller, 'Who is afraid of the crime of aggression?' (2021) 19 JICJ 999–1016 at 1001.

The crime of aggression then, unlike the other core crimes, is a macro-level criminalisation of a decision by the leadership of a State to go to war. It should, if the tenets of criminal deterrence are operationally effective, serve to make such leaders think again before conducting an aggressive war. That deterrence should in principle mean that the 2017 criminalisation of aggression creates a statutory footing for punishing someone who disrupts the international peace, which is the very aspiration underpinning the UN Charter. On this reading, 15 December 2017 should have been a red-letter day for those interested in the settlement of international disputes. It should have marked the beginning of the end of military belligerence. The settlement of international disputes by force should be much reduced or eliminated by such methods being subject to criminal sanction. Leaders will now think twice before engaging in military aggression, and this risk of prosecution will have a deterrent effect, one might hope.

However, there is not much hope for a deterrent effect in relation to the crime of aggression. The two principal reasons for this are in the definition of and the jurisdiction over the crime of aggression. The definition, set out in Article 8*bis* of the Rome Statute, restricts the liability for the offence to leaders who 'control or direct' the aggression itself.[61] This is a more restrictive approach than found within ICL more generally and is a product of great compromises that were needed to achieve a definition that was sufficiently acceptable to become an amendment to the Statute. However, it is more restrictive than the standards adopted at Nuremberg. It excludes many who are influential on policy and decision-making and significantly reduces the number of people who could be found guilty of aggression.[62] International disputes involving aggression usually require significant work, from planning to operations, of many senior and middle-ranking functionaries. The restrictive definition of aggression leaves many such operatives outside the purview of criminal sanction. This, Heller argues, reduces the value of the provisions by casting the net far too narrowly and not catching aggressive conduct that is deserving of criminal sanction.

The restrictive definition is matched with a highly restrictive jurisdictional framework. The jurisdictional problems can be seen in Article 15*bis* and 15*ter* of the Statute. In short, with the exceptions of referrals from the Security Council, the crime of aggression can only be prosecuted when both the aggressor and victim States are State parties to the Statute *and* the aggression amendments.[63] It is no protection for a State with an aggressive neighbour to

61 Rome Statute, Art 8*bis*(1).

62 Kevin Jon Heller, 'Retreat from Nuremberg: The leadership requirement in the crime of aggression' (2007) 18 EJIL 477–97.

63 Heller, 'Who is afraid of the crime of aggression?'

ratify the amendment if their neighbour does not wish to do so. This is a much higher jurisdictional hurdle for prosecution than that imposed on the Statute's other three core crimes. Heller argues that the circumscribed definition and limited jurisdiction of the crime of aggression mean that it is almost certain never to be prosecuted and unlikely to alter the decision-making of any senior political or military leader with the capacity to breach it.[64]

The crime of aggression could be imagined to have made an impact on international dispute settlement. Perhaps more than any of the other core crimes, it could make clear that international disputes are to be settled peacefully, and a failure to do so will result in individual punishment. Yet, the peculiar jurisdictional arrangements and the relatively small number of signatories to the amendment mean that it is something of a dead letter. Although it is great progress for humanity that the criminal definition has now been settled upon, the likelihood of a prosecution for many of the most blatant acts of aggression in today's world is very slim.

Having said that, there is a denunciatory value to the achievement of this definition. Defining and bringing into force the ban on aggression, even within a circumscribed jurisdiction, is a statement of progress when compared to the international community's inability to confirm a definition for such a crime in the preceding decades.

12.3.3 *The Former Yugoslavia and the Impact of ICL on Post-conflict Reconciliation*

The Former Yugoslavia is a useful case study for understanding how ICL can contribute to post-conflict reconciliation as a component of international dispute settlement. There are a number of reasons for this. First, it is the longest standing dispute to be subject to contemporary ICL. Therefore, it has more jurisprudence, data, and history to help with understanding the impact of ICL on the conflict. The second reason is that in criminal justice terms, the ICTY has been reasonably successful. It has convicted and punished many senior operatives for their roles in atrocity crimes. This has included imposing many life sentences. It has secured convictions of senior leaders and the unprecedented indictment and trial of a former head of State (Slobodan Milošević, who however died in custody before a verdict was reached). The penal successes may be down to the individual skills and commitment of early professionals,[65] significant resources supporting the process, and the

[64] Ibid.

[65] John Hagan and Ron Levi, 'Social skill, the Milosevic indictment, and the rebirth of international criminal justice' (2004) 1 EJC 445–75.

requirement of cooperation with the Tribunal for later governments to commence the long process of accession to the European Union.[66] This success in criminal law terms does not mean that it has been a success in its international law aims, such as fostering peace or improving global security.

Clark's work on Bosnia and Herzegovina (BiH) is instructive in assessing the impact of ICL on the international disputes which are ongoing in the region. She has conducted a substantial piece of qualitative research in BiH in 2009 to look at some of the claims made for the impact of ICL and how they apply specifically to BiH.[67] For Clark, post-conflict reconciliation as part of a move towards an established and sustainable peace requires more than retributive justice.

In her research, she takes as her starting point the claims by Cassese that international criminal accountability has four positive effects: it dissipates calls for revenge, individualises guilt, establishes a historical record, and contributes to reconciliation.[68] These are plausible positive effects from international criminal justice and in line with the aims set out above. There is a logic as to why imposing penalties after trial on those found guilty of serious international crimes would lead to these outcomes. Logical as it may be, there is not a lot of evidence to support this proposition, however. Clark's evidence suggests that the only one of these things which the ICTY achieved successfully was the second: individualising guilt. Having interviewed over 170 residents in BiH on all sides of the conflict, Clark concluded that in the specific context of that part of the conflict which related to BiH, evidence does not sustain the argument that the ICTY had a reconciliatory effect.

Milanović takes this further. Using opinion polling conducted in Serbia, Kosovo, Croatia, and BiH, he argues that 'denialism and revisionism are not just alive and well in the Former Yugoslavia – they are thriving'.[69] While the ICTY has made a 'positive net contribution' to individualised justice, it has failed on other significant counts, such as deterrence and reconciliation. For the former, Milanović notes that the ICTY's establishment in 1993 did not deter the Srebrenica genocide in 1995. For the latter, he uses the polling data to show that only one-fifth of Bosnians believe any crime (let alone genocide) was committed at Srebrenica. His conclusion from the detailed data is that the ICTY has failed to convince the people of the Former Yugoslavia – its most

66 Iavor Rangelov, 'EU conditionality and transitional justice in the Former Yugoslavia' (2006) 2 Croat Yearb Eur Law Policy 365–75.

67 Janine Natalya Clark, 'The limits of retributive justice: Findings of an empirical study in Bosnia and Hercegovina' (2009) 7 JICJ 463–87.

68 Cassese, cited in Clark, 'Limits of retributive justice', p. 464.

69 Marko Milanović, 'The impact of the ICTY on the Former Yugoslavia: An anticipatory postmortem' (2016) 110 AJIL 233–59.

important target audience for its message – that the contents of its judgments are true.

In a later work, Milanović goes on to consider why this aspect of the Tribunal's work is such a failure.[70] He takes a social psychology lens to theorise the way many in the Former Yugoslavia have so doggedly resisted internalising the Tribunal's findings of fact. He argues that 'the causes of the ICTY's ineffectiveness are complex, turning on an interplay between subjective and objective limitations on individuals' processing of information about war crimes'.[71]

Both Clark and Milanović argue persuasively that the data do not support the idea that the ICTY has contributed much, if anything, to post-conflict reconciliation or mutual understanding. There may be an absence of war, but there is no positive peace.

This is consistent with our understandings of criminal justice on the national level. Although there are greater moves towards transformative justice and restorative justice in individual domestic jurisdictions, the traditional punitive model, upon which ICL is based, cannot credibly be argued to be reconciliatory. Victims of serious assaults, or the families of murder victims, may find some closure at the end of the domestic criminal process, but without further intervention, it is rare that they would be reconciled with the perpetrator. This is a limitation of the criminal process that court users should be aware of if they are honest with themselves about the value of the process. To a domestic criminal practitioner, claims relating to reconciliation would likely appear grandiose and unrealistic. The criminal process, domestic or international, may be good at testing evidence, ensuring procedural fairness, individualising guilt, and balancing factors at sentence, but it is not built to mediate, reconcile, or heal.

Clark's research shows that transposing the punitive criminal model to the international sphere brings with it the problems associated with retributive justice. The ICTY then needs to be looked at for what it has achieved as a criminal court. It has worked to provide some form of accountability in the wake of a painful conflict, but it should not be oversold as a great contributor to the resolution of the dispute at the heart of the conflict. To do so is to do the ICTY a disservice. By understanding it and the ICL process for what they are, it should be more straightforward to justify their use in future conflicts and get the most out of them when we do.

[70] Marko Milanović, 'Establishing the facts about mass atrocities: Accounting for the failure of the ICTY to persuade target audiences' (2016) 47 Geo J Int'l L 1321–78.

[71] Ibid., 1327.

12.4 CONCLUSION

While a lot of claims have been made about what ICL can do to settle disputes, this chapter has sought to temper these aspirations. There are certain things which ICL can do very well. These generally derive from the criminal law aspect of the processes which comprise the jurisdiction. It has been argued in this chapter that ICL is well suited to retributive justice.

Looking at the international law aims of ICL as set out in the founding documents of its major tribunals, its aspirations are global peace and security. ICL is expected to attain these aims by using the tools and philosophies of the criminal process (inter alia retribution, deterrence, denunciation, rehabilitation, incapacitation, and reparative justice along with their contributions to post-conflict reconciliation). This chapter has argued that some of the theories of punishment relied upon by the tribunals, notably deterrence, may appear reasonable in the abstract, but are not supported by evidence to prove they are effective in practice.

The chapter also looked at the crime of aggression, which was added to the Rome Statute's core crimes in 2017. Here again great hopes were pinned on the criminalisation of the overarching super-crime of the core crimes. Yet, it is clear that the definition and its associated jurisdictional hurdles make it highly unlikely that anyone will ever be prosecuted for aggression.

Evidence from the Former Yugoslavia suggests that many of the claimed effects of ICL, beyond those grounded in retributive justice, are not borne out by empirical study. These two points make clear that there is little evidence to support major parts of the claims about ICL's capacity to resolve international disputes: that it deters international crimes and that it aids reconciliation.

The contribution, then, of ICL to international dispute resolution can only be described as minimal. Criminal courts can prosecute and punish, but their ability to resolve, reconcile, or rehabilitate are limited, even if often oversold.

International disputes that involve international crimes, such as aggression, genocide, or war crimes, are incredibly varied and complex. Perhaps the only characteristic that can be said to link them is that they are all *sui generis*. In such circumstances, it is extremely hard to make a claim that ICL can have an impact on the underlying international dispute, and it is even harder to predict what that impact might be. Thus, notwithstanding some grand claims about its potential, ICL is not a great contributor to the resolution of international disputes.

PART III

New Opportunities and the Future of International Dispute Settlement

13

Mediation and the International Law Commission's Draft Articles on the Protection of Persons in the Event of Disasters

A Case of Untapped Potential

THERESE O'DONNELL

13.1 INTRODUCTION

The 2016 International Law Commission's (ILC) Draft Articles on the Protection of Persons in the Event of Disasters[1] (hereinafter the draft Articles) evolved over a decade under the careful stewardship of Special Rapporteur Eduardo Valencia-Ospina, who noted that '[i]t is in the solidarity inspired by human suffering that the Commission's mandate finds *telos*, as an expression of our common heritage in a global context'.[2] The ILC focused on the rights and needs of disaster-stricken persons and the removal of obstacles compromising these imperatives. The final instrument was warmly received, with subsequent UN General Assembly Resolutions urging States to be mindful of the ILC's recommendations for an eventual treaty.[3]

Despite their comprehensive approach to addressing legal issues arising during disasters, the draft Articles are notably silent on dispute settlement methods, simply implying the use of pre-existing mechanisms.[4] This omission may indicate desires to highlight the ILC project's codificatory and

[1] ILC, 'Draft articles on the protection of persons in the event of disasters, with commentaries', in *Yearbook of the International Law Commission. 2016, Volume II, Part Two: Report of the Commission to the General Assembly on the Work of Its Sixty-Eighth Session (A/71/10)* (New York: UN, 2016).

[2] UNGA, 'Second report on the protection of persons in the event of disasters by Eduardo Valencia-Ospina, Special Rapporteur' (7 May 2009) UN Doc. A/CN.4/615, para. 50.

[3] UNGA Res. 71/141 (13 December 2016) UN Doc. A/RES/71/141; UNGA Res. 73/209 (20 December 2018) UN Doc. A/RES/73/209. See also UNGA, 'Protection of persons in the event of disasters: Report of the Secretary-General' (21 July 2020) UN Doc. A/75/214.

[4] Notwithstanding the survey of disaster dispute settlement methods in UNGA, 'Protection of persons in the event of disasters: Memorandum by the Secretariat' (11 December 2007) UN Doc. A/CN.4/590 paras 237–41. The 2011 ILC discussions in plenary do not mention dispute

synthesising dimensions over its more progressive aspects.[5] Sufficient existential angst existed regarding international disaster response law's nebulous and chaotic nature, without the ILC fuelling anxieties that it had extensive developmental pretensions regarding dispute settlement mechanisms. Nevertheless, this apparent reticence slightly jars with the ILC's stated aim of codifying and clarifying this area, given that provisions on dispute settlement in disaster-related instruments wildly differ in approach.[6] Further, certain high-profile disaster aid refusals have generated considerable political controversy and opposition, thereby highlighting how pressing this issue might become.

As calamitous events that cause widespread loss and disrupt the normal functioning of societies,[7] disasters present challenges to even the most developed States which may need external assistance in order to provide relief. However, some external assistance offers have been either actively refused by the stricken State or simply met with silence. Indeed, sometimes disaster-affected States simply make no call for assistance, despite satellite and seismic readings making the catastrophe's scale clear, raising concerns internationally as to the well-being of local populations. Currently the main articulation of a duty to not arbitrarily refuse offers of disaster assistance lies in soft law.[8] By drawing on this material along with norms from human rights law and international humanitarian law, the ILC has emphasised that disaster-stricken States should not arbitrarily refuse aid.[9] However, this pronouncement alone will not resolve conflicts regarding aid refusals.

While the ICJ has never adjudicated a dispute concerning disaster assistance refusal, in 2008, following Cyclone Nargis in Myanmar, the UN Security Council was confronted with such a matter. Myanmar had initially made no call for

settlement despite it receiving extensive attention during simultaneous ILC deliberations on reservations to treaties (ILC, 'Summary record of the 3103rd meeting' (12 July 2011) UN Doc. A/CN.4/3103; ILC, 'Summary record of the 3104th meeting' (13 July 2021) UN Doc. A/CN.4/3104). The Special Rapporteur's fourth report mentions the 1907 Hague Convention but only regarding external actors' rights to offer assistance (ILC, 'Summary record of the 3102nd meeting' (11 July 2011) UN Doc. A/CN.4/3102, para. 35, referencing UNGA, 'Fourth report on the protection of persons in the event of disasters by Eduardo Valencia-Ospina, Special Rapporteur' (11 May 2011) UN Doc. A/CN.4/643, paras 84 and 85).

5 UNGA, 'Preliminary report on the protection of persons in the event of disasters by Mr Eduardo Valencia-Ospina, Special Rapporteur' (5 May 2008) UN Doc. A/CN.4/598, 11; UNGA, 'Report of the International Law Commission: Sixty-third session (26 April–3 June and 4 July–12 August 2011)' (2011) UN Doc. A/66/10, para. 285.

6 UNGA, 'Memorandum by the Secretariat', paras 237–41.

7 Draft Art 3(a).

8 Institute of International Law, 'Bruges resolution on humanitarian assistance', 2 September 2003, www.idi-iil.org/app/uploads/2017/06/2003_bru_03_en.pdf (accessed 18 August 2022), para. VIII.

9 Draft Art 13(2).

assistance. France, which was extremely keen to gain access to deliver aid, invoked familiar arguments regarding Myanmar's obligations, referring to human rights law and prohibitions on crimes against humanity. It also sought to draw in international involvement (possibly involving force) via the Responsibility to Protect doctrine.[10] Myanmar argued that a French navy ship carrying around 1,000 tonnes of humanitarian equipment to the waters off the Irrawaddy delta was a warship.[11] Ultimately, the issue was resolved diplomatically. However, this *ad hoc* solution offered no guarantees for a similarly positive outcome in subsequent disasters.

Notwithstanding radical differences between the twenty-first century and the Cold War era, peaceful international dispute settlement remains a cornerstone of global relations,[12] with data suggesting that mediation is an 'increasingly common tool of crisis management'.[13] Indeed, while the ILC pondered questions regarding arbitrary refusals of disaster assistance,[14] another 2011 ILC working paper on peaceful settlement of disputes referenced mediation's importance, potential lessons from the practice of regional bodies, and possibilities of elaborating model rules.[15] Mediation holds particular appeal in disaster aid stand-offs because, as Merrills notes, parties retain control over processes in delicate circumstances and can negotiate face-saving compromises (often more difficult in direct negotiations).[16]

In brief, this chapter argues that mediation is an appropriate method for settling disputes regarding external disaster assistance. Section 13.2 provides a contextual analysis of disputes regarding external disaster assistance and the complexities often involved. Section 13.3 analyses the particular hallmarks

[10] Bernard Kouchner, 'Birmaine: morale de l'extrême urgence', *Le Monde*, 19 May 2008, www.lemonde.fr/asie-pacifique/article/2008/05/19/birmanie-morale-de-l-extreme-urgence-par-bernard-kouchner_1046630_3216.html (accessed 18 August 2022); Anon., 'Update report no. 4: Myanmar', *Security Council Report*, 14 May 2008, www.securitycouncilreport.org/update-report/lookup_c_glkwlemtisg_b_4130257.php (accessed 18 August 2022).

[11] Anon., 'Tension entre la Birmanie et la France autour de la mission humanitaire du "Mistral"', *Le Monde*, 17 May 2008, www.lemonde.fr/asie-pacifique/article/2008/05/17/tension-entre-la-birmanie-et-la-france-autour-de-le-mission-humanitaire-du-mistral_1046232_3216.html (accessed 30 September 2022).

[12] Jacob Bercovitch and Richard Jackson, *Conflict Resolution in the Twenty-First Century: Principles, Methods, and Approaches* (Ann Arbor: University of Michigan Press, 2009).

[13] Jonathan Wilkenfeld et al., 'Mediating international crises: Cross-national and experimental perspectives' (2003) 47 J Conflict Resol 279–301 at 285.

[14] UNGA, 'Report of the ILC: Sixty-third session'.

[15] UNGA, 'Peaceful settlement of disputes: Working paper prepared by Sir Michael Wood' (30 March 2011) UN Doc. A/CN.4/641, referencing a subject note by the Secretariat (UNGA, 'Settlement of disputes clauses: Note by the Secretariat' (15 March 2010) UN Doc. A/CN.4/623).

[16] John G. Merrills, *International Dispute Settlement*, 6th ed. (Cambridge: Cambridge University Press, 2017), pp. 26–27.

and positioning of contemporary international mediation processes[17] and their relevance in disasters.[18] Section 13.4 examines the regulatory context of disaster assistance refusals. It pays particular attention to ILC draft Article 13 which fetters the rights of disaster-affected States to refuse external assistance and the difficulties that may generate, especially given the lack of explicit provision for dispute settlement. The capacity of the draft Articles to give substance to dispute settlement opportunities in disasters is then analysed. ILC draft Article 7 recalls the general international obligation to co-operate, broadly stressing the importance of disaster cooperation. More unusually, draft Article 8 lists forms of disaster cooperation, thereby fleshing out a concept often derided for its vagueness. The non-exhaustive nature of this iteration allows for dispute settlement, and mediation in particular, to be unearthed as a form of disaster cooperation. It will become clear that mediation's distinctively collaborative nature, even in the most fraught circumstances, complements the overall ideology and practice of the ILC provisions while also fortifying them and giving them impetus. Taken all together, this analysis provides the broad terrain in Section 13.5 for pondering the potential features of disaster mediation models, including their modes, underpinning values, and participatory reach. Mediation can move beyond its habitual realm of armed conflicts to assist in challenging post-disaster situations. It could, and should, be explicitly recognised for such capabilities via interpretations and usage of the ILC draft Articles, or within any eventual treaty regulating disasters.

13.2 THE CONTEXT OF DISASTER ASSISTANCE REFUSALS

The ILC draft Articles emphasise incontrovertibly that disaster-affected persons are entitled to respect for their human rights.[19] The donation and receipt of immediate post-disaster assistance is generally assumed to be motivated by 'common humanity' and is accordingly uncontroversial. However, this is often articulated rhetorically, with such assertions deriving authority from intuitive, liberal understandings of morality. More secularly, strongly embedded normative allegiances to, for example, international

[17] See UNGA, 'Strengthening the role of mediation in the peaceful settlement of disputes, conflict prevention and resolution: Report of the Secretary-General' (25 June 2012) UN Doc. A/66/811, and the associated UN Guidance in Annex I thereof.

[18] Johan Galtung and Dietrich Fischer, *Johan Galtung: Pioneer of Peace Research* (Berlin: Springer, 2013), pp. 59–70; Martti Ahtisaari and Kristiina Rintakoski, 'Mediation', in Andrew F. Cooper, Jorge Heine, and Ramesh C. Thakur (eds.), *The Oxford Handbook of Modern Diplomacy* (Oxford: Oxford University Press, 2013), p. 337.

[19] Draft Art 5.

human rights law in general terms are also assumed to constrain unbridled exercises of sovereign will and prompt aid acceptance. These assumptions endure despite, or perhaps due to, legal standards and duties in disasters traditionally being difficult to discern. Somewhat unsurprisingly, suspicion and anger are often aroused when apparently well-intentioned external offers are refused.

However, conceptions of disasters as moments of innocence for casting aside politics have been roundly challenged.[20] Disasters can be highly politicised moments[21] presenting ample opportunities for instrumentalisation[22] and performativity.[23] Further, despite presumptions of unconditional receptiveness to post-disaster aid offers, aid refusals are not, and have not been, uncommon.[24] A 2020 study that assessed sixty-six disasters between 2004 and 2012 established thirty-two instances of government-rejected aid.[25] However, not all aid refusals are the same.[26] Some result from specific political antagonisms. Others are generalised and undiscerning.[27] Refusals

[20] Praful Bidwai, 'Tsunami impact: Loss of innocence in the politics of aid', *Transnational Institute*, 1 May 2006, www.tni.org/en/article/tsunami-impact (accessed 18 August 2022); B. P. C. Bose, 'The politics of disasters' (1994) 55 IJPS 119–34; Kaiting Jessica Hsu and Mark Schuller, 'Humanitarian aid and local power structures: Lessons from Haiti's "shadow disaster"' (2020) 44 Disasters 641–65.

[21] Henry Rosario, 'Humanitarian disaster response: Understanding aid rejection', May 2020, https://centreforhumanitarianleadership.org/research/publications/humanitarian-disaster-response-understanding-aid-rejection (accessed 18 August 2022), p. 11; Olivier Rubin, 'Natural disasters and politics', in Rasmus Dahlberg, Olivier Rubin, and Morten T. Vendelø (eds.), *Disaster Research: Multidisciplinary and International Perspectives* (Routledge: Abingdon, 2017), p. 82.

[22] Away from strictly needs-based approaches in favour of those strengthening political, military, or economic interests. Charlotte Dany, 'Beyond principles vs. politics: Humanitarian aid in the European Union', *ARENA*, November 2014, www.sv.uio.no/arena/english/research/publications/arena-working-papers/2014/wp11-14.pdf (accessed 18 August 2022).

[23] Jonathan Fenton-Harvey, 'Performative humanitarianism: Saudi's aid diplomacy in Yemen', *Gulf International Forum*, 17 June 2020, https://gulfif.org/performative-humanitarianism-saudis-aid-diplomacy-in-yemen (accessed 18 August 2022); Suzanne Ruth Little, 'Floods and earthquakes: The transformation and performativity of trauma cultures', conference paper, June 2011, www.researchgate.net/publication/308204193_Floods_and_Earthquakes_The_Transformation_and_Performativity_of_Trauma_Cultures (accessed 18 August 2022).

[24] Charlotte Dany, 'Why is humanitarian aid rejected? Comparing the motives of democratic and autocratic states', *7th ECPR General Conference*, Bordeaux, 4–7 September 2013, https://ecpr.eu/Events/Event/PaperDetails/3291 (accessed 19 August 2022).

[25] Allison Carnegie and Lindsay R. Dolan, 'The effects of rejecting aid on recipients' reputations: Evidence from natural disaster responses' (2021) 16 Rev Int Organ 495–519.

[26] Craig Allan and Thérèse O'Donnell, 'An offer you cannot refuse? Natural disasters, the politics of aid refusal and potential legal implications' (2013) 5 ALF 36–63.

[27] Rosario, 'Humanitarian disaster response', p. 9.

may be status-motivated, aimed at cultivating images of self-sufficiency.[28] They may involve diverse anxieties about, varyingly, 'Trojan horses',[29] unwanted foreign influences,[30] indirect assertions by donors of regional interests,[31] inabilities to cope with deluges of (often inappropriate) aid, misdirected aid due to donor dispersal restrictions,[32] or potentially devastating consequences of aid.[33] There may be general suspicions that external assistance seeks to remould recipients in a donor's image. Oftentimes, refusals will result from a mélange of these reasons,[34] and disaster-struck States are perhaps less likely to accept external offers carrying unmanageable 'level[s] of political risk'.[35]

Specific examples evidence the aforementioned conclusions. In 1990, after a devastating July earthquake, Iran's leaders indicated a general willingness to accept relief assistance, but not from Israel and South Africa[36] (a partially enduring antipathy[37]). In 1999, following a devastating flood, Venezuela rejected US navy offers of emergency aid (despite ships holding aid supplies already being anchored at the Venezuelan coast) on the basis that national

28 Carnegie and Dolan, 'The effects of rejecting aid', pp. 496–500.

29 Travis Nelson, 'Rejecting the gift horse: International politics of disaster aid refusal' (2010) 10 Confl Secur Dev 379–402; Andrew Selth, 'Even paranoids have enemies: Cyclone Nargis and Myanmar's fears of invasion' (2008) 30 Contemp Southeast Asia 379–402.

30 Kendra Dupuy, James Ron, and Aseem Prakash, 'Hands off my regime! Governments' restrictions on foreign aid to non-governmental organizations in poor and middle-income countries' (2016) 84 World Dev 299–311.

31 Bidwai, 'Tsunami impact'.

32 Patrick Worsnip, 'Tsunami aid often bypassed conflict victims: Report', *Reuters*, 25 April 2009, www.reuters.com/article/us-un-tsunami-idUSTRE53N77H20090425 (accessed 19 August 2022); Tsunami Global Lessons Learned Project Steering Committee, 'The tsunami legacy: Innovation, breakthroughs and change', 2009, https://reliefweb.int/report/indonesia/tsunami-legacy-innovation-breakthroughs-and-change (accessed 19 August 2022).

33 William Reville, 'Was the aid worse than the tsunami?', *Irish Times*, 15 October 2020, www.irishtimes.com/news/science/was-the-aid-worse-than-the-tsunami-1.4372619 (accessed 19 August 2022); Ajay Saini, 'Disaster, aid and the Nicobarese "crisis heterotopia"' (2016) 12 Northeast Window 2.

34 Julie Belanger and Richard Horsey, 'Negotiating humanitarian access to cyclone-affected areas of Myanmar: A review' (2008) 41 Humanitarian Exchange 2–5.

35 Rosario, 'Humanitarian disaster response', p. 4.

36 Lisa Beyer, 'Iran: The politics of humanitarianism', *Time*, 9 July 1990, https://content.time.com/time/subscriber/article/0,33009,970582-1,00.html (accessed 19 August 2022).

37 Raphael Ahren, 'Israel offers quake help to Iran, Iraq, but immediately turned down', *Times of Israel*, 14 November 2017, www.timesofisrael.com/israel-offers-medical-aid-to-iran-iraq-after-quake-rocks-region (accessed 19 August 2022); Andrew Tobin, 'Iran, Iraq reject Israel's offer of aid for earthquake victims', *Forward*, 15 November 2017, https://forward.com/fast-forward/387649/iran-and-iraq-reject-israel-s-offer-of-aid-for-earthquake-victims (accessed 19 August 2022).

sovereignty was at stake.[38] The twenty-first century has witnessed many examples of aid refusals. The 2008 post-Cyclone Nargis controversy has already been mentioned. In 2011, Japan rejected all international aid for two days following the Fukushima disaster, relenting only to accept single aid offers. After one month, it had rejected 148 out of 172 aid offers.[39] In 2012, Iran initially rejected all international aid after an earthquake.[40] Similarly, Pakistan refused aid aimed at alleviating the effects of devastating floods[41] and refused international aid agencies' entry into earthquake-affected areas of Balochistan in 2013. This comprised an area of considerable underdevelopment and separatist insurgency, perhaps fuelling Pakistan governmental anxieties regarding relief efforts.[42] In August 2018, Indonesia rejected external aid after the Lombok earthquake, but the following month, following an initial refusal, accepted aid after an earthquake and tsunami affected Sulawesi.[43] Sometimes generalised rejections become particularised. After Hurricane Katrina, the US rejected all international aid offers. It then relented, only maintaining a refusal of Cuban offers.[44] Similar motivations explained post-

38 Dany, 'Why is humanitarian aid rejected?', p. 3, citing Jorge Olavarría, 'Los barcos que no llegaron', 2000, www.analitica.com/va/politica/opinion/9388990.asp (accessed 1 February 2020).

39 Ministry of Foreign Affairs of Japan, 'Nuclear accident at the Fukushima Dai-ichi Nuclear Power Station', 9 April 2011, www.cn.emb-japan.go.jp/dataI.PDF (accessed 19 August 2022), referenced in Dany 'Why is humanitarian aid rejected?'

40 Anon., 'Iran U-turn opens door to foreign quake aid', *The Guardian*, 14 August 2012, www.theguardian.com/world/2012/aug/14/iran-uturn-welcomes-foreign-quake-aid (accessed 19 August 2022).

41 Rob Crilly, 'Two million at risk but Pakistan "refused to allow aid agencies to help after floods"', *The Telegraph*, 16 February 2012, www.telegraph.co.uk/news/worldnews/asia/pakistan/9084203/EMBARGOED-GMT-0001-Pakistan-floods-Oxfam-and-Save-The-Children-report-accuse-Pakistan-of-delaying-aid-agency-help-after-disaster.html (accessed 19 August 2022).

42 Anon., 'Unnecessary refusal: Aid for earthquake victims', *Dawn*, 10 October 2013, www.dawn.com/news/1048732/newspaper/newspaper/column (accessed 19 August 2022).

43 Editorial Board, 'Indonesia's gift-horse response to post-tsunami aid', *Christian Science Monitor*, 3 October 2018, www.csmonitor.com/Commentary/the-monitors-view/2018/1003/Indonesia-s-gift-horse-response-to-post-tsunami-aid (accessed 19 August 2022). See also Simon Lawry-White, Brenda Langdon, and Umi Hanik, 'Real-time response review of the 2018 Indonesia Tsunami Appeal Disasters Emergency Committee and Swiss solidarity', 1 March 2019, www.alnap.org/help-library/dec-sws-indonesia-tsunami-appeal-real-time-response-review (accessed 19 August 2022).

44 Mary Murray, 'Katrina aid from Cuba? No thanks, says U.S.', *NBC News*, 12 September 2005, www.nbcnews.com/id/wbna9311876 (accessed 19 August 2022); Walter Brasch, 'The politics of humanitarian aid', *Pacific Views*, 2 June 2008, www.pacificviews.org/weblog/archives/019343.php (accessed 19 August 2022).

Hurricane Sandy rejections of Iranian Red Crescent offers.[45] States' positions can also change. In December 2004, months after having accepted bilateral aid following flooding in Bihar's plains, India began to reject 'unnecessary' aid[46] and emphasised its changed position by providing aid to neighbours enduring disasters also affecting India.[47] This continuing approach[48] has been rationalised as a bolstering strategy, whereby a former aid recipient re-presents itself as having 'ascended the ranks' to become an aid donor.[49] Rejections of disaster assistance are clearly not exceptional, and motivations are often very complex. However, when refusals challenge firm, confident, assertive offers of assistance which cite altruistic solidarity and an assortment of legal provisions as their basis, conflict is almost inevitable.

Writing in 1962, Hans Morgenthau was clear that foreign aid, just like 'diplomatic or military policy or propaganda', was a weapon in a nation's 'political armoury',[50] and even aid delivered by proxy NGOs would be attributed by recipients to sponsoring governments.[51] Disaster assistance is no

[45] Thomas Erdbrink, 'Iran offers to send emergency aid team to stricken New York', *New York Times*, 31 October 2012, www.nytimes.com/2012/11/01/world/middleeast/iran-offers-to-send-emergency-aid-team-to-hurricane-stricken-new-york.html?_r=2& (accessed 19 August 2022), referred to in Dany 'Why is humanitarian aid rejected?'

[46] See also 2013 refusals of US and Japanese aid when Uttarakhand flooding killed thousands, and 2014 refusals of UN assistance after Kashmir floods displaced 150,000 people. Carnegie and Dolan, 'The effects of rejecting aid'; Charu Sudan Kasturi, 'Foreign aid? No, thanks', *Telegraph India*, 7 July 2013, www.telegraphindia.com/india/foreign-aid-no-thanks/cid/278963 (accessed 19 August 2022).

[47] Carnegie and Dolan, 'The effects of rejecting aid', citing Kasturi, 'Foreign aid?', and Murali Krishnan, 'Disaster management: India's big challenge', *Deutsche Welle*, 22 September 2014, www.dw.com/en/disaster-management-indias-big-challenge/a-17940229 (accessed 19 August 2022).

[48] Regarding the 2018 Kerala floods, see Nirmala Ganapathy, 'Delhi's refusal of foreign aid in flood crisis sparks debate', *Straits Times*, 29 August 2018, www.straitstimes.com/asia/south-asia/delhis-refusal-of-foreign-aid-in-flood-crisis-sparks-debate (accessed 19 August 2022); and A. Kazmin, 'India's rejection of $100m foreign flooding aid sparks anger in Kerala', *Financial Times*, 27 August 2008, www.ft.com/content/86e4bb4e-a785-11e8-8ecf-a7ae1beff35b (accessed 19 August 2022).

[49] Carnegie and Dolan, 'The effects of rejecting aid', citing Bidwai, 'Tsunami impact'. Although see challenges to donor/recipient binaries: Robert J. Bookmiller and Kirsten Nakjavani Bookmiller, 'Donor countries as aid recipients: The USA, New Zealand and the lessons of Hurricane Katrina' (2016) 12 Int J Emerg Manag 263–83; Jonathan Watts and Julian Borger, 'Tsunami pushes Japan from major aid donor to leading recipient', *The Guardian*, 11 May 2011, www.theguardian.com/world/2011/may/11/tsunami-japan-aid-donor-recipient (accessed 19 August 2022).

[50] Hans Morgenthau, 'A political theory of foreign aid' (1962) 56 Am Pol Sc Rev 301–9 at 309.

[51] Ibid., 301.

different and can inspire scepticism in stricken States doubting donors' intentions. Undoubtedly such apprehensions or paranoia may produce resistance to assistance potentially of benefit to stricken populations. However, the importance of perspective and sensitivity when it comes to external assistance should not be underplayed. Simplistic assertions that politics should be put aside often overlook the reality that after an acute, physical, large-scale rupture in a State's fabric, its sense of sovereignty may also be tender. Given the ample supporting empirical evidence, the pressing issue becomes the navigation of resulting impasses.

In 2008, it was not courts or threats of force at the United Nations Security Council (UNSC) which breached the post-Nargis impasse. Instead, the quiet diplomacy of the Association of Southeast Asian Nations (ASEAN) and the UN (led by Dr Noeleen Heyzer, UN Under Secretary-General and Executive Secretary of the UN Economic and Social Commission for Asia and the Pacific (UNESCAP))[52] brokered an agreement facilitating an international collaboration which enabled delivery of humanitarian assistance. ASEAN's Humanitarian Task Force for the Victims of Cyclone Nargis remained in place for two years, and the UN Under Secretary-General for Humanitarian Affairs and Emergency Relief, Sir John Holmes, was unequivocal that 'persistent negotiation and dialogue' had been effective at securing an agreement.[53] International assistance with a regional character was also likely 'less threatening, and provided a face-saving way for the Myanmar leadership to accept an international relief operation',[54] directly recalling Merrills' account of mediation's benefits. As well as ameliorating the increasingly hawkish public diplomacy, the UN/ASEAN/Myanmar communications actually achieved assistance for the Myanmarese people. This understated but truly effective approach forced an unflattering re-evaluation of both highly performative public diplomacy which rhetorically invoked 'humanity', and significant legal gaps including those concerning dispute settlement.[55]

52 Craig Allan and Thérèse O'Donnell, 'A call to alms? Natural disasters, R2P, duties of cooperation and uncharted consequences' (2012) 17 JC&SL 337–71; ASEAN, *Charting a New Course: ASEAN-UN Post-Nargis Partnership* (Jakarta: ASEAN, 2010), p. 20.

53 John Holmes, 'Disaster lessons', *Washington Post*, 6 August 2008, https://reliefweb.int/report/myanmar/myanmar-disaster-lessons (accessed 19 August 2022).

54 Belanger and Horsey, 'Negotiating humanitarian access'.

55 Following her successful tenure at UNESCAP, Dr Heyzer joined the UN Secretary-General's High-Level Advisory Board on Mediation in 2017.

13.3 MEDIATION

Mediation may be considered a political route that does not invoke law's authority for its power.[56] However, both law and mediations are tied to notions of good faith and justice,[57] with mediations tending to be legally facilitated and structured.[58] Mediation classically combines diplomacy's discretion with a reassuring ethos of impartiality and non-judgment regarding the importance and claims of each disputant. Further, mediation's capacity to be a predictably available, and textually provided for, method of dispute settlement beyond the material preferences of third parties emphasises its attractiveness.

13.3.1 *Mediation in International Law*

Mediation has a distinguished pedigree in international law.[59] The 1899 and 1907 Hague Conventions on Dispute Settlement foregrounded modern international mediation. The 1907 treaty noted that third-party States can, and indeed should, 'on their own initiative, and as far as circumstances allow, offer their good offices or mediation' to disputing States, and that such offers, even from disputants, can never be regarded as an unfriendly act.[60] Mediation's fundamentally consensual and advisory nature was also stressed.[61] Article 2(3) of the UN Charter obliges all member States to settle disputes peacefully and in sustainable ways, with Article 33 specifically identifying mediation's utility.

[56] Cindy Daase, 'The law of the peacemaker: The role of mediators in peace negotiations and lawmaking' (2012) 1 CJICL 107–35. For some thoughts on law and diplomacy, see David Clinton, 'Diplomacy and international law', *Oxford Research Encyclopedia of International Studies*, 30 November 2017, https://oxfordre.com/internationalstudies/internationalstudies/view/10.1093/acrefore/9780190846626.001.0001/acrefore-9780190846626-e-152 (accessed 19 August 2022); Iakovos Iakovidis, 'International law and diplomacy', in Rossana Deplano and Nikolaus Tsagourias (eds.), *Research Methods in International Law: A Handbook* (Cheltenham: Edward Elgar, 2021), pp. 488–503.

[57] Art 2(3) of the Charter of the United Nations, San Francisco, 26 June 1945, in force 24 October 1945, 1 UNTS 16.

[58] Michal Alberstein, 'Forms of mediation and law: Cultures of dispute resolution' (2007) 22 Ohio St J Disp Res 321–75 at 322.

[59] Jacob Bercovitch and Allison Houston, 'The study of international mediation: Theoretical issues and empirical evidence', in Jacob Bercovitch (ed.), *Theory and Practice of International Mediation: Selected Essays* (London: Routledge, 2011), p. 35.

[60] Art 3 of the Hague Convention on the Pacific Settlement of International Disputes, The Hague, 18 October 1907, in force 26 January 1910, (1907) 205 CTS 277.

[61] Art 6 of the 1907 Hague Convention. This system was further developed by the League of Nations Covenant (Versailles, 28 June 1919, in force 10 January 1920, (1919) 225 CTS 195) and the 1928 General Act (Pacific Settlement of International Disputes) (Geneva, 26 September 1928, in force 16 August 1929, 93 LNTS 343).

It is one option that the UNSC can call upon disputing parties to use in situations that are likely to endanger peace and security.[62] Any third party engaged will offer no binding decision or even final suggestion.[63] This model finds reiteration in other instruments, including the 1970 UN General Assembly (UNGA) Declaration on Principles of International Law Concerning Friendly Relations and Cooperation among States, and the 1982 Manila Declaration on the Peaceful Settlement of International Disputes.[64] The latter, in particular, stresses that States are to seek, in good faith and in a spirit of cooperation, an early and equitable settlement of their international disputes by a variety of peaceable means, including mediation.[65]

Mediation's utility in international disputes can be attributed to the expanding categories of personality resulting in disputes between different actors and at different levels.[66] Its effectiveness has been particularly noticeable in environmental law, with its success being attributed to its voluntariness and disputants' control over processes and personnel involved.[67] Mediation has also had conspicuous success in resolving armed conflicts, notably in Northern Ireland and Colombia. In such international crises, as noted, mediation processes classically envisage the disputing parties either seeking or accepting an offer of help from a third party (including an individual, group, State, or organisation) to settle a conflict or resolve their differences without resorting to physical force or invoking the authority of the law.[68]

Although focused on armed conflicts, the influential UN Guidance for Effective Mediation is instructive for disaster scenarios (particularly given the R2P arguments often in play). It thoughtfully identifies important factors in

[62] See also Arts 35, 36, and 38 of the UN Charter regarding the roles of the UNGA and UNSC.

[63] Christian Djeffal, 'Mediation in international law: Mapping its specifics for comparison', in Cássius Guimarães Chai, Alberto Poletti Adorno, and Christian Djeffal (eds.), *International Conflicts and Mediation* (Rio: Global Mediation, 2014), pp. 24–25.

[64] John G. Merrills, 'The peaceful settlement of disputes', in Colin Warbrick and Vaughan Lowe (eds.), *The United Nations and the Principles of International Law: Essays in Memory of Michael Akehurst* (London: Routledge, 1994), p. 49.

[65] Annex to UNGA, 'Manila declaration on the peaceful settlement of international disputes' (15 November 1982) UN Doc. A/RES/37/10. Individual bodies may also have their own particular rules. Djeffal, 'Mediation in international law', p. 21.

[66] Djeffal, 'Mediation in international law', pp. 17–18.

[67] Christina Simokat, 'Environmental mediation clauses in international legal mechanisms', *Mediate*, 31 January 2008, www.mediate.com//articles/simokatC1.cfm (accessed 19 August 2022).

[68] Jacob Bercovitch, J. Theodore Anagnoson, and Donnette L. Wille, 'Some conceptual issues and empirical trends in the study of successful mediation in international relations' (1991) 28 J Peace Res 7–17 at 8; Kyle Beardsley, *The Mediation Dilemma* (Ithaca, NY: Cornell University Press, 2011).

mediation processes: preparedness, impartiality, inclusivity, national ownership, international law and normative frameworks, coherence, co-ordination and complementarity, and quality agreements.[69] This emphasis on inclusivity has led to mediation attracting international plaudits,[70] most notably via the award of the 2015 Nobel Peace Prize to the Tunisian National Dialogue Quartet.[71] The Quartet's all-embracing approach and representation of different national sectors and values endowed it with crucial moral authority and political credibility. More broadly, the recently developed 2019 Singapore Convention on Mediation with its focus on trade suggests that non–armed conflict international mediation may be on the rise.

Although the categories of peaceful dispute settlement often overlap, mediators are less passive than those simply contributing good offices. Unlike conciliators, who may conduct their own investigations and present formal proposals for resolution, mediators tend to focus on active listening, offering informal, recommendatory proposals based on the information supplied by participants. This sense of participation and 'ownership', as well as its particular alertness to cultural difference, heightens mediation's appeal in the disaster context, and indeed its presence is referenced in some regional and bilateral disaster agreements.[72]

Given the fast-moving post-disaster context, stricken States should make timely decisions regarding external offers of assistance, and as will be noted, delays in doing so may influence impressions and assessments of a refusal's arbitrariness.[73] Arguably, the delicate, and often protracted, timeframes involved in mediations negate its viability in disasters. This could certainly be a potential danger if these processes are resorted to in an *ad hoc* real-time fashion. However, if mediation is flagged early on, and emphasised, as relevant to disaster disputes (via eventual treaty provision or interpretations of the ILC

[69] UN Guidance annexed to UNGA, 'Strengthening the role of mediation', paras 48–52.

[70] Molly M. Melin, 'When states mediate' (2013) 2 Penn State Journal of Law and International Affairs 78–90.

[71] Kaci Kullmann Five, 'Award ceremony speech: Presentation speech by the chair of the Norwegian Nobel Committee', *Nobel Prize*, 10 December 2015, www.nobelprize.org/prizes/peace/2015/ceremony-speech (accessed 19 August 2022).

[72] For details see UNGA, 'Memorandum by the Secretariat', fns 716 and 717.

[73] Commentaries to draft Art 13(3), in particular para. 7. The ILC cites UNGA, 'Humanitarian assistance to victims of natural disasters and similar emergency situations' (8 December 1988) UN Doc. A/RES/43/131, and UNGA, 'Humanitarian assistance to victims of natural disasters and similar emergency situations' (14 December 1990) UN Doc. A/RES/45/100, stressing the need for 'rapid relief' to avoid further harm (including mortalities), and the Framework Convention on Civil Defence Assistance, Geneva, 22 May 2000, in force 23 September 2001, 2172 UNTS 213: '[Offers of, or requests for, assistance should be] examined and responded to by recipient states within the shortest possible time.'

draft Articles), then the drawbacks of delay might be diminished. Raising the foreseeability of such processes opens up opportunities for developing and streamlining them to ensure that stricken populations avoid unnecessary suffering.

13.3.2 *Mediation and Disasters*

Disasters have traditionally provided contexts for mediations rather than their substantive subject matter. For example, after the 2005 Indian Ocean tsunami, the disaster prompted the peace-making mediation in Sri Lanka without being its raison d'être.[74] However, disaster aid refusals will continue, and complaints by external States that their offers are refused or left unheeded (potentially resulting in human rights abuses or international crimes) present fertile mediatory opportunities. Disaster disputes are not too niche or intractable for mediation's agile capabilities and can provide disputants with a 'political safe harbor for the transmission and rationalization of the compromises needed for settlement'.[75] Mediation's shepherding technique and essentially optimistic outlook holds that given 'the right environment . . . parties can improve their relationships and move towards cooperation'.[76] This chimes with the thrust and terms of the ILC project (discussed imminently) and positions mediation's appropriateness in disasters.

It might be assumed that the underpinning goal of disaster mediations will always be the admittance of externally offered aid and assistance, and that a mediation's focus will concentrate on delivery processes. However, given that many of the sensitivities analysed in Section 13.2 specifically address contentions that aid is not necessary or appropriate or aims to politically undermine States and the like, a credible mediation cannot close off potential conclusions that an aid refusal is legitimate. This possibility is even acknowledged by the draft Articles. Equally, there is an explicit recognition that disasters occur against a background of disaster law, international human rights, and international humanitarian law (IHL) norms which cohere around the protection of vulnerable populations. Consequently, the incontrovertible goal and fundamental value that cannot be mediated away is that the essential needs of

74 Seden Akcinaroglu, Jonathan M. DiCicco, and Elizabeth Radziszewski, 'Avalanches and olive branches: A multimethod analysis of disasters and peacemaking in interstate rivalries' (2011) 64 Pol Res Q. 260–75; Joakim Kurtz, 'From tremors to talks: Do natural disasters produce ripe moments for resolving separatist conflicts?' (2012) 38 Int Interact 482–502.

75 Gary S. Mendoza, 'Mediation as an instrument of international crisis management: Cyprus – A case study' (1981) 7 Yale J World Pub Ord 244–86.

76 UN Guidance annexed to UNGA, 'Strengthening the role of mediation', p. 4.

disaster-affected populations (as measured against the applicable international legal standards) must be met. This could be the converging incentive (for disputants and mediating third parties) that optimises any mediation's prospects.[77] Mediations concerning aid refusals would therefore focus on whether those needs are being met by the disaster-affected State or are of such a magnitude that external assistance is necessary.

13.4 THE REGULATORY CONTEXT OF DISASTER ASSISTANCE REFUSALS

As noted, international disaster law (IDL) and its sub-specialism – international disaster response law (IDRL) – have undergone an exponential growth[78] in the last thirty years,[79] and the ILC has contributed enormously to its clarification. Responding to previous calls[80] and treading where others had failed,[81] the ILC contended with a dizzying array of instruments and practices emerging from multiple bodies from across the wide strata of international society.[82] A myriad of treaties,[83] State practice, national laws, and an extensive aggregation of soft law (including numerous UNGA Resolutions) littered the route. Paradoxically, 'yawning gap[s]' also bedevilled IDRL,[84] producing seriously limiting weaknesses.[85] Consequently, the mere existence,

77 Jonathan Wilkenfeld, Kyle Beardsley, and David Quinn (eds.), *Research Handbook on Mediating International Crises* (Cheltenham: Edward Elgar, 2019), p. 1.

78 Eduardo Valencia-Ospina, 'The work of the International Law Commission on the "protection of persons in the event of disasters"' (2018) 1 YB Int'l Disaster L 5–27.

79 See, in particular, IFRC, 'Guidelines for the domestic facilitation and regulation of international disaster relief and initial recovery assistance', 2007, www.icrc.org/en/doc/assets/files/red-cross-crescent-movement/31st-international-conference/idrl-guidelines-en.pdf (accessed 19 August 2022).

80 See the Institute of International Law's 2003 urgings for legal development to prevent/mitigate disaster suffering: 'Bruges resolution', preamble.

81 See UNGA, 'Memorandum by the Secretariat', paras 3–4 in particular, regarding the failed Convention Establishing an International Relief Union, Geneva, 12 July 1927, in force 27 December 1932, 135 UNTS 247, and the unsuccessful UNDRO, 'Draft Convention on Expediting the Delivery of Emergency Assistance', 1984, https://disasterlaw.ifrc.org/media/1110 (accessed 19 August 2022).

82 See UNGA, 'Memorandum by the Secretariat'.

83 E.g., the Tampere Convention on the Provision of Telecommunication Resources for Disaster Mitigation and Relief Operations, Tampere, 18 Jun 1998, in force 8 January 2005, 2296 UNTS 5, and the Framework Convention on Civil Defence Assistance, 22 May 2000, in force 23 September 2001 2172 UNTS 213.

84 IFRC, *World Disasters Report 2000: Focus on Public Health* (Geneva: IFRC, 2000), p. 145.

85 Katrien Beeckman, 'International response to non-armed conflict disasters: Legal challenges encountered in light of the current regulatory framework' (2006) 25 Refug Surv Q 129–37.

and impressive substance, of the draft Articles testifies to the ILC's phenomenal success in synthesising, systematising, codifying, and progressing this complex area.

The draft Articles' preamble highlights their focus on the 'essential needs' and rights of disaster-affected persons, that solidarity is a 'fundamental value', and that strengthening international cooperation in the overall disaster cycle[86] is vital. The ILC also notes that the sovereignty and prerogatives of disaster-affected States and their primary roles in providing relief remain undiminished.[87] While these various imperatives should be in harmony, friction endures. This section examines the draft Articles to highlight the ILC's governance structure regarding aid refusals. It will become apparent that this scheme contains gaps that leave open considerable possibilities for disputes. These gaps could be closed by making allowance for mediation processes which could be accommodated within the more general draft Articles concerning disaster-affected States' responsibilities and duties to co-operate.

13.4.1 *The Legal Framework Concerning Disaster Assistance Refusals*[88]

Under draft Article 10, a disaster-affected State has a duty of ensuring the protection of persons and provision of disaster relief assistance in its territory. It also retains a primary role in the direction, control, co-ordination, and supervision of such assistance. Under draft Article 11, a stricken State has a duty to seek external assistance if its national resources are overwhelmed.[89] Article 13 reflects these provisions by initially proclaiming the core principle that implementing international relief assistance is contingent upon the stricken State's consent[90] and then qualifying that power by stating in draft Article 13 (2) that such consent must not be withheld arbitrarily. Draft Article 13(3) then articulates the affected State's duty to make known, whenever possible, decisions regarding external offers in a timely manner. Taken together, the draft Articles reflect wider contemporary understandings of sovereignty's conceptual envelopment of both rights and obligations. The ILC's priorities may be deducible from the fact that draft Article 13's commentaries allow two paragraphs of attention to the consent requirement and eleven paragraphs

86 Draft Articles preamble and commentary to preamble, para. 5.

87 Ibid., paras 3 and 6.

88 Allan and O'Donnell, 'A call to alms?', see also Sandesh Sivakumaran, 'Arbitrary withholding of consent to humanitarian assistance in situations of disaster' (2015) 64 ICLQ 501–31.

89 From, as appropriate, other States, the UN and other potential assisting actors.

90 See also draft Art 10(2).

justifying the qualified regime. More prosaically, it is possible that considerable explanation was needed for Article 13(2) because it had no specifically relevant, hard law antecedents. Rather, the ILC recalled with approval UNGA Resolutions[91] articulating that 'abandonment' of disaster victims 'without humanitarian assistance' threatens life and offends human dignity.[92] The ILC also cited the warm reception afforded to, and similar terms of, the 1998 UN Guiding Principles on Internal Displacement.[93] It also drew upon two Institute of International Law Resolutions in 1989 and 2003, the latter of which particularly asserts that disaster-affected States are obliged to 'not arbitrarily and unjustifiably' reject bona fide offers 'exclusively intended to provide humanitarian assistance, nor to refuse access to victims'.[94] While these sources gave substance to the norm, they carried the standard weaknesses of soft law in not providing for any enforcement mechanism or deliberative body. The 2003 Resolution attempted to bridge this gap by stating that, in particular, offers or access to victims could not be refused if that was likely to endanger victims' fundamental human rights or amount to a violation of the IHL ban on starving civilians,[95] perhaps indirectly invoking those regimes' systems of deliberation. However, as well as highlighting how draft Article 13(2) drew considerably from indirectly relevant areas of law, the analysis also reveals how the consequences of disputes were little addressed.

Taking the matter of human rights law first, disasters certainly compromise the right to life. An explicit emphasis on the importance of disaster-stricken people's dignity and human rights is given in draft Articles 4 and 5, respectively, noting that the affected States have duties of ensuring protection and assistance, which include preserving lives.[96] Conceiving these responsibilities in positive, proactive terms in disasters implies guaranteed access to humanitarian assistance for populations, whether sourced nationally or via

[91] UNGA, 'Humanitarian assistance', UN Doc. A/RES/43/131; 'Humanitarian assistance', UN Doc. A/RES/45/100.

[92] Notably, the ILC recalled this stirring sentiment in draft Art 13 but not in draft Art 12 which left external offers of assistance as discretionary.

[93] ECOSOC, 'Guiding principles on internal displacement' (11 February 1998) UN Doc. E/CN.4/1998/53/Add.2.Draft Article 13, commentary, para. 5. See the positive reception from human rights bodies, the UNGA (in unanimously adopted resolutions), and the UN Secretary-General.

[94] Institute of International Law, 'Bruges resolution', Art VIII.

[95] For disasters occurring during armed conflicts.

[96] Art 6 of the International Covenant on Civil and Political Rights (ICCPR), New York, 16 December 1966, in force 23 March 1976, 999 UNTS 171; Art 2 of the European Convention on Human Rights (ECHR), Rome, 4 November 1950, in force 3 September 1953, 213 UNTS 222; Art. 4 of the African Charter on Human and Peoples' Rights (ACHPR), Nairobi, 27 June 1981, in force 21 October 1986, 1520 UNTS 217.

international assistance. As the ILC notes, an offer of assistance that is met with refusal might thus, under certain conditions, violate the right to life under the 1966 International Covenant on Civil and Political Rights.[97] This seems straightforward, but entails somewhat general and vague obligations being reframed, without much detail, for disaster contexts. It is also unclear how a body such as the UN Human Rights Committee, which essentially receives information about breaches long after their occurrence, can be well placed to manage any real-time disputes over access to stricken populations.

The other key source upon which draft Article 13(2) draws is IHL. It takes a particular cue from Article 59 of Geneva Convention IV, which ordains an occupying power to agree to, and facilitate by all means at its disposal, relief schemes on behalf of an occupied population if the whole or part of that population is 'inadequately supplied'. In non-international armed conflicts, Article 18(2) of Additional Protocol II stipulates that where civilian populations are enduring undue hardships owing to shortages of essential supplies for survival,[98] relief actions of an exclusively humanitarian and impartial nature, conducted without any adverse distinction, shall be undertaken. Although this is subject to the relevant High Contracting party's consent, that consent is circumscribed. If a population's survival is threatened and a humanitarian organisation[99] (often the Red Cross) can remedy this situation, relief actions must take place. The authorities responsible for safeguarding the population cannot refuse such relief without good grounds,[100] as populations cannot be left to deliberately die of hunger without any measures being taken.[101] Again, the role of real-time monitoring and enforcement apparently falls to no particular body.

In practical terms, the UNSC has frequently called upon warring parties to grant humanitarian access and adopted measures relating to humanitarian

97 Draft Art 13, para. 4.

98 Such as foodstuffs and medical supplies.

99 Acting in an impartial and non-discriminatory way.

100 Protocol Additional to the Geneva Conventions of 12 August 1949, and Relating to the Protection of Victims of Non-international Armed Conflicts (Protocol II), Geneva, 8 June 1977, in force 7 December 1978, 1125 UNTS 609, Art 14; Protocol Additional to the Geneva Conventions of 12 August 1949, and Relating to the Protection of Victims of International Armed Conflicts (Protocol I), Geneva, 8 June 1977, in force 7 December 1978, 1125 UNTS 3, Art 54. See Jean-Marie Henckaerts and Louise Doswald-Beck, *Customary International Humanitarian Law* (Cambridge: Cambridge University Press, 2005), particularly the commentary to Rule 55.

101 Protocol Additional to the Geneva Conventions of 12 August 1949, and Relating to the Protection of Victims of Non-international Armed Conflicts (Protocol II), Geneva, 8 June 1977, in force 7 December 1978, 1125 UNTS 609, commentary, para. 4885 relating to Art 18 (2).

relief operations. It condemned the 'arbitrary denial of humanitarian access and depriving civilians of objects indispensable to their survival, including wilfully impeding relief supply and access' in Syria.[102] The UNSC also authorised UN humanitarian agencies and their implementing partners (with notification to Syrian authorities) to use routes across conflict lines and specified border crossings where humanitarian assistance could most effectively be provided.[103] The UNSC's role in the Syrian context was apposite given there existed an ongoing non-international armed conflict. That rationale might also extend to its intervention where a disaster is part of a complex emergency. However, it is unclear that it would always be appropriate for the UNSC to intercede in a peacetime disaster, and as noted, its involvement in Myanmar in 2008 bore little fruit.

13.4.2 *Difficulties in Determining the Arbitrariness of Disaster Assistance Refusals*

Determining the arbitrariness of disaster assistance refusals will not be simple. The ILC suggests that determinations proceed 'on a case-by-case basis',[104] saying that refusals will not be arbitrary where affected States are capable of and willing to provide an adequate and effective disaster response utilising their own resources. Particular issues regarding fact-finding and evidence (and the role of different mediation participants) are discussed in Section 13.5. Withholding consent from one external offer of assistance is also not arbitrary if appropriate and sufficient assistance has come from elsewhere. Thirdly, if the relevant offer is not made in accordance with the ILC draft Articles (notably according to the principles of humanity,[105] neutrality,[106] impartiality,[107] and on the basis of non-discrimination[108]), its non-acceptance

[102] UNSC Res 2139 (22 February 2014) UN Doc. S/RES/2139(2014).

[103] UNSC Res 2165 (14 July 2014) UN Doc. S/RES/2165(2014).

[104] Draft Art 6, commentary, para. 8.

[105] 'In the specific context of disaster relief, ... the principle of humanity requires that "human suffering must be addressed wherever it is found".' Commentary to draft Art 6, para. 3.

[106] '[P]rovision of assistance [to] be independent of any given political, religious, ethnic or ideological context.' Commentary to draft Art 6, para. 4.

[107] Impartiality encompasses three principles: non-discrimination (assistance to be delivered on a needs basis), proportionality (operating as a distributive mechanism, with attention for the most urgent needs), and impartiality proper (no subjective distinctions to be drawn among individuals in disaster responses): commentary to draft Art 6, para. 5.

[108] As well as referencing traditionally prohibited grounds for discrimination (ethnic origin, sex, nationality, political opinions, race, religion, and disability), the commentaries note that non-discrimination should be an autonomous principle given its importance in disasters and its iteration in pre-existing disaster instruments. This principle allows for the prospect of 'positive

will not be arbitrary. Helpful as these signposts might be, the real difficulty is establishing when a refusal *is* arbitrary, how that is benchmarked, which body decides, and, very importantly, what the consequences might be. The ILC offers one example that articulates the converse of the third situation iterated. If an offer of assistance is made in accordance with the draft Articles and no alternate sources of assistance exist, then non-acceptance would carry a strong inference of arbitrariness.[109]

The draft Articles' commentaries make approving reference to a study commissioned by the UN Office for the Co-ordination of Humanitarian Affairs (UNOCHA), which analysed arbitrary withholdings of consent in armed conflicts (hereinafter the Oxford Guidance).[110] Notwithstanding the differing factual and legal issues raised by disasters and armed conflicts, it was smoothly asserted that the 'subjacent legal issue' was sufficiently similar, with the Oxford Guidance offering 'valuable insights'. The three examples of arbitrary refusal offered in the Oxford Guidance involve situations where (1) consent is withheld in circumstances resulting in a State violating its international legal obligations; or (2) withholding consent violates the principles of necessity and proportionality; or (3) consent is withheld in a manner that is unreasonable, unjust, lacking in predictability, or that is otherwise inappropriate.[111] Although the Oxford Guidance focuses on IHL, the first criterion raises clear connections with international human rights law standards generally (notably regarding the right to life,[112] rights to an adequate standard of living and to health[113]) and, in certain scenarios, may particularly engage those relating to discrimination. The second situation arises where consent is withheld for valid reasons, but is rendered arbitrary if it becomes disproportionate by exceeding what is necessary in the circumstances. A refusing State seeking to impose limitations on relief operations (in terms of time, duration, location, and affected goods and services) would be prohibited from going beyond what was absolutely necessary to achieve the legitimate aim.[114] However,

discrimination' as appropriate, and indeed 'the needs of the particularly vulnerable' are specifically referenced. See commentary to draft Art 6, paras 6–7.

109 Ibid.

110 Draft Art 13, commentary, para. 9; Dapo Akande and Emanuela-Chiara Gillard, 'Oxford guidance on the law regulating humanitarian relief operations in situations of armed conflict', *UNOCHA*, 2016, www.unocha.org/sites/unocha/files/Oxford%20Guidance%20pdf.pdf (accessed 19 August 2022) (hereinafter the Oxford Guidance).

111 Ibid, paras 49–53.

112 ICCPR, Art 6; ECHR, Art 2.

113 International Covenant on Economic, Social, and Cultural Rights, New York, 16 December 1966, in force 3 January 1976, 993 UNTS 3, Arts 11 and 12.

114 Akande and Gillard, 'Oxford guidance', para. 52.

proportionality determinations are notoriously challenging, particularly so in highly charged post-disaster settings. Leaving silent where such determinations might be analysed, or even aired, seems incomplete.

The third wide-ranging scenario arguably raises more questions than it answers. If a State did not offer any reason for its decision, and such inscrutability rendered impossible an assessment of the refusal's validity, a rebuttable presumption of arbitrariness would arise. Interestingly, the Oxford Guidance draws authority from a 2011 ILC report regarding a previous incarnation of draft Article 13, which emphasised the importance of good faith in an affected State's exercise of discretion.[115] Much of this remains in the final ILC commentaries.[116] This tautological reasoning and circular invocation of authority, of a singular illustrative example, still leaves considerable room for debate as to what constitutes arbitrary refusals. The ILC stresses the importance of good faith on the part of a disaster-affected State in assessing the severity of a disaster and the limits of its national response capacity. It sees this as an element of the State's duty to protect and provide for its population.[117] The ILC notes that good faith 'serves as an outer limit of sovereignty and the exercise of discretion', particularly in cases where a State's decision must countenance political factors. This latter point resonates with the often complicated perspectives of stricken States. The stricken State is expected to make an honest and realistic assessment of its resources and seek external assistance if these resources are insufficient to tackle the disaster. Even the best prepared States will be under stress when making assessments under an international spotlight and possibly facing growing calls for international intervention. However, the mechanics of this process, including whether and where it would be subject to international review, are left unarticulated. Currently nowhere can debates over aid refusals occur in ways that are measured and productive. Mediations might usefully step into this gap. Both the ILC and mediation processes stress the importance of good faith. When combined with mediation's emphasis upon context sensitivity and legally sound outcomes, its potential contribution in the disaster milieu becomes manifest. Furthermore, while refusing States may baulk at offering any explanations for their decisions, rejecting a mediation process is drastic and would likely cast an unfavourable impression on that refusal. Thus, the likelihood of their

115 Ibid., para. 54; see also original para. 8 of commentary to previous draft Art 11; UNGA, 'Report of the ILC: Sixty-third session', pp. 160–62.

116 Draft Art 13, commentary, para. 10.

117 Commentary to draft Art 11, para. 7, recalling the terms of UNGA, 'The declaration on principles of international law concerning friendly relations and co-operation among states' (24 October 1970) UN Doc. A/RES/2625(XXV), Annex.

participation increases because, as Merrills notes, intransigence would be 'too expensive politically for a blank refusal of mediation to be feasible'.[118]

13.4.3 *The Capacity of the ILC Draft Articles to Give Substance to Dispute Settlement in Disasters via Conceptions of Cooperation*

The option of mediation for resolving disaster disputes can be derived from the draft Articles, in particular those concerning the duty to co-operate and the forms that such cooperation might take. ILC draft Article 7 ordains States to co-operate 'among themselves, with the United Nations, with the components of the Red Cross and Red Crescent Movement, and with other assisting actors'.

This draft provision was clearly influenced by, among many other instruments,[119] the landmark 1991 UNGA Resolution 46/182, which stresses co-operation's particular importance when disaster-affected States are overwhelmed, noting that this duty goes beyond merely an inter-State duty to include cooperation with intergovernmental organisations (IGOs) and NGOs.[120] Similar provisions appear in Article 11 of the 2006 Convention on the Rights of Persons with Disabilities, the influential Tampere Convention,[121] and the Sendai Framework for Disaster Reduction,[122] with these documents themselves reflecting a 'vast' number of disaster-related instruments.[123] Despite the term 'cooperation' lacking an extensive definition, Wolfrum concludes that an analysis of the 1970 Friendly Relations Declaration indicates that '[cooperation] ... describes the voluntary co-ordinated action of two or more States which takes place under a legal regime

[118] John G. Merrills, 'The means of dispute settlement', in Malcolm D. Evans (ed.), *International Law*, 5th ed. (Oxford: Oxford University Press, 2018), p. 552.

[119] Draft Art 7, commentary, paras 7 and 8.

[120] UNGA, 'Strengthening of the coordination of humanitarian emergency assistance of the United Nations' (19 December 1991) UN Doc. A/RES/46/182, Annex para. 5. Draft Art 8's commentary also makes reference to ECOSOC, 'Strengthening of the coordination of emergency humanitarian assistance of the United Nations' (25 July 2008) UN Doc. E/RES/2008/36, stressing cross-sectoral co-operation and specifically referencing the International Red Cross/Red Crescent Movement.

[121] The Tampere Convention, and the Framework Convention on Civil Defence Assistance, preamble, para. 21.

[122] UNISDR, 'Sendai framework for disaster risk reduction 2015–2030', 2015, www.undrr.org/publication/sendai-framework-disaster-risk-reduction-2015-2030 (accessed 19 August 2022), para. 19(a).

[123] Draft Art 7, commentary, para. 3.

and serves a specific objective'.[124] As regards post-disaster responses, the legal regime would be the ILC draft Articles (and any subsequent treaty), and the specific objective would be the protection of disaster-stricken populations. As regards dispute settlement, cooperation entails expectations that disputing States co-operate during proceedings and with the body to which the dispute has been submitted. Generally speaking, less institutionalised procedures, like mediation, rely on the general obligation to co-operate.[125] Mediation slots into the terms of draft Article 7 and the prevailing aim of the ILC draft Articles. Its invocation is a manifest application of general duties of co-operation[126] and more specific duties emanating from particularly relevant human rights law.[127] Draft Article 7 also notes that repeated and forceful articulation of the co-operative duty does not diminish the affected State's primary responsibility.[128] This chimes with mediation's particular appeal as lying in its non-binding (co-operative) quality which protects sovereignty,[129] a sensitive issue in disasters, as noted.

Draft Article 8 outlines forms of disaster cooperation as embracing humanitarian assistance; co-ordination of international relief actions and communications; and making available relief personnel, equipment and goods, and scientific, medical, and technical resources.[130] The ILC had no intention of creating additional legal obligations for either affected States or other assisting

[124] Rüdiger Wolfrum, 'International law of co-operation', in Petra Minnerop, Rüdiger Wolfrum, and Frauke Lachenmann (eds.), *International Development Law: The Max Planck Encyclopedia of Public International Law* (Oxford: Oxford University Press, 2019), p. 241, para. 2.

[125] Ibid., p. 249, para. 38.

[126] See Arts 1, 3, 55, and 56 of the UN Charter.

[127] Notably regarding the rights to housing, health, and water. See CESCR, 'General comment no. 2: International technical assistance measures (Art 2 of the Covenant)' (2 February 1990) UN Doc. E/1990/23; CESCR, 'General comment no. 3: The nature of States parties' obligations (Art 2, para. 1, of the Covenant)' (14 December 1990) UN Doc. E/1991/23; CESCR, 'General comment no. 7: The right to adequate housing (Art 11.1): Forced evictions' (20 May 1997) UN Doc. E/1998/22; CESCR, 'General comment no. 14: The right to the highest attainable standard of health (Art 12 of the Covenant)' (11 August 2000) UN Doc. E/C.12/2000/4; CESCR, 'General comment no. 15: The right to water (Arts 11 and 12 of the Covenant)' (20 January 2003) UN Doc. E/C.12/2002/11.

[128] Draft Art 7, commentary, para. 4; and draft Art 10.

[129] Anne Peters, 'International dispute settlement: A network of cooperational duties' (2003) 14 EJIL 1–34 at 6.

[130] See the influence of ASEAN, 'ASEAN declaration on mutual assistance on natural disasters, Manila, 26 June 1976', https://asean.org/speechandstatement/asean-declaration-on-mutual-assistance-on-natural-disasters-manila-26-june-1976 (accessed 19 August 2022); UNGA, 'Strengthening of the coordination of humanitarian emergency assistance', UN Doc. A/RES/46/182, Annex para. 27. Draft Art 8's commentaries are keen to stress that this is an illustrative, non-exhaustive list, outlining further possible examples (para. 4).

actors to engage in certain activities.[131] This might be thought to exclude anything perceived as adding in duties (or expectations) to provide for, or engage with, mediation. However, first, draft Article 8's list is illustrative and non-exhaustive. Secondly, and as noted above, disaster cooperation occurs within, and as a result of, existing obligations to settle disputes peacefully. The draft Articles need not impose further, unexpected commitments. Clarifying that forms of cooperation can include dispute settlement processes, such as mediation, would explicitly remind disputants of their existing obligations while simultaneously operationalising the ILC's goals.

This analysis complements the ILC's own understanding of draft Article 8, which notes that appropriate forms of cooperation are bespoke to particular disasters, needs of affected populations, and the capacities of affected States and other assisting actors. It notes that the principles and forms of cooperation are reciprocal and collaborative. Draft Article 8 is not about listing activities but recognising 'areas in which harmonization of efforts through consultation on the part of both the affected State and other assisting actors may be appropriate'.[132]

This spirit of engagement, consultation, and co-ordination in pursuit of bespoke outcomes mirrors mediation's strides towards 'negotiated harmony'. Mediation is a natural form of cooperation, particularly given the clear expectation of engaging States, NGOs, and international organisations as appropriate. Early explicit articulation of this form of cooperation could be achieved within a UNGA Resolution.[133]

13.5 MODELLING DISASTER MEDIATION

This chapter cannot predetermine which post-disaster mediation model is appropriate in any particular circumstance. That is an enormously complex, hugely context-dependent design project. The intention is merely to highlight mediation's potential, outline conventional mediation models, and highlight key factors which any disaster mediation needs to consider. The key values of mediation in disasters will be addressed initially with analysis before moving to possible mediators best suited to disaster contexts.

[131] Draft Art. 8, commentary, para. 5.

[132] Ibid., para. 6, cross-referencing draft Art 7, commentary, para. 6, which refers to co-operation 'as appropriate'.

[133] Including possible referencing of the UN Mediation Support Unit.

13.5.1 *Mediation Models*

As Daase notes, in international mediations, mediators might merely facilitate dialogue and negotiation in 'politically and legally set framework[s]', or instead set processes with a view to future control, possibly by legally 'coding the deal'.[134] Research and practice concludes that both ends of the spectrum and all points in between are possible. Facilitative mediation is bureaucratic and passive. It organises inter-disputant communication non-directively, aiming to elicit underlying interests and needs behind the stated demands and positions, but without making suggestions or recommendations.[135] Formulative approaches move beyond shuttling, with mediators making more substantive contributions, perhaps in developing and drafting of proposals (but lacking powers to nudge actors to endorse particular outcomes). More pejoratively termed 'manipulative' or 'power-based' mediations envisage more directive mediators who can leverage their power, directly and conclusively influencing agreements 'through setting incentives and disincentives'.[136] Alternative taxonomies focus on the effects sought by mediators[137] with distinctions being drawn between 'communication-facilitation' strategies, 'procedural strategies' (focusing on the structural aspects of meetings, media publicity, and communications processes), and 'directive strategies' whereby mediators affect the content and substance of bargaining, echoing the aforementioned power mediation. Differences between models are not always clear-cut, and perhaps more concerningly, variations may be combined and deployed at different stages of mediation processes. Ultimately, and regardless of the model adopted, mediations involve considerable reflexivity. Mediation processes must consider the disputants' political contexts (including whether or not they are democracies); their relative power status; previous relations between disputants; the dispute's nature; the timing, duration, and nature of

[134] Daase, 'Law of the peacemaker', pp. 109, 134.

[135] See 'Federal Government of Germany Guidelines on Preventing Crises, Resolving Conflicts, Building Peace', www.auswaertiges-amt.de/blob/1214246/057f794cd35937 63ea556897972574fd/preventing-crises-data.pdf (accessed 21 June 2023), pp. 77–83.

[136] Daase, 'Law of the peacemaker', p. 112; UN Guidance annexed to UNGA, 'Strengthening the role of mediation', para. 13. See also Djeffal, 'Mediation in international law', citing Loraleigh Keashly and Ronald J. Fisher, 'A contingency perspective on conflict interventions: Theoretical and practical considerations', in Jacob Bercovitch (ed.), *Resolving International Conflicts: The Theory and Practice of Mediation* (Boulder, CO: Lynne Rienner, 1996), p. 241.

[137] Djeffal, 'Mediation in international law', p. 26, drawing on Jacob Bercovitch, 'Mediation and conflict resolution', in Jacob Bercovitch, Viktor A. Kremenyuk, and Ira William Zartman (eds.), *The Sage Handbook of Conflict Resolution* (Los Angeles, CA: Sage, 2007), p. 347.

the mediation; the mediator's identity (and any history with the disputants); the mediation environment (neutral ground, mediator territory); and, given the disaster context, the intensity of harm, including the number of actual and likely fatalities.[138]

Any disaster mediation must proceed on an evidence-led basis. Early assessment is critical for investigating and evaluating available resources within the territory and prioritising needs.[139] The mechanics of this complex process entail prior planning (particularly regarding which actors are tasked with garnering and assessment duties) and could fit within the international standards determining States' disaster planning and mitigation responsibilities. This is already alluded to in draft Article 9 regarding duties of disaster preparedness, the primary responsibilities of affected States, and the aforementioned Sendai regime.[140] This also highlights and reinforces expectations of co-ordination at national/international level, which would be crucial preconditions to any potential mediation.[141] Duties of assessing the evidence of national resources could initially be discharged by affected States (while appraising their coping capabilities). If the stricken State's capacity is disputed, matters could then be elevated to the international level with well-structured and well-constituted mediation performing a vital, expert role. Clarifying the rules of engagement increases foreseeability and encourages early, beneficial buy-in from key actors whose contributions are analysed latterly.

Measuring a mediation's 'success' is complicated. Directive mediation may change participants' behaviour in the immediate term. However, it can produce feelings of alienation or resentment towards mediators (particularly perilous if this is the UN or a regional partner) or other parties,[142] ultimately undoing the benefits achieved. Stability testifies to a mediation's favourable outcome, suggesting parties' satisfaction with the outcome and its likely sustainability.[143] Given the importance of stability in disasters, in both the short term (in respect of efficiently providing for stricken populations and safeguarding aid providers[144]) and the long term (communicating exemplars

[138] Bercovitch and Houston, 'Study of international mediation', pp. 39–48. For an interesting analysis, see Fleur Johns, *Non-legality in International Law: Unruly Law* (Cambridge: Cambridge University Press, 2013), pp. 185–214.

[139] Mel Rubin, 'Disaster mediation: Lessons in conflict coordination and collaboration' (2008) 9 Cardozo J Conflict Resol 351–70 at 357.

[140] UNISDR, 'Sendai framework'.

[141] Rubin, 'Disaster mediation', p. 369.

[142] Wilkenfeld et al., 'Mediating international crises', pp. 297–98.

[143] Jacob Bercovitch, 'Mediation success or failure: A search for the elusive criteria' (2006) 7 Cardozo J Conflict Res 289–302.

[144] See draft Arts 15 and 16.

to pre-empt similar future disputes), this would appear as an appropriate measure of a disaster mediation's success.

13.5.2 *Disaster Mediation and Key Values: Consent, Impartiality, Neutrality, and Confidentiality*

Given that consent is both an ethos and a pragmatic necessity in mediation,[145] it becomes necessary to inquire as to how disputing States could opt in to disaster mediations. In practical terms, treaties can contain pre-judicial obligations regarding mediation.[146] If the ILC draft Articles form part of an eventual treaty, an appropriate provision could be inserted, with State parties' accession then representing consent to any particular process. Alternatively, as already suggested, the adoption (preferably by consensus) of a UNGA Resolution endorsing the ILC draft Articles and positing mediation's attractions would also evidence States' willing commitment. This would complement general UN Charter obligations already mentioned. In the meantime, drawing disputants towards disaster mediation processes might best be sought in an incremental fashion, with consent being cultivated and developed via assurances as to process integrity.[147]

Consent to participate may be influenced by external (f)actors which might embrace 'political, ideological or psychological considerations'[148] and international alliances. For example, there were widespread expectations that China could helpfully intercede regarding Myanmar's post-Nargis response. However, care is required, as any 'nudging' towards mediation could foster latent acrimony endangering a mediation's outcomes (if not its actual occurrence). It could even subsequently undermine or vitiate consent and derail an in-progress disaster assistance programme. Traditional approaches to exploring disaster assistance delivery have employed diplomatic intercessions in a linear fashion. These have struck bargains, issued threats, and sometimes generated ill-feeling. More sustainable arrangements might result from back-channel diplomacy (possibly via the UNOCHA or relevant regional organisations) with limited, but crucial, 'prequel' functions with disputants engaging equally and with certain procedural safeguards.

145 UN Guidance annexed to UNGA, 'Strengthening the role of mediation', paras 21–25.

146 Making mediation a more integrative or interdependent form of dispute settlement. Djeffal, 'Mediation in international law', pp. 15, 38.

147 Including confidentiality and credible mediators. Djeffal, 'Mediation in international law', pp. 15, 38.

148 Ibid., p. 8.

Impartiality is universally identified as a conceptual cornerstone of mediation.[149] Even mere perceptions of bias are damaging. However, defining precisely what the impartiality linchpin entails, beyond the intuitive, is complex. Mainstream approaches insist that effective mediators must be able to engage with all relevant actors and be capable of running balanced, fair processes, without personal interests in the outcome. The 1907 Hague Convention calls for a sensitive approach, with mediators 'reconciling ... opposing claims and appeasing ... feelings of resentment' between opposing States.[150] UN mediators must not accept conditions for support from external actors that compromise process impartiality, and should avoid associations with punitive measures against disputants by other actors.[151] Theoretically, this could include threats of sanctions or force by States against disaster-affected States.

However, impartiality and neutrality are not synonymous. Mediators are not value-free, and there is a distinction between material (economic or political) interests and constraining normative schemes. Unlike the pre-1945 scheme which bestowed considerable autonomy upon mediators, UN mediators, in particular, are 'typically mandated to uphold certain universal principles and values and may need to make them explicitly known to the parties'.[152] Some of these goals/values may be abstract and communal (such as the pursuit of peace), some more specific (UN Charter safeguards).

As noted in Section 13.3, the underpinning value in disaster mediations must be that the needs of stricken populations are met. The mediator's impartiality is not impugned by this. Process neutrality is qualified only in terms already agreed to by all UN member States, including the most disaster-prone ones. Reconstructing a disaster mediator's aim as general and communitarian, rather than particular and local, is clear, non-compromising, and uncovers a disaster mediation's more generalised, relational dimension. Furthermore, this notion of an inhibiting meta-framework resonates with the ILC project's proclaimed Vattelian imperative of solidarity.[153] This is reflected

[149] See discussion in Merrills, *International Dispute Settlement*, pp. 32–33.

[150] Art 4 of the 1907 Hague Convention. See also Art 8 regarding 'special mediation processes' for seriously peace-endangering situations whereby 'powers' specially chosen by disputants would directly engage. Djeffal, 'Mediation in international law'.

[151] Mediators feeling unable to maintain balance and impartiality should hand over to other mediators. UN Guidance annexed to UNGA, 'Strengthening the role of mediation', para. 28.

[152] Djeffal, 'Mediation in international law', p. 18.

[153] UNGA, 'Preliminary report on the protection of persons', p. 147; Thérèse O'Donnell and Craig Allan, 'Identifying solidarity: The ILC project on the protection of persons in disasters and human rights' (2017) 49 Geo Wash L Rev 53–95.

in its sets of 'guiding stars' emphasising human dignity, human rights of stricken populations, and fundamentally principled disaster responses.[154] These principles and values could underpin and delimit any disaster mediation process without favouring any particular material or political interests. Being honest with relevant actors (via effective communication) as to these 'rules of engagement' would underwrite and safeguard the integrity of the process, doing so without exerting political leverage.

It has been suggested that even actors with certain indirect involvement in disputes (even perhaps involving active support of one or other party) can act as mediators. This is on the basis that they could arguably act as fully informed, influential mediators and prompt outcomes fitting an international context.[155] Despite serious concerns about blurring the lines between mediation and direct involvement,[156] this might not be a valueless proposition, particularly if there was more than one such third party or, more attractively, the third party represented a collective. During disasters, a UN mediation partnered with a regional organisation, such as ASEAN (notably an expert in the disasters field, as will be discussed later), might tread that fine line between being informed and effective without toxic meddling.

Of course, mediation has its limits and can be instrumentalised in bad faith. This seems particularly apposite in contexts akin to the perceived 2008 Myanmarese obstructiveness. Mediation processes could be manipulated (by disputants themselves or by external forces) to delay or derail aid delivery. Mediators would have to be able to pause or withdraw their involvement, particularly if the evolving solution conflicted with international legal obligations (a particularly thorny problem to assess in disasters). As with any mediation, assessing withdrawal risks against continuing in floundering and increasingly desperate processes is onerous, stressful, and with potentially far-reaching, maybe fatal consequences.[157] There is no way around this.

Finally, confidentiality is a hallmark of mediations, but it struggles against calls for transparency. Indeed, in the disaster context, there is often relentless focus 'on deficiencies in the delivery of relief supplies'[158] via unceasing news coverage and pervasive social media. International mediations traditionally eschew public criticism of parties in favour of frankness in private. While these

[154] Draft Art 6.
[155] Merrills, *International Dispute Settlement*, p. 33.
[156] Djeffal, 'Mediation in international law', pp. 34–37.
[157] UN Guidance annexed to UNGA, 'Strengthening the role of mediation', para. 14.
[158] Louise Fréchette, 'Foreword', in Andrew F. Cooper, Jorge Heine, and Ramesh C. Thakur (eds.), *The Oxford Handbook of Modern Diplomacy* (Oxford: Oxford University Press, 2013), p. xxxi.

'protected zones' might ameliorate deleterious influences, they can arouse suspicions about diplomatic power plays and compromised processes. The experience in peace negotiations shows it may be possible to offset such anxieties via carefully calibrated, inclusive participation processes.

13.5.3 *Disaster Mediators and Mediation Participants*

While mediation often exists alongside facilitation, good offices, and dialogue efforts, it has a distinctive logic and approach, uniquely focusing on active listening. Mediators should be authoritative and selected because of their experience, skills, knowledge, cultural/contextual sensitivities, and insights into whether disputes require discreet engagement or more high-profile initiatives.[159] Mediators must possess significant political and social capital and be able to identify and connect (rather than sympathise) with key actors (often emanating from non-elite levels). International mediators comprise a wide-ranging grouping, including international and regional organisations, individuals, NGOs, and States. This section focuses on potential contributions from international organisations and NGOs. Without belittling the input of States and individuals,[160] the chosen focus builds on relations predating a disaster's onset and those actors with particular disaster expertise. It also acknowledges research findings that active strategies, supported by resources, enhance a mediation's prospects.[161]

Mediation processes must afford all parties opportunities to be heard and to access mediation process resources. Good intentions alone are insufficient; disaster contexts must be understood.[162] Mediations and disasters represent complex cultural encounters with contrasting worldviews, increasing the potential for 'stressful and destructive consequences'.[163] This cultural variable

[159] UN Guidance annexed to UNGA, 'Strengthening the role of mediation', paras 16–20.

[160] UN, 'An agenda for peace: Preventive diplomacy, peacemaking and peace-keeping. Report of the Secretary-General pursuant to the statement adopted by the Summit Meeting of the Security Council on 31 January 1992' (17 June 1992) UN Doc. A/47/277–S/24111 para. 37; Gilbert M. Khadiagala, 'The conflict-mediation role of elder-statespersons', in Katharina P. Coleman and Thomas K. Tieku (eds.), *African Actors in International Security* (Boulder, CO: Lynne Rienner, 2018).

[161] Bercovitch and Houston, 'Study of international mediation', p. 48.

[162] Anthony Oliver-Smith, *Natural Disasters and Cultural Responses* (Williamsburg, VA: Department of Anthropology, College of William and Mary, 1986); Anthony Oliver-Smith, 'Anthropological research on hazards and disasters' (1996) 25 Annu Rev Anthropol 303–28.

[163] Anthony J. Marsella and Michael A. Christopher, 'Ethnocultural considerations in disasters: An overview of research, issues, and directions' (2004) 27 Psychiatr Clin North Am 521–39 at 523–24; Jacob Bercovitch and Ole Elgström, 'Culture and international mediation: An

implies that cultural similarities between disputants optimise their prospects.[164] Similarly, disaster response programmes are more likely to be receptively considered, and effective, if affected communities have some sense of control and partnership and feel 'seen'.[165] Well-chosen mediators can help bridge gaps in these particularly social processes. They must be capable of attracting participation from key stakeholders across relevant national and international societies[166] (including country/regional experts), those possessing disaster expertise, and, most crucially, local civil society actors.[167]

13.5.3.1 International Organisations

Among the most prominent international organisations undertaking mediation are the European Union (EU), the Organisation for Economic Cooperation and Development (OECD), and the UN (including specialised agencies and subsidiary programmes such as the World Food Programme).[168] The UN's significant track record dates from the 1949 Indo-Pakistan ceasefire through to the December 2018 Hudaydah truce in Yemen.[169] Partnerships with regional bodies[170] and civil society actors[171] try to ensure clarity and avoid 'overlap and institutional rivalry'. Although, as noted, the mediatory capabilities of the UNSC and UNGA are mentioned in Chapter VI of the UN Charter, the directive nature of the former and the complex and diverse composition of the latter[172] potentially compromise their suitability as disaster mediators. By contrast, the UN Secretary-General retains a renowned mediatory role (both personally and via Special Envoys),[173] arguably working best

empirical assessment', in Jacob Bercovitch (ed.), *Theory and Practice of International Mediation: Selected Essays* (London: Routledge, 2011), p. 228.

164 Bercovitch and Elgström, 'Culture and international mediation', pp. 236, 239.

165 Marsella and Christopher, 'Ethnocultural considerations', p. 523.

166 Rubin, 'Disaster mediation', p. 357.

167 UNGA, 'Strengthening the role of mediation', paras 16–18, and the annexed UN Guidance, paras 30–34.

168 World Food Programme, 'One step forward, two steps back', 2 December 2020, www.wfp.org/stories/one-step-forward-two-steps-back (accessed 21 August 2022).

169 UN, 'Agenda for peace', para. 67; Muriel Asseburg, Wolfram Lacher, and Mareike Transfeld, 'Mission impossible? UN mediation in Libya, Syria and Yemen', *Stiftung Wissenschaft und Politik*, October 2018, www.swp-berlin.org/publications/products/research_papers/2018RP08_Ass_EtAl.pdf (accessed 21 August 2022).

170 Magnus Lundgren, 'Mediation in Syria: Initiatives, strategies, and obstacles, 2011-2016' (2016) 37 Contemp Sec Pol'y 273–88.

171 Marie-Joëlle Zahar and Sara Helmüller, 'UN-led mediation in Syria and civil society' (2019) 28 Accord 84–87.

172 Djeffal, 'Mediation in international law', pp. 27–28.

173 See UN Charter, Arts 98 and 99.

when operating independently of the deliberative bodies.[174] Increased professionalisation of UN mediation arrived with the 2006 establishment of the Mediation Support Unit (MSU)[175] and its Standby Team of Senior Mediation Advisers. These developments were paralleled by the 2010 founding of the Group of Friends Mediation (co-chaired by Finland and Turkey). Currently comprising fifty-two member States, the UN and eight regional organisations, as well as other international organisations, its goal is to promote, advance, and develop mediation's use.[176] Ongoing UN endorsement[177] of the group's efforts indicates a velocity to mediation's wider and increasing profile.

While UN mediations have principally focused on resolving armed conflicts, the UNOCHA has recognised that humanitarian crises can also benefit from such efforts.[178] Overlaps between armed conflicts, disasters, and humanitarian crises arise when disasters aggravate pre-existing tensions and/or create political opportunities for particular antagonists in armed conflicts.[179] Given UN success in mediating humanitarian access even in these intractable situations, its capacity to contribute in disasters *simpliciter* is unarguable and likely to become more pressing given accelerating climate change.[180] The UNOCHA drove forward the Guiding Principles on Internal Displacement and commissioned the Oxford Guidance, discussed in Section 13.4. Even if

[174] Although extensive interplay between the UN's main organs, offices, and relevant States enables overview and holistic approaches. Christof H. Heyns and Karen Stefiszyn (eds.), *Human Rights, Peace and Justice in Africa: A Reader* (Pretoria: Pretoria University Law Press, 2006), p. 324.

[175] Within the Policy and Mediation Division of the UN Department of Political and Peacebuilding Affairs.

[176] UN Peacemaker, 'Group of friends of mediation', https://peacemaker.un.org/friendsofmediation (accessed 21 August 2022).

[177] UNGA, 'Strengthening the role of mediation in the peaceful settlement of disputes, conflict prevention and resolution' (28 July 2011) UN Doc. A/RES/65/283; 'Strengthening the role of mediation in the peaceful settlement of disputes, conflict prevention and resolution' (15 October 2012) UN Doc. A/RES/66/291; 'United Nations activities in support of mediation: Report of the Secretary-General' (27 June 2017) UN Doc. A/72/115; 'Letter dated 21 November 2019 from the Permanent Representative of Turkey to the United Nations addressed to the Secretary-General' (25 November 2019) UN Doc. A/74/561.

[178] Anon., 'UN urges greater aid access for Gaza, "intensification of mediation efforts" to end Israel-Palestine violence', *UN News*, 18 May 2021, https://news.un.org/en/story/2021/05/1092172 (accessed 21 August 2022); Jan Egeland, 'Humanitarian diplomacy', in Andrew F. Cooper, Jorge Heine, and Ramesh C. Thakur (eds.), *The Oxford Handbook of Modern Diplomacy* (Oxford: Oxford University Press, 2013), p. 352.

[179] Katie Harris, David Keen, and Tom Mitchell, *When Disasters and Conflicts Collide: Improving Links between Disaster Resilience and Conflict Prevention* (London: Overseas Development Institute, 2013).

[180] Carl-Friedrich Schleussner et al., 'Armed-conflict risks enhanced by climate-related disasters in ethnically fractionalized countries' (2016) 113 PNAS (2016) 9216–21.

this background militates against the perceptions of UNOCHA's impartiality regarding aid refusals, this need not totally discount wider – or partnered – UN engagement in disaster mediations. Given that mediations can impact wider regional and international dynamics, they should countenance the roots and dynamics of disputes, broader societal needs, and regional and international environments.[181] This comprehensive and inclusive approach complements and reflects the trend away from mediations led exclusively by the UN or 'great powers' towards the involvement of regional organisations.[182] The UN's pre-existing relationships with such bodies highlight a rich seam for potential mediation partnerships, possibly with regional bodies such as ASEAN.

Diplomatic humanitarianism is growing in the ASEAN region,[183] and its particularly rich experience offers an instructive example for hitherto hesitant regional bodies to adopt more proactive roles in this field.[184] ASEAN has had success in facilitating disaster assistance, even where there were initial hesitancies, as evidenced in 2008 in Myanmar, and following the 2018 Indonesian earthquakes and tsunami.[185] Its long-established dispute settlement mechanisms include mediation,[186] and its pioneering prioritisation of international disaster cooperation is conspicuous in the 2005 ASEAN Agreement on Disaster Management and Emergency Response (AADMER). Widely considered a leading disaster instrument,[187] it provided for an 'operational

181 UN Guidance annexed to UNGA, 'Strengthening the role of mediation', para. 11.

182 Teresa Whitfield, *Working with Groups of Friends* (Washington, DC: Unites States Institute of Peace Press, 2010).

183 Claire Q. Smith and Susannah G. Williams, 'Why Indonesia adopted "quiet diplomacy" over R2P in the Rohingya crisis: The roles of Islamic humanitarianism, civil-military relations, and ASEAN' (2021) 13 GR2P 158–85.

184 Yves-Kim Creach and Lilianne Fan, 'ASEAN's role in the Cyclone Nargis response: Implications, lessons and opportunities', *Humanitarian Practice Network*, December 2008, https://odihpn.org/publication/asean%C2%92s-role-in-the-cyclone-nargis-response-implications-lessons-and-opportunities (accessed 19 September 2022).

185 IFRC, 'Real-time evaluation Indonesia: Earthquakes and tsunami (Lombok, Sulawesi) 2018 – Final report', 23 January 2019, https://reliefweb.int/report/indonesia/real-time-evaluation-indonesia-earthquakes-and-tsunami-lombok-sulawesi-2018-final (accessed 19 September 2022).

186 The ASEAN Treaty on Amity and Co-operation in Southeast Asia, Bali, 24 February 1976, in force 15 July 1976, 1025 UNTS 297, Art 15 specifically mentions mediation; ASEAN Protocol on Enhanced Dispute Settlement Mechanism, Vientiane, 29 November 2004, in force 29 November 2004, Art 4.

187 UNGA, 'Preliminary report on the protection of persons'. For scepticism regarding the importance of the treaty's terms rather than its existence (and the 'politics of a treaty commitment'), see Gabrielle Simm, 'Disaster response in Southeast Asia: The ASEAN Agreement on Disaster Response and Emergency Management' (2018) 8 Asian JIL 116–42 at 133, 140.

engine'[188] in the ASEAN Co-ordinating Centre for Humanitarian Assistance (the AHA Centre),[189] which facilitates cooperation and co-ordination among ASEAN members and with relevant UN offices[190] and IGOs in promoting regional collaboration in disaster management. While respecting a disaster-affected State's primary role, the AHA will offer assistance if required, including in directing requests to any 'Assisting Entity'. Indeed, the AHA can act as an intermediary regarding decisions on requests for, and offers of, assistance and the scope and terms of such assistance.[191] This role equips the AHA to cope very well with the demands and thrust of ILC draft Article 13 and to enable, at a minimum, facilitative, 'shuttle' mediations.

The 'ASEAN Way' was traditionally characterised by the key principles of consensus decision-making, non-interference, and non-use of force.[192] Although increasingly maligned as overly State-centric and inappropriate in a progressively interdependent world,[193] its underlying ethos that eschews confrontation and embarrassment, in favour of discreet communication[194] and agile, constructive engagement,[195] fits extremely well with mediation's mode. A review of ASEAN's comparative performances after Cyclone Nargis

[188] ASEAN, 'ASEAN vision 2025 on disaster management', https://ahacentre.org/publication/asean-vision-2025-on-disaster-management (accessed 21 August 2022), p. 8.

[189] Agreement on the establishment of the ASEAN Co-ordinating Centre for Humanitarian Assistance on Disaster Management, Bali, 17 November 2011, in force 7 April 2014, https://ahacentre.org/publication/the-agreement-of-the-establishment-of-the-aha-centre (accessed 21 August 2022).

[190] See also ASEAN, 'Joint declaration on ASEAN-UN collaboration in disaster management, Ha Noi, 30 October 2010', https://asean.org/joint-declaration-on-asean-un-collaboration-in-disaster-management (accessed 21 August 2022). For a reflective experiential report, see Angelo Paulo L. Trias and Alistair D. B. Cook, 'Recalibrating disaster governance in ASEAN: Implications of the 2018 Central Sulawesi earthquake and tsunami – Policy report', *S. Rajaratnam School of International Studies*, December 2019, www.rsis.edu.sg/wp-content/uploads/2019/12/PR191206_Recalibrating-Disaster-Governance-in-ASEAN_v3.pdf (accessed 21 August 2022).

[191] ASEAN Agreement on Disaster Management and Emergency Response, Vientiane, 26 July 2005, in force 24 December 2009, https://disasterlaw.ifrc.org/media/494 (accessed 21 August 2022), Art 11(4) and (5).

[192] Taku Yukawa, 'The ASEAN way as a symbol: An analysis of discourses on the ASEAN norms' (2018) 31 Pacific Rev 298–314, although it has relaxed the original unanimity approach (see p. 309).

[193] ASEAN Secretariat, 'Report of the Eminent Persons Group on the ASEAN Charter', 2006, www.asean.org/wp-content/uploads/images/archive/19247.pdf (accessed 21 August 2022), para. 12.

[194] Rodion Ebbighausen, 'The ASEAN way: Where is it leading?', *Deutsche Welle*, 7 August 2017, www.dw.com/en/the-asean-way-where-is-it-leading/a-39998187 (accessed 21 August 2022).

[195] Logan Masilamani and Jimmy Peterson, 'The "ASEAN way": The structural underpinnings of constructive engagement', *Foreign Policy Journal*, 15 October 2014, www.foreignpolicyjournal

and Typhoon Haiyan/Yolanda in the Philippines suggested that since ASEAN was neither an operational aid agency nor responsible for distributing ground-level assistance; it should instead focus on its facilitative role, particularly at the intergovernmental level.[196] Its expertise and capacity for 'gap-filling, bridging divides … and convening a wide range of actors to build a more coordinated humanitarian community' makes it well equipped for mediating in a highly disaster-vulnerable region,[197] with the potential to develop a portfolio of best practices. Further traction is lent to partnership by the ASEAN Vision 2025 on Disaster Management, which specially emphasises the contributions of civil society.[198] This reflects a contemporary understanding that single operating mediators, functioning hierarchically, are less likely to succeed than 'open architecture' processes that demonstrate a readiness to engage with diversely experienced third-party partners.[199] ASEAN's clear receptiveness to wider engagement ideally positions it to occupy a particular niche[200] in the disaster/humanitarian space, potentially setting a useful precedent for other regional organisations.

13.5.3.2 Non-governmental Organisations

Given their avowed activism, NGOs might be thought to lack the requisite neutrality for chairing mediations, with a lack of material resources posing an additional impediment. However, this lack of material interests, and their perceived independence (compared to States and IGOs), can increase the attractiveness of NGO mediators. Furthermore, the perception that NGOs are less likely to lose interest in disputes once the outside pressure disappears (unlike States and some IGOs) enhances their appeal. Indeed, the UN

.com/wp-content/uploads/2014/10/141015-Masilamani-Peterson-ASEAN.pdf (accessed 21 August 2022), pp. 1, 7, 12–13.

196 Lilianne Fan and Hanna B. Krebs, 'Regional organisations and humanitarian action: The case of ASEAN – HPG Working Paper', *Overseas Development Institute*, September 2014, https://cdn.odi.org/media/documents/9207.pdf (accessed 21 August 2022), p. 18.

197 Ibid.

198 ASEAN, 'ASEAN vision 2025', p. 17.

199 Chester A. Crocker, Fen Osler Hampson, and Pamela Aall, 'Mediation in the emerging international environment: From hierarchy to improvisation', in Jonathan Wilkenfeld, Kyle Beardsley, and David Quinn (eds.), *Research Handbook on Mediating International Crises* (Cheltenham: Edward Elgar, 2019), pp. 50, 61.

200 ASEAN Secretariat, *AADMER Work Programme, 2016–2020* (Jakarta: ASEAN Secretariat, 2016), p. 127.

Secretariat Memorandum, prepared in support of the ILC project, noted the historical mediatory contributions of NGOs in establishing aid corridors.[201]

Given the importance of cultural sensitivity in disasters, involving local civil society actors in mediations is crucial and complements their recognised contributions to disaster risk reduction[202] and recovery.[203] They are particularly helpful in pre-formal process settings,[204] and their inclusion could diminish anxieties that NGO involvement favours Global North over Global South organisations.[205] Local faith and youth organisations and those supporting marginalised social groups are more likely to understand the immediate needs of vulnerable populations, grasp local and national politics, and make vital contributions to fact-finding. Of course, there is always the danger that in seeking to enhance the legitimacy of mediation processes, such extensive assemblages may generate incoherence and chaos. However, not all actors need to intervene in proceedings at the same level all the time, and carefully designed and staged processes could diminish potential disarray.

Although not strictly an NGO, the Red Cross Movement is an obvious candidate to involve in disaster mediations given its focus on bridging communication gaps[206] through acting as an impartial and neutral intermediary.[207] Evidence shows that early Red Cross involvement in a crisis enhances its capacity to gain parties' confidence and establish ground rules. Its record of combining soundly informed perseverance with a reasonable amount of

[201] UNGA, 'Memorandum by the Secretariat', fn. 818.

[202] Jonatan A. Lassa et al., 'Civil society roles in governing disaster reduction at national and local levels in Indonesia – IRGSC Working Paper 6', June 2013, www.irgsc.org/pubs/wp/IRGSCWP006civilsocietyindrr.pdf (accessed 21 August 2022).

[203] Daniel P. Aldrich, 'The emergence of civil society: Networks in disasters, mitigation, and recovery', in Urbano Fra Paleo (ed.), *Risk Governance: The Articulation of Hazard, Politics and Ecology* (Dordrecht: Springer, 2015), p. 135.

[204] Molly M. Melin and Paul Olander, 'Supply-side incentives for mediation: Which actors mediate international crises and why?', in Jonathan Wilkenfeld, Kyle Beardsley, and David Quinn (eds.), *Research Handbook on Mediating International Crises* (Cheltenham: Edward Elgar, 2019), pp. 94, 100–1.

[205] Elena Evangelidis and Thérèse O'Donnell, 'NGOs and the International Law Commission draft Articles on the Protection of Persons in the Event of Disasters: A relationship of mutual or grudging respect?' (2018) 1 YB Int'l Disaster L 116–47.

[206] Statutes of the International Red Cross and Red Crescent Movement, Geneva, October 1986, in force 22 June 2006, www.icrc.org/en/doc/assets/files/other/statutes-en-a5.pdf (accessed 21 August 2022), Art 5(3).

[207] See explicit recognition in Art 5(3) of Additional Protocol I to the Geneva Conventions; ICRC, 'The neutral intermediary role of the ICRC: At the heart of humanitarian action', 7 July 2008, www.icrc.org/en/doc/resources/documents/interview/neutral-intermediary-interview-070708.htm (accessed 21 August 2022).

pragmatism and flexibility speaks well for its mediatory capabilities.[208] The Red Cross has particular experience and credibility in disasters, notably via IFRC efforts in aid delivery and developing pertinent rules.[209] It partners with regional organisations, such as ASEAN, and recognises the crucial role of other civil society actors, both in the immediate term and in ensuring the sustainability of a mediation's positive outcomes. Given that the ILC draft Articles also already explicitly recognise the Red Cross Movement's key role in the co-operative duty of draft Article 7, its mediatory involvement would seem a natural articulated fit between actor, process, and goal.

13.6 CONCLUSION

Given mediation's generally increasing usage, its potential for widening participation, its contextual sensitivity and discretion, and its proven success rate even in the most fraught environments, it is clearly an untapped resource for resolving disputes concerning external disaster assistance. The inevitable afterlife of the draft Articles can explore this potential. It is important to acknowledge (in neutral terms) that disputes over disaster aid occur, and that processes which allow States, international entities, and civil society to interface and work through such conflicts are necessary. Disaster aid disputes must be mapped and the legitimacy of goals explored using law, human rights, and basic needs.[210] Rather than proving a hindrance, mediation has a capacity to enable the ILC's goals and to do so in a way which eschews the civics of statecraft in favour of partnered outcomes.

[208] Such as establishing humanitarian corridors in Syria and facilitating the return of guerrilla-kidnapped Colombian soldiers. Thomas Jenatsch, 'The ICRC as a humanitarian mediator in the Colombian conflict: Possibilities and limits' (1998) 323 Int Rev Red Cross 303–18.

[209] IFRC, 'Guidelines for the domestic facilitation and regulation of international disaster relief and initial recovery assistance'.

[210] Johan Galtung, 'The TRANSCEND method in conflict mediation across levels' (2010) 15 Eur Psychol 82–90, particularly cases 5, 6, and 10.

14

The Peaceful Settlement of Space Disputes

Prospects and Challenges

ROSSANA DEPLANO

14.1 INTRODUCTION

International space law (also known as the law of outer space) is a specialised field of international law of relatively recent origin. Its building blocks developed within the United Nations (UN) at the height of the Cold War, initially in the form of soft law.[1] The *corpus juris spatialis* now consists of five multilateral Treaties[2] and several Resolutions adopted by the UN General Assembly.[3] As a specialised field, international space law is governed by general international law, including the rules on treaty interpretation codified

[1] The first document on outer space adopted by the United Nations is the UNGA, 'Declaration of legal principles governing the activities of States in the exploration and use of outer space' (13 December 1963) UN Doc. A/RES/1962(XVIII) (hereinafter referred to as the Declaration on Legal Principles).

[2] Treaty on Principles Governing the Activities of States in the Exploration and Use of Outer Space, Including the Moon and Other Celestial Bodies, Washington, Moscow, London, 27 January 1967, in force 10 October 1967, 610 UNTS 205 (hereinafter referred to as the Outer Space Treaty); Agreement on the Rescue of Astronauts, the Return of Astronauts, and the Return of Objects Launched into Outer Space, Washington, Moscow, London, 19 December 1967, in force 3 December 1968, 672 UNTS 119; Convention on International Liability for Damage Caused by Space Objects, Washington, Moscow, London, 29 March 1972, in force 1 September 1972, 961 UNTS 187 (hereinafter referred to as the Liability Convention); Convention on Registration of Objects Launched into Outer Space, New York, 12 November 1974, in force 15 September 1976, 1023 UNTS 15; Agreement Governing Activities of States on the Moon and Other Celestial Bodies, New York, 5 December 1979, in force 11 July 1984, 1363 UNTS 3 (hereinafter referred to as the Moon Agreement).

[3] They include UNGA, 'Principles governing the use by States of artificial Earth satellites for international direct television broadcasting' (10 December 1982) UN Doc. A/RES/37/92 (herein after referred to as the Principles on Direct Television Broadcasting); UNGA, 'Principles relating to remote sensing of the Earth from outer space' (3 December 1986) UN Doc. A/RES/41/65 (hereinafter referred to as the Principles on Remote Sensing of the Earth); and UNGA, 'Declaration on international cooperation in the exploration and use of outer space for the benefit and in the interest of all States, taking into particular account the needs of

by the Vienna Convention on the Law of Treaties[4] and customary international law. At the same time, it possesses unique features. Firstly, it is a field entirely driven by technological developments. For instance, the prospects of utilising space resources in support of scientific exploration missions (as well as for purely commercial purposes) have become an imminent reality due to significant advancements in material processing and robotic technology. In response, the UN Committee on the Peaceful Uses of Outer Space (COPUOS) is currently elaborating a law and policy framework for space resource utilisation.[5] Secondly, due to its historical origins, international space law is a field sensitive to political and diplomatic interactions among States. Consequently, it has so far developed through consensus, as expressed in multilateral fora such as COPUOS.

The normative framework for the peaceful settlement of space disputes reflects the nature of international space law as a specialised yet unique field of international law. Such a framework builds on the concept of conflict avoidance, which attempts to reduce the possibility of disagreements emerging from space activities.[6] In the event of a dispute, States are encouraged to seek a diplomatic solution before contemplating recourse to other dispute settlement mechanisms. As a result, the peaceful settlement of space disputes has remained an underdeveloped area of international law.[7] The general position among scholars is that the UN treaty framework is unsatisfactory, if not inadequate, to meet the demands of the growing commercialisation of outer space and the disputes that may arise.[8] The main problem appears to lie in the

developing countries' (4 February 1997) UN Doc. A/RES/51/122 (hereinafter referred to as the Declaration on Benefit Sharing).

4 Vienna Convention on the Law of Treaties, Vienna, 23 May 1969, in force 27 January 1980, 1155 UNTS 331; (1969) 8 ILM 679.

5 COPUOS Legal Subcommittee, 'Working group on legal aspects of space resources activities', 2022, www.unoosa.org/oosa/en/ourwork/copuos/lsc/space-resources/index.html (accessed 8 August 2022).

6 Gérardine Meishan Goh, *Dispute Settlement in International Space Law: A Multi-door Courthouse for Outer Space* (Leiden: Nijhoff, 2007), p. 18; Susan Cone Kilgore, 'Arbitration rules for disputes arising from outer space activity' (2018) Fed Law 58–63 at 59; Hanneke van Traa-Engelman, 'Settlement of space law disputes' (1990) 3 LJIL 139–55 at 143.

7 Most notably, it does not feature in the academic textbooks in this field.

8 See, e.g., Fabio Tronchetti, 'The PCA rules for dispute settlement in outer space: A significant step forward' (2013) 29 Space Policy 181–89 at 182; Jan Frohloff, '*Per arbitrum ad astra*' (2020) 37 J Int'l Arb 721–30 (arguing that the Outer Space Treaty does not contain a dispute resolution mechanism to claim the rights it stipulates); Stefan Pislevik, 'Law without gravity: Arbitrating space disputes at the Permanent Court of Arbitration and the relevance of adverse inferences' (2019) 43 J Space L 280–308 at 280 ('the international community has been unable to develop, much less, implement, a space-specific permanent form of dispute settlement despite discussing its utility for decades'). According to an isolated position, public

absence of a specialised dispute settlement mechanism endowed with enforcement powers.

This chapter examines the UN treaty framework for the peaceful settlement of space disputes and subsequent developments with a view to determining whether the current mechanisms are adequate to resolve various types of space disputes, including those likely to stem from the growing commercialisation of outer space, or whether they require reform. Scholarly works have provided an overview of the available dispute settlement mechanisms for space activities[9] and of proposals for reform.[10] This chapter takes a different approach. Section 14.2 analyses the legal principles underpinning the peaceful settlement of space disputes contained in the UN outer space treaties. It shows that the principles underpinning the Outer Space Treaty and the Moon Agreement offer a wide range of options to the parties in settling their disputes by peaceful means. However, they do not compel the parties to settle their disputes through one of the recognised mechanisms. Nor do they address the issue of enforcement of the settlement's outcome.

Yet, a lack of enforcement power does not necessarily amount to an inherent inefficiency of a dispute settlement mechanism. Therefore, Section 14.3 examines the extent to which the existent means for the settlement of space disputes provide effective redress for different types of disputes. To that end, it builds a taxonomy of space disputes, including the ones that are likely to be generated by new space activities, such as space mining. Section 14.4 critically evaluates the proposals for reform advanced by scholars with a view to making the settlement mechanisms for space disputes more streamlined and efficient. It shows that, by introducing compulsory requirements to settle disputes and enforce their outcomes, they go beyond the letter of the UN space treaties, effectively replacing the principle of State consent as the basis of obligation in international law.

Building on the preceding analysis, Section 14.5 reframes the debate about the need for a specialised dispute settlement mechanism for outer space. It proposes a functional approach focusing on the type of legal claims raised by the parties rather than the type of space activity involved in the dispute. It

international law cannot provide a suitable mechanism for the peaceful settlement of space disputes. Tare Brisibe, 'Settlement of disputes and resolution of conflicts', in Ram S. Jakhu and Paul Stephen Dempsey (eds.), *Routledge Handbook of Space Law* (New York: Routledge, 2017), p. 95.

9 Meishan Goh, *Dispute Settlement in International Space Law*.

10 For an overview, see Maureen Williams, 'Dispute resolution regarding space activities', in Frans G. von der Dunk and Fabio Tronchetti (eds.), *Handbook of Space Law* (Cheltenham: Edward Elgar, 2015), p. 995.

shows that a specialised dispute settlement mechanism endowed with interpretative and enforcement powers is neither necessary nor desirable to address the legal claims raised by the parties to a dispute. Complex space activities, such as space mining, consist of a bundle of operations, some of which are not regulated by positive international law. Hence the need to allow State practice to flexibly shape the direction of the progressive development of international space law. Section 14.6 provides some final remarks.

14.2 PRINCIPLES GOVERNING THE PEACEFUL SETTLEMENT OF DISPUTES IN THE UN SPACE TREATIES

International space law aims at fostering international cooperation in space activities.[11] Accordingly, the Outer Space Treaty and the Moon Agreement establish that the exploration and use of outer space 'shall be the province of mankind',[12] meaning that States have an equal right to access outer space for the purposes of its peaceful exploration and use. Considering that the conduct of space activities may be a source of conflict, the two treaties contain provisions aimed at facilitating dialogue and cooperation among States, resulting in a system largely grounded on the principles of conflict avoidance and free choice of means for the settlement of disputes. Notably, neither treaty creates a specialised dispute settlement mechanism for outer space.

This begs the question: what is the role and place of the concept of dispute settlement in outer space treaties? Given the nature of international space law as a specialised and technology-driven branch of international law, the answer requires a two-step analysis. Firstly, the inquiry into the concept of peaceful settlement of space disputes presupposes an assessment of its relationship with the principle of conflict avoidance (Subsection 14.2.1). Secondly, the nature (voluntary or compulsory) of the available dispute settlement mechanisms coexists with the freedom of choice of the means that the parties consider suitable to settle their disputes. An analysis of the relevant treaty provisions is essential to clarify whether the obligation imposed on States is one of conduct – that is to say, an obligation to attempt to settle the dispute through available mechanisms, irrespective of the outcome – or one of result, meaning an obligation to have a dispute settled and the outcome enforced (Subsection 14.2.2).

[11] Outer Space Treaty, Art III (referring to the promotion of international cooperation and understanding).

[12] Ibid., Art I, first para.; Moon Agreement, Art 4(1).

14.2.1 *Relationship between Conflict Avoidance and Dispute Settlement for Outer Space*

The principle of conflict avoidance finds expression in several provisions of both the Outer Space Treaty and the Moon Agreement. There are four main aspects to it: the duty to consult; the duty to notify the details of current and planned space activities; the duty to avoid harmful interference with the activities of other States; and the duty of due regard for other States' activities in outer space.

In relation to the duty to consult, Article IX of the Outer Space Treaty requires States to enter into consultation with each other if they have a reason to believe that an activity conducted in outer space by a State party may cause harmful interference with the activities of another State party. The Moon Agreement contains a provision of equivalent content.[13] Similarly, Article XII of the Outer Space Treaty requires States willing to visit 'stations, installations, equipment and vehicles' on celestial bodies to give reasonable advance notice in order to allow consultations to take place. Article 15(1) of the Moon Agreement contains an identical provision. Finally, Article XIII, second paragraph, of the Outer Space Treaty contains an indirect obligation for States to consult. It states that 'any practical question' arising in connection with activities in outer space carried out by international organisations shall be resolved by the State parties to the Outer Space Treaty directly with the international organisation or with one or more member States of the international organisation which are also parties to the Outer Space Treaty. There is no equivalent provision in the Moon Agreement.

Taken together, the provisions of the Outer Space Treaty and the Moon Agreement require States to adopt a precautionary approach aimed at preserving the freedom of exploration and use of outer space to its full extent on the basis of equality. Effectively they treat outer space exploration as a sovereign decision to conduct activities in an inclusive environment – that is to say, an area beyond State jurisdiction immune from property claims (whether cast by individual States or jointly).[14]

[13] Moon Agreement, Art 8(3).

[14] Philip De Man, *Exclusive Use in an Inclusive Environment: The Meaning of the Non-appropriation Principle for Space Resource Exploitation* (Cham: Springer, 2016). It is noteworthy that the Moon Agreement describes the Moon and its resources as the common heritage of mankind. However, the specific meaning of this qualification is to be established in a future agreement on the exploitation of the resources of the Moon. See Moon Agreement, Art 11(1).

The second aspect of the principle of conflict avoidance is the duty to inform the UN Secretary-General, the public, and the international scientific community about 'the nature, conduct, locations, and results' of the activities of States in outer space.[15] A similar duty of notification includes the requirement of the Moon Agreement that States notify the same actors of the discovery of any phenomena which could endanger human life or health.[16] Arguably, the two provisions aim at fostering transparency in the conduct of space activities with a view to reducing the risk of potential conflicts.[17]

The third aspect of the principle of conflict avoidance is the duty to avoid harmful contamination of outer space as well as 'adverse changes in the environment of the Earth resulting from the introduction of extraterrestrial matter'.[18] The Moon Agreement contains an identical provision.[19] The preventive principle in environmental matters, as recognised in international case law,[20] arguably applies to State activities in outer space as well. The immediate consequence is that these provisions of the UN space treaties serve a deterrent function, since they eliminate the discretion of States to conduct hazardous activities or experiments in outer space, including for scientific purposes.

The fourth aspect of the principle of conflict avoidance is the duty of States to conduct their space activities 'with due regard to the corresponding interests of all other States Parties'.[21] The UN Convention on the Law of the Sea (UNCLOS) contains an equivalent provision.[22] However, the Moon Agreement significantly extends the scope of this duty by referring to due regard that is to be paid to 'the interests of present and future generations as

15 Outer Space Treaty, Art X. See also Moon Agreement, Art 5(1) (referring to the duty of States to provide information about 'the time, purpose, locations, orbital parameters and duration' of any mission to the Moon).

16 Moon Agreement, Art 5(3).

17 Brisibe, 'Settlement of disputes', p. 98 (acknowledging 'a tendency towards dispute avoidance in the space sector alongside reluctance to employ adversarial dispute-settlement mechanisms').

18 Outer Space Treaty, Art IX.

19 Moon Agreement, Art 7(1).

20 See, e.g., *Case Concerning Pulp Mills on the River Uruguay (Argentina* v. *Uruguay)* (Judgment) [2010] ICJ Rep. 14 at p. 425, para. 101 (recognising the obligation of States to avoid activities, whether in their territory or in any area under their jurisdiction, which can cause significant damage to the environment of another State).

21 Outer Space Treaty, Art IX. The Moon Agreement contains an identical provision in Art 2.

22 United Nations Convention on the Law of the Sea, Montego Bay, 10 December 1982, in force 16 November 1994, 1833 UNTS 397 (UNCLOS), Art 87(2) (acknowledging that the freedoms of the high seas must be exercised with due regard for the interests of other States in the exercise of the freedoms of the high seas).

well as to the need to promote higher standards of living and conditions of economic and social progress and development in accordance with the Charter of the United Nations'.[23] As formulated, the duty of due regard in the UN space treaties raises two conceptual issues.

The first one is the vagueness of the content of the obligation. The Outer Space Treaty does not provide a definition of due regard. International case law suggests that the connotations of the concept of due regard are context-specific, hence not amenable to abstract generalisations. For example, in the *Chagos* case, the Permanent Court of Arbitration (PCA) held that the principle of due regard acquires meaning in relation to the circumstances of the case and the nature of the rights involved. As a result, the Court declined to find 'any universal rule of conduct'.[24] In the *Norstar* case, the International Tribunal for the Law of the Sea (ITLOS) simply denied the violation of the principle of due regard in the case at hand without discussing the criteria for assessment.[25]

The second conceptual issue is the scope of the obligation. The Moon Agreement changes the object of the duty from due regard to the corresponding interests of other States operating in outer space, to due regard to intergenerational equity. Yet, it does not provide any equitable criteria against which to assess space activities having an adverse impact on future generations. The language used in the Moon Agreement is reminiscent of Article 140(2) of UNCLOS, which states that the International Seabed Authority (ISA) 'shall provide for the equitable sharing of the financial and other economic benefits derived from activities in the Area through any appropriate mechanisms'. Article 160(2)(f)(i) of UNCLOS further stipulates that the ISA Assembly is the organ competent to approve 'the rules, regulations, and procedures' on equitable sharing, upon the recommendation of the ISA Council. Accordingly, the ISA Council's Finance Committee has carried out a study on the equitable sharing of financial and economic benefits stemming from deep-seabed mining.[26]

In relation to intergenerational equity, the Finance Committee concludes that it is impossible to write criteria for securing benefits across generations.[27]

[23] Moon Agreement, Art 4(1).

[24] *Chagos Marine Protected Area Arbitration (Mauritius* v. *United Kingdom)* (Final Award of 18 March 2015) PCA Case No. 2011-03 at p. 202, para. 519.

[25] *M/V 'Norstar' Case (Panama* v. *Italy)* (Judgment of 10 April 2019) ITLOS Reports 2018–19, 10 at p. 60, para. 214.

[26] ISA, *Equitable Sharing of Financial and Other Economic Benefits from Deep-Seabed Mining: ISA Technical Study No.* 31 (Kingston: ISA, 2021).

[27] Ibid., p. 27.

Applying this conclusion to the Moon Agreement suggests that the duty of due regard contains an inherently vague obligation requiring a case-by-case assessment, rather than preconceived criteria, to be fulfilled. This is so irrespective of the means of dispute resolution selected. The UN Declaration on Benefit Sharing confirms that, while State cooperation in the exploration and use of outer space must be arranged on an equitable and mutually acceptable basis,[28] it should be conducted 'in the modes that are considered most effective and appropriate by the countries concerned'.[29] The latter requires a case-by-case assessment not based on any preconceived sharing criteria.

Taken together, the considerations above suggest that the UN treaties on outer space acknowledge that controversies about the exploration and use of outer space are likely to arise. Hence, given the difficulties of operating in outer space, they place emphasis on preventing the emergence of disputes. Yet, they acknowledge the importance of the availability of dispute settlement mechanisms as a means to preserve the use of outer space only for peaceful purposes, thus showing that the principle of conflict avoidance and the concept of dispute settlement are not mutually exclusive in the UN space treaties.

14.2.2 *Freedom of Choice in Relation to the Means for Dispute Settlement*

The Outer Space Treaty recognises that States are free to choose their preferred means of dispute settlement. Article III thereof states that the exploration and use of outer space must be conducted 'in accordance with international law, including the Charter of the United Nations'. Effectively, it incorporates the existent means for the peaceful settlement of disputes listed in Article 33 of the UN Charter,[30] namely, negotiation, enquiry, mediation, conciliation, arbitration, judicial settlement (including adjudication by the International Court of Justice [ICJ]),[31] resort to regional agencies or arrangements, or other peaceful means chosen by the parties.[32] The provision in Article III is not unique. For instance, it is replicated in Article 2 of the Moon Agreement as well as three soft law instruments, namely, the Principles on

[28] Declaration on Benefit Sharing, paras 2–3.

[29] Ibid., para. 4.

[30] Meishan Goh, *Dispute Settlement in International Space Law*, p. 22.

[31] Charter of the United Nations, San Francisco, 26 June 1945, in force 24 October 1945, 1 UNTS 16, Art 94.

[32] Other provisions of the UN Charter contain a generic reference to the peaceful settlement of disputes, in particular Arts 1(1) and 3(3).

Remote Sensing of the Earth,[33] the Principles on Direct Television Broadcasting,[34] and the Principles on the Use of Nuclear Power in Outer Space.[35] Outside the field of space law, Article XI(1) of the Antarctic Treaty contains a provision of equivalent content.[36]

Despite the comprehensive nature of the list, scholars argue that Article 33 of the UN Charter does not provide an adequate means for the effective settlement of disputes in general, and space disputes in particular – the main reason being that the invocation of the principles of international law and the reference to the UN Charter do not impose any obligation on States to resolve their controversies through any of the mentioned dispute settlement mechanisms.[37] Other scholars argue that the Outer Space Treaty possesses a rudimentary and inadequate dispute settlement system due to its lack of enforcement powers.[38]

Be that as it may, the Outer Space Treaty establishes a relationship of priority between the principle of conflict avoidance (much emphasised in the text of the treaty)[39] and recourse to the dispute settlement means listed in Article 33 of the UN Charter as a last-resort measure failing consultation. This shows that, contrary to certain scholarly positions, the Outer Space Treaty acknowledges the concept of peaceful settlement of disputes as an integral part of the law of outer space. Yet, it does not create a specialised system for space disputes. Nor does it envision resort to a binding mechanism, thus preserving the inherently co-operative, political nature of space exploration.

Article 15 of the Moon Agreement outlines a more detailed procedure for the peaceful settlement of disputes. Paragraph 2 thereof establishes a duty of consultation in relation to any potential breach of obligations contained in the Moon Agreement. It states:

> A State Party which has reason to believe that another State Party is not fulfilling the obligations incumbent upon it pursuant to this Agreement or that another State Party is interfering with the rights which the former State has under this Agreement may request consultations with a State Party. A State Party receiving such a request shall enter into consultations without

33 Principles on Remote Sensing of the Earth, Principles III and XV.
34 Principles on Direct Television Broadcasting, Principle E.
35 UNGA, 'Principles relevant to the use of nuclear power sources in outer space' (23 February 1993) UN Doc. A/RES/47/68, Principle 10.
36 The Antarctic Treaty, Washington, 1 December 1959, in force 23 June 1961, 402 UNTS 71.
37 See, e.g., Meishan Goh, *Dispute Settlement in International Space Law*, p. 26.
38 See also Cone Kilgore, 'Arbitration rules', p. 60 (arguing that international space law lacks a system for the settlement of disputes).
39 As discussed in Subsection 14.2.1.

> delay. Any other State Party which requests to do so shall be entitled to take part in consultations.

Failing consultations, States must seek a diplomatic solution to the controversy.

> Each State party participating in such consultations *shall seek* a mutually acceptable resolution of any controversy and shall bear in mind the rights and interests of all States Parties. The Secretary-General of the United Nations shall be informed of the results of the consultations and shall transmit the information received to all States Parties concerned.[40]

The Moon Agreement further states that, in the event of failure to produce a mutually agreed outcome through diplomatic negotiations, the parties are expected to 'take all measures to settle their disputes by other peaceful means of their choice appropriate to the circumstances and the nature of the dispute'. Alternatively, they may seek assistance from the UN Secretary-General.[41] This suggests that the Moon Agreement only imposes a duty to attempt the peaceful settlement of disputes when the awareness of the existence of a dispute between States arises. Conversely, like Article III of the Outer Space Treaty, it does not require States to have their dispute settled. In this respect, the provisions of the Moon Agreement align with Article 283(1) of UNCLOS, which establishes that the parties to a dispute must 'proceed expeditiously to an exchange of views' as to the means for dispute settlement they intend to adopt.[42] In the *Chagos* case, the arbitral tribunal clarified that Article 283 of UNCLOS imposes only an obligation to exchange views regarding the selection of the means for dispute settlement. Conversely,

> it does not require the Parties to in fact engage in negotiations or other forms of peaceful dispute resolution. As a matter of textual construction, the Tribunal considers that Article 283 cannot be understood as an obligation to negotiate the substance of the dispute.[43]

Subsequent case law has reaffirmed this interpretation.[44]

[40] Moon Agreement, Art 15(2) (emphasis added).

[41] Ibid., Art 15(3). It is also noteworthy that, according to Art 37(1) of the UN Charter, failure to settle a dispute through the means indicated in Art 33 thereof requires States to refer their dispute to the UN Security Council.

[42] Likewise, it may be argued that the Moon Agreement also aligns with Art 33 of the UN Charter, which contains an obligation of conduct rather than result.

[43] *Chagos Marine Protected Area Arbitration* (Final Award), para. 378.

[44] See, e.g., *South China Sea Arbitration (Philippines* v. *China)* (Award on Jurisdiction and Admissibility of 29 October 2015) PCA Case No. 2013-19 at para. 332 ff; *The Arctic Sunrise*

The preceding analysis shows that the treaty regime for the peaceful settlement of space disputes aims at preserving international cooperation. Consequently, it contains provisions aimed at preventing disputes and fostering amicable solutions. Such provisions do not exclude recourse to dispute settlement mechanisms. Nor do they prevent States from creating specialised mechanisms if they so wish. The following Section examines the two specialised dispute settlement mechanisms currently in force and evaluates their adequacy to deal with new types of space disputes, such as those likely to arise from space mining.

14.3 TYPES OF SPACE DISPUTES AND DISPUTE SETTLEMENT MECHANISMS FOR SPACE ACTIVITIES: NORMATIVE FRAMEWORKS AND DOCTRINAL CHALLENGES

The UN space treaties envision recourse to the dispute settlement mechanisms listed in Article 33 of the UN Charter for resolving any space-related dispute. At the time of adoption of the Outer Space Treaty, the types of disputes likely to arise from State activities in outer space largely mirrored familiar types of disputes on Earth. Based on the state of technological capabilities for space exploration available in the late 1960s, Sloup provides a classification of space disputes by both subject matter (Table 14.1)[45] and parties to a dispute (Table 14.2).[46]

According to Sloup, the Outer Space Treaty is not equipped with the means required to handle space disputes.[47] As other scholars have also pointed out, an indirect reference to the dispute settlement mechanisms listed in the UN Charter does not amount to establishing a dispute settlement system for space activities.[48] Adopted in 1971, the Liability Convention, the third UN treaty on outer space, partly addresses this issue by establishing a mechanism to resolve disputes involving liability for damage caused by space objects.

An innovation by the standards of the time, the Liability Convention addresses only one typology of space disputes.[49] With the development of space technology and the contextual growth of space activities conducted by

Arbitration (Kingdom of the Netherlands v. *The Russian Federation)* (Award on Merits of 14 August 2015) PCA Case No. 2014-02 at para. 151.

45 George Paul Sloup, 'Peaceful resolution of outer space conflicts through the International Court of Justice: The line of last resistance' (1971) 20 DePaul L Rev 618–98 at 632.

46 Ibid., p. 633.

47 Ibid., p. 680.

48 As discussed in Subsection 14.2.2.

49 See Table 14.1, point 1.

TABLE 14.1 *Sloup's classification of space disputes by subject matter*

1. Liability for personal injury and property damage caused by space activities
2. Appropriation and use of space resources
3. Appropriation and use of outer space *qua* space
4. Problems related to the legal distinction between national airspace and outer space, such as the delimitation line
5. Jurisdictional issues
6. Maintenance of peace and security in outer space
7. Pollution, interference with communications, invasion of privacy, and other cause by technological advancements
8. Problems not capable of being defined at present

TABLE 14.2 *Sloup's classification of space disputes by parties to a dispute*

1. States
2. International organisations
3. Corporations
4. Individuals
5. Possibly other forms of sentient life

States in partnership with private, commercial actors throughout the 1980s and 1990s, a perception of inadequacy of the UN space treaty provisions to secure timely and effective settlement of disputes arising from an increasingly diverse range of space activities arose. In response, in 2011, the PCA adopted the Optional Rules for Arbitration of Disputes Relating to Outer Space Activities (hereinafter referred to as the PCA Rules).[50] Heralded as the most significant innovation in the field of peaceful settlement of space disputes, the PCA Rules have a broad scope, potentially applying to any type of space-related dispute.[51]

However, the imminent start of mining activities on celestial bodies, in turn, questions the suitability of the PCA Rules to settle new types of space

[50] PCA, 'Optional rules for arbitration of disputes relating to outer space activities', 6 December 2011, https://docs.pca-cpa.org/2016/01/Permanent-Court-of-Arbitration-Optional-Rules-for-Arbitration-of-Disputes-Relating-to-Outer-Space-Activities.pdf (accessed 8 August 2022) (hereinafter referred to as the PCA Rules).

[51] PCA Rules, Art 1.

disputes that will likely arise from such activities. Considering that the Outer Space Treaty remains silent on the issue of space resource utilisation, and while the Moon Agreement subordinates the regulation of the exploitation of the resources of the Moon to a future agreement and that this is unlikely to be adopted in the near future,[52] a new range of space disputes is expected to arise from space mining operations. They can be divided into two categories: disputes relating to the interpretation and application of UN space treaties, such as disputes on property rights over space resources; and disputes relating to space mining operations, such as the production of space debris on or around the mined celestial bodies. However, it remains unclear whether the settlement of disputes arising from space mining activities requires the creation of a new, specialised mechanism.

The following subsections examine the structure, effectiveness, and limitations of the existent specialised mechanisms for the settlement of space disputes – namely, the procedure for claiming compensation for damage caused by space objects established by the Liability Convention (Subsection 14.3.1) and the PCA Rules (Subsection 14.3.2) – as well as the proposals for the creation of a specialised mechanism for the settlement of space mining disputes (Subsection 14.3.3).

14.3.1 *Compensation Claims*

The Liability Convention establishes a procedure for the settlement of disputes involving damage caused by space objects. Divided into two phases, such a procedure aims at 'contribut[ing] to the strengthening of international cooperation' in space exploration.[53] This section examines the substantive and procedural aspects underpinning the submission of a claim for compensation (Subsection 14.3.1.1). It then evaluates the efficiency of the claims for damage procedure in the light of past practice and scholarly commentary (Subsection 14.3.1.2).

14.3.1.1 The Claims for Damage Procedure in Outline

The procedure for claiming compensation consists of two stages: diplomatic negotiation and the Claims Commission arbitration.[54] The availability of the

[52] Moon Agreement, Art 11(5). The Moon Agreement has been ratified by 18 States. None of them is a major spacefaring actor. The main obstacle to ratification appears to be the qualification of the Moon and its resources as the common heritage of mankind.

[53] Liability Convention, Preamble, second para.

[54] Henry R. Hertzfeld and Timothy G. Nelson, 'Binding arbitration as an effective means of dispute settlement for accidents in outer space' (2013) Proc IISL 129–42 at 136 (describing it as 'quasi-arbitration' due to its non-binding nature).

settlement of disputes through diplomatic negotiations is limited to States[55] and international organisations.[56] Private actors, such as companies and individuals, can only present a claim through their State of nationality. Absent such intervention, the State in whose territory a foreign national (natural or juridical person) has sustained damage may present a compensation claim to the launching State on their behalf.[57] As a last resort, another State may present a compensation claim to the launching State in respect of damage sustained by permanent residents in its territory.[58] The reason for the restricted personal scope of the compensation procedure rests in the Liability Convention's requirement that claims for compensation are presented exclusively through diplomatic channels.[59] If no settlement is reached through diplomatic negotiation, either party may request the establishment of a Claims Commission.[60]

Composed of three members,[61] the Claims Commission decides the merits of the dispute and the amount of compensation[62] by majority vote.[63] The procedure has strict time limits. Article X of the Liability Convention requires that a claim for compensation be presented within one year of the date of occurrence or discovery of the damage or the identification of the liable launching State.[64] Although there is no requirement for prior exhaustion of any local remedies,[65] States may decide to do so. However, Article XI(2) of the Liability Convention prohibits the contemporaneous pursuit of the same claim for damage. In terms of applicable law, Article XII of the Liability Convention only states that compensation 'shall be determined in accordance with international law and the principles of justice and equity' with a view to restoring the claimant to the condition which would have existed if the damage had not occurred.

55 Liability Convention, Art VIII(1).

56 Art XXII(3) of the Liability Convention establishes that international organisations and its member States which are also parties to the Liability Convention remain jointly and severally liable.

57 Liability Convention, Art VIII(2).

58 Ibid., Art VIII(3).

59 Ibid., Art IX.

60 Ibid., Art XV.

61 Ibid. (one member nominated by each party and the chairman nominated jointly or, absent agreement, by the UN Secretary-General upon request of either party).

62 Ibid., Art XVIII.

63 Ibid., Art XVI(5).

64 Ibid., Art X.

65 Ibid., Art XI(1).

The decisions of the Claims Commission are binding only if the parties have so agreed.[66] Absent the parties' consent, the Claims Commission issues a recommendatory award, which the parties must consider in good faith.[67] The decision or award is public and must be rendered within one year of the establishment of the Claims Commission.[68]

14.3.1.2 A Strained Relationship? Balancing Theoretical Strengths and Practical Weaknesses of the Claims for Damage Procedure

As *lex specialis*, the Liability Convention contains two theoretical innovations. In terms of scope, it elaborates on the provision of Article VII of the Outer Space Treaty – which establishes that the launching State is internationally liable for damage caused by space objects[69] – by introducing the distinction between absolute and fault liability as well as a two-step procedure for claiming compensation. It thus raises substantive and procedural issues that may affect State reliance on it.

In terms of substantive issues, the Liability Convention distinguishes between two types of liability for damage caused by space objects – absolute and fault liability. Both types of liability operate at the State level, as they do not contemplate liability for non-State actors.

Absolute liability arises in relation to damage caused by space objects 'on the surface of the Earth or to aircraft in flight'.[70] According to the Liability Convention, the launching State[71] has an obligation to pay full compensation to the claimant State without the need for the latter to provide any evidence in support of its claim. The only exoneration from absolute liability is granted for damage resulting from either gross negligence or intentional omission on the part of the claimant State.[72] The exoneration does not apply if the activities conducted by the launching State are not in conformity with international law.[73] Equally, the provision does not apply to damage caused to the nationals

66 Ibid., Art XIX(2).

67 Ibid.

68 Ibid., Art XIX(3)–(4).

69 In turn, Art VII of the Outer Space Treaty restates verbatim the provision in para. 8 of the Declaration on Legal Principles.

70 Liability Convention, Art II.

71 Art I(c) of the Liability Convention describes the launching State as either 'a state which launches or procures the launching of a space object' or 'a state from whose territory or facility a space object is launched'.

72 Liability Convention, Art V(1).

73 Ibid., Art VI(2).

of the launching State or foreign nationals participating in the operations of the space object.[74]

The concept of absolute liability has no counterpart in other areas of international law.[75] Mindful of the hazardous nature of space activities,[76] it offers a greater level of protection than the Outer Space Treaty to the victims of damage by requiring the launching State to pay compensation for damage caused by a space object which may be operated by another State while in outer space until re-entry on Earth.[77] In addition, by removing the requirement of proof of damage and presuming the launching State as liable in principle, the concept of absolute liability departs from the established principle according to which State responsibility under international law stems from an unlawful act, if it can be attributed to a State.[78]

Fault liability arises in relation to damage caused by the spacecraft in outer space. It entails the payment of compensation by the launching State, provided the damage 'is due to its fault or the fault of persons for whom it is responsible'.[79] Such a requirement is problematic in two respects. Firstly, it requires the claimant State to produce evidence of the damage. This is a very onerous task given the characteristics of outer space environment and the absence of past practice.[80] Secondly, the Liability Convention does not provide a definition of fault.[81] Nor does it clarify the applicable law to decide a claim. It only states that compensation for damage must be decided in accordance with international law and the principles of justice and equity,[82] without providing guidance on how damages should be

74 Ibid., Art VII.

75 Pablo Mendes and Hanneke van Traa, 'Space law', in André Nollkaemper and Ilias Plakokefalos (eds.), *The Practice of Shared Responsibility in International Law* (Cambridge: Cambridge University Press, 2017), pp. 453, 456.

76 Tanja L. Masson-Zwaan and Mahulena Hofmann, *Introduction to Space Law*, 4th ed. (Alphen aan den Rijn: Kluwer, 2019), p. 27.

77 Stephen Gorove, '*Cosmos* 954: Issues of law and policy' (1978) 6 J Space L 137–46 at 142–43.

78 ILC, 'Responsibility of States for internationally wrongful acts', in *Yearbook of the International Law Commission 2001, Volume II, Part Two: Report of the Commission to the General Assembly on the Work of Its Fifty-Third Session* (New York: UN, 2005), https://legal.un.org/ilc/texts/instruments/english/draft_articles/9_6_2001.pdf, ch. 1; Mendes and van Traa, 'Space law', p. 457.

79 Liability Convention, Art III.

80 Hertzfeld and Nelson, 'Binding arbitration', p. 135.

81 Caroline Arbaugh, 'Gravitating toward sensible resolutions: The PCA Optional Rules for the Arbitration of Disputes Relating to Outer Space Activities' (2014) 42 Ga J Int'l & Comp L 825–50 at 834.

82 Liability Convention, Art XII.

measured.[83] Such omissions leave key terms of the compensation for damage procedure open to interpretation.

In terms of procedural issues, scholars have pointed out that the Liability Convention has three main limitations. Firstly, access to the dispute settlement mechanisms is restricted to States. It thus prevents non-State actors, including commercial companies, from using the Claims Commission procedure.[84] Secondly, given the hazardous nature of space activities, providing evidence of fault can be challenging, especially in the absence of past practice as to the process of acquisition and submission of evidence.[85] Thirdly, the decisions of the Claims Commission are of a recommendatory character; they become binding only if States have agreed in advance to treat the outcome of the claims for compensation procedure as binding.[86] This has led scholars to suggest that, in order to secure compliance with the decision outcome, the Liability Convention should contemplate recourse to a court rather than the Claims Commission.[87] It is also noteworthy that the Moon Agreement, the latest of the UN outer space treaties to be adopted, recognises the limits – substantive and procedural – of the Liability Convention and invites States to consider adopting additional arrangements for damage caused by the likely proliferation of space activities on the Moon.[88]

Taking stock of the preceding analysis, the question arises as to whether the Liability Convention provides an effective mechanism to secure compensation for damage. As a matter of fact, the *Cosmos 954* incident is the only instance in which it has been invoked by a State. On 27 January 1978, a Russian satellite carrying a nuclear reactor (the *Cosmos 954*) disintegrated on re-entry, eventually crashing on the northwest territories of Canada. The incident did not cause damage to people or their properties. However, it scattered radioactive materials across a vast land area. This prompted Canada to conduct search-and-recovery operations aimed at removing the radioactive debris on its territory and put in place precautionary measures to avoid potential risks for human health and the environment. Such operations generated 6 million dollars in expenses for Canada, which declared its intention to pursue a claim for compensation under the Liability

83 Ronald E. Alexander, 'Measuring damages under the Convention on International Liability for Damage Caused by Space Objects' (1978) 6 J Space L 151–60 at 152.

84 Tronchetti, 'The PCA Rules', pp. 181–82.

85 Ibid.

86 Meishan Goh, *Dispute Settlement in International Space Law*, p. 38; Karl-Heinz Böckstiegel, 'Settlement of disputes regarding space activities' (1993) 21 J Space L 1–10 at 3.

87 Pislevik, 'Law without gravity', p. 283.

88 Moon Agreement, Art 14(2).

Convention. However, in the absence of any actual damage, the USSR refused to engage with the dispute settlement procedures of the Liability Convention. Instead, it granted a sum of money covering half of the expenses incurred by Canada and presented it as a gesture of goodwill.

The *Cosmos 954* incident shows the limitations of the dispute settlement procedure set forth in the Liability Convention. In terms of scope, it proved unable to secure the recovery of search-and-rescue costs in the absence of actual damage, effectively imparting a restrictive meaning to the interpretation of the term 'damage'.[89] This also shows that, for all practical purposes, absolute liability requires a proof of actual damage to be successfully invoked by a State.[90] On balance, it appears that the Liability Convention does not fully offset the risks inherent in operating space objects against its stated 'victim-oriented approach'[91] to compensation for damage.

14.3.2 *Arbitral Proceedings for Space Disputes*

Adopted in 2011, the PCA Rules provide a flexible mechanism to settle space-related legal disputes, whether contractual or not. Modelled after the 2010 UNCITRAL Arbitration Rules,[92] they were elaborated by a group of international experts working in collaboration with the PCA International Bureau with a view to overcoming the substantive and procedural limitations of the Outer Space Treaty and the Liability Convention.[93] This section examines the content and scope of the PCA Rules (Subsection 14.3.2.1). It then evaluates the extent to which the PCA Rules provide an effective means for the peaceful settlement of space disputes (Subsection 14.3.2.2).

89 Gorove, '*Cosmos 954*', p. 143.

90 Ibid.; Peter C. P. Haanappel, 'Some observations on the crash of the *Cosmos 954*' (1978) 6 J Space L 147–50 at 148.

91 Masson-Zwaan and Hofmann, *Introduction to Space Law*, p. 27.

92 For a detailed reconstruction of the differences and similarities between the PCA Rules and the 2010 UNCITRAL Rules (UN, 'UNCITRAL Arbitration Rules (as revised in 2010)', 2011, https://uncitral.un.org/sites/uncitral.un.org/files/media-documents/uncitral/en/arb-rules-revised-2010-e.pdf (accessed 9 August 2022)), see Jesse Baez, 'The PCA's Optional Rules for Arbitration of Disputes Relating to Outer Space Activities: Bringing arbitration to infinity and beyond' (2012) 4 Yb Arbitrat Mediat 218–24.

93 For an overview of the drafting history, see Fausto Pocar, 'An introduction to the PCA's Optional Rules for Arbitration of Disputes Relating to Outer Space Activities' (2012) 38 J Space L 171–210 at 177–84; Stephan Hobe, 'Optional Rules for Arbitration of Disputes Relating to Outer Space: Permanent Court of Arbitration (PCA)', in *Max Planck Encyclopedia of Procedural International Law* (Oxford: Oxford University Press, 2019).

14.3.2.1 Overview of the Procedural Aspects

In terms of structure, the PCA Rules provide a simple arbitral procedure aimed at preserving party autonomy and confidentiality. They address four main aspects: the institution of proceedings (Articles 2–6), the appointment of arbitrators (Articles 7–16), the compulsory requirements of the arbitral proceedings (Articles 17–32) and the legally binding character of the award (Articles 33–43). In general, the arbitral proceedings involve three parties: the claimant, the respondent and the PCA International Bureau serving as the registry for the proceedings while providing secretarial services.[94]

The arbitral proceedings begin with the transmission of written notice by the claimant to both the respondent and the PCA International Bureau.[95] The notice of arbitration must provide details of the arbitration agreement that is invoked as well as the legal basis of the dispute.[96] The arbitration panel consists of three arbitrators: one appointed by each party and the presiding arbitrator chosen by the two appointed arbitrators.[97] The parties may also decide to appoint a sole arbitrator[98] or a five-member arbitral tribunal.[99] Irrespective of the composition of the arbitration panel, the appointed arbitrators must provide a statement about their impartiality and independence.[100] Arbitrators also determine the place of arbitration[101] and the language(s) to be used in the proceedings.[102] The arbitral tribunal has a power to decide on jurisdiction[103] and grant interim measures.[104]

Two principles inform the conduct of arbitral proceedings – the equal treatment of the parties and the reasonable opportunity for the parties to present their claims.[105] Within these limits, arbitrators have a discretion in the ways they decide to conduct the arbitration.[106] For example, they may choose to hold hearings for the presentation of evidence by witnesses or for

[94] PCA Rules, Art 1(3).
[95] Ibid., Arts 2–3.
[96] Ibid., Art 3(d) (referring to the 'identification of any rule, decision, agreement, contract, convention, treaty, constituent instrument of an organization or agency, or relationship out of, or in relation to which, the dispute arises').
[97] PCA Rules, Art 9(1).
[98] Ibid., Art 8.
[99] Ibid., Art 9.
[100] Ibid., Art 11.
[101] Ibid., Art 18.
[102] Ibid., Art 19.
[103] Ibid., Art 23.
[104] Ibid., Art 26.
[105] Ibid., Art 17(1).
[106] Ibid.

oral argument.[107] They may also appoint an expert to provide classified information to the tribunal without compromising the confidentiality of the information invoked by a party.[108] Likewise, arbitrators may appoint a 'confidentiality advisor' to report on the basis of confidential information on specific issues, as designated by the arbitrators, without disclosing the confidential information.[109] In addition, the tribunal may request the parties to produce a non-technical document clarifying any technical or specialised information which the tribunal considers necessary to decide the case.[110] It may also appoint independent experts to report to about specific issues.[111]

Decisions are taken by majority vote[112] and the award is final and binding on the parties, which must carry it out without delay.[113] In deciding the dispute, the arbitral tribunal applies the law designated by the parties or, failing such designation, the applicable national and international law.[114] In addition, the parties may request the tribunal to provide an interpretation of the award, which will form an integral part of the award itself.[115]

Compared to the UN space treaties, the PCA Rules introduce three novel aspects. Firstly, they apply to any space-related dispute without any restriction in terms of scope.[116] As such, they depart from the single-issue approach of the Liability Convention, which applies only to disputes involving damage caused by space objects. The PCA Rules may also be adapted by the parties to suit their needs, effectively guaranteeing a sufficient understanding of technical issues while preserving the confidentiality of information.[117] Secondly, the PCA Rules are available to States, international organisations and private actors alike.[118] The enlargement of the parties to a space dispute to include non-State actors, such as private companies and individuals, is a significant shift away from the State-centred approach to dispute settlement characterising the UN space treaties,[119] which encourage diplomatic negotiation as the

[107] Ibid., Art 17(3).
[108] Ibid., Art 17(6).
[109] Ibid., Art 17(8).
[110] Ibid., Art 27(4).
[111] Ibid., Art 29(1).
[112] Ibid., Art 33(1).
[113] Ibid., Art 34(2). The award also includes the allocation of costs; see Art 40.
[114] Ibid., Art 35(1).
[115] Ibid., Art 37.
[116] Ibid., Art 1(1).
[117] Ibid.; see also Gunjan Sharma, 'Extraterrestrial litigation: What every space operator should know about potential disputes' (2021) May/June Satellite Evolut 32–36.
[118] PCA Rules, Art 1(1).
[119] Hobe, 'Optional Rules for Arbitration', para. 6.

preferred means to settle space disputes. In connection with this, the PCA Rules further state that acceptance by the parties to submit the dispute to arbitration amounts to a waiver of any right of State immunity from jurisdiction.[120] Thirdly, the arbitral award is binding on the parties. A recommendatory award, like the one decided by the Claims Commission established under the Liability Convention, is not contemplated.

14.3.2.2 Binding Arbitration: The Ultimate Solution for Space Disputes?

While generally well received, the PCA Rules have been criticised as providing a modest improvement to the treaty-based space dispute settlement mechanisms. Some scholars write that the confidentiality safeguards may allow the parties to withhold information on grounds of security or protection of commercial interests.[121] Other scholars argue that the PCA Rules, especially the rules on confidentiality, are more suited to inter-State arbitration than proceedings involving private parties, since the latter may require stricter rules on confidentiality and may decide to avail themselves of commercial arbitration.[122] Another possible downside of the PCA Rules is costs, since parties to a space dispute have to pay for the PCA Secretary-General's services as the appointing authority, the PCA International Bureau's registry and secretarial services as well as the arbitrators. Overall, it is an expensive procedure.[123]

Although designed as a voluntary means for the settlement of space disputes leading to a binding outcome,[124] in practice the PCA Rules have never been used. The reasons for this are not known. However, from a legal perspective, recourse to the PCA Rules has two main implications, which may have hindered the confidence of space actors to rely on them, at least to a certain extent.

The first implication stems from the binding character of the arbitration award. Scholars argue that, while the PCA Rules apply only to States that have

[120] PCA Rules, Art 1(2). Conversely, a waiver of immunity from execution of the arbitral award is not automatic and must be clearly stated. Both types of immunities – from jurisdiction and from execution – represent an innovation in another respect as well, since they depart from the 2010 UNCITRAL Arbitration Rules.

[121] Pislevik, 'Law without gravity', p. 280.

[122] Frohloff, '*Per arbitrum ad astra*', p. 725.

[123] Baez, 'PCA's Optional Rules', p. 224.

[124] Pocar, 'Introduction to the PCA's Optional Rules', pp. 171, 177–78 (arguing that the voluntary aspect of arbitration is important, since States are more willing to agree to a binding mechanism under discrete agreements rather than a treaty mechanism). See also Hobe, 'Optional Rules for Arbitration', para. 2 (arguing that the PCA Rules take into account the distinctive features of space law).

consented to it,[125] the final and binding nature of the award contributes to legal certainty in relation to individual disputes.[126] In addition, the PCA Rules allow the parties to a dispute to request the interpretation of the provisions of a treaty. As a result, the award may contribute to the development of international space law through precedent.[127] While possible in theory, consolidated practice at the COPUOS Legal Subcommittee shows that, contrary to the scholarly literature, States do not support the prospects of treaty interpretation by international institutions on space law matters.

For instance, while recognising that the rules on interpretation applicable to space treaties are those contained in the Vienna Convention on the Law of Treaties (1969),[128] States have consistently maintained that only the State parties to a treaty can provide an authoritative interpretation to that treaty.[129] As a result, neither COPUOS, including its Legal Subcommittee, nor the working groups established within it can provide authoritative interpretations of the UN space treaties.[130] The UN General Assembly has acknowledged this long-standing view within COPUOS,[131] thus suggesting that States may be reluctant to accept interpretations of the UN space treaties provided by an arbitral tribunal. Effectively, the possibility to ask for authoritative interpretations is a deterrent to the use of the PCA Rules by space actors.

The second implication is that, given its voluntary nature, the simple availability of a dispute settlement method leading to a binding outcome does

[125] Arbaugh, 'Gravitating toward sensible resolutions', p. 848. In contrast, see Cone Kilgore, 'Arbitration rules', p. 60 (listing the requirement of consent as a valuable feature of arbitration in general).

[126] Hobe, 'Optional Rules for Arbitration', para. 10.

[127] Tronchetti, 'The PCA Rules', p. 186; Camilo Guzman Gomez, 'The Optional Rules of Arbitration of Disputes Relating to Outer Space Activities of the Permanent Court of Arbitration: A real option for the solution of conflicts in space matters?' *63rd International Astronautical Congress*, October 2012, https://hal.archives-ouvertes.fr/hal-01919267/document (accessed 9 August 2022), p. 4 (arguing that arbitration tribunals will become 'the leading interpreters of the UN treaties [on outer space]').

[128] See, e.g., UNGA, 'Report of the legal subcommittee on the work of its forty-third session' (16 April 2004) UN Doc. A/AC.105/826, p. 16, para. 93.

[129] See, e.g., UNGA, 'Report of the legal subcommittee on its forty-fourth session' (28 April 2005) UN Doc. A/AC.105/850, p. 8, para. 35; UNGA, 'Report of the legal subcommittee on the work of its thirty-ninth session' (20 April 2000) UN Doc. A/AC.105/738, p. 11, para. 81.

[130] See, e.g., UNGA, 'Report of the legal subcommittee on the work of its thirty-ninth session' (20 April 2000) UN Doc. A/AC.105/738, Annex II, p. 19, paras 8 and 12 – statement by the Russian Federation.

[131] See, e.g., UNGA, 'Application of the concept of the "launching State"' (25 January 2005) UN Doc. A/RES/59/115, Preamble, para. 4 ('nothing in the conclusions of the Working Group or in the present resolution constitutes an authoritative interpretation of ... the Registration Convention or the Liability Convention').

not necessarily facilitate reliance on that method by space actors. The fact that they have never used the PCA Rules proves it, effectively suggesting that the PCA Rules do not, and cannot, overcome the perceived problem underlying the Liability Convention, that is to say, the discretionary power of States to avoid recourse to binding settlements.[132] It follows that the PCA Rules are better seen as an innovative method for the peaceful settlement of space disputes rather than a one-size-fits-all solution for all types of disputes involving a space actor (whether public or private).

14.3.3 *Peaceful Settlement of New Space Disputes: The Case of Space Mining*

New technological advancements allow new activities in outer space by States and private actors. From a legal perspective, this amounts to saying that the availability of new technology allows new uses of outer space. The immediate repercussion is that, as space activities diversify, the likelihood that new types of space disputes will arise also increases. This begs the question of whether the dispute settlement mechanisms available under the UN space treaties and the PCA Rules can address the types of disputes expected to arise from new space activities.

Space mining is a prime example of a new type of space activity made possible by technological developments. It entails the extraction, collection and processing of natural resources, such as minerals, from a celestial body. While not directly regulated by the UN space treaties, space mining constitutes a use of space and, as such, falls within the remit of the Outer Space Treaty. In practice, in addition to the traditional types of disputes,[133] such as compensation for damage caused by space objects, two novel types of disputes may arise from space mining activities, namely disputes related to the interpretation of the UN space treaties and disputes related to space mining operations.

On the one hand, activities aimed at the utilisation of space resources raise issues of compatibility with the UN space treaties: are they lawful activities? The international community remains divided on this issue. As a result, the COPUOS Legal Subcommittee has created a Working Group on Legal Aspects of Space Resource Activities to provide guidance to States. The Working Group is expected to conclude its work in 2027, when it will submit the text of a draft Resolution outlining the guiding principles on space

[132] As discussed in Subsection 14.3.2.
[133] See Table 14.1.

resource utilisation to the UN General Assembly for consideration.[134] Both the outcome of the Working Group and the possible Resolution of the UN General Assembly will have a recommendatory character, meaning that States remain free to interpret the provisions of the UN space treaties they have ratified and, within that framework, assess the lawfulness of space resource utilisation.

On the other hand, in the absence of a clear legal position on this subject matter, the planning of space mining operations by public and private actors is already at an advanced stage. For example, the forthcoming US-led Artemis missions aim at establishing a long-term human presence on the Moon and, in perspective, Mars.[135] They contemplate space resource utilisation in support of scientific research. For example, one of the Artemis mission's goals is to extract oxygen and hydrogen from the lunar soil (known as regolith).[136] Oxygen and hydrogen can provide life support in the form of breathable air and drinking water; they are also the basic elements of propellants, which are essential for space travel.[137] At the same time, private companies are making plans to mine metal-rich asteroids with a view to selling the extracted resources.[138] The latter have manifold applications, both in space as construction materials for space installations (to be moulded via 3D printing) and on Earth as a greener alternative to terrestrial mining.

Given their level of complexity, space mining operations raise three potential types of disputes. Firstly, every State (and private actor within its jurisdiction) has the right to use any part of outer space.[139] This entails that States are entitled to start space mining operations in any celestial body or parts thereof on a first-come, first-served basis. In order to preserve the peaceful uses of outer space, States will likely invoke priority rights – that is to say, they will notify the

[134] UNOOSA, 'Co-chairs' proposed five years workplan and methods of work for the Working Group on Legal Aspects of Space Resource Activities', 5 April 2022, www.unoosa.org/documents/pdf/copuos/lsc/space-resources/Co-Chairs_Proposed_Workplan_as_at_5_April.pdf (accessed 9 August 2022).

[135] NASA, 'Artemis Plan: NASA's lunar exploration program overview', September 2020, www.nasa.gov/specials/artemis (accessed 9 August 2022). For an overview of the exploration program, see Manfred von Ehrenfried, *The Artemis Lunar Program: Returning People to the Moon* (Chichester: Springer, 2020). For an analysis of the legal aspects, see Rossana Deplano, 'The Artemis Plan: A paradigm shift in international space law? (2022) 46 J Space L 101–133.

[136] Deplano, 'Artemis Plan', p. 102.

[137] Angel Abbud-Madrid, 'Space resource utilization', in *Oxford Research Encyclopaedia of Planetary Science* (Oxford: Oxford University Press, 2021), pp. 42–49.

[138] For instance, Asteroid Mining Corporation Ltd. (UK) is planning to mine near-Earth asteroids containing platinum group metals (M-type asteroids). Further information is available at AMC, 'Redefining mining', https://asteroidminingcorporation.co.uk (accessed 9 August 2022).

[139] Outer Space Treaty, Arts I–II.

international community of their intention to perform space mining activities in a specific location for a limited period of time; in turn, they will expect other States not to plan or perform overlapping space activities.[140] In this sense, priority rights derive from the duty of notification of space activities contained in Article XI of the Outer Space Treaty. Hence, disputes relating to priority rights appear to be suited to diplomatic and conciliatory dispute mechanisms, as recognised in the Outer Space Treaty.[141]

Secondly, the execution of space mining operations entails the use of the surface of a celestial body. However, given the physical characteristics of outer space, the area required for a space mining operation is greater than that of the excavation site. In the absence of an atmosphere and low gravity on the mined celestial bodies, the excavation activities will generate a plume effect, scattering debris over a vast area.[142] As a protective measure, space mining operators will claim a safety zone – that is to say, an area surrounding the excavation site where the space activities of other actors may be affected by the presence of floating debris or frequency interference with their equipment; likewise, activities within the claimed safety zone may affect the excavation activities of the actor who first arrived.[143]

In practice, safety zones only require notification and consultation prior to the start of the activities within the protection area. They do not constitute exclusion zones, as that would amount to a violation of the principle of non-appropriation set forth in Article II of the Outer Space Treaty.[144] Consequently, disputes arising from safety zones can be settled via diplomatic means and, in the case of compensation for damage, the Claims Commission under the Liability Convention or the PCA Rules.[145]

Thirdly, space mining operators are planning to sell the extracted resources.[146] Claiming property rights over outer space is prohibited by Article II of the Outer Space Treaty. In the absence of a definition of space

[140] Olavo de Oliveira Bittencourt Neto et al. (eds.), *Building Blocks for the Development of an International Framework for the Governance of Space Resource Activities: A Commentary* (The Hague: Eleven International, 2020), pp. 46–48.

[141] Outer Space Treaty, Art III.

[142] Abbud-Madrid, 'Space resource utilization', p. 34.

[143] Bittencourt Neto et al., *Building Blocks*, pp. 64–70.

[144] For an analysis of the concept of safety zones, as envisioned in the Artemis program, see Jack Wright Nelson, 'Safety zones: A near-term legal issue on the Moon' (2020) 44 J Space L 604–23.

[145] Arbaugh, 'Gravitating toward sensible resolutions', p. 846 (arguing that the PCA Rules may be invoked to settle disputes about space debris).

[146] See, e.g., the mission statement of Asteroid Mining Corporation Ltd. (UK) (AMC, 'Redefining mining').

resources in the UN space treaties, the same principle arguably applies to the extracted resources as well. However, the domestic legislation of several countries grants property rights over the space resources extracted by their nationals. For example, the US Commercial Space Launch Competitiveness Act recognises the right of US citizens to 'own, transport, use, and sell' space resources.[147] Similarly, the Exploration and Use of Space Resources of Luxembourg establishes that 'space resources are capable of being owned'.[148] It follows that, as a matter of national law, space mining operators can transfer property rights over the recovered space resources. This raises issues of recognition of rights in foreign jurisdictions as well as potential State responsibility under international law for the violation of Article II of the Outer Space Treaty. As a result, domestic and international litigation as well as arbitration appear suitable for this kind of disputes.

Taken together, the considerations above suggest that all the existent means for the peaceful settlement of space disputes are available to the actors performing new space activities, such as space mining operations. The next section examines whether the creation of a permanent, specialised tribunal for outer space disputes is necessary or desirable to deal with traditional and new space activities.

14.4 TOWARDS AN INTERNATIONAL TRIBUNAL FOR SPACE DISPUTES?

While the UN space treaties do not provide for a comprehensive dispute settlement mechanism, a decentralised system for the peaceful settlement of space disputes under international law, nonetheless, exists. In addition, specialised dispute settlement mechanisms for space disputes are available within the framework of international organisations. For example, the constitutive instruments of both the European Space Agency (ESA)[149] and the International Telecommunications Union (ITU) refer to arbitration as the preferred means for the settlement of disputes among member States.[150]

[147] Commercial Space Launch Competitiveness Act of 2015, Public Law 114–90 (25 November 2015), ch. 513, §51303.

[148] Law of 20 July 2017 on the Exploration and Use of Space Resources, Official Journal, Mémorial A No. 674 (28 July 2017), Art 1.

[149] Convention for the Establishment of a European Space Agency, Paris, 30 May 1975, in force 30 October 1980, (1975) 14 ILM 864, Arts XVIII and XXV.

[150] Constitution of the International Telecommunications Union, Geneva, 22 December 1992, in force 1 July 1994, 1825 UNTS 31251; Optional Protocol on the Compulsory Settlement of Disputes Relating to the Constitution of the International Telecommunications Union and to

Empirical evidence also shows that the majority of space-related disputes concerning commercial disputes, such as disputes involving the execution of commercial contracts in the satellite industry, are usually resolved through *ad hoc* arbitration.[151] This suggests that the provisions of the UN space treaties on dispute settlement are part of a broader picture, which includes dispute settlement mechanisms regulating space activities under general international law and specialised mechanisms. However, whether the current arrangements are adequate to meet the demands of the growing privatisation and commercialisation of space activities remains the subject of academic debate. Proposals revolve around two main, and often overlapping, issues: the need to create a unified body for the settlement of space disputes[152] and the need to provide access to dispute settlement mechanisms for State and non-State actors alike.[153]

The earliest attempt to create an International Tribunal for Space Law through a multilateral treaty is the work of the International Law Association leading to a Draft Convention on the Settlement of Space Law Disputes.[154] Aimed at creating the conditions for private entities to have recourse to dispute settlement mechanisms on an equal footing with States,[155] the Draft Convention covers activities in outer space or 'with effects in outer space'.[156] In terms of scope, States may limit the applicability of the Draft Convention by issuing a declaration. For example, they can exclude specific space activities or the applicability of the Draft Convention altogether when they agree to

the Administrative Regulations, Geneva, 22 December 1992, in force 1 July 1994, 1825 UNTS 31251.

151 Viva Dadwal and Madeleine Macdonald, 'Arbitration of space-related disputes: Case trends and analysis', *71st International Astronautical Congress*, 12–14 October 2020, www.mcgill.ca/iasl/files/iasl/arbitration_of_space-related_disputes.pdf (accessed 9 August 2022), p. 6.

152 Arthad Kurlekar, 'Space – The final frontier: Analysing challenges of dispute resolution relating to outer space' (2016) 33 J Int'l Arb 379–415 at 395 and 396 (advocating the creation of 'an all-encompassing dispute resolution mechanism dealing with outer space law'). See also Frans G. von der Dunk, 'Space for dispute settlement mechanisms – Dispute resolution mechanisms for space? A few legal considerations' (2001) *Proc 44th Colloquium Law Outer Space* 442–52 at 452 (advocating the creation of a mechanism ensuring coherence in the dispute settlement for space).

153 Pislevik, 'Law without gravity', p. 285.

154 ILA, *Report of the Sixty-Eighth Conference Held at Taipei, Taiwan, Republic of China: 24–30 May 1998* (London: ILA, 1998), pp. 239–75 (hereinafter referred to as the ILA Draft Convention).

155 Lotta Viikari, 'Towards more effective settlement of disputes in the space sector' (2011) 1 Lapland L Rev 226–51 at 233.

156 ILA Draft Convention, Art 1(1).

submit their dispute to another procedure for peaceful settlement entailing a binding decision.[157]

In terms of dispute settlement procedures, the Draft Convention envisages conciliation and, failing that, binding settlement after previous exhaustion of local remedies.[158] The options for binding settlement include an International Tribunal for Space Law, the ICJ and arbitration. The parties select their preferred option by means of a written declaration.[159] However, in the absence of a declaration, they are deemed to have accepted the arbitration.[160] Similarly, when the parties to a dispute do not select the same procedure, arbitration becomes the compulsory means.[161] While the three options for the binding settlement are available to States, private parties have direct access only to the International Tribunal for Space Law and arbitration.

On balance, the Draft Convention provides a flexible mechanism where parties have an option to rely upon the established methods of dispute settlement, such as adjudication and arbitration as well as a specialised means, that is to say, the International Tribunal for Space Law.[162] Equally, it subordinates the availability of these options to the consent of States to ratify or accede to the Draft Convention, effectively making it a voluntary means for the settlement of space disputes rather than a comprehensive dispute settlement mechanism for the law of outer space. As a result, scholars have put forward similar proposals for the creation of a dispute settlement mechanism combining adjudication by a court and arbitration,[163] that is to say, a compulsory and binding third-party mechanism that is able to provide the parties with the flexibility to select the method of their preference.[164] Both the Draft Convention and these similar proposals are modelled after UNCLOS,[165]

[157] Ibid., Art 1(2)(b).

[158] Ibid., Arts 3–4.

[159] Ibid., Art 6.

[160] Ibid., Art 6(4).

[161] Ibid.

[162] Karl-Heinz Böckstiegel, 'Proposed Draft Convention on the Settlement of Space Law Disputes' (1985) 12 J Space L 136–62 at 140.

[163] Viikari, 'Towards more effective settlement', p. 238. See also Karl-Heinz Böckstiegel, 'Some reflections on dispute settlement in air, space and telecommunications law', in Kaj Hobér, Annette Magnusson, and Marie Öhrström (eds.), *Between East and West: Essays in Honour of Ulf Franke* (Huntington: Juris, 2010), p. 49 (stating that this model is particularly suited for disputes among States); Meishan Goh, *Dispute Settlement in International Space Law*, p. 7.

[164] Viikari, 'Towards more effective settlement', p. 239. A limitation of the proposal is the acknowledgement that arbitration is not well suited for disputes involving highly political or military aspects (see p. 246).

[165] van Traa-Engelman, 'Settlement of space law disputes', p. 151.

whose Part XV contemplates voluntary as well as compulsory means of dispute settlement.

In particular, Article 286 of UNCLOS establishes that, where parties have not reached a settlement through voluntary means, they must submit the dispute to the ITLOS, the ICJ, or an arbitral tribunal. However, there are ways to avoid the application of Article 286 of UNCLOS. On the one hand, the parties to a dispute may select a different method of dispute settlement under Part XV, Section 1 of UNCLOS. That would satisfy the requirement of Article 283(1) of UNCLOS, which requires the parties to a dispute to 'proceed expeditiously to an exchange of views'.[166] On the other hand, the parties to a dispute may invoke an exception.[167] This suggests that any dispute settlement mechanism modelled after UNCLOS fails to compel the parties to reach a settlement.[168] As recognised in the *Southern Bluefin Tuna* case, 'UNCLOS falls significantly short of establishing a truly comprehensive regime of compulsory jurisdiction entailing binding decisions'.[169]

As of today, no State has ratified the Draft Convention. However, scholars have put forward alternative proposals for the creation of an international institution, such as an International Space Agency,[170] a Global Space Organisation serving as 'a centralized space dispute resolution and governance body',[171] or an independent institution for the settlement of outer space disputes.[172] Such

[166] As discussed in Subsection 14.2.2.

[167] As listed in Pt XV, s. 3 of the UNCLOS.

[168] Eric De Brabandere, *Merrills' International Dispute Settlement*, 7th ed. (Cambridge: Cambridge University Press, 2022), p. 305 (arguing that the UNCLOS provisions on compulsory dispute settlement fail to restrict the freedom of choice of method by States); Alan E. Boyle, 'Dispute settlement and the Law of the Sea Convention: Problems of fragmentation and jurisdiction' (1997) 46 ICLQ 37–54 at 40–41 (describing the UNCLOS provisions on compulsory dispute settlement as the 'cafeteria' approach to dispute settlement).

[169] *Southern Bluefin Tuna (New Zealand* v. *Japan, Australia* v. *Japan)* (Jurisdiction and Admissibility, Award of 4 August 2000) (2000) 23 RIAA 45, reprinted in (2009) 39 ILM 1359, para. 62.

[170] van Traa-Engelman, 'Settlement of space law disputes', pp. 154–55.

[171] Matthew J. P. Horton, 'Consolidating space: A proposal to establish a central forum for the settlement of space-related disputes' (2020) 22 Vand J Ent Tech L 627–61 at 656–57 (arguing that the GSO's decisions should be public, establish a binding precedent, and be supported by an enforcement mechanism; the GSO should also include an appeals system); Christina Isnardi, 'Problems with enforcing international space law on private actors' (2020) 50 Colum J Transnat'l L 489–530 at 525 (advocating the creation of a new specialised agency endowed with a dispute resolution organ requiring member States to enforce its decisions within their jurisdictions).

[172] Rachael O'Grady, 'Star wars: The launch of extranational arbitration?' (2016) 82 CIARb Arbitrat J 1–9 at 1, 2, 8–9, www.mayerbrown.com/en/perspectives-events/publications/2016/11/star-wars-the-launch-of-extranational-arbitration (advocating the adoption of an International Convention on the Settlement of Outer-Space Disputes, which would create an

proposals rest on the premise that outer space is a global commons, like the oceans and Antarctica. For instance, Horton writes that outer space is 'a sovereignless international commons, as stated in the Outer Space Treaty'.[173] Consequently, the selection of arbitrators of the proposed Global Space Organisation must be inclusive, ensuring the presence of 'persons whose origins lay outside of the major spacefaring States'.[174] Similarly, Arbaugh argues that the Outer Space Treaty defines outer space as a global commons,[175] while Isnardi writes that a World Space Organisation should benefit developing and non-spacefaring countries alike, since the Outer Space Treaty states that outer space is 'the province of *all* mankind'.[176] While clearly articulate, such statements are rooted on a misconception: the Outer Space Treaty states that 'the exploration and use of outer space' – not 'outer space' – is the province of mankind. By granting States the right to access outer space on terms of equality, it presents outer space as an inclusive environment not capable of appropriation, not a global commons (which is a contested concept that may be interpreted as implying collective property rights).[177]

In an attempt to eliminate State discretion in the selection of the means of settlement, scholars have also proposed the creation of a multi-door courthouse for space disputes. Derived from the alternative dispute resolution movement,[178] the multi-door courthouse consists of an independent body performing an assessment of the best method for the settlement of disputes submitted to it for consideration.[179] However, the proposal has been criticised, since it gives the screener too much power in deciding the appropriate mode of dispute settlement, effectively encroaching upon State sovereignty.[180] As a model designed for domestic law, the multi-door courthouse does not fit the

International Centre for the Settlement of Outer-Space Disputes, the ICSOD Centre. The latter would allow private entities to bring a claim against States in relation to outer space activities. Access to the ICSOD Centre would be granted through the ratification of the ICSOD Convention followed by a bilateral or multilateral agreement between States on an *ad hoc* basis. The ICSOD Centre's decisions would be final and binding).

173 Horton, 'Consolidating space', p. 645.

174 Ibid., p. 656.

175 Arbaugh, 'Gravitating toward sensible resolutions', pp. 835–36.

176 Isnardi, 'Problems with enforcing international space law', p. 525 (emphasis original).

177 For example, the United States Executive Order 13914 of 6 April 2020 denies that outer space is a global commons. For a commentary of the historical and intellectual background of the Executive Order, see John S. Goehring, 'Why isn't outer space a global commons?' (2021) 11 J Nat'l Sec L & Pol 573–90.

178 Meishan Goh, *Dispute Settlement in International Space Law*, p. 7.

179 Ibid.

180 Kurlekar, 'Space – the final frontier', pp. 394–95.

decentralised structure of the international legal system.[181] As a result, it has never been used.

In addition, there have been attempts by private actors to create alternative mechanisms for the peaceful settlement of space disputes. The oldest one dates back to 1994, when the French Society of Air and Space Law established an International Court of Aviation and Space Arbitration (ICASA).[182] The ICASA aims to provide an avenue for individuals (whether public or private legal entities) to settle disputes arising out of aviation and space activities. However, its governing Rules are inspired by the principle of 'absolute secrecy' of the proceedings,[183] which is incompatible with the principle of transparency underpinning the Outer Space Treaty.[184] Ultimately, the ICASA Rules have never been used.[185]

A more recent project is the Dubai Courts of Space, a hub for commercial arbitration yet to become operative.[186] Started in 2021 as part of the Courts of the Future initiative, the Dubai Courts of Space offer a common law jurisdiction through an opt-in mechanism.[187] Notably, the distinctive feature of the Dubai Courts of Space is the provision of mandatory expert training for perspective arbitrators aimed at equipping them with the required expertise to arbitrate both traditional and new types of space disputes.

The review of proposals conducted in this section shows that no comprehensive system for space disputes settlement exists, and it is unlikely that one will be established. Attempts to circumvent the principle of State sovereignty under international law through the establishment of third-party compulsory mechanisms are not supported by States, effectively relegating them to the realm of theoretical speculation. The following section adds a different perspective to the debate about the need to create a compulsory system for the settlement of space disputes.

14.5 REORIENTING THE DEBATE: A FUNCTIONAL APPROACH

The UN space treaties do not envision any mechanism for the enforcement of space law on space actors. Accordingly, some scholars argue that the UN

181 Ibid., p. 395.

182 The text of the ICASA Rules is available in (1995) *Revue Française de Droit Aérien at Spatial* 29ff.

183 ICASA Rules, Art 3.

184 O'Grady, 'Star wars', pp. 5–6.

185 Pislevik, 'Law without gravity', pp. 288–89.

186 More information is available on the official website: Courts of the Future, 'Courts of space', www.courtsofthefuture.org/courts-of-space (accessed 9 August 2022).

187 See ibid. for the text of the opt-in clause.

treaties do not sufficiently consider the procedural aspects underpinning the peaceful settlement of space disputes.[188] For instance, Hertzfeld and Nelson argue that accidents in space involving the award of damages should be submitted to binding arbitration, either *ad hoc* arbitration or a decentralised arbitral network. Such a network would be based on two conditions: an arbitration clause contained in the launch licence and the publication of the consent to arbitration by the launching State.[189] Similarly, Sloup proposes that, as an interim measure until a specialised dispute settlement system is created,[190] all space disputes involving questions of international law should be decided by the ICJ[191] with assistance from a panel of scientific and technological experts.[192] Yet, other scholars argue that 'there is no indication that a centralized institution nor a more specialized legal regime is warranted at this time'.[193]

The existent scholarly positions have some merit, as they recognise the need for legal certainty in space operations. At the same time, they remain a theoretical endeavour largely detached from practical developments. Space activities are complex operations, and it may not be desirable to commit to a single dispute mechanism in advance. For instance, space mining operations consist of three phases: prospecting, exploration and exploitation. The disputes arising in each phase may contain different legal claims not necessarily suited to a single dispute settlement mechanism.

The prospecting phase essentially consists of remote sensing of the target celestial body for determining its size, shape and composition. Possible disputes arising from prospecting include claims of intellectual property rights over the collected data or collision with another space object. The former is most suitable to be decided by national courts while the latter by a Claims Commission under the Liability Convention or arbitration (whether *ad hoc* or based on the PCA Rules). The exploration phase consists of the extraction and analysis of samples of *in situ* resources. Potential conflicts include the violation of safety zones and breach of priority rights, both of which appear suited for diplomatic negotiation. Finally, the exploitation phase consists of the extraction of resources of a celestial body at a scale larger than that of sampling. Potential legal disputes arising from exploitation include claims of

[188] van Traa-Engelmann, 'Settlement of space law disputes', p. 139; Karl-Heinz Böckstiegel, 'Arbitration and adjudication regarding activities in outer space' (1978) 6 J Space L 3–18 at 17.
[189] Hertzfeld and Nelson, 'Binding arbitration', pp. 137–38.
[190] Sloup, 'Peaceful resolution of outer space conflicts', p. 697.
[191] Ibid., p. 688.
[192] Ibid., p. 693.
[193] Dadwal and Macdonald, 'Arbitration of space-related disputes', p. 7.

property rights over the extracted resources (suitable to be settled through national and international adjudication as well as arbitration); violation of safety zones and breach of property rights (suitable for diplomatic negotiation); as well as damage caused by space debris generated by the extraction activity (suitable for the Claims Commission under the Liability Convention or arbitration).

Adopting a functional approach to the peaceful settlement of space disputes – that is to say, matching the legal claims to the most suitable dispute settlement mechanisms – requires flexibility in the choice of available means as disputes arise. Contrary to a scholarly position,[194] committing in advance to a specialised dispute settlement mechanism for types of space activities (such as space mining) may not necessarily be an optimal solution for space actors. In this respect, the argument that arbitration is the most appropriate means of dispute settlement involving private actors is not convincing.[195] Space exploration activities often involve public–private partnerships, making it difficult to draw a neat line between private activities suitable to arbitration and public activities suitable to other potential means of dispute resolution. In addition, the same type of space activity can be carried out by public or private actors, including space mining with its bundle of potential legal claims.

Likewise, committing in advance to a specialised dispute settlement mechanism may not be a solution to the perceived weaknesses of the dispute settlement mechanisms for space activities currently available, namely the lack of enforcement powers against recalcitrant space actors. International space law is a specialised field of international law, which is largely State-centred. Article VI of the Outer Space Treaty establishes that '[States] shall bear international responsibility for national activities in outer space … whether such activities are carried out by governmental agencies or non-governmental entities'. Accordingly, it requires that the activities of non-State actors in outer space are authorised and continuously supervised by States.[196] Effectively, private actors operate in outer space on behalf of States, which must ensure compliance with the space treaties they have ratified. The consequence is that any attempt to impose a decision on private actors requires the consent of States. For example, enforcing a decision on a

[194] I. H. Ph. Diederiks-Verschoor, 'The settlement of disputes in space: New developments' (1998) 26 J Space L 41–50 at 49 (arguing that 'in space law disputes between private parties, arbitration is the only means of settlement').

[195] Ibid.

[196] Outer Space Treaty, Art VI.

private company requires an intervention of the State of nationality (or incorporation), including through its courts.

By virtue of Article VI of the Outer Space Treaty, international space law preserves State consent as the basis of obligation in international law, as reflected in the principles governing the peaceful settlement of space disputes, including those listed in Article 33 of the UN Charter. Whether this is considered a weakness or not,[197] it demonstrates that the creation of a specialised settlement mechanism for space disputes does not per se affect the sovereign right of States to abide by only those obligations they have consented to. In this respect, the enforcement powers of any dispute settlement mechanism can only be effective within the framework of bilateral or multilateral agreements concluded by States (including with and within international organisations) to the extent that such agreements offer incentives to States to abide by them, effectively inviting a recourse to binding mechanisms to settle their disputes for the violation of the agreements' provisions. At the same time, such agreements must not alter the foundational principles of international space law contained in the Outer Space Treaty – including the principles of conflict avoidance and the freedom of choice in relation to dispute settlement means – by imposing a single, predetermined method of dispute settlement for all types of claims arising from activities in outer space.

A functional and flexible approach to the settlement of space disputes preserves both the letter and the spirit of the Outer Space Treaty while creating the conditions for the availability of both voluntary and binding dispute settlement mechanisms – provided they are agreed upon by States – in relation to the binding effects of the decisions. For example, the national licence to perform space resource extraction could stipulate that any dispute relating to property rights over space resources will be decided through adjudication or arbitration, since enforcement of a national piece of legislation is the competence of domestic courts. Equally, it may constitute the applicable law for an arbitration, should the parties so agree, together with the relevant treaty obligations on outer space. A similar stipulation could be inserted in a contractual clause (if domestic legislation grants property rights over space resources) or even in a future treaty on space resource utilisation.

Absent State consent, proposals to reform the currently unstructured framework for the peaceful settlement of space disputes are doomed to fail, as the

[197] Böckstiegel, 'Settlement of disputes', p. 2 ('It is a well-known weakness of public international law that, contrary to national law, rights and duties of a party cannot automatically be enforced against another party by access to and decision by courts').

cases of the ILA Draft Convention and the PCA Rules demonstrate. In international space law, the pragmatic approach to dispute settlement is as important as the doctrinal one. A perfect theoretical framework may not necessarily suit the needs and interests of States related to the exploration and use of outer space. As the experience with the law of the sea shows,[198] States have a duty to attempt a peaceful settlement of their disputes through a means of their choice. This does not necessarily equate with a duty to have a dispute settled. To minimise the risk of failure to settle space disputes, the Outer Space Treaty embraces the principle of dispute avoidance, which requires States to act transparently and cooperatively in outer space. Conflict avoidance is a legally binding obligation of conduct under the Outer Space Treaty carrying diplomatic connotations as well. By allowing States to compromise on their respective positions, the likelihood that space disputes remain unsettled decreases, as the case of the *Cosmos* 954 demonstrates. At the same time, State conduct outside the boundaries of the Outer Space Treaty is likely to be condemned in multilateral fora, such as COPUOS, possibly leading to diplomatic backlash and retaliation.

While the current system for the peaceful settlement of space disputes is neither comprehensive nor specialised, a functional approach to space disputes on a case-by-case basis appears a sensible compromise between the need to respect the sovereign decision of States to conduct space activities and the risk of arbitrary or unlawful State conduct in outer space leading to conflict, as opposed to transparency and cooperation. In this respect, the peaceful settlement of outer space disputes can be seen as a corollary of the principle of cooperation in outer space activities, which is by its nature open to interpretation as to its scope and flexibility in terms of means of implementation.

14.6 CONCLUSION

Informed by the principle of conflict avoidance, the UN space treaties do not establish a comprehensive framework for the peaceful settlement of space disputes. Except for the Claims Commission established under the Liability Convention, the means for the settlement of space disputes (both voluntary and binding) are those available under general international law.

Scholars have criticised the lack of a specialised dispute settlement system for space law as a sign of weakness. They argue that, in the absence of enforcement powers, the recognised mechanisms under the UN space treaties

[198] As discussed in Subsection 14.2.1.

are not able to compel the parties to settle their disputes. Contrary to this view, this chapter has argued that the lack of enforcement powers is not synonymous with the inefficiency of the current mechanisms for the settlement of space disputes. An examination of the relationship between the principle of conflict avoidance and the concept of dispute settlement showed that the current UN treaty framework does not prevent the creation of specialised dispute settlement mechanisms for space activities. It subsequently evaluated the two existent specialised dispute settlement means – namely, the Claims Commission and the PCA Rules for arbitration – and showed that, because their binding outcome can contribute to legal certainty by establishing a precedent, they run the risk of depriving States of the power of interpretation of space treaties. As a result, they have not gained the confidence of space actors and have never been used.

The chapter also evaluated whether the available dispute settlement mechanisms can address the disputes that are likely to arise from new space activities, such as space mining. Having reached a positive conclusion, it considered whether the creation of a specialised tribunal for space disputes is necessary or desirable. It showed that, if created, such a tribunal would not be able to circumvent the principle of State consent to submit a dispute to such tribunal and be bound by its decision.

Given the complex and hazardous nature of space activities, the chapter concluded that a flexible approach to the peaceful settlement of space disputes is desirable. Rather than committing to a single means in advance, States are better off choosing the most suitable mechanisms for the settlement of space disputes based on the type of legal claims originating from the dispute rather than on the nature – voluntary or binding – of the selected mechanism. Matching legal claims to the most suitable dispute settlement mechanism effectively constitutes a functional approach to the peaceful settlement of space disputes. It also acknowledges the principle of freedom of choice of the means for the peaceful settlement of disputes, including those listed in Article 33 of the UN Charter.

15

Fact-Finding and Cyber Attribution

NICHOLAS TSAGOURIAS AND FIONA MIDDLETON

15.1 INTRODUCTION

As our societies become increasingly reliant on cyberspace, they also become vulnerable to cyberattacks[1] committed by States or non-State actors either independently or in collaboration with each other. States and non-State actors exploit this complex environment and the anonymity, speed, and interconnectivity it affords to cause harm. Attribution is important in such a context because it concerns the process of assigning a cyberattack to its source, which is a prerequisite for any remedial action and for establishing responsibility.

In international law, attribution refers to the legal process of assigning an act or omission to a State (or another subject of international law), and it is one of the constitutive elements of the law of State responsibility. A State can incur responsibility only if a wrongful act or omission is attributed to it according to the criteria established in the law of State responsibility. A cyberattack can thus be attributed to a State according to the criteria contained in Articles 4–11 of the International Law Commission's Draft Articles on Responsibility of States for Internationally Wrongful Acts (2001) and engage its responsibility if it constitutes a breach of one of its obligations.[2]

That said, attribution, in general, and cyber attribution, in particular, have also a factual dimension. The factual dimension of cyber attribution refers to the attribution of a cyberattack to its source based on technical facts. This requires technical investigations conducted mainly by cyber forensics experts.[3]

[1] The term 'cyberattack' is used here generically to refer to malicious cyber operations.

[2] ILC, 'Draft articles on responsibility of states for internationally wrongful acts', in *Yearbook of the International Law Commission 2001, Volume II, Part Two: Report of the Commission to the General Assembly on the Work of Its Fifty-Third Session* (New York: UN, 2001), Art 2.

[3] Nicholas Tsagourias and Michael Farrell, 'Cyber attribution: Technical and legal approaches and challenges' (2020) 31 EJIL 941–67.

The two processes of attribution (legal and factual/technical) cannot be clearly decoupled because legal attribution is fact-dependent. To explain, facts need to be discovered and assessed according to the legal criteria of attribution in order to assign a particular cyberattack to a State for legal purposes.

It is for this reason that attribution claims are often accompanied by reports containing supporting evidence. These reports are compiled by the State making the attribution claim, often assisted by private cybersecurity companies.[4] However, in most cases these reports are quite thin on evidence and do not always explain how facts were assessed.[5] Consequently, accused States, and sometimes third States, contest the attribution claims by disputing the facts and the supporting evidence.

For example, the US attributed the Democratic National Committee (DNC) hack to Russia, which dismissed it as demanding 'some proof'.[6] China dismissed the attribution of the intrusion into the Office of Personnel Management as 'groundless'.[7] Germany attributed the intrusion into its Bundestag in April 2015 to Russia on the basis of 'hard evidence',[8] but, following the arrest warrant issued against a Russian operative, Russia's First Deputy Foreign Minister said that no evidence was provided to prove his involvement in the hack.[9] The UK and partner States attributed malicious

[4] See, e.g., FireEye Intelligence, 'Anatomy of Russia's 2016 Influence Operations', *Internet Archive*, October 2017, https://archive.org/details/2017-10-fireeye-anatomy (accessed 10 July 2022).

[5] Donald J. Trump, 'National Cyber Strategy of the United States of America', September 2018, https://trumpwhitehouse.archives.gov/wp-content/uploads/2018/09/National-Cyber-Strategy.pdf (accessed 10 July 2022), p. 21; NATO, 'Brussels Summit Declaration, issued by the heads of State and government participating in the meeting of the North Atlantic Council in Brussels 11–12 July 2018, Press release (2018) 074', 11 July 2018, www.nato.int/cps/en/natohq/official_texts_156624.htm (accessed 10 July 2022).

[6] Laura Smith-Spark, 'Russia challenges us to prove campaign hacking claims or shut up', *CNN*, 16 December 2016, https://edition.cnn.com/2016/12/16/europe/russia-us-hacking-claims-peskov/index.html (accessed 10 July 2022).

[7] Kristin Finklea et al., 'Cyber intrusion into U.S. Office of Personnel Management: In brief', *Congressional Research Service*, 17 July 2015, https://digitial.library.unt.edu/ark:/67531/metadc743551/m1/1/hig-res-d/R44111_2015Jul17.pdf (accessed 10 July 2022), p. 3.

[8] Anon., 'Merkel says Germany has "hard evidence" of Russian hacking', *Euronews*, 13 May 2020, www.euronews.com/2020/05/13/merkel-says-germany-has-hard-evidence-of-russian-hacking (accessed 10 July 2022).

[9] Catalln Clmpanu, 'Russia says Germany has not provided any evidence of Bundestag hack', *ZDNet*, 12 June 2020, www.zdnet.com/article/russia-says-germany-has-not-provided-any-evidence-of-bundestag-hack (accessed 10 July 2022). According to Foreign Ministry Spokeswoman Maria Zakharova, 'we strongly reject Germany's proofless allegations about the involvement of Russian government entities in a hacker attack on the German Bundestag in 2015'. See also Anon., 'Russia rejects claims it was behind cyberattack on Bundestag in 2015 – Diplomat', *TASS*, 4 June 2020, https://tass.com/politics/1164165 (accessed 10 July 2022).

cyber operations against the postponed 2020 Tokyo Olympic Games and the 2018 Paralympic Games in South Korea to Russia. The UK's National Cyber Security Centre assessed 'with high confidence that these attacks were carried out by the GRU's Main Centre for Specialist Technologies (GTsST), also known as Sandworm and VoodooBear'.[10] Russia, however, denied the allegations.[11] When Norway accused Russia of trying to foment discord in the country,[12] the Russian embassy responded by saying that 'as normal there are [*sic*] no evidence, just general speculations'.[13] When Norway accused Russia of interference during NATO war games that took place in Norway, the Norwegian Defence Minister reportedly said: 'Russia asked (us) to give proof. We gave them the proof'; 'Russia said "thank you, we will come back when our experts review that"'; 'To have such an answer from Russia is a positive thing'.[14] However, Russia never came back. Also, when Norway blamed Russia for a cyberattack against its parliament in 2020, the Russian embassy branded the allegation unacceptable and claimed that no evidence was provided.[15] Last but not least, the US attributed the SolarWinds hacking to

According to Maria Zakharova, 'since 2015, the German side has not only failed to furnish any proof of Russia's guilt, but it has also failed to explain even once what the accusations hurled at our country are based on'. She said, 'Now, the German authorities are referring to certain "reliable evidence" obtained by Berlin, according to German media, from – and here's the thing – the US'. The diplomat also added that 'Russia is ready to look into the data obtained by Germany from the US regarding a cyberattack on the Bundestag in 2015, if it does exist'.

10 Anon., 'UK and partners condemn GRU cyber attacks against Olympic and Paralympic Games', *National Cyber Security Centre*, 19 October 2020, www.ncsc.gov.uk/news/uk-and-partners-condemn-gru-cyber-attacks-against-olympic-an-paralympic-games (accessed 10 July 2022); UK Foreign, Commonwealth, and Development Office and Dominic Raab, 'UK exposes series of Russian cyber attacks against Olympic and Paralympic Games', *UK Government*, 19 October 2020, www.gov.uk/government/news/uk-exposes-series-of-russian-cyber-attacks-against-olympic-and-paralympic-games (accessed 10 July 2022). See also *United States of America* v. *Yuriy Sergeyevich Andrienko et al.*, United States District Court for the Western District of Pennsylvania, Case No. 20-CR-316 (15 October 2020).

11 Reuters, 'Kremlin denies Olympics hacking allegations', 19 October 2020, www.reuters.com/article/us-olympics-2020-cyber-russia-kremlin-idUSKBN2751IR (accessed 10 July 2022).

12 Thomas Nilsen, 'Russian influence ops seek to fuel discord between Arctic Norway and Oslo, Norwegian intelligence service says', *Barents Observer*, 10 February 2020, https://thebarentsobserver.com/en/security/2020/02/chief-nis-says-russian-influence-operations-fuel-disagreements-between-north-and (accessed 10 July 2022).

13 Thomas Nilsen, 'Russian Embassy denies accusations of influence operations in Norway', *Barents Observer*, 13 February 2020, https://thebarentsobserver.com/en/security/2020/02/russian-embassy-denies-accusations-influence-operations-norway (accessed 10 July 2022).

14 Reuters, 'Norway says it proved Russian GPS interference during NATO exercises', 18 March 2019, www.reuters.com/article/us-norway-defence-russia-idUSKCN1QZ1WN (accessed 10 July 2022).

15 Dafina Shala, 'Datainnbruddet mot Stortinget er ferdig etterforsket', *PST*, 8 December 2020, www.pst.no/alle-artikler/pressemeldinger/datainnbruddet-mot-stortinget-er-ferdig-etterforsket

Russia's Foreign Intelligence Service. As was stated in a White House brief, 'the U.S. Intelligence Community has high confidence in its assessment of attribution to the SVR [Foreign Intelligence Service]'.[16] Russia rejected such claims as baseless.[17]

By contesting the facts, States not only challenge implicitly or explicitly the attribution claim, but they also dispute the legal claim that can be drawn from attribution, for example, a legal claim that international law has been breached and responsibility is incurred. This is because legal inferences and valuations are drawn from facts or, to put it differently, because facts are law-dispositive.

When a dispute arises, States have an obligation to settle it peacefully.[18] This obligation is fundamental because it is indispensable for maintaining international peace and security.[19] States can, to that effect, employ a variety of dispute settlement mechanisms, with fact-finding being one such mechanism in and of itself or as part of another dispute settlement mechanism.[20]

The question this chapter aims to answer is whether a fact-finding mechanism (FFM) to establish the facts underpinning cyber attribution claims can contribute to the peaceful settlement of an attribution dispute and facilitate

(accessed 10 July 2022); Anon., 'Norway blames Russia for cyber-attack on parliament', *BBC News*, 13 October 2020, www.bbc.co.uk/news/world-europe-54518106 (accessed 10 July 2022); Catalln Clmpanu, 'Norway says Russian hacking group APT28 is behind August 2020 Parliament hack', *ZDNet*, 8 December 2020, www.zdnet.com/article/norway-says-russian-hacking-group-apt28-is-behind-august-2020-parliament-hack (accessed 10 July 2022); Reuters, '"Flattered" Russian spy chief denies SolarWinds attack – BBC', 18 May 2021, www.reuters.com/technology/russian-spy-chief-denies-svr-was-behind-solarwinds-cyber-attack-bbc-2021-05-18 (accessed 10 July 2022).

16 The White House, 'Fact sheet: Imposing costs for harmful foreign activities by the Russian government', 15 April 2021, www.whitehouse.gov/briefing-room/statements-releases/2021/04/15/fact-sheet-imposing-costs-for-harmful-foreign-activities-by-the-russian-government (accessed 10 July 2022). The UK government also attributed the hacking to Russia. UK Foreign, Commonwealth, and Development Office and Dominic Raab, 'Russia: UK and US expose global campaign of malign activity by Russian intelligence services', *UK Government*, 15 April 2021, www.gov.uk/government/news/russia-uk-and-us-expose-global-campaigns-of-malign-activity-by-russian-intelligence-services (accessed 10 July 2022).

17 Graig Graziosi, 'Russia denies claims it was responsible for massive hacking campaign targeting US government and private companies', *Independent*, 15 December 2020, www.independent.co.uk/news/world/russia-hack-us-government-b1773987.html (accessed 10 July 2022).

18 Charter of the United Nations, San Francisco, 26 June 1945, in force 24 October 1945, 1 UNTS 16, Art 2(3).

19 Russell Buchan, 'Quo vadis? Commissions of inquiry and their implications for the coherence of international law', in Christian Henderson (ed.), *Commissions of Inquiry: Problems and Prospects* (London: Bloomsbury, 2017), pp. 257–58.

20 UN Charter, Art 33. In this chapter, fact-finding commission, fact-finding mission, and fact-finding mechanism (FFM) will be used interchangeably.

the settlement of a broader dispute of which the cyber attribution dispute may be a part.

The chapter attempts to answer this question by first discussing in Section 15.2 the role of fact-finding in international dispute settlement as well as its legal, institutional, structural, and methodological modalities. In Section 15.3, the chapter will identify several challenges fact-finding is currently facing. These two sections provide the background for the discussion that will follow in Section 15.4 of fact-finding for purposes of cyber attribution. Section 15.4 will thus explain the notion of cyber facts; discuss the legal, institutional, structural, and methodological modalities of a cyber attribution FFM; and cast a critical eye on certain proposals envisaging the establishment of a cyber attribution FFM. The chapter concludes in Section 15.5 by presenting the configuration of a cyber attribution FFM which, in the opinion of the authors, would enable it to perform its fact-finding tasks effectively and contribute to dispute settlement.

15.2 FACT-FINDING AND INTERNATIONAL DISPUTE SETTLEMENT

Fact-finding as a method of dispute settlement has been recognised in the 1899 Hague Convention for the Pacific Settlement of International Disputes and is also mentioned in Article 33 of the UN Charter.[21] Its importance for the peaceful settlement of disputes and for maintaining international peace was also stressed by the UN General Assembly (UNGA) in several Resolutions.[22]

The primary aim of fact-finding is to 'elucidate' facts underlying a dispute by locating, identifying, verifying, corroborating, and analysing them.[23] The assumption is that by resolving factual controversies, it is not only the factual

[21] Arts 9–14 of the Convention for the Pacific Settlement of International Disputes, The Hague, 29 July 1899, in force 4 September 1990, (1899) 187 CTS 410 (Hague I); UN Charter, Art 33.

[22] See UNGA Res 2329(XXII) (18 December 1967) UN Doc. A/RES/2330(XXII); UNGA, 'Manila declaration on the peaceful settlement of international disputes' (15 November 1982) UN Doc. A/RES/37/10; UNGA, 'Declaration on fact-finding by the United Nations in the field of the maintenance of international peace and security' (9 December 1991) UN Doc. A/RES/46/59.

[23] Art 9, Hague I; John G. Merrills, *International Dispute Settlement*, 5th ed. (Cambridge: Cambridge University Press, 2011), p. 41; Marina Akensova and Morten Bergsmo, 'Non-criminal justice work in the age of accountability', in Morten Bergsmo (ed.), *Quality Control in Fact-Finding* (Florence: Torkel Opsahl, 2013), p. 30; Agnieszka Jachec-Neale, 'Fact finding', in *Max Planck Encyclopaedia of International Law* (Oxford: Oxford University Press, 2009). According to the UNGA, 'Declaration on fact-finding', para. 2: 'Fact-finding means any activity designed to obtain detailed knowledge of the relevant facts of any dispute.'

dispute that will be settled, but also that legal disputes linked to the facts will be prevented, accommodated, or settled.

Although fact-finding was envisaged as an objective and impartial mechanism of ascertaining facts, it evolved over the years to address a range of different situations and issues.[24] For example, fact-finding missions have been endowed with monitoring, alerting, and recommendatory tasks. They have also exercised adjudicative functions by identifying violations of international law or determining the applicability of specific legal rules,[25] and in this way, fact-finding contributed directly or indirectly to accountability at the individual or State level.[26] This meant that the nature of fact-finding changed from investigating facts to acquiring a juridical dimension either directly or indirectly because facts cannot be disentangled easily from law.[27] As a result of such changes, fact-finding has sometimes exacerbated existing disputes or triggered additional disputes about fact-finding itself.[28]

15.2.1 *Forming an FFM*

There are different routes through which FFMs can be created. In the first place, disputing States can establish an FFM based on agreement, but relevant

24 Christian Henderson, 'Commissions of inquiry: Flexible temporariness or permanent predictability?' (2014) 45 NYIL 287–310.

25 See, e.g., the UN Human Rights Council, 'Commission of Inquiry in Burundi' (5 October 2016) UN Doc. A/HRC/RES/33/24, or the International Commission of Inquiry on Darfur, 'Report of the International Commission of Inquiry on Darfur to the United Nations Secretary-General, pursuant to Security Council Resolution 1564 of 18 September 2004', January 2005, www.un.org/ruleoflaw/files/com_inq_darfur.pdf (accessed 11 July 2022). According to a survey of sixty-six missions, 'only seventeen (25 percent) mandates included reference to "fact-finding" in their mandate, and the mandate of only one mission included reference to ascertaining the "truth"'. Shiri Krebs, 'The legalization of truth in international fact-finding' (2017) 18 Chi J Int'l L 83–163 at 96.

26 Cecilie Hellestveit, 'International fact-finding mechanisms: Lighting candles or cursing darkness?', in Cecilia M. Bailliet and Kjetil M. Larsen (eds.), *Promoting Peace through International Law* (Oxford: Oxford University Press, 2015), p. 380.

27 According, however, to Art 14, Hague I, the fact-finding report does not have the character of an arbitral award.

28 See, e.g., the controversy surrounding the UN Human Rights Council, 'Report of the United Nations Fact-Finding Mission on the Gaza Conflict' (25 September 2009) UN Doc. A/HRC/12/48 (the Goldstone Report). Israel Ministry of Foreign Affairs, 'Initial Response to Report of the Fact Finding Mission on Gaza', 24 September 2009, www.gov.il/en/Departments/General/initial-response-to-report-of-the-fact-finding-mission-on-gaza (accessed 20 July 2022); Richard Goldstone, 'Reconsidering the Goldstone Report on Israel and war crimes', 11 April 2011, www.washingtonpost.com/opinions/reconsidering-the-goldstone-report-on-israel-and-war-crimes/2011/04/01/AFg111JC_story.html (accessed 20 July 2022).

practice is quite thin in this regard.[29] FFM can alternatively be established by international organisations in relation to issues falling within their competence. The UN is the most active organisation in this regard due to its far-reaching competence in the field of international peace and security.[30] According to Chapter VI of the UN Charter, the UN Security Council (UNSC) can intervene directly or indirectly in the settlement of inter-State disputes that may endanger international peace and security. To this effect, the UNSC can call upon States to settle their disputes peacefully in which case it is for the State parties to the dispute to employ any of the available dispute settlement methods,[31] or the UNSC can recommend an appropriate dispute settlement method which may also include fact-finding.[32] The UNSC can also investigate any dispute endangering international peace and security *proprio motu* by establishing an FFM.[33] Fact-finding in this case plays a diagnostic and preventive role.[34] It allows the UNSC to take appropriate action to de-escalate the dispute or facilitate its settlement through the use of other dispute settlement mechanisms.[35] Moving now to Chapter VII, although the power to establish an FFM is not mentioned expressly in the UN Charter, it falls within the UNSC's implied powers under this Chapter. The UNSC can thus recommend an FFM pursuant to Articles 39 and 40 of the UN Charter in which case the States involved in the dispute should agree on its establishment and deployment. The UNSC can also use its mandatory

[29] See, e.g., *The Red Crusader Inquiry (Denmark* v. *United Kingdom)* (1962) 35 ILR 485.

[30] See UN Library and Archives, 'International commissions of inquiry, fact-finding missions: Home', *UN Research Guides*, https://libraryresources.unog.ch/factfinding (accessed 11 July 2022).

[31] UN Charter, Art 33(2).

[32] Ibid., Art 36(1).

[33] Ibid., Art 34. In relation to the events in Greece in the 1940s, the UNSC decided 'under Article 34 of the Charter establish a Commission of Investigation to ascertain the facts relating to the alleged border violations along the frontier between Greece on the one hand and Albania, Bulgaria and Yugoslavia'. UNSC Res 15 (19 December 1946) UN Doc. S/RES/15/1946.

[34] Larissa van den Herick, 'An inquiry into the role of commissions of inquiry in international law: Navigating the tensions between fact-finding and international law-application', Grotius Centre Working Paper 2014/031-ICL, https://papers.ssrn.com/sol3/Delivery.cfm/SSRN_ID2586997_code1405039.pdf (accessed 11 July 2022), pp. 19–20. See also Chapter 11 by Nigel White in this volume.

[35] For example, the UNSC established an International Independent Investigative Committee (IIIC) to examine the exact circumstances of the 14 February 2005 terrorist bombing in Beirut. It mandated all States, including Syria, to co-operate with the IIIC and later established a special criminal tribunal to try those involved. See UNSC Res 1595 (7 April 2005) UN Doc. S/RES/1595; UNSC Res 1636 (31 October 2005) UN Doc. S/RES/1636; and UNSC Res 1757 (30 May 2007) UN Doc. S/RES/1757.

powers under Articles 39 and 41 of the UN Charter to create an FFM and instruct parties to co-operate with it.[36] In order to operate under Chapter VII, the UNSC should first determine that the dispute constitutes a threat to the peace, a breach of the peace, or an act of aggression,[37] even if the dispute has been referred to the UNSC by the States concerned.[38] This may limit the ability of the UNSC to act because its decisions are subject to veto.

Regarding the UNGA, it does not have expressed powers to establish FFMs, but such a power can be implied from Articles 10, 11, 14, and 22 of the UN Charter which give the UNGA general powers in peace and security and in all matters falling within the Charter. The UNGA does not, however, have binding powers, and therefore dispatching a fact-finding mission requires State consent.[39]

The UN Secretary-General (UNSG) can establish an FFM if requested by States or delegated by the UNSC or UNGA.[40] The UNSG can also establish FFM *proprio motu*.[41]

Aside from these organs, other UN organs, such as the Human Rights Council, have implied powers to form FFMs.[42] Their mandates are, however, narrower than the ones established by the UNGA, UNSC, or UNSG because they should fall within the parent organ's competences and powers, which are more limited. For example, FFMs established by the Human Rights Council focus on human rights violations only.

36 See, e.g., in relation to Syria, UNSC Res 2118 (27 September 2013) UN Doc. S/RES/2118 para. 7 and UNSC Res 2235 (7 August 2015) UN Doc. S/RES/2235 para. 5. Also UNSC Res 2231 (20 July 2015) UN Doc. S/RES/2231 paras 3, 19, and 26 in relation to Iran's nuclear programme.

37 UN Charter, Art. 39.

38 Ibid., Arts 35 and 37.

39 UNGA, 'International, impartial and independent mechanism to assist in the investigation and prosecution of persons responsible for the most serious crimes under international law committed in the Syrian Arab Republic since March 2011' (21 December 2016) UN Doc. A/RES/71/248 (IIIM), p. 4.

40 UN Charter, Art 98; UNGA, 'Declaration on fact-finding', para. 15; UNSC Res 2379 (21 September 2017) UN Doc. S/RES/2379 which, in para. 2, delegated the UNSC 'to establish an Investigative Team, headed by a Special Adviser, to support domestic efforts to hold ISIL (Da'esh) accountable by collecting, preserving, and storing evidence in Iraq of acts that may amount to war crimes, crimes against humanity and genocide committed by the terrorist group ISIL (Da'esh) in Iraq'.

41 UN Charter, Art 99. See UNGA, 'Declaration on fact-finding', para. 13.

42 For information on all Human Rights Council commissions of inquiry, see UN Library and Archives, 'International commissions of inquiry, fact-finding missions: Mandating authority', *UN Research Guides*, https://libraryresources.unog.ch/c.php?g=462695&p=3162812 (accessed 11 July 2022).

Outside the UN system, regional organisations can establish FFMs based on expressed or implied powers. Examples include the decision of the African Commission of Human and Peoples Rights to deploy a fact-finding mission to Sudan[43] and that of the Council of the European Union to establish an independent international fact-finding mission to investigate the conflict in Georgia.[44]

Regarding more specialised organisations, the Organisation for the Prohibition of Chemical Weapons (OPCW) stressed the 'value of the Secretariat conducting an independent investigation of an alleged use of chemical weapons with a view to facilitating universal attribution of all chemical weapons attacks' and for this reason granted its Director-General the power to 'provide technical expertise to identify those who were perpetrators, organisers, sponsors or otherwise involved in the use of chemicals as weapons'.[45] In 2014, the OPCW deployed a fact-finding mission 'to establish facts surrounding allegations of the use of toxic chemicals, reportedly chlorine, for hostile purposes in the Syrian Arab Republic',[46] whereas the OPCW–UN Joint Investigative Mechanism was established in 2015 to identify the perpetrators of chemical weapon attacks in Syria, whose mandate expired in 2017.[47] Since then, the OPCW established the Investigation and Identification Team (IIT) to identify the perpetrators of the use of chemical weapons in the Syrian Arab Republic.[48]

The OPCW also provided technical assistance to the UK in relation to the Salisbury incident of 2018. The request for assistance was made in accordance

43 African Commission on Human and Peoples' Rights, 'Resolution on Darfur, ACHPR/Res.68 (XXXV)03', 4 June 2004, https://achpr.org/sessions/resolutions?id=73 (accessed 11 July 2022).

44 Council of the European Union, 'Council Decision 2008/901/CFSP of 2 December 2008 concerning an independent international fact-finding mission on the conflict in Georgia, 2008/901/CFSP', 2 December 2008, www.legislation.gov.uk/en/eudn/2008/901 (accessed 11 July 2022).

45 OPCW Conference of the State Parties, 'Decision addressing the threat from chemical weapons use, C-SS-4/DEC.3', 27 June 2018, www.opcw.org/sites/default/files/documents/CSP/C-SS-4/en/css4dec3_e_.doc.pdf (accessed 11 July 2022), paras 19–20. See, however, Russia's strong criticism of the decision related to attribution. OPCW Conference of the State Parties, 'Russian Federation statement by Mr O. N. Ryazantsev, Head of the Delegation of the Russian Federation, Deputy Minister of Industry and Trade of the Russian Federation, at the twenty-fourth session of the Conference of the States Parties, C-24/NAT.55', 25 November 2019, www.opcw.org/sites/default/files/documents/2020/02/c24nat55%28e%29.pdf (accessed 11 July 2022).

46 See OPCW, 'Fact-finding mission', www.opcw.org/fact-finding-mission (accessed 11 July 2022).

47 UNSC Res 2235 (7 August 2015) UN Doc. S/RES/2235.

48 OPCW, 'Decision addressing the threat from chemical weapons use'. For Russia's opposition, see OPCW, 'Russian Federation statement'.

with Article VIII 38(e) of the Chemical Weapons Convention.[49] The UK government's final assessment was that it was highly likely that Russia was behind the poisoning, but this was denied by Russia.[50]

The International Atomic Energy Agency (IAEA) is another organisation conducting on-site inspections.[51] These can be *ad hoc*, routine, or special inspections.[52] For example, the IAEA has carried out on-site inspections of Iran's nuclear facilities.[53]

We should also mention here the International Humanitarian Fact-Finding Commission, whose mandate it is to investigate violations of international humanitarian law and, through its reporting and recommendations, to ensure respect of humanitarian law. Although it is treaty-based, its operation depends on State consent.[54]

[49] OPCW Technical Secretariat, 'Note by the Technical Secretariat: Summary of the report on activities carried out in support of a request for technical assistance by the United Kingdom of Great Britain and Northern Ireland (Technical Assistance Visit TAV/02/18), S/1612/2018', 12 April 2018, www.opcw.org/sites/default/files/documents/S_series/2018/en/s-1612-2018_e_.pdf (accessed 12 July 2022). See also OPCW Technical Secretariat, 'Note by the Technical Secretariat: Summary of the report on activities carried out in support of a request for technical assistance by the United Kingdom of Great Britain and Northern Ireland (Technical Assistance Visit Tav/03/18 and Tav/03b/18 "Amesbury incident") S/1671/2018', 4 September 2018, www.opcw.org/sites/default/files/documents/2018/09/s-1671-2018%28e%29_0.pdf (accessed 12 July 2022).

[50] Theresa May, 'PM Commons statement on Salisbury incident response', *UK Government*, 13 March 2018, www.gov.uk/government/speeches/pm-commons-statement-on-salisbury-incident-response-14-march-2018 (accessed 12 July 2022); John Foggo, 'Statement to the Organisation for the Prohibition of Chemical Weapons on the Salisbury attack: 4 April 2018', *UK Government*, 5 April 2018, www.gov.uk/government/speeches/statement-from-the-organisation-for-the-prohibition-of-chemical-weapons-on-the-salisbury-attack-4-april-2018 (accessed 12 July 2022).

[51] Art XII(6) of the Statute of the International Atomic Energy Agency, New York, 26 October 1956, in force 29 July 2957, 276 UNTS 3; International Atomic Energy Agency, 'Model protocol additional to the agreement(s) between State(s) and the International Atomic Energy Agency for the application of safeguards, IAEA Doc. INFCIRC/540.Corr', September 1997, www.iaea.org/sites/default/files/infcirc540c.pdf (accessed 12 July 2022).

[52] IAEA, 'IAEA safeguards overview', www.iaea.org/publications/factsheets/iaea-safeguards-overview (accessed 12 July 2022).

[53] IAEA, 'Verification and monitoring in Iran', www.iaea.org/newscenter/focus/iran (accessed 12 July 2022). UNSC Res 1737 (23 December 2006) UN Doc. S/RES/1737; and UNSC Res 2231 (20 July 2015) UN Doc. S/RES/2231.

[54] Art 90 of the Protocol Additional to the Geneva Conventions of 12 August 1949, and Relating to the Protection of Victims of International Armed Conflicts (Protocol I), Geneva, 8 June 1977, in force 7 December 1978, 1125 UNTS 3.

In addition to international organisations, NGOs have also formed FFMs in relation to specific incidents and, more generally, to collect evidence.[55] An example is the Independent Civil Society Fact-Finding Mission in Libya which was created by the Arab Organisation for Human Rights in cooperation with the Palestinian Centre for Human Rights. The objective of this fact-finding mission was to investigate widespread violations of international law in Libya.[56]

What all this shows is that in addition to States, a vast array of organisations – intergovernmental, nongovernmental, general, specialised – have created and deployed FFMs. Their power to do so is either expressed or implied, and such fact-finding missions are either *ad hoc* creations or permanent features of the organisation.

15.2.2 *Fact-Finding Structure and Methodology*

A FFM's structure and methodology includes, among others, matters concerning membership, mandates, resources, and working methods; the timescale and territorial scope of the investigations; the type of evidence that will be used and how it will be gathered, handled, and assessed; the applicable standard of proof; and reporting and communication mechanisms. It may also include information about the applicable international law framework.[57]

These matters are key for the proper functioning of the FFM, for the credibility, reliability, objectivity, and legitimacy of its process and findings, and eventually for the success of the FFM.[58] How they are dealt with depends on the FFM's mandate, goals, and institutional basis; the wishes of the parties; and international law as the overarching regulatory tool – but what is important to stress is that fact-finding missions should have clear and transparent provisions to that effect.

[55] Wolfgang Kaleck and Carolijn Terwindt, 'Non-governmental organisation fact-work: Not only a technical problem', in Morten Bergsmo (ed.), *Quality Control in Fact Finding* (Florence: Torkel Opsahl, 2013), p. 409.

[56] Marina Aksenova, Morten Bergsmo, and Carsten Stahn, 'Non-criminal justice fact work in the age of accountability', in Morten Bergsmo and Carsten Stahn (eds.), *Quality Control in Fact-Finding*, 2nd ed. (Brussels: Torkel Opsahl, 2020), p. 15.

[57] See OHCHR, *Commissions of Inquiry and Fact-Finding Missions on International Human Rights and Humanitarian Law: Guidance and Practice* (Geneva: OHCHR, 2015), p. 65.

[58] Alison Bisset, 'Procedural fairness and commissions of inquiry', in Christian Henderson (ed.), *Commissions of Inquiry: Problems and Prospects* (London: Bloomsbury, 2017), pp. 309–35; Marco Odello, 'The interplay between international human rights law and international humanitarian law in the practice of commissions of inquiry', in Christian Henderson (ed.), *Commissions of Inquiry: Problems and Prospects* (London: Bloomsbury, 2017), pp. 199–230.

15.3 CURRENT CHALLENGES TO FACT-FINDING AS DISPUTE SETTLEMENT MECHANISM

15.3.1 *State Consent*

The consent of the States involved in the dispute is important for the deployment of FFMs, their legitimacy, and the effective performance of their tasks. However, international organisations have often departed from this principle by relying on their competence to establish such an FFM as provided in their constitutive treaties to which States consented.[59]

Such an approach is formally correct but causes two main difficulties. The first concerns the legal basis upon which the FFM can perform its tasks within the disputing States. As we saw, international organisations may recommend an FFM in which case the consent of the States involved in the dispute is critical for its deployment. However, even if an international organisation has been granted the power to establish an FFM, its deployment on the territory of a particular State, or its investigations without State consent, may amount to a violation of that State's sovereignty or an unlawful intervention.[60] Article 2(7) of the UN Charter, for example, prohibits UN intervention in the domestic jurisdiction of its member States, except for Chapter VII enforcement action. Fact-finding is not, however, enforcement action, even if it is established under Chapter VII. Even if one could say that States have granted a priori consent by becoming members of an international organisation, and even if the organisation can instruct States to accept the deployment of an FFM, if States oppose its actual deployment, the only option is to enforce the deployment of the FFM, something that may require military support.

This leads to the second difficulty which relates to the effectiveness of fact-finding. If States give their consent, the FFM will be able to access and gather information,[61] which will make its work and findings more credible and reliable. In contrast, if States are forced to admit an FFM, they may obstruct its work or fail to co-operate fully. If States refuse to admit an FFM or refuse access to certain sources, an FFM may be forced to gather evidence from secondary or external sources, which may impact the reliability and credibility

[59] Rob Grace, 'From design to implementation: The interpretation of fact-finding mandates' (2015) 20 JC&SL 27–60 at 31; Alexander Orakhelashvili, 'Commission of inquiry and traditional mechanisms of dispute settlement', in Christian Henderson (ed.), *Commissions of Inquiry: Problems and Prospects* (London: Bloomsbury, 2017), p. 130.

[60] *Case Concerning Military and Paramilitary Activities in and against Nicaragua (Nicaragua* v. *United States of America)* (Merits, Judgment) [1986] ICJ Rep. 14 at para. 108.

[61] OHCHR, *Commissions of Inquiry*, pp. 64–65.

of its work and findings. If its credibility and reliability are questioned, fact-finding will not only fail in its purpose, but it can aggravate an existing dispute or even add another layer to an existing dispute involving the fact-finding mission itself.

15.3.2 *Fact-Finding Structure and Methodology*

As said before, having a clear and transparent structure and methodology is important, but existing practice indicates that FFMs are often deficient in this regard. For example, mandates or working methods are not always stated in clear or explicit terms.[62] Membership is often political or, at least, politicised,[63] and, more critically, the expertise or the capacity of members to handle complex facts is often questioned.

Furthermore, FFMs do not always state which standard of proof they apply when assessing evidence, and different commissions apply different standards. They include, inter alia, standards of reasonable suspicion, reasonable grounds, sufficient credible and reliable information, and sufficiently substantiated and overwhelming evidence.[64] Even if variation is to be expected given that each FFM is an independent institution having its own mandate, stating what is the applicable standard and applying it consistently is critical for the reliability and credibility of the fact-finding process and determinations, particularly if they are used for accountability purposes. Otherwise determinations may be contested or used arbitrarily by one of the parties to reaffirm its own version of facts.

62 The Goldstone Report.

63 Richard Goldstone, 'Quality control in international fact-finding outside criminal justice for core international crimes', in Morten Bergsmo (ed.), *Quality Control in Fact Finding* (Florence: Torkel Opsahl, 2013), p. 46.

64 Selectively see International Commission of Inquiry on Darfur, 'Report', pp. 11–12; the Goldstone Report, p. 24; UN Human Rights Council, 'Report of the International Commission of Inquiry on Libya' (8 March 2012) UN Doc. A/HRC/19/68, para. 6; OPCW, 'First report by the OPCW Investigation and Identification Team pursuant to paragraph 10 of Decision C-SS-4/Dec.3 "Addressing the threat from chemical weapons use" Ltamenah (Syrian Arab Republic) 24, 25, and 30 March 2017, S/1867/2020', 8 April 2020, www.opcw.org/iit/first-report-iit (accessed 13 July 2022), para. 2.18: 'The IIT will only reach conclusions on the identification of perpetrators on the basis of a sufficient and reliable body of information which, consistent with other information, would allow an ordinarily prudent person to reasonably believe that an individual or entity was involved in the use of chemical weapons (i.e., "reasonable grounds")'. See also Stephen Wilkinson, 'Standards of proof in international humanitarian and human rights fact-finding and inquiry missions', *Geneva Academy of International Humanitarian Law and Human Rights*, 2014, www.geneva-academy.ch/joomlatools-files/docman-files/Standards%20of%20Proof%20in%20Fact-Finding.pdf (accessed 13 July 2022).

In addition, there is often no clear guidance as to how mandates are to be interpreted because there has been, as we said, a mandate creep and because facts cannot easily be disentangled from law. One can say that because the instrument establishing an FFM is an international law instrument, international law provides the requisite interpretative context. However, due to the diverse composition, mandates, and institutional allegiances of FFMs, but also due to existing interpretative variations in international law, the interpretation or application of international law often differs among FFMs or between them and other international law institutions.[65] To give an example, which facts should be collected and which facts should be considered relevant in establishing a cyber armed attack depends on how an armed attack is legally defined, in general, and by the FFM, in particular, but views differ.[66] This state of affairs is particularly worrying when FFMs perform adjudicatory functions or when individual or State responsibility is explicitly or implicitly invoked based on facts. As a result, disputes may arise about the FFM's international law interpretations, which can extend to disputes over the determination of the underlying facts. What is more worrying, though, is the systemic effects of the international law interpretations conducted by FFMs, because they can increase the unpredictability of international law rules.

15.4 CYBER ATTRIBUTION AND FACT-FINDING

Following a short presentation of fact-finding, this section discusses the contours of fact-finding in the context of cyber attribution. More specifically, it considers what types of facts are pertinent for cyber attribution purposes and the methodology a cyber attribution FFM should apply to ascertain the facts. It then considers how such an FFM can be established, and, in this respect, it also assesses the proposed cyber attribution mechanisms.

15.4.1 *Cyber Facts and Cyber Fact-Finding Methodology*

According to the *Dictionary of Law*, a fact is 'an event or state of affairs known to have happened or existed'.[67] It was also said about 'facts' that 'the fundamental concept is that of a thing as existing, or being true. It is not limited to what is tangible, or visible, or in any way the object of sense; things invisible,

65 Henderson, 'Commissions of inquiry', p. 306.

66 Michael N. Schmitt (ed.), *Tallinn Manual 2.0 on the International Law Applicable to Cyber Operations*, 2nd ed. (Cambridge: Cambridge University Press, 2017), Rules 68–75.

67 Jonathan Law (ed.), *A Dictionary of Law*, 10th ed. (Oxford: Oxford University Press, 2022).

mere thoughts, intentions, fancies of the mind, propositions, when conceived of as existing or being true, are conceived of as facts. The question of whether a thing be a fact or not, is the question of whether it is, whether it exists, whether it be true.'[68] Facts are ascertained by evidence, defined as 'that which tends to prove the existence or nonexistence of some fact'.[69] Consequently, facts can be established on the basis of direct evidence, but they can also be derived from the evaluation or interpretation of facts through inferences or presumptions.[70]

In relation to cyber attribution, the notion of facts differs in certain respects from the types of facts that FFMs usually ascertain. FFMs usually ascertain physical facts by relying on physical, observable evidence, or testimonies[71] which they retrieve from on-site visits, investigations, and interviews with people.

Although facts ascertained through such evidence and methods are also relevant to cyber attribution in order, for example, to determine the physical location of cyberattacks or their effects, the bulk of cyber facts are technical. They are also ascertained on the basis of technical evidence following technical (forensic) investigations.

Technical evidence consists of artefacts drawn from the tools, techniques, and procedures used for the cyberattack.[72] It includes, among others, command-and-control servers, IP addresses, websites, activity logs, time stamps, malware and their design, names, and pseudonyms, software programmes, e-mails, instructions, language strings, documents, and so on.[73] Technical evidence can be collected through technical investigations from different points of the cyberattack cycle: preparation, reconnaissance, exploitation, execution, and post-execution phase.[74]

It thus becomes evident that the bulk of investigations to find such evidence will be carried out within the victim State's networks and cyber infrastructure, or within networks or cyber infrastructure belonging to a threat actor or third States. Evidence can also be gathered from other sources such as service

68 James Thayer, '"Law and fact" in jury trials' (1890) 4 Harv L Rev 147–75 at 151–52.

69 Law, *Dictionary of Law*.

70 Richard M. Mosk, 'The role of facts in international dispute settlement' (2003) 304 Collected Courses Hague Acad Int'l L 9–179 at 33.

71 UN Human Rights Council, 'Report of the International Commission of Inquiry on Libya', para. 6: 'where possible on its own observations and first-hand accounts'.

72 Florian Skopik and Timea Pahi, 'Under false flag: Using technical artifacts for cyber attack attribution' (2020) 3 Cybersecurity 1–20 at 1, https://doi.org/10.1186/s42400-020-00048-4.

73 John S. Davis et al., *Stateless Attribution: Toward International Accountability in Cyberspace* (Santa Monica, CA: RAND Corporation, 2017), p. 11.

74 Tsagourias and Farrell, 'Cyber attribution', p. 947.

providers. This is due to the interconnectedness of networks and the private ownership of cyber infrastructure. Other evidence, including non-technical evidence, can be collected from within the jurisdiction of the victim State but also that of third States.

Given that threat actors often hide or fake their identity or use deceptive tools to cover up their traces, the tactics, techniques, and tools[75] used for a cyberattack are often compared in order to identify common traits and attribute the attack to a particular actor.[76]

Considering the above, a cyber attribution FFM should first perform technical attribution, but, unless the mandate of the FFM is strictly limited to establishing the disputed technical facts, technical attribution is not sufficient in itself to attribute a cyberattack to a State because there is a difference between identifying facts and assigning them to a computer, and assigning them to a State. What is needed in this case is to link the technical facts to an individual, group, or entity and then link the individual, group, or entity to a particular State.[77] For this to happen, more and different types of facts need to be gathered and assessed. For example, documents, legislation, or administrative acts can be used as evidence in this regard.[78] Yet, the links between threat actors (individuals or groups) and States are not always formal or apparent. For this reason, all source intelligence should be used to identify

[75] See Catalln Clmpanu, 'US Cyber Command starts uploading foreign APT malware to VirusTotal', *ZDNet*, 8 November 2018, www.zdnet.com/article/us-cyber-command-starts-uploading-foreign-apt-malware-to-virustotal (accessed 13 July 2022); Anon., 'NSA and NCSC release joint advisory on Turla Group Activity', *CISA*, 21 October 2019, https://us-cert.cisa.gov/ncas/current-activity/2019/10/21/nsa-and-ncsc-release-joint-advisory-turla-group-activity (accessed 13 July 2022).

[76] NCSC and NSA, 'Advisory: Turla group exploits Iranian APT to expand coverage of victims', *NCSC*, 21 October 2019, www.ncsc.gov.uk/news/turla-group-exploits-iran-apt-to-expand-coverage-of-victims (accessed 13 July 2022). See also *United States of America* v. *Park Jin Hyok*, United States District Court for the Central District of California, Case No. MJ 18-1479, Criminal Complaint (8 June 2018) at para. 230, where the similarities of WannaCry versions 0, 1, and 2 supported attribution to Mr Park.

[77] For example, the NSA developed the Territorial Dispute programme, or TeDi, to track nation State attackers. See Kim Zetter, 'Leaked files show how the NSA tracks other countries', *The Intercept*, 7 March 2018, https://theintercept.com/2018/03/06/leaked-files-show-how-nsa-tracks-other-countries-hackers (accessed 13 July 2022); *Yeager* v. *Islamic Republic of Iran*, 17 Iran-U.S. Cl. Trib. Rep. 92 (1987) at 101–2: 'To attribute an act to the State, it is necessary to identify with reasonable certainty the actors and their association with the State.'

[78] According to the Permanent Court of International Justice, 'municipal laws are merely facts which express the will and constitute the activities of States, in the same manner as do legal decisions or administrative measures'. *Case Concerning Certain German Interests in Polish Upper Silesia (Germany* v. *Polish Republic)* (The Merits) [1926] PCIJ Rep. Series A No. 7 at p. 19.

such links. This includes information collected from open sources such as the internet or social media, human sources, and signals intelligence, such as intercepted messages.

All this indicates that fact-finding for cyber attribution purposes is a more holistic process. It has a strong technical component in that the facts and methods according to which facts are located, retrieved, ascertained, and assessed are primarily technical, but other non-technical facts should also be factored in.

Inevitably, this poses many challenges to fact-finding. A primary challenge is jurisdictional and refers to the ability and competence of the FFM to access evidence. Although, arguably, using cyber means and methods facilitates investigations – because it extends their reach, makes access to cyber evidence easier by not requiring physical presence, and surpasses impediments caused by geography, war, or unrest – legal jurisdictional impediments still exist. Investigations, even remote ones, require direct access to networks, and, therefore, the consent of the State or party that owns the network is needed, but access may be denied or restricted. Moreover, investigations may need to take place outside the jurisdiction of the disputing States because of the interconnected nature of cyber infrastructure and the ability of threat actors to operate from within different jurisdictions. If consent is denied, withdrawn, or restricted, fact-finding (on-site or remotely conducted) will be hindered. If the FFM carries out investigations without State consent, it may face accusations of having violated international law. If, in the absence of a direct access, it relies on external and secondary sources, the credibility, reliability, and legitimacy of its findings may be contested.

Besides jurisdictional limitations, another challenge concerns the diagnostic capacity of the FFM. For example, the FFM will need to have the appropriate technical resources, know-how, and skills in order to be able to gather and assess technical evidence. If such resources are not available or are limited, the FFM will not be able to perform these tasks efficiently or with the required degree of confidence. The immediate question is whether, in order to overcome this challenge, fact-finding can be delegated to expert third parties such as private security companies. If technical fact-finding is delegated to third parties, questions about the neutrality and impartiality of fact-finding may be raised, alongside questions about the credibility and reliability of the findings because of the inability of the FFM to scrutinise the determinations of third parties due to lack of resources, knowledge, and expertise.

This leads to another challenge, which concerns the applicable methodology. FFMs have their own rules, standards, and methods of identifying, analysing, establishing, ascertaining, probing, and using facts. The

2015 Group of Governmental Experts report stated that attribution claims should be substantiated,[79] but it did not lay down any standard. As we also said, FFMs do not apply any uniform standard, which raises questions about the applicable standard of proof. Even more critically, as indicated above, there are many difficulties in collecting and tracing cyber evidence which are compounded by the fact that an FFM cannot demand the production of evidence or use judicial or police mechanisms to obtain evidence unless this is provided in their constitutive document. What value should be placed then on secondary evidence to corroborate facts if primary evidence is hard to obtain?

In addition, the timescale within which the FFM can deliver its report is also important. Cyber fact-finding may take longer because of its complexity, the technical resources required due to the pace of developments in this area, and the jurisdictional hurdles that must be overcome. A thorough but longer investigation may increase the reliability and credibility of fact-finding, but may undermine its functions in cases where a swift action is needed. A faster fact-finding process may be more useful but less reliable. If a fact-finding mission's report is issued after action has been taken, it may reignite and escalate the dispute.

15.4.2 *Creating a Cyber Attribution FFM*

As explained in Section 15.2, there are different ways according to which a cyber attribution FFM can be established. In the first place, the States involved in a cyber attribution dispute can create an FFM. In doing so, States can configure its composition, mandate, and methodology. State consent can, in principle, enhance the legitimacy and effectiveness of FFMs because it will engender cooperation.[80] Yet, States may put forward national security or other justifications to limit the scope of their cooperation because, as we said, the investigation is internal to a State's cyber infrastructure. For instance, States may deny or limit access to the components of their cyber infrastructure or certain data. They may also demand that the investigation and the mission's findings remain confidential[81] in order not to reveal

79 UNGA, 'Report of the Group of Governmental Experts on Developments in the Field of Information and Telecommunications in the Context of International Security' (22 July 2015) UN Doc. A/70/174, p. 13.

80 Art 12, Hague I.

81 OPCW Conference of the State Parties, 'OPCW Policy on Confidentiality, in C-I/DEC.13/Rev.2', 30 November 2017, www.opcw.org/sites/default/files/documents/2019/05/cidec13r2%28e%29.pdf (accessed 14 July 2022). However, this does not guarantee that there will be no

sensitive information or vulnerabilities. Since the attribution may also require other information, States may withhold such information or manipulate the available information.[82] Even if States would co-operate, the FFM may need to extend its investigation into other States' networks, but these States may deny or limit such access. As a result, its work may be obstructed, and the credibility and reliability of its findings may be contested.

Another way of establishing an FFM is through the UNSC based on its Chapter VI and VII powers. As we said in Section 15.2, a Chapter VI FFM requires State consent as does an FFM established under Article 40 of the UN Charter pursuant to a UNSC recommendation. For an FFM binding under Chapter VII, the UNSC should qualify the cyber attribution dispute as a threat to international peace. This requires the affirmative vote of the permanent members, which may not be forthcoming in view of the fact that they are involved in acute cyber antagonism. That withstanding, a question that may also be asked is whether a cyber attribution dispute can reach such a level of seriousness and intensity and acquire an international dimension as to fall within the Article 39 qualifiers. Although the UNSC has discretionary powers in this respect, existing disputes over cyber attribution indicate that they hardly reach such a level, although this may change in the future. The UNSC can instead qualify as a threat to peace, the underlying dispute of which the cyber attribution dispute is just an aspect. For example, a dispute over territory or a military dispute may also have a cyber attribution dimension. In such instances, cyber attribution fact-finding may not be necessary because what is mainly needed is to settle the main dispute or to investigate the facts underlying the main dispute. Considering the above, it can be said with reason that a UNSC-created cyber attribution FFM is equally a quite remote possibility. Regarding the UNGA, as we said, it can recommend the establishment of a cyber attribution FFM, but its actual establishment and deployment

breach of confidentiality. See OPCW Technical Secretariat, 'Report of the investigation into possible breaches of confidentiality, S/1839/2020', 6 February 2020, www.opcw.org/sites/default/files/documents/2020/02/s-1839-2020%28e%29.pdf (accessed 14 July 2022).

82 'The Intelligence Community rarely can publicly reveal the full extent of its knowledge or the precise bases for its assessments, as the release of such information would reveal sensitive sources or methods and imperil the ability to collect critical foreign intelligence in the future. Thus, while the conclusions in the report are all reflected in the classified assessment, the declassified report does not and cannot include the full supporting information, including specific intelligence and sources and methods.' Office of the Director of National Intelligence, 'Background to "Assessing Russian activities and intentions in recent US elections": The analytic process and cyber incident attribution', 2017, www.dni.gov/files/documents/ICA_2017_01.pdf (accessed 14 July 2022), p. 1.

is subject to State consent, which poses the same challenges discussed in the preceding paragraph.

In order to circumvent these problems and in view of the 'newness' of cyberspace, several proposals were put forward envisaging the creation of an attribution agency whose mandate will be to establish facts and perform attribution. We are not going to consider the merits of each proposal, but rather categorise these proposals into those envisaging an intergovernmental cyber attribution agency and those envisaging a private cyber attribution agency and assess them accordingly.

15.4.2.1 Intergovernmental Cyber Attribution Agency

The creation of an intergovernmental cyber attribution agency was proposed by the Atlantic Council. More specifically, it proposed the establishment of a Multilateral Cyber Adjudication and Attribution Council (MCAAC) with mixed (public and private) membership.[83]

The underlying idea is that an intergovernmental cyber attribution agency grounded on State consent and operating on the basis of agreed standards and processes will overcome States' reservations and legitimise its standing, operation, and findings. Whether an international intergovernmental attribution agency is viable at this moment in time is doubtful.

First, States treat cyber attribution as a sovereign prerogative and have repeatedly said that they have no obligation to disclose evidence.[84]

[83] Atlantic Council, 'Confidence-building measures in cyberspace: A multistakeholder approach for stability and security', 5 November 2014, www.atlanticcouncil.org/in-depth-research-reports/report/confidence-building-measures-in-cyberspace-a-multistakeholder-approach-for-stability-and-security (accessed 14 July 2022). Commentators have also proposed the creation of an independent, international cyber court or arbitrage to deal with government-level cyber conflicts without the participation of the private sector. See Elena Chernenko, Oleg Demidov, and Fyodor Lukyanov, 'Increasing international cooperation in cybersecurity and adapting cyber norms', *Council on Foreign Relations*, 23 February 2018, www.cfr.org/report/increasing-international-cooperation-cybersecurity-and-adapting-cyber-norms (accessed 14 July 2022).

[84] Brian Egan, 'Remarks on international law and stability in cyberspace (lecture at Berkeley Law School, Berkeley, CA)', 10 November 2016, www.justsecurity.org/wp-content/uploads/2016/11/Brian-J.-Egan-International-Law-and-Stability-in-Cyberspace-Berkeley-Nov-2016.pdf (accessed 14 July 2022), p. 19; UK Attorney General's Office and Jeremy Wright, 'Cyber and international law in the 21st century', *UK Government*, 23 May 2018, www.gov.uk/government/speeches/cyber-and-international-law-in-the-21st-century (accessed 14 July 2022); New Zealand, 'The application of international law to State activity in cyberspace', *Department of the Prime Minister and Cabinet*, 1 December 2020, https://dpmc.govt.nz/sites/default/files/2020-12/The%20Application%20of%20International%20Law%20to%20State%20Activity%20in%20Cyberspace.pdf (accessed 14 July 2022), para. 20: 'While any legal attribution should be underpinned by a sound evidential basis, there is no general obligation

Cyberspace is also a strategic domain where States pursue goals such as prevention or deterrence, or more specific political, military, or economic interests. In such an environment, the role of a permanent international FFM is quite peripheral in States' thinking because it may restrict their freedom to attribute when they want and for the reasons they want.[85] For example, in a situation of inter-State conflict or tensions, a State may decide not to attribute, even if it possesses the relevant facts, in order not to aggravate the situation, avoid domestic pressure to take action, or not to attract retaliation. In contrast, a State may decide to attribute, even if it does not hold all the facts, if important interests are endangered and the State has decided to act. As Nicolas Politis has observed, fact-finding was envisaged for disputes where the essential interests of a State were not at stake.[86]

Second, States have asymmetric cyber capabilities, with certain States having very sophisticated and robust attribution technologies and mechanisms. Consequently, the benefits of an agency performing attribution on their behalf are negligible, and there are no benefits in sharing their attribution technology with such an agency which will then antagonise them.

Third, the findings of such an agency, but also any legal conclusions that can be inferred, may be contested due to the absence of a firm legal framework regarding the scope and content of States' international law obligations in cyberspace, or due to the controversies surrounding the attribution criteria in the law of State responsibility. For example, what constitutes a cyber armed attack, whether sovereignty is a rule that applies to cyberspace, and whether 'overall control' is an attribution criterion are subject to debate. As a result, such controversies will lead to further controversies about the type and calibre of evidence and the applicable standard of proof.

on the attributing State to disclose that basis. However, a State may choose as a matter of policy to disclose specific information that it considered in making its attribution decision, and may be required to defend any such decision as part of international legal proceedings'; Switzerland, 'Switzerland's position paper on the application of international law in cyberspace, Annex UN GGE 2019/2021', www.eda.admin.ch/content/dam/eda/en/documents/aussenpolitik/voelkerrecht/20210527-Schweiz-Annex-UN-GGE-Cybersecurity-2019-2021_EN.pdf (accessed 14 July 2022), p. 6: 'The decision to attribute conduct is at the discretion of the injured State and there is no obligation under international law to disclose the information leading to such a decision.'

85 The UK, for example, will 'attribute specific cyber identities publicly', when it is judged 'in the national interest to do so'. HM Government, 'National Cyber Security Strategy 2016–2021', *UK Government*, 2016, https://assets.publishing.service.gov.uk/government/uploads/system/uploads/attachment_data/file/567242/national_cyber_security_strategy_2016.pdf (accessed 14 July 2022), p. 50 at s. 6.3.3.

86 Nicolas Politis, 'Les commissions internationales d'enquête' (1912) 19 RGDIP 149–88 at 153.

Fourth, such an agency is compared to existing international mechanisms performing inspection and verification functions, such as those under the IAEA or OPCW. However, there is a critical difference between them and the proposed agency. Whereas the IAEA and OPCW have established a comprehensive regulatory regime where inspections are integral to securing compliance with States' obligations,[87] no such regime exists for cyberspace to which fact-finding can be attached.

All these issues make the creation of an intergovernmental cyber attribution agency quite unlikely, at least in the foreseeable future. However, even if such an attribution agency is eventually created, it will still confront several challenges.

Its membership will most likely be limited due to States' diverse cyber capabilities and the rivalry that currently characterises their relations. Technologically developed States or cyber powers, in general, may chose to remain outside such an agency because of the limited benefits they will receive. This immediately raises questions about the agency's resources and its mandate. If the agency's resources are inadequate, will its mandate be limited and, in this case, what will be its added value? If important cyber powers are not members, will its findings be reliable and credible? Also, what will be its leverage to conduct investigations into third States, or States that have isolated their cyberspace? If technologically developed States do participate, would that create an imbalance and invite accusations of bias regarding its findings? If a State is frequently accused of cyberattacks, is there any benefit in participating in such an agency?

An intergovernmental cyber attribution agency will also face certain methodological challenges, such as regarding the criteria according to which attribution incidents will be investigated and the type of attribution it will perform, for example, technical and/or legal. These issues need to be determined in advance, but it is doubtful whether that will be possible due to the permanent and general competence of such an agency, the dynamic nature of cyber incidents, the difficulty in disentangling law from facts, and the inherent power of institutions to interpret and determine their mandate in view of new circumstances.

Another critical question is who will conduct the fact-finding. If fact-finding is to be performed by State officials, the process may be politicised. If it is to be performed by the agency's staff, recruited because of their qualifications and professional experience, the agency will need to build its own fact-finding

87 OPCW, 'Decision addressing the threat from chemical weapons use', paras 19–20.

capabilities and expertise, but the immediate question is who is going to provide the resources, know-how, and training. As we said, States may be reluctant to share their technical attribution tools and knowledge, and, in general, they may not be ready to support and fund the development of attribution expertise by such an agency which can then compete with them. If investigations or capacity-building is delegated to third parties, such as the private sector, instead, it may affect the legitimacy, impartiality, and reliability of an agency, as mentioned previously.

Other methodological challenges include the applicable standard of proof; the legal framework governing the agency's investigations such as human rights law or intellectual property law; the availability of review mechanisms; and the manner in which and to whom findings will be communicated, for example, whether they will be made public or remain confidential.

How an agency will make decisions presents another challenge. Consensus-based decisions may be more acceptable,[88] but trying to build consensus may impact the ability of the agency to make quick decisions, or may affect the quality and transparency of its decisions. If decisions are majority-based, division and accusations may follow.

Ensuring the accountability of such an agency is another challenge. Its findings may be relied upon by States to act, which raises the question of whether the agency can be held responsible for incorrect determinations, or for assisting in the commission of unlawful acts. If a State, for instance, relies on the agency's findings to take countermeasures against another State which contends that the countermeasures were unlawful because the attribution was mistaken, can the agency be held responsible for incorrect findings, or for aiding in the commission of wrongful acts? If the matter is brought before a court or an arbitration tribunal, what value should be placed on the findings of such an agency? For example, should that court or tribunal treat them as mitigating circumstances when considering damages?

There is also the fundamental question of the status of the agency. If it is consultative, its contribution to dispute settlement may be negligible because States may employ other mechanisms or use their own judgment to settle their cyber attribution disputes. However, even in this case, there is still a danger of aggravating an existing dispute because its findings, even if non-binding, may be used by States to validate or disprove attribution claims, thus providing no closure to the dispute. If its status is adjudicatory and its findings are binding

[88] See, e.g., Russia's criticism to OPCW. OPCW, 'Russian Federation statement'.

on States, this would require transparent working methods but also accountability, which pose their own challenges, as mentioned above.

15.4.2.2 A Private Cyber Attribution Agency

A proposal for the creation of a private cyber attribution agency was put forward by RAND. More specifically, it proposed the creation of a Global Cyber Attribution Consortium whose role would be to attribute major cyberattacks with a high degree of confidence and release the evidence and its findings to the public.[89]

According to the proposal, the agency's membership will be multistakeholder, consisting of technical, legal, and policy experts from academia, research organisations, and cybersecurity and information technology companies, but State representatives will be excluded. The agency will also follow a standardised methodology regarding the collection of evidence, assessment, standard of proof, review, notification, and publication of findings.

It is claimed that the private character of such an agency will remove suspicions of politicisation, and its findings will contribute to dispute settlement by making attribution neutral, credible, and reliable. According to RAND, the consortium can only derive its legitimacy over time from 'the reputation and credibility gained from the technical expertise of its diverse global membership and its commitment to objectivity and transparency in its attribution findings'.[90]

Although the proposal tries to circumvent State reluctance or suspicion towards an intergovernmental attribution agency, it is reasonable to ask whether it is appropriate and viable to exclude States to the extent that attribution determinations, even if they are exclusively factual, may affect State interests and decisions or have legal consequences, for example, the imposition of sanctions.[91] Questions may also be asked about the competence and ability of such an agency to conduct investigations when States involved

89 Davis et al., *Stateless Attribution*. Microsoft has also put forward various proposals, but their nature is not clear. It first proposed a non-governmental organisation made up of experts. See Microsoft, 'An attribution organization to strengthen trust online', https://query.prod.cms.rt.microsoft.com/cms/api/am/binary/RW67QI (accessed 14 July 2022). Later it proposed an international organisation with public–private membership to investigate technically nation State attacks resembling the IAEA. Scott Charney et al., 'From articulation to implementation: Enabling progress on cybersecurity norms', *Microsoft*, June 2016, https://query.prod.cms.rt.microsoft.com/cms/api/am/binary/REVmc8 (accessed 14 July 2022).

90 Davis et al., *Stateless Attribution*, p. 30.

91 Council of the European Union, 'Council Decision (CFSP) 2020/1127 of 30 July 2020 amending Decision (CFSP) 2019/797 concerning restrictive measures against cyber-attacks threatening the Union or its Member States' 2020 OJ (L246) 12.

in a dispute refuse to co-operate. The private character of such an agency does not ensure that States will co-operate or disclose information. Furthermore, depending on how information is gathered, handled, assessed, and communicated by such an agency, the credibility and reliability of its findings can be challenged for lack of evidence or faulty methodology.

There are several other challenges facing a private attribution agency. First, whereas the participation of private security companies can boost the technical capabilities of the agency, how they will be selected is critical for the credibility of the agency. Secondly, these companies will continue to operate independently and often compete with the agency, which will raise questions about their commitment to the work of the agency. Third, in a competitive cybersecurity market, other private cybersecurity companies may challenge the agency's findings, which can create confusion and lower the level of confidence in the agency. Fourth, the private sector is not equally developed in all States, and States have different views about its role in cyber governance, which may create suspicion or even opposition to the involvement of the private sector.

Another challenge concerns the accountability of this agency for the same reasons mentioned above, but with an additional twist. If the agency does not operate under international law, it will not be subject to international law's accountability mechanisms. This immediately raises the question of whether national accountability mechanisms will be used against the agency or its individual members. If that is to happen, it will have a chilling effect on the agency and create confusion and uncertainty.

Finally, the private character of such an agency may pose a systemic challenge to international law because it will antagonise or even undermine States which, as we said, want to preserve their power to perform attribution and settle their disputes as they see fit. Such an agency may also undermine States' control over the international law process of rule creation, application, and interpretation if it is involved, explicitly or implicitly, in the interpretation or application of international law or in laying down new standards. In addition, another systemic challenge should be mentioned. The proliferation of attribution mechanisms may cause more confusion and conflict and aggravate disputes further instead of settling them.

All this means that such an agency's claim to neutrality, reliability, and legality may not be fully supported.

15.5 MOVING FORWARD: AN FFM FOR CYBER ATTRIBUTION?

In the preceding sections, we identified several institutional, structural, and methodological challenges that affect cyber attribution fact-finding. That said, cyber attribution disputes exist and, if not settled, may aggravate or exacerbate the underlying political and legal disputes. Thus, the question of how to establish the facts underlying a cyber attribution claim cannot go away. For this reason, in this section we will present the key features and attributes of a cyber attribution FFM which, in our opinion, could address many of the aforementioned challenges.

In the first place, such an FFM should be created by States voluntarily and on an *ad hoc* basis in relation to a particular cyber attribution dispute.[92] States' involvement in its creation and design will demonstrate their determination to settle the attribution dispute. It will also elicit their cooperation and compliance since the FFM will be entangled with the particular interests and expectations of the disputing States. Finally, it will contribute to the credibility, legitimacy, and effectiveness of the FFM. This does not contradict what we said previously, namely that States view cyber attribution as their sovereign prerogative and claim that they have no obligation to disclose evidence, or that they use attribution for strategic purposes. These remain true, but they are more pertinent in relation to fact-finding performed by permanent international institutions over which disputing States have little control, or in relation to demands to publicly disclose information. However, if States determine that settling a cyber attribution dispute is more important than letting the dispute linger or aggravate, and that settling it through an FFM is appropriate, effective, and serves their interests, they may go ahead to create such an FFM and co-operate with it. As a matter of fact, this is not against their sovereignty but confirmation of their sovereignty.

From a broader perspective, this approach to FFMs accords with the fact that States are the primary creators and designers of dispute settlement mechanisms, and that fact-finding was originally envisaged as a bilateral mechanism of dispute settlement and not as an institutional one.

Since being created by States, the FFM should be treaty-based. States will thus be able to specify in its constitutive instrument its composition, mandate, and methodology.

The composition of the FFM should be determined by the States concerned, depending on the nature and mandate of the FFM. Members can be State officials, staff borrowed from international organisations, individuals drawn from the private sector, or NGOs. Their expertise can also cover different fields, for example, technology and/or law. We are thus not prescriptive as existing proposals are, and we do not place value on a certain type of membership, but believe that membership should reflect the interests and needs of the States which establish the FFM.

[92] UNGA, 'Declaration on fact-finding', paras 6 and 21.

Insofar as its mandate is concerned, it should again be determined by States. In the first place, the constitutive instrument should specify the subject matter of the investigation. It should specify, for example, which incident(s) will be investigated and under what circumstances other related incidents will be investigated. It should also specify what type of facts it will gather and assess, and whether the FFM will perform only technical and/or legal attribution. This is important because it has implications for the methodology the FFM will follow. In addition to the above, the FFM's constitutive instrument should specify the location of the investigations, for example, which and whose networks it will investigate, and under what circumstances it will extend its investigations to connected networks. It should also specify the timeframe of investigations; the processes and conditions of gathering, storing, handling, or sharing evidence; the process according to which evidence will be assessed; and the means of establishing their authenticity and reliability.

Furthermore, the constitutive instrument should specify the applicable standard of proof depending on the type of attribution it will perform, and whether the FFM will have an adjudicatory or consultative function. It should also state how and by whom its findings will be reviewed.

There are several other issues that the FFM's constitutive instrument should specify. It should specify the terms and words used in the mandate, such as attribution, networks, and non-State actors. It should specify the guiding principles of the FFM, for example, its adherence to the principles of transparency, fairness, neutrality, and accountability. It should specify the law that will apply to the FFM and its investigations, for example, whether the investigations will be conducted according to international law.

Regarding the decision-making process, the constitutive instrument should state whether decisions will be consensual or majority-based. It should also explain the reporting and communication process, including whether the findings will remain private and confidential, or made public, and whether, in the latter case, evidence will be made public. This is important because it will have implications on the applicable methodology.

The constitutive instrument should make provisions for a continuous supply of financial,[93] technical, or any other resources required for the performance of the FFM's duties.

93 To give an example, Russia refused to fund the OPCW's IIT tasked with finding those responsible for the use of chemical weapons in the Syrian Arab Republic. See Ministry of Foreign Affairs of the Russian Federation, 'On the first report of the OPCW Investigation and Identification Team on chemical incidents in Al Lataminah (SAR)', 22 April 2020, www.mid.ru/en/foreign_policy/international_organizations/1430837 (accessed 20 July 2021).

Finally, the constitutive instrument should establish internal and/or external accountability mechanisms.

We believe that, if States create a cyber attribution FFM which addresses all these issues with the requisite care, the FFM will be able to operate smoothly and efficiently and establish the facts underpinning cyber attribution disputes in a credible and reliable manner. It can thus contribute to dispute resolution without becoming itself the subject of a dispute.

15.6 CONCLUSION

This chapter has considered the role of fact-finding as a mechanism for settling cyber attribution disputes. In this respect, it discussed its merits but also identified several challenges it is facing relating to its legal basis, institutional nature, structure, and methodology. The chapter then went on to present certain key features a cyber attribution FFM should exhibit, which will enable it, in the view of the authors, to perform its fact-finding tasks effectively. In our opinion, if fact-finding is calibrated appropriately, it can contribute to the peaceful settlement of cyber attribution disputes.

16

International Dispute Settlement

Digital Evidence and Online Dispute Resolution

ANTONIO SEGURA SERRANO

16.1 INTRODUCTION

Cyberspace and new technologies have an intriguing relationship with international law, in particular with international dispute settlement. On the one hand, it is a challenging relationship because applying international law to activities carried out in cyberspace faces many challenges, such as whether or how extant international law rules apply to cyberspace; the legal character of cyberspace; the extension of State jurisdiction to cyberspace; the attribution of cyberattacks to States, including those launched by non-State actors; and the development of norms through treaty rules or other mechanisms, to mention just a few. On the other hand, it is a relationship full of opportunities and potential because of the benefits cyberspace and new technologies bring to international law, such as those flowing from the availability of digital evidence, the convenience of online proceedings, the use of online dispute resolution (ODR) mechanisms, and the benefits derived from the use of artificial intelligence.

These issues will be discussed in this chapter with regard to inter-State dispute settlement. Section 16.2 will consider three main challenges posed by cyberspace to inter-State dispute settlement. The first concerns the need for a dispute settlement body to determine which international law rules or regimes are applicable to the dispute before it becomes the object of interpretation. The second concerns the complex jurisdictional questions that cyber disputes give rise to and which a dispute settlement body needs to solve to establish its jurisdiction. Finally, there is the problem of attribution that a dispute settlement mechanism will need to settle to be able to adjudicate on the dispute.

Regarding the opportunities presented by cyberspace and digitalisation in general to the settlement of inter-State disputes, there are two issues that will be considered in Section 16.3. First, there is the issue of digital evidence. New technologies facilitate the collection of evidence, giving rise to what has been termed the democratisation of evidence collection.[1] The second issue is online dispute settlement as an option for solving inter-State disputes. In this respect, I will first assess the feasibility of online proceedings before international courts and, secondly, assess the practice of ODR systems already in place for online transactions among individuals (both private and public systems) in order to identify any features that can be transposed to inter-State dispute settlement. I will conclude by saying that these systems, in particular the use of algorithms, offer some important lessons for State-to-State dispute settlement.

16.2 CHALLENGES POSED TO DISPUTE SETTLEMENT BY CYBERSPACE

In this section, I address certain challenges posed by cyberspace to international law, which are already the object of intense commentary, but which are particularly critical to the settlement of cyber disputes. As mentioned in the introduction, the first challenge relates to the applicability of international law to cyberspace, which is fundamental for dispute settlement. There is consensus on the application of international law in cyberspace as stated by the United Nations Group of Governmental Experts (UN GGE) in 2013, 2015, and 2021[2] and the 2021 report of the Open-Ended Working Group (OEWG), whose work will be continued by the new OEWG 2021–25.[3] However, States have been reluctant to agree on the specifics of its applicability. Indeed, the aforementioned reports are very general, embodying a global consensus on the applicability of extant international customary law, but are devoid of details as to how these rules apply to cyber operations. Conversely, the Tallinn Manual contains very specific rules allegedly representing

1 Molly K. Land, 'Democratizing human rights fact-finding', in Phillip Alston and Sarah Knuckey (eds.), *The Transformation of Human Rights Fact-Finding* (New York: Oxford University Press, 2016), pp. 399, 402.

2 UNGA, 'Report of the Group of Governmental Experts on Developments in the Field of Information and Telecommunications in the Context of International Security' (24 June 2013) UN Doc. A/68/98; 'Report of the Group of Governmental Experts on Developments in the Field of Information and Telecommunications in the Context of International Security' (22 July 2015) UN Doc. A/70/174; 'Report of the Group of Governmental Experts on Advancing Responsible State Behaviour in Cyberspace in the Context of International Security' (14 July 2021) UN Doc. A/76/135.

3 UNGA, 'Final Substantive Report, Open-Ended Working Group on Developments in the Field of Information and Telecommunications in the Context of International Security' (10 March 2021) UN Doc. A/AC.290/2021/CRP.2.

lex lata.[4] Although the Tallinn Manual is the result of the work of a group of experts and, therefore, may be considered only as a private endeavour, it is also evident that it is representative of the legal arguments and positions held mostly by Western governments, that is, those extant international law rules are sufficient to govern international relations in cyberspace. However, scholars have already tried to assess whether the Tallinn Manual is actually followed by States and have expressed their reservations.[5] It seems that States are not willing to delegate the function of norm production, especially in the field of cyberspace, to others, and they are still in the process of determining the content and scope of international law rules as they apply to cyberspace, which means that rule consolidation will take place only gradually and slowly.[6]

Jurisdiction is another thorny issue that may present significant difficulties to the settlement of a cyber dispute by a dispute settlement body. It is true that malicious cyber activities, such as cybercrime, attributable to non-State actors are to be dealt with by State authorities through the application of domestic law. Yet, international law's jurisdictional rules on the collection of evidence may be unsatisfactory in this regard. Indeed, facing the upsurge in cybercrime, State authorities are eager to obtain digital evidence remotely from within other jurisdictions for law enforcement purposes. Such operations are subject to the authorisation of the target State (as provided by mutual legal assistance treaties (MLATs)) and, consequently, unilateral searches are not allowed under current international law, even if the question of whether such operations may violate a State's sovereignty is not yet settled.[7] As a result, norm

4 Michael N. Schmitt (ed.), *Tallinn Manual 2.0 on the International Law Applicable to Cyber Operations* (Cambridge: Cambridge University Press, 2017), pp. 2–3; Michael N. Schmitt (ed.), *Tallinn Manual on the International Law Applicable to Cyber Warfare* (Cambridge: Cambridge University Press, 2013).

5 Dan Efrony and Yuval Shany, in 'A rule book on the shelf? Tallin Manual 2.0 on cyberoperations and subsequent State practice' (2018) 112 AJIL 583–657 at 653, are critical of the Tallinn Manual, as they believe that it is not being followed by States in their most recent practice, given the wait-and-see strategy that these States have adopted. However, this remark does not go as far as to conclude that the Tallinn Manual's rules are rejected outright by States or do not represent their views at all.

6 Nicholas Tsagourias, 'The slow process of normativizing cyberspace' (2019) 113 AJIL Unbound 71–75 at 74–75.

7 There is an emerging trend, led by the US and the UK, stating that sovereignty is not a rule but only a principle so that unilateral searches in cyberspace would not be wrongful. See, e.g., Kevin J. Heller, 'In defense of pure sovereignty in cyberspace' (2021) 97 Int Law Stud 1432–99; Przemyslaw Roguski, 'Violations of territorial sovereignty in cyberspace: An intrusion-based approach', in Denis Broeders and Bibi Van den Berg (eds.), *Governing Cyberspace: Behavior, Power, and Diplomacy* (Lanham, MD: Rowman & Littlefield, 2020), pp. 65–84.

development has been crucial in this field in order to speed up the process that MLATs involve, with the Budapest Convention on Cybercrime as the main case in point.[8] However, because of the limited effectiveness of international legal cooperation as provided for by the Budapest Convention,[9] States resort to unilateral mechanisms to deal with the phenomenon of transnational cybercrime. One of those unilateral mechanisms is cross-border hacking for counterterrorism purposes or other activities.[10] Cybercrime scholars believe such methods have been used,[11] but, so far, no State has formally accused other States of this type of practice. There is also another unilateral mechanism to access digital evidence for law enforcement purposes – through a direct collaboration of foreign internet service providers. The advantage of this option is that it makes the intervention of the authorities of the destination or territorial State unnecessary (and so too of MLATs). This possibility is provided by the 2018 US Cloud Act[12] through the adoption of executive agreements to that effect,[13] and it is also envisaged in the proposed E-Evidence Regulation and Directive, which includes a European Production Order.[14] A Second Additional Protocol to the Budapest Convention on enhanced cooperation and the disclosure of electronic evidence, adopted in November 2021, is another norm development step pointing in this

[8] Antonio Segura-Serrano, 'Cybersecurity and cybercrime: Dynamic application versus norm-development' (2021) 81 Heidelberg J Int L 701–31 at 718.

[9] UNODC, *Comprehensive Study on Cybercrime* (New York: UN, 2013), p. 201, according to which, in transnational cybercrime cases, 'only in 25 per cent of cases were international and regional instruments cited as the legal basis'.

[10] Heller, 'In defense of pure sovereignty', p. 1435, stating: 'A striking example is Operation Glowing Symphony, in which U.S. Cyber Command hacked into computer systems used by ISIS in as many as thirty different States, making it "the largest and longest offensive cyber operation in US military history".'

[11] Phillipe Jougleux, Tatiana E. Synodinou, and Lilian Mitrou, 'Criminalization of attacks against information systems', in Ioannis Iglezakis (ed.), *The Legal Regulation of Cyber Attacks* (Alphen aan den Rijn: Kluwer Law, 2020), p. 116.

[12] Austin Gillett, 'First data sharing agreement under CLOUD Act reassures some, leaves others concerned', *New York University Journal of Legislation & Public Policy*, 31 January 2020, https://nyujlpp.org/quorum/gillett-first-data-sharing-agreement-under-cloud-act (accessed 10 August 2022).

[13] The US has already adopted CLOUD Act agreements with the UK and Australia. See US Department of Justice, 'CLOUD Act resources', 2022, www.justice.gov/dag/cloudact (accessed 10 August 2022).

[14] European Commission, 'E-evidence: Cross-border access to electronic evidence', https://ec.europa.eu/info/policies/justice-and-fundamental-rights/criminal-justice/e-evidence-cross-border-access-electronic-evidence_en#internaleurulesproposaloneevidence (accessed 10 August 2022).

direction.[15] However, this mechanism has been criticised by certain States, especially Russia and China.[16] In any case, these scenarios explicitly reveal the conundrums a dispute settlement body may face in entertaining evidence necessary to adjudicate on cyber disputes if unilateral remote searches were to amount to a wrongful act.

The third challenge relates to the question of attribution. As was said, one of the main difficulties in establishing international responsibility in cyberspace is attribution, due to the prevalence of anonymity on the internet. This anonymity can be achieved in various ways: through virtual private networks (VPNs), proxy servers, onion routing, and so on. In fact, the 2013, 2015, and 2021 UN GGE reports have included a prohibition on the use of third parties by States to commit internationally wrongful acts through information and communications technologies (ICTs). However, leaving aside the widespread practice of States of using intermediaries to carry out clandestine acts on the Web,[17] the operation of attribution itself is complicated by the diversity of actors present in cyberspace.[18] International legal responsibility may be engaged according to the secondary rules contained in the International Law Commission's Articles on Responsibility of States for International Wrongful Acts (ARSIWA) only if a wrongful act is attributed to a State.[19] However, legal attribution is not sufficient. There is a preceding technical attribution task that must be fulfilled in order to arrive at legal attribution determination.[20] Unfortunately, for the time being, attribution is a critical issue which extant international law has not yet addressed satisfactorily.[21] To explain, State practice shows that, so far, legal attribution and responsibility at the inter-State level has not been invoked, probably due to the prudential policy adopted by States together with the uncertainty regarding the extent to

[15] Council of Europe, 'Second Additional Protocol to the Cybercrime Convention adopted by the Committee of Ministers of the Council of Europe', 17 November 2021, www.coe.int/en/web/cybercrime/-/second-additional-protocol-to-the-cybercrime-convention-adopted-by-the-committee-of-ministers-of-the-council-of-europe (accessed 10 August 2022).

[16] Paul de Hert, Cihan Parlar, and Juraj Sajfert, 'The Cybercrime Convention Committee's 2017 Guidance Note on Production Orders: Unilateralist transborder access to electronic evidence promoted via soft law' (2018) 34 CLSR 327–36.

[17] Tim Maurer, '"Proxies" and cyberspace' (2016) 21 JC&SL 383–403.

[18] Michael N. Schmitt and Linus Vihul, 'Proxy wars in cyber space: The evolving international law of attribution' (2014) 1 FSR 55–73.

[19] ILC, 'Draft articles on responsibility of States for internationally wrongful acts', in *Yearbook of the International Law Commission 2001, Volume II, Part Two: Report of the Commission to the General Assembly on the Work of Its Fifty-Third Session* (New York: UN, 2008), p. 31.

[20] Nicholas Tsagourias, 'Cyber attacks, self-defence and the problem of attribution' (2012) 17 JC&SL 229–44 at 233.

[21] Segura-Serrano, 'Cybersecurity and cybercrime', pp. 706ff.

which international law obligations apply in cyberspace.[22] There are also difficulties in setting up the types of evidence and standards of proof needed to establish attribution,[23] and more so since States such as the US, UK, France, and the Netherlands[24] have departed from the consensus reached by the UN GGE 2015 Report, which states that 'the accusations of organising and implementing wrongful acts brought against States should be substantiated'.[25] There are also difficulties in the application of legal determinants of attribution to cyber operations.[26] To overcome this problem, part of the literature promotes attribution by non-State actors,[27] while other commentators support the setting up of a centralised international attribution mechanism[28] – though difficult to implement in the short run[29] – or propose the revision of the attribution determinants contained in Article 8 of ILC Draft Articles.[30] These proposals are in line with other proposals to internationalise the process of attribution, such as those put forward by Microsoft[31] and

[22] Efrony and Shany, 'Rule book on the shelf?' p. 594.

[23] Marco Roscini, 'Evidentiary issues in international disputes related to State responsibility for cyber operations' (2015) 50 Tex Int'l L J 233–73.

[24] Brian J. Egan, 'International law and stability in cyberspace' (2017) 35 Berkeley J Int'l L 169–80 at 177; UK Attorney General's Office and Jeremy Wright, 'Cyber and international law in the 21st century', *UK Government*, 23 May 2018, www.gov.uk/government/speeches/cyber-and-international-law-in-the-21st-century (accessed 11 August 2022); Ministère des Armées, 'Droit international appliqué aux opérations dans le cyberespace', 2019, www.justsecurity.org/wp-content/uploads/2019/09/droit-internat-appliqué-aux-opérations-cyberespace-france.pdf (accessed 11 August 2022), p. 11; Government of The Netherlands, 'Letter to the Parliament on the international legal order in cyberspace – Appendix: International law in cyberspace', 5 July 2019, www.government.nl/documents/parliamentary-documents/2019/09/26/letter-to-the-parliament-on-the-international-legal-order-in-cyberspace (accessed 9 December 2020), p. 6.

[25] UNGA, '2015 Report of the GGE', para. 28f.

[26] Nicholas Tsagourias and Michael Farrell, 'Cyber attribution: Technical and legal approaches and challenges' (2020) 31 EJIL 941–67.

[27] Kristen E. Eichensehr, 'Decentralized cyberattack attribution' (2019) 113 AJIL Unbound 213–17 at 217.

[28] Henning Lahmann, *Unilateral Remedies to Cyber Operations: Self-Defence, Countermeasures, Necessity, and the Question of Attribution*, (Cambridge: Cambridge University Press 2020), p. 279.

[29] Yuval Shany and Michael N. Schmitt, 'An international attribution mechanism for hostile cyber operations' (2020) 96 Int Law Stud 196–222, arguing that this mechanism would be of help in three contexts: for States facing capacity issues, for those interested in collective attribution, and in case of extant cyber-related sanctions regimes.

[30] Tsagourias and Farrell, 'Cyber attribution', p. 961.

[31] Shaun Waterman, 'Microsoft calls for UN-type body to attribute big cyberattacks', *FedScoop*, 23 June 2016, www.fedscoop.com/microsoft-wants-iaea-type-body-to-attribute-big-cyberattacks (accessed 11 August 2022).

RAND.[32] In sum, the aforementioned proposals for addressing the problem of attribution and improving the attribution process in cyberspace highlight that this is a core challenge that needs to be tackled by any international dispute settlement body adjudicating on a cyber dispute.

16.3 OPPORTUNITIES OFFERED BY CYBERSPACE AND NEW TECHNOLOGIES FOR DISPUTE SETTLEMENT

In this section, I consider the opportunities cyberspace and new technologies offer for dispute settlement. First, I reflect on digital evidence and how it can transform the process of dispute settlement, and, second, I consider the possibilities offered by online dispute settlement. In this respect, online court proceedings, but mainly ODR systems, will be analysed to assess their potential impact on inter-State litigation, including the possibility of having 'machine arbitrators or judges'.

16.3.1 *Digital Evidence and the International Court of Justice*

Evidence has been defined as 'information submitted to an international court or tribunal by parties to a case or from other sources with the view of establishing or disproving the alleged facts'.[33] Evidentiary issues are not an isolated problem confined to cyber disputes. To the contrary, difficulties relating to evidence are part and parcel of dispute settlement procedures, including those of the International Court of Justice (ICJ), because rules of evidence in international law 'have been more flexible and minimalistic than their domestic law equivalent'.[34] These problems are more demanding in cases where the legal determination of an actual use of force is at stake.[35] In what follows I discuss how evidence collection and assessment is approached by the ICJ and then – by looking at international criminal law procedures and

[32] John S. Davis et al., *Stateless Attribution: Toward International Accountability in Cyberspace* (Santa Monica, CA: RAND Corporation, 2017), pp. 25ff., calling for a Global Consortium for Cyber Attribution.

[33] Rüdiger Wolfrum and Mirka Möldner, 'International courts and tribunals, evidence', in *Max Planck Encyclopedia of Public International Law* (Oxford: Oxford University Press, 2013), para. 1.

[34] James Devaney, 'Evidence: International Court of Justice (ICJ)', in *Max Planck Encyclopedia of International Procedural Law* (Oxford: Oxford University Press, 2018), para. 2.

[35] Mary Ellen O'Connell, 'Rules of evidence for the use of force in international law's new era' (2006) ProcASIL 44–47.

human rights fact-finding mechanisms – consider to what extent digital evidence has ushered in changes in this field.

It should be noted that certain academics with expertise in this field have been very wary about the use of digital evidence in international disputes among States. In this vein, Roscini believes that 'digital evidence on its own is unlikely to play a decisive role in establishing State responsibility for cyber operations'.[36] According to him, digital evidence is, firstly, volatile and often located in foreign countries. Secondly, digital evidence is time-consuming and requires the cooperation of internet service providers, which in turn may be difficult to obtain as the cyber activity may have its origin in other States. Thirdly, even if digital evidence may be useful to detect the computer from which the cyber activity originated, it does not necessarily help identify the person or group behind the cyber activity, due to the use of hijacking or spoofing techniques. This last point is relevant to the problem of attribution, that is, the collection of digital evidence will not solve the issue of whether the activities of individuals may be attributed to a State according to international law.[37]

However, it is also quite reasonable to think that digital evidence as a means of proof will play a larger role in the future, as States will increasingly rely on digital evidence in general or use digital dispute settlement procedures to solve their cyber disputes. Therefore, it will be informative to examine the ICJ's procedure on collecting and assessing evidence in order to ascertain whether there are actual possibilities for digital evidence to be used before the Court. For this reason, although there are differences, it will be useful to look at human rights fact-finding mechanisms and the International Criminal Court (ICC) in order to consider how certain tools and techniques already applied by them can be transposed to the ICJ.

In relation to human rights fact-finding, the mechanisms recently set up by the General Assembly and the Security Council,[38] together with the

36 Roscini, 'Evidentiary issues', p. 264.

37 Ibid.

38 The International, Impartial, and Independent Mechanism for Syria (IIIM) created by the UN General Assembly in December 2016 pursuant to UNGA Res 71/248 (UNGA, 'International, impartial and independent mechanism to assist in the investigation and prosecution of persons responsible for the most serious crimes under international law committed in the Syrian Arab Republic since March 2011' (21 December 2016) UN Doc. A/RES/71/248); the Investigative Team to Promote Accountability for Crimes Committed by Da'esh/ISIL (UNITAD), created by the UN Security Council in September 2017 pursuant to UNSC Res 2379 (21 September 2017) UN Doc. S/RES/2379; and the International Independent Mechanism for Myanmar (IIMM), the sister mechanism of the IIIM, created by the UN Human Rights Council in December 2018 pursuant to UNHRC Res 39/2 (UN Human Rights Council, 'Situation of

Commissions of Inquiry for Gaza and Burundi, or the Office of the High Commissioner for Human Rights (OHCHR) investigation on Libya,[39] are examples of fact-finding bodies that are favouring the collection and use of digital evidence for the purposes of documenting human rights violations.[40] Collecting evidence by digital means has been hailed as a method that can possibly 'democratise the process of human rights fact-finding', allowing 'ordinary people' to play an increasing role.[41] Indeed, all that is needed to start collecting digital data is a smartphone with a camera and access to the internet, allowing communication with social networks like Facebook or Twitter. From the point of view of international justice, there are several advantages to the use of new technologies for evidence collection, such as partially avoiding biases identified in traditional investigative methods, monitoring of 'black hole' environments, acting as a 'force multiplier' for other evidence, or for early warning and preventive purposes.[42] The fact-finding mandate of the UN mechanisms is focused on the collection, collation, analysis, and preservation of evidence of international crimes and to make this evidence available for prosecutions. Those mechanisms have a principal role in promoting and respecting state-of-the-art standards regarding both the authenticity and integrity of digital material and its probative value, together with its archiving and storage.[43]

However, there are also downsides to the use of digital material, such as the potential widening of the digital divide, likely biases towards the digitally visible, the need of private sector cooperation, and problems with the authenticity and integrity of evidence.[44]

human rights of Rohingya Muslims and other minorities in Myanmar' (3 October 2018) UN Doc. A/HRC/RES/39/2).

39 UN Human Rights Council, 'Report of the detailed findings of the independent commission of inquiry established pursuant to the Human Rights Council Resolution S-21/1' (24 June 2015) UN Doc. A/HR/29/CRP.4, paras 79, 89, and 100; UN Human Rights Council, 'Rapport final détaillé de la Commission d'enquête sur le Burundi' (12 September 2018) UN Doc. A/HRC/36/CRP.1, para. 213; UN Human Rights Council, 'Investigation by the Office of the United Nations High Commissioner for Human Rights on Libya: Detailed findings' (23 February 2016) UN Doc. A/HRC/31/CRP.3, para. 224.

40 Elizabeth R. White, 'Towards a new normal: Digitization of international criminal law in the age of coronavirus', *Columbia Journal of Transnational Law Bulletin Notes*, 3 February 2022, www.jtl.columbia.edu/bulletin-notes/towards-a-new-normal-digitization-of-international-criminal-law-in-the-age-of-coronavirus (accessed 11 August 2022), p. 29.

41 Land, 'Democratizing human rights fact-finding', p. 402.

42 Federica D'Alessandra and Kirsty Sutherland, 'The promise and challenges of new actors and new technologies in international justice' (2021) 19 JICJ 9–34 at 14–16.

43 Ibid., pp. 23, 27.

44 Ibid., p. 21.

International criminal prosecutions have also benefited from the availability of digital data. The Rome Statute of the ICC and the ICC Rules of Procedure and Evidence do not explicitly envisage the use of digital evidence.[45] However, digital evidence is already playing an important role in current international criminal law and, therefore, 'further use of digitized data collection presents a promising opportunity to increase the efficacy and efficiency of international criminal investigations and thereby prosecutions'.[46] Specifically, four new technologies have been identified as 'candidates to propel the international justice into these new frontiers'.[47] These technologies are geospatial intelligence and remote sensing (GEOINT),[48] online open source intelligence (OSINT),[49] financial intelligence (FININT),[50] and documentation technologies, including specialised software such as EyeWitness,[51] CameraV,[52] and InformaCam,[53] which are applications that link photos and

45 Rome Statute of the International Criminal Court, Rome, 17 July 1998, in force 1 July 2002, 2187 UNTS 3; ICC, *Rules of Procedure and Evidence*, 2nd ed. (The Hague: ICC, 2013).

46 White, 'Towards a new normal', pp. 21–22.

47 D'Alessandra and Sutherland, 'Promise and challenges of new actors', p. 13.

48 This includes satellite imagery through Google Earth, USGS EarthExplorer, LandViewer, Copernicus Open Access Hub, and others.

49 Heather J. Williams and Ilana Blum, *Defining Second Generation Open Source Intelligence (OSINT) for the Defense Enterprise* (Santa Monica, CA: RAND Corporation, 2018), p. 8, stating: 'We define OSINT as publicly available information that has been discovered, determined to be of intelligence value, and disseminated by a member of the IC. This is consistent with the U.S. definition in Section 931 of Public Law 109-163 that defines OSINT as "intelligence that is produced from publicly available information and is collected, exploited, and disseminated in a timely manner to an appropriate audience for the purpose of addressing a specific intelligence requirement". OSIF (Open Source Information) is merely unclassified data available to the public, while OSINT results from applying processing and exploiting the information to validate it as relevant, accurate, and actionable for use by the consumers'. In other words, OSIF is the raw material that forms the basis for OSINT, encompassing 'all data that is publicly available and can be collected and shared without breaking laws or policies, needing a warrant, or participating in unethical practices. This includes: videos of events streamed live on YouTube, Facebook and other social media platforms; audio clips found online; and communications, instructions and commands posted on social media' (D'Alessandra and Sutherland, 'Promise and challenges of new actors', p. 13).

50 See Chainanalysis, 'Chainanalysis KYT', www.chainalysis.com/chainalysis-kyt (accessed 11 August 2022), and 'Chainanalysis Reactor', www.chainalysis.com/chainalysis-reactor (accessed 11 August 2022). See Elliptic, 'Elliptic Navigator', www.elliptic.co/solutions/crypto-transaction-monitoring (accessed 11 August 2022), and 'Elliptic Investigator', www.elliptic.co/solutions/crypto-investigations (accessed 11 August 2022).

51 eyeWitness, 'Welcome to eyeWitness', www.eyewitness.global (accessed 11 August 2022).

52 Guardian Project, 'CameraV: Secure verifiable photo & video camera', 2022, https://guardianproject.info/es/archive/camerav (accessed 12 August 2022).

53 Witness, 'Is this for real? How InformaCam improves verification of mobile media files', 2013, https://blog.witness.org/2013/01/how-informacam-improves-verification-of-mobile-media-files (accessed 12 August 2022).

videos with the metadata required to prove their validity in court. While the early cases before the ICC relied heavily on witness testimony, by 2011 the Office of the Prosecutor has developed forensic equipment to deal with digital evidence like videos taken with cell phone cameras and, later, satellite imagery and leads extracted from websites like Facebook and YouTube.[54] As stated, 'digital information from user-generated online content, consumer data from communications service providers, and geolocation data are quickly becoming essential tools of the trade for international criminal investigators'.[55]

The character of investigations before the ICC makes the use of digital evidence a particularly powerful tool because it can remedy some of the difficulties encountered by criminal investigations such as the time lapse between the commission of the crime and the start of the investigation.[56] Likewise, open source information is particularly useful as a way to discover new material relevant to the cases at hand, but also to verify and authenticate existing information.[57] Last but not least, digital evidence is very convenient in order to proceed with remote investigations, that is, due to security threats or because of difficulties in travelling, like those derived from the Covid-19 pandemic.[58] Of course, the use of online open source information presents not only advantages but also risks from a legal point of view, such as those flowing from the volatility of the digital material. Indeed, digital material is readily accessible by many, which means it is subject to change, which in turn affects its veracity.[59] Some of the most common pitfalls of open source

[54] Lindsay Freeman, 'Digital evidence and war crimes prosecutions: The impact of digital technologies on international criminal investigations and trials' (2018) 41 Fordham Int'l L J 283–335 at 288–89; Christoph Koettl, Daragh Murray, and Sam Dubberley, 'Open source investigation for human rights reporting: A brief history', in Sam Dubberley, Alexa Koenig, and Daragh Murray (eds.), *Digital Witness: Using Open Source Information for Human Rights Investigation, Documentation, and Accountability* (Oxford: Oxford University Press, 2020), p. 12.

[55] Freeman, 'Digital evidence', pp. 288–89.

[56] Lindsay Freeman, 'Prosecuting atrocity crimes with open source evidence: Lessons from the International Criminal Court', in Sam Dubberley, Alexa Koenig, and Daragh Murray (eds.), *Digital Witness: Using Open Source Information for Human Rights Investigation, Documentation, and Accountability* (Oxford: Oxford University Press, 2020), pp. 49, 57.

[57] Rebecca J. Hamilton, 'User-generated evidence' (2018) 57 Colum J Transnat'l L 1–60 at 17–18.

[58] White, 'Towards a new normal', pp. 31–32.

[59] Aric Toler, 'How to verify and authenticate user-generated content', in Sam Dubberley, Alexa Koenig, and Daragh Murray (eds.), *Digital Witness: Using Open Source Information for Human Rights Investigation, Documentation, and Accountability* (Oxford: Oxford University Press, 2020), p. 185.

information include misattribution, staging, and technical manipulation.[60] Therefore, it is not only important to gather metadata to authenticate potential evidence, but courts have to tighten the requirements for verifying data and preserving a chain of custody.[61] Research in this area, mainly by the UC Berkeley School of Law Human Rights Center, has led to the formulation of a set of core principles regarding open source information, namely preservation, transparency, legality, security, and objectivity,[62] which, in turn, led to the elaboration of the Berkeley Protocol on Digital Open Source Investigations.[63] There are also concerns regarding the role of user-generated evidence specifically. This type of evidence has been criticised because it may transfer the risk of collecting evidence from investigators to users and introduce bias and distortion and, therefore, affect fair trial rights.[64]

Having discussed the use of digital evidence by human rights fact-finding mechanisms and the ICC, I now discuss how digital evidence is collected and used by the ICJ. As is well known, a flexible approach applies to the issue of evidence in public international law.[65] Regarding the ICJ, there is still neither a comprehensive list of means of proof to be used by parties before the ICJ nor guidelines on the weight to be given to specific forms of evidence,[66] as was indeed also the case with the Permanent Court of International Justice.[67] The production of evidence before the ICJ is governed by Articles 48–52 of the ICJ Statute, the Rules of the Court adopted pursuant to the authority set out by Article 30 of the ICJ Statute, and the non-binding Practice Directions for use by States appearing before it that the ICJ adopted and amended from 2001 onwards. Although not explicitly mentioned in the Rules of the Court, the

60 Nikita Mehandru and Alexa Koenig, 'ICTs, social media, and the future of human rights' (2019) 17 Duke L & Tech 129–45 at 135.

61 Ibid., pp. 141–42.

62 Human Rights Center, UC Berkeley School of Law, 'The new forensics: Using open source information to investigate grave crimes', 1 July 2018, www.law.berkeley.edu/wp-content/uploads/2018/02/Bellagio_report_2018_9.pdf (accessed 12 August 2022), pp. 8ff.

63 Human Rights Center, UC Berkeley School of Law and OHCHR, *Berkeley Protocol on Digital Open Source Investigations: A Practical Guide on the Effective Use of Digital Open Source Information in Investigating Violations of International Criminal, Human Rights and Humanitarian Law* (Geneva: Human Rights Center and OHCHR, 2022).

64 Hamilton, 'User-generated evidence', pp. 35ff.

65 Chester Brown, *A Common Law of International Adjudication* (Oxford: Oxford University Press, 2007), p. 92; Shabtai Rosenne, *The Law and Practice of the International Court, 1920–2005*, 4th ed., 4 vols (Leiden: Martinus Nijhoff, 2006), vol. 3, p. 1245.

66 Wolfrum and Möldner, 'International courts', paras 3–4; Ruth Teitelbaum, 'Recent fact-finding developments at the International Court of Justice' (2007) 6 LPICT 119–58 at 124.

67 Durward V. Sandifer, *Evidence before International Tribunals* (Charlottesville: University Press of Virginia, 1975), p. 5.

foundation of evidentiary assessment in the ICJ is undoubtedly based on the principle of 'freedom of evidence', which means that the ICJ has limitless powers to determine what evidentiary standard it will require in any given case.[68] As the Court said in the *Nicaragua* case, 'within the limits of its Statute and Rules, [it] has freedom in estimating the value of the various elements of evidence'.[69] According to Judge Simma when considering the probative weight of evidence, the ICJ generally takes into account seven factors: its source, interest, relation to events, method, verification, contemporaneity, and procedure.[70] Therefore, by analogy, digital evidence will be subject to the same kind of probative assessment so that verification through cross-examination should not be any more difficult regarding digital evidence.

Regarding the type of evidence accepted by the ICJ, documentary evidence is the most common form accepted by the Court, and it encompasses everything which is not testimonial evidence.[71] It may include 'maps, photographs, video and other media, expert opinions, and judgments of national courts'.[72] It follows from this that digital evidence can be included within documentary evidence, that is, digital documents must be considered equivalent to physical documents, and the Court should accept that the digital evidence produced is authentic with no need of going through a formal process of authentication, unless the other party challenges its authenticity.[73] Even if there is no explicit procedure to challenge the authenticity of documents before the ICJ, the party producing the digital evidence will have to prove its authenticity in the first place.[74] A different problem concerns illegally obtained digital evidence,

[68] James A. Green, 'Fluctuating evidentiary standards for self-defence in the International Court of Justice' (2009) 58 ICLQ 163–79 at 164–66.

[69] *Case Concerning Military and Paramilitary Activities in and against Nicaragua (Nicaragua* v. *United States of America)* (Merits, Judgment) [1986] ICJ Rep. 14 at para. 60. See also *Case Concerning Armed Activities on the Territory of the Congo (Democratic Republic of the Congo* v. *Uganda)* (Judgment) [2005] ICJ Rep. 168 at para. 59.

[70] *Application of the International Convention on the Elimination of All Forms of Racial Discrimination (Georgia* v. *Russian Federation)* (Preliminary Objections, Judgments) [2011] ICJ Rep. 70 at p. 197 (Separate Opinion of Judge Simma). Also see Anna Riddell and Brendan Plant, *Evidence before the International Court of Justice* (London: British Institute of International and Comparative Law, 2009), p. 192.

[71] Wolfrum and Möldner, 'International courts', para. 26.

[72] Devaney, 'Evidence', para. 17.

[73] Marco Roscini, 'Digital evidence as a means of proof before the International Court of Justice' (2016) 21 JC&SL 541–54 at 544–45.

[74] Kubo Mačák, 'Article 43', in Andreas Zimmermann et al. (eds.), *The Statute of the International Court of Justice: A Commentary*, 3rd ed. (Oxford: Oxford University Press, 2019), p. 1251.

for example, from remote unilateral searches or cyberespionage.[75] This issue takes us back to the question of whether non-consensual penetration of a State's information technology systems to obtain digital evidence amounts to a breach of State sovereignty.[76] Regarding this question, in the *Corfu Channel* case, the ICJ seemed to accept evidence illegally collected by the UK in Albanian waters,[77] although, at the same time, the Court stated that this kind of intervention 'might easily lead to perverting the administration of international justice itself'.[78] The Court did not, however, address the question of admissibility because Albania did not challenge it.[79] Roscini opined that

> in the digital context, by analogy this means that the fact that digital evidence is stored in the computers or servers located in another State does not entitle the interested litigant to access them without authorisation from the competent authorities in order to submit the evidence in the proceedings. If the evidence is unlawfully collected, however, it is unlikely that it will be considered inadmissible by the ICJ on grounds of its illegality alone.[80]

I am not completely persuaded by this argument. Even if international adjudication is based on consent,[81] it would be difficult for the Court to accept illegally obtained evidence if it is challenged by the other party. However, the inadmissibility of that evidence should not exclude other, factually identical, circumstantial evidence.

Digital evidence, together with all other documentary evidence, should be submitted during written proceedings, although Article 56(1) and (2) allows the submission of additional documents during oral proceedings. In practice, parties have made recourse to this possibility even after the closure of oral proceedings, which prompted the Court to adopt Practice Direction IX in 2002.[82] Article 56(4) sets out an exception to Article 56(1) and (2) and provides that 'no reference may be made during the oral proceedings to the

[75] While the *Tallinn Manual* considers that cyberespionage is not prohibited per se under customary international law (Schmitt, *Tallinn Manual* 2.0, Rule 32, p. 169), there are other scholars who see cyberespionage as a wrongful act, even if the cyber penetration does not cause physical harm (Russell Buchan, *Cyber Espionage and International Law* (Oxford: Hart, 2019), p. 54).

[76] See Section 16.2.

[77] *Corfu Channel Case (United Kingdom of Great Britain and Northern Ireland* v. *Albania)* (Judgment) [1949] ICJ Rep. 4 at pp. 14–15.

[78] Ibid., p. 35.

[79] Hugh Thirlway, 'Dilemma or chimera? Admissibility of illegally obtained evidence in international adjudication' (1984) 78 AJIL 622–41 at 632.

[80] Roscini, 'Digital evidence', p. 553.

[81] Thirlway, 'Dilemma or chimera?' pp. 638–39.

[82] Wolfrum and Möldner, 'International courts', para. 29.

contents of any document which has not been produced [during the written proceedings], unless the document is part of a publication readily available'. Interestingly, Practice Direction IX*bis*, promulgated in 2006, expands on this possibility with the view not to undermine the rule provided in Article 56(1) and (2).[83] Indeed, the Court considers that for a document to be understood as 'part of a publication readily available', there are specific requirements that must be met. Regarding the first criterion, namely that it should be 'part of a publication', it must be interpreted as extant in the public domain 'in any format (printed or electronic), form (physical or online, such as posted on the internet) or on any data medium (on paper, on digital or any other media)'. Regarding the second criterion of being 'readily available', it must be interpreted as 'accessibility to the Court as well as to the other party', including accessibility in the official languages of the Court and the possibility of consultation within a reasonably short period of time.

This means that parties can use any publication which is accessible online with no need of prior notice to the Court itself or the other party because it is deemed to be in the 'public domain'. The consequences of Practice Direction IX*bis* are yet to be seen, but it is clear that the vast amount of information existing on the internet opens up the possibilities for parties to make recourse to digital data in unexpected ways,[84] including user-generated information that suddenly appears on social media platforms during the proceedings with direct relation to the facts of a case before the Court. Of course, any publication in the public domain and readily available does not make the facts public knowledge of which the Court should take judicial notice, because the facts still need to be proved, as it happens with the rest of documentary evidence. A publication readily available only relieves the party from the burden of having to produce the publication within written proceedings.[85] It should be said that there is a problem of fake news and disinformation, which may be counterproductive for streamlining digital evidence collection at the ICJ. However, the probity and authenticity of the evidence collected by digital

[83] Riddell and Plant, *Evidence before the ICJ*, p. 182.

[84] Ibid., p. 184, and Roscini, 'Digital evidence', p. 547, taking note of the second criterion put forward by the ICJ in Practice Direction IX*bis* (ICJ, 'Practice Directions', www.icj-cij.org/en/practice-directions (accessed 12 August 2022)) and arguing that the requirement 'readily available' is to be assessed not in general but with respect to the Court and the other party in each specific case, which may serve to lower the amount of online information submitted by the parties in the oral proceedings.

[85] Markus Benzing, 'Evidentiary issues', in Andreas Zimmermann et al. (eds.), *The Statute of the International Court of Justice: A Commentary*, 3rd ed. (Oxford: Oxford University Press, 2019), p. 1378.

means is subject to the same rules on veracity and chain of custody as mentioned in the case of international criminal law.[86] Therefore, the parties adducing digital evidence will have to prove that this evidence is verifiable through the corresponding metadata or otherwise, so that technical manipulation is avoided.

As noted above, audio-visual evidence is also included within documentary evidence, and so too must be digital audio-visual material, including satellite images.[87] Certain commentators have observed that the Court has generally given less probative value to audio-visual evidence than to written documents due to concerns regarding the authenticity and aim of its production.[88] Practice Direction IX*quater*, promulgated in 2013, sets out in paragraph 3 that

> a party's request to present audio-visual or photographic material must be accompanied by information as to the source of the material, the circumstances and date of its making and the extent to which it is available to the public. The party in question must also specify, wherever relevant, the geographic co-ordinates at which that material was taken.

Again, as with digital evidence generally, concerns about authenticity are behind this Practice Direction, and that is why certain apps such as EyeWitness, CameraV, and InformaCam have been developed by NGOs and other actors in the criminal law field.

If digital evidence is considered to be documentary evidence by the Court, then it will not take much time for the parties to make increasing use of new investigative and documentation technologies, which will mainly serve to attribute international wrongful acts to States and hold them responsible. This possibility has become a reality through the activities carried out by Bellingcat[89] and open source investigative journalists in eastern Ukraine which helped determine that it was a Russian military Buk missile launched from Donetsk on 17 July 2014 that hit Malaysia Airlines Flight *MH17*. A similar conclusion was reached by the official Dutch-led investigation, through the use of digital open source information, radar data, satellite imagery, telecommunications records, and data analysis, among others.[90] As

86 Roscini, 'Digital evidence', p. 545.

87 On the previous use since the 1990s of satellite images before the ICJ, see Riddell and Plant, *Evidence before the ICJ*, p. 288, and Roscini, 'Digital evidence', p. 549.

88 Riddell and Plant, *Evidence before the ICJ*, p. 287.

89 Bellingcat, 'MH17 – The open source investigation, three years later', 17 July 2017, www.bellingcat.com/news/uk-and-europe/2017/07/17/mh17-open-source-investigation-three-years-later (accessed 12 August 2022).

90 D'Alessandra and Sutherland, 'Promise and challenges of new actors', p. 17.

a result, the Netherlands brought a case against Russia before the European Court of Human Rights[91] and, very recently, together with Australia, initiated legal proceedings against the Russian Federation before the International Civil Aviation Organisation.[92] Likewise, Ukraine presented open source information, including user-generated evidence, before the ICJ in its request for provisional measures against Russia.[93] Other instances where digital evidence, mainly in the form of open source information, has been used to confirm State participation in a criminal event are the chemical weapons attack by the Syrian government in 2018[94] and the alleged violations of the Genocide Convention by Myanmar in a case brought by the Gambia before the ICJ, a case which at the time of writing is still pending.[95] The Gambia relied on satellite imagery assessed by the UN Fact-Finding Mission on Myanmar as displaying 'irrefutable documentation of the scale of destruction perpetrated' against the Rohingya. The Fact-Finding Mission on Myanmar analysed 'the vast extent of Myanmar's hate campaign against the Rohingya group' by scrutinising, among other things, Facebook posts and audio-visual materials. The Gambia relied on this digital open source material to put forward claims of 'genocidal intent'. These examples show how digital evidence can be used in assisting judicial proceedings seeking to uphold State responsibility.[96]

In conclusion, it can be said that cyber disputes between States may be brought before the ICJ with no need to change the current Rules of Procedure

[91] Government of The Netherlands, 'The Netherlands brings MH17 case against Russia before European Court of Human Rights', 10 July 2020, www.government.nl/latest/news/2020/07/10/the-netherlands-brings-mh17-case-against-russia-before-european-court-of-human-rights (accessed 12 August 2022).

[92] Minister for Foreign Affairs, Australia, 'Australia and the Netherlands initiate MH17 legal proceedings', 14 March 2022, www.foreignminister.gov.au/minister/marise-payne/media-release/australia-and-netherlands-initiate-mh17-legal-proceedings (accessed 12 August 2022).

[93] ICJ, *Application of the International Convention for the Suppression of the Financing of Terrorism and of the International Convention on the Elimination of all Forms of Racial Discrimination (Ukraine* v. *Russian Federation)* (Application Instituting Proceedings), 16 January 2017, www.icj-cij.org/public/files/case-related/166/166-20170116-APP-01-00-EN.pdf (accessed 12 August 2022).

[94] Ministry for Europe and Foreign Affairs, France, 'National assessment document on chemical attack of 7 April 2018 (Douma, Eastern Ghouta, Syria) and Syria's clandestine chemical weapons programme', 14 April 2018, www.diplomatie.gouv.fr/en/country-files/syria/news/article/national-assessment-document-on-chemical-attack-of-7-april-2018-douma-eastern (accessed 12 August 2022).

[95] ICJ, *Application of the Convention on the Prevention and Punishment of the Crime of Genocide (The Gambia* v. *Myanmar)* (Application Instituting Proceedings and Request for the Indication of Provisional Measures), 11 November 2019, www.icj-cij.org/public/files/case-related/178/178-20191111-APP-01-00-EN.pdf (accessed 12 August 2022).

[96] D'Alessandra and Sutherland, 'Promise and challenges of new actors', p. 19.

and Evidence. As for the question of who is going to produce digital evidence or how this evidence is going to be presented, the answer is that digital evidence must be produced by parties, unless they are 'part of a publication readily available', which exponentially enlarges the amount of evidence that may be relied upon by parties, including open source information. As stated, this means that almost any type of digital evidence may be accepted by the Court, no matter its source, only subject to the required proof to be provided by the respective party. Therefore, documentary evidence in the form of open source information and user-generated content, such as Facebook posts, YouTube videos, Instagram photos, and WhatsApp messages, are all valid before the Court, because they may have a role in discovering new material relevant to the cases at hand, but also to verify and authenticate existing information. In this vein, the setting up of an international agency within the UN or otherwise,[97] for attributing acts taking place in cyberspace to States,[98] may help the ICJ in the task of obtaining and filtering the digital evidence needed or produced, respectively, to decide a case on wrongful activities in cyberspace.

16.3.2 *Online Dispute Settlement*

In this section I first provide an overview of ODR practised since the beginning of the twenty-first century in certain areas involving digital transactions in order to identify issues and derive lessons which can be transposed into international law. I then go on to consider the feasibility of online proceedings in general, and the online resolution of inter-State disputes in particular.

16.3.2.1 Online Dispute Resolution

Twenty years ago, the concept of ODR was coined as an umbrella term,[99] which included many different online procedures and technological tools used in order to solve disputes.[100] ODR mechanisms are mainly to be found

[97] On the outsourcing of the fact-finding activity by the ICJ to UN organs of various sorts, see Daniel Joyce, 'Fact-finding and evidence at the International Court of Justice: Systemic crisis, change or more of the same?' (2007) 18 FYBIL 283–306 at 294; see also Devaney, 'Evidence', paras 53ff.; Teitelbaum, 'Recent fact-finding developments', p. 146.

[98] Segura-Serrano, 'Cybersecurity and cybercrime', p. 731.

[99] Ayelet Sela, 'The effect of online technologies on dispute resolution system design: Antecedents, current trends, and future directions' (2017) 21 LCLR 635–82 at 636.

[100] See generally Ethan Katsh and Janet Rifkin, *Online Dispute Resolution: Resolving Conflicts in Cyberspace* (San Francisco, CA: Jossey-Bass, 2001).

in the consumer redress realm, where they were first tested once the internet became a commercial network.[101] As stated, there are two primary pragmatic and philosophical reasons behind the evolution of ODR.[102] The first and key driver of ODR was the upsurge in online activities and services, led by the e-commerce sector and supported by technological improvements. The second driver of ODR was the 'effective access to justice' movement,[103] including the 'efficiency paradigm' and the related recourse to alternative dispute resolution (ADR) methods.

In 1999, eBay devised a new way to handle the large number of disputes arising among its platform's users. eBay selected a start-up, SquareTrade, which designed software (commonly known as 'the fourth party') that could replace a human mediator in simple cases. It would assist and collaborate with the neutral third party in any kind of case to set up an ODR that was impartial, effective, and acceptable to both parties and which eventually helped solve millions of online disputes each year.[104] Generally speaking, ODR systems learn from parties' preferences, organise communications around the most important issues in need of solution, and help structure negotiations.[105] There is a model for designing ODR processes that has been frequently used, called the Diagnosis, Negotiation, Mediation, Evaluation, and Appeal Model (DNMEA model). It describes the steps a system must take to attain an appropriate resolution process for an individual dispute type. The first two steps (Diagnosis and Negotiation) are handled by software, whereas the latter three (Mediation, Evaluation, and Appeal) are handled by humans.[106]

eBay's ODR system is able to handle over 60 million online disputes annually,[107] and nowadays technologically assisted dispute resolution is commonly used within the private sector, especially for low-value consumer disputes. Even the UN Commission on International Trade Law (UNCITRAL) has a working group on ODR seeking redress for trans-border

[101] Ethan Katsh and Orna Rabinovich-Einy, *Digital Justice: Technology and the Internet of Disputes* (New York: Oxford University Press, 2017), p. 10.

[102] Sela, 'Effect of online technologies', p. 637.

[103] J. J. Prescott, 'Improving access to justice in State courts with platform technology' (2017) 70 Vand L Rev 1993–2050, evaluating the introduction of online platform technology to improve citizen access to justice in courts.

[104] Katsh and Rabinovich-Einy, *Digital Justice*, pp. 10–11.

[105] Colin Rule, 'Technology and the future of dispute resolution' (2015) Disp Resol Mag 4–7 at 4–6.

[106] Colin Rule, 'Online dispute resolution and the future of justice' (2020) 16 Annu Rev Law Soc Sci 277–92 at 284.

[107] Sela, 'Effect of online technologies', p. 662.

consumer issues,[108] and a EU Regulation[109] requires of its member States to implement ODR for cross-border consumer cases with the framework and principles set forth by the EU ADR Directive[110] in an effort to make ODR available for all global purchases.[111] However, there is disagreement within UNCITRAL between the US and the EU regarding the enforceability of pre-dispute arbitration clauses in consumer contracts, which is widely accepted in US law as opposed to what happens in the EU.[112]

ODR systems are gaining momentum beyond the e-commerce domain. Indeed, they are already operative for disputes arising in several industries like medicine, finance, or entertainment. Some fields, however, do present challenges that need to be addressed, such as on-demand healthcare, social media, the workplace, courts, and other public institutions.[113]

ODR systems have also been introduced in litigation in certain jurisdictions. Early instances worth mentioning are the eCourtroom launched by the Federal Court of Australia and the UK 'Money Claim Online', both established in 2001. The former works as an e-mail exchange system, while the latter has been very successful in allowing online filing of claims up to £100,000 that may be executed if there is no counterclaim.[114] The British Columbia Civil Resolution Tribunal was created in 2012 as Canada's first online tribunal and the only ODR system in the world fully integrated into the justice system, in the words of its chair.[115] It uses online problem diagnosis as the first step of a progressive system of ODR processes.[116] Other innovative initiatives are the *Rechtwijzer* in the Netherlands and the *Matterhorn* in

[108] UNCITRAL, Working Group III, 'Online dispute resolution (2010–2016)', https://uncitral.un.org/working_groups/3/online_dispute (accessed 12 August 2022).

[109] Regulation (EU) 524/2013 of the European Parliament and of the Council of 21 May 2013 on online dispute resolution for consumer disputes and amending Regulation (EC) 2006/2004 and Directive 2009/22/EC, OJ 2013 No. L165/1, 18 June 2013.

[110] Directive 2013/11/EU of the European Parliament and of the Council of 21 May 2013 on alternative dispute resolution for consumer disputes and amending Regulation (EC) 2006/2004 and Directive 2009/22/EC, OJ 2013 No. L165/63, 18 June 2013.

[111] Pablo Cortes, 'A new regulatory framework for extra-judicial consumer redress: Where we are and how to move forward' (2015) 35 Leg Stud 114–41.

[112] Amy J. Schmitz, 'American exceptionalism in consumer arbitration' (2012) 10 Loy U Chi Int'l L Rev 81–103 at 95–98; Pablo Cortes, *Online Dispute Resolution for Consumers in the European Union* (London: Routledge, 2010), pp. 107–11.

[113] Katsh and Rabinovich-Einy, *Digital Justice*, pp. 57ff.

[114] Ibid., pp. 158–59.

[115] Shannon Salter, 'Online dispute resolution and justice system integration: British Columbia's Civil Resolution Tribunal' (2017) 34 Windsor Y B Access Just 112–29 at 114.

[116] Sela, 'Effect of online technologies', p. 658.

Michigan and Ohio, both built on the Modria platform.[117] The *Rechtwijzer* initially focused on family cases and aims to assist parties first with problem diagnosis and negotiation and then with mediation and arbitration offered on a secure platform. The *Matterhorn* in Michigan was meant for resolving outstanding disputes regarding traffic violations and was later extended to warrant cases and misdemeanours. It goes beyond merely providing a communication portal for parties and law enforcement, as it comprises other tools for citizens (including artificial intelligence).[118] In addition, Malaysia has established its first cybercourt in 2016 to hear cybercrime cases.[119] And, of course, China has supported the establishment of internet courts, the Beijing Internet Court being the most advanced one, as it uses artificial intelligence as part of an online litigation centre.[120] Other more recent initiatives include the upcoming introduction of the UK online court called 'Her Majesty's Online Court' for claims up to £25,000 that will entail the availability of a negotiation and settlement tool, expected to be completed in 2023.[121]

Even if there are challenges flowing from the use of new technologies in the legal realm,[122] the substitution of human intervention with algorithms has been praised not only for introducing efficiency in mass-scale consumer dispute resolution but also for overcoming the human discretion-based biases found in online ADR systems like ICANN (Internet Corporation for Assigned Names and Numbers) based on its Uniform Domain Name Dispute Resolution Policy.[123] The next move, already underway, is that of collecting, using, and reusing data in order to prevent disputes. This will give companies huge powers that could be abused as their dispute prevention activities

[117] The Modria platform evolved from technology used to power dispute resolution for e-commerce giants PayPal and eBay. See Tyler Technologies, 'Online dispute resolution powered by Modria', www.tylertech.com/products/modria (accessed 13 August 2022).

[118] Amy J. Schmitz, 'Expanding access to remedies through e-court initiatives' (2019) 67 Buff L Rev 89–163 at 106.

[119] Mireze Philippe, 'What does it take to bring justice online?' (2019) 6 IJODR 183–92 at 188.

[120] Teresa Ballesteros, 'International perspectives on online dispute resolution in the e-commerce landscape' (2021) 8 IJODR 85–101 at 93.

[121] Elina Mockeviciute, 'Online courts – HMCTS Reforms Programme', *Lexology*, 19 March 2019, www.lexology.com/library/detail.aspx?g=10651420-b002-4626-8a01-4c88411be9ff (accessed 13 August 2022).

[122] James E. Cabral et al., 'Using technology to enhance access to justice' (2012) 26 Harv J L & Tech 241–324 at 305–24.

[123] See Jacques de Werra, 'Alternative dispute resolution in cyberspace: The need to adopt global ADR mechanisms for addressing the challenges of massive online micro-justice' (2016) 26 SRIEL 289–306, proposing the Uniform Domain Name Dispute Resolution Policy as a source of guidance for global dispute resolution.

are unknown and, therefore, not subject to accountability or fairness processes.[124]

These shifts, from a face-to-face to a virtual setting, from human intervention and decision-making to automation, and from dispute resolution to dispute prevention (through collecting, using, and reusing data) are also said to be experienced in ODR systems applied in courts.[125] However, this does not necessarily mean that ODR will become the normative path for all dispute resolution in the future.[126]

Certainly, there are many reasons to advocate the introduction of ODR in low-value, massive, and repetitive consumer claims. Between justice and redress, ODR systems have inclined towards the latter so that the ODR field has seen the dominance of the 'efficiency paradigm', due to the fact that those systems are designed by private service providers.[127] Even if this situation is being changed nowadays through the introduction of greater legitimacy and greater emphasis on delivering justice, literature exists that has underlined the role that ODR can play in addressing the latent legal market.[128] It contends that a satisfactory resolution of a dispute, although it may not entail or promote justice proper, is much better than the opposite option, that is, no resolution at all, or an unbearably expensive resolution.[129] However, public courts have been slow to adopt ODR or develop e-courts.[130]

Even if courts have serious objections to the deregulation of judicial processes and the decentralisation of power stemming from the courts,[131] which may lead to a 'spiral of irrelevance',[132] there are other concerns that should be taken into account. The promise of ODR for increasing access to justice cannot be fully realised unless it is integrated into a public justice system (including all the evidentiary and procedural rules derived from legal principles and statutory provisions) and that such an integration should not create a buffer zone that ends up insulating ODR from the justice system.[133]

For this reason, certain basic tenets should be taken into account in developing valuable ODR, especially in public courts. They refer to

[124] Katsh and Rabinovich-Einy, *Digital Justice*, pp. 79–80.

[125] Ibid., p. 162.

[126] Ballesteros, 'International perspectives', p. 87.

[127] Sela, 'Effect of online technologies', p. 681.

[128] Richard Susskind, *The Future of Law: Facing the Challenges of Information Technology* (Oxford: Oxford University Press, 1998), p. 41; Richard Susskind, *The End of Lawyers? Rethinking the Nature of Legal Services* (Oxford: Oxford University Press, 2008), p. 99.

[129] Sela, 'Effect of online technologies', p. 681.

[130] Schmitz, 'Expanding access to remedies', p. 92.

[131] Ballesteros, 'International perspectives', pp. 99–100.

[132] Rule, 'Online dispute resolution', p. 283.

[133] Salter, 'Online dispute resolution', pp. 114–17.

legitimacy and due process,[134] which includes the confidentiality, impartiality, competence, and quality of the adjudicatory process.[135] There are also calls for a cautious use of artificial intelligence and algorithms: it is one thing for technology to assist in dispute resolution as a 'fourth party', and another for technology to become the only and final decision-maker.[136] It is only regulation that can ensure that an undue focus on costs and efficiency does not render access to justice and due process unfeasible.[137] Having said that, in my opinion, more complex cases should always be decided by courts.[138]

16.3.2.2 Inter-State Dispute Settlement Online?

In this subsection, I explore the possibility of instituting online proceedings before courts or arbitration tribunals as well as the possibility of automation in inter-State arbitration and adjudication processes.

In this regard, it is reasonable to say that the Covid-19 pandemic brought about the greatest change to the ICJ's procedure in the shortest period of time.[139] Although the Court initially decided to suspend all hearings and meetings until 16 April 2020,[140] it soon realised that there was no other option but to adapt itself to the new situation. Therefore, the Court issued a press release stating that 'through the use of modern technologies, the Court has made the necessary arrangements to hold virtual meetings and adapted its working methods to the need to work remotely during the Covid-19 pandemic',[141] which allowed it to hold, on 22 April 2020, the first virtual plenary meeting in its history.[142] After amending Articles 59 and 94 of the Rules of the Court to decide – for health, security, or other compelling reasons – to hold

[134] Anjanette H. Raymond and Scott J. Shackelford, 'Technology, ethics, and access to justice: Should an algorithm be deciding your case?' (2014) 35 Mich J Int'l L 485–524 at 517–18.

[135] Daniel Rainey, 'Third-party ethics in the age of the fourth party' (2014) 1 IJODR 37–56 at 42–52.

[136] Schmitz, 'Expanding access to remedies', pp. 146, 154.

[137] Raymond and Shackelford, 'Technology, ethics, and access to justice', pp. 521–22.

[138] Ballesteros, 'International perspectives', p. 101.

[139] Giulia Pinzauti and Philippa Webb, 'Litigation before the International Court of Justice during the pandemic' (2021) 34 LJIL 787–800.

[140] ICJ, 'Press Release No. 2020/9', 20 March 2020, www.icj-cij.org/public/files/press-releases/0/000-20200320-PRE-01-00-EN.pdf (accessed 13 August 2022).

[141] ICJ, 'Press Release No. 2020/11', 23 April 2020, www.icj-cij.org/public/files/press-releases/0/000-20200423-PRE-01-00-EN.pdf (accessed 13 August 2022).

[142] Ibid.

hearings and the reading of judgments entirely or in part by video link,[143] the ICJ held its first virtual hearing in the case concerning the *Arbitral Award of 3 October 1899 (Guyana* v. *Venezuela)*.[144]

Although the ICJ was a late converter to online proceedings, international criminal courts have been more sympathetic to online proceedings since before the pandemic. One issue of chief importance for international criminal courts is the right to a fair trial which encompasses the right of the accused to be present at trial, as set out, for instance, in Article 63(1) of the ICC Statute. In 2013, the new Rule 134*bis* established that an accused's presence at trial using video technology is admissible following approval by the Trial Chamber on a case-by-case basis.[145] However, virtual presence for the purposes of international criminal law trials may be problematic because it may affect the rights of the accused (Article 67 of the ICC Statute), for example, the right to a public trial, to have adequate time and facilities for the preparation of the defence, and to communicate freely with counsel of the accused's choosing in confidence. The drawbacks of virtual presence were underscored in the literature prior to the pandemic, and they mostly relate to the sense of disconnection and exhaustion or alienation that it may produce.[146] In June 2020, the ICC published a set of guidelines on the holding of court hearings during the Covid-19 pandemic;[147] however, the possibility of remote hearings and the minimum requirements for a virtual hearing were plainly stated by the defence in *Prosecutor* v. *Bosco Ntaganda*.[148] With the

[143] ICJ, 'Press Release No. 2020/16', 25 June 2020, www.icj-cij.org/public/files/press-releases/0/000-20200625-PRE-01-00-EN.pdf (accessed 13 August 2022).

[144] ICJ, 'Press Release No. 2020/18', 30 June 2020, www.icj-cij.org/public/files/case-related/171/171-20200630-PRE-01-00-EN.pdf (accessed 13 August 2022).

[145] ICC, 'Amendments to the Rules of Procedure and Evidence' (27 November 2013) UN Doc. ICC-ASP/12/Res.7.

[146] David Tait et al., 'Towards a distributed courtroom', *Western Sydney University*, 2017, https://courtofthefuture.org/wp-content/uploads/2017/07/170710_TowardsADistributedCourtroom_Compressed.pdf (accessed 13 August 2022), p. 17; Penelope Gibbs, 'Defendants on video – Conveyor belt justice or a revolution in access?', *Transform Justice*, October 2017, www.transformjustice.org.uk/wp-content/uploads/2017/10/Disconnected-Thumbnail-2.pdf (accessed 13 August 2022), p. 33. Contra Linda Mulcahy, 'Virtual poverty? What happens when criminal trials go online?', in Dave Cowan and Ann Mumford (eds.), *Pandemic Legalities: Legal Responses to COVID-19 – Justice and Social Responsibility* (Bristol: Bristol University Press, 2021), p. 41.

[147] ICC, 'Guidelines for the judiciary concerning the holding of court hearings during the Covid-19 pandemic', 23 June 2020, www.icc-cpi.int/itemsDocuments/200623-guidelines-for-court-proceedings-covid-19-eng.pdf (accessed 13 August 2022).

[148] *Situation in the Democratic Republic of the Congo, Prosecutor* v. *Bosco Ntaganda* (Corrigendum to the 'Defence submissions on the scheduled oral hearing', 5 May 2020, ICC-01/04-02/06-2524) ICC-01/04-02/06, at para. 23: '(i) public access to the hearings; (ii) display

technological challenges being addressed,[149] trials were conducted through virtual presence.[150]

A recent publication makes some very interesting recommendations regarding online proceedings before the ICJ.[151] According to this publication, the advantages of virtual hearings may be found in the easy scheduling of the hearing, quick processing of cases, economies of scale for parties, and environmental benefits due to less travel needs. However, there are certain features that seem to be important in inter-State litigation that require physical presence, such as the symbolism of adjudication, the diplomatic component, and the importance of advocacy for guiding the Bench.[152] Nevertheless, there are lessons to be learned for the ICJ. I previously mentioned the advantages of ODR (quick processing of cases or economies of scale, among others). Therefore, ODR mechanisms may become more appealing to States, as they already are an 'efficient, timely and cost-effective'[153] way of resolving disputes. In other words, ODR mechanisms may become a plausible alternative to the ICJ, and this risks side-lining the ICJ given its already (relatively) small caseload. This is also valid for other international courts. It is clear that, to remain competitive, dispute settlement before the ICJ needs to be adapted in order to attract more cases in the near future;[154] otherwise, ODR mechanisms may start to be seen by States as a reasonable alternative to adjudication by the ICJ.

Leaving aside the issue of online international proceedings, and in light of the preceding discussion regarding the ODR experience, the question, in the

of multiple images simultaneously; (iii) real-time French-English interpretation; (iv) real-time transcription in French and English; (v) privileged consultations between the Defence and Mr. Ntaganda; (vi) closed sessions for reference to confidential evidence or information; and (vi) the ability for Mr. Ntaganda to be held in a location where he could participate in both open and closed sessions, and potentially address the Appeals Chamber directly'.

149 *Situation in the Republic of Mali, Prosecutor* v. *Al Hassan* (Registry's observations on methods of work to minimise the impact of Covid-19 and related measures on the conduct of proceedings (ICC-01/12-01/18-776), 20 May 2020) ICC-01/12-01/18.

150 Liz White, 'Towards a new normal: Virtual proceedings under international criminal law in the age of Covid-19', *Columbia Journal of Transnational Law Bulletin Blog*, 22 March 2021, www.jtl.columbia.edu/bulletin-blog/towards-a-new-normal-virtual-proceedings-under-international-criminal-law-in-the-age-of-covid-19 (accessed 13 August 2022).

151 Pinzauti and Webb, 'Litigation before the ICJ', p. 798.

152 Ibid., p. 799.

153 Kun Fan, 'The impact of Covid-19 on the administration of justice', *Kluwer Arbitration Blog*, 10 July 2020, http://arbitrationblog.kluwerarbitration.com/2020/07/10/the-impact-of-covid-19-on-the-administration-of-justice (accessed 13 August 2022).

154 Pinzauti and Webb, 'Litigation before the ICJ', p. 799, also stating that 'no new cases were brought before the Court in 2020, and only one in 2021 at the time of writing'. Finally, two cases were brought to the ICJ in 2021.

words of Ashley Deeks, is the following: 'Is there a possibility of using technology to help adjudicate disputes that involve not just private commercial actors or individuals, but also States?'[155] It is true that the advent of the internet era and new computational capabilities have not led States to make huge changes in, for example, how they conclude treaties or adjudicate international legal disputes. However, the development of new technologies, especially artificial intelligence,[156] will finally affect international law, from both a substantive and a procedural point of view. As for the former, I earlier mentioned the case of digital evidence in international criminal law, but the case of autonomous vehicles in international trade law,[157] or the challenge of facial recognition software in international human rights law, should also be mentioned.[158] From a procedural point of view, it mostly concerns the creation of international law through new treaties and the resolution of international disputes.[159]

Initially applied only to domestic legal systems, machine learning tools are mainly used for document discovery, but also to create drafts of contracts, conduct progressively complex legal search, and forecast case outcomes.[160] Likewise, they may be used by international lawyers in what may be termed as data-driven international law[161] to navigate through international litigation. On the one hand, text-as-data analysis may be valuable in order to extract information about arbitral or judicial tribunals and their decision-making processes. The goal here is to understand how arbitral or judicial tribunals render their decisions, which can help States develop strategies regarding when and how to file a case or forecast the likely outcomes of a particular

[155] Ashley Deeks, 'High-tech international law' (2020) 88 Geo Wash L Rev 574–653 at 631.

[156] Asley Deeks, 'Introduction to the symposium: How will artificial intelligence affect international law?' (2020) 114 AJIL Unbound 138–40.

[157] Ching-Fu Lin, 'Public morals, trade secrets, and the dilemma of regulating automated driving systems', in Shin-yi Peng, Ching-Fu Lin, and Thomas Streinz (eds.), *Artificial Intelligence and International Economic Law: Disruption, Regulation, and Reconfiguration* (Cambridge: Cambridge University Press, 2021), p. 237.

[158] Council of Europe, 'Facial recognition: Strict regulation is needed to prevent human rights violations', *Council of Europe Newsroom*, 28 January 2021, www.coe.int/en/web/portal/-/facial-recognition-strict-regulation-is-needed-to-prevent-human-rights-violations (accessed 13 August 2022).

[159] Deeks, 'High-tech international law', pp. 578–81.

[160] John O. McGinnis and Russell G. Pearce, 'The great disruption: How machine intelligence will transform the role of lawyers in the delivery of legal services' (2014) 82 Fordham L Rev 3041–66 at 3046–55.

[161] Sergio Puig, Joost Pauwelyn, and Wolfgang Alschner, 'The data-driven future of international law', *EJIL: Talk!*, 25 July 2017, www.ejiltalk.org/the-data-driven-future-of-international-law (accessed 13 August 2022).

dispute.[162] This process of text-mining has not been put in motion in international law, with the exception of the trade and investment area,[163] where databases have been created by some scholars,[164] and the case law of the European Court of Human Rights, whose large database has been mined already.[165] This is probably because of the high volume of cases extant in those realms. However, it would be difficult to apply this sort of data analysis to the jurisprudence emanating from the ICJ or the International Tribunal for the Law of the Sea, as their number of cases are rather limited.[166]

As was also seen, ODR systems, private and public, are undergoing a transformation due to machine learning and computational text analysis, giving way to the so-called automated fourth party.[167] The potential use of 'machine arbitrators' – that is, the use of data analytics and machine learning tools in order to achieve automated decisions in arbitration cases – has already been discussed by scholars and practitioners in the field.[168] The same is true for 'machine judges', a subject that is not new,[169] although nowadays its normative acceptance seems to be growing,[170] even if certain scholars state that some human intervention is still needed.[171] At the very least, it can be said

[162] Deeks, 'High-tech international law', p. 624.

[163] Wolfgang Alschner, Joost Pauwelyn, and Sergio Puig, 'The data-driven future of international economic law' (2017) 20 J Int'l Econ L 217–31.

[164] Swiss National Foundation, 'Big data conquers legal analysis', *Science X Network*, 28 September 2017, https://phys.org/news/2017-09-big-conquers-legal-analysis.html (accessed 13 August 2022); Daniel Behn and Malcolm Langford, 'Trumping the environment? An empirical perspective on the legitimacy of investment treaty arbitration' (2017) 18 JWIT 14–61.

[165] Nikolaos Aletras et al., 'Predicting judicial decisions of the European Court of Human Rights: A natural language processing perspective', *PeerJ Computer Science*, 24 October 2016, https://peerj.com/articles/cs-93 (accessed 13 August 2022).

[166] Deeks, 'High-tech international law', pp. 629–30.

[167] See Subsection 16.3.2.1.

[168] Gizem Halis Kasap, 'Can artificial intelligence ("AI") replace human arbitrators? Technological concerns and legal implications' (2021) J Disp Resol 209–54 at 242, using the term 'machine arbitrator'; Lucas Bento, 'International arbitration and artificial intelligence: Time to tango?', *Kluwer Arbitration Blog*, 23 February 2018, http://arbitrationblog.kluwerarbitration.com/2018/02/23/international-arbitration-artificial-intelligence-time-tango (accessed 13 August 2022); José María de la Jara et al., 'Machine arbitrator: Are we ready?' *Kluwer Arbitration Blog*, 4 May 2017, http://arbitrationblog.kluwerarbitration.com/2017/05/04/machine-arbitrator-are-we-ready (accessed 13 August 2022).

[169] See, e.g., Anthony D'Amato, 'Can/should computers replace judges?' (1977) 11 Ga L Rev 1277–301.

[170] Eugene Volokh, 'Chief justice robots' (2019) 68 Duke L J 1135–92.

[171] Tim Wu, 'Will artificial intelligence eat the law? The rise of hybrid social-ordering systems' (2019) 119 Colum L Rev 2001–28 at 2001–5, purporting the use of human–machine hybrids for the time being as the only option to solve the issues of procedural fairness, explainability, and the deciding of hard cases.

that the aforementioned tools will support the work of arbitrators and the parties to extract meaning from the massive amounts of documentation that arbitration cases entail.[172] Alternative decisions will also be created through algorithms that may be checked against arbitrator's own decisions.[173] Moreover, predictive or forecasting justice is another outcome to be derived from the use of such tools, as arbitration or court decisions will be analysed in order to statistically derive probabilities about how the case at hand is going to be solved.[174] Finally, machine arbitration or adjudication entails the use of complete automated decision-making, where artificial intelligence will produce, without any human involvement, the final judgment or decision to the case. This is not without risks, such as bias, the risk of hacking, and the amplification of human mistakes, which in turn will prompt the need to use algorithms in a transparent manner in order to avoid the 'black box' problem.[175] Of course, the debate regarding the use of artificial intelligence and automation resembles the debates already taking place within other areas of international law, such as international humanitarian law, where 'human meaningful control'[176] has been commended as the only way forward for the legal approval of lethal autonomous weapons.[177] To some extent, this is what happens in ODR, like the system used by eBay and other systems commented upon above, where there is human intervention when needed to complete or oversee the final decision of the dispute at hand. Likewise, in the short run, it is probable that pure automated decision-making in inter-State arbitration or adjudication will be avoided in favour of a human-mediated system, at least for difficult or last-instance cases.[178]

[172] Hogan Lovells, 'The future of arbitration: New technologies are making a big impact – And AI robots may take on "human" roles', 21 February 2018, www.hoganlovells.com/publications/the-future-of-arbitration-ai-robots-may-take-on-human-roles (accessed 13 August 2022).

[173] Paul Cohen and Sophie Nappert, 'The march of the robots', *Global Arbitration Review*, 15 February 2017, https://globalarbitrationreview.com/the-march-of-the-robots (accessed 13 August 2022).

[174] Hogan Lovells, 'The future of arbitration'.

[175] Bento, 'International arbitration and AI'.

[176] See, e.g., Article 36, 'Killer robots: UK government policy on fully autonomous weapons', April 2013, www.article36.org/wp-content/uploads/2013/04/Policy_Paper1.pdf (accessed 13 August 2022), p. 1.

[177] See, e.g., Daniele Amoroso, *Autonomous Weapons Systems and International Law: A Study on Human–Machine Interactions in Ethically and Legally Sensitive Domains* (Naples: Edizioni Scientifiche Italiane, 2020). See also Rebecca Crootof, 'A meaningful floor for "meaningful human control"' (2016) 30 Temp Int'l & Comp L J 53–62 at 54, stating that the problem then would be *when* there is meaningful human control.

[178] Wu, 'Will artificial intelligence eat the law?' pp. 2001–5.

16.4 CONCLUSION

This chapter started from the premise that cyberspace poses several challenges to international law, and international dispute settlement more specifically. Together with the need to elucidate what part of international law is applicable in cyberspace, there are two other issues that pose challenges to dispute settlement: jurisdictional issues and the question of attribution.

However, cyberspace and new technologies are already offering new opportunities to the resolution of inter-State disputes. In the first place, digital evidence is opening up new avenues for international criminal courts and international litigation in general, especially through the use of open source and user-generated information. In particular, cyberspace disputes that entail digital evidence collection between States may be brought before the ICJ with no need to change its Rules of Procedure and Evidence. Digital evidence can be produced by parties, unless they are 'part of a publication readily available', which hugely increases the amount of evidence that may be relied upon by parties, including open source information.

Secondly, ODR systems have flourished in the commercial realm as an efficient and inexpensive way to solve disputes among private parties, making use of the possibilities now brought by cyberspace and new technologies. As noted, there are five steps that an ODR system usually undertakes to experience a suitable resolution process: the first two steps (Diagnosis and Negotiation) are handled by software, whereas the latter three (Mediation, Evaluation, and Appeal) are handled by humans. Moreover, this experience is being increasingly developed by public courts all over the world. This situation offers many insights into international dispute settlement. Certainly, international adjudication has already experienced the advantages to be derived from the setting up and expansion of online court proceedings. However, the adoption of the processes and techniques already applied in the ODR field may bring international dispute settlement to a brand-new era full of possibilities, including online arbitration or mediation. Whether States will feel inclined to making use of dispute settlement mechanisms based on the ODR system explained above in the near future is yet to be seen. There is a clear rationale for the ODR system in domestic legal systems. There is a need to provide access to justice in an efficient and cheap way in view of the massive, low-value character of consumer disputes; however, this motivation does not play a pressing role in inter-State dispute settlement. The volume of case law of the ICJ is relatively low. Having said that, States will probably take advantage of text-as-data and machine learning tools to improve their expectations from dispute settlement, including outcome prediction or forecasting. However, it is difficult to envisage complete reliance on automated decision-making, with no human involvement whatsoever in dispute settlement, as the risks associated with bias and hacking are very high, at least as of today.

17

International Dispute Settlement

A Bright or Depressing Future?

SIR MICHAEL WOOD

17.1 INTRODUCTION

I begin by paying tribute to John Merrills. Beyond Sheffield, he is perhaps best known among international lawyers for his book *International Dispute Settlement*, which has been regularly updated since it first appeared in 1984[1] and which has long been regarded as a leading general introduction to the field.[2] It is a first port of call for anyone seeking enlightenment on general questions of international dispute settlement. Like all of Merrills' writings, this work is clear, incisive, and unpretentious. He was not one to introduce novel constructions of little interest to anyone but the writer, or to mystify readers with his own secret language.[3]

1 John G. Merrills, *International Dispute Settlement*, 6th ed. (Cambridge: Cambridge University Press, 2017). See also John G. Merrills, 'The means of dispute settlement', in Malcom D. Evans (ed.), *International Law*, 5th ed. (Oxford: Oxford University Press, 2018), pp. 548–72.

2 Another up-to-date introduction is Yoshifumi Tanaka, *The Peaceful Settlement of International Disputes* (Cambridge: Cambridge University Press, 2018). Detailed entries on various aspects of international dispute settlement may be found in the *Max Planck Encyclopedias of Public International Law*, https://opil.ouplaw.com/home/mpil (accessed 31 July 2022). See also Rosalyn Higgins et al., *Oppenheim's International Law: The United Nations* (Oxford: Oxford University Press, 2017), pp. 1093–134. The relevant part of Volume 2 of *Oppenheim's International Law*, last published in 1951, is under revision. The *Handbook on the Peaceful Settlement of Disputes between States* was published thirty years ago (UN, OLA/COD/2394 (New York: UN, 1992)). A proposal to request the Secretariat to update the *Handbook* continues to be considered within the Special Committee on the Charter of the United Nations; it would be good if the proposal could be adopted at an early date.

3 In his keynote address at the 2018 European Society of International Law Annual Conference, which was also the 2018 Melland Schill lecture, Professor Jan Klabbers suggested that 'international law, in the academy, is no longer about what states do, but has become about what international lawyers do. We have lost touch with legal practice, and the discipline has become transfixed by methodological debates'. He continued: 'Instead of the fragmentation of international law being a concern, we should be worried about the fragmentation of

The theme of this volume, like that of the conference on which it is based, is the changing character of international dispute settlement.[4] How far the character of international dispute settlement has changed – or is changing – is, however, an open question. Indeed, it seems easier to see continuity. The fundamentals of inter-State disputes have changed little since 1920. Consent to third-party dispute settlement remains at the heart of the system, as does a widespread reluctance by sovereign States to give that consent, across the board, in advance of disputes arising. The Optional Clause remains unchanged after a hundred years, as does States' unwillingness to accept it or to do so without extensive reservations.

That said, there have been important developments, if not in fundamental respects. If we compare the first and latest editions of Merrills' book on international dispute settlement, we can immediately see the great expansion and changes over the years, changes that continue apace.[5] Even since the appearance of the sixth edition in 2017, there have been quite a few developments – for good or ill.[6]

The title selected for this essay – 'International dispute settlement: A bright or depressing future?' – is rather unsubtle. I doubt whether John Merrills would have set it as an exam question. Anyway, the answer, of course, is that the future of international dispute settlement is both bright and depressing, depending largely on expectations and focus. A measure of scepticism may also attach to what seems to be a widely held view that we live in challenging times for international law. It is common these days to refer to a re-emergence of nationalism (and 'populism') and to a retreat from multilateralism and international institutions. As may happen, however, such references are often

international lawyers.' Jan Klabbers, 'On epistemic universalism and the melancholy of international law' (2018) 29 EJIL 1057–69 at 1062. See also Michael Wood, 'International law in practice', in *Courses of the Summer School on Public International Law* (Moscow: International and Comparative Law Research Center, 2022), pp. 27–45 (dealing with 'Practice and theory – The place of teachings').

4 See also the Introduction.

5 The six editions appeared at regular intervals between 1984 and 2017. The 1984 edition was published by Sweet & Maxwell in their 'Modern Legal Studies' series. The volume was eminently concise and clear, comprising 187 pages of text, in a conveniently small (*duodecimo*) format. An extract from the first edition is reproduced in Jean-Pierre Gauci and Jill Barrett (eds.), *Anthology of British Contributions to International Law, 1915–2015* (Boston: Brill, 2020), pp. 1773–94. In his introductory comment, Mubarak Waseem notes that 'the book is set apart from others by its practical examples . . . the monograph provides useful insights and starting points for students and practitioners in the area. It is now a common set text for specialised courses on public international dispute settlement.'

6 A seventh edition, with Eric De Brabandere as author and entitled *Merrills' International Dispute Settlement*, was published in 2022.

exaggerated and reflect an unrealistic view of what can be expected of the law. The same is true of views on the broader crisis in international relations that are put forward, a crisis that is sometimes presented as more dramatic than it is. In any event, a crisis in international relations is not the same as a crisis in international law.

The focus of what follows is on settlement through international courts and tribunals, though, of course, these are by no means the only or the most common way of settling international disputes: negotiation has pride of place. And the focus is on inter-State dispute settlement: I shall not deal with disputes involving private parties, including investment disputes.[7] I do not deal with disputes involving international organisations (including such disputes of a private law nature), though that is an interesting topic and one the International Law Commission (ILC) has recently taken up.[8] Nor do I deal with human rights procedures, though, as we increasingly see, these may also take the form of inter-State proceedings in Strasbourg, Geneva, or The Hague.[9] Of course, human rights procedures and investment disputes are, in numerical terms, by far the most common international court proceedings and, in some respects, the most controversial. Any overall stocktaking should certainly take them into account, but this contribution is not the occasion.

17.2 CHANGE AND CHALLENGE

Perhaps the most obvious change in inter-State dispute settlement is its great expansion. In the decade leading up to 1984, when John Merrills' book first appeared, the International Court of Justice (ICJ) decided just four cases on the merits and delivered three advisory opinions.[10] In 1984, the International Tribunal for the Law of the Sea (ITLOS) did not exist – the first elections were

7 Looking beyond inter-State courts, one could speak of the malaise with investor–State disputes settlement, and with the International Criminal Court. See, in general, the chapters by Tarcisio Gazzini and Alessandra Pietrobon (Chapter 2), Eric De Brabandere (Chapter 9), James Mehigan (Chapter 12), and Aris Georgopoulos and Petros Mavroidis (Chapter 10) in this volume.

8 The Commission included the topic in its programme of work in 2022. For the syllabus for the topic, see UNGA, 'Report of the International Law Commission on the work of its sixty-eighth session (2 May–10 June and 4 July–12 August 2016)' (2016) UN Doc. A/71/10, 'Annex A: The settlement of international disputes to which international organizations are parties; see also the 2023 ILC Annual Report'. There has also been a long-standing item on the agenda of the Council of Europe's Committee of Legal Advisers on Public International Law (CAHDI) on 'Settlement of disputes of a private character to which an international organisation is a party', but rather little has been made public about the discussions.

9 See Chapter 7 by Malcolm Evans in this volume.

10 See Chapter 4 by Massimo Lando in this volume.

held in 1996; there had been no UN Convention on the Law of the Sea (UNCLOS) Annex VII arbitral tribunals (the first dates from 1999);[11] there was no World Trade Organization (WTO) Dispute Settlement Understanding (which entered into force in 1995);[12] and the expansion of regional courts had yet to take place.

The contrast with today is dramatic. The increase in the number of international courts and tribunals, both worldwide and regional,[13] which occurred mainly in the 1990s and was sometimes referred to as 'proliferation',[14] has been remarkable, though it now seems to have reached a plateau. In recent years, those who seek to promote new permanent international courts and tribunals (in such fields as the environment, investment protection, human rights, and even constitutional law) have met with little success. Together with the greatly enhanced activity of international courts and tribunals, including as a result of the entry into force of new bases of jurisdiction such as UNCLOS, this increase has led to a wider range of judges, arbitrators, and counsel, with more diversity. It now seems that the world does not need new international courts (though it may need greater and better use of existing ones).

Together with expansion came challenges. Among these, seven may merit particular mention. *First*, one of the main problems with sectoral courts is that they tend to lead to settlement procedures that artificially deal with disputes from one particular aspect rather than in the round. A similar phenomenon is seen in cases where jurisdiction is exclusively founded on one specific treaty, such as those based on the Genocide Convention, the International Convention on the Elimination of All Forms of Racial Discrimination,[15] or even sometimes on UNCLOS.[16]

Second, there has been a significant expansion of the ICJ's caseload compared with earlier decades, but there are other courts and tribunals that have

[11] See Chapter 5 by Richard Collins in this volume.

[12] See Chapter 10 by Aris Georgopoulos and Petros Mavroidis in this volume.

[13] For a recent account of the African courts, see James Thuo Gathii (ed.), *The Performance of Africa's International Courts: Using Litigation for Political, Legal, and Social Change* (Oxford: Oxford University Press, 2020).

[14] See John G. Merrills, 'The mosaic of international dispute settlement procedures: Complementary or contradictory?' (2007) 54 NILR 361–93 at 362. Many questioned whether such 'proliferation' is a good thing; I agree with those who say that it is. 'Fragmentation' of the law is no longer considered a threat, if it ever was one. See also Mads Andenas and Eirik Bjorge (eds.), *A Farewell to Fragmentation: Reassertion and Convergence in International Law* (Cambridge: Cambridge University Press, 2015).

[15] See Chapter 7 by Malcolm Evans in this volume.

[16] See Chapter 5 by Richard Collins in this volume.

had no work at all or remain greatly underused. The Organisation for Security and Cooperation in Europe (OSCE) Court of Arbitration and Conciliation, almost thirty years after its establishment, has yet to hear a case.[17] No less than six attempts by Arab States to establish regional judicial bodies have failed.[18] ITLOS has decided fewer cases than might have been expected: in the twenty-five years since it was established, as of August 2023 it has only issued seven judgments on the merits in inter-State cases, though some of its special jurisdictions have proved useful (prompt release of vessels and crews;[19] provisional measure pending the establishment of Annex VII arbitral tribunals;[20] and advisory opinions of the Seabed Disputes Chamber at the request of the Council or Assembly of the International Seabed Authority or, according to a controversial decision, of the full ITLOS at the request of other bodies[21]).

Third, the WTO appellate body is currently unable to review appeals given the ongoing inability to fill vacancies in its membership.[22] This crisis is the result of US disillusionment, which came to a head during the Trump administration, though it seems that his successor too will not allow the appellate body to function until a US reform agenda is satisfied.[23]

[17] Convention on Conciliation and Arbitration within the Conference on Security and Co-operation in Europe, Stockholm, 15 December 1992, in force 5 December 1994, 1842 UNTS 151. Among the extensive literature on this body, see Christian Tomuschat, Riccardo Pisillo Mazzeschi, and Daniel Thürer (eds.), *Conciliation in International Law: The OSCE Court of Conciliation and Arbitration* (Leiden: Brill/Nijhoff, 2017); Christian Tomuschat and Marcelo G. Kohen, *Flexibility in International Dispute Settlement: Conciliation Revisited* (Leiden: Brill/Nijhoff, 2020).

[18] Cesare P. R. Romano, 'Mirage in the desert: Regional judicialization in the Arab world', in Ignacio de la Rasilla and Jorge E. Viñuales (eds.), *Experiments in International Adjudication: Historical Accounts* (Cambridge: Cambridge University Press, 2019), pp. 169–90.

[19] United Nations Convention on the Law of the Sea, Montego Bay, 10 December 1982, in force 16 November 1994, 1833 UNTS 397, Art 292. Between 1997 and 2007, the International Tribunal for the Law of the Sea heard a series of eight prompt release cases, but there have been none since.

[20] Under Art 290(5), the ITLOS has a special jurisdiction to prescribe binding provisional measures pending the constitution and functioning of an Annex VII arbitral tribunal. Seeking provisional measures seems to be increasingly popular in inter-State cases, and between 1999 and 2019 there has been a steady stream of cases under Art 290(5).

[21] The advisory jurisdiction of the ITLOS plenary (as opposed to its Seabed Disputes Chamber) was contested, and its scope remains obscure: see note 37.

[22] See Chapter 10 by Aris Georgopoulos and Petros Mavroidis in this volume.

[23] At the monthly WTO dispute settlement body meeting on 22 February 2021, in response to a slate of proposed appellate body appointments, the US said it was 'not in a position' to support the decision, adding: 'The United States continues to have systemic concerns with the appellate body. As members know, the United States has raised and explained its systemic concerns for more than 16 years and across multiple US administrations.' Eleanor Wagg, 'Slim changes for the WTO appellate body despite US return to multilateralism', *Global Trade*

Fourth, there seems to be a resurgence of States deciding not to appear in proceedings before international courts and tribunals, whether at a particular stage or at all. These have included, over the last few years, three permanent members of the Security Council (China,[24] Russia,[25] the US[26]), as well as Venezuela[27] and Kenya.[28] Of course, however regrettable it may be,[29] it is their right not to appear, though they do so at their own risk as they are legally bound by the result, whether they appear or not. Similarly, States fail to appoint or agree on arbitrators, and otherwise treat courts with discourtesy, for example, by failing to meet deadlines without seeking an extension in good time. Even more serious is when States unilaterally reject decisions by which they have agreed to be bound.[30] Examples include Croatia's refusal to accept the arbitral award in its case with Slovenia (albeit under exceptional

Review, 3 March 2021, www.gtreview.com/news/americas/slim-chances-for-the-wto-appellate-body-despite-the-us-return-to-multilateralism (accessed 31 July 2022).

24 *The South China Sea Arbitration (The Republic of Philippines* v. *The People's Republic of China)* PCA Case No. 2013-19. China's position of non-acceptance of and non-participation in the arbitration was reaffirmed by the Chinese Ministry of Foreign Affairs in its 7 December 2014 'Position paper of the Government of the People's Republic of China on the matter of jurisdiction in the South China Sea arbitration initiated by the Republic of the Philippines' and later in two letters sent to the members of the Tribunal from the Chinese Ambassador to the Netherlands.

25 *The Arctic Sunrise Arbitration (Netherlands* v. *Russia)* PCA Case No. 2014-02; *Dispute Concerning the Detention of Ukrainian Naval Vessels and Servicemen (Ukraine* v. *the Russian Federation)* PCA Case No. 2019-28; Russia did not participate in the oral proceeding of March 2022 concerning the provisional measures requested from the ICJ in the case *Allegations of Genocide under the Convention on the Prevention and Punishment of the Crime of Genocide (Ukraine* v. *Russian Federation)*, although it did communicate to the Court a document setting out its 'position regarding the lack of competence of the Court in this case'.

26 *Relocation of the United States Embassy to Jerusalem (Palestine* v. *United States of America)* (Order of 15 November 2018) [2018] ICJ Rep. 708. By a letter dated 14 November 2019, the US confirmed its decision not to participate in the written proceedings, but transmitted a memorandum 'to assist the Court in identifying certain fundamental issues and associated information going to jurisdiction and admissibility that may not otherwise be readily apparent': *Yearbook of the International Court of Justice 2019–2020*, pp. 32–33.

27 *Arbitral Award of 3 October 1899 (Guyana* v. *Venezuela)* (Jurisdiction of the Court, Judgment) [2020] ICJ Rep. 455. Venezuela submitted to the Court a document entitled 'Memorandum of the Bolivarian Republic of Venezuela on the application filed before the International Court of Justice by the Cooperative Republic of Guyana on March 29th, 2018'.

28 *Maritime Delimitation in the Indian Ocean (Somalia* v. *Kenya)* [2021] ICJ Rep 206.

29 Ibid., para. 29.

30 Para. 11 of the UNGA, 'Manila declaration on the peaceful settlement of international disputes' (15 November 1982) UN Doc. A/RES/37/10, provides that 'States shall in accordance with international law implement in good faith all the provisions of agreements concluded by them for the settlement of their disputes'.

circumstances); China in the *South China Sea* case; and Kenya in the *Maritime Delimitation* case with Somalia.

Fifth, withdrawals from or reduced commitment to international dispute settlement also seem to be on the increase. Acceptance of the Optional Clause remains low despite regular but largely unsuccessful efforts to promote acceptances.[31] In fact, acceptance is significantly lower as a proportion of States than it was at the time of the Permanent Court of International Justice (PCIJ). Having said that, it is not obvious that the acceptance of the Optional Clause should be seen as the barometer of the acceptance by States of the jurisdiction of international courts and tribunals.

Sixth, despite the statutory provisions, States do not always have regard to the quality of those they select as candidates and elect to international courts and tribunals. It seems difficult to develop ways of improving election processes at the international level,[32] though some efforts have been made to improve national procedures in an effort to enhance the quality of candidates.[33] And the quality of reasoning in some judgments and advisory opinions has been the object of robust criticism, including from within the courts in separate and dissenting opinions.[34] This may be a serious obstacle to building and retaining confidence in the institutions concerned. (There is incidentally nothing wrong with criticising a court, preferably in a reasoned and respectful way, despite what the International Criminal Court (ICC) seemed to have thought in an inappropriate media effort following its Appeals Chamber's judgment on Jordan's appeal in the *Al-Bashir* case.[35])

[31] For a recent attempt, see 'The works of the International Round Table on *Promoting the Jurisdiction of the International Court of Justice (Bucharest, VTC, 24 June 2021)*' (2021) 25 Rom J Int'l L; Declaration on promoting the jurisdiction of the International Court of Justice, Launch Event, New York, 3 November 2021.

[32] Voting deals, even across elections, have become ubiquitous within bodies such as the UN General Assembly.

[33] Michael Wood, 'The selection of candidates for international judicial office: Recent practice', in Tafsir Malick Ndiaye and Rüdiger Wolfrum (eds.), *Law of the Sea, Environmental Law and Settlement of Disputes: Liber Amicorum Judge Thomas A. Mensah* (Leiden: Brill, 2007), pp. 357–68.

[34] See, e.g., and whatever one may think of the result, the strong criticisms of Delimitation of the maritime boundary in the Indian Ocean (Mauritius/Maldives), Preliminary Objections, Judgment, ITLOS Reports 2020–2021, p. 17.

[35] See the interventions by the spokesperson of the International Criminal Court attacking academic debate on the judgment and separate joint opinion in *The Prosecutor* v. *Omar Hassan Ahmad Al-Bashir* (Judgment in the *Jordan Referral re Al-Bashir* of 6 May 2019) ICC-02/05-01/09-397, for example, the 'Q & A Regarding Appeals Chamber's 6 May 2019 Judgment in the Jordan Referral Re Al-Bashir Appeal'.

Finally, there are some very real problems connected with the practice and procedure of advisory opinions before the ICJ.[36] And there are critical uncertainties concerning the scope of the contested advisory jurisdiction that was found to exist by the plenary of the ITLOS in its 2015 *Sub-regional Fisheries Commission* advisory opinion.[37] Recent requests for advisory opinions highlight the importance of such issues.[38] In the case of the ICJ, there are problems within the UN General Assembly both when it makes a request and receives the opinion[39] and when the request comes before the Court itself.[40] These include the potential for the abuse of the advisory procedure within the UN General Assembly, where a simple majority can ask almost any question, however one-sided; the possible circumvention of the crucial requirement of consent to jurisdiction (and the apparent reluctance or inability of the Court to uphold this principle);[41] and the random presentation of arguments (usually in alphabetical order), with the consequent inability of States to respond adequately or at all to what others have said. There is no sign

[36] See Chapter 4 by Massimo Lando in this volume.

[37] *Request for Advisory Opinion Submitted by the Sub-regional Fisheries Commission* (Advisory Opinion of 2 April 2015) ITLOS Reports 2015, p. 4. On the controversy surrounding the advisory jurisdiction of the ITLOS plenary (as opposed to its Seabed Disputes Chamber) and the uncertainties it gives rise to, see Tom Ruys and Anemoon Soete, '"Creeping" advisory jurisdiction of international courts and tribunals? The case of the International Tribunal for the Law of the Sea' (2016) 29 LJIL 155–76; Massimo Lando, 'The advisory jurisdiction of the International Tribunal for the Law of the Sea: Comments on the *Request for an Advisory Opinion Submitted by the Sub-regional Fisheries Commission*' (2016) 29 LJIL 441–61; Michael Wood, 'Understanding the advisory jurisdiction of the International Tribunal for the Law of the Sea', in *The Contribution of the International Tribunal for the Law of the Sea to the Rule of Law: 1996–2016* (Leiden: Brill, 2018), pp. 213–20.

[38] See ITLOS, *Request for an Advisory Opinion submitted by the Commission of Small Island States on Climate Change and International Law*, 16 December 2022; ICJ, *Obligations of States in respect of Climate Change*, Request for an advisory opinion, 12 April 2023.

[39] This is nothing new. See, for example, R. Higgins, 'A Comment on the Current Health of Advisory Opinions', in V. Lowe, M. Fitzmaurice (eds.), *Fifty years of the International Court of Justice: Essays in honour of Sir Robert Jennings* (Cambridge: Cambridge University Press, 1996) 567.

[40] Franklin D. Berman, 'The uses and abuses of advisory opinions', in Nisuke Ando, Edward McWhinney, and Rüdiger Wolfrum (eds.), *Liber Amicorum Judge Shiguru Oda* (Leiden: Brill, 2002), pp. 809–28; Michael Wood, 'Advisory jurisdiction: Lessons from recent practice', in Holger P. Hestermeyer et al. (eds.), *Coexistence, Cooperation and Solidarity: Liber Amicorum Rüdiger Wolfrum* (Leiden: Brill, 2012), pp. 1833–49. See also Chapter 11 by Nigel White in this volume.

[41] *Legal Consequences of the Separation of the Chagos Archipelago from Mauritius in 1965* (Advisory Opinion) [2019] ICJ Rep. 95 at pp. 261–66 (Dissenting Opinion of Judge Donoghue).

of these serious defects being remedied, for example, by a more responsible attitude towards requests for advisory opinions, including their drafting (for instance, to avoid requests that turn on what are in effect bilateral disputes), but unless these matters are addressed, they risk casting a shadow on the reputation of international courts and tribunals more generally.

Are we seeing trends or not? Are these short-term matters that will soon pass, or are they symptomatic of a longer-term disaffection? That is difficult to say. Some may indeed be short-term, such as the current fashion for non-participation; others, such as the deficiencies in the advisory process, seem more entrenched. On the whole, it is perhaps more reasonable to see such matters as being like a pendulum; they come and they go, but in the longer term, progress is made and is, at least in some respects, irreversible.

The various challenges just mentioned mostly have political origins, and it is not exclusively a matter for lawyers to seek to correct them. At the same time, it is perhaps worth reaffirming two basic propositions of the international dispute settlement system, already alluded to, which international courts and tribunals forget at their peril: that jurisdiction depends upon consent, and that the task of an international court is, in principle, no more than to settle the dispute before it.

17.3 THE JURISDICTION OF AN INTERNATIONAL COURT DEPENDS UPON CONSENT

The principle of consent to jurisdiction played an important role in the December 2020 ICJ judgment on jurisdiction in the *Arbitral Award of 3 October 1899 (Guyana* v. *Venezuela)* case.[42] The case itself illustrates the great variety of possible dispute settlement procedures in international law. It also shows how events of the past may play their part in contemporary international law disputes. The case is about the validity of an arbitral award given some 120 years ago and the interpretation of a treaty (the Geneva Agreement) which itself was negotiated in 1966 to resolve the ancient controversy, that is, well over forty years before the case was instituted before the ICJ. This is a reminder that an interest in history can be helpful to international lawyers.[43]

[42] *Arbitral Award of 3 October 1899 (Guyana* v. *Venezuela)* (Jurisdiction of the Court, Judgment) [2020] ICJ Rep. 455.

[43] For the suggestion that 'history – the history of international relations – is the most important beacon for any judge who seeks to chart the difficult shoals of customary international law', see José A. Cabranes, 'Customary international law: What it is and what it is not' (2011) 22 Duke J Comp & Int'l L 143–52 at 152.

The judgment of 18 December 2020 turned on the interpretation of Article IV, paragraph 2 of the Geneva Agreement of 1966, an unusual provision that provoked an interesting debate within the Court.[44] It turned on the question whether, by entering into the Geneva Agreement, the parties had conferred jurisdiction upon the Court such that it could be seized by unilateral application. The majority held that this was so. However, a minority, comprising four powerful dissents from Judges Abraham, Bennouna, Gaja, and Gevorgian, interpreted the provision differently. Judge Gaja's declaration sought to distinguish between a treaty obligation to resort to the ICJ and consent to the institution of proceedings, concluding that Venezuela and Guyana were

> under an obligation to resort to judicial settlement and therefore to confer jurisdiction on the Court. Pending consent to that effect, the Court does not yet have jurisdiction on the dispute.[45]

Among other points of interest in *Guyana* v. *Venezuela* are the Court's careful handling of a case where one of the parties declines to take part and how non-participating States do, in fact, participate. Similar care was taken under what, to an outsider, seemed very difficult circumstances for the Court in the *Somalia* v. *Kenya* case.[46]

The principle that the jurisdiction of an international court or tribunal over States derives from their consent was and remains central to the international legal system (though consent may be given in any form and in advance of a dispute arising). The need for consent will not disappear and, at the same time, it is unrealistic to expect States in the foreseeable future to give consent

[44] Art IV, para. 2 of the Agreement to Resolve the Controversy over the Frontier between Venezuela and British Guiana, Geneva, 17 February 1966, in force 17 February 1966 (561 UNTS 322) (Geneva Agreement), is worth quoting in full: 'If, within three months of receiving the final report, the Government of Guyana and the Government of Venezuela should not have reached agreement regarding the choice of one of the means of settlement provided in Article 33 of the Charter of the United Nations, they shall refer the decision as to the means of settlement to an appropriate international organ upon which they both agree or, failing agreement on this point, to the Secretary-General of the United Nations. If the means so chosen do not lead to a solution of the controversy, the said organ or, as the case may be, the Secretary-General of the United Nations shall choose another of the means stipulated in Article 33 of the Charter of the United Nations, and so on until the controversy has been resolved or until all the means of peaceful settlement there contemplated have been exhausted.'

[45] *Guyana* v. *Venezuela* (Jurisdiction of the Court), p. 510, para. 9.

[46] *Maritime Delimitation in the Indian Ocean (Somalia* v. *Kenya)* [2021] ICJ Rep 206.

in advance and across the board, as efforts in 1920, 1945, and subsequently have shown.[47] It is incumbent on international courts and tribunals to uphold the principle, and to do so with a degree of rigour. Nothing is more likely to undermine the confidence of States in international courts, and to undermine the legitimacy that has built up over the years, than attempts to find jurisdiction when consent has not actually been given. International courts and tribunals cannot simply rely on the *compétence de la compétence* (kompetenz-kompetenz) principle; States will feel at liberty to reject decisions which they consider to have been given in excess of jurisdiction, whatever the legal position. It is in the long-term interest of progress in international dispute settlement that courts should err on the side of caution in matters of jurisdiction.

17.4 THE TASK OF AN INTERNATIONAL COURT IS TO DECIDE THE DISPUTE SUBMITTED TO IT

It is often suggested that international courts and tribunals have multiple functions. Yet, their 'singular task' in contentious proceedings is to decide the dispute before them.[48] Their task is not to engage in making new law, however much some might wish them to do so. Even in advisory proceedings, their task is to expound the existing law.

Do international courts nonetheless have a role in the 'development' of international law? This is an old question, to which different answers can be given, depending on what is meant by 'development'.[49] At the end of the day, most commentators agree that all courts worthy of the name are bound to apply the law as they find it, not as they or others would like it to be. As the ICJ itself said in the *Namibia* opinion, it 'acts only on the basis of the law … A court functioning as a court of law can act in no other way.'[50] With regard to

[47] See note 31.

[48] David D. Caron, 'Fifth Annual Charles N. Brower Lecture on International Dispute Resolution: The multiple functions of international courts and the singular task of the adjudicator' (2017) 111 ProcASIL 231–40.

[49] See, e.g., the seminal book by Hersch Lauterpacht, *The Development of International law by the International Court* (London: Stevens & Sons, 1958), being a revised edition of Hersch Lauterpacht, *The Development of International Law by the Permanent Court of International Justice* (London: Longmans, Green, 1934); and Christian J. Tams and James Sloan (eds.), *The Development of International Law by the International Court of Justice* (Oxford: Oxford University Press, 2013).

[50] *Legal Consequences for States of the Continued Presence of South Africa in Namibia (South West Africa) Notwithstanding Security Council Resolution 276 (1970)* (Advisory Opinion) [1971] ICJ Rep. 16 at p. 23, para. 29. See also *South West Africa, Second Phase* (Judgment) [1966] ICJ Rep. 6 at p. 34, para. 49 ('[The Court] is a court of law, and can take account of moral principles only in so far as these are given a sufficient expression in legal form. Law

treaties, for example, the Court has stressed that 'it is the duty of the Court to interpret the [Peace] Treaties, not to revise them'.[51]

That is the principle, and it is important that international courts and tribunals be seen to uphold it if States are to accept the judgments addressed to them. Yet, the reality may be somewhat different: courts and tribunals do not always strictly apply the law; sometimes they do develop it, or even – so it may seem to the litigants – make it up. The ninth edition of *Oppenheim* put it quite subtly: 'Judges do not in principle make law but apply existing law.'[52] Waldock, as so often the voice of common sense and reason, explained that the ICJ performed

> the classic functions of a court in determining and clarifying what it conceived to be the existing law. In doing so, however, it threw fresh light on the considerations and the principles on which the law was based in a manner to suggest the path for future development.[53]

In deciding cases, international courts inevitably clarify the law. Together with the ILC, the ICJ has also done much to promote clarity of concepts. Terms like 'countermeasures' and 'circumstance precluding wrongfulness' have become part of our common lexicon as a result of the work of the ICJ and the ILC. Beyond this, the ICJ, like the ILC, has also played an important role in achieving a measure of agreement on the basic structure, or architecture, of international law. This includes the ICJ's significant contribution, alongside

exists, it is said, to serve a social need; but precisely for that reason it can do so only through and within the limits of its own discipline. Otherwise, it is not a legal service that would be rendered'); *Fisheries Jurisdiction Case (United Kingdom* v. *Iceland)* (Merits, Judgment) [1974] ICJ Rep. 3 at pp. 23–24, para. 53 ('The Court, as a court of law, cannot render judgment *sub specie legis ferendae*, or anticipate the law before the legislator has laid it down'); *Legality of the Threat or Use of Nuclear Weapons* (Advisory Opinion) [1996] ICJ Rep. 226 at p. 237, para. 18 ('[The Court] states the existing law and does not legislate. This is so even if, in stating and applying the law, the Court necessarily has to specify its scope and sometimes note its general trend'). As Pellet and Müller's commentary on Art 38 suggests, it may be 'inferred from the – sometimes passionate – discussions among the members [of the Advisory Committee of Jurists which drafted the PCIJ Statute] that the intention behind the final wording of [Article 38] was that jurisprudence ... [was] supposed to elucidate what the rules to be applied by the Court were, not to create them': Alain Pellet and Daniel Müller, 'Article 38', in Andreas Zimmermann et al. (eds.), *The Statute of the International Court of Justice: A Commentary*, 3rd ed. (Oxford: Oxford University Press, 2019), MN 305.

51 *Interpretation of Peace Treaties (Second Phase)* (Advisory Opinion) [1950] ICJ Rep. 221 at p. 229.

52 Robert Y. Jennings and Arthur Watts (eds.), *Oppenheim's International Law*, 9th ed. (Harlow: Longman, 1992), p. 41.

53 Humphrey Waldock, 'The International Court of Justice as seen from the bar and bench' (1983) 54 BYBIL 1–5 at 4.

the ILC, to what we now think of as 'secondary' rules of law (especially international responsibility), in relation to both States and international organisations.[54]

Beyond the determination of substantive rules, international courts and tribunals – chief among them the ICJ – have also made important contributions to the sources and methods of international law.[55] The law of treaties has been much refined by the PCIJ and the ICJ (both before and after the conclusion of the 1969 Vienna Convention), which provided guidance on such questions as what may be regarded as a treaty, the nature and impact of reservations to treaties, and how treaties are to be interpreted. A particular contribution of the Court has been in determining how far rules set forth in the Vienna Convention may be considered as rules of customary international law. This is important in practice: not only is the 1969 Vienna Convention not retroactive,[56] it still (as of August 2023) has only 116 State parties. And the Court has also shed light on the nature and legal significance of unilateral acts of States, again both inspiring and being inspired by the ILC's work.

The Court's case law has also provided invaluable guidance on the methodology for identifying the rules of customary international law. From the *Asylum* and *Right of Passage* cases, through *North Sea Continental Shelf* and *Nicaragua* v. *United States* to *Jurisdictional Immunities of the State* and the *Chagos* advisory opinion, the Court has given us important signposts pointing to how the existence or otherwise of 'a general practice accepted as law' may be established. This case law was heavily relied on by the ILC in its work on the identification of customary international law.[57]

The ICJ has yet to say much, at least not explicitly, about the third source of international law listed in its Statute: 'The general principles of law recognized by civilized nations.' The ILC, on the other hand, is working on this

54 See, generally, O. Sender, *A Partnership for Purpose: International Law-Making by the International Court of Justice and International Law Commission* (Cambridge: Cambridge University Press, forthcoming).

55 Michael Wood, 'Method and style in international law, and the International Court of Justice's contribution', in Patricia Galvão Teles and Manuel de Almeida Ribeiro (eds.), *Case-Law and the Development of International Law: Contributions by International Courts and Tribunals* (Leiden: Brill, 2021), pp. 14–28.

56 Vienna Convention on the Law of Treaties, Vienna, 23 May 1969, in force 27 January 1980, 1155 UNTS 331; (1969) 8 ILM 679, Art 4.

57 UNGA, 'Report of the International Law Commission on the work of its seventieth session (30 April–1 June and 2 July–10 August 2018)' (2018) UN Doc. A/73/10, pp. 122–56. In resolution 73/203 of 20 December 2018, the UN General Assembly took note of the conclusions (the text of which was annexed to the resolution), brought them to the attention of States and all who may be called upon to identify the rules of customary international law, and encouraged their widest possible dissemination: UN Doc. A/RES/73/203.

topic and has already introduced a measure of clarity, including on the importance of distinguishing between general principles of law and customary international law.[58] The ILC's Special Rapporteur of Ecuador, Marcelo Vásquez-Bermúdez, issued reports in 2019, 2020, and 2022.[59] And in 2023, the ILC adopted a set of 11 draft conclusions on first reading.[60]

17.5 INTERNATIONAL COURTS AND TRIBUNALS AS A SUBSIDIARY MEANS FOR DECIDING LEGAL DISPUTES

I do not here consider the decisions of courts and tribunals as a 'subsidiary means' (subsidiary but, nevertheless, important) for the determination of rules of international law within the meaning of Article 38.1(d) of the ICJ Statute.[61] Instead, I refer to the question whether international courts and tribunals are a subsidiary means for deciding legal disputes.[62]

It is all too easy for international lawyers to think that international courts and tribunals are some kind of panacea for the ills of the world. Yet, as we all know, and as Merrills' writings remind us, judicial settlement and arbitration are but two of the peaceful means of dispute settlement enumerated in Article 33 of the UN Charter. First among such means is negotiation. So, in a sense (and although no hierarchy is stipulated), the role of courts in settling disputes is a subsidiary one. As the PCIJ noted in the *Free Zones* case, 'the judicial settlement of international disputes ... is simply an alternative to the direct and friendly settlement of such disputes between the Parties'.[63] That was said in the year 1929. It remains true today.

[58] Michael Wood, 'Customary international law and the general principles of law recognized by civilized nations' (2019) 21 Int C L Rev 307–24.

[59] UNGA, 'First report on general principles of law by Marcelo Vásquez-Bermúdez, Special Rapporteur' (5 April 2019) UN Doc. A.CN.4/732; UNGA, 'Second report on general principles of law by Marcelo Vásquez-Bermúdez, Special Rapporteur' (9 April 2020) UN Doc. A/CN.4/741; UNGA, 'Third report on general principles of law by Marcelo Vásquez-Bermúdez, Special Rapporteur' (18 April 2022) UN Doc. A/CN.4/753. See also the Secretariat's 2020 memorandum: UNGA, 'General principles of law: Memorandum by the Secretariat' (12 May 2020) UN Doc. A/CN.4/742.

[60] UNGA, 'Report of the International Law Commission on the work of its seventy-fourth session (24 April-2 June and 3 July-4 August 2023)' UN Doc. A/78/10, ch. VI.

[61] See Conclusion 13 with commentary of the ILC's 2018 conclusions on the identification of customary international law: see UNGA, 'Report of the ILC' (2018), pp. 149–50.

[62] This section includes elements from the author's British Embassy Annual Lecture on International Law, titled 'International courts and tribunals: A "subsidiary means"?', delivered at The Hague on 27 June 2019.

[63] *Case of the Free Zones of Upper Savoy and the District of Gex* (Order of 19 August 1929) PCIJ Rep. Series A No. 22 at p. 13.

One illustration of recourse to a body other than a court or tribunal is the first ever 'compulsory conciliation' under UNCLOS, between Timor-Leste and Australia.[64] This ended successfully in March 2018 with the signature in New York of the Australia/Timor-Leste Treaty Establishing Their Maritime Boundaries in the Timor Sea, which entered into force on 30 August 2019.[65]

The background is worth recalling. Blocked from commencing contentious proceedings by Australia's carve-outs of maritime delimitation from UNCLOS Part XV and from its acceptance of the ICJ's jurisdiction under the Optional Clause, Timor-Leste commenced the conciliation process by an application under Article 298 of UNCLOS. Following a hearing, the Commission upheld its competence in a reasoned decision.[66] Thereafter, the Commission held several rounds with the parties between October 2016 and February 2018, leading to a four-page 'Comprehensive Package Agreement' dated 30 August 2017. On the basis of this 'Package Agreement', a rather detailed treaty text was negotiated directly between the two parties (mostly by tele- and videoconference between Dili, Canberra, London, and Lisbon).

The procedure adopted by the Conciliation Commission was essentially devised from scratch by the members of the Commission, with much assistance from the International Bureau of the Permanent Court of Arbitration (PCA). The procedure, which consisted mainly of shuttle diplomacy, is described in detail in the Commission's report, available on the PCA website.[67]

Under the Commission's auspices, the parties negotiated a treaty containing a number of innovations that enabled them to reach an agreement on the location of the boundaries. Chief amongst these are continental shelf and exclusive economic zone boundaries which are not the same in all segments; a mechanism for automatic adjustment of parts of the continental shelf

[64] Alfredo Crosato, 'Conciliation between Timor-Leste and Australia', in *Max Planck Encyclopedia of Public International Law* (Oxford: Oxford University Press, 2019); Katrina Cooper, 'Law and diplomacy in the compulsory conciliation between Australia and Timor-Leste', in M. McGuinness, D Stewart (eds.), *Research Handbook on Law and Diplomacy* (Cheltenham: Edward Elgar, 2022), pp. 41-60

[65] *Timor Sea Conciliation (Timor-Leste* v. *Australia)* (Report and Recommendations of the Compulsory Conciliation Commission of 9 May 2018) PCA Case No. 2016-10 at Annex 28: Treaty between the Democratic Republic of Timor-Leste and Australia Establishing Their Maritime Boundaries in the Timor Sea, New York, 6 March 2018, in force 30 August 2019.

[66] *Timor Sea Conciliation (Timor-Leste* v. *Australia)* (Decision on Australia's Objections to Competence of 19 September 2016) PCA Case No. 2016-10, XXXIV UNRIAA pp. 208–243.

[67] *Timor Sea Conciliation* (Report and Recommendations), available at PCA, 'Report and recommendations of the Compulsory Conciliation Commission between Timor-Leste and Australia on the Timor Sea', 9 May 2018, XXXIV UNRIAA, pp. 245–464.

boundary if necessary and once certain conditions are met; the establishment of an area of joint exercise of the parties' sovereign rights over the continental shelf; and the inextricable link between the boundary and resource arrangements as part of an overall package settlement. This is not a solution that could easily have emerged following judicial proceedings. In short, the conciliation process had two important features that contributed to the parties overcoming long-standing differences about the location of their maritime boundaries: first, it was forward-looking; and second, it focused on seeking an overall solution to the issues in dispute, rather than merely an adjudication of the parties' respective legal claims in the delimitation. Conciliation, if successful, undoubtedly has such advantages over adjudication.

The limited role of international courts and tribunals may perhaps be illustrated most vividly if we turn yet again to the Optional Clause. The battle for compulsory jurisdiction of a World Court was fought and lost in 1920; it was fought and lost again in 1945. The Optional Clause is what was left, and even that has hardly been a resounding success. As I have already said, calls for States to consider accepting the Optional Clause have gone largely unheeded. Relatively few States accept it.[68] Many States that have accepted the Clause have done so with far-reaching reservations so as to protect themselves from exposure, presumably because they feel vulnerable. Similarly, quite a few States have made maximum use of optional exceptions to compulsory jurisdiction under Article 298 of UNCLOS.[69]

All in all, there has hardly been a great vote of confidence in the settlement of international disputes by courts and tribunals. It is often remarked that since the 1980s, when both France and the US withdrew their acceptance, the UK has been the only permanent member to accept the Optional Clause, albeit with extensive reservations.[70]

The reasons for the reluctance of States to commit themselves to binding judicial settlement in general terms and in advance are obvious and understandable. But perhaps we should speak about them more openly if we want to see a more positive approach in the longer term. Then, perhaps, we may see

68 See note 31.

69 It is worth pointing out the significance of opting-out versus opting-in. It requires a conscious and specific decision to opt out, which may be both bureaucratically and politically difficult; conversely, opting in requires a conscious decision to accept compulsory dispute settlement.

70 Michael Wood, 'The United Kingdom's acceptance of the compulsory jurisdiction of the International Court of Justice', in Ole Kristian Fauchald, Henning Jakhelln, and Aslak Syse (eds.), *dog Fred er ej det Beste, Festskrift til Carl August Fleischer* (Oslo: Universitetsforlaget, 2006), reprinted in Gauci and Barrett, *Anthology of British Contributions to International Law, 1915–2015*, pp. 3261–84. The current UK acceptance is dated 22 February 2017.

more States approaching courts by agreement, as Belize and Guatemala have done in bringing their territorial dispute before the ICJ (as approved by referendum in each country).[71]

17.6 WRITINGS ON INTERNATIONAL DISPUTE SETTLEMENT

On this occasion in memory of John Merrills, it seems appropriate to conclude with a few words about the value of writings in the field of international dispute settlement and to offer some thoughts for work still to be done. As in all fields of international law, such writings have proliferated in recent years; in addition to the classic volumes, there are many new books and articles on particular aspects of the subject, as well as whole journals devoted to international dispute settlement. This seemingly overwhelming (and still growing) volume of writings, if well done, may make an important contribution to modern international dispute settlement and is, of course, of considerable assistance to practitioners.

Much has been written about modern international dispute settlement, but much remains to be written. Perhaps this is, in part, because some of the more interesting issues are and should remain confidential. Lawyers directly involved in a case may feel that they should not write about it: it may not be right to do so, at least not without the client's agreement, and it may be difficult for a participant to write objectively, or be seen to be writing objectively.[72] One way to seek to avoid this last pitfall is to write jointly with lawyers from the other side.[73]

It is easy enough these days to keep up with the ICJ and the ITLOS. This is true also of inter-State arbitrations, in so far as they are public. In most cases, there are good resources available, such as the websites of the PCA and the

[71] *Guatemala's Territorial, Insular and Maritime Claim (Guatemala/Belize)* (Special Agreement of 8 December 2008). Another recent example of a case brought before the Court by agreement is that of *Land and Maritime Delimitation and Sovereignty over Islands (Gabon/Equatorial Guinea)*.

[72] Some recent observations to this effect may be found in Daniel Bethlehem, 'Thirty-Fifth ITF Public Conference: Evidence in investor-state arbitration – Keynote address', 29 April 2021, www.biicl.org/documents/10698_bethlehem_-_evidence_in_investor-state_arbitration_final.pdf (accessed 31 July 2022).

[73] See, e.g., S. Abayasekara et al., 'Report Number 6-20 (5), Treaty between Australia and the Democratic Republic of Timor-Leste Establishing Their Maritime Boundaries in the Timor Sea', in Coalter Lathrop (ed.), *International Maritime Boundaries*, vol. 8 (Leiden: Brill, 2020), pp. 5547–603; the four co-authors were from the Australian and Timor-Leste legal teams and assumed the task of authorship with the agreement of their respective clients.

International Centre for Settlement of Investment Disputes (ICSID). But this is not the case with all international courts and tribunals.

There are matters of great interest to practitioners on which it is often hard to get accurate and up-to-date information. These include, but are by no means limited to, the following:

First, the practice of 'appointing authorities', empowered to make appointments to arbitral tribunals (e.g. when a party fails to do so), remains largely a mystery. The president of the ICJ may be given this role, as may the president of the ITLOS, the Secretary-General of the PCA, or others. Long ago there was a memorable piece by former ICJ President Muhammad Zafrulla Khan;[74] there is a rather short chapter in *Rosenne's Law and Practice*;[75] and there have been recent pieces by Jianjun Gao (on appointment under Annex VII of UNCLOS)[76] and by Peter Tzeng (more general).[77] Much of what happens in practice, however, might benefit from further exploration and analysis.

Second, the selection of *ad hoc* judges (or party-appointed arbitrators) is one of the most difficult things for a practitioner to advise on. It is often seen to be a matter of great importance, at least by clients. In the case of the ICJ, selection has not been made any easier by what are perhaps the unnecessarily strict restrictions introduced in 2002 by Practice Direction VI: that parties, when choosing a judge *ad hoc*, should refrain from nominating persons who have acted as agent, counsel, or advocate in another case before the Court in the three years preceding the date of the nomination. Again, for obvious reasons, virtually nothing has been written about the question of selection. Indeed, little has been written about the role in practice of *ad hoc* judges (or party-appointed arbitrators).[78]

74 Muhammad Zafrulla Khan, 'The appointment of arbitrators by the president of the International Court of Justice', in *Il processo internazionale: Studi in onore di Gaetano Morelli. Vol. XIV: Communicazioni e Studi* (Milan: Giuffrè, 1975), p. 1021.

75 Malcolm N. Shaw, *Rosenne's Law and Practice of the International Court, 1920–2015*, 5th ed. (Leiden: Brill, 2016), ch. 29. See also Robert Kolb, *The International Court of Justice* (Oxford: Hart, 2013), pp. 1193–97.

76 Jianjun Gao, 'Appointment of arbitrators by the president of the ITLOS pursuant to Article 3 of Annex VII to the LOS Convention: Some tentative observations' (2017) 16 Chinese JIL 723–49.

77 Peter Tzeng, 'Appointing authorities: Self-appointment, party appointment and non-appointment', in Freya Baetens (ed.), *Legitimacy of Unseen Actors in International Adjudication* (Cambridge: Cambridge University Press, 2019), pp. 164–88.

78 Judge *ad hoc* Lauterpacht's views in the *Bosnia* case give a rare insight, though he does not go into the question of selection: see *Application of the Convention on the Prevention and Punishment of the Crime of Genocide (Bosnia and Herzegovina* v. *Serbia and Montenegro)* (Order) [1993] ICJ Rep. 325, at pp. 408–9, paras 4–6 (Separate Opinion of 13 September 1993

Third, little has been written on the drafting of rules of procedure for *ad hoc* inter-State arbitral tribunals. Whenever an *ad hoc* arbitral tribunal is established, one of the first (and crucial) matters to consider is the rules of procedure. Procedural provisions in the constituent documents are often rudimentary.[79] Where does one turn for guidance? The PCA and the UN have prepared 'model rules', which are of interest, but which are rarely adopted and applied without modification. Moreover, in some cases they reflect rules that have been applied in commercial or investor–State disputes and which are not necessarily considered appropriate in inter-State arbitration or, indeed, familiar to practitioners in that field. The rules that have been adopted and applied in particular inter-State arbitrations are often – but not always – publicly available, in which case they may serve as useful precedents, as may their interpretation and application by arbitral tribunals. But the materials are not always readily available.

Fourth, the discontinuance of proceedings is a well-established procedure in inter-State proceedings, but again the decisions of international courts and tribunals (and the underlying positions of the parties to the proceedings), even if public, are not always revealing. Reference is sometimes found to the 'suspension' of proceedings, but this may involve no more than the prolongation of time limits. Not much is to be found in the books on these matters.[80]

17.7 BY WAY OF CONCLUSION

A bright or depressing future? The very fact that the contributors to this volume address such varied aspects of international dispute settlement is reason enough for optimism. There is much that is new, and many promising developments. The contributions to the volume, overall, suggest a bright future for international dispute settlement and for the study of international dispute settlement. Those studying the subject now live in an incomparably

Relating to the Further Requests for the Indication of Provisional Measures). Judge Cot did so to some extent in his essay, Jean-Pierre Cot, 'L'arrêt sur la délimitation dans la mer Noire: la perspective d'un juge *ad hoc*', in Bogdan Aurescu (ed.), *Romania and the International Court of Justice: The Works of the International Conference 'Romania and the International Court of Justice. 5 Years since the Maritime Delimitation in the Black Sea'* (Bucharest: Editura Hamangiu, 2014). See also President Donoghue's remarks on this matter in the provisional summary record of the International Law Commission's 3585th meeting (1 June 2022) UN Doc. A/CN.4/SR.3585.

79 See, e.g., Annex VII to UNCLOS.

80 Michael Wood, 'International courts and tribunals, discontinuance of cases', in *Max Planck Encyclopedia of Public International Law* (Oxford: Oxford University Press, 2017).

more active and exciting world than was the case when I first learnt about the ICJ decades ago.

Merrills had great faith in international dispute settlement, tempered with more than a touch of realism, and dispute settlement reflects much that is central in his writings. But we should not forget Merrills' many other contributions to international law, not least his teaching of generations of law students from around the world. Those taught by him were fortunate indeed: they benefitted from his deep understanding of international law and its limits.

Index

For EU product safety concerns, contact us at Calle de José Abascal, 56–1°, 28003 Madrid, Spain or eugpsr@cambridge.org.

www.ingramcontent.com/pod-product-compliance
Lightning Source LLC
LaVergne TN
LVHW021055220926
848484LV00021B/933